Eighth Edition

EVERYTHING'S AN
argument
with readings

Andrea A. Lunsford
STANFORD UNIVERSITY

John J. Ruszkiewicz
UNIVERSITY OF TEXAS AT AUSTIN

Keith Walters
PORTLAND STATE UNIVERSITY

bedford/st.martin's
Macmillan Learning
Boston | New York

For Bedford/St. Martin's

Vice President, Editorial, Macmillan Learning Humanities: Edwin Hill
Executive Program Director for English: Leasa Burton
Senior Program Manager: John E. Sullivan III
Executive Marketing Manager: Joy Fisher Williams
Director of Content Development, Humanities: Jane Knetzger
Senior Developmental Editor: Rachel Goldberg
Associate Editor: Lexi DeConti
Editorial Assistant: William Hwang
Senior Content Project Manager: Ryan Sullivan
Senior Workflow Project Manager: Jennifer Wetzel
Production Coordinator: Brianna Lester
Media Project Manager: Jodi Isman
Media Editor: Julia Domenicucci
Editorial Services: Lumina Datamatics, Inc.
Composition: Lumina Datamatics, Inc.
Cartographer: Mapping Specialists, Ltd.
Text Permissions Manager: Kalina Ingham
Text Permissions Editor: Arthur Johnson, Lumina Datamatics, Inc.
Photo Permissions Editor: Angela Boehler
Photo Researcher: Krystyna Borgen, Lumina Datamatics, Inc.
Director of Design, Content Management: Diana Blume
Text Design: Claire Seng-Niemoeller, Anna Palchik, and Graphic World, Inc.
Cover Design: William Boardman
Cover Images: (*laptop*) fStop Images/Epoxydude/Getty Images; (*polar bear*) dagsjo/Getty Images; (*vegan label*) Good_Studio/Getty Images; (*free speech sign*) Imfoto/Shutterstock; (*kids with cell phones*) Hero Images/Getty Images
Printing and Binding: LSC Communications

Manufactured in the United States of America.

1 2 3 4 5 6   23 22 21 20

For information, write: Bedford/St. Martin's, 75 Arlington Street, Boston, MA 02116

ISBN 978-1-319-36237-9

Acknowledgments

Text acknowledgments and copyrights appear at the back of the book on pages 793–94, which constitute an extension of the copyright page. Art acknowledgments and copyrights appear on the same page as the art selections they cover.

Preface

When we began work on this text in 1996 (the first edition came out in 1998), we couldn't have anticipated all the events of the next two tumultuous decades, or all the changes to public and private discourse, or the current deeply divided state of our nation. But we have tried hard, over these decades, to track such changes and the ways rhetoric and argument have evolved and responded to them.

Certainly, we recognized the increasingly important role digital culture plays in all our lives, and so with each new edition we have included more on the technologies of communication, particularly those associated with social media; and we early on recognized that, like rhetoric itself, social media can be used for good or for ill, to bring people together or to separate them.

We have also carefully tracked the forms that arguments take today, from cartoons and graphic narratives to blogs and other postings to multimodal projects of almost every conceivable kind. While argument has always surrounded us, today it does so in an amazing array of genres and forms, including aural and visual components that strengthen and amplify arguments.

The sheer proliferation of information (not to mention misinformation, disinformation, and outright lies) that bombards all writers led us to reaffirm our commitment to studying and teaching style, since (as Richard Lanham and others argue) in the age of information overload, style is the tool writers possess to try to capture and keep the attention of audiences. Attention to style reveals other changes, such as the increasing use of informal registers and conversational styles even in academic arguments.

Perhaps most important, though, a look back over the last twenty-two years reaffirms the crucial role that rhetoric can and should play in personal, work, and school lives. At its best, rhetoric is the art, theory, and practice of ethical communication, needed more sorely today than perhaps ever before. *Everything's an Argument with Readings* presents this view of rhetoric and illustrates it with a fair and wide range of perspectives and views, which we hope will inspire student writers to think of themselves as rhetors, as Quintilian's "good person, speaking well."

Key Features

Two books in one, neatly linked. Up front is a brief guide to Aristotelian, Toulmin, and Rogerian argument; common types of arguments; presenting arguments; and researching arguments. In the back is a thematically organized anthology of readings in a wide range of genres. Handy cross-references in the margins allow students to move easily from the argument chapters to specific examples in the readings and from the readings to appropriate rhetorical instruction.

Short, relatable excerpts weave in the debates that rage around us. From #metoo tweets and protest posters to essays and scholarly writing, bold-faced examples illustrate the arguments happening in politics, economics, journalism, and media, with brief student-friendly analyses.

Five thematic readings chapters that encourage students to explore complex arguments. Readings on "How Does Popular Culture Stereotype You?," "Has the Internet Destroyed Privacy?," and "How Free Should Campus Speech Be?" demand that students consider the many sides of contemporary issues across the political spectrum, going beyond a simple pro/con stance.

A real-world, full-color design that builds students' understanding of visual rhetoric. Presenting readings in the style of their original publications helps students recognize and think about the effect that design and visuals have on written and multimodal arguments.

New to This Edition

A new section on rhetorical listening in Chapter 1. The very first chapter of the eighth edition now emphasizes the importance of listening rhetorically and respectfully, encouraging readers to move beyond "echo chambers" and build bridges among all viewpoints.

Eight new full-length models in the guide provide engaging, topical arguments of fact, definition, evaluation, cause and effect, proposals, and rhetorical analysis. Legal scholar Stephen L. Carter offers a Toulmin analysis of whether racial epithets should be considered free speech, while *New York Times* columnist Nicholas Kristof presents an op-ed in defense of public wilderness.

Five new annotated student essays address topics students care about, from millennials' love of food to breaking a social media addiction.

Thirty-one engaging new readings on hot-button issues such as free speech, food, language, privacy, and stereotypes. Selections represent a range of genres and span the full gamut of social and political views, including:

- excerpts from a recent Gallup poll showing what college students think about First Amendment issues
- visual arguments and a scholarly essay supporting and critiquing the concept of racial microaggressions
- best-selling essayist Roxane Gay on the language we use to describe sexual violence
- an *Economist* blog post acknowledging that sport shooting can be, well, *fun*
- an argument against veganism . . . written by a vegan

A new introduction in the instructor's notes. Focusing on the teaching of argument, this new introduction gives experienced and first-time instructors a strong pedagogical foundation. Sample syllabi for both semester and quarter courses provide help for pacing all types of courses.

We're all in. As always.

Bedford/St. Martin's is as passionately committed to the discipline of English as ever, working hard to provide support and services that make it easier for you to teach your course your way.

Find **community support** at the Bedford/St. Martin's English Community (**community.macmillan.com**), where you can follow our *Bits* blog for new teaching ideas, download titles from our professional resource series, and review projects in the pipeline.

Choose **curriculum solutions** that offer flexible custom options, combining our carefully developed print and digital resources, acclaimed works from Macmillan's trade imprints, and your own course or program materials to provide the exact resources your students need. Our approach to customization makes it possible to create a customized project uniquely suited for your students and, based on your enrollment size, return money to your department and raise your institutional profile with a high-impact author visit through the Macmillan Author Program ("MAP").

Rely on **outstanding service** from your Bedford/St. Martin's sales representative and editorial team. Contact us or visit **macmillanlearning.com** to learn more about any of the options below.

LaunchPad for *Everything's an Argument with Readings*: Where Students Learn

LaunchPad provides engaging content and new ways to get the most out of your book. Get an interactive e-book combined with assessment tools in a fully customizable course space; then assign and mix our resources with yours.

- **Reading comprehension quizzes**, to help you quickly gauge your students' understanding of the assigned reading.

- **Interactive exercises and tutorials** for reading, writing, and research.

- **Diagnostics** provide opportunities to assess areas for improvement and assign additional exercises based on students' needs. Visual reports show performance by topic, class, and student as well as improvement over time.

- **Pre-built units**—including readings, videos, quizzes, and more—are easy to adapt and assign by adding your own materials and mixing them with our high-quality multimedia content and ready-made assessment options, such as **LearningCurve** adaptive quizzing and **Exercise Central**.

- Use LaunchPad on its own or **integrate it** with your school's learning management system so that your class is always on the same page.

LaunchPad for *Everything's an Argument with Readings* can be purchased on its own or packaged with the print book at a significant discount. An activation code is required. To order LaunchPad for *Everything's an Argument with Readings* with the print book, contact your sales representative. For more information, go to **launchpadworks.com**.

Choose from Alternative Formats of *Everything's an Argument with Readings*

Bedford/St. Martin's offers a range of formats. Choose what works best for you and your students:

- **Paperback brief edition** To order the paperback edition of *Everything's an Argument*, use ISBN 978-1-319-36238-6.
- **Popular e-book formats** For details of our e-book partners, visit **macmillanlearning.com/ebooks**.

Select Value Packages

Add value to your text by packaging a Bedford/St. Martin's resource, such as *Writer's Help* 2.0, with *Everything's an Argument with Readings* at a significant discount. Contact your sales representative for more information.

Writer's Help 2.0 is a powerful online writing resource that helps students find answers, whether they are searching for writing advice on their own or as part of an assignment.

- **Smart search.** Built on research with more than 1,600 student writers, the smart search in *Writer's Help* 2.0 provides reliable results even when students use novice terms, such as *flow* and *unstuck*.
- **Trusted content from our best-selling handbooks.** Andrea Lunsford's user-friendly tone ensures that students have clear advice and examples for all of their writing questions.
- **Diagnostics that help establish a baseline for instruction.** Assign diagnostics to identify areas of strength and areas for improvement and to help students plan a course of study. Use visual reports to track performance by topic, class, and student as well as improvement over time.
- **Adaptive exercises that engage students.** *Writer's Help* 2.0 includes LearningCurve, game-like online quizzing that adapts to what students already know and helps them focus on what they need to learn.

Student access for *Writer's Help 2.0, Lunsford Version*, is packaged with *Everything's an Argument with Readings* at a significant discount. Contact your sales representative to ensure your students have easy access to online writing support. Students who rent or buy a used book can purchase access and instructors may request free access at **macmillanlearning .com/writershelp2**.

Instructor Resources

You have a lot to do in your course. We want to make it easy for you to find the support you need—and to get it quickly.

Instructor's Notes for Everything's an Argument with Readings is available as a PDF that can be downloaded from **macmillanlearning.com**. Visit the instructor resources tab for *Everything's an Argument with Readings*. In addition to chapter overviews and teaching tips, the instructor's manual offers an introduction about teaching the argument course, sample syllabi, correlations to the Council of Writing Program Administrators' Outcomes Statement, and potential answers to the "Respond" questions in the book.

Acknowledgments

We owe a debt of gratitude to many people for making *Everything's an Argument with Readings* possible. Our first thanks must go to the thousands of people we have taught in our writing courses over nearly four decades, particularly students at the Ohio State University, Stanford University, the University of Texas at Austin, and Portland State University. Almost every chapter in this book has been informed by a classroom encounter with a student whose shrewd observation or perceptive question sent an ambitious lesson plan spiraling to the ground. (Anyone who has tried to teach claims and warrants on the fly to skeptical first-year writers will surely appreciate why we have qualified our claims in the Toulmin chapter so carefully.) But students have also provided the motive for writing this book. More than ever, they need to know how to read and write arguments effectively if they are to secure a place in a world growing ever smaller and more rhetorically challenging.

We are deeply grateful to the editors at Bedford/St. Martin's who have contributed their formidable talents to this book. In particular, we want to thank the ingenious and efficient Rachel Goldberg for guiding us so patiently and confidently—helping us locate just the right items whenever we needed fresh examples and images and gracefully recasting passage after passage to satisfy permissions mandates. Senior content project manager Ryan Sullivan was relentlessly upbeat and kind in all his communications, making the ever-more-complex stages of production almost a pleasure. We also appreciate the extensive support and help of Lexi DeConti, who kept us attuned to examples and readings that might appeal to students today. We are similarly grateful to senior program manager John Sullivan, whose support was unfailing; Kalina Ingham, Arthur Johnson, and Tom Wilcox, for text permissions; Angela Boehler and Krystyna Borgen, for art permissions; William Boardman, for our cover design; Bridget Leahy, copyeditor; and William Hwang, editorial assistant. All of you made editing the eighth edition feel fresh and creative.

We'd also like to thank the astute instructors who reviewed the seventh edition: Brigitte Anderson, University of Pikeville; Samantha Battrick, Truman State University; Kathryn Bennett, Old Dominion University; Jeanne Bohannon, Kennesaw State University; Rebecca Cepek, Duquesne University; Laura Dumin, University of Central Oklahoma; Tim Engles, Eastern Illinois University; Karen Feldman, Seminole State College of Florida; Africa Fine, Palm Beach State College; Darius Frasure, Mountain View College; Erin Gallagher, Washington State University; Ben Graydon, Daytona State College; Joseph Hernandez, Mt. San Jacinto College; Julie Moore-Felux, Northwest Vista College; Laurie Murray, Anderson University; Kolawole Olaiya, Anderson University; Leslie Rapparlie, University of Colorado; Thomas Reynolds, Northwestern State University; Loreen Smith, Isothermal Community College; Benjamin Syn, University of Colorado; Gina Szabady, Lane Community College; Amy Walton, Iowa State University; and Miriam Young, Truman State University.

Thanks, too, to Sherrie Weller of Loyola Chicago University and Valerie Duff-Stroutmann of Newbury College, who updated the instructor's notes for this eighth edition with a new introduction, new model syllabi, new points for discussion, and new classroom activities. We hope this resource will be useful as instructors build their courses. Finally, we are grateful to the students whose fine argumentative essays or materials appear in our chapters: Cameron Hauer, Kate Beispel, Jenny Kim, Laura Tarrant, Natasha Rodriguez, Caleb Wong, Juliana Chang, George Chidiac, and Charlotte Geaghan-Breiner. We hope that *Everything's an Argument with Readings* responds to what students and instructors have said they want and need.

Andrea A. Lunsford
John J. Ruszkiewicz
Keith Walters

Correlation to Council of Writing Program Administrators' (WPA) Outcomes

Everything's an Argument with Readings works with the Council of Writing Program Administrators' Outcomes Statement for first-year composition courses (last updated 2014).

2014 WPA Outcomes	Support in *Everything's an Argument with Readings*, 8e
Rhetorical Knowledge	
Learn and use key rhetorical concepts through analyzing and composing a variety of texts.	**Chapter 1, "Understanding Arguments and Reading Them Critically"** (pp. 3–31), establishes the central elements of the rhetorical situation and encourages rhetorical listening. **Chapter 6, "Rhetorical Analysis"** (pp. 97–132), further develops these concepts and teaches students how to analyze a rhetorical analysis and compose their own. Each chapter offers dozens of written, visual, and multimodal texts to analyze, in both the guide portion and the thematic reader.
Gain experience reading and composing in several genres to understand how genre conventions shape and are shaped by readers' and writers' practices and purposes.	*Everything's an Argument with Readings* provides engaging readings across genres, from academic essays and newspaper editorials to tweets and infographics. **"Respond" boxes** throughout each chapter (e.g., pp. 56–57) invite students to think critically about the material. For more genre variety, *Everything's an Argument with Readings* also contains a five-chapter thematic reader with additional multimodal genres, including an art installation, Web articles, scholarly essays, and political cartoons. Each chapter on a specific type of argument features project ideas (e.g., p. 186), giving students detailed prompts to write their own arguments of fact, arguments of definition, evaluations, causal arguments, and proposals.
Develop facility in responding to a variety of situations and contexts, calling for purposeful shifts in voice, tone, level of formality, design, medium, and/or structure.	**Chapter 13, "Style in Arguments"** (pp. 321–45), addresses word choice, tone, sentence structure, punctuation, and figurative language, with engaging examples of each. The **"Cultural Contexts for Argument"** boxes throughout the text (e.g., p. 163) address how people from other cultures might respond to different styles or structures of argument. This feature offers suggestions on how to think about argument in an unfamiliar cultural context.
Understand and use a variety of technologies to address a range of audiences.	**Chapter 16, "Multimodal Arguments"** (pp. 381–402), addresses how new media has transformed the array of choices for making arguments and reaching audiences. This chapter teaches how to analyze multimodal arguments as well as how to create them through Web sites, videos, wikis, blogs, social media, memes, posters, and comics.
Match the capacities of different environments (e.g., print & electronic) to varying rhetorical situations.	**Chapter 14, "Visual Rhetoric"** (pp. 346–62), discusses the power of visual rhetoric and how students can use visuals in their own work. **Chapter 15, "Presenting Arguments"** (pp. 363–80), includes material on incorporating various media into presentations and Webcasts. **Chapter 16, "Multimodal Arguments"** (pp. 381–402), analyzes the evolving landscape of argument across media platforms. **Chapter 17, "Academic Arguments"** (pp. 405–37), covers the conventions of academic arguments.

2014 WPA Outcomes	Support in *Everything's an Argument with Readings*, 8e
Critical Thinking, Reading, and Composing	
Use composing and reading for inquiry, learning, thinking, and communicating in various rhetorical contexts.	**Chapter 1, "Understanding Arguments and Reading Them Critically"** (pp. 3–31), features a section called **"Why Listen to Arguments Rhetorically and Respectfully"** (pp. 7–8). It teaches students to listen openly and constructively and calls attention to the need to escape "echo chambers," respectfully consider all viewpoints, and find common ground.
	Throughout *Everything's an Argument with Readings*, students are invited to delve deeper into current issues in the world around them, considering the various arguments presented in tweets, newspapers, scholarly papers, court rulings, and even bumper stickers. *Everything's an Argument with Readings* guides students in asking critical questions about these contexts and learning how to respond to and create their own compositions. Chapters dedicated to central types of argument explain how students might best approach each writing situation. The chapters close with a guide to writing arguments of that type:

	Chapter 8, "Arguments of Fact" (pp. 164–96)
	
	    Chapter 9, "Arguments of Definition" (pp. 197–223)
	
	    Chapter 10, "Evaluations" (pp. 224–54)
	
	    Chapter 11, "Causal Arguments" (pp. 255–85)
	
	    Chapter 12, "Proposals" (pp. 286–318)
	
	    Chapter 16, "Multimodal Arguments" (pp. 381–402)

Read a diverse range of texts, attending especially to relationships between assertion and evidence, to patterns of organization, to interplay between verbal and nonverbal elements, and how these features function for different audiences and situations.	**Chapter 7, "Structuring Arguments"** (pp. 135–63), examines making claims and using evidence to support those claims. It delves into the structure of Rogerian and Toulmin arguments, showing how different argument types work for different writing situations.
	Each **Guide to Writing** features sections on "Formulating a Claim" and "Thinking about Organization" (e.g., pp. 212 and 214), emphasizing the use of evidence and the structure of the argument.
Locate and evaluate primary and secondary research materials, including journal articles, essays, books, databases, and informal Internet sources.	**Chapter 18, "Finding Evidence"** (pp. 438–53), covers locating evidence from print, electronic, and field research sources.
	Chapter 19, "Evaluating Sources" (pp. 454–63), addresses how to assess those sources effectively.
Use strategies—such as interpretation, synthesis, response, critique, and design/redesign—to compose texts that integrate the writer's ideas with those from appropriate sources.	**Chapter 20, "Using Sources,"** provides detailed explanations of summary, paraphrase, and quotation and when to use each approach (pp. 467–73). The chapter discusses framing with introductory phrases and signal verbs, and it presents multiple ways to connect source material to a student's own ideas—by establishing a context, introducing a term or concept, developing a claim, highlighting differences, and avoiding "patchwriting" (pp. 480–82).
	Chapter 21, "Plagiarism and Academic Integrity" (pp. 484–93), highlights the importance of acknowledging another writer's work.
	Chapter 22, "Documenting Sources" (pp. 494–532), concludes the research section of the book with a discussion of MLA and APA documentation, including a wide range of citation models in both formats.

2014 WPA Outcomes	Support in *Everything's an Argument with Readings*, 8e
Processes	
Develop a writing project through multiple drafts.	**Chapter 17, "Academic Arguments"** (pp. 405–37), stresses the importance of working through multiple drafts of a project, using revision and peer feedback to improve the document.
Develop flexible strategies for reading, drafting, reviewing, collaboration, revising, rewriting, rereading, and editing.	Writing is a fundamental focus of *Everything's an Argument with Readings*, and students learn to critique their own work and the work of others in almost every part of the book. Each **Guide to Writing**, focusing on a specific type of argument in the **Part 2** chapters, contains step-by-step advice on drafting, researching, and organizing, as well as peer review questions about the claim being made, the evidence provided for the claim, and the organization and style of the essay.
	The **Guide to Writing** also asks students to review their spelling, punctuation, mechanics, documentation, and format.
Use composing processes and tools as a means to discover and reconsider ideas.	**Chapter 7, "Structuring Arguments"** (pp. 135–63), provides a clear explanation for how to construct an argument and support it effectively, and it includes a brief annotated model from a classic text.
	The **"Developing an Academic Argument"** section (pp. 411–18) in **Chapter 17, "Academic Arguments"** (pp. 405–37), guides students through the specific process of developing a paper in an academic setting, from selecting a topic and exploring it in depth to entering into the conversation around the chosen topic. Two annotated examples of academic arguments are provided at the end of the chapter.
Experience the collaborative and social aspects of writing processes.	Many "Respond" questions have students work in pairs or groups to analyze rhetorical situations, arguments, or appeals. See p. 36, for instance.
	In **Chapter 21, "Plagiarism and Academic Integrity"** (pp. 484–93), students learn the importance of giving credit, getting permission to use the materials of others, citing sources appropriately, and acknowledging collaboration with their peers.
Learn to give and act on productive feedback to works in progress.	Each **Guide to Writing**, focusing on a specific type of argument in the **Part 2** chapters, contains a **"Getting and Giving Response: Questions for Peer Review"** section (e.g., pp. 183–85) tailored to that argument type. These questions address the claim being made, the evidence provided for the claim, and the organization and style of the essay.
Adapt composing processes for a variety of technologies and modalities.	Awareness of technology runs throughout *Everything's an Argument with Readings*, beginning in the first chapter with an exploration of arguments made via Twitter. A particular focus on multimodal arguments is made in **Chapter 14, "Visual Rhetoric"** (pp. 346–62), which covers how effective images can be and instructs students on incorporating them to achieve specific rhetorical purposes, and in **Chapter 16, "Multimodal Arguments"** (pp. 381–402), which focuses on how technology offers new platforms and opportunities for composition, as well as some new pitfalls to avoid. These chapters provide students with tools for creating their own multimodal compositions.
Reflect on the development of composing practices and how those practices influence their work.	*Everything's an Argument with Readings* presents students with an important foundation in the purpose and history of rhetoric (e.g., **"Why We Make Arguments,"** pp. 8–9; **"The Classical Oration,"** pp. 136–39) as well as thoughtful reflections on how composition and argument have changed in an increasingly digital world (e.g., **"Old Media Transformed by New Media,"** pp. 382–83; **"Conventions in Academic Argument Are Not Static,"** p. 410).

2014 WPA Outcomes	Support in *Everything's an Argument with Readings*, 8e
Knowledge of Conventions	
Develop knowledge of linguistic structures, including grammar, punctuation, and spelling, through practice in composing and revising.	Chapter 13, "Style in Arguments" (pp. 321–45), covers sentence structure and punctuation.
	Chapter 17, "Academic Arguments" (pp. 405–37), discusses drafting, revising, and editing.
	The Guide to Writing in each Part 2 chapter asks students to review their spelling, punctuation, mechanics, documentation, and format.
Understand why genre conventions for structure, paragraphing, tone, and mechanics vary.	The argument chapters in Part 2 address genre conventions, discussing how the approach and structure of a document adapt to its genre. Each chapter also includes a Guide to Writing and Sample Arguments, which highlight differing uses of sources and tone (e.g., "Guide to Writing a Proposal," pp. 300–305).
Gain experience negotiating variations in genre conventions.	Each of the Part 2 chapters offers a section on characterizing that particular genre (e.g., "Characterizing Evaluation," pp. 229–32) as well as a section to guide students to develop a paper in that particular genre (e.g., "Developing an Evaluative Argument," pp. 233–39). These chapters pay particular attention to the nuances and variations of differing purposes and approaches.
	For more genre variety, *Everything's an Argument with Readings* also contains a five-chapter thematic reader with additional multimodal genres, including infographics, professional reports, scholarly journal articles, and comic strips.
Learn common formats and/or design features for different kinds of texts.	Part 3, "Style and Presentation in Arguments," offers four chapters on how to design an argument, paying attention to how these choices will vary depending on the student's rhetorical purpose (e.g., "Using Images and Visual Design to Create Pathos," pp. 350–52).
	The "Considering Design and Visuals" section (e.g., pp. 238–39) in each Part 2 argument chapter acquaints students with common design features and formats of that type of document.
	The Guide to Writing in each Part 2 chapter contains a "Considering Genre and Media" section that invites students to think about how to choose the appropriate format and medium for a particular argument.
Explore the concepts of intellectual property (such as fair use and copyright) that motivate documentation conventions.	Chapter 20, "Using Sources," explores the topics of summary, paraphrase, and quotation and when each approach might be most appropriate (pp. 466–73). The chapter discusses framing with introductory phrases and signal verbs, and it presents multiple ways to connect source material to a student's own ideas by establishing a context, introducing a term or concept, developing a claim, highlighting differences, and avoiding "patchwriting" (pp. 474–82).
	Chapter 21, "Plagiarism and Academic Integrity" (pp. 484–93), shines a light on the importance of acknowledging the work of another.
	The section on MLA style in Chapter 22, "Documenting Sources" (pp. 496–515), provides guidance on how to get permission for copyrighted material (including Internet sources) and how to navigate Creative Commons and fair use. It also offers an in-depth examination of in-text citations and Works Cited entries, with more than fifty examples of citation types and sample pages from a student essay.
Practice applying citation conventions systematically in their own work.	Chapter 22, "Documenting Sources" (pp. 494–532), examines in-text citations and Works Cited entries for both MLA and APA style, with more than fifty examples of citation types and sample pages from a student essay.

Brief Contents

Contents

PHOTOS TOP TO BOTTOM: Chip Somodevilla/Getty Images; Daily Beast; Steve Nease; TIM SLOAN/ Getty Images; WPA Pool/Getty Images

xix

Part 2
Writing Arguments   *133*

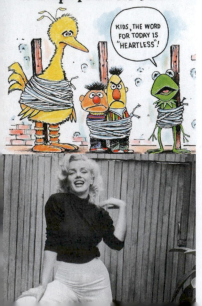

PHOTOS TOP TO BOTTOM: Caroline Kristof; World History Archive/Alamy Stock Photo; Anthony Pidgeon/Getty Images; Dave Granlund/Cagle Cartoons, Inc. © Cagle Cartoons Inc.; Alfred Eisenstaedt/Getty Images

PHOTOS TOP TO BOTTOM: Jeff Stahler/Andrews McMeel Syndication; Charles Krupa/AP Images; T3 Magazine/Getty Images; Bastiaan Slabbers/iStock/Getty Images; dpa picture alliance/Alamy

PHOTOS TOP TO BOTTOM: Jeff Barnard/AP Images; Twin Design/Shutterstock; © John Atkinson/Wrong Hands; claire norman/Shutterstock; ESB Professional/Shutterstock

Part 3
Style and Presentation in Arguments *319*

13.   Style in Arguments *321*

14.   Visual Rhetoric *346*

PHOTOS TOP TO BOTTOM: NASA/Getty Images; © Photofest, Inc.; Chronicle/Alamy Stock Photo; Lisa Benson, 2017/4/18, The Washington Post Writers Group; H. Armstrong Roberts/ClassicStock/Getty Images

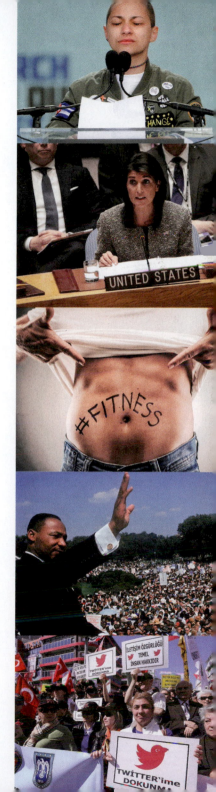

PHOTOS TOP TO BOTTOM: Chip Somodevilla/Getty Images; Drew Angerer/Getty Images; knape/Getty Images; Francis Miller/
Getty Images; ADEM ALTAN/Getty Images

Part 4
Research and Arguments *403*

PHOTOS TOP TO BOTTOM: 06photo/Shutterstock; Rogelio V. Solis/AP Images; MIKE NELSON/AFP/Getty Images; Paul Faith/
PA Wire URN:9724483 (Press Association via AP Images); J. Bicking/Shutterstock.com

"Some irresponsible gossip mongers around the office have misquoted me as calling you a 'silly goose'."

GOTLOVE?

PHOTOS TOP TO BOTTOM: AFP/Getty Images; Cartoon Resource/Shutterstock; Jutta Kuss/Getty Images; Sarah L. Voisin/The Washington Post/Getty Images; Kristen Prahl/Shutterstock

Part 5
Arguments   *533*

27. How Free Should Campus Speech Be? *729*

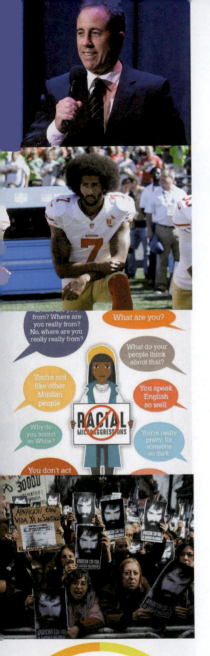

PART 1

READING AND UNDERSTANDING
arguments

1
Understanding Arguments and Reading Them Critically

LEFT TO RIGHT: Paul Archuleta/Getty Images; Daily Beast; Chelsea Guglielmino/Getty Images

On October 15, 2017, actor and activist Alyssa Milano took to Twitter to issue a call to action:

> **Alyssa Milano** ✓
> @Alyssa_Milano
>
> Follow ∨
>
> If you've been sexually harassed or assaulted write 'me too' as a reply to this tweet.
>
> Me too.
>
> Suggested by a friend: "If all the women who have been sexually harassed or assaulted wrote 'Me too.' as a status, we might give people a sense of the magnitude of the problem."
>
> 1:21 PM - 15 Oct 2017

Milano was joining the conversation surrounding a spate of revelations about very high-profile and powerful men accused of sexual harassment: Bill Cosby, Roger Ailes, Bill O'Reilly, and Harvey Weinstein. Milano's tweet argues for standing up and speaking out—in big numbers—and her message certainly hit a nerve: within 24 hours, 4.7 million people around the world had joined the "me too" conversation, with over 12 million posts and comments. Some of these comments pointed out that the "me too" movement is actually more than ten years old: it began with activist Tarana Burke, who was directing a Girls for Gender Equity program in Brooklyn, aimed at giving voice to young women of color. As Burke told CNN after Milano's tweet went viral: "It's not about a viral campaign for me. It's about a movement."

Burke's reaction to the 2017 meme makes an important point, one that was echoed in some of the responses Milano received and further elaborated by Jessi Hempel, the editorial director of Backchannel, in "The Problem with #metoo and Viral Outrage." Hempel says that "on its surface," #metoo has what looks to be the makings of an "earnest and effective social movement." But like Burke, Hempel wonders whether #metoo will actually have the power and longevity of a true social movement. She's concerned that while millions of people are weighing in, at last, on a long-ignored issue, the campaign may not culminate in real change:

> In truth, however, #MeToo is a too-perfect meme. It harnesses social media's mechanisms to drive users (that's you and me) into escalating states of outrage while exhausting us to the point where we cannot meaningfully act.

Hempel cites extensive research by Yale professor Molly Crockett that suggests that "digital technologies may be transforming the way we experience outrage, and limiting how much we can actually change social realities." In other words, expressing outrage online lets us talk the talk but not walk the walk of actual change.

In spite of these caveats, the work begun by Tarana Burke over a decade ago and given new urgency by Alyssa Milano has led to a series of high-profile firings, and some criminal convictions, in many sectors of society, from the Hollywood film industry (Weinstein's company had to declare bankruptcy) to New York's cultural scene (the Metropolitan Opera fired its conductor, James Levine) to Congress (Senator Al Franken was forced to resign his seat) to the world of sports (Olympics team doctor Larry Nassar was sentenced to 40 to 175 years in prison for assaulting as many as 160 women athletes). In short, it now looks as though #metoo does constitute a genuine movement that will continue to lead to actual, concrete changes in cultural attitudes and practices. Certainly, the argument over its effectiveness and reach will continue, much of it playing out on social media platforms.

As this example shows, arguments on social media occur on crowded, two-way channels, with claims and counterclaims whizzing by, fast and furious. Such tools reach audiences (like the 4.7 million who initially responded to #metoo) and they also create them, offering an innovative way to make and share arguments. Just as importantly, anyone, anywhere, with access to a phone, tablet, or other electronic device, can launch arguments that circle the globe in seconds. Social networking and digital tools are increasingly available to all—for better or for worse, as shown by the recent example of Facebook's allowing data from 50 million users to be used for political purposes.

Everything Is an Argument

As you know from your own experiences with social media, arguments are all around us, in every medium, in every genre, in everything we do. There may be an argument on the T-shirt you put on in the morning, in the sports column you read on the bus, in the prayers you utter before an exam, in the off-the-cuff political remarks of a teacher lecturing, on the bumper sticker on the car in front of you, in the assurances of a health center nurse that "This won't hurt one bit."

The clothes you wear, the foods you eat, and the groups you join make nuanced, sometimes unspoken assertions about who you are and what you value. So an argument can be any text—written, spoken, aural, or visual—that expresses a point of view. In fact, some theorists claim that language is inherently persuasive. When you say, "Hi, how's it going?" in one sense you're arguing that your hello deserves a response. Even humor makes an argument when it causes readers to recognize— through bursts of laughter or just a faint smile—how things are and how they might be different.

More obvious as arguments are those that make direct claims based on or drawn from evidence. Such writing often moves readers to recognize problems and to consider solutions. Persuasion of this kind is usually easy to recognize:

> The National Minimum Drinking Age Act, passed by Congress [in 1984], is a gross violation of civil liberties and must be repealed. It is absurd and unjust that young Americans can vote, marry, enter contracts, and serve in the military at 18 but cannot buy an alcoholic drink in a bar or restaurant.
>
> —Camille Paglia, "The Drinking Age Is Past Its Prime"

We will become a society of a million pictures without much memory, a society that looks forward every second to an immediate replication of what it has just done, but one that does not sustain the difficult labor of transmitting culture from one generation to the next.

—Christine Rosen, "The Image Culture"

RESPOND●

Can an argument really be any text that expresses a point of view? What kinds of arguments—if any—might be made by the following items?

a Golden State Warriors cap

Nike Air Zoom Pegasus 34

the "explicit lyrics" label on a best-selling rap CD

the health warnings on a package of cigarettes

a Tesla Model 3 electric car

a pair of Ray-Ban sunglasses

Why Read Arguments Critically and Rhetorically?

More than two millennia ago, Aristotle told students that they needed to know and understand and use the arts of rhetoric for two major reasons: to be able to get their ideas across effectively and persuasively and to protect themselves from being manipulated by others. Today, we need these abilities more than ever before: as we are inundated with "alternative facts," "fake news," mis- and disinformation, and often even outright lies, the ability to read between the lines, to become fact-checkers, to practice what media critic Howard Rheingold calls "crap detection" (see p. 459), and to read with careful attention are now survival skills.

Steve Nease

This need is so acute that new courses are springing up on college campuses, such as one at the University of Washington named (provocatively) "Calling Bullshit," which Professors Carl Bergstrom and Jevin West define as "language, statistical figures, graphics, and other forms of presentation intended to persuade by impressing and overwhelming a reader or listener with a blatant disregard for truth and logical coherence." (Search for "The Fine Art of Sniffing Out Crappy Science" on the Web.) These professors are particularly interested in the use of statistics and visual representation of data to misinform or confuse, and in showing how "big data" especially can often obscure rather than reveal valid claims, although they acknowledge the power of verbal misinformation as well.

You can practice self-defense against such misrepresentation by following some sound advice:

- Pay attention, *close* attention, to what you are reading or viewing. While it's tempting to skim, avoid the temptation, especially when the stakes are high. Keep focused on the text at hand, with your critical antenna up!
- Keep an eye out for "click bait," those subject lines or headings that scream "read me, read me" but usually lead to little information.
- Be skeptical. Check the author, publisher, sources: how reliable are they?
- Look for unstated assumptions behind claims—and question them.
- Distinguish between facts that have verifiable support and claims and those which may or may not be completely empty.
- Learn to triangulate: don't take the word of a single source but look for corroboration from other reliable sources.
- Become a fact checker! Get familiar with nonpartisan fact-checkers like Politifact, FactCheck.org, the Sunlight Foundation, and Snopes.com.

You will find additional information about reading attentively and critically throughout this book, especially in Chapters 6 and 19.

Why Listen to Arguments Rhetorically and Respectfully?

Rhetorician Krista Ratcliffe recommends that we all learn to listen rhetorically, which she defines as "a stance of openness" you can take in relation to any person, text, or culture. Taking such a stance is not easy, especially when emotions and disagreements run high, but doing so is a necessary step in understanding where other people are coming from and in acknowledging that our own stances are deeply influenced by forces we may not even be aware of. Even when we stand on the shoulders of giants, our view is limited and partial, and it's good to remember that this maxim is true for everyone.

Amid the extreme divisions in the United States today, amid the charges and countercharges, the ongoing attacks of one group on another, it's especially important to learn to listen to others, even others with whom we drastically disagree. Scholars and pundits alike have written about the "echo chambers" we often inhabit, especially online, where we hear only from people who think as we do, act as we act, believe as we believe. Such echo chambers are dangerous to a democracy. As a result, some are advocating for rhetorical listening. Oprah Winfrey, for example, brought together a group of women, half of whom supported Trump and half of whom supported Clinton, over "croissants and great jam." At first no one wanted to participate, but once Winfrey got them together and they started listening to one another's stories, the women began to find small patches of common ground. Listening openly and respectfully was the key. So it is with the website and app "Hi from the Other Side," where people can sign up to be paired with someone on another side of an issue, get guidance on how to begin a conversation, and eventually meet to pursue common ground and common interests (see https://www.hifromtheotherside.com for more information).

You can begin to practice rhetorical listening as you get to know people who differ from you on major issues, listening to their views carefully and respectfully, asking them for that same respect, and beginning to search for some common ground, no matter how small. Arguments are never won by going nowhere except "Yes I can"/"No you can't" over and over again, yet that's the way many arguments are conducted today. Learning to listen rhetorically and beginning to find some small commonality is usually a better way to argue constructively than plunging right in with accusations or dramatic claims.

Why We Make Arguments

As this discussion suggests, in the politically divided and entertainment-driven culture of the United States today, the word *argument* may well call up negative images: the hostile scowl, belligerent tweet, or shaking fist of a politician or news pundit who wants to drown out other voices and prevail at all costs. This winner-take-all view has a long history, but it often turns people off to the whole process of using reasoned conversation to identify, explore, and solve problems. Hoping to avoid perpetual standoffs with people on "the other side," many people now sidestep opportunities to speak their minds on issues shaping their lives and work. We want to counter this attitude throughout this book: we urge you to examine your values and beliefs, to understand where they come from, and to voice them clearly and cogently in arguments you make, all the while respecting the values and beliefs of others.

Some arguments, of course, *are* aimed at winning, especially those related to politics, business, and law. Two candidates for office, for example, vie for a majority of votes; the makers of one smartphone try to outsell their competitors by offering more features at a lower price; and two lawyers try to outwit each other in pleading to a judge and jury. In your college writing, you may also be called on to make arguments that appeal to a "judge" and "jury" (perhaps your instructor and classmates). You might, for instance, argue that students in every field should be required to engage in service learning projects. In doing so, you will need to offer better arguments or more convincing evidence than those with other perspectives—such as those who might regard service learning as a politicized or coercive form of education. You can do so reasonably and responsibly, no name-calling required.

There are many reasons to argue and principled ways to do so. We explore some of them in this section.

Arguments to Convince and Inform

We're stepping into an argument ourselves in drawing what we hope is a useful distinction between *convincing* and—in the next section—*persuading*. (Feel free to disagree with us!) Arguments to convince lead audiences to accept a claim as true or reasonable—based on information or evidence that seems factual and reliable; arguments to persuade then seek to move people beyond conviction to *action*. Academic arguments often combine both elements.

Many news reports and analyses, white papers, and academic articles aim to convince audiences by broadening what they know about a subject. Such fact-based arguments might have no motives beyond laying out what the facts are. Here's an opening paragraph from a 2014 news story by Anahad O'Connor in the *New York Times* that itself launched a thousand arguments (and lots of huzzahs) simply by reporting the results of a recent scientific study:

> Many of us have long been told that saturated fat, the type found in meat, butter and cheese, causes heart disease. But a large and exhaustive new analysis by a team of international scientists found no evidence that eating saturated fat increased heart attacks and other cardiac events.
> —Anahad O'Connor, "Study Questions Fat and Heart Disease Link"

Wow. You can imagine how carefully the reporter walked through the scientific data, knowing how this new information might be understood and repurposed by his readers.

Similarly, in a college paper on the viability of nuclear power as an alternative source of energy, you might compare the health and safety record of a nuclear plant to that of other forms of energy. Depending upon your findings and your interpretation of the data, the result of your fact-based presentation might be to raise or alleviate concerns readers have about nuclear energy. Of course, your decision to write the argument might be driven by your conviction that nuclear power is much safer than most people believe.

Today, images offer especially powerful arguments designed both to inform and to convince. For example, David Plunkert's cover art for the August 28, 2017, issue of the *New Yorker* is simple yet very striking.

David Plunkert/The New Yorker © Condé Nast

Plunkert, who doesn't often involve himself with political subjects, said he was prompted to do so in response to what he saw as President Trump's "weak pushback" against the hateful violence on exhibit in Charlottesville, Virginia, on August 11, 2017: "A picture does a better job showing my thoughts than words do; it can have a light touch on a subject that's extremely scary."

Arguments to Persuade

Today, climate change may be the public issue that best illustrates the chasm that sometimes separates conviction from persuasion. Although the weight of scientific research attests to the fact that the earth is warming and that humans are responsible for a good bit of that warming, convincing people to accept this evidence and persuading them to act on it still doesn't follow easily. How then does change occur? Some theorists suggest that persuasion—understood as moving people to do more than nod in agreement—is best achieved via appeals to emotions such as fear, anger, envy, pride, sympathy, or hope. We think that's an oversimplification. The fact is that persuasive arguments, whether in advertisements, political blogs, YouTube videos, tweets, or newspaper editorials, draw upon *all* the appeals of rhetoric (see p. 24) to motivate people to act— whether it be to buy a product, pull a lever for a candidate, or volunteer for a civic organization. Here, once again, is Camille Paglia driving home her argument that the 1984 federal law raising the drinking age in the United States to 21 was a catastrophic decision in need of reversal:

> What this cruel 1984 law did is deprive young people of safe spaces where they could happily drink cheap beer, socialize, chat, and flirt in a free but controlled public environment. Hence in the 1980s we immediately got the scourge of crude binge drinking at campus fraternity keg parties, cut off from the adult world. Women in that boorish free-for-all were suddenly fighting off date rape. Club drugs—Ecstasy, methamphetamine, ketamine (a veterinary tranquilizer)—surged at raves for teenagers and on the gay male circuit scene.

Paglia chooses to dramatize her argument by sharply contrasting a safer, more supportive past with a vastly more dangerous present when drinking was forced underground and young people turned to highly risky behaviors. She doesn't hesitate to name them either: binge drinking, club drugs, raves, and, most seriously, date rape. This highly rhetorical, one might say *emotional*, argument pushes readers hard to endorse a call for serious action—the repeal of the current drinking age law.

In the excerpt from his scholarly journal article, Scott O. Lilienfeld aims to persuade psychologists and other academics to put aside the term "microaggressions" because— though they may be offensive— these slights and insults aimed at minorities have not been proven to be psychologically harmful.

LINK TO P. 756

Admit it, Duchess of Cornwall. You *knew* abandoned dogs need homes, but it was heartrending photos on the Battersea Dogs & Cats Home Web site that *persuaded* you to visit the shelter.
WPA Pool/Getty Images

RESPOND•

Apply the distinction made here between convincing and persuading to the way people respond to two or three current political or social issues. Is there a useful distinction between being convinced and being persuaded? Explain your position.

Arguments to Make Decisions

Closely allied to arguments to convince and persuade are arguments to examine the options in important matters, both civil and personal—from managing out-of-control deficits to choosing careers. Arguments to make decisions occur all the time in the public arena, where they are often slow to evolve, caught up in electoral or legal squabbles, and yet driven by a genuine desire to find consensus. In recent years, for instance, Americans have argued hard to make decisions about health care, the civil rights of same-sex couples, and the status of more than 11 million undocumented immigrants in the country. Subjects so complex aren't debated in straight lines. They get haggled over in every imaginable medium by thousands of writers, politicians, and ordinary citizens working alone or via political organizations to have their ideas considered.

For college students, choosing a major can be an especially momentous personal decision, and one way to go about making that decision is to argue your way through several alternatives. By the time you've explored the pros and cons of each alternative, you should be a little closer to a reasonable and defensible decision.

Sometimes decisions, however, are not so easy to make.

Ed Fischer/CartoonStock.com

Arguments to Understand and Explore

Arguments to make decisions often begin as choices between opposing positions already set in stone. But is it possible to examine important issues in more open-ended ways? Many situations, again in civil or personal arenas, seem to call for arguments that genuinely explore possibilities without constraints or prejudices. If there's an "opponent" in such situations at all (often there is not), it's likely to be the status quo or a current trend which, for one reason or another, puzzles just about everyone. For example, in trying to sort through the extraordinary complexities of the 2011 budget debate, philosophy professor Gary Gutting was able to show how two distinguished economists—John Taylor and Paul Krugman—drew completely different conclusions from the exact same sets of facts. Exploring how such a thing could occur led Gutting to conclude that the two economists were arguing from the same facts, all right, but that they did not have *all* the facts possible. Those missing

In the excerpt from her professional report "Covering the Transgender Community," Sara Morrison explores how journalists are working to incorporate correct terminology, respect the preferred gender pronouns and identities of their transgender subjects, and address the issues that matter to transgender individuals.

LINK TO P. 580

or unknown facts allowed them to fill in the blanks as they could, thus leading them to different conclusions. By discovering the source of a paradox, Gutting potentially opened new avenues for understanding.

Exploratory arguments can also be personal, such as Zora Neale Hurston's ironic exploration of racism and of her own identity in the essay "How It Feels to Be Colored Me." If you keep a journal or blog, you have no doubt found yourself making arguments to explore issues near and dear to you. Perhaps the essential argument in any such piece is the writer's realization that a problem exists—and that the writer or reader needs to understand it and respond constructively to it if possible.

Explorations of ideas that begin by trying to understand another's perspective have been described as **invitational arguments** by researchers Sonja Foss, Cindy Griffin, and Josina Makau. Such arguments are interested in inviting others to join in mutual explorations of ideas based on discovery and respect. Another kind of argument, called **Rogerian argument** (after psychotherapist Carl Rogers), approaches audiences in similarly nonthreatening ways, finding common ground and establishing trust among those who disagree about issues. Writers who take a Rogerian approach try to see where the other person is coming from,

"You say it's a win–win, but what if you're wrong–wrong and it all goes bad–bad?"

The risks of Rogerian argument © David Sipress/The New Yorker Collection/The Cartoon Bank looking for "both/and" or "win/win" solutions whenever possible. (For more on Rogerian strategies, see Chapter 7.)

RESPOND•

What are your reasons for making arguments? Keep notes for two days about every single argument you make, using our broad definition to guide you. Then identify your reasons: How many times did you aim to convince? To inform? To persuade? To explore? To understand?

Occasions for Argument

In a fifth-century BCE textbook of **rhetoric** (the art of persuasion), the philosopher Aristotle provides an ingenious strategy for classifying arguments based on their perspective on time—past, future, and present. His ideas still help us to appreciate the role arguments play in society in the twenty-first century. As you consider Aristotle's occasions for argument, remember that all such classifications overlap (to a certain extent) and that we live in a world much different than his.

Arguments about the Past

Debates about what has happened in the past, what Aristotle called **forensic arguments**, are the red meat of government, courts, businesses, and academia. People want to know who did what in the past, for what reasons, and with what liability. When you argue a speeding ticket in court, you are making a forensic argument, claiming perhaps that you weren't over the limit or that the officer's radar was faulty. A judge will have to decide what exactly happened in the past in the unlikely case you push the issue that far.

In the aftermath of the 2016 election, many researchers both in and outside the government devoted themselves to trying to understand the effects of hacking on the election and, more specifically, the extent to which Russia was involved in such activities. Cybersecurity experts from agencies such as the CIA, FBI, and Homeland Security argued that they had extensive evidence to show that Russia had conducted a number of hacking expeditions and had manipulated messages on social media to try to disrupt the American elections. Others inside the Trump administration argued that the evidence wasn't convincing; the president even declared that it had been "made up." As this book goes to press, the argument over what happened is still raging. What hacks actually occurred in the run-up to the election? Which state voting procedures, if any, were violated? What part did the Russian government play? These are all forensic questions to be carefully investigated, argued, and answered by agencies and special counsels currently at work.

Some forensic arguments go on . . . and on and on. Consider, for example, the lingering arguments over Christopher Columbus's "discovery" of America. Are his expeditions cause for celebration or notably unhappy chapters in human history? Or some of both? Such

James B. Comey, former director of the FBI who was fired by President Trump, testifies before the Senate Intelligence Committee on June 8, 2017. Chip Somodevilla/Getty Images

arguments about past actions—heated enough to spill over into the public realm—are common in disciplines such as history, philosophy, and ethics.

Arguments about the Future

Debates about what will or should happen in the future—**deliberative arguments**—often influence policies or legislation for the future. *Should local or state governments allow or even encourage the use of self-driving cars on public roads? Should colleges and universities lend support to more dual-credit programs so that students can earn college credits while still in high school? Should coal-fired power plants be phased out of our energy grid?* These are the sorts of deliberative questions that legislatures, committees, or school boards routinely address when making laws or establishing policies.

But arguments about the future can also be speculative, advancing by means of projections and reasoned guesses, as shown in the following passage from an essay by media analyst Marc Prensky. He argues that while professors and colleges will always be responsible for teaching students to learn from the knowledge provided by print texts, it's about time for some college or university to be the first to ban physical, that is to say *paper*, books on its campus, a controversial proposal to say the least:

> So, as counterintuitive as it may sound, eliminating physical books from college campuses would be a positive step for our 21st-century students, and, I believe, for 21st-century scholarship as well. Academics, researchers, and particularly teachers need to move to the tools of the future. Artifacts belong in museums, not in our institutions of higher learning.
>
> —Marc Prensky, "In the 21st-Century University, Let's Ban Books"

Arguments about the Present

Arguments about the present—what Aristotle terms **epideictic** or **ceremonial arguments**—explore the current values of a society, affirming or challenging its widely shared beliefs and core assumptions. Epideictic arguments are often made at public and formal events such as inaugural addresses, sermons, eulogies, memorials, and graduation

In his 2016 blog post at Tedium, Ernie Smith argues that the plural pronoun *they* will and should continue to be used to represent a subject in a gender-neutral way, even though it defies conventional grammar.

LINK TO P. 650

speeches. Members of the audience listen carefully as credible speakers share their wisdom. For example, as the selection of college commencement speakers has grown increasingly contentious, Ruth J. Simmons, the first African American woman to head an Ivy League college, used the opportunity of such an address (herself standing in for a rejected speaker) to offer a timely and ringing endorsement of free speech. Her words perfectly illustrate epideictic rhetoric:

> Universities have a special obligation to protect free speech, open discourse and the value of protest. The collision of views and ideologies is in the DNA of the academic enterprise. No collision avoidance technology is needed here. The noise from this discord may cause others to criticize the legitimacy of the academic enterprise, but how can knowledge advance without the questions that overturn misconceptions, push further into previously impenetrable areas of inquiry and assure us stunning breakthroughs in human knowledge? If there is anything that colleges must encourage and protect it is the persistent questioning of the status quo. Our health as a nation, our health as women, our health as an industry requires it.
>
> —Ruth J. Simmons, Smith College, 2014

Perhaps more common than Smith's impassioned address are values arguments that examine contemporary culture, praising what's admirable and blaming what's not. In the following argument, student Latisha Chisholm looks at the state of rap music after Tupac Shakur:

> With the death of Tupac, not only did one of the most intriguing rap rivalries of all time die, but the motivation for rapping seems to have changed. Where money had always been a plus, now it is obviously more important than wanting to express the hardships of Black communities. With current rappers, the positive power that came from the desire to represent Black people is lost. One of the biggest rappers now got his big break while talking about sneakers. Others announce retirement without really having done much for the soul or for Black people's morale. I equate new rappers to NFL players that don't love the game anymore. They're only in it for the money. . . . It looks like the voice of a people has lost its heart.
>
> —Latisha Chisholm, "Has Rap Lost Its Soul?"

As in many ceremonial arguments, Chisholm here reinforces common values such as representing one's community honorably and fairly.

Are rappers since Tupac—like Jay Z—only in it for the money? Many epideictic arguments either praise or blame contemporary culture in this way. Michael N. Todaro/Getty Images

RESPOND•

In a recent magazine, newspaper, or blog, find three editorials—one that makes a forensic argument, one a deliberative argument, and one a ceremonial argument. Analyze the arguments by asking these questions: Who is arguing? What purposes are the writers trying to achieve? To whom are they directing their arguments? Then decide whether the arguments' purposes have been achieved and how you know.

Occasions for Argument

	Past	*Future*	*Present*
What is it called?	Forensic	Deliberative	Epideictic
What are its concerns?	What happened in the past?	What should be done in the future?	Who or what deserves praise or blame?
What does it look like?	Court decisions, legal briefs, legislative hearings, investigative reports, academic studies	White papers, proposals, bills, regulations, mandates	Eulogies, graduation speeches, inaugural addresses, roasts

Kinds of Argument

Yet another way of categorizing arguments is to consider their status or stasis—that is, the specific *kinds of issues they address*. This approach, called **stasis theory**, was used in ancient Greek and Roman civilizations to provide questions designed to help citizens and lawyers work their way through legal cases. The status questions were posed in sequence because each depended on answers from the preceding ones. Together, the queries helped determine the point of contention in an argument—where the parties disagreed or what exactly had to be proven. A modern version of those questions might look like the following:

- Did something happen?
- What is its nature?
- What is its quality or cause?
- What actions should be taken?

Each stasis question explores a different aspect of a problem and uses different evidence or techniques to reach conclusions. You can use these questions to explore the aspects of any topic you're considering. You'll discover that we use the stasis issues to define key types of argument in Part 2.

Did Something Happen? Arguments of Fact

There's no point in arguing a case until its basic facts are established. So an **argument of fact** usually involves a statement that can be proved or disproved with specific evidence or testimony. For example, the question of pollution of the oceans—is it really occurring?—might seem relatively easy to settle. Either scientific data prove that the oceans are being dirtied as a result of human activity, or they don't. But to settle the matter, writers and readers need to ask a number of other questions about the "facts":

- Where did the facts come from?
- Are they reliable?
- Is there a problem with the facts?
- Where did the problem begin and what caused it?

For more on arguments based on facts, see Chapters 4 and 8.

What Is the Nature of the Thing? Arguments of Definition

Some of the most hotly debated issues in American life today involve questions of definition: we argue over the nature of the human fetus, the meaning of "amnesty" for immigrants, the boundaries of sexual assault. As you might guess, issues of definition have mighty consequences, and decades of debate may nonetheless leave the matter unresolved. Here, for example, is how one type of sexual assault is defined in an important 2007 report submitted to the U.S. Department of Justice by the National Institute of Justice:

> We consider as incapacitated sexual assault any unwanted sexual contact occurring when a victim is unable to provide consent or stop what is happening because she is passed out, drugged, drunk, incapacitated, or asleep, regardless of whether the perpetrator was responsible for her substance use or whether substances were administered without her knowledge. We break down incapacitated sexual assault into four subtypes. . . .
> —"The Campus Sexual Assault (CSA) Study: Final Report"

The specifications of the definition go on for another two hundred words, each of consequence in determining how sexual assault on college campuses might be understood, measured, and addressed.

Of course many **arguments of definition** are less weighty than this, though still hotly contested: Is playing video games a sport? Can Batman be a tragic figure? Is LeBron James a hero for our age? (For more about arguments of definition, see Chapter 9.)

What Is the Quality or Cause of the Thing? Arguments of Evaluation

Arguments of evaluation present criteria and then measure individual people, ideas, or things against those standards. For instance, a 2017 article in the *Atlantic* examined "How Pixar Lost Its Way," arguing that "The golden age of Pixar is over." Chronicling the company's success from the first *Toy Story* (1995), the writer identifies what Pixar accomplished so well:

> The theme that the studio mined with greatest success during its first decade and a half was parenthood, whether real (*Finding Nemo*, *The Incredibles*) or implicit (*Monsters, Inc.*, *Up*). Pixar's distinctive insight into parent-child relations stood out from the start, in *Toy Story*, and lost none of its power in two innovative and unified sequels.
>
> —Christopher Orr, "How Pixar Lost Its Way"

As we read this article, we are bound to ask what happened: why and how did Pixar lose its way? And Christopher Orr probes further, suggesting that the sale of Pixar to Disney and the dependence on sequel after sequel led to the downturn. As he concludes his analysis of Pixar's evolution, Orr distressingly notes the announcement of plans for *Toy Story* 4, which unravels the trilogy's neat arc.

Zohar Lazar

Although evaluations differ from causal analyses, in practice the boundaries between stasis questions are often porous: particular arguments have a way of defining their own issues.

For much more about arguments of evaluation, see Chapter 10; for causal arguments, see Chapter 11.

What Actions Should Be Taken? Proposal Arguments

After facts in a controversy have been confirmed, definitions agreed on, evaluations made, and causes traced, it may be time for a **proposal argument** answering the question *Now, what do we do about all this?* For example, in developing an argument about out-of-control student fees at your college, you might use all the prior stasis questions to study the issue and determine exactly how much and for what reasons these costs are escalating. Only then will you be prepared to offer knowledgeable suggestions for action. In examining a nationwide move to eliminate remedial education in four-year colleges, John Cloud offers a notably moderate proposal to address the problem:

> Students age twenty-two and over account for 43 percent of those in remedial classrooms, according to the National Center for Developmental Education. . . . [But] 55 percent of those needing remediation must take just one course. Is it too much to ask them to pay extra for that class or take it at a community college?
> —John Cloud, "Who's Ready for College?"

For more about proposal arguments, see Chapter 12.

The No Child Left Behind Act was signed in 2002 with great hopes and bipartisan support, but it did not lead to the successes those proposing it had hoped for.
TIM SLOAN/Getty Images

STASIS QUESTIONS AT WORK

Suppose you have an opportunity to speak at a student conference on the impact of climate change. You are tentatively in favor of strengthening industrial pollution standards aimed at reducing global warming trends. But to learn more about the issue, you use the stasis questions to get started.

- **Did something happen?** Does global warming exist? *Maybe not*, say many in the oil and gas industry; at best, evidence for global warming is inconclusive. *Yes*, say most scientists and governments; climate change is real and even seems to be accelerating. To come to your conclusion, you'll weigh the facts carefully and identify problems with opposing arguments.

- **What is the nature of the thing?** Skeptics define climate change as a naturally occurring event; most scientists base their definitions on change due to human causes. You look at each definition carefully: *How do the definitions foster the goals of each group? What's at stake for each group in defining it that way?*

- **What is the quality or cause of the thing?** Exploring the differing assessments of damage done by climate change leads you to ask who will gain from such analysis: *Do oil executives want to protect their investments? Do scientists want government money for grants? Where does evidence for the dangers of global warming come from? Who benefits if the dangers are accepted as real and present, and who loses?*

- **What actions should be taken?** If climate change is occurring naturally or causing little harm, then arguably *nothing* needs to be or can be done. But if it is caused mainly by human activity and dangers, action is definitely called for (although not everyone may agree on what such action should be). As you investigate the proposals being made and the reasons behind them, you come closer to developing your own argument.

Appealing to Audiences

Exploring all the occasions and kinds of arguments available will lead you to think about the audience(s) you are addressing and the specific ways you can appeal to them. Audiences for arguments today are amazingly diverse, from the flesh-and-blood person sitting across a desk when you negotiate a student loan to your "friends" on social media, to the "ideal" reader you imagine for whatever you are writing, to the unknown people around the world who may read a blog you have posted. The figure below suggests just how many dimensions an audience can have as writers and readers negotiate their relationships with a text, whether it be oral, written, or digital.

As you see there, texts usually have **intended readers**, the people writers hope and expect to address—let's say, routine browsers of a newspaper's op-ed page. But writers also shape the responses of these actual readers in ways they imagine as appropriate or desirable—for example, maneuvering readers of editorials into making focused and knowledgeable judgments about politics and culture. Such audiences, as imagined and fashioned by writers within their texts, are called **invoked readers**.

Readers and writers in context

Making matters even more complicated, readers can respond to writers' maneuvers by choosing to join the invoked audiences, to resist them, or maybe even to ignore them. Arguments may also attract "real" readers from groups not among those that writers originally imagined or expected to reach. You may post something on the Web, for instance, and discover that people you did not intend to address are commenting on it. (For them, the experience may be like reading private email intended for someone else: they find themselves drawn to and fascinated by your ideas!) As authors of this book, we think about students like you whenever we write: you are our intended readers. But notice how in dozens of ways, from the images we choose to the tone of our language, we also invoke an audience of people who take writing arguments seriously. We want you to become that kind of reader.

So audiences are *very* complicated and subtle and challenging, and yet you somehow have to attract and even persuade them. As always, Aristotle offers an answer. He identified three time-tested appeals that speakers and writers can use to reach almost any audience, labeling them *pathos*, *ethos*, and *logos*—strategies as effective today as they were in ancient times, though we usually think of them in slightly different terms. Used in the right way and deployed at the right moment, emotional, ethical, and logical appeals have enormous power, as we'll see in subsequent chapters.

RESPOND●

You can probably provide concise descriptions of the intended audience for most textbooks you have encountered. But can you detect their invoked audiences—that is, the way their authors are imagining (and perhaps shaping) the readers they would like to have? Carefully review this entire first chapter, looking for signals and strategies that might identify the audience and readers invoked by the authors of *Everything's an Argument*.

Emotional Appeals: Pathos

Emotional appeals, or **pathos**, generate emotions (fear, pity, love, anger, jealousy) that the writer hopes will lead the audience to accept a claim. Here is an alarming sentence from a book by Barry B. LePatner arguing that Americans need to make hard decisions about repairing the country's failing infrastructure:

> When the I-35W Bridge in Minneapolis shuddered, buckled, and collapsed during the evening rush hour on Wednesday, August 1, 2007, plunging 111 vehicles into the Mississippi River and sending thirteen people to their deaths, the sudden, apparently inexplicable nature of the event at first gave the appearance of an act of God.
>
> —*Too Big to Fall: America's Failing Infrastructure and the Way Forward*

If you ever drive across a bridge, LePatner has probably gotten your attention. His sober and yet descriptive language helps readers imagine the dire consequence of neglected road maintenance and bad design decisions. Making an emotional appeal like this can dramatize an issue and sometimes even create a bond between writer and readers. (For more about emotional appeals, see Chapter 2.)

Ethical Appeals: Ethos

When writers or speakers come across as trustworthy, audiences are likely to listen to and accept their arguments. That trustworthiness (along with fairness and respect) is a mark of **ethos**, or credibility. Showing that you know what you are talking about exerts an ethical appeal, as does emphasizing that you share values with and respect your audience. Once again, here's Barry LePatner from *Too Big to Fall*, shoring up his authority for writing about problems with America's roads and bridges by invoking the ethos of people even more credible:

> For those who would seek to dismiss the facts that support the thesis of this book, I ask them to consult the many professional engineers in state transportation departments who face these problems on a daily basis. These professionals understand the physics of bridge and road design, and the real problems of ignoring what happens to steel and concrete when they are exposed to the elements without a strict regimen of ongoing maintenance.

It's a sound rhetorical move to enhance credibility this way. For more about ethical appeals, see Chapter 3.

Logical Appeals: Logos

Appeals to logic, or **logos**, are often given prominence and authority in U.S. culture: "Just the facts, ma'am," a famous early TV detective on *Dragnet* used to say. Indeed, audiences respond well to the use of reasons and evidence—to the presentation of facts, statistics, credible testimony, cogent examples, or even a narrative or story that embodies a sound reason in support of an argument. Following almost two hundred pages of facts, statistics, case studies, and arguments about the sad state of American bridges, LePatner can offer this sober, logical, and inevitable conclusion:

> We can no longer afford to ignore the fact that we are in the midst of a transportation funding crisis, which has been exacerbated by an even larger and longer-term problem: how we choose to invest in our infrastructure. It is not difficult to imagine the serious consequences that will unfold if we fail to address the deplorable conditions of our

bridges and roads, including the increasingly higher costs we will pay for goods and services that rely on that transportation network, and a concomitant reduction in our standard of living.

For more about logical appeals, see Chapter 4.

Bringing It Home: *Kairos* and the Rhetorical Situation

In Greek mythology, Kairos—the youngest son of Zeus—was the god of opportunity. He is most often depicted as running, and his most unusual characteristic is a shock of hair on his forehead. As Kairos dashes by, you have a chance to seize that lock of hair, thereby seizing the opportune moment; once he passes you by, however, you've missed your chance.

Time as Occasion (Kairos) by Italian Renaissance painter Francesco de' Rossi Heritage Images/Getty Images

Kairos is also a term used to describe the most suitable time and place for making an argument and the most opportune ways of expressing it. It is easy to point to rhetorical moments, when speakers find exactly the right words to stir—and stir up—an audience: Franklin Roosevelt's "We have nothing to fear but fear itself," Ronald Reagan's "Mr. Gorbachev, tear down this wall," and of course Martin Luther King Jr.'s majestic "I have a dream. . . ." But *kairos* matters just as much in less dramatic situations, whenever speakers or writers must size up the core elements of a rhetorical situation to decide how best to make their expertise and ethos work for a particular message aimed at a specific audience. The diagram below hints at the dynamic complexity of the rhetorical situation.

But rhetorical situations are embedded in contexts of enormous social complexity. The moment you find a subject, you inherit all the knowledge, history, culture, and technological significations that surround it. To lesser and greater degrees (depending on the subject), you also bring personal circumstances into the field—perhaps your gender, your race, your religion, your economic class, your habits of language. And all those issues weigh also upon the people you write to and for.

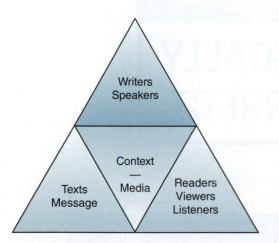

The rhetorical situation

So considering your rhetorical situation calls on you to think hard about the notion of *kairos*. Being aware of your rhetorical moment means being able to understand and take advantage of dynamic, shifting circumstances and to choose the best (most timely) proofs and evidence for a particular place, situation, and audience. It means seizing moments and enjoying opportunities, not being overwhelmed by them. Doing so might even lead you to challenge the title of this text: is everything an argument?

That's what makes writing arguments exciting.

RESPOND•

Take a look at the bumper sticker below, and then analyze it. What is its purpose? What kind of argument is it? Which of the stasis questions does it most appropriately respond to? To what audiences does it appeal? What appeals does it make and how?

filo/Getty Images

CULTURAL CONTEXTS FOR ARGUMENT

Considering What's "Normal"

If you want to communicate effectively with people across cultures, then learn about the traditions in those cultures and examine the norms guiding your own behavior:

- Explore your assumptions! Most of us regard our ways of thinking as "normal" or "right." Such assumptions guide our judgments about what works in persuasive situations. But just because it may seem natural to speak bluntly in arguments, consider that others may find such aggression startling or even alarming.

- Remember: ways of arguing differ widely across cultures. Pay attention to how people from groups or cultures other than your own argue, and be sensitive to different paths of thinking you'll encounter as well as to differences in language.

- Don't assume that all people share your cultural values, ethical principles, or political assumptions. People across the world have different ways of defining *family*, *work*, or *happiness*. As you present arguments to them, consider that they may be content with their different ways of organizing their lives and societies.

- Respect the differences among individuals *within* a given group. Don't expect that every member of a community behaves—or argues—in the same way or shares the same beliefs. Avoid thinking, for instance, that there is a single Asian, African, or Hispanic culture or that Europeans are any less diverse or more predictable than Americans or Canadians in their thinking. In other words, be skeptical of stereotypes.

2
Arguments Based on Emotion: Pathos

LEFT TO RIGHT: Piyaset/Shutterstock; Jan Martin Will/Shutterstock; Blueguy/Shutterstock

Emotional appeals (*appeals to pathos*) are powerful tools for influencing what people think and believe. We all make decisions—even including the most important ones—based on our feelings. That's what many environmental advocates are counting on when they use images like those above to warn of the catastrophic effects of global warming on the earth and its peoples. The first image shows a boy and his boat on what used to be a lake but is now cracked dry earth; the second, a polar bear stranded on a small ice floe as the oceans rise around it; and the third, a graphic design of a melting earth.

Of course, some people don't believe the warnings about climate change, arguing instead that they represent a hoax and that even if the climate is changing, it is not a result of human activities. And, as we would expect, this opposite side of the argument also uses emotionally persuasive images, like the following one from American Patriot, a news commentary YouTube channel.

EXPOSED!

The arguments packed into these four images all appeal to emotion, and research has shown us that we often make decisions based on just such appeals. So when you hear that formal or academic arguments should rely solely on facts to convince us, remember that facts alone often won't carry the day, even for a worthy cause. The largely successful case made for same-sex marriage provides a notable example of a movement that persuaded people equally by virtue of the reasonableness and the passion of its claims. Like many political and social debates, though, the issue provoked powerful emotions on every side—feelings that sometimes led to extreme words and tactics.

Recent research also shows that images that evoke fear are less effective than those that arouse interest, worry, or hope. When the Yale Center for Climate Change Communication asked both supporters and deniers of climate change what they felt when they thought about this topic, they got the following results:

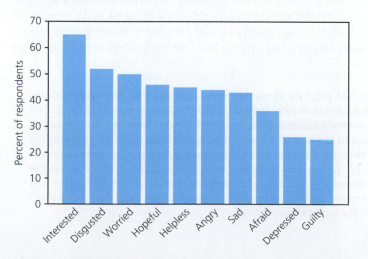

Yale Center for Climate Change Communication

In spite of the findings from such research, we don't have to look hard for arguments that appeal to fear, hatred, envy, and greed, or for campaigns intended to drive wedges between economic or social groups, making them fearful or resentful. For that reason alone, writers should not use emotional appeals rashly or casually. But used carefully and ethically, appeals to emotions—especially ones like worry or hope—can be very helpful in moving an audience to action. (For more about emotional fallacies, see p. 8.)

Reading Critically for Pathos

On February 24, 2014, Senator Tom Harkin of Iowa, fresh from two fact-finding trips to Cuba, described his experiences on the Senate floor in a speech praising that island nation's accomplishments in health care and education and urging a normalization of Cuban–American relationships, a recommendation taken up by then-President Obama and Cuban President Raul Castro, who announced on December 17, 2014, that such normalization would begin. Many in the United States applauded this move, but others, including many Cuban Americans in the Miami area, objected strenuously. Florida senator Marco Rubio was one of those speaking most passionately against normalization of relationships. Shortly after Senator Harkin's talk about the "fascinating" socialist experiment ninety miles from the coast of the United States, Rubio delivered a fifteen-minute rejoinder to Harkin without a script or teleprompter. After a sarcastic taunt ("Sounded like he had a wonderful trip visiting what he described as a real paradise"), Rubio quickly turned serious, even angry, as he offered his take on the country Harkin had toured:

> I heard him also talk about these great doctors that they have in Cuba. I have no doubt they're very talented. I've met a bunch of them. You know where I met them? In the United States because they defected. Because in Cuba, doctors would rather drive a taxi cab or work in a hotel than be a doctor. I wonder if they spoke to him about the outbreak of cholera that they've been unable to control, or about the three-tiered system of health care that exists where foreigners and government officials get health care much better than that that's available to the general population.

Language this heated and pointed has risks, especially when a young legislator is taking on a far more experienced colleague. But Rubio, the son of Cuban immigrants, isn't shy about allowing his feelings to show: in the following passage, he uses the kind of emotion-stirring verbal repetition common in oratory to drive home his major concern about Cuba, its influence on other nations:

> Let me tell you what the Cubans are really good at, because they don't know how to run their economy, they don't know how to build, they don't know how to govern a people. What they are really good at is repression. What they are really good at is shutting off information to the Internet and to radio and television and social media. That's what they're really good at. And they're not just good at it domestically, they're good exporters of these things.

When the Obama administration indeed loosened restrictions on travel to Cuba and began establishing diplomatic relations, Rubio stuck to his guns, consistently and emotionally arguing against this move. And while he was a bitter primary campaign rival of Donald Trump, who ridiculed Rubio during the campaign as "little Marco" who was always sweating ("It looked like he had just jumped into a swimming pool with his clothes on"), once Trump was elected president Rubio continued his

Senator Rubio with President Trump Lynne Sladky/AP Images

impassioned campaign to reverse policy on Cuba. So in June 2017, when President Trump announced tightening of restrictions on travel to Cuba and other changes to the Obama policy, Rubio spoke glowingly of the president, saying that "A year and a half ago, an American president landed in Havana and outstretched his hand to a regime. Today, a new president lands in Miami to reach out his hand to the people of Cuba." It's likely that we have not heard the end of this debate, and that we will continue to hear emotion-filled arguments on all sides of this contentious issue.

RESPOND•

Working with a classmate, find a speech or a print editorial that you think uses emotional appeals effectively but sparingly, in an understated way. Make a list of those appeals and briefly explain how each one appeals to an audience. What difference would it have made if the emotional appeals had been presented more forcefully and dramatically? Would doing so have been likely to appeal more strongly to the audience—and why or why not? What is at stake for the writer or speaker in such situations, in terms of credibility and ethos? What are the advantages of evoking emotions in support of your claims or ideas?

Using Emotions to Build Bridges

You may sometimes want to use emotions to connect with readers to assure them that you understand their experiences or "feel their pain," to borrow a sentiment popularized by President Bill Clinton. Such a bridge is especially important when you're writing about matters that readers regard as sensitive. Before they'll trust you, they'll want assurances that you understand the issues in depth. If you strike the right emotional note, you'll establish an important connection. That's what Apple founder Steve Jobs does in a much-admired 2005 commencement address in which he tells the audience that he doesn't have a fancy speech, just three stories from his life:

> My second story is about love and loss. I was lucky. I found what I loved to do early in life. Woz [Steve Wozniak] and I started Apple in my parents' garage when I was twenty. We worked hard and in ten

years, Apple had grown from just the two of us in a garage into a $2 billion company with over four thousand employees. We'd just released our finest creation, the Macintosh, a year earlier, and I'd just turned thirty, and then I got fired. How can you get fired from a company you started? Well, as Apple grew, we hired someone who I thought was very talented to run the company with me, and for the first year or so, things went well. But then our visions of the future began to diverge, and eventually we had a falling out. When we did, our board of directors sided with him, and so at thirty, I was out, and very publicly out. . . .

I didn't see it then, but it turned out that getting fired from Apple was the best thing that could have ever happened to me. The heaviness of being successful was replaced by the lightness of being a beginner again, less sure about everything. It freed me to enter one of the most creative periods in my life. During the next five years I started a company named NeXT, another company named Pixar and fell in love with an amazing woman who would become my wife. Pixar went on to create the world's first computer-animated feature film, *Toy Story*, and is now the most successful animation studio in the world.

—Steve Jobs, "You've Got to Find What You Love, Jobs Says"

In no obvious way is Jobs's recollection a formal argument. But it prepares his audience to accept the advice he'll give later in his speech, at least partly because he's speaking from meaningful personal experiences.

A more obvious way to build an emotional tie is simply to help readers identify with your experiences. If, like Georgina Kleege, you were blind and wanted to argue for more sensible attitudes toward blind people, you might ask readers in the first paragraph of your argument to confront their prejudices. Here Kleege, a writer and college instructor who in July 2017 was featured on PBS's "Brief but Spectacular" video series, makes an emotional point by telling a story:

I tell the class, "I am legally blind." There is a pause, a collective intake of breath. I feel them look away uncertainly and then look back. After all, I just said I couldn't see. Or did I? I had managed to get there on my own—no cane, no dog, none of the usual trappings of blindness. Eyeing me askance now, they might detect that my gaze is not quite focused. . . . They watch me glance down, or towards the door where someone's coming in late. I'm just like anyone else.

—Georgina Kleege, "Call It Blindness"

Alexandra Dal's cartoon "Questions" offers insight into what it feels like to be on the receiving end of racial microaggressions on a regular basis.

LINK TO P. 753

Given the way she narrates the first day of class, readers are as likely to identify with the students as with Kleege, imagining themselves sitting in a classroom, facing a sightless instructor, confronting their own prejudices about the blind. Kleege wants to put her audience on the edge emotionally.

Let's consider another rhetorical situation: how do you win over an audience when the logical claims that you're making are likely to go against what many in the audience believe? Once again, a slightly risky appeal to emotions on a personal level may work. That's the tack that Michael Pollan takes in bringing readers to consider that "the great moral struggle of our time will be for the rights of animals." In introducing his lengthy exploratory argument, Pollan uses personal experience to appeal to his audience:

> The first time I opened Peter Singer's *Animal Liberation*, I was dining alone at the Palm, trying to enjoy a rib-eye steak cooked medium-rare. If this sounds like a good recipe for cognitive dissonance (if not indigestion), that was sort of the idea. Preposterous as it might seem to supporters of animal rights, what I was doing was tantamount to reading *Uncle Tom's Cabin* on a plantation in the Deep South in 1852.
>
> —Michael Pollan, "An Animal's Place"

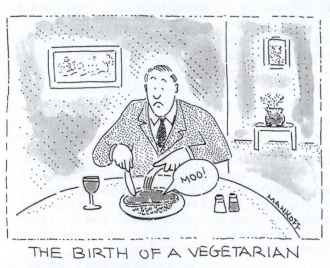

THE BIRTH OF A VEGETARIAN

A visual version of Michael Pollan's rhetorical situation
© Robert Mankoff

In creating a vivid image of his first encounter with Singer's book, Pollan's opening builds a bridge between himself as a person trying to enter into the animal rights debate in a fair and open-minded, if still skeptical, way and readers who might be passionate about either side of this argument.

Using Emotions to Sustain an Argument

You can also use emotional appeals to make logical claims stronger or more memorable. In a TV political attack ad, a video clip of a scowling, blustering candidate talking dismissively about an important issue has the potential to damage that candidate considerably. In contrast, a human face smiling or showing honest emotion can sell just about any product—that's why so many political figures now routinely smile at any camera they see. Using emotion is tricky, however, and it can sometimes backfire. Lay on too much feeling—especially sentiments like outrage, pity, or shame, which make people uncomfortable—and you may offend the very audiences you hoped to convince.

Still, strong emotions can add energy to a passage or an entire argument, as they do in Richard Lloyd Parry's *Ghosts of the Tsunami: Death and Life in Japan's Disaster Zone.* In this passage, Parry describes in vivid detail the scene that greeted one mother the day the 2011 earthquake hit:

> On the near side was Hitomi's home village of Magaki and then an expanse of paddies stretching to the Fuji lake; the polished blue and red roofs of other hamlets glittered at the edges of the hills. It was an archetypal view of the Japanese countryside: abundant nature, tamed and cultivated by man. But now she struggled to make sense of what she saw.
>
> Everything up to and in between the hills was water. There was only water: buildings and fields had gone. The water was black in the early light; floating on it were continents and trailing archipelagos of dark scummy rubble, brown in color and composed of tree trunks. Every patch of land that was not elevated had been absorbed by the river, which had been annexed in turn by the sea.
>
> In this new geography, the Fuji lake was no longer a lake. . . . The river was no longer a river. . . . Okawa Elementary School was invisible, hidden from view by the great shoulder of hills from which Hitomi looked down. But the road, the houses, and Magaki,

where Hitomi's home and family had been, were washed from the earth.

A wrecked car lies submerged in floodwaters after the earthquake and tsunami in Fukushima prefecture, Japan.
AP Photo/Wally Santana

As this example suggests, it can be difficult to gauge how much emotion will work in a given argument. Some issues—such as racism, immigration, abortion, and gun control—provoke strong feelings and, as a result, are often argued on emotional terms. But even issues that seem deadly dull—such as reform of federal student loan programs—can be argued passionately when proposed changes in these programs are set in human terms: reduce support for college loans and Kai, Riley, and Jayden end up in dead-end, low-paying jobs; don't reform the program and we're looking at another Wall Street–sized loan bailout and subsequent recession. Both alternatives might scare people into paying enough attention to take political action.

Using Humor

Humor has always played an important role in argument, sometimes as the sugar that makes the medicine go down. You can slip humor into an argument to put readers at ease, thereby making them more open to a proposal you have to offer. It's hard to say *no* when you're laughing.

Humor also makes otherwise sober people suspend their judgment and even their prejudices, perhaps because the surprise and naughtiness of wit are combustive: they provoke laughter or smiles, not reflection. Who can resist a no-holds-barred attack on a famous personality, such as this assessment of model/actor Cara Delevingne in the 2017 sci-fi flop *Valerian*:

> As played by model Cara Delevingne with a smirk that just won't quit, Laureline is way ballsier than Valerian, who still looks in need of a mother's love. She can pose and preen like an expert in her space gear—and those eyebrows!—but there's no there there.
>
> —Peter Travers, in *Rolling Stone*

Humor deployed cleverly may be why TV shows like *South Park* and *Modern Family* became popular with mainstream audiences, despite their willingness to explore controversial themes. Similarly, it's possible to make a point through humor that might not work that well in more academic writing. The subject of standardized testing, for instance, has generated much heat and light, as researchers and teachers and policy makers argue endlessly over whether it is helpful—or not. TV talk show host and satirist John Oliver took a crack at the subject in a segment of *Last Week Tonight*, arguing that the testing business in America has gotten way out of hand and that it does not help students but rather funnels money into the coffers of companies such as Pearson, who dominate the testing market.

Frederick M. Brown/Getty Images

After introducing the subject, Oliver goes on one of his signature humorous rampages, skewering the country's obsession with testing:

> Look, standardized tests are the fastest way to terrify any child with five letters outside of just whispering the word "clown."

After showing a video clip of kids rapping about the joys of testing, Oliver continues:

> Standardized tests look like amazing fun. I wish I could take one right now: bring me a pencil please—a number 2 pencil! But it just gets better, because an elementary school in Texas even held a test-themed pep rally featuring a monkey mascot.

Fade to a monkey cavorting around the auditorium stage, swooning over testing fun and yelling "here comes the monkey." Then after a video clip showing teachers describing how many students get physically sick while taking tests ("Something is wrong with our system when we just assume that a certain number of kids will vomit"), Oliver asks,

> Is it any wonder that students are sick of tests? . . . If standardized tests are bad for teachers and bad for kids, who exactly are they good for? Well, it turns out, they're operated by companies like Pearson, who control forty percent of the testing market.

Pearson, Oliver says, is

> the equivalent of Time Warner Cable: either you never had an interaction with them and don't care, or they ruined your [entire] life.

Viewers may not agree with Oliver's claims about standardized testing, but his use of humor and satire certainly gets him a large viewing audience and keeps them listening to the end.

A writer or speaker can even use humor to deal with sensitive issues. For example, sports commentator Bob Costas, given the honor of eulogizing the great baseball player Mickey Mantle, couldn't ignore problems in Mantle's life. So he argues for Mantle's greatness by admitting the man's weaknesses indirectly through humor:

> It brings to mind a story Mickey liked to tell on himself and maybe some of you have heard it. He pictured himself at the pearly gates, met by St. Peter, who shook his head and said, "Mick, we checked the record. We know some of what went on. Sorry, we can't let you in.

But before you go, God wants to know if you'd sign these six dozen baseballs."

—Bob Costas, "Eulogy for Mickey Mantle"

Similarly, politicians may use humor to deal with issues they couldn't acknowledge in any other way. Here, for example, is former president George W. Bush at the 2004 Radio and TV Correspondents' Dinner discussing his much-mocked intellect:

Those stories about my intellectual capacity do get under my skin. You know, for a while I even thought my staff believed it. There on my schedule first thing every morning it said, "Intelligence briefing."

—George W. Bush

Not all humor is well-intentioned or barb-free. In fact, among the most powerful forms of emotional argument is ridicule—humor aimed at a particular target. Eighteenth-century poet and critic Samuel Johnson was known for his stinging and humorous put-downs, such as this comment to an aspiring writer: "Your manuscript is both good and original, but the part that is good is not original and the part that is original is not good." (Expect your own writing teachers to be kinder.) In our own time, the *Onion* has earned a reputation for its mastery of both ridicule and satire, the art of using over-the-top humor to make a serious point.

But because ridicule is a double-edged sword, it requires a deft hand to wield it. Humor that reflects bad taste discredits a writer completely, as does satire that misses its mark. Unless your target deserves riposte and you can be very funny, it's usually better to steer clear of such humor.

Using Arguments Based on Emotion

You don't want to play puppet master with people's emotions when you write arguments, but it's a good idea to spend some time early in your work thinking about how you want readers to feel as they consider your persuasive claims. For example, would readers of your editorial about campus traffic policies be more inclined to agree with you if you made them envy faculty privileges, or would arousing their sense of fairness work better? What emotional appeals might persuade meat eaters to consider a vegan diet—or vice versa? Would sketches of stage props on a Web site persuade people to buy a season ticket to the theater, or would you spark more interest by featuring pictures of costumed performers?

Consider, too, the effect that a story can have on readers. Writers and journalists routinely use what are called *human-interest stories* to give presence to issues or arguments. You can do the same, using a particular incident to evoke sympathy, understanding, outrage, or amusement. Take care, though, to tell an honest story.

RESPOND●

1. To what specific emotions do the following slogans, sales pitches, and maxims appeal?

   "Make America Great Again" (Donald Trump rallying cry)

   "Just do it." (ad for Nike)

   "Think different." (ad for Apple computers)

   "Reach out and touch someone." (ad for AT&T)

   "There are some things money can't buy. For everything else, there's MasterCard." (slogan for MasterCard)

   "Have it your way." (slogan for Burger King)

   "The ultimate driving machine." (slogan for BMW)

   "It's everywhere you want to be." (slogan for Visa)

   "Don't mess with Texas!" (anti-litter campaign slogan)

   "American by Birth. Rebel by Choice." (slogan for Harley-Davidson)

2. Bring a magazine to class, and analyze the emotional appeals in as many full-page ads as you can. Then practice your critical reading skills by classifying those ads by types of emotional appeal, and see whether you can connect the appeals to the subject or target audience of the magazine. Compare your results with those of your classmates, and discuss your findings. For instance, how exactly are the ads in publications such as *Cosmopolitan*, *Wired*, *Sports Illustrated*, *Motor Trend*, and *Smithsonian* adapted to their specific audiences?

3. How do arguments based on emotion work in different media? Are such arguments more or less effective in books, articles, television (both news and entertainment shows), films, brochures, magazines, email, Web sites, the theater, street protests, and so on? You might explore how a single medium handles emotional appeals or compare

different media. For example, why do the comments sections of blogs seem to encourage angry outbursts? Are newspapers an emotionally colder source of information than television news programs? If so, why?

4. Spend some time looking for arguments that use ridicule or humor to make their point: check out your favorite Twitter feeds or blogs; watch for bumper stickers, posters, or advertisements; and listen to popular song lyrics. Bring one or two examples to class, and be ready to explain how the humor makes an emotional appeal and whether it's effective.

3

Arguments Based on Character: Ethos

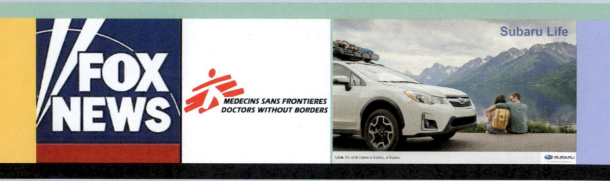

Whenever you read anything—whether it's a news article, an advertisement, a speech, or a tweet—you no doubt subconsciously analyze the message for a sense of the character and credibility of the sender: *Is this someone I know and trust? Does the Fox News reporter—or the Doctors Without Borders Web site—seem biased, and if so, how? Why should I believe an advertisement for a car? Is this scholar really an authority on the subject?* Our culture teaches us to be skeptical of most messages, especially those that bombard us with slogans, and such reasonable doubt is a crucial skill in reading and evaluating arguments.

For that reason, people and institutions that hope to influence us do everything they can to establish their character and credibility, what ancient rhetors referred to as *ethos*. And sometimes slogans such as "All the News That's Fit to Print," "The Most Trusted Name in News," or "Lean In" can be effective. At the very least, if a phrase is repeated often enough, it begins to sound plausible. Maybe Fox News really IS the most watched and most trusted news source!

But establishing character usually takes more than repetition, as marketers of all kinds know. It arises from credentials actually earned in some way. In the auto industry, for instance, Subaru builds on its customer loyalty by telling buyers that love makes a Subaru, and companies such as Toyota, General Motors, and Nissan are hustling to present themselves as environmentally responsible producers of fuel-efficient, low-emission cars—the Prius, Bolt, and Leaf. BMW, maker of "the ultimate driving machine," points to its fuel-sipping i3 and i8 cars as evidence of its commitment to "sustainable mobility." And Elon Musk (who builds rockets as well as Tesla cars) polishes his good-citizenship bona fides by releasing an affordable mass market electric car and by sharing his electric vehicle patents with other manufacturers. All of these companies realize that their future success is linked to an ability to project a convincing ethos for themselves and their products.

If corporations and institutions can establish an ethos, consider how much character matters when we think about people in the public arena. Perhaps no individual managed a more exceptional assertion of personal ethos than Jorge Mario Bergoglio did after he became Pope Francis on March 13, 2013, following the abdication of Benedict XVI—a man many found scholarly, cold, and out of touch with the modern world. James Carroll, writing for the *New Yorker*, identifies the precise moment when the world realized that it was dealing with a new sort of pope:

> "Who am I to judge?" With those five words, spoken in late July [2013] in reply to a reporter's question about the status of gay priests in the Church, Pope Francis stepped away from the disapproving tone, the explicit moralizing typical of popes and bishops.
> —James Carroll, "Who Am I to Judge?"

Carroll goes on to explain that Francis quickly established his ethos with a series of specific actions, decisions, and moments of identification with ordinary people, marking him as someone even nonbelievers might listen to and respect:

> As pope, Francis has simplified the Renaissance regalia of the papacy by abandoning fur-trimmed velvet capes, choosing to live in a two-room apartment instead of the Apostolic Palace, and replacing the papal Mercedes with a Ford Focus. Instead of the traditional red slip-ons, Francis wears ordinary black shoes. . . . Yet Francis didn't criticize the choices of other prelates. "He makes changes without attacking people," a Jesuit official told me. In his interview with *La Civiltà Cattolica*, Francis said, "My choices, including those related to the day-to-day aspects of life, like the use of a modest car, are related to a spiritual discernment that responds to a need that arises from looking at things, at people, and from reading the signs of the times."

Osservatore Romano/ZUMA Press/Vatican City/Holy See/Newscom

In that last sentence, Francis acknowledges that ethos is gained, in part, through identification with one's audience and era. And this man, movingly photographed embracing the sick and disfigured, also posed for selfies!

You can see, then, why Aristotle treats ethos as a powerful argumentative appeal. Ethos creates quick and sometimes almost irresistible connections between readers and arguments. We observe people, groups, or institutions making and defending claims all the time and inevitably ask ourselves, *Should we pay attention to them? Can we rely on them? Do we dare to trust them?* Consider, though, that the same questions will be asked about you and your work, especially in academic settings.

Thinking Critically about Arguments Based on Character

Put simply, arguments based on character (ethos) depend on *trust*. We tend to accept arguments from those we trust, and we trust them (whether individuals, groups, or institutions) in good part because of their reputations. Three main elements—credibility, authority, and unselfish or clear motives—add up to ethos.

To answer serious and important questions, we often turn to professionals (doctors, lawyers, engineers, teachers, pastors) or to experts (those with knowledge and experience) for good advice. Based on their backgrounds, such people come with their ethos already established. Thus, appeals or arguments about character often turn on claims like these:

- A person (or group or institution) is or is not trustworthy or credible on this issue.
- A person (or group or institution) does or does not have the authority to speak to this issue.
- A person (or group or institution) does or does not have unselfish or clear motives for addressing this subject.

Establishing Trustworthiness and Credibility

Trustworthiness and credibility speak to a writer's honesty, respect for an audience and its values, and plain old likability. Sometimes a sense of humor can play an important role in getting an audience to listen to or "like" you. It's no accident that all but the most serious speeches begin with a joke or funny story: the humor puts listeners at ease and helps them identify with the speaker. Writer J. K. Rowling, for example, puts her audience (and herself) at ease early in the commencement address she delivered at Harvard by getting real about such speeches, recalling her own commencement:

> The speaker that day was the distinguished British philosopher Baroness Mary Warnock. Reflecting on her speech has helped me enormously in writing this one, because it turns out that I can't remember a single word she said.
> —J. K. Rowling, "The Fringe Benefits of Failure, and the Importance of Imagination"

In just two sentences, Rowling pokes fun at herself and undercuts the expectation that graduation addresses change people's lives. For an audience well disposed toward her already, Rowling has likely lived up to expectations.

But using humor to enhance your credibility may be more common in oratory than in the kind of writing you'll do in school. Fortunately, you have many options, one being simply to make plausible claims and then back them up with evidence. Academic audiences appreciate a reasonable disposition; we will discuss this approach at greater length in the next chapter.

The UMass Amherst Information Security department uses humor in its posters reminding students that their pets' names are not the best choice for a secure password.

LINK TO P. 698

You can also establish trustworthiness by connecting your own beliefs to core principles that are well established and widely respected. This strategy is particularly effective when your position seems to be—at first glance, at least—a threat to traditional values. For example, when former Smith College president Ruth J. Simmons describes her professional self to a commencement audience, she presents her acquired reputation in terms that align perfectly with contemporary values:

> For my part, I was cast as a troublemaker in my early career and accepted the disapproval that accompanies the expression of unpopular views: unpopular views about disparate pay for women and minorities; unpopular views about sexual harassment; unpopular views about exclusionary practices in our universities.
> —Ruth J. Simmons

It's fine to be a rebel when you are on the right side of history.

Writers who establish their credibility seem trustworthy. But sometimes, to be credible, you have to admit limitations, too, as *New York Times* columnist Frank Bruni does as he positions himself in relation to issues of oppression and deep-seated bias in an editorial titled "I'm a White Man: Hear Me Out." First acknowledging his racial and socioeconomic privilege as a white man from an upper-class background (private school, backyard swimming pool), Bruni then addresses another, less-privileged facet of his identity:

> But wait. I'm gay. . . . Gay from a different, darker day, . . . when gay stereotypes went unchallenged, gay jokes drew hearty laughter and exponentially more Americans were closeted than out. . . . Then AIDS spread, and . . . our rallying cry, "silence = death," defined marginalization as well as any words could.
> —Frank Bruni, "I'm a White Man: Hear Me Out"

Making such concessions to readers sends a strong signal that you've looked critically at your own position and can therefore be trusted when you turn to arguing its merits. Speaking to readers directly, using *I* or *you* or *us*, can also help you connect with them, as can using contractions and everyday or colloquial language—both strategies employed by Bruni. In other situations, you may find that a more formal tone gives your claims greater credibility. You'll be making such choices as you search for the ethos that represents you best.

In fact, whenever you write an essay or present an idea, you are sending signals about your credibility, whether you intend to or not. If your ideas are reasonable, your sources are reliable, and your language is appropriate to the project, you suggest to academic readers that you're someone whose ideas *might* deserve attention. Details matter: helpful graphs, tables, charts, or illustrations may carry weight with readers, as will the visual attractiveness of your text, whether in print or digital form. Obviously, correct spelling, grammar, and mechanics are important too. And though you might not worry about it now, at some point you may need letters of recommendation from instructors or supervisors. How will they remember you? Often chiefly from the ethos you have established in your work. Think about that.

Claiming Authority

When you read or listen to an argument, you have every right to ask about the writer's authority: *What does he know about the subject? What experiences does she have that make her especially knowledgeable? Why should I pay attention to this person?* When you offer an argument yourself, you have to anticipate and be prepared to answer questions like these, either directly or indirectly.

How does someone construct an authoritative ethos? In an essay about John McCain's decision to vote against a Senate bill to repeal the Affordable Care Act, AP reporter Laurie Kellman notes some of McCain's experiences that help build his credibility:

> Longtime colleagues . . . say [McCain] developed his fearlessness as a navy aviator held as a prisoner for more than five years in Vietnam. Resilience, they say, has fueled his long Senate career and helped him overcome two failed presidential campaigns. For some, McCain has become the moral voice of the Republican Party.
>
> —Laurie Kellman, "Cancer Isn't Silencing McCain"

Here Kellman stresses McCain's length of service in the Senate as well as his military service and prisoner of war status, and she refers to him as a "standard bearer" and "moral voice" of the Republican Party. In doing so, she indicates that McCain's ethos is hard won and to be taken seriously.

Rob Greenfield establishes his ethos right in the title of his blog post, "An Argument against Veganism . . . from a Vegan."

LINK TO P. 609

Senator John McCain Justin Sullivan/Getty Images

Of course, writers establish their authority in various ways. Sometimes the assertion of ethos will be bold and personal, as it is when writer and activist Terry Tempest Williams attacks those who poisoned the Utah deserts with nuclear radiation. What gives her the right to speak on this subject? Not scientific expertise, but gut-wrenching personal experience:

> I belong to the Clan of One-Breasted Women. My mother, my grandmothers, and six aunts have all had mastectomies. Seven are dead. The two who survive have just completed rounds of chemotherapy and radiation.
>
> I've had my own problems: two biopsies for breast cancer and a small tumor between my ribs diagnosed as a "borderline malignancy."
>
> —Terry Tempest Williams, "The Clan of One-Breasted Women"

We are willing to listen to Williams because she has lived with the nuclear peril she will deal with in the remainder of her essay.

Other means of claiming authority are less dramatic. By simply attaching titles to their names, writers assert that they hold medical or legal or engineering degrees, or some other important credentials. Or they may mention the number of years they've worked in a given field or the distinguished positions they have held. As a reader, you'll pay more attention to an argument about sustainability offered by a professor of ecology and agriculture at the University of Minnesota than one by your Uncle Sid, who sells tools. But you'll prefer your uncle to the professor when you need advice about a reliable rotary saw.

In our current political climate, the ethos of experts—such as scientists or other academics with deep knowledge about a subject—is being questioned. Matt Grossmann and David A. Hopkins, professors of public policy and political science, identify this trend particularly at the right end of the political spectrum:

> **Data from the General Social Survey demonstrate that declining public faith in science is concentrated among conservatives. Compared to Democrats, Republicans are significantly less likely to trust what scientists say, more critical of political bias in academe and less confident in colleges and universities. Negative attitudes toward science and the media also intersect, with one-third of Republicans reporting no trust in journalists to accurately report scientific studies.**
>
> —Matt Grossmann and David A. Hopkins,
> "How Information Became Ideological"

Like the attacks on "fake news," here Grossmann and Hopkins identify an assault on the ethos of scientists and other academic experts.

When readers might be skeptical of both you and your claims, you may have to be even more specific about your credentials. That's exactly the strategy Richard Bernstein uses to establish his right to speak on the subject of "Asian culture." What gives a New York writer named Bernstein the authority to write about Asian peoples? Bernstein tells us in a sparkling example of an argument based on character:

> **The Asian culture, as it happens, is something I know a bit about, having spent five years at Harvard striving for a Ph.D. in a joint program called History and East Asian Languages and, after that, living either as a student (for one year) or a journalist (six years) in China and Southeast Asia. At least I know enough to know there is no such thing as the "Asian culture."**
>
> —Richard Bernstein, *Dictatorship of Virtue*

When you write for readers who trust you and your work, you may not have to make such an open claim to authority. But making this type of appeal is always an option.

Coming Clean about Motives

When people are trying to convince you of something, it's important (and natural) to ask: *Whose interests are they serving? How will they profit from their proposal?* Such questions go to the heart of ethical arguments.

In a hugely controversial 2014 essay published in the *Princeton Tory*, Tal Fortgang, a first-year student at the Ivy League school, argues that those on campus who used the phrase "Check your privilege" to berate white male students like him for the advantages they enjoy are, in fact, judging him according to gender and race, and not for "all the hard work I have done in my life." To challenge stereotypical assumptions about the "racist patriarchy" that supposedly paved his way to Princeton, Fortgang writes about the experiences of his ancestors, opening the paragraphs with a striking parallel structure:

> Perhaps it's the privilege my grandfather and his brother had to flee their home as teenagers when the Nazis invaded Poland, leaving their mother and five younger siblings behind, running and running. . . .
>
> Or maybe it's the privilege my grandmother had of spending weeks upon weeks on a death march through Polish forests in subzero temperatures, one of just a handful to survive. . . .
>
> Perhaps my privilege is that those two resilient individuals came to America with no money and no English, obtained citizenship, learned the language and met each other. . . .
>
> Perhaps it was my privilege that my own father worked hard enough in City College to earn a spot at a top graduate school, got a good job, and for 25 years got up well before the crack of dawn, sacrificing precious time he wanted to spend with those he valued most—his wife and kids—to earn that living.
>
> —Tal Fortgang, "Checking My Privilege: Character as the Basis of Privilege"

Fortgang thus attempts to establish his own ethos and win the argument against those who make assumptions about his roots by dramatizing the ethos of his ancestors:

> That's the problem with calling someone out for the "privilege" which you assume has defined their narrative. You don't know what their struggles have been, what they may have gone through to be where they are. Assuming they've benefitted from "power systems" or other conspiratorial imaginary institutions denies them credit for all they've

done, things of which you may not even conceive. You don't know whose father died defending your freedom. You don't know whose mother escaped oppression. You don't know who conquered their demons, or may still [be] conquering them now.

As you might imagine, the pushback to "Checking My Privilege" was enormous, some of the hundreds of comments posted to an online version accusing Fortgang himself of assuming the very ethos of victimhood against which he inveighs. Peter Finocchiaro, a reviewer on *Slate*, is especially brutal: "Only a few short months ago he was living at home with his parents. His life experience, one presumes, is fairly limited. So in that sense, he doesn't really know any better. . . . He is an ignorant 19-year-old white guy from Westchester." You can see in this debate how ethos quickly raises issues of knowledge and motives. Fortgang tries to resist the stereotype others would impose on his character, but others regard the very ethos he fashions in his essay as evidence of his naïveté about race, discrimination, and, yes, privilege.

We all, of course, have connections and interests that bind us to other human beings. It makes sense that a young man would explore his social identity, that a woman might be concerned with women's issues, that members of minority groups might define social and cultural conditions on their own terms—or even that investors might look out for their investments. It's simply good strategy, not to mention ethical, to let your audiences know where your loyalties lie when such information does, in fact, shape your work.

Using Ethos in Your Own Writing

- Establish your credibility by listening carefully to and acknowledging your audience's values, showing respect for them, and establishing common ground where (and if) possible. How will you convince your audience you are trustworthy? What will you admit about your own limitations?

- Establish your authority by showing you have done your homework and know your topic well. How will you show that you know your topic well? What appropriate personal experience can you draw on?

- Examine your motives for writing. What, if anything, do you stand to gain from your argument? How can you explain those advantages to your audience?

CULTURAL CONTEXTS FOR ARGUMENT

Ethos

In the United States, students are often asked to establish authority by drawing on personal experiences, by reporting on research they or others have conducted, and by taking a position for which they can offer strong evidence. But this expectation about student authority is by no means universal.

Some cultures regard student writers as novices who can most effectively make arguments by reflecting on what they've learned from their teachers and elders—those who hold the most important knowledge and, hence, authority. When you're arguing a point with people from cultures other than your own, ask questions like:

- Whom are you addressing, and what is your relationship with that person?

- What knowledge are you expected to have? Is it appropriate or expected for you to demonstrate that knowledge—and if so, how?

- What tone is appropriate? And remember: politeness is rarely, if ever, inappropriate.

RESPOND.

1. Consider the ethos of these public figures. Then describe one or two products that might benefit from their endorsements as well as several that would not.

   Edward Snowden—whistleblower

   Beyoncé—singer, dancer, actress

   Denzel Washington—actor

   Tom Brady—football player

   Rachel Maddow—TV news commentator

   Ariana Grande—singer

   Seth Meyers—late-night TV host

   Lin-Manuel Miranda—hip hop artist and playwright

   Venus Williams—tennis player

2. Opponents of Richard Nixon, the thirty-seventh president of the United States, once raised doubts about his integrity by asking a single

ruinous question: *Would you buy a used car from this man?* Create your own version of the argument of character. Begin by choosing an intriguing or controversial person or group and finding an image online. Then download the image into a word-processing file. Create a caption for the photo that is modeled after the question asked about Nixon: *Would you give this woman your email password? Would you share a campsite with this couple? Would you eat lasagna that this guy fixed?* Finally, write a serious 300-word argument that explores the character flaws or strengths of your subject(s).

3. Practice reading rhetorically and critically by taking a close look at your own Facebook page (or your page on any other social media site). What are some aspects of your character, true or not, that might be conveyed by the photos, videos, and messages you have posted online? Analyze the ethos or character you see projected there, using the advice in this chapter to guide your analysis.

4

Arguments Based on Facts and Reason: Logos

In 2018, it feels like facts are under siege, as these three images suggest. Cartoonists are having a field day with a "post-fact" world, while serious scientists are hard at work trying to understand "why facts don't change our minds." From Kellyanne Conway's evocation of "alternative facts" to Donald Trump's tendency to label reports that do not support his views as "fake news," we are witnessing a world in which the statement by *Through the Looking-Glass*'s White Queen that "sometimes I've believed as many as six impossible things before breakfast" seems, well, unremarkable. After the 2016 election, for example, President Trump declared that there was "serious voter fraud" in Virginia, in New Hampshire, in California, and elsewhere, although researchers could find no evidence to back up his claim, and fact-checkers across the board found the "fact" to be baseless. In June 2017, three CNN employees resigned after the network retracted a story that claimed Congress was investigating a "Russian investment fund with ties to Trump officials"; the journalists had used only one unreliable source to back up this supposedly factual claim. We could go on and on with such examples from across the political spectrum, and no doubt you could add your own to the list.

In "Why Facts Don't Change Our Minds," Elizabeth Kolbert surveys cognitive science research that's trying to understand why this is so, pointing to a series of experiments at Stanford University that found that "Even after the evidence for their beliefs had been totally refuted, people fail to make appropriate revisions to those beliefs":

> Thousands of subsequent experiments have confirmed (and elaborated on) this finding. As everyone who's followed the research—or even occasionally picked up a copy of *Psychology Today*—knows, any graduate student with a clipboard can demonstrate that reasonable-seeming people are often totally irrational. Rarely has this insight seemed more relevant than it does now.

Scientists working on this issue point to the "confirmation" or "myside" bias, the strong tendency to accept information that supports our beliefs and values and to reject information that opposes them, as well as to our tendency to think we know a whole lot more than we actually do. A study at Yale asked graduate students to rate their knowledge of everyday items, including toilets, and to write up an explanation of how such devices worked. While the graduate students rated their knowledge/understanding as high before they wrote up the explanations, that exercise showed them that they didn't really know how toilets worked, and their self-assessment dropped significantly. The researchers, Steven Sloman and Philip Fernbach, call this effect the "illusion of explanatory depth" and find that it is very widespread. "Where it gets us into trouble," they say, is in "the political domain." As Kolbert writes, "It's one thing for me to flush a toilet without knowing how it operates, and another for me to favor (or oppose) an immigration ban without knowing what I'm talking about." Sloman and Fernbach explain: "As a rule, strong feelings about issues do not emerge from deep understanding. . . . This is how a community of knowledge can become dangerous."

Such findings are important to all of us, and they suggest several steps all writers, readers, and speakers should take as they deal with arguments based on facts and reason. First, examine your own beliefs in particular facts and pieces of information: do you really know what you're talking about or are you simply echoing what others you know say or think? Second, you need to become a conscientious fact-checker, digging deep to make sure claims are backed by evidence. Doing so is especially important with information you get from social media, where misinformation, disinformation, and even outright lies may be presented as "facts" that you might retweet or post, thus perpetuating false or questionable information.

Finally, don't give up on facts. The researchers discussed above also show that, when given a choice, most people still say they respect and even prefer appeals to claims based on facts, evidence, and reason. Just make sure that the logical appeals you are using are factually correct and ethical as well.

Thinking Critically about Hard Evidence

Aristotle helps us out in classifying arguments by distinguishing two kinds:

Artistic Proofs	Arguments the writer/speaker creates	Constructed arguments	Appeals to reason; common sense
Inartistic Proofs	Arguments the writer/speaker is given	Hard evidence	Facts, statistics, testimonies, witnesses, contracts, documents

We can see these different kinds of logical appeals at work in a passage from a statement made on September 5, 2017, by Attorney General Jeff Sessions:

> Good morning. I am here today to announce that the program known as DACA that was effectuated under the Obama Administration is being rescinded. The DACA program was implemented in 2012 and essentially provided a legal status for recipients for a renewable two-year term, work authorization and other benefits, including participation in the social security program, to 800,000 mostly-adult illegal aliens. This policy was implemented unilaterally to great controversy and legal concern after Congress rejected legislative proposals to extend similar benefits on numerous occasions to this same group of illegal aliens.
>
> In other words, the executive branch, through DACA, deliberately sought to achieve what the legislative branch specifically refused to authorize on multiple occasions. Such an open-ended circumvention of immigration laws was an unconstitutional exercise of authority by the Executive Branch. The effect of this unilateral executive amnesty, among other things, contributed to a surge of unaccompanied minors

on the southern border that yielded terrible humanitarian consequences. It also denied jobs to hundreds of thousands of Americans by allowing those same jobs to go to illegal aliens.

Jeff Sessions announcing that DACA would be rescinded by the Trump administration Alex Wong/Getty Images

Sessions opens his statement with a simple "good morning" and a direct announcement of his purpose: to rescind the Deferred Action for Childhood Arrivals (DACA) program initiated by the Obama administration in 2012. In the next sentence, he uses "inartistic" evidence of what DACA provided (it was renewable and provided work authorization and other benefits) for "800,000 mostly-adult illegal aliens." Noting that Congress had refused on several occasions to extend benefits to the "same group of illegal aliens," Sessions offers the constructed argument that Obama's "open-ended circumvention of immigration laws was an unconstitutional exercise of authority." Presumably now drawing on hard evidence, Sessions argues that DACA led to "a surge of unaccompanied minors," that it denied jobs to "hundreds of thousands" of Americans, and, by neglecting the "rule of law," it subjected the United States to "the risk of crime, violence, and even terrorism."

Sessions says early on in his statement that DACA was implemented amidst "great controversy," and indeed that fact checks out. Other claims made in the statement, however, were quickly challenged. The nonpartisan FactCheck.org, for example, calls out Sessions's description of DACA recipients as "mostly-adult illegal aliens" (a label he uses several times), citing research by Professor Tom Wong of the University of California, San Diego, whose national survey of 3,063 DACA holders in summer 2017 found that "on average they were six and a half years old when they arrived in the U.S. Most of them—54 percent—were under the age of 7." So while they are adults today, they were *not* adults when they were brought to the United States. Likewise, FactCheck.org points out that Sessions's claim that DACA contributed to a "surge of unaccompanied minors" is, at best, misleading and out of context:

> It is true that there was a surge of unaccompanied children that caught the Obama administration off guard in fiscal 2012. The number of unaccompanied minors crossing the border peaked in fiscal 2014 at 68,541, dropping 42 percent to 39,970 in fiscal 2015 before rising again in fiscal year 2016 to 59,692.
>
> But the children who crossed the border illegally were not eligible for DACA. As we said earlier, the criteria for DACA is continuous residence in the United States since June 15, 2007.

If you were reading or listening to this statement and wanted to do some fact-checking of your own, you might well begin by determining whether DACA really led to the loss of hundreds of thousands of jobs. In today's political climate, in fact, it's important that every one of us read with a critical eye, refusing to accept claims without proof, constructed arguments, or even "hard evidence" that we can't fact-check for ourselves.

Two DACA "Dreamers" protesting near Trump Tower in New York the day after Sessions's statement rescinding the program
John Moore/Getty Images

RESPOND●

Discuss whether the following statements are examples of hard evidence or constructed arguments. Not all cases are clear-cut.

1. Drunk drivers are involved in more than 50 percent of traffic deaths.
2. DNA tests of skin found under the victim's fingernails suggest that the defendant was responsible for the assault.
3. A psychologist testified that teenage violence could not be blamed on video games.
4. The crowds at President Trump's inauguration were the largest on record.
5. "The only thing we have to fear is fear itself."
6. Air bags ought to be removed from vehicles because they can kill young children and small-framed adults.

Facts

Gathering factual information and transmitting it faithfully practically define what we mean by professional journalism and scholarship. Carole Cadwalladr, a reviewer for the British newspaper the *Guardian*, praises the research underlying *It's Complicated: The Networked Lives of Teens*. Drawing on almost a decade of research by assistant professor danah boyd of New York University,

> **the book is grounded in hard academic research: proper interviews conducted with actual teenagers. What comes across most strongly, more so than the various "myths" and "panics" that the author describes, is just how narrow and circumscribed many of these teenagers' lives have become.**

Here the "hard academic research" the reviewer mentions is the ethnographic research that yields an accurate description of these young people's lives.

When your facts are compelling, they might stand on their own in a low-stakes argument, supported by little more than saying where they come from. Consider the power of phrases such as "reported by the *Wall Street Journal*" or "according to FactCheck.org." Such sources gain credibility if they have reported facts accurately and reliably over time. Using such credible sources in an argument can also reflect positively on you.

In scholarly arguments, which have higher expectations for accuracy, what counts is drawing sober conclusions from the evidence turned up through detailed research or empirical studies. The language of such material may seem dryly factual to you, even when the content is inherently interesting. But presenting new knowledge dispassionately is (ideally at least) the whole point of scholarly writing, marking a contrast between it and the kind of intellectual warfare that occurs in many media forums, especially news programs and blogs. Here for example is a portion of a lengthy opening paragraph in the "Discussion and Conclusions" section of a scholarly paper arguing that people who spend a great deal of time on Facebook often frame their lives by what they observe there:

> As expected in the first hypothesis, the results show that the longer people have used Facebook, the stronger was their belief that others were happier than themselves, and the less they agreed that life is fair. Furthermore, as predicted in the second hypothesis, this research found that the more "friends" people included on their Facebook whom they did not know personally, the stronger they believed that others had better lives than themselves. In other words, looking at happy pictures of others on Facebook gives people an impression that others are "always" happy and having good lives, as evident from these pictures of happy moments.
> —Hui-Tzu Grace Chou, PhD, and Nicholas Edge, BS,
> "'They Are Happier and Having Better Lives Than I Am':
> The Impact of Using Facebook on Perceptions of Others' Lives"

There are no fireworks in this conclusion, no slanted or hot language, no unfair or selective reporting of data, just a careful attention to the facts and behaviors uncovered by the study. But one can easily imagine these facts being subsequently used to support overdramatized claims about the dangers of social networks. That's often what happens to scholarly studies when they are read and interpreted in the popular media.

Of course, arguing with facts can involve challenging even the most reputable sources if they lead to unfair or selective reporting or if the stories are presented or "framed" unfairly.

In an ideal world, good information—no matter where it comes from—would always drive out bad. But you already know that we don't live in an ideal world, so all too often bad information gets repeated in an echo chamber that amplifies the errors.

Statistics

You've probably heard the old saying "There are three kinds of lies: lies, damned lies, and statistics," and it is certainly possible to lie with numbers, even those that are accurate, because numbers rarely speak for themselves. They need to be interpreted by writers—and writers almost always have agendas that shape the interpretations.

Of course, just because they are often misused doesn't mean that statistics are meaningless, but it does suggest that you need to use them carefully and to remember that your careful reading of numbers is essential. Consider the attention-grabbing map below that went viral in June 2014. Created by Mark Gongloff of the *Huffington Post* in the wake of a school shooting in Oregon, it plotted the location of all seventy-four school shootings that had occurred in the United States since the Sandy Hook tragedy in December 2012, when twenty elementary school children and six adults were gunned down by a rifle-wielding killer. For the graphic, Gongloff drew on a list assembled by the group Everytown for Gun Safety, an organization formed by former New York City mayor and billionaire Michael Bloomberg to counter the influence of the National Rifle Association (NRA). Both the map and Everytown's sobering list of shootings received wide attention in the media, given the startling number of incidents it recorded.

It didn't take long before questions were raised about their accuracy. Were American elementary and secondary school children under such frequent assault as the map based on Everytown's list suggested? Well, yes and no. Guns were going off on and around school campuses, but the firearms weren't always aimed at children. The *Washington Post*, CNN, and other news outlets soon found themselves pulling back on

Lindsay McKenzie cites statistics in her Web article about how secure students feel in protecting themselves from cyberattacks.

LINK TO P. 698

their initial reporting, offering a more nuanced view of the controversial number. To do that, the *Washington Post* began by posing an important question:

> What constitutes a school shooting?
>
> That five-word question has no simple answer, a fact underscored by the backlash to an advocacy group's recent list of school shootings. The list, maintained by Everytown, a group that backs policies to limit gun violence, was updated last week to reflect what it identified as the 74 school shootings since the massacre in Newtown, Conn., a massacre that sparked a national debate over gun control.
>
> Multiple news outlets, including this one, reported on Everytown's data, prompting a backlash over the broad methodology used. As we wrote in our original post, the group considered any instance of a firearm discharging on school property as a shooting—thus casting a broad net that includes homicides, suicides, accidental discharges and, in a handful of cases, shootings that had no relation to the schools themselves and occurred with no students apparently present.
>
> —Niraj Chokshi, "Fight over School Shooting List
> Underscores Difficulty in Quantifying Gun Violence"

CNN followed the same path, re-evaluating its original reporting in light of criticism from groups not on the same page as Everytown for Gun Safety:

> Without a doubt, that number is startling.
>
> So . . . CNN took a closer look at the list, delving into the circumstances of each incident Everytown included. . . .
>
> CNN determined that 15 of the incidents Everytown included were situations similar to the violence in Newtown or Oregon—a minor or adult actively shooting inside or near a school. That works out to about one such shooting every five weeks, a startling figure in its own right.
>
> Some of the other incidents on Everytown's list included personal arguments, accidents and alleged gang activities and drug deals.
>
> —Ashley Fantz, Lindsey Knight, and Kevin Wang, "A Closer Look: How
> Many Newtown-like School Shootings since Sandy Hook?"

Other news organizations came up with their own revised numbers, but clearly the interpretation of a number can be as important as the statistic itself. And what were Mark Gongloff's Twitter reactions to these reassessments? They made an argument as well:

> **Mark Gongloff** ✔
> @markgongloff
> ☐ Follow
>
> Map critics unhappy not all shootings =
> madmen stalking halls. But gangs/suicides
> /accidents are OK?

> **Mark Gongloff** ✔
> @markgongloff
> ☐ Follow
>
> CNN: of 74 school shootings since Sandy
> Hook, *only* 15 were just like it. What a
> relief cnn.com/2014/06/11/us/ ...

Arguments over gun violence in schools reached a new peak in 2018 after seventeen students and staff members were killed at Marjory Stoneman Douglas High School in Florida, leading to a nationwide student walkout on March 14 and massive protests at eight hundred sites around the world on March 24 (including over half a million in Washington, D.C., alone), all organized and led by students. Articulate and media savvy, the student leaders knew to rely on "hard evidence" and solid, fact-checked statistics, and they conducted the research necessary to do so. Students across the United States learned a lesson well: when you rely on statistics in your arguments, make sure you understand where they come from, what they mean, and what their limitations might be. Check and double-check them or get help in doing so: you don't want to be accused of using fictitious data based on questionable assumptions.

RESPOND•

Statistical evidence becomes useful only when interpreted fairly and reasonably. Go to the *Business Insider* Australia Web site and look for one or more charts of the day (www.businessinsider.com/au/category/chart-of-the-day). Choose one, and use the information in it to support three different claims, at least two of which make very different points. Share your claims with classmates. (The point is not to learn to use data dishonestly but to see firsthand how the same statistics can serve a variety of arguments.)

Surveys and Polls

When they verify the popularity of an idea or a proposal, surveys and polls provide strong persuasive appeals because they come as close to expressing the will of the people as anything short of an election—the most decisive poll of all. However, surveys and polls can do much more than help politicians make decisions. They can be important elements in scientific research, documenting the complexities of human behavior. They can also provide persuasive reasons for action or intervention. When surveys show, for example, that most American sixth-graders can't locate France or Wyoming on a map—not to mention Ukraine or Afghanistan—that's an appeal for better instruction in geography. It always makes sense, however, to question poll numbers, especially when they support our own point of view. Ask who commissioned the poll, who is publishing its outcome, who was surveyed (and in what proportions), and what stakes these parties might have in its outcome.

Are we being too suspicious? Not at all, and especially not today. In fact, this sort of scrutiny is exactly what you might anticipate from your readers whenever you use (or create) surveys to explore an issue. You should be confident that enough subjects have been surveyed to be accurate, that the people chosen for the study were representative of the selected population as a whole, and that they were chosen randomly—not selected because of what they were likely to say. In a splendid article on how women can make research-based choices during pregnancy, economist Emily Oster explores, for example, whether an expectant mother might in fact be able to drink responsibly. She researches not only the results of the data, but also who was surveyed, and how their participation might have influenced the results. One 2001 study of pregnant women's drinking habits and their children's behavior years later cautioned that even a single drink per day while pregnant could cause behavioral issues. However, Oster uncovered a serious flaw in the study, noting that

> 18% of the women who didn't drink at all and 45% of the women who had one drink a day reported using cocaine during pregnancy. . . . [R]eally? Cocaine? Perhaps the problem is that cocaine, not the occasional glass of Chardonnay, makes your child more likely to have behavior problems.
>
> —Emily Oster, "Take Back Your Pregnancy"

Clearly, polls, surveys, and studies need to be examined critically. You can't take even academic research at face value until you have explored its details.

The meaning of polls and surveys is also affected by the way that questions are posed. In the past, research revealed, for example, that polling about same-sex unions got differing responses according to how questions were worded. When people were asked whether gay and lesbian couples should be eligible for the same inheritance and partner health benefits that heterosexual couples receive, a majority of those polled said yes—unless the word *marriage* appeared in the question; then the responses were primarily negative. If anything, the differences here reveal how conflicted people may have been about the issue and how quickly opinions might shift—as they have clearly done. Remember, then, to be very careful in reviewing the wording of survey or poll questions.

Finally, always keep in mind that the date of a poll may strongly affect the results—and their usefulness in an argument. In 2014, for example, a Reuters poll found that 20 percent of California residents said they supported "CalExit," a proposal for California to secede from the United States and become a country in its own right. In 2017, however, the same poll found that figure had jumped from 20 percent to 32 percent. The pollsters note, however, that the "margin of error for the California answers was plus or minus 5 percentage points." On public and political issues, you need to be sure that you are using the most timely information you can get.

RESPOND•

Choose an important issue and design a series of questions to evoke a range of responses in a poll. Try to design a question that would make people strongly inclined to agree, another question that would lead them to oppose the same proposition, and a third that tries to be more neutral. Then try out your questions on your classmates and note what you learn about how to improve your questions.

Testimonies and Narratives

Writers often support arguments by presenting human experiences in the form of narrative or testimony—particularly if those experiences are their own. When Republican Senator Orrin Hatch condemned KKK, neo-Nazi, and white nationalist protests in Charlottesville, Virginia, in August 2017, he did so by calling on personal experience:

In his article "Thick of Tongue," linguist John McWhorter shares his personal experience as a black man whom others insist "sounds white."

LINK TO P. 657

In courts, judges and juries often take into consideration detailed descriptions and narratives of exactly what occurred. In the case of *Doe v. City of Belleville*, the judges of the Seventh Circuit Court of Appeals decided, based on the testimony presented, that a man (known as H.) had been sexually harassed by other men in his workplace. The narrative, in this case, supplies the evidence, noting that one coworker

> constantly referred to H. as "queer" and "fag" and urged H. to "go back to San Francisco with the rest of the queers." . . . The verbal taunting of H. turned physical one day when [a coworker] trapped [him] against a wall, proceeded to grab H. by the testicles and, having done so, announced to the assemblage of co-workers present, "Well, I guess he's a guy."

Personal perspectives can support a claim convincingly and logically, especially if a writer has earned the trust of readers. In arguing that Tea Party supporters of a government shutdown had no business being offended when some opponents described them as "terrorists," Froma Harrop, one of the writers who used the term, argued logically and from experience why the characterization was appropriate:

> [T]he hurt the tea party writers most complained of was to their feelings. I had engaged in name-calling, they kept saying. One professing to want more civility in our national conversation, as I do, should not be flinging around the *terrorist* word.
>
>   May I presume to disagree? Civility is a subjective concept, to be sure, but hurting people's feelings in the course of making solid arguments is fair and square. The decline in the quality of our public discourse results not so much from an excess of spleen, but a deficit of well-constructed arguments. Few things upset partisans more than when the other side makes a case that bats home.

"Most of us know that effectively scoring on a point of argument opens us to the accusation of mean-spiritedness," writes Frank Partsch, who leads the National Conference of Editorial Writers' Civility Project. "It comes with the territory, and a commitment to civility should not suggest that punches will be pulled in order to avoid such accusations."

—Froma Harrop, "Hurt Feelings Can Be a Consequence of Strong Arguments"

This narrative introduction gives a rationale for supporting the claim Harrop is making: we can expect consequences when we argue ineffectively. (For more on establishing credibility with readers, see Chapter 3.)

RESPOND•

Bring to class a full review of a recent film that you either enjoyed or did not enjoy. Using testimony from that review, write a brief argument to your classmates explaining why they should see that movie (or why they should avoid it), being sure to use evidence from the review fairly and reasonably. Then exchange arguments with a classmate, and decide whether the evidence in your peer's argument helps to change your opinion about the movie. What's convincing about the evidence? If it doesn't convince you, why doesn't it?

Using Reason and Common Sense

If you don't have "hard facts," you can turn to those arguments Aristotle describes as "constructed" from reason and common sense. The formal study of such reasoning is called *logic*, and you probably recognize a famous example of deductive reasoning, called a **syllogism**:

All human beings are mortal.

Socrates is a human being.

Therefore, Socrates is mortal.

In valid syllogisms, the conclusion follows logically—and technically—from the premises that lead up to it. Many have criticized syllogistic reasoning for being limited, and others have poked fun at it, as in the cartoon on page 72.

Logic: another thing that penguins aren't very good at.

© Randy Glasbergen/glasbergen.com

But we routinely see something like syllogistic reasoning operating in public arguments, particularly when writers take the time to explain key principles. Consider the step-by-step reasoning Michael Gerson uses to explain why exactly it was wrong for the Internal Revenue Service in 2010–2011 to target specific political groups, making it more difficult for them to organize politically:

> Why does this matter deserve heightened scrutiny from the rest of us? Because crimes against democracy are particularly insidious. Representative government involves a type of trade. As citizens, we cede power to public officials for important purposes that require centralized power: defending the country, imposing order, collecting taxes to promote the common good. In exchange, we expect public institutions to be evenhanded and disinterested. When the stewards of power—biased judges or corrupt policemen or politically motivated IRS officials—act unfairly, it undermines trust in the whole system.
>
> —Michael Gerson, "An Arrogant and Lawless IRS"

Gerson's criticism of the IRS actions might be mapped out by the following sequence of statements.

> Crimes against democracy undermine trust in the system.
>
> Treating taxpayers differently because of their political beliefs is a crime against democracy.
>
> Therefore, IRS actions that target political groups undermine the American system.

Few writers, of course, think about formal deductive reasoning when they support their claims. Even Aristotle recognized that most people argue perfectly well using informal logic. To do so, they rely mostly on habits of mind and assumptions that they share with their readers or listeners—as Gerson essentially does in his paragraph.

In Chapter 7, we describe a system of informal logic that you may find useful in shaping credible appeals to reason—Toulmin argument. Here, we briefly examine some ways that people use informal logic in their everyday lives. Once again, we begin with Aristotle, who used the term **enthymeme** to describe an ordinary kind of sentence that includes both a claim and a reason but depends on the audience's agreement with an assumption that is left implicit rather than spelled out. Enthymemes can be very persuasive when most people agree with the assumptions they rest on. The following sentences are all enthymemes:

> We'd better cancel the picnic because it's going to rain.
>
> Flat taxes are fair because they treat everyone the same.
>
> I'll buy a PC instead of a Mac because it's cheaper.

Sometimes enthymemes seem so obvious that readers don't realize that they're drawing inferences when they agree with them. Consider the first example:

> We'd better cancel the picnic because it's going to rain.

Let's expand the enthymeme a bit to say more of what the speaker may mean:

> We'd better cancel the picnic this afternoon because the weather bureau is predicting a 70 percent chance of rain for the remainder of the day.

Embedded in this brief argument are all sorts of assumptions and fragments of cultural information that are left implicit but that help to make it persuasive:

Picnics are ordinarily held outdoors.

When the weather is bad, it's best to cancel picnics.

Rain is bad weather for picnics.

A 70 percent chance of rain means that rain is more likely to occur than not.

When rain is more likely to occur than not, it makes sense to cancel picnics.

For most people, the original statement carries all this information on its own; the enthymeme is a compressed argument, based on what audiences know and will accept.

CULTURAL CONTEXTS FOR ARGUMENT

Logos

In the United States, student writers are expected to draw on "hard facts" and evidence as often as possible in supporting their claims: while ethical and emotional appeals are increasingly important and often used in making decisions, logical appeals still tend to hold sway in academic writing. So statistics and facts speak volumes, as does reasoning based on time-honored values such as fairness and equity. In writing to global audiences, you need to remember that not all cultures value the same kinds of appeals. If you want to write to audiences across cultures, you need to know about the norms and values in those cultures. Chinese culture, for example, values authority and often indirect allusion over "facts" alone. Some African cultures value cooperation and community over individualism, and still other cultures value religious texts as providing compelling evidence. So think carefully about what you consider strong evidence, and pay attention to what counts as evidence to others. You can begin by asking yourself questions like:

- What evidence is most valued by your audience: Facts? Concrete examples? Firsthand experience? Religious or philosophical texts? Something else?

- Will analogies count as support? How about precedents?

- Will the testimony of experts count? If so, what kinds of experts are valued most?

But sometimes enthymemes aren't self-evident:

> Be wary of environmentalism because it's religion disguised as science.

> iPhones are undermining civil society by making us even more focused on ourselves.

> It's time to make all public toilets unisex because to do otherwise is discriminatory.

In these cases, you'll have to work much harder to defend both the claim and the implicit assumptions that it's based on by drawing out the inferences that seem self-evident in other enthymemes. And you'll likely also have to supply credible evidence; just calling something a fact doesn't make it one, so a simple declaration of fact won't suffice.

Providing Logical Structures for Argument

Some arguments depend on particular logical structures to make their points. In the following pages, we identify a few of these logical structures.

Degree

Arguments based on degree are so common that people barely notice them, nor do they pay much attention to how they work because they seem self-evident. Most audiences will readily accept that *more of a good thing* or *less of a bad thing* is good. In her novel *The Fountainhead*, Ayn Rand asks: "If physical slavery is repulsive, how much more repulsive is the concept of servility of the spirit?" Most readers immediately comprehend the point Rand intends to make about slavery of the spirit because they already know that physical slavery is cruel and would reject any forms of slavery that were even crueler on the principle that *more of a bad thing is bad*. Rand still needs to offer evidence that "servility of the spirit" is, in fact, worse than bodily servitude, but she has begun with a logical structure readers can grasp. Here are other arguments that work similarly:

> If I can get a ten-year warranty on an inexpensive Kia, shouldn't I get the same or better warranty from a more expensive Lexus?

> The health benefits from using stem cells in research will surely outweigh the ethical risks.

> Better a conventional war now than a nuclear confrontation later.

A demonstrator at an immigrants' rights rally in New York City in 2007. Arguments based on values that are widely shared within a society—such as the idea of equal rights in American culture—have a strong advantage with audiences.
AP Photo/Seth Wenig

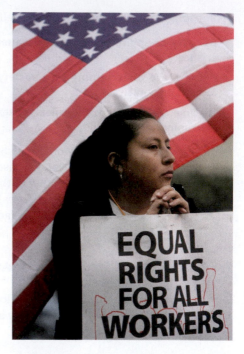

Analogies

Analogies, typically complex or extended comparisons, explain one idea or concept by comparing it to something else.

Here, writer and founder of literacy project 826 Valencia, Dave Eggers, uses an analogy in arguing that we do not value teachers as much as we should:

> When we don't get the results we want in our military endeavors, we don't blame the soldiers. We don't say, "It's these lazy soldiers and their bloated benefits plans! That's why we haven't done better in Afghanistan!" No, if the results aren't there, we blame the planners. . . . No one contemplates blaming the men and women fighting every day in the trenches for little pay and scant recognition. And yet in education we do just that. When we don't like the way our students score on international standardized tests, we blame the teachers.
>
> —Dave Eggers and Nínive Calegari,
> "The High Cost of Low Teacher Salaries"

Precedent

Arguments from **precedent** and arguments of analogy both involve comparisons. Consider an assertion like this one, which uses a comparison as a precedent:

> If motorists in most other states can pump their own gas safely, surely the state of Oregon can trust its own drivers to be as capable. It's time for Oregon to permit self-service gas stations.

You could tease out several inferences from this claim to explain its reasonableness: people in Oregon are as capable as people in other states; people with equivalent capabilities can do the same thing; pumping gas is not hard; and so forth. But you don't have to because most readers get the argument simply because of the way it is put together. In any case, that argument has begun to have traction: as of January 2018, Oregon began permitting self-service pumps in fifteen rural counties, though doing so called forth virulent pushback on social media. So the debate goes on!

Here is an excerpt from an analytical argument by Kriston Capps that examines attempts by the sculptor of Wall Street's *Charging Bull* to have a

Alli Joseph discusses the portrayal of Pacific Islanders in Disney's *Moana* and compares it to the studio's previous depictions of ethnic minorities.

LINK TO P. 537

Anadolu Agency/Getty Images

new, competing sculpture, *Fearless Girl*, removed on the basis of legal precedents supporting the rights of visual artists. Sculptor Arturo Di Modica's assertion,

> that Visbal's work infringes on his own, is unlikely to hold sway, under recent readings of the Visual Artists Rights Act. . . . The argument that *Fearless Girl* modifies or destroys *Charging Bull* by blocking its path would represent a leap that courts have been reluctant to take even in clearer cases.
>
> —Kriston Capps, "Why Wall Street's *Charging Bull* Sculptor Has No Real Case against *Fearless Girl*"

You'll encounter additional kinds of logical structures as you create your own arguments. You'll find some of them in Chapter 5, "Fallacies of Argument," and still more in Chapter 7 on Toulmin argument.

5
Fallacies of Argument

LEFT TO RIGHT: Nate Beeler, The Columbus Dispatch/Cagle Cartoons, Inc.; The Upturned Microscope

Do these cartoons ring a bell with you? The first panel skewers slippery slope arguments, which aim to thwart action by predicting dire consequences: "occupy" enough spaces and the Occupy movement looks just like the Tea Party. In the second item, an example of a straw man argument, the first author of an academic paper puts down his coauthor by shifting the subject, saying that the coauthor is an egotist who cares only for fame, not what the coauthor had said at all. And the third image provides an example of a very common fallacy, the *ad hominem* argument, in which a speaker impugns the character of an opponent rather than addressing the arguments that person raises. Rather than argue the point that human cloning is wrong, the bird says, simply, "you're an idiot."

Candidate Donald Trump made something of a specialty of the *ad hominem* argument. Rather than address their arguments directly, he attacked the characters of his opponents: Marco Rubio was always "little Marco," Hillary Clinton was always "crooked," Elizabeth Warren was "goofy," and Cruz was always "Lyin' Ted." Early on in the campaign, when asked about rival candidate Carly Fiorina's plans, he said, "Can you imagine that, the face of our next president? I mean, she's a woman and I'm not supposed to say bad things, but really, folks, come on." Classic *ad hominem*, and oftentimes such tactics work all too well!

Fallacies are argumentative moves flawed by their nature or structure. Because such tactics can make principled argument more difficult, they potentially hurt everyone involved, including the people responsible for them. The worst sorts of fallacies muck up the frank but civil conversations that people should be able to have, regardless of their differences.

Yet it's hard to deny the power in offering audiences a compelling either/or choice or a vulnerable straw man in an argument: these fallacies can have great persuasive power. For exactly that reason, it's important that you can recognize and point out fallacies in the work of others—and avoid them in your own writing. This chapter aims to help you meet these goals: here we'll introduce you to fallacies of argument classified according to the emotional, ethical, and logical appeals we've discussed earlier (see Chapters 2, 3, and 4).

Fallacies of Emotional Argument

Emotional arguments can be powerful and suitable in many circumstances, and most writers use them frequently. However, writers who pull on their readers' heartstrings or raise their blood pressure too often—or who oversentimentalize—can violate the good faith on which legitimate argument depends.

Scare Tactics

Politicians, advertisers, and public figures sometimes peddle their ideas by frightening people and exaggerating possible dangers well beyond their statistical likelihood. Such ploys work because it's easier to imagine something terrible happening than to appreciate its rarity.

Scare tactics can also be used to stampede legitimate fears into panic or prejudice. Laborers who genuinely worry about losing their jobs can be persuaded to fear immigrants who might work for less money. Seniors living on fixed incomes can be convinced that minor changes to entitlement programs represent dire threats to their well-being. Such tactics have the effect of closing off thinking because people who are scared often act irrationally. Even well-intended fear campaigns—like those directed against smoking, unprotected sex, or the use of illegal drugs—can misfire if their warnings prove too shrill or seem hysterical. People just stop listening.

Either/Or Choices

Either/or choices can be well-intentioned strategies to get something accomplished. Parents use them all the time ("Eat your broccoli, or you won't get dessert"). But they become fallacious arguments when they reduce a complicated issue to excessively simple terms (e.g., "You're either for me or against me") or when they're designed to obscure legitimate alternatives. Here, for example, is Riyad Mansour, the Palestinian representative to the United Nations, offering the nation of Israel just such a choice in an interview on PBS in January 2014:

> It is up to them [the Israelis] to decide what kind of a state they want to be. Do they want to be a democratic state where Israel will be the

A false choice? © Adam Zyglis/Cagle Cartoons, Inc.

state for all of its citizens? Or do they want to be a state for the Jewish people, therefore excluding 1.6 million Palestinian Arabs who are Israelis from their society? That debate is not our debate. That debate is their debate.

But Joel B. Pollak, writing for Breitbart News Network, describes Mansour's claim as a "false choice" since Israel already is a Jewish state that nonetheless allows Muslims to be full citizens. The either/or argument Mansour presents, according to Pollack, does not describe the realities of this complex political situation.

Slippery Slope

The **slippery slope** fallacy portrays today's tiny misstep as tomorrow's slide into disaster. Some arguments that aim at preventing dire consequences do not take the slippery slope approach (for example, the parent who corrects a child for misbehavior now is acting sensibly to prevent more serious problems as the child grows older). A slippery slope argument becomes wrongheaded when a writer exaggerates the likely consequences of an action, usually to frighten readers. As such, slippery slope arguments are also scare tactics. In recent years, the issue of gun ownership in America has evoked many slippery slope arguments. Here are two examples:

> "Universal background checks will inevitably be followed by a national registry of gun-owners which will inevitably be followed by confiscation of all their guns." Or, "A ban on assault-style weapons and thirty+ round magazines will inevitably be followed by a ban on hand guns with ten-round magazines...."
>
> —Michael Wolkowitz, "Slippery Slopes, Imagined and Real"

Social and political ideas and proposals do have consequences, but they aren't always as dire as writers fond of slippery slope tactics would have you believe.

Overly Sentimental Appeals

Overly **sentimental appeals** use tender emotions excessively to distract readers from facts. Often, such appeals are highly personal and individual and focus attention on heartwarming or heartrending situations that

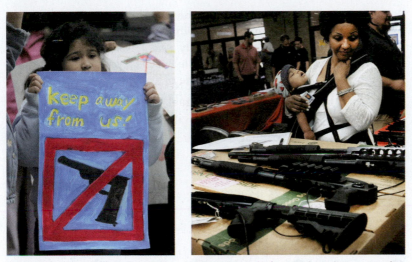

The first image, taken from a gun control protest, is designed to elicit sympathy by causing the viewer to think about the dangers guns pose to innocent children and, thus, support the cause. The second image supports the other side of the debate. Tim Boyle/Getty Images; Spencer Platt/Getty Images

make readers feel guilty if they challenge an idea, a policy, or a proposal. Emotions can become an impediment to civil discourse when they keep people from thinking clearly.

Such sentimental appeals are a major vehicle of television news, where tugging at viewers' heartstrings can mean high ratings. For example, when a camera documents the day-to-day sacrifices of a single parent trying to meet mortgage payments and keep her kids in college, the woman's on-screen struggles can seem to represent the plight of an entire class of people threatened by callous bankers and college administrators. But while such human interest stories stir genuine emotions, they seldom give a complete picture of complex social or economic issues.

Bandwagon Appeals

Bandwagon appeals urge people to follow the same path everyone else is taking. Such arguments can be relatively benign and seem harmless. But they do push people to take the easier path rather than think independently about what choices to make or where to go.

Many American parents seem to have an innate ability to refute bandwagon appeals. When their kids whine, *Everyone else is going camping without chaperones*, the parents reply, *And if everyone else jumps off a cliff (or a railroad bridge or the Empire State Building), you will too?* The children groan—and then try a different line of argument.

Advertisers use bandwagon appeals frequently, as this example of a cellphone ad demonstrates:

Unfortunately, not all bandwagon approaches are so transparent. In recent decades, bandwagon issues have included a war on drugs, the nuclear freeze movement, campaigns against drunk driving—and for freedom of speech, campaigns for immigration reform, bailouts for banks and businesses, and *many* fads in education. All these issues are too complex to permit the suspension of judgment that bandwagon tactics require.

Fallacies of Ethical Argument

Because readers give their closest attention to authors they respect or trust, writers usually want to present themselves as honest, well-informed, likable, or sympathetic. But not all the devices that writers use to gain the attention and confidence of readers are admirable. (For more on appeals based on character, see Chapter 3.)

Appeals to False Authority

Many academic research papers find and reflect on the work of reputable authorities and introduce these authorities through direct quotations or citations as credible evidence. (For more on assessing the reliability of sources, see Chapter 19.) **False authority**, however, occurs when writers offer themselves or other authorities as sufficient warrant for believing a claim:

Claim	X is true because I say so.
Warrant	What I say must be true.

Claim	X is true because Y says so.
Warrant	What Y says must be true.

Though they are seldom stated so baldly, claims of authority drive many political campaigns. American pundits and politicians are fond of citing the U.S. Constitution and its Bill of Rights (Canadians have their Charter of Rights and Freedoms, and Britain has had its Bill of Rights since the seventeenth century) as ultimate authorities, a reasonable practice when the documents are interpreted respectfully. However, the rights claimed sometimes aren't in the texts themselves or don't mean what the speakers think they do. And most constitutional matters are debatable—as volumes of court records prove. Likewise, religious believers often base arguments on books or traditions that wield great authority in a particular religious community. But the power of such texts is often limited to that group and less capable of persuading others solely on the grounds of authority.

In short, you should pay serious attention to claims supported by respected authorities, such as the Centers for Disease Control, the National Science Foundation, or the *Globe and Mail*. But don't accept information simply because it is put forth by such offices and agencies. To quote a Russian proverb made famous by Ronald Reagan, "Trust, but verify."

Dogmatism

A writer who asserts or assumes that a particular position is the *only one* that is conceivably acceptable is expressing **dogmatism**, a fallacy of character that undermines the trust that must exist between those who make and listen to arguments. When people or organizations write dogmatically, they imply that no arguments are necessary: the truth is self-evident and needs no support. Here is an extreme example of such an appeal, quoted in an *Atlantic* story by Tracy Brown Hamilton and describing an anti-smoking appeal made by the Third Reich:

> **"Brother national socialist, do you know that your Fuhrer is against smoking and thinks that every German is responsible to the whole people for all his deeds and omissions, and does not have the right to damage his body with drugs?"**
> —Tracy Brown Hamilton, "The Nazis' Forgotten
> Anti-Smoking Campaign"

Subjects or ideas that can be defended with facts, testimony, and good reasons ought not to be off the table in a free society. In general, whenever someone suggests that even raising an issue for debate is totally unacceptable—whether on the grounds that it's racist, sexist, unpatriotic, blasphemous, insensitive, or offensive in some other way—you should be suspicious.

Ad Hominem Arguments

Ad hominem (Latin for "to the man") **arguments** attack the character of a person rather than the claims he or she makes: when you destroy the credibility of your opponents, you either destroy their ability to present reasonable appeals or distract from the successful arguments they may be offering. During the 2016 presidential primary, Marco Rubio criticized rival candidate Ted Cruz for not speaking Spanish: was that a valid argument for why Cruz would not make a good president? Such attacks, of course, aren't aimed at men only, as columnist Jamie Stiehm proved when she criticized Supreme Court Justice Sonia Sotomayor for delaying an Affordable Care Act mandate objected to by the Little Sisters of the Poor, a Catholic religious order. Stiehm directly targets Sotomayor's religious beliefs:

> **Et tu, Justice Sonia Sotomayor? Really, we can't trust you on women's health and human rights? The lady from the Bronx just dropped the ball on American women and girls as surely as she did the**

sparkling ball at midnight on New Year's Eve in Times Square. Or maybe she's just a good Catholic girl.

—Jamie Stiehm, "The Catholic Supreme Court's War on Women"

Stiehm then widens her *ad hominem* assault to include Catholics in general:

Sotomayor's blow brings us to confront an uncomfortable reality. More than WASPs, Methodists, Jews, Quakers or Baptists, Catholics often try to impose their beliefs on you, me, public discourse and institutions. Especially if "you" are female.

Arguably, *ad hominem* tactics like this turn arguments into two-sided affairs with good guys and bad guys (or gals), and that's unfortunate, since character often really *does* matter in argument. Even though the norms of civic discourse were strained to the limit during and after the 2016 presidential election, most people still expect the proponent of peace to be civil, a secretary of the treasury to pay his or her taxes, the champion of family values to be a faithful spouse, and the head of the Environmental Protection Agency to advocate for protecting the environment. But it's fallacious to attack any of these people for their traits, backgrounds, looks, or other irrelevant information.

Stacking the Deck

Just as gamblers try to stack the deck by arranging cards so they are sure to win, writers **stack the deck** when they show only one side of the story—the one in their favor. In a 2016 *New Yorker* article, writer Kathryn Schulz discusses the Netflix series *Making a Murderer*. Schulz notes that the filmmakers have been accused of limiting their evidence in order to convince viewers that the accused, Steven Avery, had been framed for the crime:

Ricciardi and Demos have dismissed the idea, claiming that they simply set out to investigate Avery's case and didn't have a position on his guilt or innocence. Yet . . . the filmmakers minimize or leave out many aspects of Avery's less than savory past, including multiple alleged incidents of physical and sexual violence. They also omit important evidence against him, . . . evidence that would be nearly impossible to plant. . . . Ricciardi and Demos instead stack the deck to support their case for Avery, and, as a result, wind up mirroring the entity that they are trying to discredit.

—Kathryn Schulz, "Dead Certainty: How *Making a Murderer* Goes Wrong"

In the same way, reviewers have been critical of documentaries by Michael Moore and Dinesh D'Souza that resolutely show only one side of a story or prove highly selective in their coverage. When you stack the deck, you take a big chance that your readers will react like Schulz and decide not to trust you: that's one reason it's so important to show that you have considered alternatives in making any argument.

Fallacies of Logical Argument

You'll encounter a problem in any argument when the claims, warrants, or proofs in it are invalid, insufficient, or disconnected. In theory, such problems seem easy enough to spot, but in practice, they can be camouflaged by a skillful use of words or images. Indeed, logical fallacies pose a challenge to civil argument because they often seem reasonable and natural, especially when they appeal to people's self-interests.

Hasty Generalization

A **hasty generalization** is an inference drawn from insufficient evidence: because *my* Fiat broke down, then *all* Fiats must be junk. It also forms the basis for most stereotypes about people or institutions: because *a few* people in a large group are observed to act in a certain way, *all* members of that group are inferred to behave similarly. The resulting conclusions are usually sweeping claims of little merit: *women are bad drivers*; *men are slobs*; *English teachers are nitpicky*; *computer jocks are . . .* ; and on and on.

To draw valid inferences, you must always have sufficient evidence (see Chapter 18) and you must qualify your claims appropriately. After all, people do need generalizations to make reasonable decisions in life. Such claims can be offered legitimately if placed in context and tagged with sensible qualifiers—*some, a few, many, most, occasionally, rarely, possibly, in some cases, under certain circumstances, in my limited experience.*

Faulty Causality

In Latin, **faulty causality** is known as *post hoc, ergo propter hoc,* which translates as "after this, therefore because of this"—the faulty assumption that because one event or action follows another, the first causes

Look closely at Alexandra Dal's and the Turner Consulting Group's visual arguments showing how damaging microaggressions can be. Then compare them to Scott O. Lilienfeld's argument against the use of microaggressions. Do you see any fallacies in the trio of selections?

LINK TO PP. 752, 756

the second. Consider a lawsuit commented on in the *Wall Street Journal* in which a writer sued Coors (unsuccessfully), claiming that drinking copious amounts of the company's beer had kept him from writing a novel. This argument is sometimes referred to as the "Twinkie defense," referring to a claim that the person who shot and killed San Francisco Supervisor Harvey Milk had eaten so many Twinkies and other sugary foods that his reasoning had been impaired. The phrase is now sometimes used to label the claims of criminals that their acts were caused by something beyond their control.

Of course, some actions do produce reactions. Step on the brake pedal in your car, and you move hydraulic fluid that pushes calipers against disks to create friction that stops the vehicle. In other cases, however, a supposed connection between cause and effect turns out to be completely wrong. For example, doctors now believe that when an elderly person falls and breaks a hip or leg, the injury usually caused the fall rather than the other way around.

That's why overly simple causal claims should always be subject to scrutiny. In summer 2008, writer Nicholas Carr posed a simple causal question in a cover story for the *Atlantic*: "Is Google Making Us Stupid?" Carr essentially answered yes, arguing that "as we come to rely on computers to mediate our understanding of the world, it is our own intelligence that flattens" and that the more one is online the less he or she is able to concentrate or read deeply.

But others, like Jamais Cascio (senior fellow at the Institute for Ethics and Emerging Technologies), soon challenged that causal connection: rather than making us stupid, Cascio argues, Internet tools like Google will lead to the development of "'fluid intelligence'—the ability to find meaning in confusion and to solve new problems, independent of acquired knowledge." The final word on this contentious causal relationship—the effects on the human brain caused by new technology—has yet to be written, and will probably be available only after decades of complicated research.

Begging the Question

Most teachers have heard some version of the following argument: *You can't give me a C in this course; I'm an A student.* A member of Congress accused of taking kickbacks can make much the same argument: *I can't be guilty of accepting such bribes; I'm an honest person.*

In both cases, the claim is made on grounds that can't be accepted as true because those grounds themselves are in question. How can the accused bribe-taker defend herself on grounds of honesty when that honesty is in doubt? Looking at the arguments in Toulmin terms helps to see the fallacy:

Claim	You can't give me a C in this course . . .
Reason	. . . because I'm an A student.
Warrant	An A student is someone who can't receive Cs.
Claim	Representative X can't be guilty of accepting bribes . . .
Reason	. . . because she's an honest person.
Warrant	An honest person cannot be guilty of accepting bribes.

With the warrants stated, you can see why **begging the question**—assuming as true the very claim that's disputed—is a form of circular argument that goes nowhere. (For more on Toulmin argument, see Chapter 7.)

Equivocation

Equivocations—half truths or arguments that give lies an honest appearance—are usually based on tricks of language. Consider the plagiarist who copies a paper word for word from a source and then declares that "I wrote the entire paper myself"—meaning that she physically copied the piece on her own. But the plagiarist is using *wrote* equivocally and knows that most people understand the word to mean composing and not merely copying words.

Parsing words carefully can sometimes look like equivocation or be the thing itself. For example, during the 2016 presidential campaign, Hillary Clinton was asked regularly (some would say she was hounded) about her use of a private email server and about whether any of the emails contained classified information. Here's what she said on February 1, 2016:

> The emails that I was received were not marked classified. Now, there are disagreements among agencies on what should have been perhaps classified retroactively, but at the time that doesn't change the fact that they were not marked classified.
>
> —NPR *Morning Edition*, February 1, 2016

Many commentators at the time felt that this statement was a clear equivocation, and this controversy continued to haunt Clinton throughout her campaign.

Non Sequitur

A **non sequitur** is an argument whose claims, reasons, or warrants don't connect logically. You've probably detected a non sequitur when you react to an argument with a puzzled, "Wait, that doesn't follow." Children are adept at framing non sequiturs like this one: *You don't love me or you'd buy me a new bike.* It doesn't take a parental genius to realize that love has little connection with buying children toys.

Non sequiturs often occur when writers omit steps in an otherwise logical chain of reasoning. For example, it might be a non sequitur to argue that since postsecondary education now costs so much, it's time to move colleges and university instruction online. Such a suggestion *may* have merit, but a leap from brick-and-mortar schools to virtual ones is extreme. Numerous issues and questions must be addressed step-by-step before the proposal can be taken seriously.

Politicians sometimes resort to non sequiturs to evade thorny issues or questions. Here, for example, is Donald Trump replying to questions in a 2017 interview with Michael Scherer of *Time Magazine*:

Scherer: Mitch McConnell has said he'd rather you stop tweeting, that he sees it as a distraction.

Trump: Mitch will speak for himself. Mitch is a wonderful man. Mitch should speak for himself.

Here Trump does not respond to the claim the interviewer says Senate Majority Leader Mitch McConnell has made, but instead abruptly changes the subject, commenting instead on McConnell, saying he is a "wonderful man."

Straw Man

Those who resort to the **straw man** fallacy attack arguments that no one is really making or portray opponents' positions as more extreme or far less coherent than they actually are. The speaker or writer thus sets up an argument that is conveniently easy to knock down (like a man of straw), proceeds to do so, and then claims victory over an opponent who may not even exist.

Straw men are especially convenient devices for politicians who want to characterize the positions of their opponents as more extreme than they actually are: consider obvious memes such as "war on women" and "war on Christmas." But straw man arguments are often more subtle. For instance, Steven Novella of Yale University argues that political commentator Charles Krauthammer slips into the fallacy when he misconstrues the meaning of "settled science" in a column on climate change. Novella rebuts Krauthammer's assertion that "There is nothing more anti-scientific than the very idea that science is settled, static, impervious to challenge" by explaining why such a claim is deceptive:

> Calling something an established scientific fact means that it is reasonable to proceed with that fact as a premise, for further research or for policy. It does not mean "static, impervious to challenge." That is the straw man. Both evolution deniers and climate change deniers use this tactic to misinterpret scientific confidence as an anti-scientific resistance to new evidence or arguments. It isn't.
> —Steven Novella, *NeuroLogica Blog*, February 25, 2014

In other words, Krauthammer's definition of *science* is not one that most scientists use.

Red Herring

This fallacy gets its name from the old British hunting practice of dragging a dried herring across the path of the fox in order to throw the hounds off the trail. A **red herring** fallacy does just that: it changes the subject abruptly or introduces an irrelevant claim or fact to throw readers or listeners off the trail. For example, people skeptical about climate change will routinely note that weather is always changing and point to the fact that Vikings settled in Greenland one thousand years ago before harsher conditions drove them away. True, scientists will say, but the point is irrelevant to arguments about worldwide global warming caused by human activity.

The red herring is not only a device writers and speakers use in the arguments they create, but it's also a charge used frequently to undermine someone else's arguments. Couple the term "red herring" in a Web search to just about any political or social cause and you'll come up with numerous articles complaining of someone's use of the device.

> **climate change + red herring**
>
> **white supremacy + red herring**
>
> **immigration reform + red herring**

"Red herring" has become a convenient way of saying "I disagree with your argument" or "your point is irrelevant." And perhaps making a too-easy rebuttal like that can itself be a fallacy?

Faulty Analogy

Comparisons can help to clarify one concept by measuring it against another that is more familiar. Consider the power and humor of this comparison attributed to Mark Twain, an implicit argument for term limits in politics:

> **Politicians and diapers must be changed often, and for the same reason.**

When comparisons such as this one are extended, they become *analogies*—ways of understanding unfamiliar ideas by comparing them with something that's better known (see p. 76). But useful as such comparisons are, they may prove false if either taken on their own and pushed too far, or taken too seriously. At this point, they turn into **faulty analogies**—inaccurate or inconsequential comparisons between objects or concepts. Secretary of Education Betsy DeVos found herself in a national controversy following a statement she made after meeting with Historically Black Colleges and Universities presidents in Washington, when she made an analogy between HCBUs and her advocacy of "school choice" today:

> **They [African Americans] saw that the system wasn't working, that there was an absence of opportunity, so they took it upon themselves**

to provide the solution. HBCUs are real pioneers when it comes to school choice. They are living proof that when more options are provided to students, they are afforded greater access and greater quality. Their success has shown that more options help students flourish.

What commentators immediately pointed out was that this statement included a false analogy. HBCUs were not created to provide more choice for African American students (and thus be analogous to DeVos's push for charter schools and school "choice") but rather because these students had little to no choice; after the Civil War, African American students were barred from most white public institutions.

Paralipsis

This fallacy (sometimes spelled *paralepsis* and often compared with *occultatio*) has been so predominant in the last two years that we think it's worthy of inclusion here. Basically, this fallacy occurs when speakers

Martin Shovel/Creativity Works

or writers say they will NOT talk about something, thus doing the very thing they say they're not going to do. It's a way of getting a point into an argument obliquely, of sneaking it in while saying that you are not doing so. Although paralipsis is rampant today, it is not new: Socrates famously used it in his trial when he said he would not mention his grieving wife and children who would suffer so mightily at his death. In the 2016 presidential campaign and in the first years of his presidency, Donald Trump used paralipsis repeatedly. Here, for instance, he is at a campaign rally in Fort Dodge, Iowa, speaking about rival candidate Marco Rubio:

> I will not call him a lightweight, because I think that's a derogatory term, so I will not call him a lightweight. Is that OK with you people? I refuse to say that he's a lightweight.

Although he is the most conspicuous user of paralipsis today, Trump is by no means the only politician to use this fallacy. Here's a commentator reporting on presidential candidate Bernie Sanders at a 2016 town hall meeting in Iowa:

> Sen. Bernie Sanders (I-Vt.) on Friday called Bill Clinton's sexual scandals "totally disgraceful and unacceptable" but said he would not use the former president's infidelities against Hillary Clinton. "Hillary Clinton is not Bill Clinton. What Bill Clinton did, I think we can all acknowledge was totally, totally, totally disgraceful and unacceptable."
> —Reporter Lisa Hagen, *The Hill*

In saying he would not use the former president's scandalous behavior against Hillary Clinton, he in fact does just the opposite.

Finally, you may run across the use of paralipsis anywhere, even at the movies, as spoken here by Robert Downey Jr.'s character Tony Stark:

> I'm not saying I'm responsible for this country's longest run of uninterrupted peace in 35 years! I'm not saying that from the ashes of captivity, never has a phoenix metaphor been more personified! I'm not saying Uncle Sam can kick back on a lawn chair, sipping on an iced tea, because I haven't come across anyone man enough to go toe to toe with me on my best day. It's not about me!
> —Robert Downey Jr., *Iron Man 2* (2010)

You may be tempted to use this fallacy in your own writing, but beware: it is pretty transparent and may well backfire on you. Better to say what you believe to be the truth—and stick to it.

RESPOND •

1. Examine each of the following political slogans or phrases for logical fallacies.

   "Resistance is futile." (Borg message on *Star Trek: The Next Generation*)

   "It's the economy, stupid." (sign on the wall at Bill Clinton's campaign headquarters)

   "Make love, not war." (antiwar slogan popularized during the Vietnam War)

   "Build bridges, not walls." (attributed to Martin Luther King Jr.)

   "Stronger Together" (campaign slogan)

   "Guns don't kill, people do." (NRA slogan)

   "Dog Fighters Are Cowardly Scum." (PETA T-shirt)

   "If you can't stand the heat, get out of the kitchen." (attributed to Harry S Truman)

2. Hone your critical reading skills by choosing a paper you've written for a college class and analyze it for signs of fallacious reasoning. Then find an editorial, a syndicated column, and a news report on the same topic and look for fallacies in them. Which has the most fallacies—and what kind? What may be the role of the audience in determining when a statement is fallacious? How effective do you think the fallacies were in speaking to their intended audience?

3. Find a Web site that is sponsored by an organization (the Future of Music Coalition, perhaps), a business (Coca-Cola, Pepsi), or another group (the Democratic or Republican National Committee), and analyze the site for fallacious reasoning. Among other considerations, look at the relationship between text and graphics and between individual pages and the pages that surround or are linked to them.

4. Political blogs such as *Mother Jones* and *InstaPundit* typically provide quick responses to daily events and detailed critiques of material in other media sites, including national newspapers. Study one such blog for a few days to see whether and how the site critiques the articles, political commentary, or writers it links to. Does the blog ever point out fallacies of argument? If so, does it explain the problems with such reasoning or just assume readers will understand the fallacies? Summarize your findings in a brief oral report to your class.

6
Rhetorical Analysis

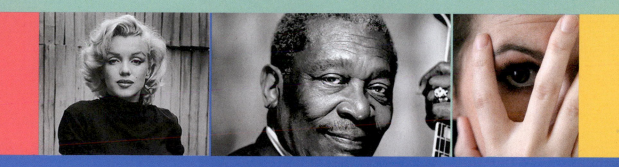

LEFT TO RIGHT: Alfred Eisenstaedt/The LIFE Picture Collection/Getty Images; Steve Debenport/Getty Images

If you watched the 2016 Super Bowl between the Carolina Panthers and the Denver Broncos, you may remember the commercial in which the images above appeared. For a full 60 seconds, "Portraits"—which celebrates the seventy-fifth birthday of Jeep—shows still photographs of the faces of a wide range of people, all of whom have had some connection with the iconic Jeep. B. B. King, one of the most influential blues musicians of all time, recorded a cover of the famous Duke Ellington song, "Jeep's Blues," and Marilyn Monroe rode in a Jeep when she visited troops in 1954. One of the noncelebrities in the commercial is a young woman holding her hands in front of her face; who knows what her connection might be? This advertisement, which won the Super Clio for the best ad of the 2016 Super Bowl, plays in black and white, flashing from one memorable face to another, as a voice speaks to viewers:

> I've seen things no man should bear and those that every man should dare, from the beaches of Normandy to the farthest reaches of the earth. In my life, I've lived millions of lives. I've outrun robots and danced with dinosaurs. I've faced the faces of fear, and of fortitude,

and witnessed great beauty in the making. I've kept the company of kings—and queens. But I'm no royalty or saint. I've traveled, trekked, wandered, and roamed only to find myself right where I belong.

As the portraits are shown, they are occasionally joined by an image of a Jeep, and the ad closes with these lines:

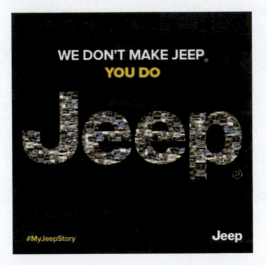

Within seconds of its showing, the ad had been viewed on YouTube over 15,000 times. So how do we account for the power of such advertisements? That would be the work of a **rhetorical analysis**, the close, critical reading of a text or, in this case, a video commercial, to figure out exactly how it functions. Certainly, Iris, the ad agency that created "Portraits," counted on the strong emotional appeal of the photographs, assuming that the faces represented would stir strong sentiments, along with the lyrical words of the voiceover.

The ad's creators pushed the envelope of convention, too, by rejecting the over-the-top, schmaltzy, or super-cute techniques of other advertisements and by the muted product connection. As Super Clio commissioner Rob Reilly put it, "I liked the restraint it showed for the Super Bowl, to not use the typical tricks. Jeep could have easily shown driving footage . . . but they chose to show very little product and tell a great story." Another Clio juror found that the ad "credits people with intelligence and asks you to decode it." (For more information on analyzing images, see Chapter 14.)

Rhetorical analysis and critical reading also probe the contexts that surround any argument or text—its impact on a society, its deeper implications, or even what it lacks or whom it excludes. Predictably, the widely admired Jeep commercial found its share of critics. In a review of the ad for *Wired*, Jenna Garrett helps viewers understand some of the choices made by the advertisers, such as the decision to show the ad in portrait format (and thus using only a third of the TV screen) in recognition that many would be watching on cell phones and tablets (indeed, she reports, the ad looks very fine on those devices). But she then turns to faults she finds with the ad:

> Some of the photos are legitimately great, taken by the likes of celebrity photographer Martin Schoeller. But others look like vacation snapshots, and many of the Jeep images were "fan photos" taken by people doing, well, whatever. Although the photos make the point that Jeep has been everywhere and loved by everyone, the ad doesn't feel cohesive. The pictures of Terminator and T-rex, for example, were jarring, particularly the Terminator's red eyes (the only splash of color in the entire ad). And speaking from a strictly technical perspective, the photos are all over the map in terms of contrast, and some of the crops are entirely too tight.
>
> —Jenna Garrett, "Why Jeep's $10M Super Bowl Ad Only Used a Third of the Screen"

Other reviewers found the advertisement over-sentimental, even saccharine; still others noted some lack of diversity.

Whenever you undertake a rhetorical analysis, do what these reviewers did: read (and view) critically, noting every detail and asking yourself how those details affect the audience, how they build agreement or adherence to the argument—or how they do not do so. And ask plenty of questions: Why does an ad for a cell phone or breakfast sandwich make people want one immediately? How does an op-ed piece in the *Washington Post* suddenly change your long-held position on immigration? Critical reading and rhetorical analysis can help you understand and answer these questions. Dig as deep as you can into the context of the item you are analyzing, especially when you encounter puzzling, troubling, or unusually successful appeals—ethical, emotional, or logical. Ask yourself what strategies a speech, editorial, opinion column, film, or ad uses to move your heart, win your trust, and change your mind—or why, maybe, it fails to do so.

Composing a Rhetorical Analysis: Reading and Viewing Critically

You perform a rhetorical analysis by analyzing how well the components of an argument work together to persuade or move an audience. You can study arguments of any kind—advertisements (as we've seen), Web sites, editorials, political cartoons, and even songs, movies, photographs, buildings, or shopping malls. In every case, you'll need to focus your rhetorical analysis on elements that stand out or make the piece intriguing or problematic. You could begin by exploring *some* of the following issues:

- What is the purpose of this argument? What does it hope to achieve?
- Who is the audience for this argument? Who is ignored or excluded?
- What appeals or techniques does the argument use—emotional, logical, ethical?
- What type of argument is it, and how does the genre affect the argument? (You might challenge the lack of evidence in editorials, but you wouldn't make the same complaint about bumper stickers.)
- Who is making the argument? What ethos does it create, and how does it do so? What values does the ethos evoke? How does it make the writer or creator seem trustworthy?
- What authorities does the argument rely on or appeal to?
- What facts, reasoning, and evidence are used in the argument? How are they presented?
- Can you detect the use of misinformation, disinformation, "fake" news, or outright lies?
- What claims does the argument make? What issues are raised—or ignored or evaded?
- What are the contexts—social, political, historical, cultural—for this argument? Whose interests does it serve? Who gains or loses by it?
- Can you identify fallacies in the argument—emotional, ethical, or logical? (See Chapter 5.)
- How is the argument organized or arranged? What media does the argument use and how effectively?
- How does the language and style of the argument work to persuade an audience?

In answering questions like these, try to show *how* the key devices in an argument actually make it succeed or fail. Quote freely from a written piece, or describe the elements in a visual argument. (Annotating a visual text is one option.) Let readers know where and why an argument makes sense and where it falls apart. If you believe that an argument startles, challenges, insults, or lulls audiences, explain why that is the case and provide evidence. Don't be surprised when your rhetorical analysis itself becomes an argument. That's what it should be.

Understanding the Purpose of Arguments You Are Analyzing

To understand how well any argument works, begin with its purpose: Is it to sell running shoes? To advocate for limits to college tuition? To push a political agenda? In many cases, that purpose may be obvious. A conservative blog will likely advance right-wing causes; ads from a baby food company will likely show happy infants delighted with stewed prunes.

But some projects may hide their persuasive intentions. Perhaps you've responded to a mail survey or telephone poll only to discover that the questions are leading you to switch your cable service or buy apartment insurance. Do such stealthy arguments succeed? Do consumers resent the intrusion? Answering questions like these provides material for useful rhetorical analyses that assess the strengths, risks, and ethics of such strategies.

Understanding Who Makes an Argument

Knowing *who* is claiming *what* is key to any rhetorical analysis. That's why persuasive appeals usually have a name attached to them. Remember the statements included in TV ads during the last federal election: "Hello, I'm X—and I approve this ad"? Federal law requires such statements so we can tell the difference between ads a candidate endorses and ones sponsored by groups not even affiliated with the campaigns. Their interests and motives might be very different.

But knowing a name is just a starting place for analysis. You need to dig deeper, and you could do worse than to Google such people or groups

Senator Elizabeth Warren endorsing Kamala Harris, who won the 2016 race to replace long-time California senator Barbara Boxer

to discover more about them. What else have they produced? Who publishes them: the *Wall Street Journal*, the blog *The Daily Kos*, or even a Live-Journal celebrity gossip site such as *Oh No They Didn't*? Check out related Web sites for information about goals, policies, contributors, and funding.

RESPOND●

Describe a persuasive moment that you can recall from a speech, an editorial, an advertisement, a YouTube clip, or a blog posting. Or research one of the following famous persuasive moments and describe the circumstances—the historical situation, the issues at stake, the purpose of the argument—that make it so memorable.

Abraham Lincoln's Gettysburg Address (1863)

Elizabeth Cady Stanton's Declaration of Sentiments at the Seneca Falls Convention (1848)

Chief Tecumseh's address to General William Henry Harrison (1810)

Winston Churchill's radio addresses to the British people during World War II (1940)

Martin Luther King Jr.'s "Letter from Birmingham Jail" (1963)

Ronald Reagan's tribute to the *Challenger* astronauts (1986)

Toni Morrison's speech accepting the Nobel Prize (1993)

Former President Obama's eulogy in memory of the worshippers killed at the Emmanuel AME Church in Charleston (2015)

Identifying and Appealing to Audiences

Most arguments are composed with specific audiences in mind, and their success depends, in part, on how well their strategies, content, tone, and language meet the expectations of that audience. So your rhetorical analysis of an argumentative piece should identify its target readers or viewers (see "Appealing to Audiences," p. 24) if possible, or make an educated guess about the audience, since most arguments suggest whom they intend to reach and in what ways.

Both a flyer stapled to a bulletin board in a college dorm ("Why you shouldn't drink and drive") and a forty-foot billboard for Bud Light might be aimed at the same general population—college students. But each will adjust its appeals for the different moods of that group in different moments. For starters, the flyer will appeal to students in a serious vein, while the beer ad will probably be visually stunning and virtually text-free.

You might also examine how a writer or an argument establishes credibility with an audience. One effective means of building credibility is to show respect for your readers or viewers, especially if they may not agree with you. In introducing an article on problems facing African American women in the workplace, editor-in-chief of *Essence* Diane Weathers considers the problems that she faced with respecting all her potential readers:

> We spent more than a minute agonizing over the provocative cover line for our feature "White Women at Work." The countless stories we had heard from women across the country told us that this was a workplace issue we had to address. From my own experience at several major magazines, it was painfully obvious to me that Black and White women are not on the same track. Sure, we might all start out in the same place. But early in the game, most sisters I know become stuck—and the reasons have little to do with intelligence or drive. At some point we bump our heads against that ceiling. And while White women may complain of a glass ceiling, for us, the ceiling is concrete.
>
> So how do we tell this story without sounding whiny and paranoid, or turning off our White-female readers, staff members, advertisers and girlfriends? Our solution: Bring together real women (several of them highly successful senior corporate executives), put them in a room, promise them anonymity and let them speak their truth.
>
> —Diane Weathers, "Speaking Our Truth"

Sara Morrison's report "Covering the Transgender Community" has a clear audience: journalists and others interested in how transgender individuals are represented in the media.

LINK TO P. 580

Both paragraphs affirm Weathers's determination to treat audiences fairly *and* to deal honestly with a difficult subject. The strategy would merit attention in any rhetorical analysis.

Look, too, for signals that writers share values with readers or at least understand an audience. In the following passage, writer Jack Solomon is clear about one value that he hopes readers have in common—a preference for "straight talk":

> There are some signs in the advertising world that Americans are getting fed up with fantasy advertisements and want to hear some straight talk. Weary of extravagant product claims . . . , consumers trained by years of advertising to distrust what they hear seem to be developing an immunity to commercials.
>
> —Jack Solomon, "Masters of Desire:
> The Culture of American Advertising"

But straight talk still requires common sense. If ever a major television ad seriously misread its audience, it may have been a spot that ran during the 2014 Winter Olympics for Cadillac's pricey new plug-in hybrid, the ELR. The company seemed to go out of its way to offend a great many people, foreign and domestic. As is typical strategy in rhetorical analyses, *Huffington Post*'s Carolyn Gregoire takes care to describe in detail the item she finds offensive—a shot of a man overlooking the pool in his backyard and asking why we work so hard, "For this? For stuff?":

> [I]t becomes clear that the answer to this rhetorical question is actually a big fat YES. And it gets worse. "Other countries, they work," he

WAL★MART
ALWAYS LOW PRICES.
Always.

Retailers like Walmart build their credibility by simple "straight talk" to shoppers: we *always* have low prices. Here the use of red, white, and blue says "we're all-American," while the simple layout and direct statement (a promise, really) say they are talking the talk as well as walking the walk.

says. "They stroll home. They stop by the cafe. They take August off. Off."

Then he reveals just what it is that makes Americans better than all those lazy, espresso-sipping foreigners.

"Why aren't you like that?" he says. "Why aren't we like that? Because we're crazy, driven, hard-working believers, that's why."

—Carolyn Gregoire, "Cadillac Made a Commercial about the American Dream, and It's a Nightmare"

Her conclusion then is blistering, showing how readily a rhetorical analysis becomes an argument—and subject to criticism itself:

> Cadillacs have long been a quintessentially American symbol of wealth and status. But as this commercial proves, no amount of wealth or status is a guarantee of good taste. Now, the luxury car company is selling a vision of the American Dream at its worst: Work yourself into the ground, take as little time off as possible, and buy expensive sh*t (specifically, a 2014 Cadillac ELR).

Examining Arguments Based on Emotion: Pathos

Some emotional appeals are just ploys to win over readers with a pretty face, figurative or real. You've seen ads promising an exciting life and attractive friends if only you drink the right soda or wear a particular brand of clothes. Are you fooled by such claims? Probably not, if you pause to think about them. But that's the strategy—to distract you from thought just long enough to make a bad choice. It's a move worth commenting on in a rhetorical analysis.

Yet emotions can add real muscle to arguments, too, and that's worth noting. For example, persuading people not to drink and drive by making them fear death, injury, or arrest seems like a fair use of an emotional appeal. Public service announcements often use emotion-laden images to remind drivers to think of the consequences.

In analyzing emotional appeals, judge whether the emotions raised—anger, sympathy, fear, envy, joy, love, lust—advance the claims offered. Look, for example, at these photographs of protests in Charlottesville, Virginia, over the possible removal of a statue of General Robert E. Lee.

The August 2017 rally in Charlottesville stirred emotions across the country, as ordinary people, commentators, and politicians weighed in on issues of white supremacy, neo-Nazism, fascism, race-based hatred,

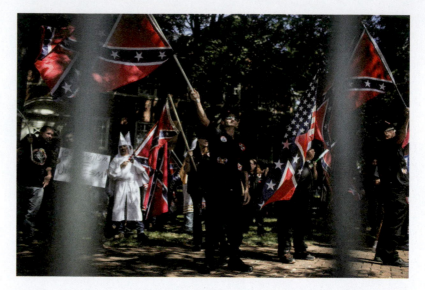

This photo shows proud members of the Loyal White Knights of the Ku Klux Klan, some carrying Confederate flags. What emotions do you think these protesters wanted to appeal to? What emotions does the photo stir in you?
Chet Strange/Getty Images

Or how about this photo, from the same rally, showing counterprotesters: again, what emotions are being appealed to? How effective do you find either of these photos in appealing to your emotions? AP Photo/Steve Helber and bigotry. President Trump at first suggested that there was plenty of blame on "all sides," but later adjusted that statement when many accused him of drawing a false equivalency between those advocating for Nazism and those who were protesting against it.

But arguments that appeal to emotions don't have to be as highly charged—and dangerous—as the Charlottesville event was. Consider, for example, how columnist Ron Rosenbaum makes the reasonable argument he offers for fatty foods all the more attractive by loading it with emotional language:

> The foods that best hit that sweet spot and "overwhelm the brain" with pleasure are high-quality fatty foods. They discourage us from overeating. A modest serving of short ribs or Peking duck will be both deeply pleasurable and self-limiting. As the brain swoons into insensate delight, you won't have to gorge a still-craving cortex with mediocre sensations. "Sensory-specific satiety" makes a slam-dunk case (it's science!) for eating reasonable servings of superbly satisfying fatty foods.
> —Ron Rosenbaum, "Let Them Eat Fat"

Does the use of evocative language ("swoons," "insensate delight," "superbly satisfying," "slam-dunk") convince you, or does it distract from considering the scientific case for "sensory-specific satiety"? Your task in a rhetorical analysis is to study an author's words, the emotions they evoke, and the claims they support and then to make this kind of judgment.

Short ribs: health food? Who does this photo appeal to—and who might it turn off? Chicago Tribune/Getty Images

RESPOND.

Browse YouTube or another Web site to find an example of a powerful emotional argument that's made visually, either alone or using words as well. In a paragraph, defend a claim about how the argument works. For example, does an image itself make a claim, or does it draw you in to consider a verbal claim? What emotion does the argument generate? How does that emotion work to persuade you?

Examining Arguments Based on Character: Ethos

It should come as no surprise: readers believe writers who seem honest, wise, and trustworthy. So in analyzing the effectiveness of an argument, look for evidence of these traits. Does the writer have the experience or authority to write on this subject? Are all claims qualified reasonably? Is evidence presented in full, not tailored to the writer's agenda? Are important objections to the author's position acknowledged and addressed? Are sources documented? Above all, does the writer sound trustworthy?

When a Norwegian anti-immigration extremist killed seventy-six innocent people in July 2011, Prime Minister Jens Stoltenberg addressed the citizens of Norway (and the world), and in doing so evoked the character or ethos of the entire nation:

> We will not let fear break us! The warmth of response from people in Norway and from the whole world makes me sure of this one thing: evil can kill a single person, but never defeat a whole people. The strongest weapon in the world—that is freedom of expression and democracy.

In analyzing this speech, you would do well to look at the way this passage deploys the deepest values of Norway—freedom of expression and democracy—to serve as a response to fear of terrorism. In doing so, Stoltenberg evokes ethical ideals to hold onto in a time of tragedy.

Or take a look at the following paragraph from a blog posting by Timothy Burke, a teacher at Swarthmore College and parent of a preschool child who is trying to think through the issue of homework for elementary school kids:

> So I've been reading a bit about homework and comparing notes with parents. There is a lot of variation across districts, not just in the amount of homework that kids are being asked to do, but in the kind of

Burke establishes his ethos by citing his reading and his talks with other parents.

homework. Some districts give kids a lot of time-consuming busywork; other districts try to concentrate on having homework assignments be substantive work that is best accomplished independently. Some give a lot from a very early point in K-12 education; some give relatively little. **As both a professional educator and an individual with personal convictions,** I'd tend to argue against excessive amounts of homework and against assigning busywork. But what has ultimately interested me more about reading various discussions of homework is how intense the feelings are swirling around the topic **and how much that intensity strikes me as a problem in and of itself. Not just as a symptom of a kind of civic illness, an inability to collectively and democratically work through complex issues, but also in some cases as evidence of an educational failure in its own right.**

> He underscores his right to address the matter.

> He expresses concern about immoderate arguments and implies that he will demonstrate an opposite approach.

In considering the role of ethos in rhetorical analyses, pay attention to the details right down to the choice of words or, in an image, the shapes and colors. The modest, tentative tone that Burke uses in his blog is an example of the kind of choice that can shape an audience's perception of ethos. But these details need your interpretation. Language that's hot and extreme can mark a writer as either passionate or loony. Work that's sober and carefully organized can paint an institution as competent or overly cautious. Technical terms and abstract phrases can make a writer seem either knowledgeable or pompous.

Examining Arguments Based on Facts and Reason: Logos

In analyzing most arguments, you'll have to decide whether an argument makes a plausible claim and offers good reasons for you to believe it. Not all arguments will package such claims in a single neat sentence, or **thesis**—nor should they. A writer may tell a story from which you have to infer the claim. Visual arguments may work the same way: viewers have to assemble the parts and draw inferences in order to get the point. Take a look, for instance, at this advertisement for GEICO insurance:

This ad draws attention with a snappy photo of a large silver watch and a headline: "That watch won't pay for itself." The smaller text below mentions other luxury items consumers may covet: designer aviators, for example, that don't "come cheap." Then the logical shift: if you want luxury things you would do well to save money. And how to save money? "So switch to GEICO and save money for the things you love." There's an implied syllogism here:

You need to save money so you can afford the things you love.

GEICO will help you save money.

GEICO will help you afford the things you love.

But a little critical thinking can lead you to question each of these implied premises. Is the reason to save money really to buy luxury items? Just exactly how will GEICO help you save money? How much is your current insurance and how does that compare to the cost of GEICO? Maybe GEICO does offer a very good deal on insurance, but you'll need to do some more research to assure yourself of that fact. (For more on analyzing visual images, see Chapter 14.)

Some print arguments (like those on an editorial page) may be perfectly obvious: writers stake out a claim and then present reasons that you should consider, or they may first present reasons and lay out a case that leads you to accept a claim in the conclusion. Consider the following example. In a tough opinion piece in *Time*, political commentator John McWhorter argues that filmmaker Spike Lee is being racist when he rails against hipsters moving into Fort Greene, a formerly all-black neighborhood in Brooklyn, New York. Lee fears that the whites are raising housing prices, pushing out old-time residents and diminishing the African American character of Fort Greene. McWhorter, an African American like Lee, sees matters differently:

> Basically, black people are getting paid more money than they've ever seen in their lives for their houses, and a once sketchy neighborhood is now quiet and pleasant. And this is a bad thing . . . why?
>
> Lee seems to think it's somehow an injustice whenever black people pick up stakes. But I doubt many of the blacks now set to pass fat inheritances on to their kids feel that way. This is not the old story of poor blacks being pushed out of neighborhoods razed down for highway construction. Lee isn't making sense.
>
> —John McWhorter, "Spike Lee's Racism Isn't Cute"

When you encounter explicit charges like these, you analyze whether and how the claims are supported by good reasons and reliable evidence. A lengthy essay may, in fact, contain a series of claims, each developed to support an even larger point. Here's McWhorter, for instance, expanding his argument by suggesting that Lee's attitudes toward whites are irreconcilable.

> "Respect the culture" when you move in, Lee growls. But again, he isn't making sense. We can be quite sure that if whites "respected" the culture by trying to participate in it, Lee would be one of the first in line to call it "appropriation." So, no whites better open up barbecue joints or spoken word cafes or try to be rappers. Yet if whites walk on by the culture in "respectful" silence, then the word on the street becomes that they want to keep blacks at a distance.

Indeed, every paragraph in an argument may develop a specific and related idea. In a rhetorical analysis, you need to identify all these separate propositions and examine the relationships among them: Are they solidly linked? Are there inconsistencies that the writer should acknowledge? Does the end of the piece support what the writer said (and promised) at the beginning?

You'll also need to examine the quality of the information presented in an argument, assessing how accurately such information is reported, how conveniently it's displayed (in charts or graphs, for example), and

See another argument on race by John McWhorter, this time on what it means when we say someone "sounds black" or "sounds white."

LINK TO P. 657 ·

An anti-fur protestor in London makes a rather specific claim.
CHARLES PLATIAU/REUTERS/Newscom

Historian Catherine Nolan-Ferrell asks us to confront the value of logos when she asks, "How do we navigate a world where many in society have lost trust in shared data?"

LINK TO P. 772

how well the sources cited represent a range of *respected* opinions on a topic. (For more information on the use of evidence, see Chapter 4.)

Knowing how to judge the quality of sources is more important now than ever before because the digital universe is full of junk. In some ways, the computer terminal has become the equivalent of a library reference room, but the sources available online vary widely in quality and have not been evaluated by a library professional. As a consequence, you must know the difference between reliable, firsthand, or fully documented sources and those that don't meet such standards. (For using and documenting sources, see Chapters 19, 20, and 22.)

Examining the Arrangement and Media of Arguments

Aristotle carved the structure of logical argument to its bare bones when he observed that it had only two parts:

- statement
- proof

You could do worse, in examining an argument, than to make sure that every claim a writer makes is backed by sufficient evidence. Some arguments are written on the fly in the heat of the moment. Most arguments that you read and write, however, will be more than mere statements followed by proofs. Some writers will lay their cards on the table immediately; others may lead you carefully through a chain of claims toward a conclusion. Writers may even interrupt their arguments to offer background information or cultural contexts for readers. Sometimes they'll tell stories or provide anecdotes that make an argumentative point. They'll qualify the arguments they make, too, and often pause to admit that other points of view are plausible.

In other words, there are no set formulas or acceptable patterns that fit all successful arguments. In writing a rhetorical analysis, you'll have to assess the organization of a persuasive text on its own merits.

It's fair, however, to complain about what may be *absent* from an argument. Most arguments of proposal (see Chapter 12), for example, include a section that defends the feasibility of a new idea, explaining how it might be funded or managed. In a rhetorical analysis, you might fault an editorial that supports a new stadium for a city without addressing feasibility issues. Similarly, analyzing a movie review that reads like an off-the-top-of-the-head opinion, you might legitimately ask what criteria of evaluation are in play (see Chapter 10).

Rhetorical analysis also calls for you to look carefully at an argument's transitions, headings and subheadings, documentation of sources, and overall tone or voice. Don't take such details for granted, since all of them contribute to the strength—or weakness—of an argument.

Nor should you ignore the way a writer or an institution uses media. Would an argument originally made in a print editorial, for instance, work better as a digital presentation (or vice versa)? Would a lengthy essay have more power if it included more illustrations—graphs, maps, photographs, and so on? Or do these images distract from a written argument's substance?

Finally, be open to the possibility of new or nontraditional structures of arguments. The visual arguments that you analyze may defy conventional principles of logic or arrangement—for example, making juxtapositions rather than logical transitions between elements or using quick cuts, fades, or other devices to link ideas. Quite often, these nontraditional structures will also resist the neatness of a thesis, leaving readers to construct at least a part of the argument in their heads. As we saw with the "Portraits" Jeep spot at the beginning of this chapter, advertisers are growing fond of soft-sell multimedia productions that can seem like something other than what they really are—product pitches. We may be asked not just to buy a product but also to live its lifestyle or embrace its ethos. Is that a reasonable or workable strategy for an argument? Your analysis might entertain such possibilities.

Looking at Style

Even a coherent argument full of sound evidence may not connect with readers if it's dull, off-key, or offensive. Readers naturally judge the credibility of arguments in part by how stylishly the case is made—even when they don't know exactly what style is (for more on style, see Chapter 13). In fact, today rhetoricians and media critics alike point out the crucial importance of style in getting and holding attention in a time when readers are drowning in an overload of information.

Consider how these simple, blunt sentences from the opening of an argument for gun control shape your image of the author and probably determine whether you're willing to continue to read the whole piece:

> Six minutes and about twenty seconds. In a little over six minutes, seventeen of our friends were taken from us. Fifteen were injured, and everyone—absolutely everyone—in [our] community was forever altered. Everyone who was there understands. Everyone who has been touched by the cold grip of gun violence understands.
>
> —Emma Gonzalez, speech delivered at March
> for Our Lives on March 24, 2018

The strong, straightforward tone, the drum-beat use of repetition, and the stark evocation of just how little time it took to take the lives of seventeen high school students and staff set the style for this speech, which led to six minutes of silence and then to prolonged, and loud, applause and cheers.

Now consider the brutally sarcastic tone of Nathaniel Stein's hilarious parody of the Harvard grading policy, a piece he wrote following up on a professor's complaint of out-of-control grade inflation at the school. Stein borrows the formal language of a typical "grading standards" sheet to mock the decline in rigor that the professor has lamented:

> The A+ grade is used only in very rare instances for the recognition of truly exceptional achievement.

For example: A term paper receiving the A+ is virtually indistinguishable from the work of a professional, both in its choice of paper stock and its font. The student's command of the topic is expert, or at the very least intermediate, or beginner. Nearly every single word in the paper is spelled correctly; those that are not can be reasoned out phonetically within minutes. Content from Wikipedia is integrated with precision. The paper contains few, if any, death threats. . . .

An overall course grade of A+ is reserved for those students who have not only demonstrated outstanding achievement in coursework but have also asked very nicely.

Finally, the A+ grade is awarded to all collages, dioramas and other art projects.

—Nathaniel Stein, "Leaked! Harvard's Grading Rubric"

Both styles probably work, but they signal that the writers are about to make very different kinds of cases. Here, style alone tells readers what to expect.

Manipulating style also enables writers to shape readers' responses to their ideas. Devices as simple as repetition, parallelism, or even paragraph length can give sentences remarkable power. Consider this brief announcement by Jason Collins, who played for the Washington Wizards:

I'm a 34-year-old NBA center. I'm black. And I'm gay.

I didn't set out to be the first openly gay athlete playing in a major American team sport. But since I am, I'm happy to start the conversation. I wish I wasn't the kid in the classroom raising his hand and saying, "I'm different." If I had my way, someone else would have already done this. Nobody has, which is why I'm raising my hand.

—Jason Collins, *Sports Illustrated*, May 6, 2013

In this passage, Collins opens with three very short, very direct, and roughly parallel sentences. He also uses repetition of first-person pronouns to hammer home that he is claiming his own identity with this statement. Doing so invites readers and listeners to listen to his experience and to walk in his shoes, even for a brief time.

In a rhetorical analysis, you can explore such stylistic choices. Why does a formal style work for discussing one type of subject matter but not another? How does a writer use humor or irony to underscore an important point or to manage a difficult concession? Do stylistic choices, even something as simple as the use of contractions or personal pronouns, bring readers close to a writer, or do technical words and an impersonal voice signal that an argument is for experts only?

Jason Collins © Gary A. Vasquez/USA Today Sports Images

To describe the stylistic effects of visual arguments, you may use a different vocabulary and talk about colors, camera angles, editing, balance, proportion, fonts, perspective, and so on. But the basic principle is this: the look of an item—whether a poster, an editorial cartoon, or a film documentary—can support the message that it carries, undermine it, or muddle it. In some cases, the look will *be* the message. In a rhetorical analysis, you can't ignore style.

Here's an award-winning poster for *Beauty and the Beast,* praised by critics for its stylistic elegance. As a commentator for DigitalSpy put it, "So chic. So stylish. So yellow."

A rhetorical analysis would note that the bright yellow dress and title evoke the sun as the image of Beauty dominates the middle of the image, while the beast's profile is superimposed on a full moon. Here the simplicity, vivid color, and careful juxtaposition suggest that these two are made for each other. (For more on analyzing visual images, see Chapter 14.)

RESPOND•

> Find a recent example of a visual argument, either in print or on the Internet. Even though you may have a copy of the image, describe it carefully in your paper on the assumption that your description is all readers may have to go on. Then make a judgment about its effectiveness, supporting your claim with clear evidence from the "text."

Examining a Rhetorical Analysis

On the following pages, well-known *New York Times* columnist Nicholas Kristof reports on his family's annual vacation, when they "run away to the mountains." He argues that we are plagued by "nature deficit disorder," that we have lost our connection with the wilderness, with the land that supports us, and that we must do our best to preserve and protect the "natural splendor that no billionaire is allowed to fence off." Responding to Kristof's argument with a careful critical reading and detailed rhetorical analysis is Cameron Hauer, a student at Portland State University.

Fleeing to the Mountains

NICHOLAS KRISTOF

Brent N. Clarke/
Getty Images

ON THE PACIFIC CREST TRAIL, NORTHWEST OF TRUCKEE, Calif. —

This will make me sound grouchy and misanthropic, but I sometimes wonder if what makes America great isn't so much its people as its trees and mountains.

In contrast to many advanced countries, we have a vast and spectacular publicly owned wilderness, mostly free and available to all. In an age of inequality, the affluent have gated neighborhoods, private schools, backup generators and greater influence on elected officials. But our most awe-inspiring wild places have remained largely a public good to be shared by all, a bastion of equality.

My family and I have been backpacking on the Pacific Crest Trail through the Sierras north of Donner Pass, enjoying magnificent splendor that no billionaire is allowed to fence off. We all have equal access, at no charge: If you can hold your own against mosquitoes and bears, the spot is yours for the night.

Yet these public lands are at risk today. More on that in a moment, but first let me tell you about the Kristofs' grand vacation. As we do each summer, we ran away from home to the mountains. We escaped the tether of email and cellphones, the tyranny of the inbox, and fled with everything we needed on our backs.

We're yanked back to a simple life. We sleep under the stars rather than in a tent; if it rains we pull out a tarp to keep dry. Dawn wakes us up, we roll up our sleeping bags and plastic ground sheet, wolf down trail mix or granola bars and start down the path. We fill our water bottles at passing streams, stop for rest and meals wherever we fancy, chat as we walk, and when dusk comes we look for a flat spot, kick aside any rocks and branches and unroll our ground sheet and sleeping bags again.

Granted, we also moan about blisters. And marauding mosquitoes. And the heat—or, sometimes, the cold. We whine a lot, but that builds family solidarity.

Caroline Kristof

This is also a spiritual experience: It's a chance to share a reverence for the ethereal scenery of America's wild places. The wilderness is nature's cathedral, and it's a thrill to worship here.

The march of civilization has been about distancing ourselves from the raw power of nature. At home, we move the thermostat up or down by a degree, and we absorb the idea that we are lords of the universe. On the trail, we are either sweating or freezing, and it always feels as if the path is mainly uphill. Nature mocks us, usefully reminding us who's boss.

If your kids are suffering from what the writer Richard Louv calls nature-deficit disorder, I recommend that you all run away from home together. Flee to the mountains. It's heaven with blisters.

There are often charges to enter much-trafficked spots like Yellowstone or Yosemite, but the wilderness is mostly free to hikers.

This is our collective patrimony, a tribute to the wisdom of Theodore Roosevelt, Gifford Pinchot and other visionaries who preserved our wild places for the future. Thank God for them. Otherwise, these lands might have been carved up and sold off as ranches for the rich.

Because of the foresight of past generations, the federal government owns one million square miles, an area three times the size of California, Oregon and Washington combined. Much of this is unspoiled, our inheritance and our shared playground.

Yet today, President Trump sees this heritage as an opportunity for development. More aggressively than past administrations, Trump's is systematically handing over America's public lands for private exploitation in ways that will scar the land forever.

The Trump administration lifted a moratorium on new coal mining leases on public land, it is drawing up plans to reduce wilderness protected as national monuments and it is rapidly opening up additional public lands to coal mining and oil and gas drilling.

A second challenge comes from our paralysis in the face of climate change, compounded by the Trump administration, and the risks this creates to our wilderness. A warmer climate has led to droughts and to the 20-year spread of the mountain pine beetle, and a result is the death of vast swaths of Western forests. Last year, 62 million trees died in California alone, the Forest Service says, and in Oregon and Washington I've watched forests turn brown and sickly. In parts of Wyoming and Colorado, the pine beetle has killed almost all the mature lodgepole pine trees, and it's arguably even worse in British Columbia.

The third risk is from gradual degradation and chronic underfunding. Even before Trump took office, wilderness trails and campgrounds were in embarrassing disrepair. How is it that we could afford to construct these trails 80 years ago in the Great Depression but cannot manage even to maintain them today?

When public lands are lost — or mined in ways that scar the landscape — something has been lost forever on our watch. A public good has been privatized, and our descendants have been robbed.

To promote an understanding of what is being lost, I encourage everyone to run away from home as well. Flee to the mountains, deserts and babbling brooks to get in touch with wild spaces, to find perspective and humility. The wilderness nourishes our souls, if we let it.

Appeal, Audience, and Narrative in Kristof's Wilderness

CAMERON HAUER

Courtesy of
Cameron Hauer

Growing up in an outdoorsy middle class family instilled a love of the outdoors in me from an early age. I joined a local Boy Scouts chapter as a pre-adolescent and spent practically every other weekend in the pristine wilderness of Washington, Idaho, and Montana. From alpine skiing in the Canadian Rockies to 50-mile backpacking treks, the wilderness was a big part of my life. I owe a lot of personal development and fond memories to America's vast and mostly public wilderness, the value of which Nicholas Kristof captures stirringly in his *New York Times* op-ed column, "Fleeing to the Mountains."

> Connects article to personal experience to create an ethical appeal

Kristof's article is principally a piece of epideictic rhetoric, extolling the virtues of America's publicly owned wilderness areas and those who created them while casting blame on those who try to undermine them. Early in the piece, Kristof connects public ownership of wild lands to a core set of American values, regarding the country's public lands as "a bastion of equality." In the wilderness, he says, "we all have equal access, no charge." Kristof warns, however, that America's wilderness is under attack.

> Provides brief overview of Kristof's argument and major claim

To bolster his case for the specialness of America's wildlands, Kristof relies heavily on ethical and emotional appeals: a lively account of his family's backpacking trips and the ways they free them from the technologically structured rigidity of modern city life. In these sections, Kristof's style ranges from breezy and playful

---

Cameron Hauer is a student at Portland State University, where he is majoring in Applied Linguistics, having returned to school after a decade spent cooking in fine dining establishments in the Pacific Northwest.

(the wilderness is "heaven with blisters") to awestruck and reverent (it is "our inheritance and shared playground"). This section also offers personal testimony; Kristof has spent a lot of time in wild places, and he is well positioned to describe their virtues. He invites readers to share this ethic, to revel in the joy provided by open spaces, but also to regard them as an almost sacred inheritance.

Transition sentence signals a shift in the argument

About halfway through the column, Kristof makes a shift to address threats facing our wilderness. He lays blame on those in power, like President Trump, who "sees this heritage as an opportunity for development" and is "systematically handing over America's public lands for private exploitation in ways that will scar the land forever." Kristof's style here becomes more somber and more reliant on verifiable facts. The primary appeal shifts to logos rather than the ethos and pathos of the earlier sections. Whereas before he was trying to evoke a particular feeling and ethic, his present goal is to convince readers that public lands in the U.S. are under threat by marshaling a series of facts about actions of the Trump Administration that Kristof believes undermine the U.S. public wilderness system. These facts include lifting a moratorium on new mining leases and opening up new lands to fossil fuel extraction. He also describes the effects of climate change, which he argues the Trump Administration ignores, and chronic underfunding, which he notes predates Trump. In the online version of the column, Kristof includes hyperlinks so readers can fact-check his evidence. This is the only section in which hyperlinks appear, underscoring again the shift to logical appeals. Note, however, that Kristof lessens the effect of what could be an abrupt shift in appeal by maintaining his established narrative, of wilderness as an inheritance.

Discusses style and use of evidence

Puts Kristof's article in rhetorical context

Several elements of Kristof's argument give special insight into the particular moment in which Kristof offers his argument as well as into the audience he is addressing. The place of Trump in Kristof's narrative is particularly significant, because what Kristof describes as a unique threat to American public lands is simply the implementation of long-standing Republican Party policy. If he had wanted to, Kristof could fairly ascribe the policies of privatization and fossil fuel extraction to the GOP as a whole. But in the rhetorical context Kristof occupies—a left-of-center newspaper in 2017—choosing Trump as the avatar of anti-environmental policies is a strong, if obvious, rhetorical move. To a liberal readership still reeling from the shock of the 2016 election, the invocation of Trump is an invitation for the audience to adopt Kristof's pro-wilderness platform as a plank of a broader anti-Trump agenda.

Analyzes author's intended audience

It is also worth noting some telling elisions in Kristof's argument. In the narrative Kristof provides, wild lands are either public and devoted to use by the people, or privatized and devoted to resource extraction and "ranches for the rich." To Kristof's invoked audience, which bristles at the rapacity of unrestrained free enterprise and its attendant inequality, this framework may be convincing, but a rural conservative who believes strongly in the primacy of property rights will probably be unmoved. While it may seem natural to progressives to regard public ownership as an unmitigated good, conservatives often view such ownership with extreme suspicion. Whereas Kristof views public ownership as a means of providing equal access for all Americans, rural conservatives may view it as a means by which potentially valuable resources are turned into playgrounds for yuppies. And whereas Kristof views private ownership as facilitating degradation and waste, conservatives may view it as a means by which hardworking people can make a decent living off the land.

Offers a critique of Kristof's position

Such considerations bring up another important evasion in Kristof's argument, one that may stand out sharply to both left and right. Kristof's characterization

Points out another flaw in Kristof's argument

of public lands as "a bastion of equality" may be true in a narrow, legal sense: most of these places are open to the public, free of charge. But to get access to wilderness requires a decent salary and paid time off, among other things. In an economic system where millions struggle to afford basic food and housing, unfettered use of America's wildlands remains out of reach.

These evasions and omissions may point to Kristof's biases and his own rhetorical stance, but they should not be regarded as damning. Even if Kristof has rejoinders to these objections — and it's likely he does — it would be hard to give them their due in the restricted format of a newspaper column. This op-ed article is, after all, crafted for a particular audience. To address the concerns of staunch conservatives would probably require Kristof to adopt very different rhetorical strategies. Kristof's readers are mostly a self-selecting group of liberals already sympathetic in some ways to his views. Thus the rhetorical goal is not to convince a group of hostile adversaries of his position but to persuade a group of amenable readers that this particular issue — and this particular ethic — is one that they should adopt as their own.

Analyzes the genre of Kristof's piece (and its limitations)

WORK CITED

Kristof, Nicholas. "Fleeing to the Mountains." *Everything's an Argument*, 8th ed., by Andrea A. Lunsford and John J. Ruszkiewicz, Bedford/St. Martin's, 2018, pp. 118–20. Reprint of "Fleeing to the Mountains," *The New York Times*, 12 August 2017.

GUIDE to writing a rhetorical analysis

● Finding a Topic

A rhetorical analysis is usually assigned: you're asked to show how an argument works and to assess its effectiveness. When you can choose your own subject for analysis, look for one or more of the following qualities:

- a complex verbal or visual argument that challenges you—or disturbs or pleases you
- a text that raises current or enduring issues of substance
- a text that you believe should be taken more seriously

Look for arguments to analyze in the editorial and op-ed pages of any newspaper, political magazines such as the *Nation* or *National Review*, Web sites of organizations and interest groups, political blogs such as *Huffington Post* or *Power Line*, corporate Web sites that post their TV ad spots, videos and statements posted to YouTube, and so on.

● Researching Your Topic

Once you've got a text to analyze, find out all you can about it. Use library or Web resources to explore:

- who the author is and what his or her credentials are
- if the author is an institution, what it does, what its sources of funding are, who its members are, and so on
- who is publishing or sponsoring the piece and what the organization typically publishes
- what the leanings or biases of the author and publisher might be, where they are coming from in the argument, and what influences may have led them to make the argument
- what the context of the argument is—what preceded or provoked it and how others have responded to it

● Formulating a Claim

Begin with a hypothesis. A full thesis might not become evident until you're well into your analysis, but your final thesis should reflect the complexity of the piece that you're studying. In developing a thesis, consider questions such as the following:

- What is the major claim of the argument? What evidence is presented in support of it?

- How can I describe what this argument achieves?

- What is the purpose, and is it accomplished?

- What audiences does the argument address and what audiences does it ignore, and why?

- Which rhetorical appeals does the argument make use of and which will likely influence readers most: ethos of the author? emotional appeals? logical progression? style, use of images or other illustrations? What aspects of the argument work better than others?

- How do the rhetorical elements of ethos, pathos, and logos interact?

Here's the hardest part for most writers of rhetorical analyses: whether you agree or disagree with an argument should not keep you from careful, meticulous analysis: you need to stay out of the fray and pay attention only to how—and to how well—the argument works.

● Examples of Possible Claims for a Rhetorical Analysis

- Some people admire the directness and plain talking of Donald Trump; others are put off by his lack of information, his tendency to stretch or ignore the truth, and his noisy bluster. A close look at several of his tweets and public appearances will illuminate both sides of this debate.

- Today's editorial in the *Daily Collegian* about campus crimes may scare first-year students, but its anecdotal reporting doesn't get down to hard numbers—and for a good reason. Those statistics don't back the position taken by the editors.

- The imageboard 4chan has been called an "Internet hate machine," yet others claim it as a great boon to creativity. A close analysis of its homepage can help to settle this debate.

- The original design of New York's Freedom Tower, with its torqued surfaces and evocative spire, made a stronger argument about American values than its replacement, a fortress-like skyscraper stripped of imagination and unable to make any statement except "I'm 1,776 feet tall."

- The controversy over speech on campuses has reached a fever pitch, with some arguing that those who spout hate and bigotry and prejudice should be barred from speaking.

● Preparing a Proposal

If your instructor asks you to prepare a proposal for your rhetorical analysis, here's a format you might use:

- Provide a copy of the work you're analyzing, whether it's a print text, a photograph, a digital image, or a URL, for instance.

- Offer a working hypothesis or tentative thesis.

- Indicate which rhetorical components seem especially compelling and worthy of detailed study and any connections between elements. For example, does the piece seem to emphasize facts and logic so much that it becomes disconnected from potential audiences? If so, hint at that possibility in your proposal.

- Indicate background information you intend to research about the author, institution, and contexts (political, economic, social, and religious) of the argument.

- Define the audience you'd like to reach. If you're responding to an assignment, you may be writing primarily for a teacher and classmates. But they make up a complex audience in themselves. If you can do so within the spirit of the assignment, imagine that your analysis will be published in a local newspaper, Web site, or blog.

- Conclude by briefly discussing the key challenges you anticipate in preparing a rhetorical analysis.

● Considering Genre and Media

Your instructor may specify that you use a particular genre and/or medium. If not, ask yourself these questions to help you make a good choice:

- What genre is most appropriate for your rhetorical analysis? Does it call for an academic essay, a report, an infographic, a poster, brochure, or something else?

- What medium is most appropriate for your analysis? Would it be best delivered orally to a live audience? Presented as an audio essay or podcast? Presented in print only or in print with illustrations?

- Will you need visuals, such as moving or still images, maps, graphs, charts—and what function will they play in your analysis? Make sure they are not just "added on" but are necessary components of the analysis.

● Thinking about Organization

Your rhetorical analysis is likely to include the following:

- Facts about the text you're analyzing: provide the author's name; the title or name of the work; its place of publication or its location; the date it was published or viewed.

- Evidence that you have read the argument carefully and critically, that you have listened closely to and understand the points it is making, and that you have been open and fair in your assessment.

- Contexts for the argument: readers need to know where the text is coming from, to what it may be responding, in what controversies it might be embroiled, and so on. Don't assume that they can infer the important contextual elements.

- A synopsis of the text that you're analyzing: if you can't attach the original argument, you must summarize it in enough detail so that a reader can imagine it. Even if you attach a copy of the piece, the analysis should include a summary.

- Some claim about the work's rhetorical effectiveness: it might be a simple evaluative claim or something more complex. The claim can come early in the paper, or you might build up to it, providing the evidence that leads toward the conclusion you've reached.

- A detailed analysis of how the argument works: although you'll probably analyze rhetorical components separately, don't let your analysis become a dull roster of emotional, ethical, and logical appeals. Your rhetorical analysis should be an argument itself that supports a claim; a simple list of rhetorical appeals won't make much of a point.

- Evidence for every point made in your analysis.

- An assessment of alternative views and counterarguments to your own analysis.

● Getting and Giving Response: Questions for Peer Response

If you have access to a writing center, discuss the text that you intend to analyze with a writing consultant before you write the analysis. Try to find people who agree with the argument and others who disagree, and take notes on their observations. Your instructor may assign you to a peer group for the purpose of reading and responding to one another's drafts; if not, share your draft with someone on your own. You can use the following questions to evaluate a draft. If you're evaluating someone else's draft, be sure to illustrate your points with examples. Specific comments are always more helpful than general observations.

The Claim

- Does the claim address the rhetorical effectiveness of the argument itself rather than the opinion or position that it takes?
- Is the claim significant enough to interest readers?
- Does the claim indicate important relationships between various rhetorical components?
- Would the claim be one that the creator of the piece would regard as serious criticism?

Evidence for the Claim

- Is enough evidence given to support all your claims? What evidence do you still need?
- Is the evidence in support of the claim simply announced, or are its significance and appropriateness analyzed? Is a more detailed discussion needed?
- Do you use appropriate evidence, drawn from the argument itself or from other materials?
- Do you address objections readers might have to the claim, criteria, or evidence?
- What kinds of sources might you use to explain the context of the argument? Do you need to use sources to check factual claims made in the argument?
- Are all quotations introduced with appropriate signal phrases (for instance, "As Áida Álvarez points out"), and do they merge smoothly into your sentences?

Organization and Style

- How are the parts of the argument organized? How effective is this organization? Would some other structure work better?
- Will readers understand the relationships among the original text, your claims, your supporting reasons, and the evidence you've gathered (from the original text and any other sources you've used)? If not, what could be done to make those connections clearer? Are more transitional words and phrases needed? Would headings or graphic devices help?

- Are the transitions or links from point to point, sentence to sentence, and paragraph to paragraph clear and effective? If not, how could they be improved?

- Is the style suited to the subject and appropriate to your audience? Is it too formal? Too casual? Too technical? Too bland or boring?

- Which sentences seem particularly effective? Which ones seem weakest, and how could they be improved? Should some short sentences be combined, or should any long ones be separated into two or more sentences?

- How effective are the paragraphs? Do any seem too skimpy or too long? Do they break the analysis at strategic points?

- Which words or phrases seem particularly effective, accurate, and powerful? Do any seem dull, vague, unclear, or inappropriate for the audience or your purpose? Are definitions provided for technical or other terms that readers might not know?

Spelling, Punctuation, Mechanics, Documentation, and Format

- Check the spelling of the author's name, and make sure that the name of any institution involved with the work is correct. Note that the names of many corporations and institutions use distinctive spelling and punctuation.

- Check the title of the text you're analyzing so you're sure to get it right.

- Look for any errors in spelling, punctuation, capitalization, and the like.

- Check the format of your assignment and make sure it matches instructions given on your original assignment.

RESPOND.

Find an argument on the editorial page or op-ed page in a recent newspaper. Read it carefully and critically, taking time to make sure you understand the claims it is making and the evidence that backs up the claim. Then analyze it rhetorically, using principles discussed in this chapter. Show how it succeeds, fails, or does something else entirely. Perhaps you can show that the author is unusually successful in connecting with readers but then has nothing to say. Or perhaps you discover that the strong logical appeal is undercut by a contradictory emotional argument. Be sure that the analysis includes a summary of the original essay and basic publication information about it (its author, place of publication, and publisher).

PART 2

WRITING
arguments

7
Structuring Arguments

I get hives after eating ice cream.
My mouth swells up when I eat cheese.
Yogurt triggers my asthma.

↓

Dairy products make me sick.

Dairy products make me sick.
Ice cream is a dairy product.

↓

Ice cream makes me sick.

These two sets of statements illustrate the most basic ways in which Western culture structures logical arguments. The first piles up specific examples and draws a conclusion from them: that's **inductive reasoning** and structure. The second sets out a general principle (the major premise of a syllogism) and applies it to a specific case (the minor premise) in order to reach a conclusion: that's **deductive reasoning** and structure. In everyday reasoning, we often omit the middle statement, resulting in what Aristotle called an *enthymeme*: "Since dairy products make me sick, I better leave that ice cream alone." (See p. 71 for more on enthymemes.)

But the arguments you will write in college call for more than just the careful critical thinking offered within inductive and deductive reasoning. You will also need to make claims, explain the contexts in which you are offering them, defend the assumptions on which they are based, offer convincing evidence, appeal to specific audiences, consider counterarguments fairly and carefully, and more. And you will have to do so using a coherent structure that moves your argument forward. This chapter introduces you to three helpful ways to structure arguments. Feel free to borrow from all of them!

The Classical Oration

The authors of this book once examined a series of engineering reports and found that—to their great surprise—these reports were generally structured in ways similar to those used by Greek and Roman rhetors two thousand years ago. Thus, this ancient structuring system is alive and well in twenty-first-century culture. The classical oration has six parts, most of which will be familiar to you, despite their Latin names:

> *Exordium:* You try to win the attention and goodwill of an audience while introducing a topic or problem.
>
> *Narratio:* You present the facts of the case, explaining what happened when, who is involved, and so on. The *narratio* puts an argument in context.
>
> *Partitio:* You divide up the topic, explaining what the claim is, what the key issues are, and in what order they will be treated.
>
> *Confirmatio:* You offer detailed support for the claim, using both logical reasoning and factual evidence.
>
> *Refutatio:* You carefully consider and respond to opposing claims or evidence.
>
> *Peroratio:* You summarize the case and move the audience to action.

This structure is powerful because it covers all the bases: readers or listeners want to know what your topic is, how you intend to cover it, and what evidence you have to offer. And you probably need a reminder to present a pleasing *ethos* when beginning a presentation and to conclude with enough *pathos* to win an audience over completely. Here, in outline form, is a five-part updated version of the classical pattern, which you may find useful on many occasions:

Introduction

- gains readers' interest and willingness to listen
- indicates your qualifications to write about your topic
- establishes some common ground with your audience
- demonstrates that you're fair and even-handed
- states your claim

Background

- presents information, including personal stories or anecdotes relevant to your argument

Lines of Argument

- present good reasons, including logical and emotional appeals, in support of your claim

Alternative Arguments

- carefully consider different points of view and opposing arguments
- note the advantages and disadvantages of these views
- explain why your view is preferable to others

Conclusion

- summarizes the argument
- elaborates on the implications of your claim
- makes clear what you want the audience to think or do
- reinforces your credibility and perhaps offers an emotional appeal

Not every piece of rhetoric, past or present, follows the structure of the oration or includes all its components. But you can identify some of its elements in successful arguments if you pay attention to their design. Here are the words of the 1776 Declaration of Independence:

> When in the Course of human events, it becomes necessary for one people to dissolve the political bands which have connected them with another, and to assume among the powers of the earth, the separate and equal station to which the Laws of Nature and of Nature's God entitle them, a decent respect to the opinions of mankind requires that they should declare the causes which impel them to the separation.
>
> We hold these truths to be self-evident, that all men are created equal, that they are endowed by their

Opens with a brief *exordium* explaining why the document is necessary, invoking a broad audience in acknowledging a need to show "a decent respect to the opinions of mankind." Important in this case, the lines that follow explain the assumptions on which the document rests.

Creator with certain unalienable Rights, that among these are Life, Liberty, and the pursuit of Happiness—that to secure these rights, Governments are instituted among Men, deriving their just powers from the consent of the governed—That whenever any Form of Government becomes destructive to these ends, it is the Right of the People to alter or to abolish it and to institute new Government, laying its Foundation on such principles and organizing its powers in such form, as to them shall seem most likely to effect their Safety and Happiness. Prudence, indeed, will dictate that Governments long established should not be changed for light and transient causes; and accordingly all experience hath shewn that mankind are more disposed to suffer, while evils are sufferable, than to right themselves by abolishing the forms to which they are accustomed. But when a long train of abuses and usurpations, pursuing invariably the same Object evinces a design to reduce them under absolute Despotism, it is their right, it is their duty, to throw off such Government and to provide new Guards for their future security. — Such has been the patient sufferance of these Colonies; and such is now the necessity which constrains them to alter their former Systems of Government. The history of the present King of Great Britain is a history of repeated injuries and usurpations, all having in direct object the establishment of an absolute Tyranny over these States. To prove this, let Facts be submitted to a candid world.

—Declaration of Independence, July 4, 1776

A *narratio* follows, offering background on the situation: because the government of George III has become destructive, the framers of the Declaration are obligated to abolish their allegiance to him.

Arguably, the *partitio* begins here, followed by the longest part of the document (not reprinted), a *confirmatio* that lists the "long train of abuses and usurpations" by George III.

The authors might have structured this argument by beginning with the last two sentences of the excerpt and then listing the facts intended to prove the king's abuse and tyranny. But by choosing first to explain the

Notice that John Hancock's defiant signature on the Declaration of Independence is still readable in this much reduced image of the original document. National Archives

purpose and "self-evident" assumptions behind their argument and only then moving on to demonstrate how these "truths" have been denied by the British, the authors forge an immediate connection with readers and build up to the memorable conclusion. The structure is both familiar and inventive—as your own use of key elements of the oration should be in the arguments you compose.

Rogerian and Invitational Arguments

In trying to find an alternative to confrontational and angry arguments like those that so often erupt in legislative bodies around the world, scholars and teachers of rhetoric have adapted the nonconfrontational principles employed by psychologist Carl Rogers in personal therapy sessions. In simple terms, Rogers argued that people involved in disputes should not respond to each other until they could fully, fairly, and even sympathetically state the other person's position. Scholars of rhetoric Richard E. Young, Alton L. Becker, and Kenneth L. Pike developed a four-part structure that is now known as Rogerian argument:

1. **Introduction:** You describe an issue, a problem, or a conflict in terms rich enough to show that you fully understand and respect any alternative position or positions.

2. **Contexts:** You describe the contexts in which alternative positions may be valid.

3. **Writer's position:** You state your position on the issue and present the circumstances in which that opinion would be valid.

4. **Benefits to opponent:** You explain to opponents how they would benefit from adopting your position.

The key to Rogerian argumentation is a willingness to think about opposing positions and to describe them fairly. In a Rogerian structure, you have to acknowledge that alternatives to your claims exist and that they might be reasonable under certain circumstances. In tone, Rogerian arguments steer clear of heated and stereotypical language, emphasizing instead how all parties in a dispute might gain from working together.

In the same vein, feminist scholars Sonja Foss and Cindy Griffin have outlined a form of argument they label "invitational," one that begins with careful attention to and respect for the person or the audience you are in conversation with. Foss and Griffin show that such listening—in effect, walking in the other person's shoes—helps you see that person's points of view more clearly and thoroughly and thus offers a basis for moving together toward new understandings. The kind of argument they describe is what rhetorician Krista Ratcliffe calls "rhetorical listening," as we saw in Chapter 1—listening that helps to establish productive connections between people and thus helps enable effective cross-cultural communications.

Invitational rhetoric has as its goal not winning over opponents but getting people and groups to work together and identify with each other; it strives for connection, collaboration, and the mutually informed creation of knowledge. As feminist scholar Sally Miller Gearhart puts it, invitational argument offers a way to disagree without hurting one another, to disagree with respect. This kind of argument is especially important in a society that increasingly depends on successful collaboration to get things done. In college, you may have opportunities to practice invitational rhetoric in peer-review sessions, when each member of a group listens carefully in order to work through problems and issues. You may also practice invitational rhetoric looking at any contested issue from other people's points of view, taking them into account, and engaging them fairly and respectfully in your own argument. Students we know who are working in high-tech industries also tell us how much such arguments are valued, since they fuel innovation and "out of the box" thinking.

Invitational arguments, then, call up structures that more resemble good two-way conversations or free-ranging dialogues than straight-line marches from thesis to conclusion. Even conventional arguments benefit from invitational strategies by giving space early on to a full range of perspectives, making sure to present them thoroughly and clearly. Remember that in such arguments your goal is enhanced understanding so that you can open up a space for new perceptions and fresh ideas.

Consider how Frederick Douglass tried to broaden the outlook of his audiences when he delivered a Fourth of July oration in 1852. Most nineteenth-century Fourth of July speeches followed a pattern of praising the Revolutionary War heroes and emphasizing freedom, democracy, and justice. Douglass, a former slave, had that tradition in mind as he delivered his address, acknowledging the "great principles" that the "glorious anniversary" celebrates. But he also asked his (white) listeners to see the occasion from another point of view:

> Fellow-citizens, pardon me, allow me to ask, why am I called upon to speak here today? What have I, or those I represent, to do with your national independence? Are the great principles of political freedom and natural justice, embodied in the Declaration of Independence, extended to us? And am I, therefore, called upon to bring our humble offering to the national altar, and to confess the benefits and express devout gratitude for the blessings resulting from your independence to us? . . . I say it with a sad sense of the disparity between us. I am not included within the pale of this glorious anniversary! Your high independence only reveals the immeasurable distance between us. The blessings in which you, this day, rejoice, are not enjoyed in common. The rich inheritance of justice, liberty, prosperity and independence, bequeathed by your fathers, is shared by you, not by me. The sunlight that brought life

Frederick Douglass World History Archive/Alamy Stock Photo

and healing to you, has brought stripes and death to me. This Fourth of July is yours, not mine. You may rejoice, I must mourn.

—Frederick Douglass, "What to the Slave Is the Fourth of July?"

Although his speech is in some ways confrontational, Douglass is also inviting his audience to see a version of reality that they could have discovered on their own had they dared to imagine the lives of African Americans living in the shadows of American liberty. Issuing that invitation, and highlighting its consequences, points a way forward in the conflict between slavery and freedom, black and white, oppression and justice, although response to Douglass's invitation was a long time in coming.

More recently, in the aftermath of Donald J. Trump's unexpected victory in the 2016 presidential election, pundits on the political left reconsidered strategies that may have distanced many working-class voters from any appeal Hillary Clinton might have made. Kevin Drum in *Mother Jones* offers what amounts to a Rogerian analysis of how liberal Democrats (like himself) might recapture middle-American voters who swung to Trump by accepting, not denigrating, their political values, such as being pro-life or owning a gun for self-defense:

> In the same way that right-wing Republicans need to learn how to talk about women's issues, Democrats need to learn how to talk about middle America. No more deplorables. No more clinging to guns and religion. Less swarming over every tin-eared comment on race.
>
> —Kevin Drum, "Less Liberal Contempt, Please," May 31, 2017

In finding validity in views held by some of middle America's working-class voters, Drum urges his fellow liberals to take the high road of respect and learn to talk with those with whom they might share common interests.

The use of invitational argument like this in contemporary political life may seem rare, but in spite of much evidence to the contrary (think of brutal clashes on Twitter and cable news shows), the public *claims* to prefer nonpartisan and invitational rhetoric to one-on-one, winner-take-all battles. The lesson to take from Rogerian or invitational argument may be that it makes good sense to learn opposing positions well enough to state them accurately and honestly, to strive to understand the points of view of your opponents, to acknowledge those views fairly in your own work, and to look for solutions that benefit as many people as possible.

RESPOND •

Dividing into groups, choose a controversial topic that is frequently in the news, and decide how you might structure an argument on the subject, using the general principles of the classical oration. Then look at the same subject from a Rogerian or invitational perspective. How might your argument differ? Which approach would work better for your topic? For the audiences you might want to address?

Toulmin Argument

In *The Uses of Argument* (1958), British philosopher Stephen Toulmin presented structures to describe the way that ordinary people make reasonable arguments. Because Toulmin's system acknowledges the complications of life—situations when we qualify our thoughts with words such as *sometimes*, *often*, *presumably*, *unless*, and *almost*—his method isn't as airtight as formal logic that uses syllogisms (see p. 135 in this chapter and p. 71 in Chapter 4). But for that reason, Toulmin logic has become a powerful and, for the most part, practical tool for understanding and shaping arguments in the real world.

Toulmin argument will help you come up with and test ideas and also figure out what goes where in many kinds of arguments. Let's take a look at the basic elements of Toulmin's structure:

Claim	the argument you wish to prove
Qualifiers	any limits you place on your claim
Reason(s)/Evidence	support for your claim
Warrants	underlying assumptions that support your claim
Backing	evidence for warrant

If you wanted to state the relationship among them in a sentence, you might say:

> My claim is true, to a qualified degree, because of the following reasons, which make sense if you consider the warrant, backed by these additional reasons.

These terms—claim, evidence, warrants, backing, and qualifiers—are the building blocks of the Toulmin argument structure. Let's take them one at a time.

Making Claims

Toulmin arguments begin with **claims**, debatable and controversial statements or assertions you hope to prove.

A claim answers the question *So what's your point?* or *Where do you stand on that?* Some writers might like to ignore these questions and avoid stating a position. But when you make a claim worth writing about, then it's worth standing up and owning it.

Is there a danger that you might oversimplify an issue by making too bold a claim? Of course. But making that sweeping claim is a logical first step toward eventually saying something more reasonable and subtle. Here are some fairly simple, undeveloped claims:

Congress should enact legislation that establishes a path to citizenship for undocumented immigrants.

It's time to treat the opioid addiction in the United States as a medical crisis.

NASA should affirm its commitment to a human expedition to Mars.

Veganism is the most responsible choice of diet.

Military insurance should not cover the cost of sex reassignment surgery for service men and women.

Good claims often spring from personal experiences. You may have relevant work or military or athletic experience—or you may know a lot about music, film, sustainable agriculture, social networking, inequities in government services—all fertile ground for authoritative, debatable, and personally relevant claims.

RESPOND.

Claims aren't always easy to find. Sometimes they're buried deep within an argument, and sometimes they're not present at all. An important skill in reading and writing arguments is the ability to identify claims, even when they aren't obvious.

In class and working in a group, collect a sample of four to six brief argumentative postings from political blogs or editorial postings (from news sites). Read each item, and then try to identify every claim that the writer makes. When you've compiled a list of claims, look carefully at the words that the writer or writers use when stating their positions. Is there a common vocabulary? Can you find terms or phrases that signal an impending claim? Which of these seem most effective? Which ones seem least effective? Why?

Offering Evidence and Good Reasons

You can begin developing a claim by drawing up a list of reasons to support it or finding **evidence** that backs up the point.

Evidence and Reason(s) ⟶ So Claim

One student writer wanted to gather good reasons in support of an assertion that his college campus needed more official spaces for parking bicycles. He did some research, gathering statistics about parking-space allocation, numbers of people using particular designated slots, and numbers of bicycles registered on campus. Before he went any further, however, he listed his primary reasons for wanting to increase bicycle parking:

- **Personal experience:** At least twice a week for two terms, he was unable to find a designated parking space for his bike.
- **Anecdotes:** Several of his friends told similar stories. One even sold her bike as a result.
- **Facts:** He found out that the ratio of car to bike parking spaces was 100 to 1, whereas the ratio of cars to bikes registered on campus was 25 to 1.
- **Authorities:** The campus police chief told the college newspaper that she believed a problem existed for students who tried to park bicycles legally.

On the basis of his preliminary listing of possible reasons in support of the claim, this student decided that his subject was worth more research. He was on the way to amassing a set of good reasons and evidence that were sufficient to support his claim.

In shaping your own arguments, try putting claims and reasons together early in the writing process to create enthymemes. Think of these enthymemes as test cases or even as topic sentences:

> Bicycle parking spaces should be expanded because the number of bikes on campus far exceeds the available spots.

> It's time to lower the driving age because I've been driving since I was fourteen and it hasn't hurt me.

> National legalization of marijuana is long overdue since it is already legal in many states, has proven to be less harmful than alcohol, and provides effective relief from pain associated with cancer.

Academic arguments such as "Playing with Prejudice: The Prevalence and Consequences of Racial Stereotypes in Video Games" by Melinda C. R. Burgess et al. often closely follow the Toulmin structure, making sure that all their claims are well supported.

LINK TO P. 567

Violent video games should be carefully evaluated and their use monitored by the industry, the government, and parents because such games cause addiction and even psychological harm to players.

As you can see, attaching a reason to a claim often spells out the major terms of an argument.

But your work is just beginning when you've put a claim together with its supporting reasons and evidence—because readers are certain to begin questioning your statement. They might ask whether the reasons and evidence that you're offering actually do support the claim: should the driving age really be changed just because you've managed to drive since you were fourteen? They might ask pointed questions about your evidence: exactly how do you know that the number of bikes on campus far exceeds the number of spaces available? Eventually, you've got to address potential questions about the quality of your assumptions and the reliability of your evidence. The connection between claim and reason(s) is a concern at the next level in Toulmin argument.

Determining Warrants

Crucial to Toulmin argument is appreciating that there must be a logical and persuasive connection between a claim and the reasons and data supporting it. Toulmin calls this connection the **warrant**. It answers the

Briahna Joy Gray argues that charges of cultural appropriation imply ownership of culture, as represented by music, costume, food, etc. What warrants lie behind this claim?

LINK TO P. 620

"I know your type, you're the type who'll make me prove every claim I make."

Anticipate challenges to your claims. © Charles Barsotti/The New Yorker Collection/The Cartoon Bank question *How exactly do I get from the data to the claim?* Like the warrant in legal situations (a search warrant, for example), a sound warrant in an argument gives you authority to proceed with your case.

The warrant tells readers what your (often unstated) assumptions are—for example, that any major medical problem should be a concern of the government. If readers accept your warrant, you can then present specific evidence to develop your claim. But if readers dispute your warrant, you'll have to defend it before you can move on to the claim itself.

Stating warrants can be tricky because they can be phrased in various ways. What you're looking for is the general principle that enables you to justify the move from a reason to a specific claim—the bridge connecting them. The warrant is the assumption that makes the claim seem believable. It's often a value or principle that you share with your readers. Here's an easy example:

Don't eat that mushroom: it's poisonous.

The warrant supporting this enthymeme can be stated in several ways, always moving from the reason (*it's poisonous*) to the claim (*Don't eat that mushroom*):

Anything that is poisonous shouldn't be eaten.

If something is poisonous, it's dangerous to eat.

Here's the relationship, diagrammed:

Perfectly obvious, you say? Exactly—and that's why the statement is so convincing. If the mushroom in question is a death cap or destroying angel (and you might still need expert testimony to prove that it is), the warrant does the rest of the work, making the claim that it supports seem logical and persuasive.

Let's look at a similar example, beginning with the argument in its basic form:

> **We'd better stop for gas because the gauge has been reading empty for more than thirty miles.**

In this case, you have evidence that is so clear (a gas gauge reading empty) that the reason for getting gas doesn't even have to be stated: the tank is almost empty. The warrant connecting the evidence to the claim is also obvious:

> **If the fuel gauge of a car has been reading empty for more than thirty miles, then that car is about to run out of gas.**

Since most readers would accept this warrant as reasonable, they would also likely accept the statement the warrant supports.

Naturally, factual information might undermine the whole argument: the fuel gauge might be broken, or the driver might know from experience that the car will go another fifty miles even though the fuel gauge reads empty. But in most cases, readers would accept the warrant.

Now let's consider how stating and then examining a warrant can help you determine the grounds on which you want to make a case. Here's a political enthymeme of a familiar sort:

> **Flat taxes are fairer than progressive taxes because they treat all taxpayers in the same way.**

A simple icon—a skull and crossbones—can make a visual argument that implies a claim, a reason, and a warrant. PhotoLink/Getty Images

Warrants that follow from this enthymeme have power because they appeal to a core American value—equal treatment under the law:

> **Treating people equitably is the American way.**
>
> **All people should be treated in the same way.**

You certainly could make an argument on these grounds. But stating the warrant should also raise a flag if you know anything about tax policy. If the principle is obvious and universal, then why do federal and some state income taxes require people at higher levels of income to pay at higher tax rates than people at lower income levels? Could the warrant not be as universally popular as it seems at first glance? To explore the argument further, try stating the contrary claim and warrants:

> **Progressive taxes are fairer than flat taxes because people with more income can afford to pay more, benefit more from government, and shelter more of their income from taxes.**
>
> **People should be taxed according to their ability to pay.**
>
> **People who benefit more from government and can shelter more of their income from taxes should be taxed at higher rates.**

Now you see how different the assumptions behind opposing positions really are. If you decided to argue in favor of flat taxes, you'd be smart to recognize that some members of your audience might have fundamental reservations about your position. Or you might even decide to shift your entire argument to an alternative rationale for flat taxes:

> **Flat taxes are preferable to progressive taxes because they simplify the tax code and reduce the likelihood of fraud.**

Here, you have two stated reasons that are supported by two new warrants:

> **Taxes that simplify the tax code are desirable.**
>
> **Taxes that reduce the likelihood of fraud are preferable.**

Whenever possible, you'll choose your warrant knowing your audience, the context of your argument, and your own feelings.

Be careful, though, not to suggest that you'll appeal to any old warrant that works to your advantage. If readers suspect that your argument for progressive taxes really amounts to *I want to stick it to people who work harder than I*, your credibility may suffer a fatal blow.

Examples of Claims, Reasons, and Warrants

E-cigarettes legitimize smoking among youth and entice children by using flavors like bubblegum.

So the federal government should ban e-cigarettes from all public places.

<u>Since</u>

The Constitution was established to "promote the general welfare," and citizens are thus entitled to protection from harmful actions by others.

The Electoral College used to elect American presidents undermines rule by the majority of voters.

So it should be abolished.

<u>Since</u>

No electoral process should subvert majority rule.

I've been drinking since age fourteen without problems.

So the legal age for drinking should be lowered.

<u>Since</u>

What works for me should work for everyone else.

RESPOND●

At their simplest, warrants can be stated as "X is good" or "X is bad." Return to the editorials or blog posts that you analyzed in the exercise on p. 144, this time looking for the warrant that is behind each claim. As a way to start, ask yourself these questions:

If I find myself agreeing with the letter writer, what assumptions about the subject matter do I share with him/her?

If I disagree, what assumptions are at the heart of that disagreement?

The list of warrants you generate will likely come from these assumptions.

Offering Evidence: Backing

The richest, most interesting part of a writer's work—backing—remains to be done after the argument has been outlined. Clearly stated claims and warrants show you how much evidence you will need. Take a look at this brief argument, which is both debatable and controversial, especially in tough economic times:

NASA should affirm its commitment to a human expedition to Mars because Americans need a unifying national goal.

Here's one version of the warrant that supports the enthymeme:

What unifies the nation ought to be a national priority.

To run with this claim and warrant, you'd first need to place both in context. Human space exploration has been debated with varying intensity following the 1957 launch of the Soviet Union's *Sputnik* satellite, after the losses of the U.S. space shuttles *Challenger* (1986) and *Columbia* (2003), and after the retirement of the Space Shuttle program in 2011. Acquiring such background knowledge through reading, conversation, and inquiry of all kinds will be necessary for making your case. (See Chapter 3 for more on gaining authority.)

There's no point in defending any claim until you've satisfied readers that questionable warrants on which

Sticker honoring the retirement of the Space Shuttle program
© Steven Barrymore

the claim is based are defensible. In Toulmin argument, evidence you offer to support a warrant is called **backing**.

Warrant

What unifies the nation ought to be a national priority.

Backing

Americans want to be part of something bigger than themselves. (Emotional appeal as evidence)

In a country as diverse as the United States, common purposes and values help make the nation stronger. (Ethical appeal as evidence)

In the past, government investments such as the Hoover Dam and the *Apollo* moon program enhanced economic progress for many—though not all—Americans. (Logical appeal as evidence)

In addition to evidence to support your warrant (backing), you'll need evidence to support your claim:

Argument in Brief (Enthymeme/Claim)

NASA should launch a human expedition to Mars because Americans now need a unifying national goal.

Evidence

The American people are politically divided along lines of race, ethnicity, religion, gender, and class. (Fact as evidence)

A common challenge or problem often unites people to accomplish great things. (Emotional appeal as evidence)

A successful Mars mission would require the cooperation of the entire nation—and generate tens of thousands of jobs. (Logical appeal as evidence)

A human expedition to Mars would be an admirable scientific project for the nation to pursue. (Appeal to values as evidence)

As these examples show, appeals to values and emotions can be just as appropriate as appeals to logic and facts, and all such claims will be stronger if a writer presents a convincing ethos. In most arguments, appeals work together rather than separately, reinforcing each other. (See Chapter 3 for more on ethos.)

Using Qualifiers

Experienced writers know that qualifying expressions make writing more precise and honest. Toulmin logic encourages you to acknowledge limitations to your argument through the effective use of **qualifiers**. You can save time if you qualify a claim early in the writing process. But you might not figure out how to limit a claim effectively until after you've explored your subject or discussed it with others.

Qualifiers

few	more or less	often
it is possible	in some cases	perhaps
rarely	many	under these conditions
it seems	typically	possibly
some	routinely	for the most part
it may be	most	if it were so
sometimes	one might argue	in general

Never assume that readers understand the limits you have in mind. Rather, spell them out as precisely as possible, as in the following examples:

Unqualified Claim	People who don't go to college earn less than those who do.
Qualified Claim	*Statistics show that in most cases,* people who don't go to college earn less than those who do.

Understanding Conditions of Rebuttal

In the Toulmin system, potential objections to an argument are called **conditions of rebuttal**. Understanding and reacting to these conditions are essential to support your own claims where they're weak and also to recognize and understand the reasonable objections of people who see the world differently. For example, you may be a big fan of the Public Broadcasting Service (PBS) and the National Endowment for the Arts (NEA) and prefer that federal tax dollars be spent on these programs. So you offer the following claim:

Claim	The federal government should support the arts.

You need reasons to support this thesis, so you decide to present the issue as a matter of values:

Argument in Brief	The federal government should support the arts because it also supports the military.

Now you've got an enthymeme and can test the warrant, or the premises of your claim:

Warrant	If the federal government can support the military, then it can also support other programs.

But the warrant seems frail: you can hear a voice over your shoulder saying, "In essence, you're saying that *Because we pay for a military, we should pay for everything!*" So you decide to revise your claim:

Revised Argument	If the federal government can spend huge amounts of money on the military, then it can afford to spend moderate amounts on arts programs.

Trump's plans for PBS ...

KIDS, THE WORD FOR TODAY IS "HEARTLESS"!

Dave Granlund/Cagle Cartoons, Inc. © Cagle Cartoons Inc.

Now you've got a new warrant, too:

Revised Warrant	A country that can fund expensive programs can also afford less expensive programs.

This is a premise that you can defend, since you believe strongly that the arts are just as essential as a strong military is to the well-being of the country. Although the warrant now seems solid, you still have to offer strong grounds to support your specific and controversial claim. So you cite statistics from reputable sources, this time comparing the federal budgets for the military and the arts. You break them down in ways that readers can visualize, demonstrating that much less than a penny of every tax dollar goes to support the arts.

But then you hear those voices again, saying that the "common defense" is a federal mandate; the government is constitutionally obligated to support a military, and support for the arts is hardly in the same league! Looks like you need to add a paragraph explaining all the benefits the arts provide for very few dollars spent, and maybe you should suggest that such funding falls under the constitutional mandate to "promote the general welfare." Though not all readers will accept these grounds, they'll appreciate that you haven't ignored their point of view: you've gained credibility by anticipating a reasonable objection.

Dealing with conditions of rebuttal is an essential part of argument. But it's important to understand rebuttal as more than mere opposition. Anticipating objections broadens your horizons, makes you more open to alternative viewpoints, and helps you understand what you need to do to support your claim.

Within Toulmin argument, conditions of rebuttal remind us that we're part of global conversations: Internet newsgroups and blogs provide potent responses to positions offered by participants in discussions; instant messaging and social networking let you respond to and challenge others; links on Web sites form networks that are infinitely variable and open. In cyberspace, conditions of rebuttal are as close as your screen.

RESPOND•

Using an essay or a project you are composing, do a Toulmin analysis of the argument. When you're done, see which elements of the Toulmin scheme are represented. Are you short of evidence to support the warrant? Have you considered the conditions of rebuttal? Have you qualified your claim adequately? Next, write a brief revision plan: How will you buttress the argument in the places where it is weakest? What additional evidence will you offer for the warrant? How can you qualify your claim to meet the conditions of rebuttal? Then show your paper to a classmate and have him/her do a Toulmin analysis: a new reader will probably see your argument in different ways and suggest revisions that may not have occurred to you.

Outline of a Toulmin Argument

Consider the claim that was mentioned on p. 150:

Claim	The federal government should ban e-cigarettes.
Qualifier	The ban would be limited to public spaces.
Good Reasons	E-cigarettes have not been proven to be harmless. E-cigarettes legitimize smoking and also are aimed at recruiting teens and children with flavors like bubblegum and cotton candy.
Warrants	The Constitution promises to "promote the general welfare." Citizens are entitled to protection from harmful actions by others.
Backing	The United States is based on a political system that is supposed to serve the basic needs of its people, including their health.
Evidence	Analysis of advertising campaigns that reveal direct appeals to children Lawsuits recently won against e-cigarette companies, citing the link between e-cigarettes and a return to regular smoking Examples of bans on e-cigarettes already imposed in many public places

Authority	Cite the FDA and medical groups on effect of e-cigarette smoking.
Conditions of Rebuttal	E-cigarette smokers have rights, too. Smoking laws should be left to the states. Such a ban could not be enforced.
Responses	The ban applies to public places; smokers can smoke in private.

A Toulmin Analysis

You might wonder how Toulmin's method holds up when applied to an argument that is longer than a few sentences. Do such arguments really work the way that Toulmin predicts? In the following column from Bloomberg Opinion (June 19, 2017), Stephen L. Carter explains why he supports a unanimous Supreme Court decision protecting offensive speech. Carter, a professor

The Slants chose their band's name to reappropriate the offensive slur. Anthony Pidgeon/Getty Images

of law at Yale, novelist, and essayist, begins by offering background information on a trademark case brought before the Supreme Court by a band called The Slants. Carter signals quite clearly (in what amounts to his core claim) that the Court was right to strike down restrictions on potentially offensive trademarks set in place during World War II. To justify his support for the new ruling, Carter helps readers understand the Constitutional rationale for defending forms of speech that some people might regard as offensive, derogatory, or racist. Carter even draws upon the remarks of two Supreme Court justices who reach the same conclusion about the unconstitutionality of the so-called "disparagement clause" through very different approaches. As you will see below, many elements of Toulmin argument are in play throughout Carter's essay, even if they don't follow a predictable sequence from claim to reason to evidence to conditions of rebuttal to response pattern.

Offensive Speech Is Free Speech.
If Only We'd Listen.

STEPHEN L. CARTER

Contextual
information
leading up to
claim
The government doesn't get to punish offensive speech. That's the resounding message of the U.S. Supreme Court's unanimous decision Monday in *Matal v. Tam*, which struck down as unconstitutional the provisions of federal trademark law allowing the denial of registration for offensive or scandalous marks. The justices were able to agree on little other than the outcome—there are three separate opinions, not one of which in its entirety commanded a majority—but they all reach the same

Claim: Carter
endorses
"happy
conclusion."
happy conclusion. The federal bureaucracy is the wrong place to adjudicate questions of offensiveness.

More context
The case involved the effort of a band to register its name, The Slants, as a federal trademark. The application was denied under what is sometimes known as the "disparagement clause" of the Trademark Act on the ground that "slants" is an offensive term for Asian Americans.[1] The band appealed. A federal appellate court held that the provision allowing the government to make such

Reaffirmation of
claim
judgments violated the First Amendment. Now, happily, the Supreme Court has agreed.

Reason
It's obvious that the band's choice of name is itself an act of speech. All of the group's members are in fact Asian American, and they have argued from the start

Reason
that they chose "The Slants" as an act of "reappropriation"—that is, they are taking a pejorative and reversing

Qualifier
its significance. But even had the band's goal been less

---

1. The disparagement clause, Section 2(a) of the 1946 Lanham Act, bans registration of marks that the Patent and Trademark Office finds "may disparage . . . persons, living or dead, institutions, beliefs, or national symbols, or bring them into contempt, or disrepute." As the court notes, the provision has not been amended since its enactment.

progressive, the constitutional problem would remain. The First Amendment protects not admirable speech or good speech or likeable speech. It protects speech.

Warrant

The court firmly rejected efforts to save the disparagement clause. "No matter how the point is phrased," wrote Justice Samuel Alito in his plurality opinion, "its unmistakable thrust is this: The Government has an interest in preventing speech expressing ideas that offend." That argument, eight justices[2] agreed, is contrary to the First Amendment.[3]

Claim

Reasons

When I wrote about the case back in January, I pointed out that the disparagement clause of federal trademark law is a relic of the post–World War II era, when the felt need to enforce a uniformity of values led to public and private efforts to curtail speech considered offensive. Comic books and movies were censored. Certain music could not be played. You could be arrested for cursing in public. Over the years the disparagement clause has been used to deny registration for hundreds of marks, including "Madonna" and "Messias" (both for wine) and "Pussy" (for nonalcoholic beverages). Most famously, the courts have recently used the disparagement clause to

Claim
Reason

Evidence

---

2. Justice Neil Gorsuch was not involved in the case.

3. In his plurality opinion (some parts of which are also the opinion of the court), Justice Alito was called upon to navigate some tricky shoals. There is not space to discuss all of them here, but one bears mention. In order to strike down the disparagement clause, the justices had to find a way to distinguish the many cases allowing the government to restrict speech that it subsidizes. Alito's answer was that the programs where the Supreme Court has allowed government to refuse to support some viewpoints and favor others all involve direct cash payments, whereas here the applicant pays the government. It is true, he wrote, that benefits arise from trademark registration, but the same is true when the state registers real estate or issues "driver's licenses, motor vehicle registrations, and hunting, fishing, and boating licenses or permits." The distinction is not entirely persuasive but it is perfectly practical and draws a clear line for later application—exactly the qualities one wants in a Supreme Court opinion.

strike down federal registration of the trademarks owned by the Washington Redskins. After Monday's decision, the team will get its marks back.

Claim

We live in an era in which expression enjoys far more robust protection than the post-war period when the disparagement clause was adopted. That's a very good

Conditions of rebuttal

thing. True, not all of the consequences of our freedom are happy. I wish the world were less coarse than it has become. I wish that our political discourse were more civil, that social media did not use outrage to chase clicks, that popular entertainment featured less vulgarity and raunch. But I shudder at the thought that clean-

Response

ing things up is the job of government.

Claim

When we try to limit speech we find offensive we put the decision into the hands of bureaucrats—exactly the

Reason

wrong place. The same power that can restrict speech that hurts can restrict speech that gladdens. Alito acknowledged this point in what was surely a signal that the courts should not look kindly on efforts to regulate so-called hate speech:

Warrant

> Speech that demeans on the basis of race, ethnicity, gender, religion, age, disability, or any other similar ground is hateful; but the proudest boast of our free speech jurisprudence is that we protect the freedom to express "the thought we hate."

Justice Anthony Kennedy, in a concurring opinion joined by three of his colleagues, put the point differ-

Reason

ently. Even speech we hate, he pointed out, can wind up teaching us:

Evidence

> The danger of viewpoint discrimination is that the government is attempting to remove certain ideas or perspectives from a broader debate. The danger is all the greater if the ideas or perspectives are ones a particular audience might think offensive, at least at first hearing. An initial reaction may prompt further reflec-

Warrant

> tion, leading to a more reasoned, more tolerant position.

This is not, perhaps, a comfortable message for the era when the instinct of the offended is to swarm forth in anger and shut down unpopular campus speakers or presentations of Shakespeare. We as a people have never been very good at tolerating what we find intolerable. Nowadays in particular, we seem unable to imagine that we might learn anything from those with whom we disagree. Instead we too often retreat childlike to intellectual bubbles and political echo chambers where nothing we believe will be disturbed or even challenged. So perhaps the true message of *Matal v. Tam* is that it's time for us to grow up.

Response

Conditions of rebuttal

What Toulmin Teaches

As Carter's essay demonstrates, few arguments you read have perfectly sequenced claims or clear warrants, so you might not think of Toulmin's terms in building your own arguments. Once you're into your subject, it's easy to forget about qualifying a claim or finessing a warrant. But remembering what Toulmin teaches will always help you strengthen your arguments:

- Claims should be clear, reasonable, and carefully qualified.

- Claims should be supported with good reasons and evidence. Remember that a Toulmin structure provides the framework of an argument, which you fill out with all kinds of data, including facts, statistics, precedents, photographs, and even stories.

- Claims and reasons should be based on assumptions your audience will likely accept. Toulmin's focus on warrants can be confusing because it asks us to state the values that underlie our arguments—something many would rather not do. Toulmin also prompts us to consider how our assumptions relate to particular audiences.

- Effective arguments respectfully anticipate objections readers might offer. Toulmin argument acknowledges that any claim can crumble under certain conditions, so it encourages complex views that don't insist on absolute or unqualified positions.

It takes considerable experience to write arguments that meet all these conditions. Using Toulmin's framework brings them into play automatically. If you learn it well enough, constructing good arguments can become a habit.

Organization

As you think about organizing your argument, remember that cultural factors are at work: patterns that you find persuasive are probably ones that are deeply embedded in your culture. In the United States, many people expect a writer to "get to the point" as directly as possible and to articulate that point efficiently and unambiguously. The organizational patterns favored by many in business hold similarities to the classical oration—a highly explicit pattern that leaves little or nothing unexplained—introduction and thesis, background, overview of the parts that follow, evidence, other viewpoints, and conclusion. If a piece of writing follows this pattern, American readers ordinarily find it "well organized."

So it's no surprise that student writers in the United States are expected to make their structures direct and their claims explicit, leaving little unspoken. Their claims usually appear early in an argument, often in the first paragraph.

But not all cultures take such an approach. Some expect any claim or thesis to be introduced subtly, indirectly, and perhaps at the end of a work, assuming that audiences will "read between the lines" to understand what's being said. Consequently, the preferred structure of arguments (and face-to-face negotiations, as well) may be elaborate, repetitive, and full of digressions. Those accustomed to such writing may find more direct Western styles naive, childish, or even rude.

When arguing across cultures, look for cues to determine how to structure your presentations effectively. Here are several points to consider:

- Do members of your audience tend to be very direct, saying explicitly what they mean? Or are they more restrained? Consider adjusting your work to the expectations of the audience.

- Do members of your audience tend to respect authority and the opinions of groups? They may find blunt approaches disrespectful or contrary to their expectations.

- Consider when to state your thesis: At the beginning? At the end? Somewhere else? Not at all?

- Consider whether digressions are a good idea, a requirement, or an element to avoid.

8

Arguments of Fact

LEFT TO RIGHT: Richard Baker/Getty Images; Alfred Eisenstaedt/Getty Images; David R. Frazier Photolibrary, Inc./Alamy Stock Photo

Some people believe that extensive use of smartphones and social media is especially harmful to children and young adults, and recent research provides disturbing evidence that they may be right.

In the past, female screen stars like Marilyn Monroe could be buxom and curvy, less concerned about their weight than actresses today. Or so the legend goes. But measuring the costumes worn by Monroe and other actresses reveals a different story.

When an instructor announces a tough new attendance policy for her course, a student objects that there is no evidence that students who regularly attend classes perform any better than those who do not. The instructor begs to differ.

Understanding Arguments of Fact

Factual arguments come in many varieties, but they all try to establish whether something is or is not so, answering questions such as *Is a historical legend true? Has a crime occurred?* or *Are the claims of a scientific study replicable?* At first glance, you might object that these aren't arguments at all but just a matter of looking things up and then writing reports. And you'd be correct to an extent: people don't usually argue factual matters that are settled or undisputed (*The earth revolves around the sun*), that might be decided with simple research (*The Mendenhall Glacier has receded 1.75 miles since 1958*), or that are the equivalent of a rule (*One mile measures 5,280 feet*). Reporting facts, you might think, should be free of the friction of argument.

But the authority of "facts" has been routinely challenged. With a full generation of contemporary philosophers insisting that reality is just a creation of language, perhaps it's not surprising that politicians and pundits now find themselves arguing over "fake news," "known facts," and "alternative facts."

Yet facts do still become arguments whenever they're controversial on their own or challenge people's conventional beliefs and lifestyles. Disagreements about childhood obesity, endangered species, or energy production ought to have a kind of clean, scientific logic to them. But that's rarely the case because the facts surrounding them must be interpreted. Those interpretations then determine what we feed children, where we can build a dam, or how we heat our homes. In other words, serious factual arguments almost always have consequences. *Can we rely on wind and solar power to solve our energy needs? Will the Social Security trust fund really go broke? Is it healthy to eat fatty foods?* People need well-reasoned factual arguments on subjects of this kind to make informed decisions. Such arguments educate the public.

For the same reason, we need arguments to challenge beliefs that are common in a society but held on the basis of inadequate or faulty information. We sometimes need help, too, noticing change that is occurring all around us. So corrective arguments appear daily in the media, often based on studies written by scientists or researchers that the public would not encounter on their own. Many people, for example, still believe that talking on a cell phone while driving is just like listening to the radio. But their intuition is not based on hard data: scientific studies show that using a cell phone in a car is comparable to driving under the influence of alcohol. That's a fact. As a result, fifteen states (and counting) have banned the use of handheld phones while driving—and almost all now ban texting while driving.

Factual arguments also routinely address broad questions about how we understand the past. For example, are the accounts that we have of the American founding—or the Civil War, Reconstruction, or the heroics of the "Greatest Generation" in World War II—accurate? Or do the "facts" that we teach today sometimes reflect the perspectives and prejudices of earlier times or ideologies? The telling of history is almost always controversial and rarely settled: the British and Americans will always tell different versions of what happened in North America in 1776.

The Internet puts mountains of information at our fingertips, but we need to be sure to confirm whether or not that information is fact, using what Howard Rheingold calls "crap detection," the ability to distinguish between accurate information and inaccurate information, misinformation, or disinformation. (For more on "crap detection," see Chapter 19, "Evaluating Sources.")

As you can see, arguments of fact do much of the heavy lifting in our world. They report on what has been recently discovered or explore the implications of that new information. They also add interest and complexity to our lives, taking what might seem simple and adding new dimensions to it. In many situations, they're the precursors to other forms of analysis, especially causal and proposal arguments. Before we can explore why things happen as they do or solve problems, we need to do our best to determine the facts.

Jeff Stahler/Andrews McMeel Syndication

RESPOND•

For each topic in the following list, decide whether the claim is worth arguing to a college audience, and explain why or why not.

> Earthquakes at Yellowstone National Park are increasing in number and intensity.
>
> Many people die annually of heart disease.
>
> The planet would benefit enormously if more people learned to eat insects.
>
> Japan might have come to terms more readily in 1945 if the Allies in World War II hadn't demanded unconditional surrender.
>
> Boys would do better in school if there were more men teaching in elementary and secondary classrooms.
>
> The benefits of increasing oil and natural gas production via fracking more than outweigh the environmental downsides of the process.
>
> There aren't enough high-paying jobs for college graduates these days.
>
> Hydrogen may never be a viable alternative to fossil fuels because it takes too much energy to change hydrogen into a usable form.

Characterizing Factual Arguments

Factual arguments are often motivated by simple human curiosity or suspicion: *Are people who earn college degrees happier than those who don't? If being fat is so unhealthy, why aren't mortality rates rising? Does it matter economically that so many young people today think of themselves as foodies?* Researchers may notice a pattern that leads them to look more closely at some phenomenon or behavior, exploring questions such as *What if?* or *How come?* Or maybe a writer first notes something new or different or unexpected and wants to draw attention to that fact: *Contrary to expectations, suicide rates are much higher in rural areas than in urban ones.*

Such observations can lead quickly to **hypotheses**—that is, toward tentative and plausible statements of fact whose merits need to be examined more closely. *Perhaps people at different educational levels define happiness differently? Maybe being a little overweight isn't as bad for people as we've been told? Maybe self-identifying as a "foodie" is really a marker of class and social aspirations?* To support such hypotheses, writers then have to uncover evidence that reaches well beyond the casual observations that triggered an initial interest—like a news reporter motivated to see whether there's a verifiable story behind a source's tip.

For instance, the authors of *Freakonomics*, Stephen J. Dubner and Steven D. Levitt, were intrigued by the National Highway Traffic Safety Administration's claim that car seats for children were 54 percent effective in preventing deaths in auto crashes for children below the age of four. In a *New York Times* op-ed column entitled "The Seat-Belt Solution," they posed an important question about that factual claim:

> **But 54 percent effective compared with what? The answer, it turns out, is this: Compared with a child's riding completely unrestrained.**

Their initial question about that claim led them to a more focused inquiry, then to a database on auto crashes, and then to a surprising conclusion: for kids above age twenty-four months, those in car seats were statistically safer than those without any protection but weren't safer than those confined by ordinary seat belts (which are much simpler, cheaper, and more readily available devices). Looking at the statistics every which way, the authors wonder if children older than two years would be just as well off physically—and their parents less stressed and better off financially—if the government mandated seat belts rather than car seats for them.

What kinds of evidence typically appear in sound factual arguments? The simple answer might be "all sorts," but a case can be made that factual arguments try to rely more on "hard evidence" than do "constructed" arguments based on logic and reason (see Chapter 4). Even so, some pieces of evidence are harder than others!

Developing a Factual Argument

Entire Web sites are dedicated to finding and posting errors from news and political sources. Some, like Media Matters for America and Accuracy in Media, take overtly partisan stands. Here's a one-day sampling of headlines from Media Matters:

> **After NASA Announces It Found Water on Mars, Rush Limbaugh Says It's Part of a Climate Change Conspiracy**

> **Trump administration met with a GOP donor and a Fox contributor about a fake story meant to distract from Russia probe**

> **Fox hosts can't keep their facts straight while praising Trump's immigration cuts**

And here's a listing from Accuracy in Media from the same day:

Major Newspapers Just Pretend to Have Conservative Columnists

Left Claims Hitler-Style "Indoctrination" in Trump's Boy Scouts Speech

***Washington Post* Reluctantly Admits Stock Market Gains Linked to Trump**

It would be hard to miss the blatant political agendas at work on these sites.

Other fact-checking organizations have better reputations when it comes to assessing the truths behind political claims and media presentations. Although both are also routinely charged with bias, Pulitzer Prize–winning PolitiFact.com and FactCheck.org at least make an effort to seem fair-minded across a broader political spectrum. FactCheck.org, for example, provides a detailed analysis of the claims it investigates in relatively neutral and denotative language, and lists the sources its researchers used—just as if its writers were doing a research paper. At its best, FactCheck.org demonstrates what one valuable kind of factual argument can accomplish.

Any factual argument that you might compose—from how you state your claim to how you present evidence and the language you use—should be similarly shaped by the occasion for the argument and a desire to serve the audiences that you hope to reach. We can offer some general advice to help you get started.

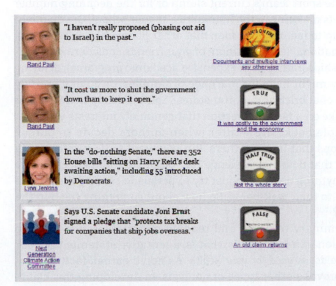

PolitiFact uses a meter to rate political claims from "True" to "Pants on Fire." Poynter Institute

RESPOND●

The Annenberg Public Policy Center at the University of Pennsylvania hosts FactCheck.org, a Web site dedicated to separating facts from opinion or falsehood in the area of politics. It claims to be politically neutral. Find a case that interests you, either a recent controversial item listed on its homepage or another from its archives. Carefully study the item. Pay attention to the devices that FactCheck.org uses to suggest or ensure objectivity and the way that it handles facts and statistics. Then offer your own brief *factual* argument about the site's objectivity.

In their report about food insecurity on college campuses, researchers James Dubick, Brandon Mathews, and Clare Cady offer an argument of fact based on more than 3,700 surveys of students on 34 college campuses.

LINK TO P. 634

Identifying an Issue

To offer a factual argument of your own, you need to identify an issue or problem that will interest you and potential readers. Look for situations or phenomena—local or national—that seem novel or out of the ordinary in the expected order of things. For instance, you might notice that many people you know are deciding not to attend college. How widespread is this change, and who are the people making this choice?

Or follow up claims that strike you as at odds with the facts as you know them or believe them. Maybe you doubt explanations being offered for your favorite sport team's current slump or for the declining number of male students majoring in the humanities at your school. Or you might give a local spin to factual questions that other people have already formulated on a national level. Are more of your friends considering technical apprenticeships (rather than expensive academic programs), delaying any plans they might have for marriage or families, or buying entirely online instead of at brick and mortar stores? You will likely write a better paper if you take on a factual question that genuinely interests you.

In fact, whole books are written when authors decide to pursue factual questions that intrigue them. But you want to be careful not to argue matters that pose no challenge for you or your audiences. You're not offering anything new if you just try to persuade readers that smoking is harmful to their well-being. So how about something fresh in the area of health?

Quick preliminary research and reading might allow you to move from an intuition to a hypothesis, that is, a tentative statement of your claim: *Having a dog is good for your health.* As noted earlier, factual arguments often provoke other types of analysis. In developing this claim, you'd need to explain what "good for your health" means, potentially an argument of definition. You'd also likely find yourself researching causes of the phenomenon if you can demonstrate that it is factual. As it turns out, your canine hypothesis would have merit if you defined "good for health" as "encouraging exercise." Here's the lede to a 2011 *New York Times* story reporting recent research:

> If you're looking for the latest in home exercise equipment, you may want to consider something with four legs and a wagging tail.
>
> Several studies now show that dogs can be powerful motivators to get people moving. Not only are dog owners more likely to take regular walks, but new research shows that dog walkers are more active overall than people who don't have dogs.
>
> —Tara Parker-Pope, "Forget the Treadmill. Get a Dog," March 14, 2011

As always, there's another side to the story: what if people likely to get dogs are the very sort already inclined to be more physically active? You could explore that possibility as well (and researchers have) and then either modify your initial hypothesis or offer a new one. That's what hypotheses are for. They are works in progress.

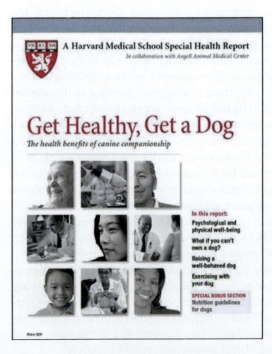

A Harvard source for your paper on dogs and health?

RESPOND•

Working with a group of colleagues, generate a list of a dozen "mysteries" regularly explored on TV shows, in blogs, or in tabloid newspapers. Here are three to get you started—the alien crash landing at Roswell, the existence of Atlantis, and the uses of Area 51 in Nevada. Then decide which—if any—of these puzzlers might be resolved or explained in a reasonable factual argument and which ones remain eternally mysterious and improbable. Why are people attracted to such topics? Would any of these items provide material for a noteworthy factual argument?

Read C. Richard King's excerpt from *Redskins: Insult and Brand* in Chapter 23. What kind of research does King use to support his argument?

LINK TO P. 554

Researching Your Hypothesis

How and where you research your subject will depend, naturally, on your subject. You'll certainly want to review Chapter 18, "Finding Evidence," Chapter 19, "Evaluating Sources," and Chapter 20, "Using Sources," before constructing an argument of fact. Libraries and the Web will provide you with deep resources on almost every subject. Your task will typically be to separate the best sources from all the rest. The word *best* here has many connotations: some reputable sources may be too technical for your audiences; some accessible sources may be pitched too low or be too far removed from the actual facts.

You'll be making judgment calls like this routinely. But do use primary sources whenever you can. For example, when gathering a comment from a source on the Web, trace it whenever possible to its original site, and read the comment in its full context. When statistics are quoted, follow them back to the source that offered them first to be sure that they're recent and reputable. Instructors and librarians can help you appreciate the differences. Understand that even sources with pronounced biases can furnish useful information, provided that you know how to use them, take their limitations into account, and then share what you know about the sources with your readers.

Sometimes, you'll be able to do primary research on your own, especially when your subject is local and you have the resources to do it. Consider conducting a competent survey of campus opinions and attitudes, for example, or study budget documents (often public) to determine trends in faculty salaries, tuition, student fees, and so on. Primary research of this sort can be challenging because even the simplest surveys or polls have to be intelligently designed and executed in a way that samples a representative population (see Chapter 4). But the work could pay off in an argument that brings new information to readers.

Refining Your Claim

As you learn more about your subject, you might revise your hypothesis to reflect what you've discovered. In most cases, these revised hypotheses will grow increasingly complex and specific. Following are three versions of essentially the same claim, with each version offering more information to help readers judge its merit:

- Americans really did land on the moon, despite what some people think!

- Since 1969, when the *Eagle* supposedly landed on the moon, some people have been unjustifiably skeptical about the success of the United States' *Apollo* program.

- Despite plentiful hard evidence to the contrary—from *Saturn V* launches witnessed by thousands to actual moon rocks tested by independent labs worldwide—some people persist in believing falsely that NASA's moon landings were filmed on deserts in the American Southwest as part of a massive propaganda fraud.

'...And, of course, there are the conspiracy theorists who say that it was all a big hoax and I didn't jump over it at all.'

KES/CartoonStock.com

The additional details about the subject might also suggest new ways to develop and support it. For example, conspiracy theorists claim that the absence of visible stars in photographs of the moon landing is evidence that it was staged, but photographers know that the camera exposure needed to capture the foreground—astronauts in their bright space suits—would have made the stars in the background too dim to see. That's a key bit of evidence for this argument.

As you advance in your research, your thesis will likely pick up even more qualifying words and expressions, which help you to make reasonable claims. Qualifiers—words and phrases such as *some, most, few, for most people, for a few users, under specific conditions, usually, occasionally, seldom,* and so on—will be among your most valuable tools in a factual argument. (See p. 153 in Chapter 7 for more on qualifiers.)

Sometimes it will be important to contextualize a factual claim for others who may find it hard to accept. Of course, you could just present the hard numbers, but research suggests that many people double down on their positions when offered contrary facts. What to do? Michael Shermer, writing in *Scientific American*, suggests these common sense strategies:

> [W]hat can we do to convince people of the error of their beliefs? From my experience, 1. keep emotions out of the exchange, 2. discuss, don't attack (no *ad hominem* and no *ad Hitlerum*), 3. listen carefully and try to articulate the other position accurately, 4. show respect, 5. acknowledge that you understand why someone might hold that opinion, and 6. try to show how changing facts does not necessarily mean changing worldviews. These strategies may not always work to change people's minds, but now that the nation has just been put through a political fact-check wringer, they may help reduce unnecessary divisiveness.
> —Michael Shermer, "How to Convince Someone When Facts Fail"

Deciding Which Evidence to Use

In this chapter, we've blurred the distinction between factual arguments for scientific and technical audiences and those for the general public (in magazines, blogs, social media sites, television documentaries, and so on). In the former kind of arguments, readers will expect specific types of evidence arranged in a formulaic way. Such reports may include a hypothesis, a review of existing research on the subject, a description of methods, a presentation of results, and finally a formal discussion of the findings. If you are thinking "lab report," you are already familiar with an academic form of a factual argument with precise standards for evidence.

Less scientific factual arguments—claims about our society, institutions, behaviors, habits, and so on—are seldom so systematic, and they may draw on evidence from a great many different media. For instance, you might need to review old newspapers, scan videos, study statistics on government Web sites, read transcripts of congressional hearings, record the words of eyewitnesses to an event, glean information by following experts on Twitter, and so on. Very often, you will assemble your arguments from material found in credible, though not always concurring, authorities and resources—drawing upon the factual findings of scientists and scholars, but perhaps using their original insights in novel ways.

For example, you might be intrigued by a much cited article from the *Atlantic* (August 5, 2017) in which author Jean M. Twenge reviews evidence that suggests that adolescents who spend more and more time on their cellphones are increasingly unhappy—to the detriment of their emotional health. Here's an important moment in her lengthy argument:

> You might expect that teens spend so much time in these new spaces because it makes them happy, but most data suggest that it does not. The Monitoring the Future survey, funded by the National Institute on Drug Abuse and designed to be nationally representative, has asked 12th-graders more than 1,000 questions every year since 1975 and queried eighth- and 10th-graders since 1991. The survey asks teens how happy they are and also how much of their leisure time they spend on various activities, including nonscreen activities such as in-person social interaction and exercise, and, in recent years, screen activities such as using social media, texting, and browsing the web. The results could not be clearer: Teens who spend more time than average on screen activities are more likely to be unhappy, and those who spend more time than average on nonscreen activities are more likely to be happy.
>
> There's not a single exception. All screen activities are linked to less happiness, and all nonscreen activities are linked to more happiness.
>
> —Jean M. Twenge, "Have Smartphones Destroyed a Generation?"

Reading such dire news (and the article reports even more frightening increases in suicide), may raise new questions for you: Are there contrary studies? Is it conceivable that time spent online has benefits? Twenge herself notes, for example, that teen pregnancies have dropped dramatically in recent years. Perhaps, too, adolescents so inwardly directed by screen use might develop into more sensitive and less violent adults? Such considerations might lead you to look for research that complicates the earlier work by bringing fresh facts or perspectives to the table.

Often, though, you may have only a limited number of words or pages in which to make an academic argument. What do you do then? You present your best evidence as powerfully as possible: you *can* make a persuasive factual case with just a few examples—three or four often suffice to make a point. Indeed, going on too long or presenting even good data in uninteresting ways can undermine a claim.

Presenting Your Evidence

In *Hard Times* (1854), British author Charles Dickens poked fun at a pedagogue he named Thomas Gradgrind, who preferred hard facts before all things human or humane. When poor Sissy Jupe (called "girl number twenty" in his awful classroom) is unable at his command to define *horse*, Gradgrind turns to his star pupil, Bitzer:

> "Bitzer," said Thomas Gradgrind. "Your definition of a horse."
> "Quadruped. Graminivorous. Forty teeth, namely twenty-four grinders, four eyeteeth, and twelve incisive. Sheds coat in the spring; in marshy countries, sheds hoofs, too. Hoofs hard, but requiring to be shod with iron. Age known by marks in mouth." Thus (and much more) Bitzer.
> "Now girl number twenty," said Mr. Gradgrind. "You know what a horse is."
>
> —Charles Dickens, *Hard Times*

But does Bitzer? Rattling off facts about a subject isn't quite the same thing as knowing it, especially when your goal is, as it is in an argument of fact, to educate and persuade audiences. So you must take care how you present your evidence.

Factual arguments, like any others, take many forms. They can be as simple and pithy as a letter to the editor (or Bitzer's definition of a horse) or as comprehensive and formal as a senior thesis or even a dissertation, meant for just two or three readers evaluating the competence of your work. But to earn the attention of readers in more public forums, you may need to work harder, affirming your expertise by offering engaging and authoritative sources, presenting your argument with grace and clarity, including tables, graphs, photographs and other visual evidence when appropriate, and documenting all your claims. Such moves will establish the ethos of your work, making it seem serious, credible, well-conceived, and worth reading.

Considering Design and Visuals

When you prepare a factual argument, consider how you can present your evidence most effectively. Precisely because factual arguments often rely on evidence that can be measured, computed, or illustrated, they benefit from thoughtful, even artful presentation of data. If you have lots of examples, you might arrange them in a list (bulleted or otherwise) and keep the language in each item roughly parallel. If you have an argument that can be translated into a table, chart, or graph (see Chapter 14), try it. On page 178, for example, are three of the six tables that accompanied Jean M. Twenge's essay on smartphones, all dramatically illustrating a decline in various adolescent behaviors following the introduction of the iPhone in 2007. And if there's a more dramatic medium for your factual argument—a Prezi slide show, a multimedia mashup, a documentary video posted via a social network—experiment with it, checking to be sure it would satisfy the assignment.

Images and photos—from technical illustrations to imaginative re-creations—have the power to document what readers might otherwise have to imagine, whether actual conditions of drought, poverty, or a disaster like Hurricane Harvey that dropped 27 trillion gallons of water on Texas and Louisiana in 2017, or the dimensions of the Roman forum as it existed in the time of Julius Caesar. Readers today expect the arguments they read to include visual elements, and there's little reason not to offer this assistance if you have the technical skills to create them.

Consider also the rapid development of the genre known as infographics—basically data presented in bold visual form. These items can be humorous and creative, but many, such as "Learning Out of Poverty" on the following page, make powerful factual arguments even when they leave it to viewers to draw their own conclusions. Just search "info-graphics" on the Web to find many examples.

For an example of how to use design effectively in a factual argument, see "How Do Your Eating Habits Differ from Your Grandparents'?" in Chapter 24. Compare the chart to the table that accompanies it. How does design impact the success of the factual argument?

LINK TO P. 601

THE SMARTPHONE GENERATION: A STATISTICAL PORTRAIT

The constant presence of the internet, particularly social media, is changing the behavior and attitudes of today's teens.

1 Not Hanging Out With Friends
Times per week teenagers go out without their parents

- 12th-graders
- 10th-graders
- 8th-graders

2 In No Rush to Drive
Percentage of 12th-graders who drive

- Drove at all in the past year
- Have a driver's license

3 Less Dating ...
Percentage of teenagers who ever go out on dates

- 12th-graders
- 10th-graders
- 8th-graders

Jean M. Twenge uses graphs to support her claims about the impact of smartphones on teenagers. © 2018 The Atlantic Media Co., as first published in The Atlantic Magazine. All rights reserved. Distributed by Tribune Content Agency, LLC.

"Learning Out of Poverty." Infographics like this one turn facts and data into arguments. USAID

GUIDE to writing an argument of fact

● Finding a Topic

You're entering an argument of fact when you:

- make a claim about fact or existence that's controversial or surprising: *Climate change is threatening species in all regions by extending the range of non-native plants and animals.*

- correct an error of fact: *The overall abortion rate is not increasing in the United States, though rates are increasing in some states.*

- challenge societal myths: *Many Mexicans fought alongside Anglos in battles that won Texas its independence from Mexico.*

- wish to discover the state of knowledge about a subject or examine a range of perspectives and points of view: *The rationales of parents who homeschool their children reveal some surprising differences.*

● Researching Your Topic

Use both a library and the Web to locate the information you need. A research librarian is often a valuable resource, as are experts or eyewitnesses. Begin research by consulting the following types of sources:

- scholarly books on your subject

- newspapers, magazines, reviews, and journals (online and print)

- online databases

- government documents and reports

- Web sites, blogs, social networking sites, and listservs or newsgroups

- experts in the field, some of whom might be right on your campus

Do field research if appropriate—a survey, a poll, or systematic observation. Or invite people with a stake in the subject to present their interpretations of the facts. Evaluate all sources carefully, making sure that each is authoritative and credible.

● Formulating a Hypothesis

Don't rush into a thesis. Instead, begin with a hypothesis that expresses your beliefs at the beginning of the project but that may change as you learn more. It's okay to start with a question to which you don't have an answer or with a broad, general interest in a subject:

- **Question:** Have higher admissions standards at BSU reduced the numbers of entering first-year students from small, rural high schools?
- **Hypothesis:** Higher admissions standards at BSU are reducing the number of students admitted from rural high schools, which tend to be smaller and less well-funded than those in suburban and urban areas.
- **Question:** Have music sites like Pandora and Spotify reduced the amount of illegal downloading of music?
- **Hypothesis:** Services like Pandora and Spotify may have done more than lawsuits by record companies to discourage illegal downloads of music.
- **Question:** How dangerous is nuclear energy, really?
- **Hypothesis:** The danger posed by nuclear power plants is far less than that attributable to other viable energy sources.
- **Question:** Why can't politicians and citizens agree about the threat posed by the huge federal deficit?
- **Hypothesis:** People with different points of view see different threats in the budget numbers and so react differently.

● Examples of Arguable Factual Claims

- A campus survey that shows that far more students have read *Harry Potter and the Prisoner of Azkaban* than *Hamlet* indicates that our current core curriculum lacks depth.
- Evidence suggests that the European conquest of the Americas may have had more to do with infectious diseases than any superiority in technology or weaponry.
- In the long run, dieting may be more harmful than moderate overeating.

Preparing a Proposal

If your instructor asks you to prepare a proposal for your project, here's a format that may help:

State your thesis or hypothesis completely. If you are having trouble doing so, try outlining it in Toulmin terms:

> Claim:
>
> Reason(s):
>
> Warrant(s):

Alternatively, you might describe the complications of a factual issue you hope to explore in your project, with the thesis perhaps coming later.

- Explain why the issue you're examining is important, and provide the context for raising the issue. Are you introducing new information, making available information better known, correcting what has been reported incorrectly, or complicating what has been understood more simply?

- Identify and describe those readers you most hope to reach with your argument. Why is this group of readers most appropriate for your project? What are their interests in the subject? How might you involve them in the paper?

- Discuss the kinds of evidence you expect to use in the project and the research the paper will require.

- Briefly discuss the key challenges you anticipate in preparing your argument.

Considering Genre and Media

Your instructor may specify that you use a particular genre and/or medium. If not, ask yourself these questions to help you make a good choice:

- What genre is most appropriate for your argument of fact? Does it call for an academic essay, a report, an infographic, a brochure, or something else?

- What medium is most appropriate for your argument? Would it be best delivered orally to a live audience? Presented as an audio essay or podcast? Presented in print only or in print with illustrations?

- Will you need visuals, such as moving or still images, maps, graphs, charts—and what function will they play in your argument? Make sure they are not just "added on" but are necessary components of the argument.

Thinking about Organization

The simplest structure for a factual argument is to make a claim and then prove it. But even a basic approach needs an introductory section that provides a context for the claim and a concluding section that assesses the implications of the argument. A factual argument that corrects an error or provides an alternative view of some familiar concept or historical event will also need a section early on explaining what the error or the common belief is. Be sure your opening section answers the *who*, *what*, *where*, *when*, *how*, and (maybe) *why* questions that readers will bring to the case.

Factual arguments offered in some academic fields follow formulas and templates. A format favored in the hard sciences and also in the social and behavioral sciences is known by its acronym, IMRAD, which stands for Introduction, Methods, Research, and Discussion. Another typical format calls for an abstract, a review of literature, a discussion of method, an analysis, and a references list. When you have flexibility in the structure of your argument, it makes sense to lead with a striking example to interest readers in your subject and then to conclude with your strongest evidence. Pay particular attention to transitions between key points.

If you are defending a specific claim, anticipate the ways people with different points of view might respond to your argument. Consider how to address such differences respectfully in the body of your argument. But don't let a factual argument with a persuasive thesis end with concessions or refutations, especially in pieces for the general public. Such a strategy leaves readers thinking about problems with your claim at precisely the point when they should be impressed by its strengths. On the other hand, if your factual argument becomes exploratory, you may find yourself simply presenting a range of positions.

Getting and Giving Response: Questions for Peer Response

Your instructor may assign you to a group for the purpose of reading and responding to each other's drafts. If not, ask for responses from serious readers or consultants at a writing center. Use the following questions to evaluate a colleague's draft. Since specific comments help more than general observations, be sure to illustrate your comments with examples. Some of the questions below assume a conventional, thesis-driven project, but more exploratory or invitational arguments of fact also need to be clearly phrased, organized, and supported with evidence.

The Claim

- Does the claim clearly raise a serious and arguable factual issue?
- Is the claim as clear and specific as possible?
- Is the claim qualified? If so, how?

Evidence for the Claim

- Is the evidence provided enough to persuade readers to believe your claim? If not, what additional evidence would help? Does any of the evidence seem inappropriate or ineffective? Why?
- Is the evidence in support of the claim simply announced, or do you explain its significance and appropriateness? Is more discussion needed?
- Are readers' potential objections to the claim or evidence addressed adequately? Are alternative positions understood thoroughly and presented fairly?
- What kinds of sources are cited? How credible and persuasive will they be to readers? What other kinds of sources might work better?
- Are all quotations introduced with appropriate signal phrases (such as "As Tyson argues, . . .") and blended smoothly into the writer's sentences?
- Are all visuals titled and labeled appropriately? Have you introduced them and commented on their significance?

Organization and Style

- How are the parts of the argument organized? Is this organization effective?
- Will readers understand the relationships among the claims, supporting reasons, warrants, and evidence? If not, how might those connections be clearer? Is the function of every visual clear? Are more transitions needed? Would headings or graphic devices help?

- Are the transitions or links from point to point, sentence to sentence, and paragraph to paragraph clear and effective? If not, how could they be improved?

- Are all visuals carefully integrated into the text? Is each visual introduced and commented on to point out its significance? Is each visual labeled as a figure or a table and given a caption as well as a citation?

- Is the style suited to the subject? Is it too formal, casual, or technical? Can it be improved?

- Which sentences seem effective? Which ones seem weaker, and how could they be improved? Should short sentences be combined, and any longer ones be broken up?

- How effective are the paragraphs? Too short or too long? How can they be improved?

- Which words or phrases seem effective? Do any seem vague or inappropriate for the audience or the writer's purpose? Are technical or unfamiliar terms defined?

Spelling, Punctuation, Mechanics, Documentation, and Format

- Are there any errors in spelling, punctuation, capitalization, and the like?

- Is an appropriate and consistent style of documentation used for parenthetical citations and the list of works cited or references? (See Chapter 22.)

- Does the paper or project follow an appropriate format? Is it appropriately designed and attractively presented? How could it be improved?

PROJECTS.

1. Turn a database of information you find in the library or online into a traditional argument or, alternatively, into a multimodal project such as an infographic that offers various ways to present a claim. FedStats, a government Web site, provides endless data, but so can the sports or financial sections of a newspaper. Once you find a rich field of study, examine the data and draw your ideas from it, perhaps amplifying these ideas with material from other related sources of information. If you decide to create an infographic, you'll find good examples online at VizWorld or Cool Infographics. Software tools you can use to create infographics include Piktochart and Google Public Data Explorer. Have fun.

2. Write an argument about a factual matter you are confident—based on personal experience or your state of knowledge—that most people get wrong, time and again. Use your expertise to correct this false impression.

3. Tough economic and political times sometimes reinforce and sometimes undermine cultural myths. With your classmates, generate a list of common beliefs about education, employment, family life, marriage, social progress, technology, and so on that seem to be under unusual scrutiny today. *Does it still pay to invest in higher education? Do two-parent households matter as much as they used to? Can children today expect to do better than their parents? Is a home still a good investment?* Pick one area to explore in depth, narrow the topic as much as you can, and then gather facts that inform it by doing research, perhaps working collaboratively to expand your findings. Turn your investigation into a factual argument.

4. Since critic and writer Nicholas Carr first asked "Is Google Making Us Stupid?" many have answered with a resounding "yes," arguing that extensive time online is reducing attention spans and leaving readers less critical than ever. Others have disagreed, saying that new technologies are doing just the opposite—expanding our brain power. Do some research on this controversy, on the Web or in the library, and consult with a wide range of people interested in the subject, perhaps gathering them together for a panel discussion. Then offer a factual argument based on what you uncover, reflecting the range of perspectives and opinions you have encountered.

The Snacktivities and Musings of a Millennial Foodie

KATE BEISPEL

It's 80 degrees and I'm breaking a sweat as I hoist my just-bought lobster roll into the air, struggling to position it in a way that focuses on the mountain of chopped lobster baking in butter, while subtly blurring out the ocean behind it. I have one goal for this picture—to make it on to the *Food in the Air* Instagram account. I've spent months of my life positioning meals in front of breathtaking backdrops and sending them in to the anonymous geniuses that run this account, with no success. This meal, I've decided, will be my big break.

Beispel draws readers in with a first-person point of view.

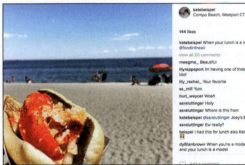

Courtesy of Kate Beispel

Kate Beispel wrote "The Snacktivities and Musings of a Millennial Foodie" for a writing class when she was a senior at the University of Texas at Austin. Drawing on both personal experience and a number of sources, this communications/journalism major argues that her generation, so uniquely and oddly focused on food and technology, is changing both business and culture. To prove her case, she draws on plentiful lifestyle evidence that members of her generation will almost certainly recognize. Beispel is pursuing a career in technology and media.

187

It turns out it wasn't. But that hasn't stopped me. I've continued to seek out amazing meals and yell "wait, wait, wait" if someone dares to take a bite before I take a picture. Trying new foods, finding something amazing, and sharing it with all of my followers is one of my hobbies. And I'm not alone.

The word *love* doesn't do justice to the relationship between Millennials and food. It's no secret—we're obsessed. It's a strange dichotomy—that a generation often perceived as unwilling to work hard in a job market with little prospects would be so invested in a gourmet lifestyle at a relatively young age. According to *Bon Appetit*, a monthly food magazine owned by Condé Nast, Millennials spend over $96 billion a year on food. Forty-four percent of the money they spend on food goes towards eating out (Peele). The numbers don't lie: this is a generation that values food and the experience that comes with dining. And of course, there's a name for them. Foodies.

"Foodies" are self-proclaimed food critics who understand the industry and all it has to offer. Or at least they think they do. They may *even* have a food blog. Foodies need neither a formal background in culinary education nor the ability to cook. Last week my friends and I decided to try poke, a Hawaiian fish salad dish that's very in right now. With no prior experience trying poke and no knowledge of what it's supposed to taste like, we critiqued our bowls as if we were Hawaiian natives. "The chunks of fish are too large," remarked my friend. "They should be about 50% smaller," someone else agreed. I couldn't help but roll my eyes and laugh at the way foodies of this generation speak of food with the confidence of seasoned chefs.

While Millennials are not the only age group who loves food, the aspects they value differ from those of other generations. Cherishing the quality of food has been a characteristic important to many diners over the years. The term "gourmet" has long been used to describe

Factual evidence from a reputable magazine supports Beispel's claim about millennials' obsession with food.

Poking fun at herself and her friends, Beispel supports her claim with an example and gains the trust of her readers.

Defining the term *gourmet*, Beispel analyzes how millennials differ from previous generations.

these food connoisseurs. Michelin star restaurants, *New York Times* restaurant reviews, and celebrities who write cookbooks aren't new to the scene either—these things have been present in food culture for decades. Yet it is hard to pin down exactly when "foodie" began to replace "gourmet" as a term to describe those with educated palettes.

Many still link an obsession with food to affluence and class, but the term foodie clearly lacks upper-class connotations. The Millennial foodie doesn't need or expect tablecloths and silver spoons, and some extremely popular restaurants today even arrive in the form of food trucks. Today, fifty percent of Millennials refer to themselves as foodies, according to a recent study conducted by advertising agency BBDO, further indicating that the food obsession and appreciation isn't just for the wealthy ("How Millennials"). Where there's a food line, there's a Millennial waiting: foodie culture is accessible to anyone who wants to be a part of it.

This paragraph builds on the previous one by expanding the analysis of millennial foodies.

Unsurprisingly, technology has signaled the difference between gourmet cultures of the past and the foodies of the present and future. In a 2014 Nielsen survey, Millennials cited technology as *the* defining characteristic of their generation ("Millennials: Technology"). For a generation obsessed with food, having the ability to share and tell stories about their meals is key. And they don't hold back. They believe that the aesthetics and presentation of a plate can't be enjoyed without photographic evidence of it first.

The importance of technology is emphasized via survey data.

Walk into a restaurant and look around—people are photographing their food before they eat. What they plan to do with this picture is anybody's guess. But there's no shortage of platforms available for Millennials to share their culinary experiences and combine their two favorite obsessions—food and technology. A Tumblr account entitled "Pictures of Hipsters Taking Pictures of Food" even exists solely to document people photographing food that they didn't cook and simply ordered (a skill in itself).

Pictures of Hipsters Taking
Pictures of Food Tumblr

Clearly, food has gone viral. Instagram is a foodie haven. Accounts like @igbrunchclub and @infatuation have upwards of 700,000 followers who tune in to see what these often non-certified and not-formally edu-cated Instagram users have to say about food. For more specialized food experiences, Instagram users can check out accounts such as @spoonuniversity or @newforkcity that tailor their accounts to college students or specific cities. Even though @tinyfoods posts only pictures of miniature food, the site still has thousands of followers. There is a luscious culinary experience for any range of tastes and interests on the 'Gram. It's hard to exit the app without feeling hungry.

Snapchat and Facebook have also jumped on the bandwagon. The food phenomenon is now global and at the tip of a foodie's fingers. Open up Snapchat and the *Food Network* Snapchat channel boasts endless recipes, hacks, and pictures. Users can even subscribe to the net-work so they never miss the carefully selected and curated content. Buzzfeed's "Tasty" videos reach tens of millions of viewers and create quick recipes on camera for users to mimic at home. The comments are full of thousands of Facebook users tagging their friends so they tune into the content as well.

And, of course, there's Yelp. I don't remember the last time I picked a restaurant or ordered a dish without Yelping it first. For those who aren't familiar, Yelp is the Wikipedia of food. Users can rate and review restaurants (among other establishments), post pictures of dishes, and provide other information and tips about dining out. Yelp enables food lovers to have additional control of their dining experience. It eliminates the questioning over whether you'll like a new restaurant or dish. You can visualize your food before you eat it and see what other people thought of it. You know the best dishes on the restaurant menu before you arrive. That's not to discount the untrustworthiness of Yelp and the type of person who would be inclined to post a review: usually someone who had a one-star or five-star experience. Generally, though, thanks to technology, there's less risk for foodies when dining out.

More important, the bizarre, distinctive, and often laughable behavior of Millennial foodies is more than a social phenomenon—this food-obsessed species has the ability to drive society in powerful directions. Food giants are now changing their core values to align with those of Millennials. For a generation that isn't particularly brand loyal and values health, convenience, and low prices, companies are launching new products and remarketing old ones. Due to poor sales, PepsiCo, for example, has dropped ingredients perceived as unhealthy. Whole Foods plans to open a chain of grocery stores directed at a 30 and under crowd, with lower prices for healthy, high-quality food. These stores will also feature smaller packaging, catering to an age group that has yet to start a family.

The effects of millennials' purchasing habits are explored.

So look around: the power of the Millennial foodies is real. They have become unpaid brand ambassadors for restaurants they prefer. They're marketers and promoters, too, for their favorite foods—just add a geotag to say whatever restaurant you're at and anyone can access your photo and opinions. Non-foodies may love to hate them, but foodies are devoted to anything and anybody who stylishly satisfies their hunger. And they've probably taken a picture of your meal while you weren't looking. The phrase "you are what you eat" has been completely redefined.

WORKS CITED

"How Millennials Are Changing the Foodie Game." *RDP Food Service*, rdpfoodservice.com/blog/millennials-changing-foodie-game/. Accessed 8 Mar. 2017.

"Millennials: Technology = Social Connection." *Nielsen*, 26 Feb. 2014, www.nielsen.com/us/en/insights/news/2014/millennials-technology-social-connection.html.

Peele, Anna. "Just How Food-Obsessed Is the Typical Millennial?" *Bon Appetit*, 16 Feb. 2016, www.bonappetit.com/entertaining-style/pop-culture/article/millennials-and-food.

Pictures of Hipsters Taking Pictures of Food, Tumblr, pohtpof.tumblr.com/. Accessed 8 Mar. 2017.

Beispel concludes her argument with a new spin on an old adage.

Don't Believe Facebook: The Demise of the Written Word Is Very Far Off

MICHAEL HILTZIK

June 17, 2016

Facebook executive Nicola Mendelsohn shook up the online-o-sphere earlier this week with one of those offhand declarations that sound superficially profound for a moment or two but are vacuous at their core. In five years, she told a *Fortune* conference in London, her platform will probably be "all video," and the written word will be essentially dead.

"I just think if we look already, we're seeing a year-on-year decline on text," she said. "If I was having a bet, I would say: video, video, video." That's because "the best way to tell stories in this world, where so much information is coming at us, actually is video. It conveys so much more information in a much quicker period. So actually the trend helps us to digest much more information."

This is, of course, exactly wrong. We don't mean her prediction about Facebook; in that respect she's talking her own book, since Facebook has made a big commercial bet on video. It's her assertion that video conveys more information—and faster—than text that's upside-down.

We'll outsource the initial pushback to Kevin Drum of Mother Jones, who observes, "Video has many benefits, but information density generally isn't one of them. . . . I can read the transcript of a one-hour speech in about five or 10 minutes and easily pick out precisely what's interesting and what's not. With video, I have to slog through the full hour." That's why his policy is never to click a link that goes to video.

Michael Hiltzik's argument originally appeared in the *Los Angeles Times*, where he is a columnist who ordinarily writes about financial issues. You'll see that orientation in his reflections on why the written word will likely thrive in the digital era. The piece includes no endnotes, but we've underlined where the online text provides links to source materials.

Drum's most salient point applies to the definition of the "information" people are seeking when they're accessing video or text. "I read/view stuff on the Web in order to gather actual information that I can comment on," he writes. Plainly, video is hopelessly overmatched by text in conveying hard information—facts, figures, data. A given video may arguably convey more "information" in bulk, but most of that is self-reinforcing context—color, motion, sound. The underlying factual information is relatively meager, in the same sense that the energy capacity of an electric-car battery can't match that of an average gasoline fuel tank (the range of a fully charged Tesla Model S is about 250 miles, while that of a typical gasoline-fueled sedan can exceed 400).

Then there's the challenge of extracting usable information from video vs. text. Video is a linear medium: You have to allow it to unspool frame by frame to glean what it's saying. Text can be absorbed in blocks; the eye searches for keywords or names or other pointers such as quotation marks. Text is generally searchable online. Some programs can convert some videos to searchable form, but more often, the search is done via a transcript keyed to points in the video. Here, for example, is the <u>full transcript</u> of "Meet the Press" for May 29. Below is the video of the entire show. If your task was to find the moment when Chuck Todd first mentioned Trump University, which would you use to find it? (We're not even counting the five commercial breaks.) [A *video appears here in Hiltzik's original text*.]

Give up? It's at about the 24:43 mark.

The demise of text is often predicted, but the horizon seems to perpetually recede. Tech writer Tim Carmody puts his finger on the reasons why "text is surprisingly resilient" <u>in an essay at Kottket.org</u>: "It's cheap, it's flexible, it's discreet. Human brains process it absurdly well considering there's nothing really built-in for it. Plenty of people can deal with text better than they can spoken language, whether as a matter of preference or necessity. And it's endlessly computable—you can search it, code it. . . . In short, all of the same technological advances that enable more and more video, audio, and immersive VR entertainment also enable more and more text. We will see more of all of them as the technological bottlenecks open up."

He concludes that "nothing has proved as invincible as writing and literacy. Because text is just so malleable. Because it fits into any container we put it in. Because our world is supersaturated in it, indoors and out. Because we have so much invested in it. . . . Unless our civilization fundamentally collapses, we will never give up writing and reading."

In predicting a world overtaken by video, Mendelsohn seems to be making a category error; she's conflating visual with video. Facebook and other online platforms understand that their users are accessing their sites for their visual offerings, but that's not the same as saying they're doing nothing but watching clips.

That notion is contradicted by the findings of Oxford University's Reuters Institute for the Study of Journalism in its just-released <u>Digital News Report for 2016</u>.

The study found that most consumers of online news (59%) still gravitate to news articles—that is, text; only 24% said they accessed news video in the week before they were polled. "One surprise in this year's data," the report's authors found, "is that online news video appears to be growing more slowly than might be expected." The 24% figure "represents surprisingly weak growth given the explosive growth and prominence on the supply side." In other words, there's more video than ever before, but it's not attracting a commensurately large audience.

Why not? For the same reasons Drum mentioned:

They take too long to load and unspool, and extracting the sought-after information is slower and more inconvenient than reading the written word. The number-two complaint—"Pre-roll ads put me off"—is another artifact of the linear nature of video, compounded by the cleverness of video providers in forcing you to watch through an entire ad, or three, before the clip even starts.

The secret underlying Mendelsohn's claim is that there is something at which video is better than text: marketing.

The goal of advertising is not to impart information, but to keep it from the audience—to distract viewers from thinking too hard or asking questions. Video is ideal for that because that color, movement, noise, and light is all distraction. Video is entertainment, often of the empty-calorie variety. People love circuses, but they don't normally go there to study zoology.

Indeed, it seems that most of the articles (yes, articles) written about the coming dominance of video look at the phenomenon from the marketer's standpoint: "A recent campaign from Volkswagen," <u>the *Guardian* reported</u>

last year, "saw a trio of its videos viewed a combined 155 million times." Here's a safe bet: those videos weren't produced to explain why the car company had been <u>faking emissions data</u>, but to entice viewers to buy their cars. Mendelsohn, by the way, came to Facebook from the advertising industry.

Certainly text and the written word will change to meet the demands of the new technologies through which we do our reading. That's always been the case. Novels tended to be structured as a series of cliffhangers when they were read in monthly installments in a popular magazine; and in a different narrative form when they began to be printed in books sized to fit conveniently in a saddlebag, or valise, or before the fireplace. The length of news articles began to shrink when the reading audience began to migrate from newspapers that arrived on the stoop in the morning and were kept around to be perused at leisure, and toward smartphones and pads to be read between elevator stops.

That's a testament to the infinite malleability of text. Text can conform to the relentless shrinkage of people's attention spans; video can't. Who will have time in the future to watch even a five-minute video, when they can learn so much more by scanning five paragraphs of text? "Bet for better video, bet for better speech, bet for better things we can't imagine," Carmody writes, "but if you bet against text, you will lose."

9

Arguments of Definition

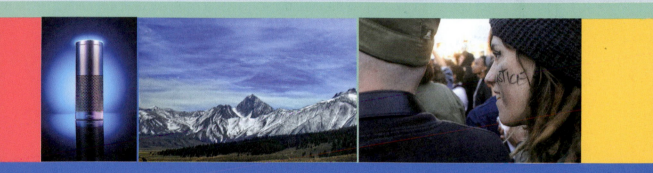

Everyone seems convinced that products like Amazon's Alexa and Apple's Homekit are redefining the way people live in and control their homes. But what exactly do these products do? What defines *them*?

A panel of judges must decide whether computer-enhanced images must be identified as such in a contest for landscape photography. At what point is an electronically manipulated image no longer a *photograph*—or does it even matter?

A conservative student group accuses the student government on campus of sponsoring a lecture series featuring a disproportionate number of "social justice warrior types." A spokesperson for the student government defends its program by questioning whether the term actually means anything.

Understanding Arguments of Definition

Definitions matter. Just ask scientists, mathematicians, engineers, judges—or people who want to use restrooms consistent with their gender identification. Looking back, in 1996 the Congress passed, and President Clinton signed, the Defense of Marriage Act (DOMA), which defined marriage in federal law this way:

> In determining the meaning of any Act of Congress, or of any ruling, regulation, or interpretation of the various administrative bureaus and agencies of the United States, the word "marriage" means only a legal union between one man and one woman as husband and wife, and the word "spouse" refers only to a person of the opposite sex who is a husband or a wife. 1 U.S.C. 7.

This decision and its definitions of *marriage* and *spouse* have been challenged over and over again in the ensuing decades, leading eventually to another Supreme Court decision, in the summer of 2013, that declared DOMA unconstitutional. The majority opinion, written by Justice Kennedy, found that the earlier law was discriminatory and that it labeled same-sex unions as "less worthy than the marriage of others." In so ruling, the court affirmed that the federal government cannot differentiate between a "marriage" of heterosexuals and one of homosexuals. Debates over laws that involve definitions of marriage and, more recently, gender are still ongoing, and you might want to check the status of such controversies in your own state.

Cases like these demonstrate that arguments of definition aren't abstract academic exercises: they often have important consequences for ordinary people—that's why farmers, landowners, Congress, and the Environmental Protection Agency have battled for decades over how that agency defines "wetlands," which Congress long ago gave it power to regulate. And why it was so controversial when in *Citizens United v. Federal Election Commission* (2010) the Supreme Court decided that individuals in association—such as unions or corporations—are equivalent to individual citizens when it comes to the exercise of free speech rights and thus have no limit on their spending in election campaigns. Opponents of the decision argue that it enhances the power of monied interests in American politics; others see it as affirming free speech in the face of increasing government censorship.

Arguments about definition even sometimes decide what someone or something is or can be. Such arguments can both include or exclude:

A wolf in Montana either is an endangered species or it isn't. An unsolicited kiss is or is not sexual harassment. A person merits official political refugee status in the United States or doesn't. Another way of approaching definitional arguments, however, is to think of what falls between *is* and *is not* in a definitional claim. In fact, many definitional disputes occur in that murky realm.

Consider the controversy over how to define *human intelligence.* Some argue that human intelligence is a capacity that is measured by tests of verbal and mathematical reasoning. In other words, it's defined by IQ and SAT scores. Others define *intelligence* as the ability to perform specific practical tasks. Still others interpret *intelligence* in emotional terms as a competence in relating to other people. Any of these positions could be defended reasonably, but perhaps the wisest approach would be to construct a definition of *intelligence* that is rich enough to incorporate all these perspectives—and maybe more.

The fact is that crucial political, social, and scientific terms—such as *intelligence, justice, free speech,* or *gender*—are reargued, reshaped, and updated for the times.

Why not just consult a dictionary when the meanings of terms are disputed? It doesn't work that way, no matter how up to date or authoritative a dictionary might be. In fact, dictionaries (almost by definition!) inevitably reflect the way individual groups of people use words at a specified time and place. And like any form of writing, these reference books mirror the interests and prejudices of their makers—as shown, perhaps most famously, in the entries of lexicographer Samuel Johnson (1709–1784), who gave the English language its first great dictionary. No

> **sail·ing** (sā′ling), 1. *n.* the fine art of getting wet and becoming ill while slowly going nowhere at great expense.
>
> A DICTIONARY FOR LANDLUBBERS, OLD SALTS, & ARMCHAIR DRIFTERS • BY HENRY BEARD & ROY McKIE •

The *Dictionary for Landlubbers* defines words according to their point of view! Excerpted from *SAILING: A Dictionary for Landlubbers, Old Salts, & Armchair Drifters.* Copyright © 1981 by Henry Beard and Roy McKie. Used by permission of Workman Publishing Co., Inc., New York, All Rights Reserved.

friend of the Scots, Johnson defined *oats* as "a grain which in England is generally given to horses, but in Scotland supports the people." (To be fair, he also defined *lexicographer* as "a writer of dictionaries, a harmless drudge.") Thus, it's possible to disagree with dictionary definitions or to regard them merely as starting points for arguments.

RESPOND●

Briefly discuss how you might define the italicized terms in the following controversial claims of definition. Compare your definitions of the terms with those of your classmates.

Graphic novels can be *serious literature*.

Burning a nation's flag is a *hate crime*.

Neither Matt Drudge nor Rachel Maddow is a *journalist*.

College sports programs have become *big businesses*.

Plagiarism can be an act of *civil disobedience*.

The menus at Taco Bell and Panda Express illustrate *cultural appropriation*.

Satanism is a *religion* properly protected by the First Amendment.

The District of Columbia should not have all the privileges of an American *state*.

Polyamorists should have the option of *marriage*.

Kinds of Definition

Because there are various kinds of definitions, there are also different ways to make a definition argument. Fortunately, identifying a particular type of definition is less important than appreciating when an issue of meaning is at stake. Let's explore some common definitional issues.

Formal Definitions

Formal definitions are what you find in dictionaries. Such definitions place a term in its proper **genus** and **species**—first determining its class and then identifying the features or criteria that distinguish it from other members of that class. That sounds complicated, but an example will help you see the principle. To define *electric car*, for example, you might first place it in a general class—*passenger vehicles*. Then you define its species. Here's how the U.S. Department of Energy does that, explaining specific differences between cars powered by electricity (EVs):

> Just as there are a variety of technologies available in conventional vehicles, plug-in electric vehicles (also known as electric cars or EVs) have different capabilities that can accommodate different drivers' needs. A major feature of EVs is that drivers can plug them in to charge from an off-board electric power source. This distinguishes them from hybrid electric vehicles, which supplement an internal combustion engine with battery power but cannot be plugged in.

Got that? It gets even more complicated (or precise) as the government goes on to distinguish among plug-in hybrid electric vehicles (PHEVs), all-electric vehicles (AEVs), battery electric vehicles (BEVs), and even fuel cell electric vehicles (FCEVs).

But all these definitional distinctions can actually make matters clearer. For instance, suppose that you are considering a new car and prefer an electric one this time. Quickly, the definitional question becomes—*what kind?* A Toyota Prius, or maybe a Tesla Model 3? How do they differ? Both are clearly passenger cars—one might even add four-door sedans, so the *genus* raises no question. But the Prius is an electrically *assisted* version of a regular gasoline car while the Tesla is fully electric—just battery and motor, no engine. That's the *species* difference, which obviously has consequences for consumers concerned, let's say, either about range or about CO_2 emissions. (Or maybe it just comes down to good looks?)

Tesla Model 3 dpa picture alliance/Alamy

Consider how Ben Schwartz defines *funny* in his response to claims of a "humor crisis" in America.

LINK TO P. 746

Operational Definitions

Operational definitions identify an object or idea by what it does or by what conditions create it. For example, someone's offensive sexual imposition on another person may not meet the technical definition of *harassment* unless it is considered *unwanted*, *unsolicited*, and *repeated*. These three conditions then define what makes an act that might be acceptable in some situations turn into harassment. But they might also then become part of a highly contentious debate: were the conditions actually present in a given case? For example, could an offensive act be harassment if the accused believed sexual interest was mutual and therefore solicited?

As you might imagine, arguments arise from operational definitions whenever people disagree about what the conditions define or whether these conditions have been fulfilled. Here are some examples of those types of questions:

Questions Related to Conditions

- Can institutional racism occur in the absence of specific and individual acts of racism?
- Can people paid for their community service still be called volunteers?
- Does academic dishonesty occur if a student accepts wording suggested by a writing center tutor?

Questions Related to Fulfillment of Conditions

- Has an institution supported traditions or policies that have led to widespread racial inequities?
- Was the compensation given to volunteers really "pay" or simply "reimbursement" for expenses?
- Did the student actually copy down what the tutor said with the intention of using it?

RESPOND•

This chapter opens with three rhetorical situations that center on definitional issues: What is Alexa? What is a photograph? What defines a social justice warrior (SJW)? Select one of these situations, and then address it, using the strategies either of formal definitions or of operational ones. For example, might a formal definition help to explain what products like Alexa or Home-kit are? (You may have to do some quick research.) Would an operational definition work to explain or defend what SJWs allegedly do or don't do?

THE PRINCE RECONSIDERS:

IS WAKING SLEEPING BEAUTY WITH A KISS SEXUAL HARASSMENT?

Prince Charming considers whether an action would fulfill the conditions for an operational definition. Cartoonstock Ltd./CartoonStock.com

Definitions by Example

Resembling operational definitions are **definitions by example**, which define a class by listing its individual members. Such definitions can be helpful when it is easier to illustrate or show what related people or things have in common than to explain each one in precise detail. For example, one might define the broad category of *virtual reality products* by listing the major examples of these items or define *Libertarian Democrat* by naming politicians or thinkers associated with that title.

Arguments of this sort may focus on who or what may be included in a list that defines a category—*classic movies, worst natural disasters,*

An app like Discovr Music defines musical styles by example when it connects specific artists or groups to others who make similar sounds. David McKinney

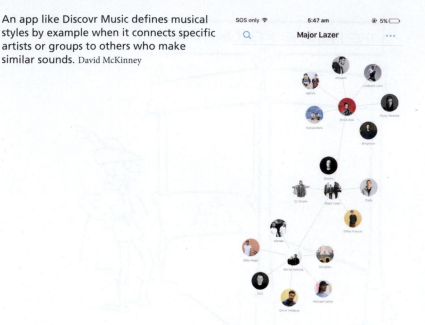

groundbreaking painters, acts of terror. Such arguments often involve comparisons and contrasts with the items that most readers would agree belong in this list. One could ask why Washington, D.C., is denied the status of a state: how does it differ from the fifty recognized American states? Or one might wonder why the status of planet is denied to asteroids, when both planets and asteroids are bodies that orbit the sun. A comparison between planets and asteroids might suggest that size is one essential feature of the eight recognized planets that asteroids don't meet. (In 2006, in a famous exercise in definitional argument, astronomers decided to deny poor Pluto its planetary classification.)

Negative Definitions

Definitional arguments sometimes involve explaining what a person, thing, or concept is by defining what it is *not* or explaining with what it should be contrasted. Such strategies of definition play a substantial role in politics today, as individuals or political groups craft public images that show them in the best light—as *not* radicals, *not* fascists, *not* Alt-Right, *not* Antifa, *not* coastal elitists, *not* one-percenters, and so on. But this strategy of argument has other uses as well, especially when a writer wants to counter stereotypes or change expectations. For a thoughtful—and particularly apropos—example, see Rob Jenkins's "Defining the Relationship" at the end of this chapter.

Developing a Definitional Argument

Definitional arguments don't just appear out of the blue; they often evolve from daily life. You might get into an argument over the definition of *ordinary wear and tear* when you return a rental car with some soiled upholstery. Or you might be asked to write a job description for a new position to be created in your workplace: you have to define the job position in a way that doesn't step on anyone else's turf. Or maybe employees at your school object to being defined as *temporary workers* when they've held their same jobs for years. Or someone derides one of your best friends as *fake woke* and you're unsure how to read the term. In a dozen ways every day, you encounter situations that are questions of definition. They're so inevitable that you barely notice them for what they are.

Legal scholar John Palfrey's discussion of free speech on college campuses depends on the definition and limits of free expression.

LINK TO P. 731

Formulating Claims

In addressing a question of definition, you'll likely formulate a *tentative claim*—a declarative statement that represents your first response to such situations. Note that such initial claims usually don't follow a single definitional formula.

Claims of Definition

A person paid to do public service is not a *volunteer*.

Institutional racism can exist—maybe even thrive—in the absence of overt civil rights violations.

Climate change is not the same thing as *global warming*.

Political bias has been routinely practiced by some media outlets.

Theatergoers shouldn't confuse *musicals* with *operas*.

None of the statements listed here could stand on its own because it likely reflects a first impression and gut reaction. But that's fine because making a claim of definition is typically a starting point, a cocky moment that doesn't last much beyond the first serious rebuttal or challenge. Statements like these aren't arguments until they're attached to reasons, data, warrants, and evidence (see Chapter 7).

Finding good reasons to support a claim of definition usually requires formulating a general definition by which to explore the subject. To be persuasive, the definition must be broad and not tailored to the specific controversy:

> A volunteer is . . .
>
> Institutional racism is . . .
>
> Climate change is . . . but global warming is . . .
>
> Political bias is . . .
>
> A musical is . . . but an opera is . . .

Now consider how the following claims might be expanded with a general definition to become full-fledged definitional arguments:

Arguments of Definition

> Someone paid to do public service is not a volunteer because volunteers are people who . . .
>
> Institutional racism can exist even in the absence of overt violations of civil rights because, by definition, institutional racism is . . .
>
> Climate change differs from global warming because . . .
>
> Political bias in media outlets is evident whenever . . .
>
> Musicals focus on words first while operas . . .

Notice, too, that some of the issues can involve comparisons between things—such as operas and musicals.

Crafting Definitions

Imagine that you decide to tackle the concept of *paid volunteer* in the following way:

> Participants in the federal AmeriCorps program are not really volunteers because they receive "education awards" for their public service. Volunteers are people who work for a cause without receiving compensation.

In Toulmin terms, as explained in Chapter 7, the argument looks like this:

Claim	Participants in AmeriCorps aren't volunteers . . .
Reason	. . . because they are paid for their service.
Warrant	People who are compensated for their services are, ordinarily, employees.

As you can see, the definition of *volunteers* will be crucial to the shape of the argument. In fact, you might think you've settled the matter with this tight little formulation. But now it's time to listen to the readers over your shoulder (again, see Chapter 7), who are pushing you further. Do the terms of your definition account for all pertinent cases of volunteerism—in particular, any related to the types of public service AmeriCorps members might be involved in? What do you do with unpaid interns: how do they affect your definition of *volunteers*? Consider, too, the word *cause* in your original claim of the definition:

> **Volunteers are people who work for a cause without receiving compensation.**

Cause has political connotations that you may or may not intend. You'd better clarify what you mean by *cause* when you discuss its definition in your paper. Might a phrase such as *the public good* be a more comprehensive or appropriate substitute for *a cause*? And then there's the matter of *compensation* in the second half of your definition:

> **Volunteers are people who work for a cause without receiving compensation.**

Aren't people who volunteer to serve on boards, committees, and commissions sometimes paid, especially for their expenses? What about members of the so-called all-volunteer military? They're financially compensated during their years of service, and they enjoy benefits after they complete their tours of duty.

As you can see, you can't just offer up a definition as part of an argument and expect that readers will accept it. Every part of a definition has to be interrogated, critiqued, and defended. So investigate your subject in the library, on the Internet, and in conversation with others, especially *genuine* experts if you can. You might then be able to present your definition in a single paragraph, or you may have to spend several pages coming to terms with the complexity of the core issue.

After conducting research of this kind, you'll be in a better position to write an extended definition that explains to your readers what you believe makes a volunteer a volunteer, how to identify institutional racism, or how to distinguish between a musical and an opera.

Matching Claims to Definitions

Once you've formulated a definition that readers will accept—a demanding task in itself—you might need to look at your particular subject to see if it fits your general definition. It should provide evidence of one of the following:

- It is a clear example of the class defined.
- It clearly falls outside the defined class.
- It falls between two closely related classes or fulfills some conditions of the defined class but not others.
- It defies existing classes and categories and requires an entirely new definition.

How do you make this key move in an argument? Here's an example from an article by Anthony Tommasini entitled "Opera? Musical? Please Respect the Difference." Early in the piece, Tommasini argues that a key element separates the two musical forms:

> Both genres seek to combine words and music in dynamic, felicitous and, to invoke that all-purpose term, artistic ways. But in opera, music is the driving force; in musical theater, words come first.
>
> This explains why for centuries opera-goers have revered works written in languages they do not speak.

Tommasini's claim of definition (or of difference) makes sense because it clarifies aspects of the two genres.

If evidence you've gathered while developing an argument of definition suggests that similar limitations may be necessary, don't hesitate to modify your claim. It's amazing how often seemingly cut-and-dried matters of definition become blurry—and open to compromise and accommodation—as you learn more about them. That has proved to be the case as various campuses across the country have tried to define *hate speech* or *internship*—tricky matters indeed. And even the Supreme Court has never said exactly what *pornography* is. Just when matters seem to be settled, new legal twists develop. Should virtual child pornography created with software be illegal, as is the real thing? Or is a virtual image—even a lewd one—an artistic expression that is protected (as other works of art are) by the First Amendment?

Considering Design and Visuals

In thinking about how to present your argument of definition, you may find a simple visual helpful, such as the Venn diagram below from Wikimedia Commons that defines *sustainability* as the place where our society and its economy intersect with the environment. Such a visual might even suggest a structure for an oral presentation.

Remember too that visuals like photographs, charts, and graphs can also help you make your case. Such items could demonstrate that the conditions for a definition have been met—for example, a widely circulated photograph of children in Flint, Michigan, carrying bottled water (see p. 210) might define *crisis* or *civic collapse*. Or you might create a graphic yourself to illustrate a concept you are defining, perhaps through comparison and contrast.

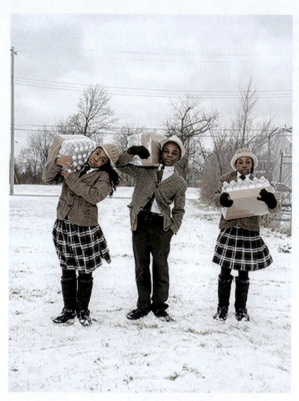

Wayne Lawrence

Finally, don't forget that basic design elements—such as boldface and italics, headings, or links in online text—can contribute to (or detract from) the credibility and persuasiveness of your argument of definition. (See Chapter 14 for more on "Visual Rhetoric.")

GUIDE to writing an argument of definition

● Finding a Topic

You're entering an argument of definition when you:

- formulate a controversial or provocative definition: *Cultural appropriation is the disrespectful borrowing of the ideas, history, cultural achievements, dress, music, traditions, foods, or any other cultural artifacts of an exploited or marginalized group by a more powerful one.*

- challenge a definition: *For many Americans today, cultural appropriation is an idea that runs counter to the melting-pot ideal of American assimilation.*

- try to determine whether something fits an existing definition: *Dining at Taco Bell or Panda Express is (or is not) an act of cultural appropriation.*

- seek to broaden an existing definition or create a new definition to accommodate wider or differing perspectives: *In a world where cultural information is shared so fluidly via social media, it may be time to explore alternative representations of cultural appropriation.*

Look for issues of definition in your everyday affairs—for instance, in the way that jobs are classified at work, that key terms are used in your academic major, that politicians visually represent social issues that concern you, and so on. Be especially alert to definitional arguments that arise when you or others deploy adjectives such as *true, real, actual,* or *genuine: a true patriot, real reform, authentic Kombucha tea.*

● Researching Your Topic

You can research issues of definition by using the following sources:

- college dictionaries and encyclopedias
- unabridged dictionaries
- specialized reference works and handbooks, such as legal and medical dictionaries
- your textbooks (check their glossaries)
- Web articles and blogs that focus on particular topics, especially political ones

- community or advocacy groups focused on legal or social issues
- social media postings by experts you respect

Browse in your library reference room and use the electronic indexes and databases to determine how often disputed or contentious terms or phrases occur in influential online newspapers, journals, and Web sites.

When dealing with definitions, ask librarians about the most appropriate and reliable sources. For instance, to find the definition of a legal term, *Black's Law Dictionary* or a database such as FindLaw may help. Check USA.gov for how the government defines terms.

● Formulating a Claim

After exploring your subject, try to formulate a thesis that lets readers know where you stand or what issues are at stake. Begin with the following types of questions:

- questions related to genus: *Is assisting in suicide a crime?*
- questions related to species: *Is marijuana a harmful addictive drug or a useful medical treatment?*
- questions related to conditions: *Must the imposition of sexual attention be both unwanted and unsolicited to be considered sexual harassment?*
- questions related to fulfillment of conditions: *Has our college kept in place traditions or policies that might embody forms of racial privilege?*
- questions related to membership in a named class: *Can a story put together out of thirty-one retweets be called a novel, or even a short story?*

If you start with a thesis, it should be a complete statement that makes a claim of definition and states the reasons supporting it. You may later decide to separate the claim from its supporting reasons. But a working thesis should be a fully articulated thought that spells out all the details and qualifications: *Who? What? Where? When? How many? How regularly? How completely?*

However, since arguments of definition are often exploratory and tentative, an initial thesis (if you have one) may simply describe problems in formulating a particular definition: *What we mean by X is likely to remain unsettled until we can agree more fully about Y and Z; The key to understanding what constitutes X may lie in appreciating how different groups approach Y and Z.*

● Examples of Definitional Claims

- Assisting a gravely ill person in committing suicide should not be considered *murder* when the motive for the act is to ease a person's suffering and not to benefit from the death.

- Although somewhat addictive, marijuana should not be classified as a *dangerous drug* because it damages individuals and society less than heroin or cocaine and because it helps people with life-threatening diseases live more comfortably.

- Giving college admission preference to all racial minorities can be an example of *class discrimination* because such policies may favor middle- and upper-class students who are already advantaged.

- Attempts to define the concept of *free speech* need to take into account the way the term is understood in cultures worldwide, not just in the countries of Western Europe and North America.

● Preparing a Proposal

If your instructor asks you to prepare a proposal for your project, here's a format that may help:

State your thesis or hypothesis completely. If you're having trouble doing so, try outlining it in Toulmin terms:

Claim:

Reason(s):

Warrant(s):

Alternatively, you might describe the complications of a definitional issue you hope to explore in your project, with the thesis perhaps coming later.

- Explain why this argument of definition deserves attention. What's at stake? Why is it important for your readers to consider?

- Identify whom you hope to reach through your argument and why these readers would be interested in it. How might you involve them in the paper?

- Briefly discuss the key challenges that you anticipate in preparing your argument.

- Determine what sources you expect to consult: Social media? Databases? Dictionaries? Encyclopedias? Periodicals?
- Determine what visuals to include in your definitional argument.

● Considering Genre and Media

Your instructor may specify that you use a particular genre. If not, ask yourself these questions to help you make a good choice:

- What format is most appropriate for your argument of definition? Does it call for an academic essay, report, infographic, poster, or something else?
- What medium is most appropriate for your argument? Would it be best delivered orally to a live audience? Presented as an audio essay or podcast? Presented in print only or in print with illustrations?
- Will you need visuals, such as moving or still images, maps, graphs, charts—and what function will they play in your argument? Make sure they are not just "added on" but are necessary components of the argument.

● Thinking about Organization

An argument of definition is likely to include some of the following parts:

- a claim involving a question of definition
- a general definition of some key concept
- a careful look at your subject in terms of that general definition
- evidence for every part of the argument, including visual evidence if appropriate
- a careful consideration of alternative views and counterarguments
- a conclusion drawing out the implications of the argument

It's impossible, however, to predict what emphasis each of those parts might receive or what the ultimate shape of an argument of definition will be. Try to account for the ways people with different points of view will likely respond to your argument. Then, consider how to address such differences civilly in the body of your argument.

● **Getting and Giving Response: Questions for Peer Response**

Your instructor may assign you to a group for the purpose of reading and responding to each other's drafts. If not, ask for responses from serious readers or consultants at a writing center. Use the following questions to evaluate a colleague's draft. Be sure to illustrate your comments with examples; specific comments help more than general observations.

The Claim

- Is the claim clearly an issue of definition?

- Is the claim significant enough to interest readers?

- Are clear and specific criteria established for the concept being defined? Do the criteria define the term adequately? Using this definition, could most readers identify what's being defined and distinguish it from other related concepts?

Evidence for the Claim

- Is enough evidence furnished to explain or support the definition? If not, what kind of additional evidence is needed?

- Is the evidence in support of the claim simply announced, or are its significance and appropriateness analyzed? Is a more detailed discussion needed?

- Are all the conditions of the definition met in the concept being examined?

- Are any objections readers might have to the claim, criteria, evidence, or way the definition is formulated adequately addressed? Have you represented other points of view completely and fairly?

- What kinds of sources are cited? How credible and persuasive will they be to readers? What other kinds of sources might work better?

- Are all quotations introduced with appropriate signal phrases (such as "As Tyson argues, . . .") and blended smoothly into the writer's sentences?

- Are all visual sources labeled, introduced, and commented upon?

Organization and Style

- How are the parts of the argument organized or presented? Is this organization effective?

- Will readers understand the relationships among the claims, supporting reasons, warrants, and evidence? If not, how might those connections be clearer? Does every visual serve a clear purpose? Are more transitions (verbal or visual) needed? Would headings help?

- Are the transitions or links from point to point, sentence to sentence, and paragraph to paragraph clear and effective? If not, how could they be improved?

- Are all visuals (or other elements such as audio or video clips) carefully integrated into the text? Is each visual introduced and commented on to point out its significance? If your argument of definition is an academic essay, is each visual labeled as a figure or a table and given a caption as well as a citation?

- Is the style suited to the subject? Is it too formal, casual, or technical? Can it be improved?

- Which sentences seem effective? Which ones seem weaker, and how could they be improved? Should short sentences be combined, and any longer ones be broken up?

- How effective are the paragraphs? Too short or too long? How can they be improved?

- Which words or phrases seem effective? Do any seem vague or inappropriate for the audience or the writer's purpose? Are technical or unfamiliar terms defined?

Spelling, Punctuation, Mechanics, Documentation, and Format

- Are there any errors in spelling, punctuation, capitalization, and the like?

- Is the documentation appropriate and consistent? (See Chapter 22.)

- Does the paper or project follow an appropriate format? Is it appropriately designed and attractively presented?

PROJECTS•

1. Write an argument of definition about a term such as *fake news* or *intersectionality* that has suddenly become culturally significant or recently changed in some important way. Either defend the way the term has come to be defined or raise questions about its appropriateness, offensiveness, accuracy, and so on. Consider words or expressions such as *Antifa, big data, deep state, disruptive technology, Islamophobia, machine learning, marginalization, white nationalist,* etc.

2. Write an essay in which you compare or contrast the meaning of two related terms, explaining the differences between them by using one or more methods of definition: formal definition, operational definition, definition by example. Be clever in your choice of the initial terms: look for a pairing in which the differences might not be immediately apparent to people unfamiliar with how the terms are used in specific communities. Consider terms such as *liberal/progressive, classy/cool, lead soprano/prima donna, student athlete/jock, highbrow/intellectual, manual laborer/blue collar worker, babysitter/nanny,* and so on.

3. In an essay at the end of this chapter, Natasha Rodriguez explores the adjective *underprivileged,* trying to understand why this label bothers her so much. She concludes that needing financial aid should not be conflated with being disadvantaged. After reading this selection carefully, respond to Rodriguez's argument in an argument of definition of your own—either an academic essay or a multimodal presentation, combining various media such as audio, video, posters, etc. Alternatively, explore a concept similar to "underprivileged" with the same intensity that Rodriguez brings to her project. Look for a term to define and analyze either from your major or from an area of interest to you.

4. Because arguments of definition can have such important consequences, it helps to develop one by first getting input from lots of "stakeholders," that is, from people or groups likely to be affected by any change in the way a term is defined. Working with a small group, identify a term in your school or wider community that might need a fresh formulation or a close review. It could be a familiar campus word or phrase such as *nontraditional student, diversity, scholastic dishonesty,* or *social justice*; or it may be a term that has newly entered the local environment, perhaps reflecting an issue of law enforcement, safety, transportation, health, or even entertainment. Once you have settled on a significant term, identify a full range of stakeholders. Then, through some systematic field research (interviews, questionnaires) or by examining existing documents and materials (such as library sources, Web sites, pamphlets, publications), try to understand how the term currently functions in your community. Your definitional argument will, in effect, be what you can learn about the meanings that word or phrase has today for a wide variety of people.

Who Are You Calling Underprivileged?

NATASHA RODRIGUEZ

I have come to loathe the word "underprivileged." When I filled out my college applications, I checked off the Latino/Hispanic box whenever I was asked to give my ethnicity. My parents in turn indicated their income, hoping that we would qualify for financial aid. But while I waited for acceptances and rejections, several colleges I was considering sent me material that made me feel worthless rather than excited about attending those institutions.

The first mailing I received was a brochure that featured a photograph of African-American, Asian, and Latino teens standing around in a cluster, their faces full of laughter and joy. The title of the brochure was "Help for Underprivileged Students." At first I was confused: "Underprivileged" was not a word that I associated with myself. But there was the handout, with my name printed boldly on the surface.

The author questions the connotations of underprivileged.

The text went on to inform me that, since I was a student who had experienced an underprivileged life, I could qualify for several kinds of financial aid and scholarships. While I appreciated the intent, I was turned off by that one word—"underprivileged."

I had never been called that before. The word made me question how I saw myself in the world. Yes, I needed financial aid, and I had received generous scholarships to help me attend a private high school on the Upper East Side of New York. Surely that didn't mean that I had lived a less-privileged life than others. My upbringing had been very happy.

Natasha Rodriguez wrote this argument while a student at Sarah Lawrence College. She went on to do graduate work in journalism at Columbia University.

What does "underprivileged" actually mean? According to most dictionaries, the word refers to a person who does not enjoy the same standard of living or rights as a majority of people in a society. I don't fit that definition. Even though my family does not have a lot of money, we have always had enough to get by, and I have received an excellent education.

What angered me most about the label was why colleges would ever use such a term. Who wants to be called underprivileged? I'm sure that even those who have had no opportunities would not want their social status rubbed in their faces so blatantly. People should be referred to as underprivileged only if they're the ones who are calling themselves that.

Misfortune, like beauty, is in the eye of the beholder. It's not appropriate to slap labels on people that they might not like or even agree with. Social research has found that those who are negatively labeled usually have lower self-esteem than others who are not labeled in that way. So why does the label of "underprivileged" persist?

Most colleges brag about the diversity of their students. But I don't want to be bragged about if my ethnicity is automatically associated with "underprivileged." Several colleges that had not even received information on my parents' finances just assumed that I was underprivileged because I had checked "Latino/Hispanic" on their applications.

That kind of labeling has to stop. Brochures and handouts could be titled "Help for Students in Need" rather than "Help for Underprivileged Students." I am sure that many people, myself included, are more than willing to admit that they require financial aid, and would feel fine about a college that referred to them as a student in need.

That's a definition I can agree with. I am a student in need; I'm just not an underprivileged one.

The author then gives a standard definition for underprivileged *and explains why she refuses the label.*

The author examines the assumptions colleges make based on ethnicity and income.

The essay concludes with the author's own self-definition.

Defining the Relationship

ROB JENKINS

August 9, 2016

Dear Students: I think it's time we had the talk. You know, the one couples who've been together for a while sometimes have to review boundaries and expectations? Your generation calls this "DTR"—short for "defining the relationship."

We definitely need to define our relationship because, first of all, it is a long-term relationship—maybe not between you and me, specifically, but between people like you (students) and people like me (professors). And, second, it appears to need some defining, or redefining. I used to think the boundaries and expectations were clear on both sides, but that no longer seems to be the case.

The truth is, I wonder if college students today truly understand the nature of their relationship to professors. Perhaps their experiences with other authority figures—high-school teachers, parents, and bosses—have led them to make assumptions that aren't quite accurate. Or perhaps students are just not too thrilled with authority figures in general. That's always been the case, to some extent. But it seems to me, after 31 years of college teaching, that the lines have grown blurrier, the misconceptions more profound.

So I'd like to take a few moments to define the professor-student relationship. And if no one has ever put it to you quite this way before—well, that just highlights the need for a DTR.

And by the way, please keep in mind that I'm not trying to offend you or tick you off. I actually like you quite a bit, or I wouldn't even bother having this discussion.

I don't work for you. Students (or their parents), when they're unhappy with something I've said or done, occasionally try throwing this line in my face: "You work for me." They mean that by paying tuition and taxes, they pay my salary and I should, therefore, be responsive in the way they desire.

Let's dismiss that old canard right off the bat. Yes, as a professor at a state institution, I am a public employee. But that's precisely the point: I'm

Rob Jenkins is an associate professor of English at Georgia State University–Perimeter College and a regular contributor to the *Chronicle of Higher Education,* where this argument was published.

employed by the college and by the public, not by any particular member of the public. My duty—to the institution and to the people of this state—is to ensure that students in my courses meet the standards set by the college's faculty and are well-prepared for further study and for life.

You're not a customer, and I'm not a clerk. Unfortunately, too many students have been told for too long that they are "customers" of the institution—which means, of course, that they're always right. Right?

Wrong. This is not Wal-Mart. You are not a customer, and I don't even own a blue smock. Our relationship is much more like that of doctor and patient. My only obligation: to tell you what you need to hear (not what you want to hear) and to do what I think is best (not what you think is best).

I'm not a cable network or streaming site. What you get out of this relationship is that you'll be better equipped to succeed in this and other college courses, and life in general. What I get is a great deal of professional and personal satisfaction.

Natives of today's social-media-fueled digital universe have come to expect that everything they want will be available whenever they want it, on demand. That includes, or ought to include, their professors. I mean, we have email, don't we? And cellphones?

Consider this official notice that I have opted out of the on-demand world. My office hours are listed on my syllabus. If for some reason I can't be in my office during those hours, I'll let you know beforehand if possible or post a note on my door. But I'm usually there.

As for email, yes, I have it and I check it often, but not constantly. I do have a life outside this classroom—a wife, kids, hobbies, other professional obligations. That's why I don't give out my private cell number. If you need me after hours, email me and I'll probably see it and respond within 24 to 48 hours.

I'm not a high-school teacher. A common refrain among first-year college students is, "But my high-school teacher said. . . ."

Those teachers did their best to prepare you for college and tell you what to expect. Unfortunately, some of their information was outdated or just plain wrong. For example, not every essay has exactly five paragraphs, and it's OK, in certain situations, to begin a sentence with "because." One of the main differences between them and me is that I'm not telling you how you're going to do things "once you get to college." This is college, and this is how we do things.

Plus, because of something called "academic freedom," which most college professors enjoy but most high-school teachers don't, I'm not nearly as easy to intimidate when you think you deserved an A. I'm sure you (or your parents) would never dream of trying anything like that, but I thought I'd go ahead and mention it, just in case.

I'm not your boss. Please don't misunderstand: I don't take a "my way or the highway" approach to teaching. In my view, that's not what education, and certainly not higher education, is all about. I'm here to help you learn. Whether you choose to accept that help—ultimately, whether you choose to learn anything—is up to you.

My role is not to tell you what to do, like your shift manager at the fast-food restaurant. Rather, I will provide information, explain how to do certain things, and give you regular assignments and assessments designed to help you internalize that knowledge and master those skills. Internalizing and mastering are your responsibility. I can't "fire" you, any more than you can get me fired. But I can and will evaluate the quality and timeliness of your work, and that evaluation will be reflected in your final grade.

I'm not your parent. Some of my colleagues (especially among the administration) believe the institution should act "in loco parentis," which means "in the place of a parent." In other words, when you're away from your parents, we become your parents.

I've never really subscribed to that theory, at least not in the classroom. I suppose there are certain areas of the college, like student services, that have some parental-like obligation to students. But as a professor, I don't. And what that means, more than anything else, is that I'm not going to treat you like a child.

I'm not your BFF. When I first started teaching, I was only a few years older than many of my students. It was tempting, at times, to want to be friends with some of them. I occasionally struggled to maintain an appropriate professional distance.

Not anymore. I've been doing this for a while now—over 30 years—and I'm no longer young. (Sadly, I'm no longer mistaken for a student, either.) I try to be friendly and approachable, but if by "friendly" you think I mean "someone to hang out with," I don't. I regret that we cannot actually be friends.

That applies to virtual friendship, too. Even if you happen to track me down on Facebook, I will not accept your friend request. You're welcome to follow me on Twitter, if you like, but I won't follow you back. And I don't do Instagram or Snapchat or, um, whatever else there is.

I'm not your adversary. Just because we're not best buds, please don't think I'm your enemy. Nothing could be further from the truth. In fact, if by "friend" you mean someone who cares about your well-being and success, then I guess I am a friend after all.

Yet there is always a degree of tension in the student-professor relationship. You may at times feel that I am behaving in an adversarial manner—questioning the quality and relevance of your work, making judgments that you perceive as negative. Understand that is only because I do want you to succeed. It's not personal, on my end, and you must learn not to take it personally.

I'd like to be your partner. More than anything, I'd like for us to form a mutually beneficial alliance in this endeavor we call education.

I pledge to do my part. I will:

- Stay abreast of the latest ideas in my field.
- Teach you what I believe you need to know, with all the enthusiasm I possess.
- Invite your comments and questions and respond constructively.
- Make myself available to you outside of class (within reason).
- Evaluate your work carefully and return it promptly with feedback.
- Be as fair, respectful, and understanding as I can humanly be.
- If you need help beyond the scope of this course, I will do my best to provide it or see that you get it.

In return, I expect you to:

- Show up for class each day or let me know (preferably in advance) if you have some good reason to be absent.
- Do your reading and other assignments outside of class and be prepared for each class meeting.
- Focus during class on the work we're doing and not on extraneous matters (like whoever or whatever is on your phone at the moment).
- Participate in class discussions.
- Be respectful of your fellow students and their points of view.
- In short, I expect you to devote as much effort to learning as I devote to teaching.

What you get out of this relationship is that you'll be better equipped to succeed in this and other college courses, work-related assignments, and life in general. What I get is a great deal of professional and personal satisfaction. Because I do really like you guys and want the best for you.

All in all, that's not a bad deal. It's a shame more relationships aren't like ours.

10
Evaluations

"We don't want to go there for coffee. Their beans aren't fair trade, the drinks are high in calories, and the stuff is *way* overpriced."

The campus storytelling project has just won a competition sponsored by NPR, and everyone involved is thrilled. Then they realize that this year all but one of the leaders of this project will graduate and that they have very few new recruits. So they put their heads together to figure out what qualities they need in new recruits that will help maintain the excellence of their project.

Orson Welles's masterpiece *Citizen Kane* is playing at the Student Union for only one more night, but the new Marvel *Avengers* epic is featured across the street in 3-D. Guess which movie your roomie wants to see? You intend to set her straight.

Understanding Evaluations

Evaluations are everyday arguments. By the time you leave home in the morning, you've likely made a dozen informal evaluations: You've selected neat but informal clothes because you have a job interview with a manufacturing company looking for machinists. You've chosen low-fat yogurt and fruit over the pancakes you really love. You've queued up the perfect playlist on your iPhone for your hike to campus. In each case, you've applied criteria to a particular problem and then made a decision. That's evaluating on the fly.

Some professional evaluations require more elaborate standards, evidence, and paperwork (imagine an aircraft manufacturer certifying a new jet for passenger service), but they don't differ structurally from the simpler choices that people make all the time. People love to voice their opinions, and they always have. In fact, a mode of ancient rhetoric—called the *ceremonial* or *epideictic* (see Chapter 1)—was devoted entirely to speeches of praise and blame.

Today, rituals of praise and (mostly) blame are a significant part of American life. Adults who would choke at the notion of debating causal or definitional claims will happily spend hours appraising the Oakland Raiders, Boston Red Sox, or Pittsburgh Penguins. Other evaluative spectacles in our culture include awards shows, late-night comedy shows, most-valuable-player presentations, lists of best-dressed or worst-dressed celebrities, literary prizes, consumer product magazines, and—the ultimate formal public gesture of evaluation—elections. Indeed, making evaluations is a form of entertainment in America and generates big audiences (think of *The Voice*) and revenues.

Arguments about sports are usually evaluations of some kind. Erik Williams/AP Images

RESPOND•

The last ten years have seen a proliferation of "reality" talent shows around the world—*Dancing with the Stars*, *So You Think You Can Dance*, *American* (or *Canadian* or *Australian* or many other) *Idol*, *America's Got Talent*, *The Voice*, and so on. Write a short opinion piece assessing the merits of a particular "talent" show. What should a proper event of this kind accomplish? Does the event you're reviewing do so?

Criteria of Evaluation

Arguments of evaluation can produce simple rankings and winners or can lead to profound decisions about our lives, but they always involve standards. The particular standards we establish for judging anything—whether a political candidate, consumer product, work of art, or career strategy—are called **criteria of evaluation**. Sometimes criteria are self-evident: a truck that gets nine miles per gallon is a gas hog, and a piece of fish that smells even a little off shouldn't be eaten. But criteria get complicated when a subject is abstract: *What constitutes a fair wage? What are the qualities of a classic song? What makes an event worthy of news coverage?* Struggling to identify such amorphous criteria of evaluation can lead to important insights into your values, motives, and preferences.

Why make such a big deal about criteria when many acts of evaluation seem effortless? Because we should be suspicious of opinions we offer too casually. Spontaneous quips and snap judgments can't carry the same weight as well-informed and well-argued opinions. Serious evaluations require reflection, and when we look deeply into our judgments, we sometimes discover important questions that typically go unasked, many prefaced by *why*:

- You challenge the grade you received in a course, but you don't question the practice of grading.
- You argue passionately that a Democratic Congress is better for America than a Republican one, but you fail to consider why voters get only two choices.
- You argue that news coverage is biased, but it doesn't occur to you to ask what makes an event worthy of news coverage.

Push an argument of evaluation hard enough and even simple judgments become challenging and intriguing.

In fact, for many writers, grappling with criteria is the toughest step in producing an evaluation. When you offer an opinion about a topic you know well, readers ought to learn something from your argument. So you need to formulate and then justify the criteria for your opinions, whatever the subject.

Do you think, for instance, that you could explain what (if anything) makes a veggie burger good? Though many people have eaten veggie burgers, they probably haven't spent much time thinking about them. Moreover it wouldn't be enough merely to assert that a proper one should be juicy or tasty—such observations are trite, uninteresting, and obvious. The following criteria offered on the *Cook's Illustrated* Web site show what happens when experts give the matter their attention:

> We wanted to create veggie burgers that even meat eaters would love. We didn't want them to taste like hamburgers, but we did want them to act like hamburgers, *having a modicum of chew, a harmonious blend of savory ingredients, and the ability to go from grill to bun without falling apart.* [emphasis added]
>
> —*Cook's Illustrated*

After a lot of experimenting, *Cook's Illustrated* came up with a recipe that met these criteria.

Criteria of evaluation aren't static, either. They may evolve over time depending upon audience. Much market research, for example, is

What criteria of evaluation are embedded in this visual argument? Ildi Papp/AGE Fotostock

designed to find out what particular consumers want now or may want in the future—what their criteria are for choosing a product or service. In good economic times, people may demand homes with soaring entryways, lots of space, and premium appliances. In tougher times, they may care more about quality insulation and energy-efficient stoves and dishwashers. Shifts in values, attitudes, and criteria happen all the time.

Criteria can also reveal biases we hardly notice. In a *Current Affairs* column (July 28, 2017), Nathan J. Robinson, citing a 2007 study featured on the Our World In Data Web site, argues that we are blind to an especially insidious omission in mainstream American news coverage—the unspoken and often racially motivated criteria networks use to decide what merits public attention at all. Robinson contends that only "the purest kind of subconscious prejudice" is at work in determining whose death is worth reporting. Looking closely at 700,000 major network news stories, the researchers found that

> **the loss of 1 European life was equivalent to the loss of 45 African lives, in terms of the amount of coverage generated. Deaths in Europe and the Americas were given tens of times more weight than Asian, African, and Pacific lives.**

Robinson is clearly asking news providers and consumers alike to reconsider how they evaluate newsworthiness.

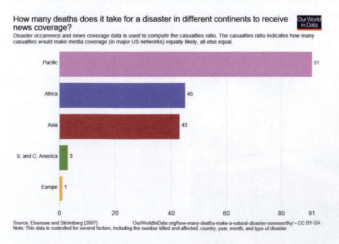

A graph from the Our World In Data Web site shows significant disparities in news coverage given to loss of life in different parts of the world. Our World in Data

RESPOND•

Choose one item from the following list that you understand well enough to evaluate (or choose a category of your own). Develop several criteria of evaluation that you could defend to distinguish excellence from mediocrity in the area. Then choose an item that you don't know much about and explain the research you might do to discover reasonable criteria of evaluation for it.

smartwatches	U.S. vice presidents
NFL quarterbacks	organic vegetables
social media sites	electric cars
TV journalists	spoken word poetry
video games	specialty coffee
virtual reality products	country music bands
Navajo rugs	superhero films

Characterizing Evaluation

One way of understanding evaluative arguments is to consider the types of evidence they use. A distinction explored in Chapter 4 between hard evidence and constructed arguments based on reason is helpful here: we defined **hard evidence** as facts, statistics, testimony, and other kinds of arguments that can be measured, recorded, or even found—the so-called smoking gun in a criminal investigation. We defined constructed arguments based on reason as those that are shaped by language and various kinds of logic.

We can talk about arguments of evaluation the same way, looking at some as quantitative and others as qualitative. **Quantitative arguments** of evaluation employ criteria that can be measured, counted, or demonstrated in some mechanical fashion (something is taller, faster, smoother, quieter, or more powerful than something else). In contrast, **qualitative arguments** rely on criteria that must be explained through language and media, alluding to such matters as values, traditions, and emotions (something is more ethical, more beneficial, more handsome, or more noble than something else). A claim of evaluation might be supported by arguments of both sorts.

Quantitative Evaluations

At first glance, quantitative evaluations seem to hold all the cards, especially in a society as enamored of science and technology as our own is. Making judgments should be easy if all it involves is measuring and counting—and in some cases, that's the way things work out. *Who's the tallest or oldest or loudest person in your class?* If your classmates allow themselves to be measured, you could find out easily enough, using the right equipment and internationally sanctioned standards of measurement—the meter, the calendar, or the decibel.

But what if you were to ask, *Who's the smartest person in class?* You could answer this more complex question quantitatively, using IQ tests or college entrance examinations that report results numerically. In fact, almost all college-bound students in the United States submit to this kind of evaluation, taking either the SAT or the ACT to demonstrate their verbal and mathematical prowess. Such measures are widely accepted by educators and institutions, but they are also vigorously challenged. What do they actually measure? They predict likely academic success only in college, which is one kind of intelligence. As you might guess, quantitative measures of evaluation have limits. Devised to measure only certain criteria and ignore others, they have an inevitably limited perspective.

And yet quantitative evaluations may still be full of insight. For example, even if you are not concerned with finding a mate at this point, you might be interested to know what people are looking for in a potential partner. Good looks? Of course—according to a *Business Wire* story, 51 percent of the people on online dating services value attractiveness in a potential mate. Others look for modesty (39 percent), ambition (50 percent), and a sense of humor (67 percent). But what trumps all these qualities is something you might not have thought much about at this point: your credit rating. Fully 69 percent of those surveyed thought a good credit score was important or very important in considering whom they might date. An odd criterion? Not at all. Dr. Helen Fischer, chief scientific advisor for Match.com, explains why:

> When it comes to dating, a good credit score ups your mate value, helping you win a responsible, long-term partner, more so than some

other qualities that online daters might highlight on their profile. Money talks, but your credit score can speak more about who you are as a person, and singles agree that those with good credit tend to be conscientious and reliable.

—"Online Daters Say a Good Credit Score Is More Attractive Than a Fancy Car," *Business Wire*, August 21, 2017

Something to remember when your next credit card bill comes due?

Qualitative Evaluations

Many issues of evaluation that are closest to people's hearts aren't subject to quantification. *What makes a movie great or significant?* If you suggested a quantitative measure like length, your friends would probably hoot, "Get serious!" But what about box-office receipts, adjusted for inflation? Would films that made the most money—an easily quantifiable measure—be the "best pictures"? That select group would include movies such as *Star Wars*, *The Sound of Music*, *Gone with the Wind*, *Titanic*, *Avatar*, and E.T. An interesting group of films—but the best?

To define the criteria for "significant movie," you'd more likely look for the standards and evidence that serious critics explore in their arguments, abstract or complicated issues such as their societal impact, cinematic technique, dramatic structures, intelligent casting, and so on. Most of these markers of quality could be defined or identified with some precision but not actually measured or counted. You'd also have to make your case rhetorically, convincing the audience to accept the benchmarks of quality you are offering and yet appreciating that they might not.

Indeed, a movie reviewer (or anyone else) making strong qualitative judgments might spend as much time defending criteria of evaluation as providing evidence that these standards are present in a particular film. And putting those standards into action can be what makes a review attention getting or, even better, worth reading. Here's a paragraph from Mehera Bonner, an entertainment editor for *Marie Claire* who is not shy about applying a feminist perspective to Christopher Nolan's World War II epic *Dunkirk* (2017), depicting the evacuation of more than 300,000 allied soldiers trapped by German forces on the coast of France at the outset of the conflict:

[M]y main issue with *Dunkirk* is that it's so clearly designed for men to man-out over. And look, it's not like I need every movie to have "strong female leads." *Wonder Woman* can probably tide me over for at least a year, and I understand that this war was dominated by brave male soldiers. I get that. But the packaging of the film, the general vibe, and the tenor of the people applauding it just screams "men-only"—and specifically seems to cater to a certain type of very pretentious man who would love nothing more than to explain to me why I'm wrong about not liking it. . . . [T]o me, *Dunkirk* felt like an excuse for men to celebrate maleness.

—Mehera Bonner, "I Think *Dunkirk* Was Mediocre at Best, and It's Not Because I'm Some Naïve Woman Who Doesn't Get It"

RESPOND •

For examples of powerful evaluation arguments, search the Web for eulogies or obituaries of famous, recently deceased individuals. Try to locate at least one such item, and then analyze the types of claims it makes about the accomplishments of the deceased. What types of criteria of evaluation hold the obituary or eulogy together? Why should we respect or admire the person?

Web sites such as Netflix and Rotten Tomatoes offer recommendations for films based on users' past selections and the ratings of other users and critics. Sometimes those judgments are at odds. Then whom do you trust?
Kaspars Grinvalds/Shutterstock

Developing an Evaluative Argument

Developing an argument of evaluation can seem like a simple process, especially if you already know what your claim is likely to be. To continue the movie theme for one more example:

> *Citizen Kane* **is likely the finest film ever made by an American director.**

Having established a claim, you would then explore the implications of your belief, drawing out the reasons, warrants, and evidence that might support it:

Claim	*Citizen Kane* is the finest film ever made by an American director . . .
Reason	. . . because it revolutionizes the way we see the world.
Warrant	Great films change viewers in fundamental ways.
Evidence	Shot after shot, *Citizen Kane* presents the life of its protagonist through cinematic images that viewers can never forget.

The warrant here is, in effect, an implied statement of criteria—in this case, the quality that defines "great film" for the writer. It may be important for the writer to share that assumption with readers and perhaps to identify other great films that similarly make viewers appreciate new perspectives.

As you can see, in developing an evaluative argument, you'll want to pay special attention to criteria, claims, and evidence.

Formulating Criteria

Although even casual evaluations (*This band sucks!*) might be traced to reasonable criteria, most people don't defend their positions until they are challenged (*Oh yeah?*). Writers who address readers with whom they share core values rarely discuss their criteria in great detail. Similarly, critics with established reputations in their fields aren't expected to restate all their principles every time they write reviews. They assume audiences will—over time—come to appreciate their standards. Indeed,

What criteria does Deanna Hartley use in evaluating what makes some candidates more successful than others in how they use social media during a job search?

LINK TO P. 709

the expertise they command becomes a part of their persuasive ethos (see Chapter 3). Still, criteria can make or break a piece.

So spend time developing your criteria of evaluation. What exactly makes a shortstop an all-star? What marks a standardized test as an unreliable measure of intelligence? What distinguishes an inspired rapper from a run-of-the-mill one? In cases like these, list the possibilities and then pare them down to the essential qualities. If you propose vague, dull, or unsupportable principles, expect to be challenged.

You're most likely to be vague about your beliefs when you haven't thought, read, or experienced enough about your subject. Push yourself at least as far as you imagine readers will. Anticipate readers looking over your shoulder, asking difficult questions. Say, for example, that you intend to argue that anyone who wants to stay on the cutting edge of personal technology will obviously want Microsoft's latest Surface Pro because it does so many amazing things. But what does that mean exactly? What makes the device "amazing"? Is it that it offers the flexibility of a touch screen, boasts an astonishing high-resolution screen, and gives artists the ability to draw with a stylus? These are particular features of the device. But can you identify a more fundamental quality to explain the product's appeal, such as a Surface user's experience, enjoyment, or productivity? You'll often want to raise your evaluation to a higher level of generality like this so that your appraisal of a product, book, performance, or political figure works as a coherent argument, and not just as a list of random observations.

Be certain, too, that your criteria of evaluation apply to more than just your topic of the moment. Your standards should make sense on their own merits and apply across the board. If you tailor your criteria to get the outcome you want, you are doing what is called "special pleading." You might be pleased when you prove that the home team is awesome, but it won't take skeptics long to figure out how you've cooked the books.

RESPOND●

Local news and entertainment magazines often publish "best of" issues or articles that catalog their readers' and editors' favorites in such categories as "best place to go on a first date," "best ice cream sundae," and "best dentist." Sometimes the categories are specific: "best places to say 'I was retro before retro was cool'" or "best movie theater seats." Imagine that you're the editor of your own local magazine and that you want to put out a "best of" issue tailored to your hometown. Develop five categories for evaluation. For each category, list the evaluative criteria that you would use to make your judgment. Next, consider that because your criteria are warrants, they're especially tied to audience. (The criteria for "best dentist," for example, might be tailored to people whose major concern is avoiding pain, to those whose children will be regular patients, or to those who want the cheapest possible dental care.) For several of the evaluative categories, imagine that you have to justify your judgments to a completely different audience. Write a new set of criteria for that audience.

Making Claims

In evaluations, claims can be stated directly or, more rarely, strongly implied. For most writers, strong and specific statements followed by reasonable qualifications work best. Consider the differences between the following three claims and how much greater the burden of proof is for the first claim:

> J. R. R. Tolkien is the best writer of fantasy ever.

> J. R. R. Tolkien's *The Lord of the Rings* is a better fantasy series than J. K. Rowling's Harry Potter series, even for children.

> For most readers, J. R. R. Tolkien's *The Return of the King* offers, arguably, a more profound examination of evil than J. K. Rowling's *Harry Potter and the Deathly Hallows*.

Here's a second set of examples demonstrating the same principle, that knowledgeable qualifications generally make a claim of evaluation easier to deal with and smarter:

> Chicago mayor Rahm Emanuel's recent suggestion for a new graduation requirement for high school seniors in his city sure is dumb!

> A proposal by Mayor Rahm Emanuel of Chicago that students in his city's schools not receive high school diplomas unless they've been admitted to college, joined the military, or are already employed, might do more harm than good.

> While praiseworthy in its goal to make high school seniors think about their futures, Mayor Emanuel's proposed graduation requirement might force many working-class students into making the wrong choices—going to trade school, joining the military, enrolling in second-rate online schools—just to claim a high school diploma they've already earned.

Food blogger Jess Kapadia makes a strong evaluative claim when she asserts that, for example, the best Indian food she ever ate was not in India but in Singapore.

LINK TO P. 615

The point of qualifying theses like these isn't to make evaluative claims bland but to make them responsible and reasonable. Consider how Reagan Tankersley uses the criticisms of a musical genre he enjoys to frame an assertion he makes in its defense:

> Structurally, dubstep is a simple musical form, with formulaic progressions and beats, something that gives a musically tuned ear little to grasp or analyze. For this reason, a majority of traditionally trained musicians find the genre to be a waste of time. These people have a legitimate position. . . . However, I hold that it is the simplicity of dubstep that makes it special: the primal nature of the song is what digs so deeply into fans. It accesses the most primitive area in our brains that connects to the uniquely human love of music.
>
> —Reagan Tankersley, "Dubstep: Why People Dance"

Tankersley doesn't pretend that dubstep is a subtle or sophisticated musical form, nor does he expect his argument to win over traditionally minded critics. Yet he still makes a claim worth considering.

One tip: Nothing adds more depth to an opinion than letting others challenge it. When you can, use the resources of the Internet or local discussion boards to get responses to your opinions or topic proposals. It can be eye-opening to realize how strongly people react to ideas or points of view that you regard as perfectly normal. Share your claim and then, when you're ready, your first draft with friends, classmates, or

Dubstep band Dope D.O.D. performing live in Moscow in 2015 hurricanehank/Shutterstock

tutors at the writing center, asking them to identify places where your ideas need additional support, either in the discussion of criteria or in the presentation of evidence.

Presenting Evidence

Generally, the more evidence in an evaluation the better, provided that the evidence is relevant. For example, in evaluating the performance of two laptops, the speed of their processors would be essential; the quality of their keyboards or the availability of service might be less crucial yet still worth mentioning. But you have to decide how much detail your readers want in your argument. For technical subjects, you might make your basic case briefly and then attach additional support- ing documents at the end—tables, graphs, charts—for those who want more data.

Just as important as relevance in selecting evidence is presentation. Not all pieces of evidence are equally convincing, nor should they be treated as such. Select evidence that is most likely to influence your readers, and then arrange the argument to build toward your strongest points. In most cases, that best material will be evidence that's specific, detailed, memorable, and derived from credible sources. The following example comes from a celebratory defense of art and artists by musi- cian, songwriter, and producer T Bone Burnett, delivered at the 2016 AmericanaFest music festival in Nashville. The energy of his language and the memorable examples likely solidify the case that music is foun- dational to the American mythology:

> This is the story of the United States: a kid walks out of his home with a song and nothing else, and conquers the world. We have replicated that phenomenon over and over: Elvis Presley, ... Rosetta Tharpe, Johnny Cash, Howlin Wolf, Mahalia Jackson, Bob Dylan, John Coltrane, Billie Holiday.
>
> —T Bone Burnett, Nashville, TN, September 22, 2016

In evaluation arguments, don't be afraid to concede a point when evidence goes contrary to the overall claim you wish to make. If you're really skillful, you can even turn a problem into an argumentative asset, as Bob Costas does in acknowledging the flaws of baseball great Mickey Mantle in the process of praising him:

T Bone Burnett gave the keynote speech at the AmericanaFest (Americana Music Festival & Conference) in Nashville. Anna Webber/Getty Images

> None of us, Mickey included, would want to be held to account for every moment of our lives. But how many of us could say that our best moments were as magnificent as his?
>
> —Bob Costas, "Eulogy for Mickey Mantle"

Considering Design and Visuals

Visual components play a significant role in many kinds of evaluation arguments, especially during political campaigns—as the image on the following page suggests. But they can also be important in more technical arguments as well (see for instance the Our World In Data graph on p. 228). As soon as numbers are involved in supporting your claim, think about ways to arrange quantitative information in tables, charts, graphs, or infographics to make the information more accessible to readers. Visual elements are especially helpful when comparing items. The facts can seem to speak for themselves if they are presented with care and deliberation.

But don't ignore other basic design features of a text—such as headings for the different criteria you're using or, in online evaluations, links to material related to your subject.

RESPOND ▪

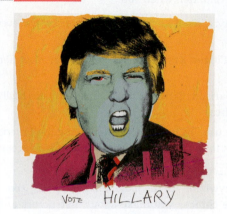

Vote Hillary by Deborah Kass © 2018
Deborah Kass/Artists Rights Society (ARS),
New York

Take a close look at what artist Deborah Kass described in July 2016 as her "official fundraising screen print" for the presidential campaign of Hillary Clinton. In what ways did it make an argument of evaluation designed to make Americans consider voting for the Democratic candidate rather than for Republican Donald Trump? Would any elements in it make some voters perhaps less likely to support Clinton? Explain your assessment of the image.

GUIDE to writing an evaluation

● Finding a Topic

You're entering an argument of evaluation when you:

- make a judgment about quality: Citizen Kane *is probably the finest film ever made by an American director.*
- challenge such a judgment: Citizen Kane *is vastly overrated by most film critics.*
- construct a ranking or comparison: Citizen Kane *is a more intellectually challenging movie than* Casablanca.
- explore criteria that might be used in making critical judgments: *Criteria for judging films are evolving as the production and audiences of films become ever more international.*

Issues of evaluation crop up everywhere—in the judgments you make about public figures or policies; in the choices you make about instructors and courses; in the recommendations you offer about books, films, or television programs; in the preferences you exercise in choosing products, activities, or charities. Evaluations typically use terms or images that indicate value or rank—*good/bad, effective/ineffective, best/worst, competent/incompetent, successful/ unsuccessful.* When you can choose a topic for an evaluation, consider writing about something on which others regularly ask your opinion or advice.

● Researching Your Topic

You can research issues of evaluation by using the following sources:

- journals, reviews, and magazines (for current political and social issues)
- books (for assessing judgments about history, policy, etc.)
- biographies (for assessing people)
- research reports and scientific studies
- books, magazines, and Web sites for consumers
- periodicals and Web sites that cover entertainment and sports
- blogs and social media sites that explore current topics

Surveys and polls can be useful in uncovering public attitudes: *What kinds of movies are young people seeing today? Who are the most admired people in the country? What activities or businesses are thriving or waning?* You'll discover that Web sites, newsgroups, and blogs thrive on evaluation. (Ever receive an invitation to "like" something on social media?) Browse these public forums for ideas, and, when possible, explore your own topic ideas there. But remember that all sources need to be critically assessed themselves; examine each source carefully, making sure that it is legitimate and credible.

● Formulating a Claim

After exploring your subject, try to draw up a full and specific claim that lets readers know where you stand and on what criteria you'll base your judgments. Come up with a thesis that's challenging enough to attract readers' attention. In developing a thesis, you might begin with questions like these:

- What exactly is my opinion? Where do I stand?
- Can I make my judgment more clear-cut?
- Do I need to narrow or qualify my claim?
- By what standards will I make my judgment?
- Will readers or viewers accept my criteria, or will I have to defend them, too? What criteria might others offer?
- What evidence or major reasons can I offer in support of my evaluation?

For a conventional evaluation, such as a book or restaurant review, your thesis should be a complete statement. In one sentence, make a claim of evaluation and state the reasons that support it. Be sure your claim is specific. Anticipate the questions readers might have: *Who? What? Where? Under what conditions? With what exceptions? In all cases?* Don't expect readers to guess where you stand.

For a more exploratory argument, you might begin (and even end) with questions about the process of evaluation itself. *What are the qualities we seek—or ought to—in our political leaders? What does it say about our cultural values when we find so many viewers entertained by so-called reality shows on television? What might be the criteria for collegiate athletic programs consistent with the values of higher education?* Projects that explore topics like these might not begin with straightforward theses or have the intention to persuade readers.

● Examples of Evaluative Claims

- Though they may never receive Oscars for their work, Tom Cruise and Angela Bassett deserve credit as actors who have succeeded in a wider range of film roles than most of their contemporaries.

- The much-vaunted population shift back to urban areas in the United States has really been mostly among rich, educated, and childless people who can afford the high costs of living there.

- The most remarkable aspect of Elon Musk as an entrepreneur is the way he blatantly uses public money to build his companies—from Tesla to SpaceX.

- Jimmy Carter has been highly praised for his work as a former president of the United States, but history may show that even his much-derided term in office laid the groundwork for the foreign policy and economic successes now attributed to later administrations.

- Young adults today are shying away from diving into the housing market because they no longer believe that homeownership is a key element in economic success.

● Preparing a Proposal

If your instructor asks you to prepare a proposal for your project, here's a format that may help:

State your thesis completely. If you're having trouble doing so, try outlining it in Toulmin terms:

    Claim:

    Reason(s):

    Warrant(s):

Alternatively, you might describe your intention to explore a particular question of evaluation in your project, with the thesis perhaps coming later.

- Explain why this issue deserves attention. What's at stake?

- Identify whom you hope to reach through your argument and why these readers would be interested in it.

- Briefly discuss the key challenges you anticipate in preparing your argument.
- Determine what research strategies you'll use. What sources do you expect to consult?

Considering Genre and Media

Your instructor may specify that you use a particular genre and/or medium. If not, ask yourself these questions to help you make a good choice:

- What genre is most appropriate for your argument of evaluation? Does it call for an academic essay, a report, an infographic, a video, or something else?
- What medium is most appropriate for your argument? Would it be best delivered orally to a live audience? Presented as an audio essay or podcast? Presented in print only or in print with illustrations?
- Will you need visuals, such as moving or still images, maps, graphs, charts— and what function will they play in your argument? Make sure they are not just "added on" but are necessary components of the argument.

Thinking about Organization

Your evaluation will likely include elements such as the following:

- an evaluative claim that makes a judgment about a person, idea, or object
- the criterion or criteria by which you'll measure your subject
- an explanation or justification of the criteria (if necessary)
- evidence that the particular subject meets or falls short of the stated criteria
- consideration of alternative views and counterarguments

All these elements may be present in arguments of evaluation, but they won't follow a specific order. In addition, you'll often need an opening paragraph to explain what you're evaluating and why. Tell readers why they should care about your subject and take your opinion seriously.

Getting and Giving Response: Questions for Peer Response

Your instructor may assign you to a group for the purpose of reading and responding to each other's drafts. If not, ask for responses from serious readers or consultants at a writing center. Use the following questions to evaluate a colleague's draft. Be sure to illustrate your comments with examples; specific comments help more than general observations.

The Claim

- Is the claim an argument of evaluation? Does it make a critical judgment about something?
- Does the claim establish clearly what's being evaluated?
- Is the claim too sweeping or too narrow? Does it need to be qualified or expanded?
- Will the criteria used in the evaluation be clear to readers? Do the criteria need to be defined more precisely?
- Are the criteria appropriate ones to use for this evaluation? Are they controversial? Should they be defended?

Evidence for the Claim

- Is enough evidence provided to show that what's being evaluated meets the established criteria? If not, what additional evidence is needed?
- Is the evidence in support of the claim simply announced, or are its significance and appropriateness analyzed? Is more detailed discussion needed?
- Are any objections readers might have to the claim, criteria, or evidence adequately addressed?
- What kinds of sources are cited? How credible and persuasive will they be to readers? What other kinds of sources might work better?
- Are all quotations introduced with appropriate signal phrases (such as "As Tyson argues, . . .") and blended smoothly into the writer's sentences?
- Are all visual sources labeled, introduced, and commented upon?

Organization and Style

- How are the parts of the argument organized? Is this organization effective?
- Will readers understand the relationships among the claims, supporting reasons, warrants, and evidence? If not, how might those connections be clearer? Does every visual serve a clear purpose? Are more transitions needed? Would headings or graphic devices help?

- Are the transitions or links from point to point, sentence to sentence, and paragraph to paragraph clear and effective? If not, how could they be improved?

- Are all visuals carefully integrated into the text? Is each visual introduced and commented on to point out its significance? Is each visual labeled as a figure or a table and given a caption as well as a citation?

- Is the style suited to the subject? Is it too formal, casual, or technical? Can it be improved?

- Which sentences seem effective? Which ones seem weaker, and how could they be improved? Should short sentences be combined, and any longer ones be broken up?

- How effective are the paragraphs? Too short or too long? How can they be improved?

- Which words or phrases seem effective? Do any seem vague or inappropriate for the audience or the writer's purpose? Are technical or unfamiliar terms defined?

Spelling, Punctuation, Mechanics, Documentation, and Format

- Are there any errors in spelling, punctuation, capitalization, and the like?

- Is the documentation appropriate and consistent? (See Chapter 22.)

- Does the paper or project follow an appropriate format? Is it well designed and attractively presented?

PROJECTS

1. What kinds of reviews or evaluations do you read or consult most often—those of TV shows, sports teams, video games, fashions, fishing gear, political figures? Try composing an argument of evaluation in your favorite genre: make and defend a claim about the quality of some object, item, work, or person within your area of interest or special knowledge. Let the project demonstrate an expertise you have gained. If it helps, model your evaluation upon the work of a reviewer or expert you particularly respect and choose the medium that you think works best.

2. Prepare a project in which you challenge what you regard as a wrong-headed evaluation, providing sound reasons and solid evidence for challenging this existing and perhaps commonly held view. Maybe you believe that a classic novel you had to read in high school is over-rated or that people who criticize a particular social media platform really don't understand it. Explain why the subject of your evaluation needs to be reconsidered and provide reasons, evidence, and, if necessary, different criteria of evaluation for doing so. For an example of this type of (re)evaluation, see Becca Stanek's "I took vitamins every day for a decade. Then I found out they're useless," on pp. 252–54.

3. Write an evaluation in which you compare or assess the contributions or achievements of two or three notable people working within the same field or occupation. They may be educators, entrepreneurs, public officials, artists, legislators, editorial cartoonists, fashion designers, programmers, athletes, faculty at your school, or employees where you work. While your first instinct might be to rank these individuals and pick a "winner," you could also aim to help readers appreciate the different paths by which your subjects have achieved distinction.

4. Within this chapter, the authors claim that criteria of evaluation can change depending on times and circumstances: "In good economic times, people may demand homes with soaring entryways, lots of space, and premium appliances. In tougher times, they may care more about quality insulation and energy-efficient stoves and dishwashers." Working in a group, discuss several scenarios of change and then explore how those circumstances could alter the way we evaluate particular objects, activities, or productions. For example, what impact might global warming have upon the way we determine desirable places to live or vacation? How might growing resistance worldwide to immigration or open borders affect political alliances or cultural diversity? If people across the globe continue to put on weight, how might standards of personal beauty or fashion alter? If media and news outlets continue to fall in public esteem, how might we change the way we make political decisions? Following the discussion, write a paper or prepare a project in which you explore how one scenario for change might revise customary values and standards of evaluation.

The Toxicity in Learning

Sang Young Kim

JENNY KIM

My eyes burst open. My body is shaking and my palms are sweaty. 528—perfect score; 521—the start of the 99th percentile; 516—minimum score needed for top tier medical schools, that is, 129 on all four sections. How do I compare to my peers? To those Ivy League applicants? Everything is a competition, and I need to be perfect. I must be crazy. Two weeks away from the most important test of my life to date, I'm suffering from insomnia.

In fact, I was convinced that I was crazy until I talked to my fellow peers who'd also fallen prey to one of the most demoralizing tests created: the MCAT. Of the fourteen people I talked to, thirteen of them had experienced nightmares and insomnia as the test drew near, and two of them continued to have trouble sleeping weeks after their exam! MCAT PTSD? Surely, that doesn't exist.

Opening paragraphs focus on the emotional trauma of anticipating the MCAT—the Medical College Admission Test.

Perhaps MCAT PTSD isn't a real disease, but there has been a rise in an obsession with academic perfection that has led to increased suicide rates among students and the development of mental disorders (Duriez). To make matters worse, this preoccupation with scores and perfection is not limited to pre-med candidates. Across all disciplines, there is an unhealthy infatuation with a 4.0 GPA that detracts from true learning.

Many of the skills and materials picked up in school *can* be integrated in innovative ways to tackle world problems, and it is a student's duty to acquire such skills

---

Jenny Kim, a biochemistry/pre-med major at the University of Texas at Austin, wrote "The Toxicity of Learning" for an Advanced Writing class when she was a junior—contrasting two styles of learning. In a topic proposal, she wrote, "I want to argue the importance of learning as opposed to getting 'good grades.' Although there is an overlap between the two, I do believe there is a fine line between going to school to learn and going to school to get a 4.0."

A thesis contrasts two modes of experiencing college: studying for the test and genuine learning for professional life.

and eventually advance their professions. But that is an impossible feat if students are immersed in a culture that emphasizes short-term memorization and immediate forgetfulness rather than careful analysis and the steady accumulation of knowledge. Unfortunately much of academia has adopted the habit of regurgitation. Despite the ubiquity of this toxic culture, college students should strive to escape it and yearn for something more: an insatiable curiosity and profound understanding of a field they're passionate about.

Recalling high school, I can see why many students are inclined to memorize and forget. Back then, I took all the advanced placement courses and excelled in them. But it was often enough just to memorize definitions and plug numbers into equations. Fast forward a few years. It is my second semester in college and my first in a research lab. I am standing beside four fellow freshmen on our first day. Before this, I'd never been given the opportunity to perform "actual research." The entirety of my lab experiences prior to college were disorganized AP Chemistry labs taught by a clueless but kind microbiology teacher. But that day, the professor running the lab, a researcher/educator, asked us a question regarding the biotechnology used to express antibiotics. My chest tightened. I had no idea what he was talking about, but the terms sounded familiar. True to our high school roots, the four other freshmen and I began blurting out definitions and random facts regarding PCR, bacteria, and selectivity. I had no idea what these concepts meant, much less how they related to one another, but assumed that if I included "buzz words" and science jargon in my answer, I would at least appear smart. I have never been so wrong. All five of us received a long, well-deserved lecture that day, and it was not pleasant.

Still in high-school mode, the author learns a painful lesson in her first college lab.

My desire to appear intelligent would be a classical example of surface motive. According to Dr. Bernardo Lopez, a professor and the vice dean faculty of philosophy and science at the University of Valencia, two questions arise when a student begins an academic task: "What do I want to accomplish with this? What can I do to accomplish it?" (Lopez). The answers to these questions are divided into two categories: surface and deep. Surface motive and learning are marked by short-term gratification and a lack of scholarly drive, such as my fruitless attempt to impress the professor. Deep motive and learning are characterized by a desire to apply oneself meaningfully at a higher conceptual level, with genuine curiosity for the subject at hand. In other words, it's the difference between memorizing to get a 4.0 as opposed to learning to build upon a pre-existing knowledge base.

Kim introduces technical terms to evaluate two contrasting styles of learning: surface motive and deep motive.

The research of Dr. Lopez comparing deep and surface learning revealed a correlation between deep learning motives/strategies and academic success. In his study, a greater portion of excellent students—defined as those scoring in the 90th percentile on a university-wide exam—were found to use deep strategy and have deep motive when compared to average students. On the other hand, average students were found to use more surface strategy and have more surface motive than their more academically accomplished peers (Lopez).

Almost by definition, students with deep learning motives succeed in their courses.

Now, earning a 4.0 isn't necessarily bad. However, taking easy college classes just to "boost GPA" is a grand waste of time. The purpose of an education is to become more knowledgeable in an area of interest and develop practical skills to excel in said field. When tempted to take a pointless GPA booster or memorize their way into an A, college students should remind themselves why they're paying thousands of dollars and spending hundreds of sleepless nights to get an "education."

Merely going through the motions can earn high grades, but doesn't produce actual learning.

That being said, the first steps to escaping the regurgitation culture is for students to pursue a field *they're* drawn to and develop a desire to push that field forward. When asked by adults to justify their choice of major, most students mention passion, talent, or interest. But how can that be the case when many students lack a fundamental understanding of their area of study? What makes a good writer, a good biologist, or a good musician? Memorizing procedures and facts surely doesn't. Anyone can learn to read music, given a few days and a book, so what is it that distinguishes a true musician from a biology, English, or even a music major?

As an experienced tutor myself, I know that one of the most frustrating moments of teaching occurs when you realize your student has not learned anything from the past few lessons. There is a fine line between memorizing disconnected fragments and constructing a full roadmap in one's head. This is exactly the problem Dr. Eric Mazur, a physics professor at Harvard University, ran into when he decided to give a conceptual problem to test his students' understanding. When asked about Newton's third law of motion, the students could recite it word for word. However, when it came time to apply the concept, Newton's third law had conveniently transformed into a novel and bewildering idea. He found that very few of his students could even set up a simple quantitative problem based on the principles of the law (Weimer).

What differentiates a musician from a biology or English major, and even a "surface-driven" music major is not the capacity to read music, or the knowledge of when to use a détatché as opposed to a legato bow stroke. The difference lies in the musician's ability to express the distinct personas of different composers, or illustrate the variation within a single composer's work: charming the audience with celebratory birds in Spring then making the audience tremble from the harsh extreme of Winter while maintaining Vivaldi's sprightly sense of style throughout the entirety of *The Four Seasons*. It's only through motivated practice and careful analyses that a music major can consolidate fragments of knowledge into a whole and become an actual musician. Being able to play violin means nothing if the intonation, style,

> Mere knowledge does not translate into passion for a subject.

> An elaborate comparison explains the difference between rote learning and the real thing.

tone, volume, rhythm, and phrasing, among other things, aren't present.

There are many college courses in which students can earn an A through sheer memorization or repetition. There are other college courses that will guarantee them an A on their transcript. But, students should remind themselves that they're acquiring an education. Surface motives and strategy may earn them gold stars and a 4.0 on their transcripts, but how will they memorize their way through an open heart surgery, their first novel, or a concert with the New York Symphony? And if that isn't enough to deter students from a toxic obsession with a 4.0, is a perfect GPA worth all those nervous breakdowns and panic attacks? Surely not. Passion for a field is one thing, obsession over scores and competition is another. Weimer offers this advice: "Don't aim for success if you want it; just do what you love and believe in, and it will come naturally." Now, excuse me while I check the average MCAT scores for my top medical schools.

WORKS CITED

Duriez, Kara. "Grade Obsession and Why It's a Serious Problem." sites.psu.edu/siowfa15/2015/09/17/grade-obsession-and-why-its-a-serious-problem/.

Lopez, Bernardo, et al. "Learning Styles and Approaches to Learning in Excellent and Average First-Year University Students." *European Journal of Psychology of Education*, vol. 28, no. 4, pp. 1361–79.

Weimer, Maryellen. "Do Your Students Understand the Material, or Just Memorize and Forget?" *Faculty Focus*, www.facultyfocus.com/articles/teaching-professor-blog/do-your-students-understand-the-material-or-just-memorize-and-forget/.

I took vitamins every day for a decade. Then I found out they're useless.

BECCA STANEK

March 22, 2017

Save for a few lapses in my irresponsible college days, I've popped a multivitamin every single day since middle school.

First it was the chalky multivitamins that left a lump in my throat for minutes after I'd gulped one down. Then it was the slightly grainy, massive pills that my mom bought in bulk at Costco. (They were technically for post-menopausal women, but my mother assured me they would be just fine for my 17-year-old self.) Then last year, tired of big, bad-tasting pills, I bought gummy vitamins. Who doesn't like noshing on some candy that holds the promise of great health?

Well, last week I threw my vitamins away. I'll miss that sugary, fruity taste—but, according to my doctor, that's about all I'll be missing.

At my appointment last Wednesday, my doctor bluntly informed me that my multivitamins weren't doing a darn thing for me. Though the idea of getting just a little bit more of all the most important vitamins may seem like a foolproof idea, she informed me that more isn't necessarily better. Few people have vitamin deficiencies. Moreover, for those who do have a deficiency in, say, Vitamin D or Vitamin B12, those little grape-shaped gummies—or any multivitamin, for that matter—don't pack anywhere near enough of any one vitamin to correct that deficiency, she explained.

That could be passed off as just one doctor's opinion . . . except there are a plethora of studies out there that back up her argument. A much buzzed-about study published in *Annals of Internal Medicine* in 2013, for instance, came to this clear-cut conclusion after reviewing three trials of

---

Becca Stanek, a writer for *TheWeek.com*, explains exactly why she gave up a habit common to many Americans—taking multivitamins. Citing ample research, she argues that most people don't need them and people with genuine vitamin deficiencies need something more potent than an over-the-counter pill. We've underlined the hyperlinked words and phrases to give you an idea of how a professional writer backs up important claims in an evaluative argument. You can find the piece online.

multivitamin supplements and 24 trials of "single or paired vitamins that randomly assigned more than 40,000 participants":

> Evidence is sufficient to advise against routine supplementation, and we should translate null and negative findings into action. The message is simple: Most supplements do not prevent chronic disease or death, their use is not justified, and they should be avoided. This message is especially true for the general population with no clear evidence of micronutrient deficiencies, who represent most supplement users in the United States and in other countries. [_Annals of Internal Medicine_]

Specifically, the study found vitamins to be ineffective when it comes to reducing the risk of heart disease, cancer, declines in cognitive ability, and premature death. And, Quartz noted, some vitamins can even be "harmful in high enough quantities":

> Our bodies can easily get rid of excess vitamins that dissolve in water, like vitamin C, all the B vitamins, and folate, but they hold onto the ones that are fat soluble. Buildup of vitamin A, K, E, or D—all of which are necessary in low levels—can cause problems with your heart and kidneys, and can even be fatal in some cases. [Quartz]

Though the FDA says on its vitamins information page that there "are many good reasons to consider taking supplements," it indicates vitamins only "may be useful when they fill a specific identified nutrient gap that cannot or is not otherwise being met by the individuals' intake of food." The CDC estimated in 2014 that "nine out of 10 people in the U.S. are indeed getting enough of some important vitamins and nutrients."

So why are so many Americans still taking multivitamins? Steven Salzberg, a medicine professor at Johns Hopkins, told NPR multivitamins are "a great example of how our intuition leads us astray." "It seems reasonable that if a little bit of something is good for you, then more should be better for you. It's not true," Salzberg said. "Supplementation with extra vitamins or micronutrients doesn't really benefit you if you don't have a deficiency."

Americans' abysmally bad diets also give vitamin companies some marketing ammunition. When the average American is eating just one or two servings of fruits and veggies a day (experts recommend as many as 10 servings of fruits and veggies a day for maximum benefits), a little boost of vitamins might seem like a good idea. But popping a pill isn't going to make up for all those lost servings. "Food contains thousands of phyto-chemicals, fiber, and more that work together to promote good health that cannot be duplicated with a pill," said nutritionist Karen Ansel.

And if it's those tasty gummy vitamins we're falling back on, there's an even better chance we're not offsetting our sugar- and fat-laden diets. The women's gummy multivitamins I was taking pack three grams of sugar per gummy. A serving size is two gummies. Even before breakfast, I was consuming six grams of sugar—almost a quarter of the American Heart Association's recommended maximum sugar intake for women.

So why, if there are so many signs pointing to no on multivitamins, had I never really heard any of them until that fateful visit to the doctor? Pediatrician Paul Offit explained in a 2013 *New York Times* opinion article that it might have something to do with a bill introduced in the 1970s:

> In December 1972, concerned that people were consuming larger and larger quantities of vitamins, the FDA announced a plan to regulate vitamin supplements containing more than 150 percent of the recommended daily allowance. Vitamin makers would now have to prove that these "megavitamins" were safe before selling them. Not surprisingly, the vitamin industry saw this as a threat, and set out to destroy the bill. In the end, it did far more than that.
>
> Industry executives recruited William Proxmire, a Democratic senator from Wisconsin, to introduce a bill preventing the FDA from regulating megavitamins. [Paul Offit, via the *New York Times*]

That bill became law in 1976. Some 30 years later, almost a third of Americans were still taking a daily multivitamin. But count this gal out.

11
Causal Arguments

LEFT TO RIGHT: claire norman/Shutterstock; Jeff Barnard/AP Images; Katie Orlinsky/Getty Images

Although they have thrived for over fifty million years, several decades ago colonies of bees started dying . . . and dying. Are pesticides the cause? Or perhaps it's the move agriculture has made from planting cover crops like alfalfa and clover that create natural fertilizers to using synthetic fertilizers. Or has the decline been triggered by viruses transmitted by the varroa mite, which infested the United States beginning in the mid-1980s? Scientists believe a combination of these factors accounts for a continuing decline in bees.

Somewhat unexpectedly, marijuana prices have declined sharply in locales that have recently legalized pot. As a result, state governments have not enjoyed the tax bonanzas they anticipated, but at least they've enjoyed a reduction in law enforcement costs.

Despite attempts to raise oil prices by cutting production, OPEC (Organization of Petroleum Exporting Countries) has discovered that fracking techniques pioneered in the United States—which will likely spread around the world—have broken the power the cartel once held over petroleum markets.

Understanding Causal Arguments

Americans seem to be getting fatter, so fat in fact that we hear often about the "obesity crisis" in the United States. But what is behind this rise in weight? Rachel Berl, writing for *U.S. News and World Report*, points to the combination of unhealthy foods and a sedentary lifestyle. Berl quotes Harvard nutrition professor Walter Willett, who notes that individuals with lower income and lower education are more likely to buy inexpensive foods high in refined sugar and starch:

> **"There is no single, simple answer to explain the obesity patterns" in America, says Willett. . . . "More deeply, [obesity] also reflects lower public investment in education, public transportation, and recreational facilities," he says. The bottom line: cheap, unhealthy foods mixed with a sedentary lifestyle have made obesity the new normal in America.**
>
> —Rachel Pomerance Berl

Many others agree that as processed fast food and other things such as colas have gotten more and more affordable, consumption of them has gone up, along with weight. But others offer different theories for the rise in obesity.

Whatever the reasons for our increased weight, the consequences can be measured by everything from the width of airliner seats to the rise of diabetes in the general population. Scientists, social critics, and

Bartomeu Amengual/AGE Fotostock

health gurus offer many explanations, and some are challenged or refuted. But figuring out exactly what's going on is a national concern — and an important example of cause-and-effect argument.

Causal arguments—from the causes of an opioid addiction crisis in many American communities to the consequences of ocean pollution around the globe—are at the heart of many major policy decisions, both national and international. But arguments about causes and effects also inform choices that people make every day. Suppose that you need to petition for a grade change because you were unable to turn in a final project on time. You'd probably enumerate the reasons for your failure—the illness of your hamster, followed by an attack of the hives, followed by a crash of your computer—hoping that an associate dean reading the petition might see these explanations as tragic enough to change your grade. In identifying the causes of the situation, you're implicitly arguing that the effect (your failure to submit the project on time) should be considered in a new light. Unfortunately, the administrator might accuse you of faulty causality (see p. 89) and propose that your failure to complete the project is due more to procrastination than to the reasons you offer—a causal analysis of her own.

Causal arguments exist in many forms and frequently appear as part of other arguments (such as evaluations or proposals). It may help focus your work on causal arguments to separate them into three major categories:

Arguments that state a cause and then examine its effects

Cause A ⟶ leads to → Effect B / Effect C / Effect D

Arguments that state an effect and then trace the effect back to its causes

Effect D ⟶ stems from → Cause A / Cause B / Cause C

Arguments that move through a series of links: A causes B, which leads to C and perhaps to D

Cause A → leads to Cause B → leads to Cause C → leads to Effect D

Arguments That State a Cause and Then Examine Its Effects

What would happen if Congress ever came together and passed immigration reform that gave millions of people in the United States a legal pathway to citizenship? Before such legislation could be enacted, the possible consequences of this "cause" would have to be examined in detail and argued intensely. In fact, groups on all sides of this hot-button issue have been doing so for decades now, and they generally posit different outcomes. In this debate, you'd be successful if you could convincingly describe the consequences of such a change and make people see them as beneficial. Alternatively, you could challenge the causal explanations made by groups you don't agree with. But, either way, speculation about causes and effects can be dicey simply because life is complicated.

Consider the following passage from an essay in the *Chronicle of Higher Education* by political scientist and self-identifying liberal Mark Lilla, in which he describes the effects that he believes follow from focusing too single-mindedly on "identity politics," especially in higher education:

> Identity politics on the left was at first about large classes of people—African-Americans, women, gays—seeking to redress major historical wrongs by mobilizing and then working through our political institutions to secure their rights. But by the 1980s it had given way to a pseudo-politics of self-regard and increasingly narrow and exclusionary self-definition that is now cultivated in our colleges and universities. The main result has been to turn young people back onto themselves, rather than turning them outward toward the wider world they share with others. It has left them unprepared to think about the common good in non-identity terms and what must be done practically to secure it—especially the hard and unglamorous task of persuading people very different from themselves to join a common effort. Every advance of liberal identity consciousness has marked a retreat of effective liberal political consciousness.
>
> —Mark Lilla, "How Colleges Are Strangling Liberalism"

Predictably, Professor Lilla's causal analysis received much attention and criticism, but he raised issues and described consequences that merit serious discussion.

Arguments That State an Effect and Then Trace the Effect Back to Its Causes

This type of argument might begin with a specific effect (an unprecedented drop in sales of traditional four-door sedans) and then trace it to its most likely causes (the popularity of crossover SUVs, availability of all-wheel drive SUVs, cheaper gas). Or you might examine the reasons auto manufacturers offer for the sales decline of their once most popular models—Honda Accords and Toyota Camrys—and decide whether their causal explanations pass muster.

Like other types of causal arguments, those tracing effects to a cause can offer provocative insights. You can see that in a 2017 *Atlantic* article by Jean M. Twenge, already excerpted in Chapter 8. In the piece, Twenge, a professor at San Diego State University, examines research that documents disturbing behaviors she'd been noticing in post-millennial children and adolescents. She begins the piece describing those effects (generally) before going on to propose a not entirely surprising cause:

> I've been researching generational differences for 25 years, starting when I was a 22-year-old doctoral student in psychology. Typically, the characteristics that come to define a generation appear gradually, and along a continuum. Beliefs and behaviors that were already rising simply continue to do so. Millennials, for instance, are a highly individualistic generation, but individualism had been increasing since the Baby Boomers turned on, tuned in, and dropped out. I had grown accustomed to line graphs of trends that looked like modest hills and valleys. Then I began studying [the current] generation.
>
> Around 2012, I noticed abrupt shifts in teen behaviors and emotional states. The gentle slopes of the line graphs became steep mountains and sheer cliffs, and many of the distinctive characteristics of the Millennial generation began to disappear. In all my analyses of generational data—some reaching back to the 1930s—I had never seen anything like it.
>
> At first I presumed these might be blips, but the trends persisted, across several years and a series of national surveys. The changes weren't just in degree, but in kind. The biggest difference between the Millennials and their predecessors was in how they viewed the world; teens today differ from the Millennials not just in their views but in how they spend their time. The experiences they have every day are radically different from those of the generation that came of age just a few years before them.
>
> What happened in 2012 to cause such dramatic shifts in behavior? It was after the Great Recession, which officially lasted from 2007 to 2009 and had a starker effect on Millennials trying to find a place in a sputtering economy. But it was exactly the moment when the proportion of Americans who owned a smartphone surpassed 50 percent.
>
> —Jean M. Twenge, "Have Smartphones Destroyed a Generation?"

Twin Design/Shutterstock

Twenge goes on to connect the iPhone (and its clones) to a host of specific effects, some positive, but most negative: fewer auto accidents; less drinking; higher rates of depression and suicide; declines in dating and sexual activity; avoidance of adult responsibilities. Needless to say, her analysis caused a stir, likely because many readers found the evidence she cited compelling.

Arguments That Move through a Series of Links: A Causes B, Which Leads to C and Perhaps to D

As you might guess, entire arguments can be structured around a series of linked causal connections. But you can see that structure within individual paragraphs too when writers want to draw out the consequences of their cause/effect studies. Here are two such paragraphs near the end of Twenge's essay (described above) on how smartphones have damaged a whole generation of children; note how she uses the causal links to emphasize the consequences over time of that addiction:

> The correlations between depression and smartphone use are strong enough to suggest that more parents should be telling their kids to put down their phone. As the technology writer Nick Bilton has reported, it's a policy some Silicon Valley executives follow. Even Steve Jobs limited his kids' use of the devices he brought into the world.
>
> What's at stake isn't just how kids experience adolescence. The constant presence of smartphones is likely to affect them well into adulthood. Among people who suffer an episode of depression, at

least half become depressed again later in life. Adolescence is a key time for developing social skills; as teens spend less time with their friends face-to-face, they have fewer opportunities to practice them. In the next decade, we may see more adults who know just the right emoji for a situation, but not the right facial expression.

What is happening now, Twenge argues, has predictable implications for the future.

RESPOND•

The causes of the following events and phenomena are well known and frequently discussed. But do you understand these causes well enough to spell them out to someone else? Working in a group, see how well (and in how much detail) you can explain these events or phenomena. Which explanations are relatively clear, and which seem more open to debate?

earthquakes/tsunamis

swelling caused by a bee sting

sharp rises in reported cases of autism or asthma

fake news

climate change

popularity of the Netflix series *13 Reasons Why*

increasing post-graduation debt for college students

outcome of the 2016 presidential election

controversies in schools and online over free speech

© John Atkinson/Wrong Hands

Characterizing Causal Arguments

Causal arguments tend to share several characteristics.

They Are Often Part of Other Arguments

Many stand-alone causal arguments address questions that are fundamental to our well-being: *What accounts for the rise of violent extremist political groups—left and right—in the United States? What will happen as space travel moves into the private sector, thanks to companies like SpaceX, Blue Origin, and Virgin Galactic? How will the American middle class adjust to its diminishing status? What will happen to Europe or Japan if birthrates there continue to decline?*

But causal analyses often work to support other types of arguments—especially proposals. For example, a proposal to limit the time that people spend on social media (see p. 307) might begin with evidence establishing that too much time on Facebook and Instagram can have dire psychological consequences. This initial causal analysis then provides a rationale for the proposal argument that follows.

They Are Almost Always Complex

The complexity of most causal relationships makes it difficult to establish causes and effects. For example, in 2011 researchers at Northwestern University reported a startling correlation: youths who participated in church activities were far more likely to grow into obese adults than their counterparts who were not engaged in religious activities. How does one even begin to explain such a peculiar and unexpected finding? Too many church socials? Unhealthy food at potluck meals? More regular social engagement? Perhaps.

Or consider the complexity of analyzing cause and effect when it relates to consuming specific foods. In Chapter 4 we mentioned a *Wall Street Journal* article by economist Emily Oster examining the research behind many of the dietary prohibitions pregnant women routinely face. When she took the time to read the actual research behind the advice, Oster made interesting discoveries. Some of the causal connections stood up to scrutiny, but other claims were more ambiguous. The claim that light drinking could cause behavior problems in children was complicated by the fact that 45 percent of the women in the study who had one drink a day also used cocaine. As Oster wryly observed, "Perhaps the

C. Richard King examines the complex network of cause and effect surrounding the racial slur and professional football team name "redskin," wondering if the slur is the result of racism or its cause—or both.

LINK TO P. 554

problem is that cocaine, not the occasional glass of Chardonnay, makes your child more likely to have behavior problems."

With all its careful details and qualifications, what Oster's article illustrates—and it's worth reading in its entirety—is that causal claims, even those you have heard routinely, are rarely simple or beyond scrutiny.

They Are Often Definition Based

One reason that causal arguments are complex is that they often depend on careful definitions. Recent figures from the U.S. Department of Education, for example, show that the number of high school dropouts is rising and that this rise has caused an increase in youth unemployment. But exactly how does the study define *dropout*? A closer look may suggest that some students (perhaps a lot) who drop out later "drop back in" and complete high school or that some who drop out become successful entrepreneurs or business owners. Further, how does the study define *employment*? Until you can provide definitions for all key terms in a causal claim, you should proceed cautiously with your argument.

They Usually Yield Probable Rather Than Absolute Conclusions

Because causal relationships are almost always complex or subtle, they seldom can yield more than a high degree of probability. Consequently,

"The rise in unemployment, however, which was somewhat offset by an expanding job market, was countered by an upturn in part-time dropouts, which, in turn, was diminished by seasonal factors, the anticipated summer slump, and, over-all, a small but perceptible rise in actual employment."

Causal arguments can also be confusing. Ed Arno/The New Yorker Collection/The Cartoon Bank they are almost always subject to criticism or open to charges of false causality. (We all know smokers who defy the odds to live long, cancer-free lives.) Scientists in particular are wary when making causal claims.

Even after an event, proving precisely what caused it can be hard. During the student riots of the late 1960s, for example, a commission was charged with determining the causes of riots on a particular campus. After two years of work and almost a thousand pages of evidence and reports, the commission was unable to pinpoint anything but a broad network of contributing causes and related conditions. And how many years is it likely to take to unravel all the factors responsible for the extended recession and economic decline in the United States that began in 2008? After all, serious scholars are still arguing about the forces responsible for the Great Depression of 1929.

To demonstrate that X caused Y, you must find the strongest possible evidence and subject it to the toughest scrutiny. But a causal argument doesn't fail just because you can't find a single compelling cause. In fact, causal arguments are often most effective when they help readers appreciate how tangled our lives and landscapes really are.

Developing Causal Arguments

Exploring Possible Claims

To begin creating a strong causal claim, try listing some of the effects—events or phenomena—that you'd like to know the causes of:

- Why do college and university tuition costs so greatly outstrip the rate of inflation?
- Why are almost all the mothers in animated movies either dead to begin with or quickly killed off?
- Why have American schools largely abandoned technical training programs that, in the past, led to successful blue-collar careers?
- Why do so few younger Americans vote, even in major elections?

Or try moving in the opposite direction, listing some phenomena or causes you're interested in and then hypothesizing what kinds of effects they may produce:

In her essay "The Careless Language of Sexual Violence," Roxane Gay looks closely at the cultural and linguistic causes and effects of "rape culture"—the way male violence toward women has become expected and even accepted.

LINK TO P. 682

- What effect is fracking having on the development of alternative energy sources?
- What consequences will follow from the politicization of traditional news organizations?
- What will be the consequences if more liberal (or conservative) judges are appointed to the U.S. Supreme Court?
- What will happen as China and India become dominant industrialized nations?

Read a little about the causal issues that interest you most, and then try them out on friends and colleagues. They might suggest ways to refocus or clarify what you want to do or offer leads to finding information about your subject. After some initial research, map out the causal relationship you want to explore in simple form:

X might cause (or might be caused by) Y for the following reasons:

1.

2.

3. **(add more as needed)**

Such a statement should be tentative because writing a causal argument should be an exercise in which you uncover facts, not assume them to be true. Often, your early assumptions (*Tuition was raised to renovate the stadium*) might be undermined by the facts you later discover (*Tuition doesn't fund the construction or maintenance of campus buildings*).

You might even decide to write a wildly exaggerated or parodic causal argument for humorous purposes. Humorist Dave Barry does this when he explains the causes of El Niño and other weather phenomena: "So we see that the true cause of bad weather, contrary to what they have been claiming all these years, is TV weather forecasters, who have also single-handedly destroyed the ozone layer via overuse of hair spray." Most of the causal reasoning you do, however, will take a serious approach to subjects that you, your family, and your friends care about.

RESPOND.

Working with a group, write a big *Why?* on a sheet of paper or computer screen, and then generate a list of *why* questions. Don't be too critical of the initial list:

Why

—*do people laugh?*

—*do swans mate for life?*

—*do college students binge drink?*

—*do teenagers no longer care about getting driver's licenses?*

—*do babies cry?*

—*do politicians, celebrities, or journalists take risks on social media?*

Generate as lengthy a list as you can in fifteen minutes. Then decide which of the questions might make plausible starting points for intriguing causal arguments.

© Bill Coster/ardea./AGE Fotostock

Defining the Causal Relationships

In developing a causal claim, examine the various types of causes and effects in play in a given argument and define their relationship. Begin by listing all the plausible causes or effects you need to consider. Then decide which are the most important for you to analyze or the easiest to defend or critique. The following chart on "Causes" may help you to appreciate some important terms and relationships.

Type of Cause	What It Is or Does	What It Looks Like
Sufficient cause	Enough for something to occur on its own	Lack of oxygen is sufficient to cause death Cheating on an exam is sufficient to fail a course
Necessary cause	Required for something to occur (but in combination with other factors)	Fuel is necessary for fire Capital is necessary for economic growth
Precipitating cause	Brings on a change	Protest march ignites a strike by workers Plane flies into strong thunderstorms
Proximate cause	Immediately present or visible cause of action	Strike causes company to declare bankruptcy Powerful wind shear causes plane to crash
Remote cause	Indirect or underlying explanation for action	Company was losing money on bad designs and inept manufacturing Wind shear warning failed to sound in cockpit
Reciprocal causes	One factor leads to a second, which reinforces the first, creating a cycle	Lack of good schools in a neighborhood leads to poverty, which further weakens education, which leads to even fewer opportunities . . .

Even the most everyday causal analysis can draw on such distinctions among reasons and causes. What factors might persuade a student in choosing a post-secondary school? *Proximate* reasons might be the location of the school or its excellent track record of graduate employment. But what are the *necessary* reasons—the ones without which your choice of that college could not occur? Adequate financial support? Good test scores and academic record? The expectations of a parent?

Once you've identified a causal claim, you can draw out the reasons, warrants, and evidence that can support it most effectively:

Claim   Certain career patterns cause women to be paid less than men.

Reason   Women's career patterns differ from men's.

Warrant   Successful careers are made during the period between ages twenty-five and thirty-five.

Evidence   Women often drop out of or reduce work during the decade between ages twenty-five and thirty-five to raise families.

Claim	Lack of community and alumni support caused the football coach to lose his job.
Reason	Ticket sales and alumni support have declined for three seasons in a row despite a respectable team record.
Warrant	Winning over fans is as important as winning games for college coaches in smaller athletic programs.
Evidence	Over the last ten years, coaches at several programs have been sacked because of declining support and revenues.

RESPOND●

Here's a schematic causal analysis of one event, exploring the difference among precipitating, necessary, and sufficient causes. Critique and revise the analysis as you see fit. Then create another of your own, beginning with a different event, phenomenon, incident, fad, or effect.

Event: Traffic fatality at an intersection

Precipitating cause: A pickup truck that runs a red light, totals a Miata, and injures its driver

Necessary cause: Two drivers who are navigating Friday rush-hour traffic (if no driving, then no accident)

Sufficient cause: A truck driver who is distracted by a cell-phone conversation

Supporting Your Point

In drafting your causal argument, you'll want to do the following:

- Show that the causes and effects you've suggested are highly probable and backed by evidence, or show what's wrong with the faulty causal reasoning you may be critiquing.

- Assess any links between causal relationships (what leads to or follows from what).

- Show that your explanations of any causal chains are accurate, or identify where links in a causal chain break down.

- Show that plausible cause-and-effect explanations haven't been ignored or that the possibility of multiple causes or effects has been considered.

In other words, you will need to examine your subject carefully and find appropriate ways to support your claims. There are different ways to accomplish that goal.

For example, in studying effects that are physical and measurable (as they would be with diseases or climate conditions), you can usually offer and test *hypotheses*, or theories about possible causes. That means exploring such topics thoroughly to draw upon authorities and research articles for your explanations and evidence. (See Chapter 17, "Academic Arguments," and Chapter 18, "Finding Evidence.") Don't be surprised if you find yourself debating which among conflicting authorities make the most plausible causal or explanatory arguments. Your achievement as a writer may be simply that you present these differences in an essay, leaving it to readers to make judgments of their own.

But not all the evidence in compelling causal arguments needs to be strictly scientific or scholarly. Many causal arguments rely on **ethnographic observations**—the systematic study of ordinary people in their daily routines. How would you explain, for example, why some people step aside when they encounter someone head-on and others do not? In an argument that attempts to account for such behavior, investigators Frank Willis, Joseph Gier, and David Smith observed "1,038 displacements involving 3,141 persons" at a Kansas City shopping mall. In results that surprised the investigators, "gallantry" seemed to play a significant role in causing people to step aside for one another—more so than other causes that the investigators had anticipated (such as deferring to someone who's physically stronger or higher in status). Doubtless you've read of other such studies, perhaps in psychology or sociology courses. You may even decide to do a little fieldwork on your own—which raises the possibility of using personal experiences in support of a causal argument.

Indeed, people's experiences generally lead them to draw causal conclusions about things they know well. Personal experience can also help build your credibility as a writer, gain the empathy of listeners, and thus support a causal claim. Although one person's experiences cannot ordinarily be universalized, they can still argue eloquently for causal relationships. Listen to Sara Barbour, writing in 2011 as a student at Columbia University and drawing upon her own carefully described experiences to bemoan what may happen when e-readers finally displace printed books:

> In eliminating a book's physical existence, something crucial is lost forever. Trapped in a Kindle, the story remains but the book can no longer be scribbled in, hoarded, burned, given, or received. We may be able to read it, but we can't share it with others in the same way, and its ability to connect us to people, places, and ideas is that much less powerful.

I know the Kindle will eventually carry the day—an electronic reader means no more embarrassing coffee stains, no more library holds and renewals, no more frantic flipping through pages for a lost quote, or going to three bookstores in one afternoon to track down an evasive title. Who am I to advocate the doom of millions of trees when the swipe of a finger can deliver all 838 pages of *Middlemarch* into my waiting hands?

But once we all power up our Kindles something will be gone, a kind of language. Books communicate with us as readers—but as important, we communicate with each other through books themselves. When that connection is lost, the experience of reading—and our lives—will be forever altered.

—Sara Barbour, "Kindle vs. Books: The Dead Trees Society,"
Los Angeles Times, June 17, 2011

All these strategies—testing hypotheses, presenting experimental evidence, and offering personal experience—can help you support a causal argument or undermine a causal claim you regard as faulty.

RESPOND•

One of the fallacies of argument discussed in Chapter 5 is the *post hoc, ergo propter hoc* ("after this, therefore because of this") fallacy. Causal arguments are particularly prone to this kind of fallacious reasoning, in which a writer asserts a causal relationship between two entirely unconnected events. When Angelina Jolie gave birth to twins in 2008, for instance, the stock market rallied by nearly six hundred points, but it would be difficult to argue that either event is related to the other.

Because causal arguments can easily fall prey to this fallacy, you might find it instructive to create and defend an absurd connection of this kind. Begin by asserting a causal link between two events or phenomena that likely have no relationship: *Isn't it more likely that rising sea levels, usually attributed to global warming, are due to the water displaced by ever larger ocean-going cargo vessels and by more numerous cruise ships filled with much heavier passengers?* Then spend a page or two spinning out an imaginative argument to defend the claim. It's OK to have fun with this assignment exercise, but see how convincing you can be at generating plausibly implausible arguments.

Sharp Increase in Opioid Prescriptions ➡ Increase in Deaths

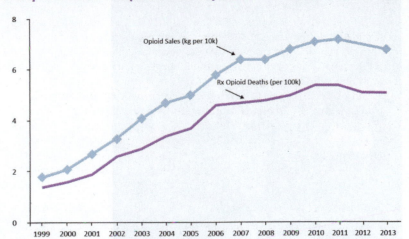

A graph can provide visual evidence for a causal claim—in this case, the link between opioid prescriptions and opioid deaths. National Vital Statistics System, DEA's Automation of Reports and Consolidated Orders System

Considering Design and Visuals

You may find that the best way to illustrate a causal relationship is to present it visually. Even a simple bar graph or chart can demonstrate a relationship between two variables that might be related to a specific cause, like the one above suggesting a connection between the rise in opioid prescriptions and the rise in opioid deaths. The report accompanying the graph, published by the Centers for Disease Control and Prevention, sets out guidelines for prescribing opioids to relieve chronic pain without increasing the likelihood of addiction and overdose.

Or you may decide that the most dramatic way to present important causal information about a single issue or problem is via an infographic, cartoon, or public service announcement. Our arresting example is part of a campaign by People for the Ethical Treatment of Animals (PETA). An organization that advocates for animal rights, PETA promotes campaigns

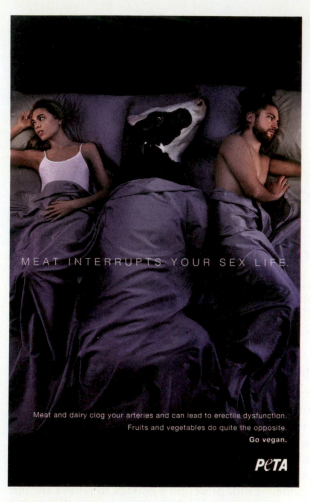

"Meat interrupts your sex life." This PETA ad campaign
makes a causal argument that's hard to ignore. PETA

that typically try to sway people to adopt vegetarian diets by depicting
the practices of the agriculture industry as cruel. But in this item, they
make a very different causal argument, connect eating meat to . . . well,
you'll see if you check the fine print.

GUIDE to writing a causal argument

● Finding a Topic

You're entering a causal argument when you:

- state a cause and then examine its effects: *An enduring economic downturn in many blue-collar areas of the country changed the political landscape in 2016.*

- describe an effect and trace it back to its causes: *There has been a recent decline in migration to the U.S., likely due to questions about what immigration policies will look like in the immediate future.*

- trace a string of causes to figure out why something happened: *The housing and financial markets collapsed in 2008 after government mandates to encourage homeownership led banks to invent questionable financial schemes in order to offer subprime mortgages to borrowers who bought homes they could not afford with loans they could not pay back.*

- explore plausible consequences (intended or not) of a particular action, policy, or change: *The ban on incandescent lightbulbs may draw more attention to climate change than any previous government action.*

Spend time brainstorming possibilities for causal arguments. Many public issues lend themselves to causal analysis and argument: browse the homepage of a newspaper or news source on any given day to discover plausible topics. Consider topics that grow from your own experiences.

It's fair game, too, to question the accuracy or adequacy of existing arguments about causality. You can write a strong paper by raising doubts about the facts or assumptions that others have made and perhaps offering a better causal explanation on your own.

● Researching Your Topic

Causal arguments will lead you to many different resources:

- current news media—especially magazines, newspapers (online or in print), and news networks

- online databases and search engines

- scholarly journals

- books written on your subject (here you can do a keyword search, either in your library or online)
- social media

In addition, why not carry out some field research? Conduct interviews with appropriate authorities on your subject, create a questionnaire aimed at establishing a range of opinions on your subject, or arrange a discussion forum among people with a stake in the issue. The information you get from interviews, questionnaires, or open-ended dialogue might provide ideas to enrich your argument or evidence to back up your claims.

● Formulating a Claim

For a conventional causal analysis, try to formulate a claim that lets readers know where you stand on some issue involving causes and effects. First, identify the kind of causal argument that you expect to make (see pp. 256–61 for a review of these kinds of arguments) or decide whether you intend, instead, to debunk an existing cause-and-effect claim. Then explore your relationship to the claim. What do you know about the subject and its causes and effects? Why do you favor (or disagree with) the claim? What significant reasons can you offer in support of your position?

End this process by formulating a thesis—a complete sentence that says, in effect, *A causes (or does not cause or is caused by) B*, followed by a summary of the reasons supporting this causal relationship. Make your thesis as specific as possible and be sure that it's sufficiently controversial or intriguing to hold a reader's interest. Of course, feel free to revise any such claim as you learn more about a subject.

For causal topics that are more open-ended and exploratory, you may not want to take a strong position, particularly at the outset. Instead, your argument might simply present a variety of reasonable (and possibly competing) explanations and scenarios.

● Examples of Causal Claims

- Right-to-carry gun laws have led to increased rates of violent crime in states that have approved such legislation.
- Sophisticated use of social media like Twitter is now a must for any political candidate who hopes to win.
- Grade inflation is lowering the value of a college education.

- The proliferation of images in film, television, and education is changing the way we read and use information.
- The disappearance of rewarding blue-collar jobs and careers will likely further polarize the country between haves and have-nots.

Preparing a Proposal

If your instructor asks you to prepare a proposal for your project, here's a format that may help:

State your thesis completely. If you're having trouble doing so, try outlining it in Toulmin terms:

Claim:

Reason(s):

Warrant(s):

Alternatively, you might indicate an intention to explore a particular causal question in your project, with the thesis perhaps coming later.

- Explain why this issue deserves attention. What's at stake?
- Identify whom you hope to reach through your argument and why this group of readers would be interested in it.
- Briefly discuss the key challenges you anticipate in preparing your argument.
- Determine what research strategies you'll use. What sources do you expect to consult?
- Briefly identify and explore the major stakeholders in your argument and what alternative perspectives you may need to consider as you formulate your argument.

Considering Genre and Media

Your instructor may specify that you use a particular genre and/or medium. If not, ask yourself these questions to help you make a good choice:

- What genre is most appropriate for your causal argument? Does it call for an academic essay, a report, an infographic, a video, or something else?

- What medium is most appropriate for your argument? Would it be best delivered orally to a live audience? Presented as an audio essay or podcast? Presented in print only or in print with illustrations?

- Will you need visuals, such as moving or still images, maps, graphs, charts—and what function will they play in your argument? Make sure they are not just "added on" but are necessary components of the argument.

● Thinking about Organization

Your causal argument will likely include elements such as the following:

- a specific causal claim somewhere in the paper—or the identification of a significant causal issue

- an explanation of the claim's significance or importance

- evidence sufficient to support each cause or effect—or, in an argument based on a series of causal links, evidence to support the relationships among the links

- a consideration of other plausible causes and effects, and evidence that you have thought carefully about these alternatives before offering your own ideas

● Getting and Giving Response: Questions for Peer Response

Your instructor may assign you to a group for the purpose of reading and responding to each other's drafts. If not, ask for responses from serious readers or consultants at a writing center. Use the following questions to evaluate a colleague's draft. Be sure to illustrate your comments with examples; specific comments help more than general observations.

The Claim

- Does the claim state a causal argument?

- Does the claim identify clearly what causes and effects are being examined?

- What about the claim will make it appeal to readers?

- Is the claim too sweeping? Does it need to be qualified? How might it be narrowed and focused?

- How strong is the relationship between the claim and the reasons given to support it? How could that relationship be made more explicit?

Evidence for the Claim

- What's the strongest evidence offered for the claim? What, if any, evidence needs to be strengthened?

- Is enough evidence offered to show that these causes are responsible for the identified effect, that these effects result from the identified cause, or that a series of causes and effects are linked? If not, what additional evidence is needed? What kinds of sources might provide this evidence?

- How credible will the sources be to potential readers? What other sources might be more persuasive?

- Is evidence in support of the claim analyzed logically? Is more discussion needed?

- Have alternative causes and effects been considered? Have objections to the claim been carefully considered and presented fairly? Have these objections been discussed?

Organization and Style

- How are the parts of the argument organized? Is this organization effective?

- Will readers understand the relationships among the claims, supporting reasons, warrants, and evidence? If not, how might those connections be clearer? Does every visual serve a clear purpose? Are more transitions needed? Would headings or graphic devices help?

- Are the transitions or links from point to point, sentence to sentence, and paragraph to paragraph effective? If not, how could they be improved?

- Are all visuals (or other elements such as audio or video clips) carefully integrated into the text? Is each visual introduced and commented on to point out its significance? Is each visual labeled as a figure or a table and given a caption as well as a citation?

- Is the style suited to the subject? Is it too formal, casual, or technical? Can it be improved?

- Which sentences seem effective? Which ones seem weaker, and how could they be improved? Should short sentences be combined, and any longer ones be broken up?

- How effective are the paragraphs? Too short or too long? How can they be improved?

- Which words or phrases seem effective? Do any seem vague or inappropriate for the audience or the writer's purpose? Are technical or unfamiliar terms defined?

Spelling, Punctuation, Mechanics, Documentation, and Format

- Are there any errors in spelling, punctuation, capitalization, and the like?
- Is the documentation appropriate and consistent? (See Chapter 22.)
- Does the paper or project follow an appropriate format? Is it appropriately designed and attractively presented?

PROJECTS

1. Develop an argument exploring one of the cause-and-effect topics
   mentioned in this chapter. Just a few of those topics are listed below:

   Disappearance of honeybees in the United States

   The implications of fracking in the United States on the global oil
   market

   Increasing numbers of obese children and/or adults

   Ramifications of identity politics on efforts to build consensus

   Long-term consequences of food or healthcare choices

   Psychological influences of smartphones on people who have
   grown up with them

   How career patterns affect professional achievement and income

   What is lost/gained as paper books disappear

2. Write a causal argument about a subject you know well, even if the
   topic does not strike you as particularly "academic": *What accounts for
   the popularity of superhero movie franchises or series on streaming services
   like Netflix or Hulu? What are the likely consequences of students living more
   of their lives via social media? How are video games changing the way students you know learn or interact? Why do women love shoes?* In this argument, be sure to separate precipitating or proximate causes from
   sufficient or necessary ones. In other words, do a deep and revealing
   causal analysis about your subject, giving readers new insights.

3. In "Forever Alone (and Perfectly Fine)" (see p. 280), Laura Tarrant argues
   that remaining single is a valid option many people choose for many
   different reasons. In a project of your own, describe and analyze caus-
   ally the trends in personal relationships that you have experienced or
   seen among your family, friends, coworkers, or neighbors, including
   such choices as remaining single, living with a significant other, getting married, remaining childless by choice, choosing to have children,
   etc. Why are people making these decisions? Clearly, Tarrant is comfortable being single, but you or those around you may feel differently
   about your own relationship or family status.

4. Pascal-Emmanuel Gobry's essay "America's Birthrate Is Now a National
   Emergency" (see pp. 284–85) explores some of the consequences for societies that produce fewer children. After reading the Gobry piece, list any
   comparable situations you know of where a largely unnoticed change
   may have long-term consequences. The changes you list need not be as
   consequential as the one Gobry has identified. Choose your most intriguing situation, do the necessary research, and write or present a causal
   argument about it, using whatever media work best to make your point.

Forever Alone (and Perfectly Fine)

LAURA TARRANT

Sean Tarrant

An introductory section analyzes attitudes toward singleness that suggest it is an unhappy or aberrant choice.

April 12, 2017

I've been single all my life, and so far it's worked out. It's not as if I'm by myself; I have great friends, a loving family, some interesting pets, and an entire church behind me. No dating means I can focus on school and work with few distractions. Even better, there isn't very much drama around to kill my good vibes. But over time, I've found singleness to be, well, rather lonely: nobody else seems to be nearly as happy about being single as I am. Apparently, I'm not supposed to *want* this lifestyle.

If you google the phrase "being single," the most popular links take you to fun, cheery blogs and Web sites that tell you "How to Embrace Your Time Being Single" or the "9 Surprising Benefits of Being Single." These articles (if you can call them that) all advocate the same sort of view: use your single days to go crazy, experiment, date around, find yourself, and work out whatever identity issues you might have so that one day, *one day* you can settle down and be in a successful relationship. *Carpe diem,* I guess.

Then, if you google "being single forever," things get downright depressing. The top search results, like "12 Signs You Might be Permanently Solo" invite you to examine why you've become such a bitter, closed-off person with unrealistic expectations, who won't give new people a chance, and who is hopelessly incompetent in even the most simple dating situations. A forum on the popular site Reddit, "Accept that you might be alone for the rest of your life," talks about coming to terms with your singleness as you would a death or loss:

Laura Tarrant is an undergraduate Rhetoric and Writing major at the University of Texas at Austin. She wrote her causal analysis of relationship choices for an Advanced Writing course.

the denial, anger, bargaining, and depression you've experienced in your love life lead to the eventual acceptance that you're just not relationship material. How uplifting.

But there's something terribly unsatisfactory about those descriptions. Are these really the only classifications that single can fall under—waiting or discouraged? Aren't there perfectly happy, healthy, and sane individuals who just aren't interested in romantic relationships? If the Internet is to be believed, those types of people are emotionally underdeveloped in some way: they're either not ready to be in a secure relationship (still "finding themselves," presumably), or there's some combination of negative emotions blocking them from the dating scene.

Yet if significant numbers of Americans are choosing the single life, they must have reasons.

But that seems unlikely. According to the Census Bureau, the number of single people in the U.S. made up 45% of the adult population as of 2014. It just doesn't feel right to assume that an entire demographic, 107 million people, are single only because they're still looking or they've given up. There are plenty of other reasons, not discussed in your favorite blog, for why singleness has become the lifestyle of choice for so many people.

The essay examines various reasons people choose a single life.

First, choices besides romantic relationships can provide emotional fulfillment. If you decide not to take a romantic partner, you give yourself the opportunity to focus on many other types of relationships, activities, and community roles. Eric Klinenberg, author of *Going Solo: The Extraordinary Rise and Surprising Appeal of Living Alone,* found in his research that singles, not couples, are more likely to "volunteer in civic organizations . . . and spend time with friends and neighbors." Another study by social scientist Bella DePaulo PhD found, in addition to results like Klinenberg's, singles are also more likely to "help friends, neighbors and coworkers [with] transportation, errands, shopping . . . advice, encouragement, and moral and emotional support." The examples continue: singles tend to be giving with their time and money,

Sources are identified within the essay itself rather than in footnotes.

more active in the social scenes of their cities, and are more likely to take on the long-term care of their elderly parents. All noble pursuits, all fulfilling, and not at all romantic. To suggest then that a large percentage of single people are somehow emotionally deficient therefore doesn't hold. Why would a demographic allegedly full of jaded, emotionally stunted people give so willingly of themselves?

Second, many people choose to be single because they have no interest in dating, not because they aren't emotionally mature or otherwise incapable of connection. In a piece on Splinter entitled "Meet the people who want to be single forever," Laura Feinstein interviews people who had made the decision to abstain from romantic relationships. One woman, Deborah, knew "in [her] bones" that she didn't want to be married from the age of 16. Another woman, Kristen, told of how she "played 'runaway,'" a game in which she pretended to live on her own, while other children her age played house. Due to social pressure, both women tried and failed to sustain long-term relationships. Deborah's relationships "always felt really *odd*." Kirsten knew when she got married "that [she'd] made a terrible mistake." Both eventually returned to permanent singleness later in life, and both were better off because of it. Other testimonies in the article read much the same way. Men and women alike who elect to be single usually do so because they feel it's right for them. If anything, it's a sign of emotional maturity that these people know themselves well enough to choose a lifestyle more suited to their personalities, and to stop forcing relationships against their better judgment. Emotional maturity, then, isn't attached to any particular relationship status, but rather a complete understanding of one's emotional needs.

Finally, being single sometimes is more in accord with an individual's personal goals, regardless of emotional needs. This one's an old concept. In his letters to the Corinthians, the Apostle Paul gave a compelling reason

The single life makes sense when the reasons people make that choice are understood.

to stay single: The married person has their interests necessarily divided between the demands of their personal calling and the demands and responsibilities of marriage. Essentially, whether or not people should be in committed relationships depends on the direction of their lives. If you feel a strong, single-minded call to the ministry, public service, or any such career that requires great personal sacrifice, it might be better to go it alone. In doing so you avoid the strain and turmoil that divided priorities might cause. Could Paul have devoted himself so fully to his ministry, and been as successful as he was, if he'd also had to worry about a spouse, and his responsibilities to her? No, by his own admission. Therefore, the choice today to be single or not is an ethical one. Can you responsibly pursue a relationship if you have other, deeply important obligations in your life? If the answer is no, then singleness might be the correct path for you, just as being in a relationship may be the correct path for someone else.

So, even if the lifestyle of singleness might not be for everyone, it is certainly an acceptable way to live. Singleness doesn't have to be a steppingstone on the way to a relationship, nor does it have to result from some emotional deficiency. Rather, singleness is its own alternative lifestyle. The direction that lifestyle takes you in is entirely up to you.

America's Birthrate Is Now a National Emergency

PASCAL-EMMANUEL GOBRY

August 12, 2016

The new birth rate numbers are out, and they're a disaster. There are now only 59.6 births per 1,000 women, the lowest rate ever recorded in the United States. Some of the decrease is due to good news, which is the continuing decline of teen pregnancies, but most of it is due to people getting married later and choosing to have fewer children. And the worst part is, everyone is treating this news with a shrug.

It wasn't always this way. It used to be taken for granted that the best indicator of a nation's health was its citizens' desire and capacity to reproduce. And it should still seem self-evident that people's willingness to have children is not only a sign of confidence in the future, but a sign of cultural health. It's a signal that people are willing to commit to the most enduring responsibility on Earth, which is raising a child.

But reproduction is also a sign of national health in a more dollars-and-cents way. The more productive people you have in your society, the healthier your country's economy. It's an idea that was obvious back in the 17th century, when economist Jean Bodin wrote "the only wealth is people."

Today we see the problems wrought by the decline in productive populations all over the industrialized world, where polities are ripping each other to shreds over how to pay for various forms of entitlements, especially for old people. The debates play out in different ways in different countries, but in other ways they are exactly the same. That's because they are ruled by the same ruthless math: The fewer young, productive people you have to pay for entitlements for old, unproductive people, the steeper the bill for the entire society becomes. This basic problem is strangling Europe's economies. And while the United States is among the least bad of the bunch, it is still headed in the wrong direction.

Pascal-Emmanuel Gobry, who has written for *Forbes*, the *Atlantic*, *Commentary*, and the *National Review*, among other publications, is a fellow at the Ethics and Public Policy Center.

It doesn't have to be this way. While the evidence for government programs that encourage people to have more children is mixed, the fact of the matter is that in contemporary America, 40 percent of women have fewer children than they want to.

And there are plenty of policies that could help close that gap, whether from the left or from the right. Not just pro-maternity policies, but also policies that encourage healthy child-rearing, like child tax credits, family savings accounts, and tax-free children savings accounts. Or education reforms that would make fewer parents feel that they have to pony up for private school to give their kids a decent shot at life. Perhaps one of the biggest things we could do is to reduce the countless state and local regulations that make housing expensive.

But put policy aside for a second. The United States literally exports more oil than Saudi Arabia and has the world's top expertise in both renewable and traditional energy forms. It is the world's biggest food producer and a gargantuan country with very little density. There is no reason for the United States to have a weak birth rate—and it is a national emergency that it does.

Yet no one seems worried. And that might be the biggest worry of all.

12
Proposals

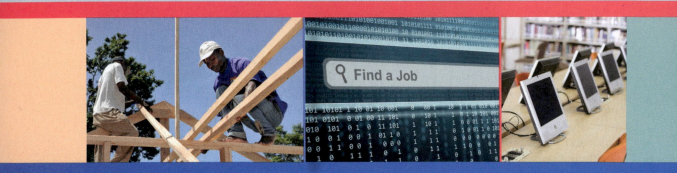

LEFT TO RIGHT: Florian Kopp/imageBROKER/AGE Fotostock; spaxiax/Shutterstock; ESB Professional/Shutterstock

A student looking forward to spring break proposes to two friends that they join a group that will spend the vacation helping to build a school in a Haitian village.

Members of a business club at a community college talk about their common need to create informative, appealing, interactive résumés. After much discussion, three members suggest that the club develop a résumé app designed especially for students looking for a first job.

A project team at a large architectural firm works for three months developing a response to an RFP (request for proposal) to convert a university library into a digital learning center.

Understanding and Categorizing Proposals

We live in an era of big proposals—complex schemes for reforming health care, bold dreams to privatize space exploration, multibillion-dollar prototypes for hyperloop transport systems, serious calls for free post-secondary education, and so many other such ideas usually shot down to earth by budget realities. As a result, there's often more talk than action because persuading people (or legislatures) to do something—or *anything!*—is always hard. But that's what *proposal arguments* do: they provide compelling reasons for supporting or sometimes resisting change.

Such arguments, whether national or local, formal or casual, are important not only on the national scene but also in all of our lives. How many proposals do you make or respond to in one day to address problems and offer solutions? A neighbor might suggest that you volunteer to help revitalize a neglected city park; a campus group might demand more reasonably priced student/staff parking; a supervisor might ask for employee suggestions to improve customer satisfaction at a restaurant; or you might propose to a friend that you both invest in a vinyl record outlet. In each case, the proposal implies that there are good reasons for new action or that you've found a solution to a problem.

In their simplest form, proposal arguments look something like this:

A should do B because of C.

```
┌──────── A ────────┐┌────────── B ──────────────┐
```
Our student government should endorse the Academic Bill of Rights
```
┌─────────────────── C ──────────────────────────┐
```
because students should not be punished in their courses for their personal political views.

Proposals come at us so routinely that it's not surprising that they cover a dizzyingly wide range of possibilities. So it may help to think of proposal arguments as divided roughly into two kinds—those that focus on specific practices and those that focus on broad matters of policy. Here are several examples of each kind:

Proposals about Practices

- The college should allow students to pay tuition on a month-by-month basis.
- Conventional businesses should learn to compete with nontraditional competitors like Airbnb and Uber within the sharing economy.
- College athletes should be paid for the entertainment they provide.

Proposals about Policies

- The college should guarantee that in any disciplinary hearings students charged with serious misconduct be assured of regular due-process protections.
- The United Nations should make saving the oceans from pollution a global priority.
- Major Silicon Valley firms should routinely reveal the demographic makeup of their workforces.

RESPOND•

People write proposal arguments to address problems and to change the way things are. But problems aren't always obvious: what troubles some people might be no big deal to others. To get an idea of the range of issues people face at your school (some of which you may not even have thought of as problems), divide into groups and brainstorm about things that annoy you about your institution, including things such as complex or restrictive registration procedures, poor scheduling of lab courses, and convoluted paperwork for student aid applications. Ask each group to aim for at least a half dozen gripes. Then choose three problems and, as a group, discuss how you'd prepare a proposal to deal with them.

Characterizing Proposals

1. They call for change, often in response to a problem.
2. They focus on the future.
3. They center on the audience.

Proposals always call for some kind of action. They aim at getting something done—or sometimes at *preventing* something from being done. Proposals marshal evidence and arguments to persuade people to choose a course of action: *Let's make the campus safer for people taking night courses. Let's create an organization for first-generation or working-class students. Let's ban drones from local airspace, especially at sporting and entertainment venues. Let's investigate incentives for supporting small business start-ups in our community.* But you know the old saying, "You can lead a horse to water, but you can't make it drink." It's usually easier to *convince* audiences what a good course of action is than to *persuade* them to take it (or pay for it). Even if you present a cogent proposal, you may still have work to do.

Proposal arguments must appeal to more than good sense. Ethos matters, too. It helps if a writer suggesting a change carries a certain *gravitas* earned by experience or supported by knowledge and research. If your word and credentials carry weight, then an audience is more likely to listen to your proposal. So when the commanders of three *Apollo* moon missions, Neil Armstrong, James Lovell, and Eugene Cernan, wrote an open letter to President Obama in 2010 expressing their dismay at his administration's decision to cancel NASA's plans for advanced spacecraft and new lunar missions, they won a wide audience:

> For the United States, the leading space faring nation for nearly half a century, to be without carriage to low Earth orbit and with no human exploration capability to go beyond Earth orbit for an indeterminate time into the future, destines our nation to become one of second or even third rate stature. While the President's plan envisages humans traveling away from Earth and perhaps toward Mars at some time in the future, the lack of developed rockets and spacecraft will assure that ability will not be available for many years.

But even their considerable ethos was not enough to carry the day with the space agency or the man who made the decision. Entrepreneurs like Elon Musk and Jeff Bezos have since acted on their own to privatize (at least partially) what had been a government monopoly, offering new proposals for innovative rockets and spacecraft.

Who thought *this* crazy idea could work? A fourteen-story tall SpaceX first-stage booster rocket successfully lands on a barge at sea after helping to launch a supply mission to the International Space Station (April 8, 2016). NASA/Getty Images

Yet, as the photo demonstrates, proposal arguments inevitably focus on the future—what individuals, institutions, or entire governments should do over the upcoming weeks, months, or even decades. This orientation toward the future presents special challenges, since few of us have crystal balls. Proposal arguments must therefore offer the best evidence available to suggest that actions we recommend can achieve what they promise.

Proposals must also be tailored to reach and convince audiences to support, possibly approve, and quite often pay for them. Not surprisingly, politicians making public policy proposals not infrequently exaggerate the benefits and minimize the costs or disadvantages.

It makes sense that proposals aimed at general audiences make straightforward and relatively simple points, avoid technical language, and use visuals like charts, graphs, and tables to make supporting data comprehensible. You can find such arguments, for example, in newspaper editorials, letters to the editor, and actual proposal documents. Such appeals to broad groups make sense when a project—say, to finance new toll roads or build a sports arena—must surf on waves of community support.

But just as often, proposals need to win support from specific groups or individuals (such as bankers, developers, public officials, and legislators) who have power to make change actually happen. Arguments to them will usually be far more technical, detailed, and comprehensive than those aimed at the general public because such people likely know the subject already and they may be responsible eventually for implementing or financing the proposal. You can expect these experts or professionals—engineers, designers, administrators, bureaucrats—to have specific questions and, possibly, formidable objections.

So identifying your potential and most powerful audiences is critical to the success of any proposal. On your own campus, for example, a plan to alter admissions policies might be directed both to students in general and (perhaps in a different form) to the university president and provost, members of the faculty council, and admissions officers.

An effective proposal also has to be compatible with the values of the audience. Some ideas sound appealing, but cannot be enacted immediately—as California legislators discovered when in 2017 they first tried to implement single-payer, universal health care for that state. Citizens favored the idea, but legislators blanched at the considerable costs. Or consider a less complicated matter: many American towns and suburbs have a significant problem with expanding deer populations.

Adrian Raeside

Without natural predators, the deer are moving closer to homes, dining on gardens and shrubbery, and endangering traffic. Yet one obvious and feasible solution—culling the herds through hunting—is usually not saleable to communities (perhaps too many people remember *Bambi*).

RESPOND•

Work in a group to identify about half a dozen problems on your campus or in the local community, looking for a wide range of issues. (Don't focus on problems in individual academic classes.) Once you have settled on these issues, then use various resources—social media, the phone book (if you can find one), a campus directory—to locate specific people, groups, or offices whom you might address or influence to deal with the issues you have identified.

Developing Proposals

In developing a proposal, you will have to do some or all of the following:

- Define a problem that lacks a good solution or describe a need that is not currently addressed—and convince audiences the matter deserves attention.
- Make a strong claim that addresses the problem or need. Your solution should be an action directed at the future.
- Show why your proposal will fix the problem or address the need.
- Demonstrate that your proposal is feasible.

This might sound easy, but writing a proposal argument can be a process of discovery. At the outset, you think you know exactly what ought to be done, but by the end, you may see (and even recommend) other options.

Defining a Need or Problem

To make a proposal, first establish that a need or problem exists. You'll typically dramatize the problem that you intend to fix at the beginning of your project and then lead up to a specific claim that attempts to solve it. But in some cases, you could put the need or problem right after your claim as the major reason for adopting the proposal:

> **Let's ban cell phones for students walking (or biking!) across college property. Why? Because we've become dangerous zombies. The few students not browsing the Web or chatting have to dodge their clueless and self-absorbed colleagues. Worse, no one speaks to or even acknowledges the people they pass on campus. We are no longer a functional community.**

How can you make readers care about the problem you hope to address? Following are some strategies:

- Paint a vivid picture of the need or problem.
- Show how the need or problem affects people, both those in the immediate audience and the general public as well.
- Underscore why the need or problem is significant and pressing.
- Explain why previous attempts to address the issue may have failed.

For example, were you to propose that the military draft be restored in the United States or that all young men and women give two years to national service (a tough sell!), you might begin by drawing a picture of a younger generation that is self-absorbed, demands instant gratification, and doesn't understand what it means to participate as a full member of society. Or you might note how many young people today fail to develop the life skills they need to strike out on their own. Or you could define the issue as a matter of fairness, arguing that the current all-volunteer army shifts the burden of national service to a small and unrepresentative sample of the American population. Of course, you would want to cite authorities and statistics to prove that any problem you're diagnosing is real and that it touches your likely audience. Then readers *may* be willing to hear your proposal.

In compiling their report "Hunger on Campus: The Challenge of Food Insecurity for College Students," the researchers used surveys at thirty-four colleges and universities to identify the problem of food insecurity. Their study found that 48 percent of students surveyed were food insecure in the previous month.

LINK TO P. 634

In describing a problem that your proposal argument intends to solve, be sure to review earlier attempts to fix it. Many issues have a long history that you can't afford to ignore (or be ignorant of). Understand too that some problems seem to grow worse every time someone tinkers with them. You might think twice before proposing any new attempt to change the current system of financing federal election campaigns when you discover that previous reforms have resulted in more bureaucracy, more restrictions on political expression, and more unregulated money flowing into the system. *"Enough is enough"* can be a potent argument when faced with such a mess.

RESPOND•

If you review "My Free-Range Kids Manifesto" at the end of this chapter (p. 313), a proposal by blogger and columnist Lenore Skenazy, you'll see that she spends quite a bit of time arguing that American children had more fun and learned more life skills in the past, when parents were (in general) less protective than she believes they are today. Chances are, you grew up in the highly protective environment she describes. If so, do you relate to the problem she defines in her manifesto? Or does the piece fail to engage your interest? If so, why?

Making a Strong and Clear Claim

After you've described and analyzed a problem, you're prepared to offer a fix. Begin with your claim (a proposal of what X or Y should do), followed by the reason(s) that X or Y should act and the effects of adopting the proposal:

Claim   Americans should encourage and support more scientists running for political office.

Reason   Scientists are trained to think more systematically and globally and may have greater respect for facts than the lifelong politicians who currently dominate American government.

Effects   Scientists will move our governments at all levels (local, state, federal) to make decisions based on facts and evidence rather than on emotions or the politics of the moment.

In "The Power of Words," the Japanese American Citizens League advocates using precise, clear terms instead of euphemisms to describe the experience of Japanese Americans during World War II. Instead of "relocation," for instance, they recommend "forced removal."

LINK TO P. 667

Having established a claim, you can explore its implications by drawing out the reasons, warrants, and evidence that can support it most effectively:

Claim	In light of a recent U.S. Supreme Court decision that ruled that federal drug laws cannot be used to prosecute doctors who prescribe drugs for use in suicide, our state should immediately pass a bill legalizing physician-assisted suicide for patients who are terminally ill.
Reason	Physician-assisted suicide can relieve the suffering of those who are terminally ill and will die soon.
Warrant	The relief of suffering is desirable.
Evidence	Oregon voters have twice approved the state's Death with Dignity Act, which has been in effect since 1997, and to date the suicide rate has not risen sharply, nor have doctors given out a large number of prescriptions for death-inducing drugs. At least four other states, as well as the District of Columbia, have legalized physician-assisted suicide.

The *reason* sets up the need for the proposal, whereas the *warrant* and *evidence* demonstrate that the proposal is just and could meet its objective. Your actual argument would develop each point in detail.

RESPOND•

For each problem and solution below, make a list of readers' likely objections to the solution offered. Then propose a solution of your own, and explain why you think it's more workable than the original.

Problem	Future deficits in the Social Security system
Solution	Raise the age of retirement to seventy-two.
Problem	Severe grade inflation in college courses
Solution	Require a prescribed distribution of grades in every class: 10% A; 20% B; 40% C; 20% D; 10% F.
Problem	Increasing rates of obesity in the general population
Solution	Ban the sale of high-fat sandwiches and entrees in fast-food restaurants.
Problem	Increase in sexual assaults on and around campus
Solution	Establish a 10:00 p.m. curfew on weekends.

A proposal argument in four panels © Andy Singer/ Cagle Cartoons, Inc.

Showing That the Proposal Addresses the Need or Problem

An important but tricky part of making a successful proposal lies in relating the claim to the need or problem that it addresses. Facts and probability are your best allies. Take the time to show precisely how your solution will fix a problem or at least improve upon the current situation. Sometimes an emotional appeal is fair play, too. Here, for example, is a paragraph from a group called YesCalifornia backing a referendum for that state to secede from the United States, a proposal that gained traction after the 2016 presidential election. The group explains what type of government California might expect after it leaves the United States:

> [O]ur referendum is a way to gauge the sense of the people on whether we Californians prefer the status quo of statehood, or if we want to see a change towards nationhood. Voting yes on the referendum is essentially voting yes to reform our system of government as well as our political and elections process to guarantee a more responsible and

> responsive government; move away from a two-party system; reduce the influence of big money in elections; restore the principle of one person, one vote; establish a system of proportional representation; and, engage disenfranchised voters. These are goals Californians and others are currently fighting for, yet under the corrupt U.S. political system, they are unlikely to be achieved.

The advocacy group seems to be claiming that an independent California would guarantee a more responsive government and a more engaged citizenry no longer swayed by big-money elections and two-party politics. Wishful thinking perhaps, but powerful rationale for change?

Alternatively, when you oppose an idea, these strategies work just as well in reverse: if a proposal doesn't fix a problem, you have to show exactly why. Perhaps you are skeptical about a proposal mentioned earlier in this chapter to reinstate a military draft in the United States. You might ask for proof that forced military conscription would, in fact, improve the moral fiber of young Americans. Or you might raise doubts about whether any new draft could operate without loopholes for well-connected or favored groups. Or, like Doug Bandow writing for *Forbes*, you might focus on the monetary and social costs of a restored draft: "Better to make people do grunt work than to pay them to do it? Force poorer young people into uniform in order to save richer old people tax dollars. . . . It would be a bad bargain by any measure."

Finally, if your own experience backs up your claim or demonstrates the need or problem that your proposal aims to address, then consider using it to develop your proposal. Consider the following questions in deciding when to include your own experiences in showing that a proposal is needed or will in fact do what it claims:

- Is your experience directly related to the need or problem that you seek to address or to your proposal about it?

- Will your experience be appropriate and speak convincingly to the audience? Will the audience immediately understand its significance, or will it require explanation?

- Does your personal experience fit logically with the other reasons that you're using to support your claim?

Be careful. If a proposal seems crafted to serve mainly your own interests, you won't get far.

Showing That the Proposal Is Feasible

To be effective, proposals must be *feasible*—that is, the action proposed can be carried out in a reasonable way. Demonstrating feasibility calls on you to present evidence—from similar cases, from personal experience, from observational data, from interview or survey data, from Internet research, or from any other sources—showing that what you propose can indeed be done with the resources available. "Resources available" is key: if the proposal calls for funds, personnel, or skills beyond reach or reason, your audience is unlikely to accept it. When that's the case, it's time to reassess your proposal, modify it, and test any new ideas against these revised criteria. This is also when you can reconsider proposals that others might suggest are better, more effective, or more workable than yours. There's no shame in admitting that you may have been wrong. When drafting a proposal, ask friends to think of counterproposals. If your own proposal can stand up to such challenges, it's likely a strong one.

Considering Design and Visuals

Because proposals often address specific audiences, they can take a number of forms—a letter, a memo, a Web page, a feasibility report, an infographic, a video, a prospectus, or even an editorial cartoon (see Andy Singer's "No Exit" item on p. 295). Each form has different design requirements. Indeed, the form of a proposal may determine its effectiveness.

For example, formal reports on paper or slides typically use straightforward headings to identify the stages of the presentation, terms such as Introduction, Nature of the Problem, Current Approaches or Previous Solutions, Proposal/Recommendations, Advantages, Counterarguments, Feasibility, Implementation, and so on. Important data may be arrayed in tables and charts, all of them clearly labeled. Infographics making proposals will be more visually intense, with their claims and data presented in ways designed to grab readers and then hold their attention as they move through panels or pages. So before you produce a final copy of any proposal, be sure its overall design complements and enhances its messages.

Proposal arguments, especially those aimed at wide audiences, may rely on a wide range of graphic materials that to convey information—photographs, pie charts, scatter charts, timelines, maps, artist's renderings, and so on. Such items help readers visualize problems and then (if need be) imagine solutions. Any such items you find or create should be

The proposed design of the National Museum of African American History & Culture Courtesy of NMAAHC and Freelon Adjaye Bond/SmithGroup

carefully designed, incorporated, and credited when you borrow them: they will contribute to your ethos.

Images also make proposals more interesting. Architects, engineers, and government agencies know this. For example, the rendering above helped viewers imagine what a future National Museum of African American History & Culture might look like on the Mall in Washington, D.C.—its structure suggesting the shape of African baskets. This winning proposal was offered in 2009 by designer David Adjaye, architect Philip Freelon, and the Freelon Adjaye Bond/Smith Group.

But the building did evolve, gaining a third terrace and a bronze color to suggest other themes. Here's how the Smithsonian Web site describes the ideas evoked by the finished structure, which opened on September 24, 2016:

> From one perspective, the building's architecture follows classical Greco-Roman form in its use of a base and shaft, topped by a capital or corona. For our Museum, the corona is inspired by the three-tiered crowns used in Yoruban art from West Africa. Moreover, the building's main entrance is a welcoming porch, which has architectural roots in Africa and throughout the African Diaspora, especially the American

The completed version Ian Dagnall/Alamy Stock Photo

South and Caribbean. Finally, by wrapping the entire building in an ornamental bronze-colored metal lattice, Adjaye pays homage to the intricate ironwork crafted by enslaved African Americans in Louisiana, South Carolina, and elsewhere.

GUIDE | to writing a proposal

● Finding a Topic or Identifying a Problem

You're entering a proposal argument when you:

- make a claim that supports a change in practice: *Bottled water should carry a warning label describing the environmental impact of plastic.*
- make a claim that supports a change in policy: *Government workers, especially legislators and administrative officials, should never be exempt from laws or programs imposed on other citizens.*
- make a claim that resists suggested changes in practice or policy: *The surest way to guarantee that HOV lanes on freeways improve traffic flow is not to build any.*
- explore options for addressing existing issues or investigate opportunities for change: *Urban planners need to examine the long-term impact digital technologies may have on transportation, work habits, housing patterns, power usage, and entertainment opportunities in cities of the future.*

Since your everyday experience often calls on you to consider problems and to make proposals, begin your brainstorming with practical topics related to your life, education, major, or job. Or make an informal list of proposals that you would like to explore in broader academic or cultural areas—problems you see in your field or in the society around you. Or do some freewriting on a subject of political concern, and see if it leads to a call for action.

● Researching Your Topic

For many proposals, you can begin your research by consulting the following types of sources:

- newspapers, magazines, reviews, and journals (online and print)
- television or radio news reports
- online databases
- government documents and reports
- Web sites, blogs, social media
- books
- experts in the field, some of whom might be right on your campus

Consider doing some field research, if appropriate—a survey of student opinions on Internet accessibility, for example, or interviews with people who have experienced the problem you are trying to fix.

Finally, remember that your proposal's success can depend on the credibility of the sources you use to support it, so evaluate each source carefully (see Chapter 19).

● Formulating a Claim

As you think about and explore your topic, begin formulating a claim about it. To do so, come up with a clear thesis that makes a proposal and states the reasons that this proposal should be adopted. To start formulating a claim, explore and respond to the following questions:

- What do I know about the proposal that I'm making?
- What reasons can I offer to support my proposal?
- What evidence do I have that implementing my proposal will lead to the results I want?

Rather than make a specific proposal, you may sometimes want to explore the range of possibilities for addressing a particular situation or circumstance (see, for instance, the last bullet in the following section). In that case, a set of open-ended questions might be a more productive starting point than a focused thesis, suggesting, for instance, what goals any plausible proposal might have to meet.

● Examples of Proposal Claims

- Because the one-time costs for a host city/nation staging the Olympics have become staggering, the International Olympics Committee should consider moving the summer games to a permanent site—in Athens, Greece.
- Every home should be equipped with a well-stocked emergency kit that can sustain inhabitants for at least three days in a natural disaster.
- Congress should repeal the Copyright Extension Act, since it disrupts the balance between incentives for creators and the right of the public to information as set forth in the U.S. Constitution.
- To simplify the lives of the soon-to-be significant number of people driving electric cars, manufacturers should quickly settle upon a universal charging system that all e-cars can share rather than the individual systems now in place.

- People from different economic classes, age groups, political philosophies, and power groups (government, Main Street, Wall Street, blue collar labor, immigrants) all have a stake in reforming current budget and tax policies. But how do we get them to speak and to listen to each other? That is the challenge we face if we hope to solve our national economic problems.

● Preparing a Proposal

If your instructor asks you to prepare a proposal for your project, here's a format that may help:

State the thesis of your proposal completely. If you're having trouble doing so, try outlining it in Toulmin terms (see Chapter 7 for more on the Toulmin approach):

> Claim:
> Reason(s):
> Warrant(s):

Alternatively, you might describe your intention to explore a particular problem in your project, with the actual proposal (and thesis) coming later.

- Explain why this issue deserves attention. What's at stake?
- Identify and describe those readers whom you hope to reach with your proposal. Why is this group of readers appropriate? Can you identify individuals who can actually fix a problem?
- Briefly discuss the major difficulties that you foresee for your proposal. How will you demonstrate that the action you propose is necessary and workable? Persuade the audience to act? Pay for the proposal?
- Determine what research strategies you'll use. What sources do you expect to consult?

● Considering Genre and Media

Your instructor may specify that you use a particular genre and/or medium. If not, ask yourself these questions to help you make a good choice:

- What genre is most appropriate for your proposal? Does the problem call for an academic essay, a report, an infographic, a brochure, or something else?

- What medium is most appropriate for your argument? Would it be best delivered orally to a live audience? Presented as an audio essay or podcast? Presented in print only or in print with illustrations?
- Will you need visuals, such as moving or still images, maps, graphs, charts—and what function will they play in your argument? Make sure they are not just "added on" but are necessary components of the argument.

● Thinking about Organization

Proposals can take many different forms but generally include the following elements:

- a description of the problem you intend to address or the state of affairs that leads you to propose the action
- a strong and specific proposal, identifying the key reasons for taking the proposed action and the effects that taking this action will have
- a clear connection between the proposal and a significant need or problem
- a demonstration of ways in which the proposal addresses the need
- evidence that the proposal will achieve the desired outcome
- a consideration of alternative ways to achieve the desired outcome and a discussion of why these may not be feasible
- a demonstration that the proposal is feasible and an explanation of how it may be implemented

● Getting and Giving Response: Questions for Peer Response

Your instructor may assign you to a group for the purpose of reading and responding to each other's drafts. If not, ask for responses from serious readers or consultants at a writing center. Use the following questions to evaluate a colleague's draft or project. Since specific comments help more than general observations, be sure to illustrate your comments with examples. Some of the questions below assume a conventional, thesis-driven project, but more exploratory, open-ended proposal arguments in various media also need to be clearly presented, organized, and supported with evidence.

The Claim

- Does the claim clearly call for action? Is the proposal as clear and specific as possible? Is it realistic or possible to accomplish?

- Is the proposal too sweeping? Does it need to be qualified? If so, how?

- Does the proposal clearly address the problem that it intends to solve? If not, how could the connection be strengthened?

- Is the claim likely to get the audience to act rather than just to agree? If not, how could it be revised to do so?

Evidence for the Claim

- Is enough evidence furnished to get the audience to support the proposal? If not, what kind of additional evidence is needed? Does any of the evidence provided seem inappropriate or otherwise ineffective? Why?

- Is the evidence in support of the claim simply announced, or are its significance and appropriateness analyzed? Is a more detailed discussion needed?

- Are objections that readers might have to the claim or evidence adequately and fairly addressed?

- What kinds of sources are cited? How credible and persuasive will they be to readers? What other kinds of sources might work better?

- Are all quotations introduced with appropriate signal phrases (such as "As Tyson argues, . . .") and blended smoothly into the writer's sentences?

- Are all visual sources labeled, introduced, and commented upon?

Organization and Style

- How are the parts of the argument organized? Is this organization or design effective?

- Will readers understand the relationships among the claims, supporting reasons, warrants, and evidence? If not, how might those connections be clearer? Is the function of every visual clear? Are more transitions needed? Would headings or graphic devices help?

- Are the transitions or links from point to point, sentence to sentence, and paragraph to paragraph clear and effective? Are transitions evident and helpful in oral presentations or speeches, videos, infographics, or other media? If not, how could they be improved?

- Are all visuals carefully integrated into the text? Is each visual introduced and commented on to point out its significance? Is each visual labeled as a figure or a table and given a caption as well as a citation?

- Is the style suited to the subject? Is it too formal, casual, or technical? Can it be improved?

- Which sentences seem effective? Which ones seem weaker, and how could they be improved? Should short sentences be combined, and any longer ones be broken up?

- How effective are the paragraphs or sections? Too short or too long? How can they be improved?

- Which words or phrases seem effective? Do any seem vague or inappropriate for the audience or the writer's purpose? Are technical or unfamiliar terms defined?

Spelling, Punctuation, Mechanics, Documentation, and Format

- Are there any errors in spelling, punctuation, capitalization, and the like?

- Is the documentation appropriate and consistent? (See Chapter 22.)

- Does the paper or project follow an appropriate format or design? Is it appropriately formatted and attractively presented?

PROJECTS.

1. Identify a proposal currently in the news or one advocated unrelent-ingly by the media that you *really* don't like. It may be a political initia-tive, a cultural innovation, a transportation alternative, or a lifestyle change. Spend time studying the idea more carefully than you have before. And then compose a proposal argument based on your deeper understanding of the proposal. You may still explain why you think it's a bad idea. Or you may endorse it, using your new information and your interesting perspective as a former dissenter.

2. As should be evident from readings throughout this book, the uses and abuses of technology and media—from smartphones and smart-watches to social networks—seem to be on everyone's mind. Write a proposal argument about some pressing dilemma caused by the tech-nological tools and devices that are changing (ruining? improving?) our lives. You might want to explain how to bring traditional instruc-tors into the digital age, or establish etiquette for people installing surveillance equipment in and around their homes, or make sugges-tions for people discovering the self-driving features in their new cars. Or maybe you want to keep parents off social networks. Or maybe you have a great idea for separating professional and private lives online. Make your proposal in some pertinent medium: print op-ed, cartoon, photo essay, infographic, set of PowerPoint or Prezi slides, TED talk.

3. Write a proposal to yourself diagnosing some minor issue you would like to address, odd personal behavior you'd like to change, or obsession you'd like to curb. Explore the reasons behind your mania and the prob-lems it causes you and others. Then come up with a proposal to resolve the issue and prove that you can do it. Make the paper hilarious.

4. Working in a group initially, come up with a list of problems—local, national, or international—that seem just about insoluble, from per-suading nations to cut down on their CO_2 emissions to figuring out how to keep tuition or textbook costs in check. After some discussion, focus on just one or two of these matters and then discuss not the issues themselves but the general reasons that the problems have proven intractable. What exactly keeps people from agreeing on solu-tions? Are some people content with the status quo? Do some groups profit from the current arrangements? Are alternatives to the status quo just too costly or not feasible for other reasons? Do people find change uncomfortable? Following the discussion, work alone or col-laboratively on an argument that examines the general issue of *change*: What makes it possible in any given case? What makes it difficult? Use the problems you have discussed as examples to illustrate your argument. Your challenge as a writer may be to make such an open-ended discussion interesting to general readers.

Addiction to Social Media: How to Overcome It

CALEB WONG

Sean McElligott

I was broken. I applied to become a member of a student society—unlike many others, it seemed like the right fit—and I got an interview. Then I didn't get in, so I hurt myself. Succumbing to my worst instincts, I spent several hours on Facebook and Twitter, looking though the society's accounts and those of its members. I saw the gleam of their uniforms and the casual perfection of their lives, the heads of state they greeted and the inspirational quotations they tweeted. Social media invited me to view, at a distance, worlds in which I didn't belong, worlds I had been rejected from. "A-Plus human" read a comment on a post for students who were admitted into the organization. I went to bed feeling disappointed and terrible—basically, a D-minus human—and I decided to make a change that I had pondered and abandoned time and time again: deleting the social media apps from my phone. I realized I was addicted to a virtual life I wanted but couldn't have.

Apparently, I'm not alone in this predicament: struggling with an addiction to social media. Social media use is widespread; a Pew Research Center study found that nearly eight out of ten online American adults use Facebook, and 76 percent of those users use the site daily (Greenwood et al., 2016). Smaller but still significant percentages also use Twitter and Instagram. Misery loves virtual company; another report by Mixpanel, a mobile analytics company, says that 50 percent of people who use social apps are on them for more than five hours

The paper opens with a personal anecdote describing an issue: social media addiction.

Evidence for social media addiction is offered from a variety of sources.

Caleb Wong wrote this proposal paper for an Advanced Writing class while a junior at the University of Texas at Austin.

a day—and the top 20 percent of users spent more than eight hours on these social apps (Mixpanel Trends, 2017). Social media has come to define my generation not only through selfies, posts, tweets, likes, and other online social activity, but also in terms of what a sinkhole it has become. The distractions never end—bottomless Facebook, Twitter, and Instagram are eerily and endlessly personalized—for our own lives. Much can be said about the shallowness and corrosive effect of social media on civic life, but the most compelling argument against social media may be that it significantly hurts productivity. The computer science professor and productivity expert Cal Newport wrote in a *New York Times* column that the "ability to concentrate without distractions on hard tasks is becoming increasingly important in an increasingly complicated society" (Newport, 2016).

The network effect—the digital web of contacts, pictures, videos, and posts—characterizes our connections to each other in the digital sphere. In terms of social media, it has created a powerful cue—a desire for a distraction—that draws us into an endless vortex of content. We see successful people posting pictures of the camaraderie they share on service projects or the fun times they have on the weekend at a party. When overdone, the network effect is not benign: a 2011 literature review found that it incorporates "classic" addiction symptoms such as mood modification, emotional preoccupation, tolerance as usage increases, withdrawal symptoms, and relapse (Kuss & Griffiths, 2011). In the most addicted people, this desire to use social media is so ingrained that they feel the euphoric high that comes from the anticipation of sharing a "buzzy" message before it's even sent.

So how do we understand this addiction? Like tooth-brushing and nail-biting, using social media regularly is a habit. There are three parts to a habit: a cue, a routine, and a reward (Duhigg, 2016, p. 58). A cue is an automatic impulse that directs us to perform some action; that impulse could be a twitch to talk to someone or a desire to see the latest gossip. And then there's the routine: an action you take, whether it be physical, mental, or emotional. Swiping left or right on Tinder, scrolling through an Instagram or Facebook feed, obsessively checking mentions on Twitter—these are all examples of actions that might follow up on a social media cue. And then there's the reward, the pleasure we gain from performing the routine. Perhaps we forget our troubles for a moment or learn something new about our friends' lives.

So what's the solution? To change an addiction routine, you have to find out what your cue is and figure out how to get the same reward through a different response. For example, my desire for a momentary distraction from the humdrum of everyday life makes me wander into the voyeurism of social media for the reward of relaxation. But recognizing that cue, I realize that calling a friend or reading a print book, for example, would also help me relax, avoiding the addiction of social media. It's not easy; a recent study by Duke University researchers suggests that habits prime us to feed our cravings by leaving specific marks in our brain (Chi, 2016). But it's certainly possible to change a habit—and hence your life—through this step.

Another key means of breaking the social media habit is to find a community to help you stick with new routines. Scientists from the Alcohol Research Group found that Alcoholics Anonymous attendance was "significantly associated with increased abstinence and reductions in drinking intensity," suggesting in particular that relationships with others can reinforce good habits (Tonigan, Miller & Schermer, 2002). As Lee Ann Kaskutas, a psychological scientist from AA, explains in an interview with Duhigg,

> At some point, people in AA look around the room and think, *if it worked for that guy, I guess it can work for me.* There's something really powerful about groups and shared experiences. People might be skeptical about

The paper offers specific solutions to the problem of social media addiction.

their ability to change if they're by themselves, but a group will convince them to suspend disbelief. A community creates belief. (p. 85)

In scale and approach, some social addiction therapy resembles drug recovery programs.

Sound like rehab? It should. There are now Internet addiction camps which claim to foster self-efficacy in their clients through close, one-on-one therapy and recreational activities and group exercises. At a cost of about $20,000 for a 45-day program at reSTART, an Internet recovery retreat in Seattle, participants in the program attend individual and group therapy sessions, as well as go on group outings together such as feeding the homeless or hiking in a national park (Hepburn, 2013). Independent data is sparse on how well these recovery programs work, but according to a self-conducted 2015 Treatment Outcomes survey, the retreat found that more than 93 percent of participants in the program were unable to control their Internet usage before they came to camp; three to four years after completing the program, though, 57.14 percent of them were "extremely, likely or slightly likely" to control their social media use (reSTART, 2015). Clearly, the emphasis on connections with counselors and peers helps the participants respond in a healthier way to their cues. Instead of turning to social media or the other addictive properties of the Internet, they learn to get the same reward through a different routine, such as talking to real-life people or reading books or picking up other hobbies.

Author suggests that app designers can play a role in reducing social media abuse.

App designers, too, can play a role in making their social media apps less addicting. Tristan Harris, a design ethicist and a former "product philosopher" at Google, argues in a blog post that designers should stop exploiting the psychological vulnerabilities of users by helping them set boundaries (Harris, 2016). For example, the Facebook app might send reminders to people in the top percentile of its users to perhaps dial back on their usage. Also, Harris argues that apps should stop auto-playing videos, one after other to create a natural stopping point for social media use. Comparing addiction to slot machines, he writes that these apps seduce users by offering them different rewards—like a Tinder match or seeing a nice picture on Facebook—every time they use the app, keeping them coming back for the novelty.

Of course, advertisers are incentivized to keep us addicted because their income is tied to time spent on these social media applications. On average, most Facebook users are on the app 50 minutes a day, which correlates with its record-breaking net income of $1.5 billion in the first financial quarter of 2016, according to a *New York Times* article (Stewart, 2016). (If this the average amount of time spent on Facebook, imagine how much time the most addicted users spend on the app.)

As individuals and a nation, we might support a congressional investigation or a citizen's commission to investigate the pernicious effects of social media addiction. We should also insist that businesses endorse the responsible use of their products. There may be a free market for our minds, but our national mental health must be preserved for the sake of productivity and sanity. We prosecute dealers who sell heroin or cocaine or prescription drugs on the street because of their dangerous potential for abuse; we need to rein in the power of social media for the same reason. As a society, we must not just focus on treating individuals, but also the whole system to adequately address this problem. Without fear or favor, our government must examine how we can take back our lives from social media so we use it in moderation, not in excess. In the meantime, the causes of social media addiction, the habit sequence—cues, routines, and rewards—and the process of forming good habits must be taught in the workplace, school, and the home. When addicts are finally freed from the soft tyranny of their virtual feeds, they will be empowered to engage once again with the hard reality of the world around them.

Author acknowledges that social media apps are deliberately addicting.

Final proposal is for civic action of the kind applied to other societal problems.

Sources are cited in a references list, per APA style.

REFERENCES

Chi, K. R. (2016, January 21). Why are habits so hard to break? [Press release]. Retrieved from Duke University website: https://today.duke.edu/2016/01/habits

Duhigg, C. (2012). *The power of habit*. New York, NY: Random House.

Greenwood, S., Perrin, A., & Duggan, M. (2016). *Social media update 2016*. Retrieved from Pew Research Center website: http://www.pewinternet.org/2016/11/11/social-media -update-2016/

Harris, T. (2016, May). How technology hijacks people's minds [Blog post]. Retrieved from http://www.tristanharris .com/2016/05/how-technology-hijacks-peoples-minds %E2%80%8A-%E2%80%8Afrom-a-magician-and-googles -design-ethicist/

Hepburn, N. (2013, January 24). Life in the age of internet addiction. *The Week*. Retrieved from http://theweek.com /articles/468363/life-age-internet-addiction

Kuss, D. J., & Griffiths, M. D. (2011). Online social networking and addiction—a review of the psychological literature. *International Journal of Environmental Research and Public Health, 8*(9), 3528–3552. http://doi.org/10.3390/ijerph8093528

Mixpanel Trends. (2017, March 30). Addiction [Blog post]. Retrieved from https://mixpanel.com/blog/2014/03/06 /addiction/

Newport, C. (2016, November 19). Quit social media. Your career may depend on it. [Editorial]. *The New York Times*. Retrieved from https://nyti.ms/2jAKBYj

reSTART (2015). *2015 treatment outcome results*. Retrieved from https://netaddictionrecovery.com/programs/outcome -research/where-are-they-now/640-2015-treatment -outcome-results.html

Stewart, J. B. (2016, May 5). Facebook has 50 minutes of your time each day. It wants more. *The New York Times*. Retrieved from https://nyti.ms/2kpxL0j

Tonigan, J. S., Miller, W. R., & Schermer, C. (2002). Atheists, agnostics and Alcoholics Anonymous. *Journal of Studies on Alcohol, 63*(5), 534–541. Retrieved from https://www.jsad .com/

My Free-Range Parenting Manifesto

LENORE SKENAZY

July 22, 2015

Back in 2009, the parenting site Babble listed the top 50 "mom" blogs in America—funniest, most fashionable, etc., and "most controversial."

That would be my blog, Free-Range Kids. Then it was voted most controversial again, a year later.

What crazy idea was I pushing? Don't vaccinate your kids? Clobber them when they cry? Teach them to play piano by threatening to burn their stuffed animals? Actually, my message was—and is—this: Our kids are just as safe and smart as we were when we were young. There's no reason to suddenly be afraid of everything they do, see, eat, wear, hear, touch, read, watch, lick, play or hug.

That idea runs smack up against the big, basic belief of our era: That our kids are in constant danger. It's an erroneous idea that is crippling our children and enslaving us parents.

Luckily, there's new pushback in the Capitol. Last week, Sen. Mike Lee introduced the first federal legislation in support of free-range parenting.

* * *

You've heard of me. I'm the New York City mom who let her 9-year-old ride the subway alone back in 2008. I wrote a column about it and two days later ended up on *The Today Show*, MSNBC, Fox News and (for contrast) NPR, defending myself as NOT "America's Worst Mom." But if you search that phrase you'll find me there for 77 Google pages.

I started my blog the weekend after the column ran to explain that I love safety—helmets, carseats, seatbelts—I just don't believe kids need a security detail every time they leave the house. As people found the site, I started hearing just how little we let kids do at all.

For instance, thanks to a mistaken belief that "We can't let our kids play outside like we did because times have changed!" only 13 percent of

---

Lenore Skenazy offers a proposal argument with passion, humor, and what used to be called common sense. Blogger, writer, and columnist, Skenazy became famous in 2008 when she allowed her nine-year-old son to ride by himself in a New York City subway. He survived.

kids walk to school. One study found that in a typical week, only 6 percent of kids 9–13 play outside unsupervised. And *Foreign Policy* recently ran a piece about how army recruits are showing up for basic training not knowing to skip or do a somersault. It's like they totally missed the physical, frolicking part of childhood—along with its lessons. How are they going to roll away from an explosion, or skip over a landmine? And then of course there's the rise in childhood obesity, diabetes and depression.

That rise does not strike me as a coincidence. But here's the killer irony: The crime rate today is actually lower than it was when we were growing up. (And it's not lower because of helicopter parenting. We don't helicopter adults and yet crimes against them—murder, rape, assault—are all down.) We're back to the crime rate of 1963. So if it wasn't crazy for our parents to let us play outside, it is even less crazy today. But gripped by the fear of extremely rare and random tragedies hammered home by a hyperventilating news cycle, we are actually putting our kids at risk for increasingly common health risks.

Beyond those, however, there is something even sadder happening to the kids we keep indoors, or in adult-run activities "for their safety." By having their every moment supervised, kids don't get a chance to play the way we did—free play, without a coach or trophy or parents screaming from the bleachers.

This is catastrophic. Free play turns out to be one of the most important things a kid can do to develop into the kind of adult who's resilient, entrepreneurial—and a pleasure to be around.

You see, when kids play on their own, they first of all have to come up with something to do. That's called problem solving: "We don't have a ball, so what can we play?" They take matters into their own hands. Then, if they don't all agree, they have to learn to compromise—another good skill to have.

If there are a bunch of kids, someone has to make the teams. Leadership! If there's a little kid, the big kids have to throw the ball more gently. Empathy! For their part, the little kids want to earn the big kids' respect. So they act more mature, which is how they become more mature. They rise to the occasion. Responsibility!

And here's the most important lesson that kids who are "just" playing learn. How to lose. Say a kid strikes out. Now he has a choice. He can throw a tantrum—and look like a baby. He can storm off—and not get to play anymore. Or he can hold it together, however hard that is, and go to the back of the line.

Because play is so fun, a kid will usually choose the latter. And in doing that difficult deed—taking his lumps—the child is learning to control himself even when things are not going his way. The term for this is "executive function."

It's the crucial skill all parents want their kids to learn, and the easiest way to learn it is through play. In fact, Penny Wilson, a thought leader on play in Britain, calls fun the "orgasm" of play. Kids play because it's fun—not realizing that really they are actually ensuring the success of the species by learning how to function as a society.

Unfortunately, thanks to the belief that kids are in danger any second we're not watching them, this kind of play has all but evaporated. Walk to your local park the next sunny Saturday and take a look: Is there any child there who isn't a toddler with a caregiver, or a kid in uniform with a team?

Instead of letting our kids make their own fun, we enroll them in programs (fearful they'd otherwise "waste" some teachable time), or we keep them inside (fearful they'd otherwise be kidnapped). And if we do boldly say, "Go out and play!" often there's no one else out there for them to play with.

Can you imagine a country full of people who have been listening to Mozart since they were in the womb, but have no idea how to organize a neighborhood ballgame? My friend was recently telling a high school-age cousin about how he used to play pick-up basketball in the park, and the cousin couldn't understand how this was possible without supervision. "What happened if someone decided to cheat and fouled all the time?" the kid asked. "We just wouldn't play with him anymore," my friend replied. Said the cousin: "That's exclusion!" and that, he added, was a "form of" bullying.

Agghh! We are crippling kids by convincing them they can't solve any issues on their own. And as depressing as all this is, now there's another barrier to free play: The government.

You've all heard the story of the Alexander and Danielle Meitiv, the parents investigated by child protective services not once but twice for letting their kids walk home from the playground in Silver Spring, Maryland. While they were eventually found not guilty on both accounts, it seemed to require massive public outrage before the authorities let them go. Maryland has since "clarified" its CPS policy, which now states, "It is not the department's role to pick and choose among child-rearing philosophies and practices."

It sure isn't. But the authorities have a habit of doing just that. A mom in Austin was visited by the cops for letting her 6-year-old play within sight of the house. A mom in Chicago is on the child abuse registry for letting her children 11, 9 and 5 play in the park literally across the street from her house—even though she peeked out at them every 10 minutes. And I've heard from parents investigated for letting their kids walk to the library, the post office and the pizza shop.

Want more tales from the annals of government overprotection? Last year, four Rhode Island legislators proposed a bill that would make it illegal for a school bus to let off any children under 7th grade—that's age 11—unless there was an adult waiting there to walk them home from the bus stop. Naturally this was presented as just another new measure to keep kids safe. Fortunately—and perhaps just a bit due to agitation by the "most controversial" blog in America—the bill ended up shelved.

Another triumph: A library in Boulder, Colorado, had actually prohibited anyone under age 12 to be there without a guardian, because, "Children may encounter hazards such as stairs, elevators, doors, furniture, electrical equipment, or, other library patrons." Ah, yes, kids and furniture. What a recipe for disaster!

But that library regulation was beaten back, too.

The biggest ray of hope to date? Republican Sen. Mike Lee from Utah just added a groundbreaking "Free-Range" provision to the Every Child Achieves Act. It would permit kids to walk or ride their bikes to school at an age their parents deem appropriate, without the threat of criminal or civil action—provided this doesn't pre-empt state or local laws. "'Helicopter parents' should be free to hover over their own kids, but more 'Free-Range' parents have the exact same rights," the senator told me. "And government at all levels should trust loving moms and dads to make those decisions for their own families."

The Act, including Lee's amendment, passed the Senate on Thursday (although in the end Lee could not support the final version of the bill) and now must be reconciled with the House version.

Support for Lee's provision was bi-partisan. So if Free-Range was once "controversial," now it is the people's will. We are sick of seeing childhood through the kaleidoscope of doom. Sick of thinking, "A stranger near the school? Abduction!" "A child waiting in the car while mom returns a book? Instant death!" "A non-organic grape? That kid's a goner!"

Enough! It is time to stop making ourselves crazy with fear. All we need to do is adopt a new skepticism whenever we hear the words "for the safety of our precious children."

Those words precede grandstanding and bad laws. They precede sanctimony and scapegoating. They turn rational parents into outlaws and exuberant children into gelatinous lumps on the couch.

The way to keep kids safe is not by forbidding them to go outside. It's by giving them the freedom we loved when we were kids, to play, explore, goof up, run around, take responsibility and get lost in every sense of the expression. Here, then, is The Free-Range Kids' and Parents' Bill of Rights:

"Our kids have the right to some unsupervised time (with our permission) and parents have the right to give it to them without getting arrested."

Take this bill to your local legislators, or Congress, or the president (or his "Let's Move!" wife), and remind them: This is how we grew up. Why are we denying our kids a healthy, all-American upbringing?

It's time to save childhood—and the country. How can we be the home of the brave when we're too scared to let our kids go out and become smart, successful, resilient, resourceful and independent by doing what we all did at their age?

Playing.

PART 3

STYLE AND PRESENTATION IN arguments

13
Style in Arguments

The images above all reflect the notable styles of musicians from different times and musical traditions: Yo-Yo Ma, Count Basie, Kiss, and Beyoncé. One could argue that these performers craft images to define their stage personalities, but how they present themselves also reflects the music they play and the audiences they perform for. Imagine Yo-Yo Ma appearing in Kiss makeup at Carnegie Hall. Weird!

Writers, too, create styles that express their ethos and life experiences. But in persuasive situations, style is also a matter of the specific choices they make—strategically and self-consciously—to influence audiences. And today, style is arguably more important than ever before in getting messages across. In a time when we are overcome with a veritable fire-hose of information 24 hours a day, getting and holding an audience's attention is often difficult. So what can do the job for writers today? STYLE.

It's not surprising, then, that writers take questions of style very seriously, that they adapt their voices to a range of rhetorical situations, from very formal to very casual. At the formal and professional end of

321

the scale, consider the opening paragraph of a dissent by Justice Sonia Sotomayor to a Supreme Court decision affecting affirmative action in Michigan public universities. Writing doesn't get much more consequential than this, and that earnestness is reflected in the justice's sober, authoritative, but utterly clear style:

> We are fortunate to live in a democratic society. But without checks, democratically approved legislation can oppress minority groups. For that reason, our Constitution places limits on what a majority of the people may do. This case implicates one such limit: the guarantee of equal protection of the laws. Although that guarantee is traditionally understood to prohibit intentional discrimination under existing laws, equal protection does not end there. Another fundamental strand of our equal protection jurisprudence focuses on process, securing to all citizens the right to participate meaningfully and equally in self-government. That right is the bedrock of our democracy, for it preserves all other rights.
>
> —Sonia Sotomayor, dissenting opinion, April 22, 2014

Contrast this formal style with the far more casual style in a blog item by *Huffington Post* book editor Claire Fallon, arguing (tongue-in-cheek) that Shakespeare's Romeo is one of those literary figures readers just love to hate. The range of Fallon's vocabulary choices—from "most romantic dude" to "penchant for wallowing"—suggests the (Beyoncé-like?) playfulness of the exercise. Style is obviously a big part of Fallon's game:

> Romeo, Romeo, wherefore art thou such a wishy-washy doofus? . . . [Romeo] spends his first scene in the play insisting he's heartbroken over a girl he goes on to completely forget about the second he catches a glimpse of Juliet! . . . Romeo's apparent penchant for wallowing in the romantic misery of unrequited love finds a new target in naive Juliet, who then dies for a guy who probably would have forgotten about her as soon as their honeymoon ended.
>
> —Claire Fallon, "11 Unlikeable Classical Book Characters We Love to Hate"

These examples use different styles but are written in standard English, with a bit of slang mixed into the blog post. In the multilingual, polyglot world we live in today, however, writers are also mixing languages (as Gloria Anzaldúa does when she shifts from English to Spanish to Spanglish in her book *Borderlands: La Frontera*) as well as mixing dialects and languages. This translingual turn recognizes that English itself exists in many forms (Singaporean English, Canadian English, New Zealand English, and so on), that many writers of English speak and write a variety of other languages, and that many if not most writers "code mesh," a term scholar Suresh Canagarajah defines as "a strategy for merging local varieties with standard written Englishes in a move toward more gradually pluralizing academic writing and developing multilingual competence for transnational relationships" ("The Place of World Englishes in Composition," CCC, June 2006). Here is an example of code-meshing in an article by Professor Donald McCrary:

> Like my students, I know the value of my native language, black English, and the significance it has played in both my public and private life. However, many would challenge my claim that black English is both a public and private language. For example, in "Aria: A Memoir of a Bilingual Childhood," Richard Rodriguez argues for the separation of home and school languages because he believes the former is private while the latter is public. . . . I, however, view black English as a public language because it is the language with which I learned about the world, including the perils of racism, the importance of education, and the consequences of improper conduct. When Moms told me, "Don't go showin' your ass when I take you in this store," I knew she was telling me to behave respectfully, and I knew what would happen if I didn't. The black English I learned at home is the same black English I used outside the home. It got black people through slavery, and it saved my black behind a thousand times.
>
> Hold up. I know what you gonna say. Talkin' that black English is okay at home and with your friends, but don't be speakin' that foolishness in school or at the j-o-b. And don't be tellin' no students they can speak that mess either. You want people (read: white) to think they ignorant? Right.
>
> Right. I hear you. I hear you. But let's be real. America loves itself some black English. Half the announcers on ESPN speak it, and I'm talking about the white dudes, too. Americans know more black English than they like to admit. Black English is intelligible and intelligent, and just because somebody tells you different, don't necessarily make it so. And that's what I want the academy to understand. My students don't speak no broken English. They speak a legitimate dialect that conveys legitimate meanings.
>
> —Donald McCrary, "Represent, Representin', Representation: The Efficacy of Hybrid Texts in the Writing Classroom"

McCrary, who teaches at Long Island University, "meshes" elements of African American language with "standard" written English to create a style that speaks to both academic and nonacademic audiences. His use of colloquialisms ("I hear you"), features of spoken English ("at the j-o-b"), and what he refers to as "black English" establish a connection between speaker and listener ("But let's be real") as he argues for a more pluralistic and inclusive "translingual approach" to language.

RESPOND●

Write a paragraph or two (or three!) about your own use of languages and dialects. In what ways do you ordinarily "mesh" features of different dialects and/or languages? What languages did you grow up speaking and hearing and how do those languages enter into your writing today? How would you describe your own style of writing (and speaking)?

As you might guess from these examples, style always involves making choices about language across a wide range of situations. Style can be public or personal, conventional or creative, and everything in between. When you write, you'll find that you have innumerable tools and options for expressing yourself exactly as you need to. This chapter introduces you to some of them.

In her essay about the language we use to describe sexual violence, Roxane Gay presents a compelling example of the impact of subtle stylistic choices.

LINK TO P. 682

Style and Word Choice

Words matter—and those you choose will define the style of your arguments.

In spite of the extensive work on translingualism and code meshing, many academic arguments today still call for a formal or professional style using standard written English. Such language can sound weighty, and it usually is. It often uses technical terms and conventional vocabulary because that's what readers of academic journals or serious magazines and newspapers generally expect. Formal writing also typically avoids contractions, phrases that mimic speech, and sometimes even the pronoun *I*. (For information about the use of pronouns in contemporary writing, see p. 326.) But what may be most remarkable about the style is how little it draws attention to itself—and that's usually deliberate. Here's a paragraph from Annette Vee's *Coding Literacy: How Computer Programming Is Changing Writing*, published by MIT Press in 2017:

> [T]he concept of coding literacy helps to expand access, or to support "transformative access" to programming in the words of rhetorician Adam Banks.[24] For Banks, transformative access allows people "to

both change the interfaces of that system and fundamentally change the codes that determine how the system works."[25] Changing the "interface" of programming might entail more widespread education on programming. But changing "how the system works" would move beyond material access to education and into a critical examination of the values and ideologies embedded in that education. Programming as defined by computer science or software engineering is bound to echo the values of those contexts. But a concept of coding literacy suggests programming is a literacy practice with many applications beyond a profession defined by a limited set of values. The webmaster, game maker, tinkerer, scientist, and citizen activist can benefit from coding as a means to achieve their goals. As I argue in this book, we must think of programming more broadly—as coding literacy—if the ability to program is to become distributed more broadly. Thinking this way can help change "how the system works."

In this passage, Vee uses conventional standard written English, fairly complex syntax, and abstract terms (transformative access, interfaces, coding literacy) that she expects her readers will make sense of, though she draws the line at employing highly technical terms that only computer scientists would be familiar with. Also note the two footnote markers that identify her sources, also a staple of formal academic discourse. The tone is efficient and cool, the style academic and somewhat distanced.

Colloquial words and phrases, *slang*, and even first- and second-person pronouns (*I, me, we, you*) can create relationships with audiences that feel much more intimate. When you use everyday language in arguments, readers are more likely to identify with you personally and, possibly, with the ideas you represent or advocate. In effect, such vocabulary choices lessen the distance between you and readers.

Admittedly, some colloquial terms simply bewilder readers not tuned in to them. A movie review in *Rolling Stone* or a music review in *Spin* might leave your parents (or some authors) scratching their heads. Writing for the music Web site Pitchfork, Meaghan Garvey has this to say about Spanish R&B singer Bad Gyal's 2018 release:

> On "Blink," slow-winding dancehall rhythms with pulsing bass and staccato hand-claps climax in thumping reggaeton with hypnotic synth washes. Bad Gyal's voice stutters and chops along with the dembow drum loops, her melodies evoking an R-rated lullaby as she sings sweetly about grinding the club ("Me gusta el perreo").
> —Meaghan Garvey, "Bad Gyal, 'Blink'"

Huh? we say. But you probably get it.

CULTURAL CONTEXTS FOR ARGUMENT

A Note on Pronoun Preference

Conventions about personal pronouns are in flux right now, and particularly traditional third-person singular pronouns. You may have been asked what pronouns you prefer, since many people identify with neither of the traditional personal pronouns, namely *he* and *she*. For this reason, writers and speakers are sensitive to members of their audiences, realizing that some may prefer the use of singular *they* as in "Jamie called me and I called them back." Others prefer to use an alternate gender-neutral pronoun such as *ze* or *zir*. Linguist Peter Smagorinsky notes that it was only several decades ago that women, tired of having to be either *Mrs.* or *Miss*, coined the title *Ms.* It took some time, but eventually caught on:

It may well be that "ze" and "zir" will replace current pronouns over time. For those who reject "they" as grammatically improper while also recognizing that "he" and "she" are inadequate, it may become a reasonable development.

And of course, still others are just fine with the traditional *he* or *she*. The important point for writers and speakers is to be sensitive to these differences and to choose terms appropriately.

You will want to be careful, as Annette Vee is, with the use of *jargon*, the special vocabulary of members of a profession, trade, or field. Although jargon serves as shorthand for experts, it can alienate readers who don't recognize technical words or acronyms.

Another verbal key to an argument's style is its control of **connotation**, the associations that surround many words. Consider the straightforward connotative differences among the following three statements:

Students from the Labor Action Committee (LAC) carried out a hunger strike to call attention to the below-minimum wages that are being paid to campus temporary workers, saying, "The university must pay a living wage to all its workers."

Left-wing agitators and radicals tried to use self-induced starvation to stampede the university into caving in to their demands.

Champions of human rights put their bodies on the line to protest the university's tightfisted policy of paying temporary workers scandalously low wages.

The style of the first sentence is the most neutral, presenting facts and offering a quotation from one of the students. The second sentence uses loaded terms like *agitators, radicals,* and *stampede* to create a negative image of this event, while the final sentence uses other loaded words to create a positive view. As these examples demonstrate, the words you choose can change everything about a sentence.

Watch how Jason Collins, the first openly gay NBA star (see p. 116), uses the connotations of a common sports term to explain why he decided to come out:

> Now I'm a free agent, literally and figuratively. I've reached that enviable state in life in which I can do pretty much what I want. And what I want is to continue to play basketball. . . . At the same time, I want to be genuine and authentic and truthful.

Collins plays on the professional and figurative meanings of "free agent" to illustrate his desire to be honest about his sexual orientation.

RESPOND●

Exercise your critical reading muscles by reviewing the excerpts in this section and choose one or two words or phrases that you think are admirably selected or unusually interesting choices. Then explore the meanings and possibly the connotations of the word or words in a nicely developed paragraph or two.

Sentence Structure and Argument

Writers of effective arguments know that "variety is the spice of life" when it comes to stylish sentences. A strategy as simple as *varying sentence length* can keep readers attentive and interested. For instance, the paragraph from *Coding Literacy* in the preceding section (pp. 324–25) has sentences as short as ten words and as lengthy as twenty-seven. Now the author almost certainly didn't pause as she wrote and think, hmm, I need a little variation here. Instead, as an experienced writer, she simply made sure that her sentences complemented the flow of her ideas and also kept readers engaged.

Sentences, you see, offer you more options and special effects than you can ever exhaust. To pull examples from selections earlier in this chapter, just consider how dramatic, punchy, or even comic short sentences can be:

> **Hold up. I know what you gonna say.**
>
> —Donald McCrary

Longer sentences can explain ideas, build drama, or sweep readers along:

> **I, however, view black English as a public language because it is the language with which I learned about the world, including the perils of racism, the importance of education, and the consequences of improper conduct.**
>
> —Donald McCrary

> **Bad Gyal's voice stutters and chops along with the dembow drum loops, her melodies evoking an R-rated lullaby as she sings sweetly about grinding the club ("Me gusta el perreo").**
>
> —Meaghan Garvey, "Bad Gyal, 'Blink'"

Meanwhile, sentences of medium length handle just about any task assigned without a fuss. They are whatever you need them to be: serviceable, discrete, thoughtful, playful. And they pair up nicely with companions:

> **But without checks, democratically approved legislation can oppress minority groups. For that reason, our Constitution places limits on what a majority of the people may do.**
>
> —Sonia Sotomayor

Balanced or parallel sentences, in which clauses or phrases are deliberately matched, as highlighted in the following example, draw attention to ideas and relationships:

> *Ulysses* can be finished. The Internet is never finished.
>
> —Alexis C. Madrigal

And sentences that alternate sentence length can work especially well in much writing. For example, after one or more long sentences, the punch of a short sentence can be dramatic:

> **Previously, Ms. Collins was the first woman at *The Times* to hold the post of editorial page editor. The author of six books, she took time off in 2007—between the editorial page editor job and her column—and returned to write about the 2008 presidential election. She's been at it ever since.**
>
> —Susan Lehman, *The New York Times*, March 22, 2016

Sentences with complicated structures or interruptions make you pay attention to their motions and, therefore, their ideas:

> **As other voting requirements were gradually stripped away—location of birth, property ownership, race, and later sex—literacy and education began to stand in for those qualities in defining what it meant to be an American citizen.**
>
> **—Annette Vee**

Even sentence fragments—which don't meet all the requirements for full sentence status—have their place when used for a specific effect:

> **Right. Right. —Donald McCrary**

You see, then, that there's *much* more to the rhetoric of sentences than just choosing subjects, verbs, and objects—and far more than we can explain in one section. But you can learn a lot about the power of sentences simply by observing how the writers you admire engineer them—and maybe imitating some of those sentences yourself. You might also make it a habit to read and re-read your own sentences aloud (or in your head) as you compose them to gauge whether words and phrases are meshing with your ideas. And then tinker, tinker, tinker—until the sentences feel and sound right.

RESPOND.

Working with a classmate, first find a paragraph you both admire, perhaps in one of the selections in Part 2 of this book, and read it carefully and critically, making sure you understand its structure, syntax, and word choice. Then, individually write paragraphs of your own that imitate the sentences within it—making sure that both these new items are on subjects different from that of the original paragraph. When you are done, compare your paragraphs and pick out a few sentences you think are especially effective.

Punctuation and Argument

In a memorable comment, actor and director Clint Eastwood said, "You can show a lot with a look. . . . It's punctuation." He's certainly right about punctuation's effect, and it is important that as you read and write arguments, you consider punctuation closely.

"You can show a lot with a look. . . . It's punctuation." © Warner Bros./Photofest, Inc.

Eastwood may have been talking about the dramatic effect of end punctuation: the finality of periods; the tentativeness of ellipses (. . .); the query, disbelief, or uncertainty in question marks; or the jolt in the now-appearing-almost-everywhere exclamation point! Yet even exclamations can help create tone if used strategically. In an argument about the treatment of prisoners at Guantánamo, consider how Jane Mayer evokes the sense of desperation in some of the suspected terrorists:

> As we reached the end of the cell-block, hysterical shouts, in broken English, erupted from a caged exercise area nearby. "Come here!" a man screamed. "See here! They are liars! . . . No sleep!" he yelled. "No food! No medicine! No doctor! Everybody sick here!"
> —Jane Mayer, "The Experiment"

Punctuation that works within sentences can also do much to enhance meaning and style. The *semicolon*, for instance, marks a pause that is stronger than a comma but not as strong as a period. Semicolons function like "plus signs"; used correctly, they join items that are alike in structure, conveying a sense of balance, similarity, or even contrast. Do you recall Nathaniel Stein's parody of grading standards at Harvard University (see pp. 114–15)? Watch as he uses a semicolon to enhance the humor in his description of what an A+ paper achieves:

> Nearly every single word in the paper is spelled correctly; those that are not can be reasoned out phonetically within minutes.
> —Nathaniel Stein, "Leaked! Harvard's Grading Rubric"

In many situations, however, semicolons, with their emphasis on symmetry and balance, can feel stodgy, formal, and maybe even old-fashioned, and lots of writers avoid them, perhaps because they are very difficult to get right. Check a writing handbook before you get too friendly with semicolons.

Much easier to manage are colons, which function like pointers within sentences: they say *pay attention to this.* Philip Womack's London *Telegraph* review of *Harry Potter and the Deathly Hallows, Part 2* demonstrates how a colon enables a writer to introduce a lengthy illustration clearly and elegantly:

> The first scene of David Yates's film picks up where his previous installment left off: with a shot of the dark lord Voldemort's noseless face in triumph as he steals the most powerful magic wand in the world from the tomb of Harry's protector, Professor Dumbledore.
> —Philip Womack

And Paul Krugman of the *New York Times* shows how to use a colon to catch a reader's attention:

> Recently two research teams, working independently and using different methods, reached an alarming conclusion: The West Antarctic ice sheet is doomed.
> —Paul Krugman, "Point of No Return"

Colons can serve as lead-ins for complete sentences, complex phrases, or even single words. As such, they are versatile and potentially dramatic pieces of punctuation.

Like colons, dashes help readers focus on important, sometimes additional details. But they have even greater flexibility since they can be used singly or in pairs. Alone, dashes function much like colons to add information. Here's the *Washington Post*'s Eugene Robinson commenting pessimistically on a political situation in Iraq, using a single dash to extend his thoughts:

> The aim of U.S. policy at this point should be minimizing the calamity, not chasing rainbows of a unified, democratic, pluralistic Iraq—which, sadly, is something the power brokers in Iraq do not want.
> —Eugene Robinson, "The 'Ungrateful Volcano' of Iraq"

And here are paired dashes used to insert such information in the opening of the Philip Womack review of *Deathly Hallows* 2 cited earlier:

> *Harry Potter and the Deathly Hallows, Part 2*—the eighth and final film in the blockbusting series—begins with our teenage heroes fighting for their lives, and for their entire world.

As these examples illustrate, punctuation often enhances the rhythm of an argument. Take a look at how Maya Angelou uses a dash along with another punctuation mark—ellipsis points—to create a pause or hesitation, in this case one that builds anticipation:

> Then the voice, husky and familiar, came to wash over us—"The winnah, and still heavyweight champeen of the world . . . Joe Louis."
> —Maya Angelou, "Champion of the World"

It's probably worth mentioning that today we are seeing an upsurge in the use of ellipses on social media—a virtual onslaught of these little dots. Of course, in the very informal style of many texts and tweets, writers may be likely to omit end punctuation entirely. The use of ellipsis dots can signal a trailing off of a thought, leave open the possibility of further communication, or mimic conversational-style pauses. But they can also be a sign of laziness, as Matthew J. X. Malady points out in "Why Everyone and Your Mother Started Using Ellipses . . . Everywhere":

> Ellipses, then, . . . can help carefully structure a bit of written communication so that it mimics some of the more subtle, meaningful elements of face-to-face conversation. But when we want to be lazy, they also allow us to avoid thinking too much while crafting a message.

RESPOND.

First, read several movie reviews carefully and critically. Then try writing a brief movie review for your campus newspaper, experimenting with punctuation as one way to create an effective style. See if using a series of questions might have a strong effect, whether exclamation points would add or detract from the message you want to send, and so on. When you've finished the review, compare it to one written by a classmate, and look for similarities and differences in your choices of punctuation.

Special Effects: Figurative Language

You don't have to look hard to find examples of figurative language adding style to arguments. When a writing teacher suggests you take a weed whacker to your prose, she's using a figure of speech (in this case, a *metaphor*) to suggest you cut the wordiness. To indicate how little he trusts the testimony of John Koskinen, head of the Internal Revenue Service, political pundit Michael Gerson takes the metaphor of a "witch hunt" and flips it on the bureaucrat, relying on readers to recognize an *allusion* to Shakespeare's *Macbeth*:

> Democrats were left to complain about a Republican "witch hunt"—while Koskinen set up a caldron, added some eye of newt and toe of frog and hailed the Thane of Cawdor.
> —Michael Gerson, "An Arrogant and Lawless IRS"

Figurative language like this—indispensable to our ability to communicate effectively—dramatizes ideas, either by clarifying or enhancing the

The three witches from *Macbeth*, at their cauldron Chronicle/ Alamy Stock Photo

thoughts themselves or by framing them in language that makes them stand out. As a result, figurative language makes arguments attractive, memorable, and powerful. An apt simile, a timely rhetorical question, or a wicked understatement might do a better job bringing an argument home than whole paragraphs of evidence. Figurative language is not the icing on the cake: it's the cake itself!

Figures of speech are usually classified into two main types: **tropes**, which involve a change in the ordinary meaning of a word or phrase; and **schemes**, which involve a special arrangement of words. Here is a brief alphabetical listing—with examples—of some of the most familiar kinds.

Tropes

To create tropes, you often have to think of one idea or claim in relationship to others. Some of the most powerful—one might even say *inevitable*—tropes involve making purposeful comparisons between ideas: analogies, metaphors, and similes. Other tropes such as irony, signifying, and understatement are tools for expressing attitudes toward ideas: you might use them to shape the way you want your audience to think about a claim that you or someone else has made.

Allusion

An **allusion** is a connection that illuminates one situation by comparing it to another similar but usually more famous one, often with historical or literary connections. Allusions work with events, people, or concepts—expanding and enlarging them so readers better appreciate their significance. For example, a person who makes a career-ending blunder might be said to have met her *Waterloo*, the famous battle that terminated Napoleon's ambitions. Similarly, every impropriety in Washington brings up mentions of *Watergate*, the only scandal to lead to a presidential resignation; any daring venture becomes a *moon shot*, paralleling the ambitious program that led to a lunar landing in 1969. Using allusions can be tricky: they work only if readers get the connection. But when they do, they can pack a wallop. When on page 333 Michael Gerson mentions "eye of newt" and "toe of frog" in the same breath as IRS chief John Koskinen, he knows what fans of *Macbeth* are thinking. But other readers might be left clueless.

Analogy

Analogies compare two things, often point by point, either to show similarity or to suggest that if two concepts, phenomena, events, or even people are alike in one way, they are probably alike in other ways as well. Often extended in length, analogies can clarify or emphasize points of comparison, thereby supporting particular claims.

Here's the first paragraph of an essay in which a writer who is also a runner thinks deeply about the analogies between the two tough activities:

> When people ask me what running and writing have in common, I tend to look at the ground and say it might have something to do with discipline: You do both of those things when you don't feel like it, and make them part of your regular routine. You know some days will be harder than others, and on some you won't hit your mark and will want to quit. But you don't. You force yourself into a practice; the practice becomes habit and then simply part of your identity. A surprising amount of success, as Woody Allen once said, comes from just showing up.
>
> —Rachel Toor, "What Writing and Running Have in Common"

This cartoon creates an analogy in the way it depicts the relationship between North Korea and the United States. Lisa Benson, 2017/4/18, The Washington Post Writers Group

To be effective, an analogy has to make a good point and hold up to scrutiny. If it doesn't, it can be criticized as a faulty analogy, a fallacy of argument (see p. 93).

Antonomasia

Antonomasia is an intriguing trope that simply involves substituting a descriptive phrase for a proper name. It is probably most familiar to you from sports or entertainment figures: "His Airness" still means Michael Jordan; Aretha Franklin remains "The Queen of Soul"; Cleveland Cavaliers star LeBron James is "the King"; and Superman, of course, is "The Man of Steel." In politics, antonomasia is sometimes used neutrally (Ronald Reagan as "The Gipper"), sometimes as a backhanded compliment (Margaret Thatcher as "The Iron Lady"), and occasionally as a crude and racist put-down (Elizabeth Warren as "Pocahontas"). As you well know if you have one, nicknames can pack potent arguments into just one phrase.

Hyperbole

Hyperbole is the use of overstatement for special effect, a kind of fireworks in prose. The tabloid gossip magazines that scream at you in the checkout line survive by hyperbole. Everyone has seen these overstated arguments and perhaps marveled at the way they sell.

Hyperbole can, however, serve both writers and audiences when very strong opinions need to be registered. One senses exasperation in this excerpt from a list of the worst movies of 2017, which ranks *Pirates of the Caribbean: Dead Men Tell No Tales* as one of the most boring and worst films of that year:

> The (sigh) fifth movie in Disney's deathless series finds Johnny Depp and co. dead in the water. Remember when we loved the star's loose-and-boozy portrayal of Capt. Jack Sparrow, so fresh and charismatic 14 years ago? He was a joy. Now, you just want to smack the tricornered hat off his head and see him stranded on a godforsaken rock somewhere near the Marianas Trench.
>
> —John Serba, mlive.com

Irony

Irony is a complex trope in which words convey meanings that are in tension with or even opposite to their literal meanings. Readers who catch the irony realize that a writer is asking them (or someone else) to think about all the potential connotations in their language. One of the most famous uses of satiric irony in literature occurs in Shakespeare's *Julius Caesar* when Antony punctuates his condemnation of Caesar's assassins with the repeated word *honourable*. He begins by admitting, "So are they all, honourable men" but ends railing against "the honourable men / Whose daggers have stabb'd Caesar." Within just a few lines, Antony's funeral speech has altered the meaning of the term.

In popular culture, irony often takes a humorous bent in publications such as the *Onion* and the appropriately named *Ironic Times*. Yet even serious critics of society and politics use satiric devices to undercut celebrities and politicians, particularly when such public figures ignore the irony in their own positions.

Louise Linton, the Scottish actress, made news on Monday when she posted a photo to her Instagram account showing her and her husband [Secretary of the Treasury Steven Mnuchin] deplaning on an official trip to Kentucky. In her white wide-legged trousers and slim blouse,

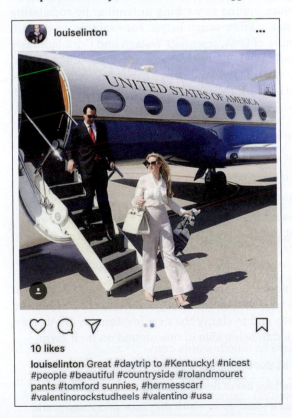

louiselinton ···

10 likes

louiselinton Great #daytrip to #Kentucky! #nicest #people #beautiful #countryside #rolandmouret pants #tomford sunnies, #hermesscarf #valentinorockstudheels #valentino #usa handbag held as though being presented in the crook of her arm, she looked every bit the jet-setting style-grammer. As any aspiring social media celebrity would, she took the opportunity to let her followers know not only what she thought of the bluegrass state, but also who she was wearing.

—Tony Bravo, "Louise Linton's Fashion Instagram
Post Reveals Her Entitlement"

The ironically negative responses to Linton came instantly: "Glad we could pay for your little getaway," Instagram user @jennimiller29 replied to Linton, ending with the hashtag "#deplorable." "Please don't tag your Hermes scarf," @emily.e.dickey responded, calling the hashtagging "Distasteful."

Metaphor

A bedrock of our language, **metaphor** creates or implies a comparison between two things, illuminating something unfamiliar by correlating it to something we usually know much better. For example, to explain the complicated structure of DNA, scientists Watson and Crick famously used items people would likely recognize: a helix (spiral) and a zipper. Metaphors can clarify and enliven arguments. In the following passage, novelist and poet Benjamin Sáenz uses several metaphors (highlighted) to describe his relationship to the southern border of the United States:

> It seems obvious to me now that I remained always a son of the border, a boy never quite comfortable in an American skin, and certainly not comfortable in a Mexican one. My entire life, I have lived in a liminal space, and that space has both defined and confined me. That liminal space wrote and invented me. It has been my prison, and it has also been my only piece of sky.

—Benjamin Sáenz, "Notes from Another Country"

In an example from Andrew Sullivan's blog, he quotes an 1896 issue of *Munsey's Magazine* that uses a metaphor to explain what, at that time, the bicycle meant to women and to clarify the new freedom it gave women who weren't accustomed to being able to ride around on their own:

> To men, the bicycle in the beginning was merely a new toy, another machine added to the long list of devices they knew in their work and play. To women, it was a steed upon which they rode into a new world.

And here is Kurt Andersen in the *Atlantic* writing about what he calls America's "lurch toward fantasy":

> For all the fun, and all the many salutary effects of the 1960s—the main decade of my childhood—I saw that those years had also been the big-bang moment for truthiness. And if the '60s amounted to a national nervous breakdown, we are probably mistaken to consider ourselves over it.

Metonymy

Metonymy is a rhetorical trope in which a writer uses a particular object to stand for a general concept. You'll recognize the move immediately in the expression "The *pen* is mightier than the *sword*"—which obviously is not about Bics and sabers. Metonyms are vivid and concrete ways of compacting big concepts into expressive packages for argument: the term *Wall Street* can embody the nation's whole complicated banking and investment system, while all the offices and officials of the U.S. military become the *Pentagon*. You can quickly think of dozens of expressions that represent larger, more complex concepts: *Nashville, Hollywood, Big Pharma, the Press, the Oval Office*, even perhaps *the electorate*.

Oxymoron

Oxymoron is a rhetorical trope that states a paradox or contradiction. John Milton created a classic example when he described Hell as a place of "darkness visible." We may be less poetic today, but we nevertheless

It's not just a street; it's a metonym!
Martin Lehmann/
Shutterstock

appreciate the creativity (or arrogance) in expressions such as *light beer*, *sports utility vehicle*, *expressway gridlock*, or *negative economic growth*. You might not have much cause to use this figure in your writing, but you'll get credit for noting and commenting on oxymoronic ideas or behaviors.

Rhetorical Question

Rhetorical questions, which we use frequently, are questions posed by a speaker or writer that don't really require answers. Instead, an answer is implied or unimportant. When you say "Who cares?" or "What difference does it make?" you're using such questions.

Rhetorical questions show up in arguments for many reasons, most often perhaps to direct readers' attention to the issues a writer intends to explore. For example, Erin Biba asks a provocative, open-ended rhetorical question in her analysis of Facebook "friending":

> So if we're spending most of our time online talking to people we don't even know, how deep can the conversation ever get?
>
> —Erin Biba, "Friendship Has Its Limits"

Signifying

Signifying, in which a speaker or writer cleverly and often humorously needles another person, is a distinctive trope found extensively in African American English. In the following passage, two African American men (Grave Digger and Coffin Ed) signify on their white supervisor (Anderson), who has ordered them to discover the originators of a riot:

> "I take it you've discovered who started the riot," Anderson said.
> "We knew who he was all along," Grave Digger said.
> "It's just nothing we can do to him," Coffin Ed echoed.
> "Why not, for God's sake?"
> "He's dead," Coffin Ed said.
> "Who?"
> "Lincoln," Grave Digger said.
> "He hadn't ought to have freed us if he didn't want to make provisions to feed us," Coffin Ed said. "Anyone could have told him that."
>
> —Chester Himes, *Hot Day, Hot Night*

Coffin Ed and Grave Digger demonstrate the major characteristics of effective signifying—indirection, ironic humor, fluid rhythm, and a surprising twist at the end. Rather than insulting Anderson directly by pointing out that he's asked a dumb question, they criticize the question

In these *Boondocks* strips, Huey signifies on Jazmine, using indirection, ironic humor, and two surprising twists. © THE BOONDOCKS © 1999 Aaron McGruder. Dist. By UNIVERSAL UCLICK. Reprinted with permission. All rights reserved.

indirectly by ultimately blaming a white man for the riot (and not just any white man, but one they're supposed to revere). This twist leaves the supervisor speechless, teaching him something and giving Grave Digger and Coffin Ed the last word—and last laugh.

Take a look at the example of signifying from a *Boondocks* cartoon (see above). Note how Huey seems to be sympathizing with Jazmine and then, in two surprising twists, reveals that he has been needling her all along.

Simile

A **simile** uses *like* or *as* to compare two things. Here's a simile from an essay about visiting Montana in the August 2017 *Hemispheres Magazine*:

> By now we've driven the cows to an open pasture. The wranglers teach me how to cut a cow from the herd, as real cowboys do. I find it's a lot like parallel parking, except the curb keeps moving to join the other curbs, and my car has lost respect for me.

> —Jacob Baynham, "Three Perfect Days: Montana"

And here is a series of similes, from an excerpt of a *Wired* magazine review of a new magazine for women:

> Women's magazines occupy a special niche in the cluttered info-scape of modern media. Ask any *Vogue* junkie: no girl-themed Web site or CNN segment on women's health can replace the guilty pleasure of slipping a glossy fashion rag into your shopping cart. Smooth as a pint of chocolate Häagen-Dazs, feckless as a thousand-dollar slip dress, women's magazines wrap culture, trends, health, and trash in a single, decadent package. But like the diet dessert recipes they print, these slick publications can leave a bad taste in your mouth.
>
> —Tiffany Lee Brown, "En Vogue"

Here, three similes—*smooth as a pint of chocolate Häagen-Dazs* and *feckless as a thousand-dollar slip dress* in the third sentence, and *like the diet dessert recipes* in the fourth—add to the image of women's magazines as a mishmash of "trash" and "trends."

Understatement

Understatement uses a quiet message to make its point. In her memoir, Rosa Parks—the civil rights activist who made history in 1955 by refusing to give up her bus seat to a white passenger—uses understatement so often that it becomes a hallmark of her style. She refers to her lifelong efforts to advance civil rights as just a small way of "carrying on."

Understatement can be particularly effective in arguments that might seem to call for its opposite. Outraged that New York's Metropolitan Opera has decided to stage *The Death of Klinghoffer*, a work depicting the murder by terrorists of a wheelchair-bound Jewish passenger on a cruise ship in 1985, writer Eve Epstein in particular points to an aria in which a terrorist named Rambo blames all the world's problems on Jews, and then, following an evocative dash, she makes a quiet observation:

> Rambo's aria echoes the views of *Der Stürmer*, Julius Streicher's Nazi newspaper, without a hint of irony or condemnation. The leitmotif of the morally and physically crippled Jew who should be disposed of has been heard before—and it did not end well.
>
> —Eve Epstein, "The Met's Staging of *Klinghoffer* Should Be Scrapped"

"It did not end well" alludes, of course, to the Holocaust.

RESPOND•

Use online sources (such as American Rhetoric's Top 100 Speeches at **americanrhetoric.com/top100speechesall.html**) to find the text of an essay or a speech by someone who uses figures of speech liberally. Pick a paragraph that is rich in figures and read it carefully and critically. Then rewrite it, eliminating every bit of figurative language. Then read the original and your revised version aloud to your class. Can you imagine a rhetorical situation in which your pared-down version would be more appropriate?

Schemes

Schemes are rhetorical figures that manipulate the actual word order of phrases, sentences, or paragraphs to achieve specific effects, adding stylistic power or "zing" to arguments. The variety of such devices is beyond the scope of this work. Following are schemes that you're likely to see most often, again in alphabetical order.

Anaphora

Anaphora, or effective repetition, can act like a drumbeat in an argument, bringing the point home. Sometimes an anaphora can be quite obvious, especially when the repeated expressions occur at the beginning of a series of sentences or clauses. Here is President Lyndon Johnson urging Congress in 1965 to pass voting rights legislation:

> There is no constitutional issue here. The command of the Constitution is plain.
> There is no moral issue. It is wrong—deadly wrong—to deny any of your fellow Americans the right to vote in this country.
> There is no issue of States rights or national rights. There is only the struggle for human rights.
> I have not the slightest doubt what will be your answer.

Repetitions can occur within sentences or paragraphs as well. Here, in an argument about the future of Chicago, Lerone Bennett Jr. uses repetition to link Chicago to innovation and creativity:

> [Chicago]'s the place where organized Black history was born, where gospel music was born, where jazz and the blues were reborn, where the Beatles and the Rolling Stones went up to the mountaintop to get the new musical commandments from Chuck Berry and the rock'n'roll apostles.
> —Lerone Bennett Jr. "Blacks in Chicago"

Antithesis

Antithesis is the use of parallel words or sentence structures to highlight contrasts or opposition:

> Marriage has many pains, but celibacy has no pleasures.
> —Samuel Johnson

> Those who kill people are called murderers; those who kill animals, sportsmen.

Inverted Word Order

Inverted word order is a comparatively rare scheme in which the parts of a sentence or clause are not in the usual subject-verb-object order. It can help make arguments particularly memorable:

> Into this grey lake plopped the thought, I know this man, don't I?
> —Doris Lessing

> Hard to see, the dark side is.
> —Yoda

Parallelism

Parallelism involves the use of grammatically similar phrases or clauses for special effect. Among the most common of rhetorical effects, parallelism can be used to underscore the relationships between ideas in phrases, clauses, complete sentences, or even paragraphs. You probably recognize the famous parallel clauses that open Charles Dickens's *A Tale of Two Cities*:

> It was the best of times,
>
> it was the worst of times . . .

The author's paralleled clauses and sentences go on and on through more than a half-dozen pairings, their rhythm unforgettable. Or consider how this unattributed line from the 2008 presidential campaign season resonates because of its elaborate and sequential parallel structure:

> Rosa sat so that Martin could walk. Martin walked so that Obama could run. Obama ran so that our children could fly.

RESPOND•

Identify the figurative language used in the following slogans. Note that some slogans may use more than one device.

"A day without orange juice is like a day without sunshine." (Florida Orange Juice)

"Taste the Feeling" (Coca-Cola)

"Be all that you can be." (U.S. Army)

"Breakfast of champions." (Wheaties)

"America runs on Dunkin'." (Dunkin' Donuts)

"Like a rock." (Chevrolet trucks)

CULTURAL CONTEXTS FOR ARGUMENT

Levels of Formality and Other Issues of Style

At least one important style question needs to be asked when arguing across cultures: what level of formality is most appropriate? In the United States, a fairly informal style is often acceptable and even appreciated. Many cultures, however, tend to value formality. If in doubt, err on the side of formality:

- Take care to use proper titles as appropriate (*Ms.*, *Mr.*, *Dr.*, etc.).
- Don't use first names unless you've been invited to do so.
- Steer clear of slang and jargon. When you're communicating with members of other cultures, slang may not be understood, or it may be seen as disrespectful.
- Avoid potentially puzzling pop cultural allusions, such as sports analogies or musical references, if your audience might not understand them.

When arguing across cultures or languages, another stylistic issue might be clarity. When communicating with people whose native languages are different from your own, analogies and similes almost always aid in understanding. Likening something unknown to something familiar can help make your argument forceful—and understandable.

14
Visual Rhetoric

LEFT TO RIGHT: H. Armstrong Roberts/ClassicStock/Getty Images; Junior Gonzalez/Getty Images; Grzegorz Knec/Alamy Stock Photo

During the summer of 2017, protesters and counterprotesters and counter-counterprotesters gathered across the United States in attempts to "unite the right," to "say no to white supremacy," to "make fascists afraid again," to rally for "blood and soil," to claim that "you will not replace us." Often the protesters carried symbols or flags, including the three depicted above: the American flag, the Confederate flag, and the flag of Nazi Germany (others carried a wide range of flags or banners, from Black Lives Matter and the Anti-Defamation League's "No Place for Hate" to the National Socialist Movement flag, the Southern Nationalist Flag, and the Identity Evropa flag, all three associated with white nationalism).

These banners and flags are powerful examples of visual rhetoric and the arguments such images can make. Even so small a sampling of visual rhetoric underscores what you doubtless already know: images grab and hold our attention, stir our emotions, tease our imaginations, provoke intense responses, and make arguments. In short, they have clout.

RESPOND.

Choose a flag or banner that speaks strongly to you and then study it carefully. What arguments—implicit and explicit—does the banner or flag make? What are its appeals and who does it seem to address? How do you respond to the image or symbol, and why? Are your responses based primarily on emotion, on logic and reason, on ethical considerations? Then write a paragraph in which you analyze your connection to this imagery.

The Power of Visual Arguments

Even in everyday situations, images—from T-shirts to billboards to animated films and computer screens—influence us. Media analyst Kevin Kelly ponders the role screens and their images now play in our lives:

> Everywhere we look, we see screens. The other day I watched clips from a movie as I pumped gas into my car. The other night I saw a movie on the backseat of a plane. We will watch anywhere. Screens playing video pop up in the most unexpected places—like ATM machines and supermarket checkout lines and tiny phones; some movie fans watch entire films in between calls. These ever-present screens have created an audience for very short moving pictures, as brief as three minutes, while cheap digital creation tools have empowered a new generation of filmmakers, who are rapidly filling up those screens. We are headed toward screen ubiquity.
>
> —Kevin Kelly, "Becoming Screen Literate"

Of course, visual arguments weren't invented by YouTube, and their power isn't novel either. The pharaohs of Egypt lined the banks of the Nile River with statues of themselves to assert their authority, and there is no shortage of monumental effigies in Washington, D.C., today.

Still, the ease with which all of us make and share images is unprecedented: people are uploading three billion shots a *day* to Snapchat. And most of us have easily adjusted to instantaneous multichannel, multimedia connectivity (see Chapter 16). We expect it to be seamless too. The prophet of this era was Marshall McLuhan, who nearly fifty years ago proclaimed that "the medium is the massage," with the play on *message* and *massage* intentional. As McLuhan says, "We shape our tools and afterwards our tools shape us. All media works us over completely."

Artist Sonny Assu uses the seemingly lighthearted medium and familiar iconography of breakfast cereals to make a serious claim about the victimization of Native Americans.

LINK TO P. 577

Not only the high and mighty: sculpture of a Great Depression–era breadline at the Franklin Delano Roosevelt Memorial in Washington, D.C. © Mel Longhurst/Photoshot

McLuhan was certainly prescient, as legendary filmmaker Werner Herzog makes clear in his 2016 documentary, *Lo and Behold: Reveries of the Connected World*. Herzog conducted interviews with a range of people— from computer scientists at UCLA and Carnegie Mellon to Silicon Valley denizens like Elon Musk and Sebastian Thrun to ordinary citizens caught up in use, abuse, and overuse—associated with the Internet. Herzog's instantly recognizable voice-over narrates the film's ten sections: as a reviewer for the *New Yorker* puts it, "It should be impossible to sound simultaneously droning and clipped, but somehow Herzog manages it, and it's delicious to watch the expressions on the faces of neuroscientists as he inquires, 'Could it be that the Internet starts to dream of itself?'"

The poster on the facing page aims to capture the complexity of "the connected world" as well as to suggest that we may well have lost our minds in the enormously complex, hugely wired world that now seems to "work us over" perhaps more than even McLuhan imagined. Take a close look at the poster and do some critical thinking about it and its effects. Note the four stars at the top under the heading, the figure dominating the poster (which appears to be a male wearing a suit and tie), the use of color to highlight the scramble in our Internet-filled heads, the change in font in the title, and the bottom caption "The human side of the digital revolution." How do image and text work together to create an argument and how would you express that argument? Certainly the poster intends to entice viewers to take in Herzog's film, but what other arguments can you detect there? Look back to Chapter 6 for more information on analyzing texts and images.

"Herzog weaves a fantastical tale. For those looking for a ride through our modern technological world, or indeed a preview of what is to come, this is it."

RESPOND•

Find an advertisement, poster, or flyer—either print or digital—that uses both verbal and visual elements. Analyze its argument first by pointing out the claims the ad makes (or implies) and then by identifying the ways it supports them verbally and/or visually. (If it helps, go over the questions about multimodal texts offered in Chapter 16 on pp. 388–91.) Then switch ads with a classmate and discuss his/her analysis. Compare your responses to the two ads. If they're different—and they probably will be—how might you account for the differences?

Using Visuals in Your Own Arguments

Given the power of images, it's only natural that you would use them in your own composing. In fact, many college instructors now expect projects for their courses to be posted to the Web, where digital photos, videos, and design elements are native. Other instructors invite or even require students to do multimedia reports or to use videos, photo collages, cartoons, or other media to make arguments. Using visual media in your academic writing can have all the reach and versatility of more conventional verbal appeals to pathos, ethos, and logos. Often even more.

Using Images and Visual Design to Create Pathos

Many advertisements, YouTube videos, political posters, rallies, marches, and even church services use visual images to trigger emotions. You can't flip through a magazine, watch a video, or browse the Web without being cajoled or seduced by figures or design elements of all kinds—most of them fashioned in some way to attract your eye and attention.

Technology has also made it incredibly easy for you to create on-the-spot photographs and videos that you can use for making arguments of your own. With a GoPro camera strapped to your head, you could document transportation problems in and around campus and then present your visual evidence in a paper or an oral report. You don't have to be a professional these days to produce poignant, stirring, or even satirical visual texts.

Yet just because images are powerful doesn't mean they always work. When you compose visually, you have to be certain to generate impressions that support your arguments, not weigh against them.

Consider the design choices made by the creators of the information security posters in Chapter 26. Which ones are most effective?

LINK TO P. 699

Shape Visuals to Convey Appropriate Feelings

To appeal visually to your readers' emotions, think first of the goal of your writing: you want every image or use of multimedia to advance that purpose. Consider, for a moment, the iconic *Apollo 8* "earthrise" photograph of our planet hanging above the horizon of the moon. You could adapt this image to introduce an appeal for additional investment in the space program. Or it might become part of an argument about the need to preserve frail natural environments, or a stirring appeal against nationalism: *From space, we are one world.* Any of these claims might be supported successfully without the image, but the photograph—like most visuals—will probably touch members of your audience more strongly than words alone could.

Still striking almost fifty years later, this 1968 *Apollo 8* photograph of the earth shining over the moon can support many kinds of arguments. NASA

Consider Emotional Responses to Color

As the "earthrise" photo demonstrates, color can have great power too: the beautiful blue earth floating in deep black space carries a message of its own. Indeed, our response to color is part of our biological and cultural makeup. So it makes sense to consider what shades are especially effective with the kinds of arguments you're making, whether they occur in images themselves or in elements such as headings, fonts, backgrounds, screens, banners, and so on. And remember that a black-and-white image can also be a memorable design choice.

Here's an image of the box cover for one of the iconic Zelda games for Nintendo. Note its simplicity and the use of vivid color: red dominates, signaling strength and adventure; the gold background and the gold-emblazoned shield and sword suggest fantasy. This particular game (*A Link to the Past*) was released in the United States in 1992.

Compare the 1992 box cover art with the most recent Zelda game, *Breath of the Wild* (2017). Here the cooler green and blue colors speak of the natural world and the adventures Link will encounter there.

When you think about using images like these in your writing, do some critical analysis of the image before you definitely decide on it. How does the image, and its use of color, help to support the argument you are making? Is it a good fit?

If you are creating images of your own, let your selection of colors be guided by your own good taste, by designs you admire, or by the advice of friends or helpful professionals. Some design and presentation software will even help you choose colors by offering dependable "default" shades or an array of pre-existing designs and compatible colors (for example, of presentation slides). To be emotionally effective, the colors you choose for a design should follow certain commonsense principles. If you're using background colors on a political poster, Web site, or slide, the contrast between words and background should be vivid enough to make reading easy. For example, white letters on a yellow background

Eve Arnold took this powerful black-and-white photograph in 1958 at a party in Virginia for students being introduced to mixed-race schools. How might a full-color image have changed the impact of the scene? © Eve Arnold/Magnum Photos

are not usually legible. Similarly, bright background colors should be avoided for long documents because reading is easiest with dark letters against a light or white background. Avoid complex patterns; even though they might look interesting and be easy to create, they often interfere with other more important elements of a presentation.

When you use visuals—either ones you've created or those you have taken from other sources—in your college projects, test them on prospective readers. That's what professionals do because they appreciate how delicate the choices of visual and multimedia texts can be. These responses will help you analyze your own arguments and improve your success with them.

Using Images to Establish Ethos

If you are on Instagram, Twitter, LinkedIn, or other social networking sites, you no doubt chose photographs for those sites with an eye to creating a sense of who you are, what you value, and how you wish to be perceived. You fashioned a self-image. So it shouldn't come as a surprise that you can boost your credibility as a writer by using visual design strategically: we know one person whose Facebook presentation of images and media so impressed a prospective employer that she got a job on the spot. So whether you are using photographs, videos, or other media on your personal pages or in your college work, it pays to attend to how they construct your ethos.

Understand How Images Enhance Credibility and Authority

You might have noticed that just about every company, organization, institution, government agency, or club now sports a logo or an emblem. Whether it's the Red Cross, the Canadian Olympic Committee, or perhaps the school you attend, such groups use carefully crafted images to signal their authority and trustworthiness. An emblem or a logo can also carry a wealth of cultural and historical implications. That's why university Web sites typically include the seal of the institution somewhere on the homepage (and always on its letterhead) or why the president of the United States travels with a presidential seal to hang on the speaker's podium.

What do the following posters, which circulated during the 2016 presidential election, suggest about each candidate's ethos? Based on these images, how would you describe each candidate as a politician?

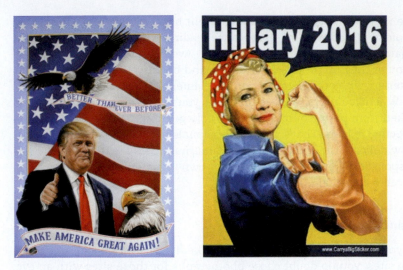

Posters from the 2016 election

Though you probably don't have a personal logo or trademark, your personal ethos functions the same way when you make an argument. You can establish it by offering visual evidence of your knowledge or competence. In an essay on safety issues in competitive biking, you might include a photo of yourself in a key race, embed a video showing how often serious accidents occur, or include an audio file of an interview with an injured biker. The photo proves that you have personal experience with biking, while the video and audio files show that you have done research and know your subject well, thus helping to affirm your credibility.

Predictably, your choice of *medium* also says something important about you. Making an appeal on a Web site sends signals about your technical skills, contemporary orientation, and personality. So if you direct people to a Facebook or Flickr page, be sure that any materials there present you favorably. Be just as careful in a classroom that any handouts or slides you use for an oral report demonstrate your competence. And remember that you don't always have to be high-tech to be effective: when reporting on a children's story that you're writing, the most sensible medium of presentation might be cardboard and paper made into an oversized book and illustrated by hand.

You demonstrate your ethos simply by showing an awareness of the basic design conventions for any kind of writing you're doing. It's no

Take a look at these three government logos, each of which intends to convey credibility, authority, and maybe more. Do they accomplish their goals? Why or why not?

accident that lab reports for science courses are sober and unembellished. Visually, they reinforce the professional ethos of scientific work. The same is true of a college research paper. So whether you're composing an essay, a résumé, a film, an animated comic, or a Web site, look for successful models and follow their design cues.

Consider How Details of Design Reflect Your Ethos

As we have just suggested, almost every design element you use in a paper or project sends signals about character and ethos. You might resent the tediousness of placing page numbers in the appropriate corner, aligning long quotations just so, and putting footnotes in the right place, but these details prove that you are paying attention. Gestures as simple as writing on official stationery (if, for example, you are representing a club or campus organization) or dressing up for an oral presentation matter too: suddenly you seem more mature and competent.

Even the type fonts that you select for a document can mark you as warm and inviting or as efficient and contemporary. The warm and inviting fonts often belong to a family called *serif*. The serifs are those little flourishes at the ends of the strokes that make the fonts seem handcrafted and artful:

warm and inviting (Bookman Old Style)

warm and inviting (Times New Roman)

warm and inviting (Georgia)

Cleaner, modern fonts go without those little flourishes and are called *sans serif*. These fonts are cooler, simpler, and, some argue, more readable on a computer screen (depending on screen resolution):

efficient and contemporary (Helvetica)

efficient and contemporary (Verdana)

efficient and contemporary (Comic Sans MS)

Other typographic elements send messages as well. The size of type can make a difference. If your text or headings are in boldface and too large, you'll seem to be shouting:

LOSE WEIGHT! PAY NOTHING!*

Tiny type, on the other hand, might make you seem evasive:

*Excludes the costs of enrollment and required meal purchases. Minimum contract: 12 months.

Finally, don't ignore the signals you send through your choice of *illustrations* and *photographs* themselves. Images communicate your preferences, sensitivities, and inclusiveness—sometimes inadvertently.

In March 2017, journalist Tim Murphy asked, "Who's missing from this photo of politicians deciding the future of women's health?" Notice anyone other than white men here?

Conference planners, for example, are careful to create brochures that represent all participants, and they make sure that the brochure photos don't show only women, only men, or only members of one racial or ethnic group.

RESPOND•

Choose a project or an essay you have written recently and read it critically for how well *visually* it establishes your credibility and how well it is designed. Ask a classmate or friend to look at it and describe the ethos you convey through the item. Then go back to the drawing board with a memo to yourself about how you might use images or media to improve it.

Using Visual Images to Support Logos

To celebrate the Fourth of July in 2017, ancestry.com, the online company that helps people identify their ancestors through DNA, aired a commercial called "Declaration Descendants." A still from one of the frames appears below.

In the commercial, people from a wide range of ethnicities recite parts of the American Declaration of Independence. At the conclusion, viewers learn that each of those readers is a descendent of someone who signed the Declaration. As the CEO of ancestry.com Vineet Mehra said about the advertisement, "We're all much more similar than you think. And we're using facts and data to prove it. This is not fluffy marketing. These are facts." Thus an online ancestry service uses images, facts, and data to support its major claim.

As this example shows, we get information from visual images of all kinds, including commercials we see on television and online every day. Today, much information comes to us in graphic presentations that use images along with words. Such images work well to gather information efficiently and persuasively. In fact, readers now expect evidence to be presented graphically, and we are learning to read such graphic representations more and more critically.

Organize Information Visually

Graphic presentation calls for design that enables readers and viewers to look at an item and understand what it does. A brilliant, much-copied example of such an intuitive design is a seat adjuster invented many years ago by Mercedes-Benz (see below). It's shaped like a tiny seat. Push any element of the control, and the real seat moves in that direction— back and forth, up and down. No instructions are necessary.

Good visual design can work the same way in an argument by conveying evidence, data, and other information without elaborate instructions. Titles, headings, subheadings, enlarged quotations, running heads, and boxes are some common visual signals:

Mercedes-Benz's seat adjuster
© Ron Kimball/KimballStock

- Use headings to guide your readers through your print or electronic document. For long and complex pieces, use subheadings as well, and make sure they are parallel.

- Use type font, size, and color to show related information among headings.

- Arrange headings or text on a page to enforce relationships among comparable items, ideas, or bits of evidence.

- Use a list or a box to set off material for emphasis or to show that it differs from the rest of the presentation. You can also use shading, color, and typography for emphasis.

- Place your images and illustrations strategically. What you position front and center will appear more important than items in less conspicuous places. Images of comparable size will be treated as equally important.

Remember, too, that design principles evolve and change from medium to medium. A printed text or presentation slide, for example, ordinarily works best when its elements are easy to read, simply organized, and surrounded by restful white space. But some electronic texts thrive on visual clutter, packing a grab bag of data into a limited space (see the "Infographic of Infographics" below). Look closely, though, and you'll probably find the logic in these designs.

Use Visuals to Convey Data Efficiently

Words are capable of great precision and subtlety, but some information is conveyed far more effectively by charts, graphs, drawings, maps, or photos—as several items in Chapter 4 illustrate. When making an argument, especially to a large group, consider what information might be more persuasive and memorable in nonverbal form.

A *pie chart* is an effective way of comparing parts to the whole. You might use a pie chart to illustrate the ethnic composition of your school,

An infographic © Ivan Cash, CashStudios.com

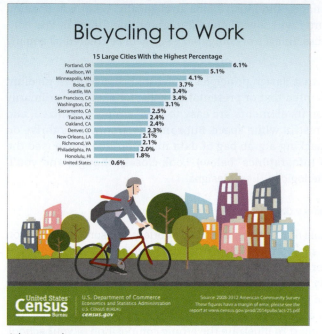

A bar graph

the percentage of taxes paid by people at different income levels, or the consumption of energy by different nations. Pie charts depict such information memorably.

A *graph* is an efficient device for comparing items over time or according to other variables. You could use a graph to trace the rise and fall of test scores over several decades, to show college enrollment by sex, race, and Hispanic origin, or to track bicycle usage in the United States, as in the bar graph above.

Diagrams or *drawings* are useful for attracting attention to details. Use drawings to illustrate complex physical processes or designs of all sorts. After the 2001 attack on the World Trade Center, for example, engineers prepared drawings and diagrams to help citizens understand precisely what led to the total collapse of the buildings.

You can use *maps* to illustrate location and spatial relationships—something as simple as the distribution of office space in your student union or as complex as poverty in the United States, as in the map

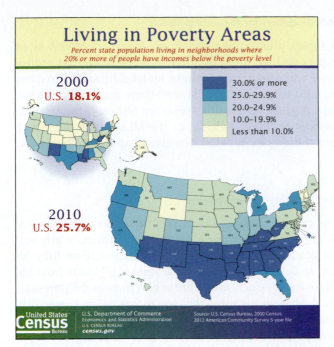

Living in Poverty Areas

*Percent state population living in neighborhoods where
20% or more of people have incomes below the poverty level*

2000
U.S. **18.1%**

2010
U.S. **25.7%**

- 30.0% or more
- 25.0–29.9%
- 20.0–24.9%
- 10.0–19.9%
- Less than 10.0%

United States Census Bureau
U.S. Department of Commerce
Economics and Statistics Administration
U.S. CENSUS BUREAU
census.gov

Source: U.S. Census Bureau, 2000 Census.
2012 American Community Survey 5-year file

A map

shown here. In fact, scholars in many fields now use geographic information system (GIS) technology to merge maps with databases in all
fields to offer new kinds of arguments about everything from traffic
patterns and health care trends to character movements in literary
works. Plotting data this way yields information far different from
what might be offered in words alone. You can find more about GIS
applications online.

Timelines allow you to represent the passage of time graphically, and
online tools like Sutori or Our Story or Office Timeline can help you create them for insertion into your documents. Similarly, Web pages can
make for valuable illustrations. Programs like ShrinkTheWeb's Snapito
let you create snapshots of Web sites that can then be inserted easily
into your writing. And when you want to combine a variety of graphs,
charts, and other texts into a single visual argument, you might create
an *infographic* using free software such as Canva Infographic Maker,
Google Charts, Easel.ly, Venngage, or Pictochart.

Follow Professional Guidelines for Presenting Visuals

Charts, graphs, tables, illustrations, timelines, snapshots of Web sites, and video clips play such an important role in many fields that professional groups have come up with guidelines for labeling and formatting these items. You need to become familiar with those conventions as you advance in a field. A guide such as the *Publication Manual of the American Psychological Association*, Sixth Edition, or the *MLA Handbook*, Eighth Edition, describes these rules in detail. See also Chapter 15, "Presenting Arguments."

Remember to Check for Copyrighted Material

You also must be careful to respect copyright rules when using visual items that were created by someone else. If you do introduce any borrowed items into academic work, be careful to document them fully. It's relatively easy these days to download visual texts of all kinds from the Web. Some of these items—such as clip art or government documents—may be in the *public domain*, meaning that you're free to use them without requesting permission or paying a royalty. But other visual texts may require permission, especially if you intend to publish your work or use the item commercially. Remember: anything you place on a Web site is considered "published." (See Chapter 21 for more on intellectual property and fair use.)

15
Presenting Arguments

LEFT TO RIGHT: Teach For America, Inc.; Drew Angerer/Getty Images

For some arguments you make in college, the format you've used since middle school is still a sensible choice—a traditional paper with double spacing, correct margins, MLA- or APA-style notes, and so on. Printed texts like these offer a methodical way to explain abstract ideas or to set down complicated chains of reasoning. Even spruced up with images or presented online (to enable color, media, and Web links), such conventional arguments—whether presented as essays, newsletters, or brochures—are cheap to create and easy to reproduce and share. You will find examples of printed texts throughout this book and especially in Part 4 on "Research and Arguments."

But print isn't your only medium for advancing arguments. Increasingly, you'll need to make a case orally, drawing on the visual or multimedia strategies discussed in previous chapters. Like Clint Smith, author of *How to Raise a Black Son in America*, delivering a TED talk, you might need illustrations or slides to back up a lecture; or, like Ambassador Nikki Haley, speaking on North Korea at the United Nations, you may find yourself engaged in serious discussions; or, maybe like college

363

sophomore Michael Bereket, you might receive an award for original research presented orally. Knowing how to speak eloquently to a point is a basic rhetorical skill.

Class and Public Discussions

No doubt you find yourself arguing all the time at school, maybe over a piece of code with a classmate in a computer science course, or perhaps with a teaching assistant whose interpretation of economic trends you're sure is flat wrong. Or maybe you spoke up at a campus meeting against the administration's latest policy on "free speech zones"—*or wish you had.* The fact is, lots of people are shy about joining class discussions or public debates, even those that interest them: indeed, the National Institute of Mental Health finds that Americans dread public speaking more than almost anything else!

Even if you are a little shy about jumping into a discussion or being part of a spirited debate, you can improve your participation in such situations by observing both effective and ineffective speakers. Watch how the participants who enliven a discussion stay on topic, add new information or ideas, and pay attention to all members of the group. Notice, too, that less successful speakers often can't stop talking, somehow make all discussions about themselves, or just play the smart aleck when they don't know much about a topic. We know you can do better than that!

You can start just by joining in on conversations whenever you can. If speaking is a problem, take it slow at first—a comment or two,

In "Balancing Classroom Civility and Free Speech," historian Catherine Nolan-Ferrell describes the heated political discussions that her students engage in, both in and out of the classroom.

LINK TO P. 772

1999, Dilbert by Scott Adams/Andrews McMeel Syndication

something as simple as "That's a really good idea!" or "I wonder how accurate this data is?" The more that you hear your own voice in discussions, the more comfortable you'll be offering your opinions in detail. Here are some more tips:

- Do the required reading in a class so that you know what you're talking about. That alone will give you a leg up in most groups.
- Listen carefully, purposefully, and respectfully, and jot down important points.
- Speak briefly to the point under discussion so that your comments are relevant. Don't do all the talking.
- Ask questions about issues that bother you: others probably have the same thoughts.
- Occasionally, summarize points that have already been made to make sure that everyone is "on the same page." Keep the summary brief.
- Respond to questions or comments by others in specific rather than vague terms.
- Try to learn the names of people in a discussion, and then use them.
- When you're already a player in a discussion, invite others to join in.

National Public Radio reporter Jorge Encinas sheds light on how Spanish-speaking baseball players are often depicted negatively in the press because of their lack of native English skills.

LINK TO P. 689

CULTURAL CONTEXTS FOR ARGUMENT

Speaking Up in Class

Speaking up in class is viewed as inappropriate or even rude in some cultures. In North America, however, doing so is expected and encouraged. Some instructors even assign credit for such class participation.

Reconsidering Confrontation

Be aware that while North Americans often like to get straight to the point, even if it means being confrontational, a number of cultures find such tactics aggressive, rude, and ineffective. East Asians, for example, generally prefer working behind the scenes to reach accord, if possible. Rather than employing direct confrontation with such an audience, experts on cross-cultural communication suggest drawing attention to issues or concerns through the use of stories, analogies, or metaphors.

Preparing a Presentation

You've probably already been asked to deliver a presentation in one or more of your college classes. That's partly because the ability to explain material clearly to an audience is a skill much admired by potential employers and partly because so much information today is shared orally, online or off. Unfortunately, instructors sometimes give little practical advice about how to hone that talent, which is not a natural gift for most of us. While it's hard to generalize here, capable presenters attribute their success to the following strategies and perceptions:

- They make sure they know their subjects thoroughly.
- They pay attention to the values, ideas, and needs of their listeners.
- They use language, patterns, gestures, eye contact, and style to make their spoken arguments easy to follow.
- They realize that oral arguments are interactive. (Live audiences can argue back!)
- They appreciate that most oral presentations involve visuals, and they plan accordingly. (We'll address multimedia presentations in the next chapter.)
- They practice, practice—and then practice some more.

We suggest a few additional moves for when you are specifically required to make a formal argument or presentation in class (or on the job): assess the rhetorical situation you face, nail down the details of the presentation, fashion a script or plan, choose media to fit your subject, and then deliver a good show.

Assess the Rhetorical Situation

Whether asked to make a formal oral report in class, to speak to the general public, or to join a panel discussion, ask yourself the same questions about rhetorical choices that you face whenever you make an argument.

Understanding Purpose. Figure out the major purpose of the assignment or situation. Is it to inform and enlighten your audience? To convince or persuade them? To explore a concept or principle? To stimulate discussion? To encourage a decision? Something else? Very important in school, will you be speaking to share your expertise or to prove that you have it (as you might in a class report)?

Assessing the Audience. Determine who will be listening to your talk. Just an instructor and classmates? Interested observers at a public meeting? People who know more about the subject than you do—or less? Or will you be a peer of the audience members—typically, a classmate? What mix of age groups, of gender, of political and religious affiliation, of rank, etc., will be in the group? What expectations will listeners bring to the talk, and what opinions are they likely to hold? Will this audience be invited to ask questions after the event?

Deciding on Content. What exactly is the topic for the presentation? What is its general scope? Are you expected to make a narrow and specific argument drawn from a research assignment? Are you expected to argue facts, definitions, causes and effects? Will you be offering an evaluation or perhaps a proposal? What degree of detail is necessary, and how much evidence should you provide for your claims?

Choosing Structure and Style. Nancy Duarte, who consults with and coaches speakers, did an extensive study of great presentations—hundreds and hundreds of them. After analyzing their structures, she found that most of the very successful presenters used a basic two-part structure, beginning with describing the current problem or situation (the status quo), and then moving to what the solution(s) might be, going back and forth between the status quo and what could and should be the case.

Rob Greenfield pays careful attention to the different audiences of his blog post, "An Argument against Veganism … from a Vegan," addressing the needs and values of both vegans and meat eaters.

LINK TO P. 609 ....

Here are students who are attending a House of Representatives session of the Mississippi State legislature and who look pretty darned bored: what might some of the speakers do to re-engage them? Rogelio V. Solis/AP Images

She also found that successful speakers embedded this structure in a story or stories and that they concluded with a call to action. You might keep these findings in mind, especially if your instructor does not specify a particular structure or type of presentation. Or perhaps your instructor will tell you that your talk should include an introduction, background information, thesis, evidence, refutation, discussion, conclusion. If so, look for other presentations you have heard or public events you have attended to look for models. What tone will your audience expect? Serious? Friendly and colloquial? Perhaps even funny? And finally, what are the standards by which your presentation will be evaluated?

Following are three excerpts from a detailed, three-page outline that sophomore George Chidiac worked up to prepare for a fifteen-minute oral presentation on Thomas More's "Petition for Free Speech" (1523)—an important document on the path to establishing free speech as a natural right. Chidiac's outline of rhetorical issues and concerns prepped him well enough to deliver the entire presentation without notes. His thesis is highlighted, but also notice the question Chidiac asks at the very end: *So what?* He recognizes an obligation to explain why his report should matter to his audience.

Oral Presentation Outline

Requirements: 15 minutes; share what I've learned in my research; help colleagues appreciate the research I've done

Introduction: Introduce myself and my agenda; define free speech: the right to express any opinions without censorship or restraint

> Set the stage: From history of free speech, we are going to micro-focus: Renaissance > 16th-century England > April 18, 1523, in the House of Commons
>
> Present a dilemma: The king called all his advisers and those able to enact legislation to raise funds to go to war. You are the intermediary between the main legislative body and the king. You have three obligations: one to truth, one to the king, and one to the body you're representing. The king wants money, the legislative body cannot object, and you want truth and the best outcome to win out. How do you *reconcile* this?

What:

What's my message? What's the focal point of my presentation?

> To provide a snapshot in time of the evolution of free speech:
>
> Thomas More, in his *Petition for Free Speech,* incrementally advanced free speech as a duty and a right.

Who:

Who made this happen? Who was involved?

> Thomas More: (before he became Speaker → Chancellor of England, friend of King Henry VIII, theologian, poet, father)
>
> Henry VIII
>
> William Roper (minor role—son-in-law and chief biographer)

Why:

Why was More's Petition "successful"? Why did Henry VIII accept the petition?

> Henry VIII's character as a humanist; spirit of *amicitia*—friendship with counsel
>
> Parliamentary expectations; relationship between king and Parliament; by accepting the petition, Henry acknowledged that while not all parliamentary speech should be *permitted*, not all speech critical of monarchy is *slanderous*

SO WHAT?

What do I want my colleagues to take away from this?

> Freedom of speech we have today wasn't always enjoyed.

Nail Down the Specific Details

Big-picture rhetorical considerations are obviously important in an oral presentation, but so are the details. Pay attention to exactly how much time you have to prepare for an event, a lecture, or a panel session, and how long the actual presentation should be: *never* infringe on the time of other speakers. Determine what visual aids, slides, or handouts might make the presentation successful. Will you need a laptop and "clicker" to move between slides, an overhead projector, a flip chart, a whiteboard? Decide whether presentation software, such as PowerPoint, Keynote, or Prezi, will help you make a stronger presentation. Then figure out where to acquire the equipment as well as the expertise to use it. If you run into problems, especially with classroom presentations, ask your instructor and fellow students for help. If possible, check out where your presentation will take place. In a classroom with fixed chairs? A lecture or assembly hall? An informal sitting area? Will you have a lectern? Other equipment? Will you sit or stand (research shows that standing makes for a stronger performance)? Remain in one place or move around? What will the lighting be, and can you adjust it? Take nothing for granted, and if you plan to use media equipment, be ready with a backup strategy if a projector bulb dies or a Web site won't load.

Not infrequently, oral presentations are group efforts. When that's the case, plan and practice accordingly. The work should be divvied up according to the strengths of the participants: you will need to figure out who speaks when, who handles the equipment, who takes the questions, and so on.

Fashion a Script Designed to Be Heard by an Audience

Unless you are presenting a formal lecture (pretty rare in college), most oral presentations are delivered from notes. But even if you do deliver a live presentation from a printed text, be sure to compose a script that is designed to be *heard* rather than *read*. Such a text—whether in the form of note cards, an overhead list, or a fully written-out paper—should feature a strong introduction and conclusion, an unambiguous structure with helpful transitions and signposts, concrete diction, and straightforward syntax.

Strong Introductions and Conclusions. Like readers, listeners remember beginnings and endings best. Work hard, therefore, to make these elements of your spoken argument memorable and personable. Consider including a provocative or puzzling statement, opinion, or question; a memorable anecdote; a powerful quotation; or a strong visual image. If you can connect your report directly to the interests or experiences of your listeners in the introduction or conclusion, then do so.

Meet Juliana Chang, who provides a strong opening to her research-based presentation. She opens her talk with a slide announcing the title and occasion, then plunges into her topic with a vivid second slide showing a photo of her mother holding her:

The title slide of Juliana's presentation
Juliana Chang

Baby Juliana and her mother
Juliana Chang

This is a photo of my mother and me at our very first home in America. My family immigrated to the U.S. when I was six months old. My mother was 36. Even though she spoke no English when she first arrived, she dedicated the next two decades of her life to raising my brother and me as Americans. Although Mandarin was my first language growing up, by the time I got to high school, I had forgotten almost everything. My mother and I could still communicate, but it was on a basic level. I could tell her what I wanted for dinner but not what I wanted to do with my life. She could tell me how messy my room was but not how devastated she felt after the 2016 election. I had lost my language and in turn lost an invaluable part of our relationship.

My name is Juliana Chang and today I'd like to talk with you about Heritage Language Loss in Second Generation East Asian Americans.

Speaking to a group of instructors and peers, Juliana begins with a vivid photo and a personal anecdote that aims to pull the audience into her talk and keep their attention. Note that she uses straightforward vocabulary, simple syntax, and concrete examples to lead up to her title and suggest her (at this point implied) thesis: East Asian Americans should do everything they can to hold onto their heritage language while also becoming totally fluent in English.

Like Juliana, be sure that your introduction clearly explains what your presentation will cover, what your focus will be, and perhaps even how the presentation will be arranged. Give listeners a mental map of where you are taking them. If you are using presentation software, a bare-bones outline sometimes makes sense, especially when the argument is a straightforward academic presentation: thesis + evidence.

The conclusion should drive home and reinforce your main point. You can summarize the key arguments you have made (again, a simple slide could do some of the work), but you don't want to end with just a rehash, especially when the presentation is short. Instead, conclude by underscoring the *implications* of your report: what do you want your audience to be thinking and feeling at the end?

In her conclusion, Juliana Chang says she wants to "close the way I opened, with a story," and shows another photo of her as an infant, this time with her beloved grandmother in Taiwan.

She then recites a poem written for the occasion, called "This is What Language Loss Looks Like," part of which says

How could I have known what I was giving up? She holds my hand and asks me a question I can no longer understand. When I shake my head and offer her a blank smile, she falters. Here is the part when I wish I

Juliana ends her presentation with a treasured photo. Juliana Chang

knew how to say I'm sorry. Remember the street with the Taro and thick, thick rain? Remember how we got lost? Remember how I talked all the way home?

The body of Juliana's presentation was full of evidence drawn from her extensive research—lots of logical proof in the form of facts and figures—all of which contributes to and supports her thesis. But for her opening and closing, she leans in on pathos and emotional appeals, painting a picture of her young self with her mother and grandmother—and what losing her first language has meant. The contrast she paints with the words of her conclusion, of her recently standing mute by her grandmother's side but of her "talking all the way home" as a child tells us "what language loss looks like."

Citations

Alba, R., Logan, J., Lutz, A., & Stults, B. (2002). Only english by the third generation? loss and preservation of the mother tongue among the grandchildren of contemporary immigrants. Demography, 39(3), 467-484.

Birner, B. (2016). Bilingualism The Linguistic Society of America.

Brown, C. L. (2009). Heritage language and ethnic identity: A case study of korean-american college students. International Journal of Multicultural Education, 11(1)

Crawford, J. (1992). Language loyalties: A source book on the official english controversy University of Chicago Press.

Gudykunst, W. B. (1999). Asian american ethnicity and communication. London: Sage Publications.

Huynh, Q. (2011). Perpetual foreigner in one's own land: Potential implications for identity and psychological adjustment. J Soc Clin Psych, 30(2)

Jo, H. Y. (2002). Negotiating ethnic identity in the college korean language classes. Identities: Global Studies in Culture and Power,

Kent, Mary & Lalasz, Robert. (2006). In the news: Speaking english in the united states. Population Reference Bureau,

Juliana's presentation ends with her cited sources. Juliana Chang

Clear Structures and Signposts. For a spoken argument, you want your organizational structure to be crystal clear. So make sure that you have a sharply delineated beginning, middle, and end and share the structure with listeners. You can do that by remembering to pause between major points of your presentation and to offer *signposts* marking your movement from one topic to the next. They can be transitions as obvious as *next, on the contrary,* or *finally.* Such words act as memory points in your spoken argument and thus should be explicit and concrete: *The second crisis point in the breakup of the Soviet Union occurred hard on the heels of the first,* rather than just *The breakup of the Soviet Union led to another crisis.*

You can also keep listeners on track by repeating key words and concepts and by using unambiguous topic sentences to introduce each new idea. These transitions can also be highlighted as you come to them on a whiteboard or on presentation slides.

Straightforward Syntax and Concrete Diction. Avoid long, complicated sentences in an oral presentation and use straightforward syntax (subject-verb-object, for instance, rather than an inversion of that order). Remember, too, that listeners can grasp concrete verbs and nouns more easily than they can mentally process a steady stream of abstractions. When you need to deal with abstract ideas, illustrate them with concrete examples.

Take a look at the following text that student Ben McCorkle wrote about *The Simpsons*, first as he prepared it for an essay and then as he adapted it for a live oral and multimedia presentation:

Print Version

The Simpson family has occasionally been described as a *nuclear* family, which obviously has a double meaning: first, the family consists of two parents and three children, and, second, Homer works at a nuclear power plant with very relaxed safety codes. The overused label "dysfunctional," when applied to the Simpsons, suddenly takes on new meaning. Every episode seems to include a scene in which son Bart is being choked by his father, the baby is being neglected, or Homer is sitting in a drunken stupor transfixed by the television screen. The comedy in these scenes comes from the exaggeration of commonplace household events (although some talk shows and news programs would have us believe that these exaggerations are not confined to the madcap world of cartoons).

—Ben McCorkle, "*The Simpsons*: A Mirror of Society"

Oral Version (with a visual illustration)

What does it mean to describe the Simpsons as a *nuclear* family? Clearly, a double meaning is at work. First, the Simpsons fit the dictionary meaning—a family unit consisting of two parents and some children. The second meaning, however, packs more of a punch. You see, Homer works at a nuclear power plant [pause here] with *very* relaxed safety codes!

Still another overused family label describes the Simpsons. Did everyone guess I was going to say *dysfunctional*? And like *nuclear*, when it comes to the Simpsons, *dysfunctional* takes on a whole new meaning.

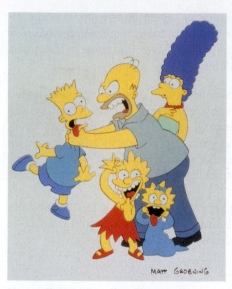

Homer Simpson in a typical pose © Fox/
Photofest, Inc.

Remember the scene when Bart is being choked by his father?

How about the many times the baby is being neglected?

Or the classic view—Homer sitting in a stupor transfixed by the TV screen!

My point here is that the comedy in these scenes often comes from double meanings—and from a lot of exaggeration of every-day household events.

Note that the second version presents the same information as the first, but this time it's written to be *heard*. The revision uses simpler syntax, so the argument is easy to listen to, and employs signposts, repetition, a list, and italicized words to prompt the speaker to give special emphasis where needed.

RESPOND.

Take three or four paragraphs from an essay that you've recently written. Then, following the guidelines in this chapter, rewrite the passage to be heard by a live audience. Finally, make a list of every change that you made.

The Power of Silence. As you work on your delivery, consider the role that pauses, or silences, may play in helping to get your point across. In her oral presentation on language loss, Juliana Chang paused dramatically during her conclusion, marking off the closing questions with a pause before each one. These silent moments held her audience's attention and created anticipation for what was coming next. During the March for Our Lives in the spring of 2018, following the killing of seventeen Florida high school students and staff members, high school senior Emma Gonzalez stood before the huge rally in Washington, D.C., called out the names of the seventeen who died, and then stood, in silence, for the length of time it had taken the shooter to take those lives. Broadcast on national television, it was a riveting, moving, and *silent* call to action.

Emma Gonzalez's moment of silence at March of Our Lives made a powerful statement. Chip Somodevilla/Getty Images

Repetition, Parallelism, and Climactic Order. Whether they're used alone or in combination, repetition, parallelism, and climactic order are especially appropriate for spoken arguments that sound a call to arms or that seek to rouse the emotions of an audience. Perhaps no person in the twentieth century used them more effectively than Martin Luther King Jr., whose sermons and speeches helped to spearhead the civil rights movement. Standing on the steps of the Lincoln Memorial in Washington, D.C., on August 23, 1963, with hundreds of thousands of marchers before him, King called on the nation to make good on the "promissory note" represented by the Emancipation Proclamation.

Look at the way that King uses repetition, parallelism, and climactic order in the following paragraph to invoke a nation to action:

> It is obvious today that America has defaulted on this promissory note insofar as her citizens of color are concerned. Instead of honoring this sacred obligation, America has given the Negro people a bad *check* which has come back marked "*insufficient funds.*" But *we* refuse to believe that the bank of justice is bankrupt. *We* refuse to believe that there are *insufficient funds* in the great vaults of opportunity of this nation. So *we have come* to cash this *check*—a *check* that will give us upon demand the riches of freedom and the security of justice. We *have also come* to this hallowed spot to remind America of the fierce urgency of now. There is no time to engage in the luxury of cooling off or to take the tranquillizing drug of gradualism. *Now* is the time *to rise* from the dark and desolate valley of segregation to the sunlit path of racial justice. *Now* is the time *to open* the doors of opportunity to all of

Francis Miller/Getty Images

God's children. *Now* is the time *to lift* our nation from the quicksands
of racial injustice to the solid rock of brotherhood.
                                   —Martin Luther King Jr., "I Have a Dream" (emphasis added)

The italicized words highlight the way that King uses repetition to drum
home his theme and a series of powerful verb phrases (*to rise*, *to open*,
to lift) to build to a strong climax. These stylistic choices, together with
the vivid image of the "bad check," help to make King's speech powerful,
persuasive—and memorable.

    You don't have to be as highly skilled and as eloquent as King to
take advantage of the power of repetition and parallelism. Simply
repeating a key word in your argument can impress it on your audience
(as Juliana Chang does at the end of her presentation when she repeats
"remember"), as can arranging parts of sentences or items in a list in
parallel order.

Choose Media to Fit Your Subject

Visual materials—charts, graphs, posters, and presentation slides—are
major tools for conveying your message and supporting your claims.

People are so accustomed to visual (and aural) texts that they genuinely expect to see them in most oral presentations. And, in many cases, a picture, video, or graph can truly be worth a thousand words. (For more about visual argument, see Chapter 14.)

Successful Use of Visuals. Be certain that any visuals that you use are large enough to be seen by all members of your audience. If you use slides or overhead projections, the information on each frame should be simple, clear, and easy to process. For slides, use 24-point type for major headings, 18 point for subheadings, and at least 14 point for other text. Remember, too, to limit the number of words per slide. The same rules of clarity and simplicity hold true for posters, flip charts, and whiteboards. (Note that if your presentation is based on source materials—either text or images—remember to include a slide that lists all those sources at the end of the presentation.)

Use appropriate software to furnish an overview for a presentation or lecture and to give visual information and signposts to listeners. Audiences will be grateful to see the people you are discussing, the key data points you are addressing, the movement of your argument as it develops. But if you've watched many oral presentations, you're sure to have seen some bad ones. Perhaps nothing is deadlier than a speaker who stands up and just reads from each screen—and we've all heard those jokes about "death by PowerPoint." Do this and you'll just put people to sleep. Also remember not to turn your back on your audience when you refer to these visuals. And if you prepare supplementary materials (such as bibliographies or other handouts), don't distribute them until the audience actually needs them, or wait until the end of the presentation so that they don't distract listeners from your spoken arguments. (For advice on creating multimodal arguments, see Chapter 16.)

The best way to test the effectiveness of any images, slides, or other visuals is to try them out on friends, family members, classmates, or

Presentation woes by Dr. Jorge Cham

roommates. If they don't get the meaning of the visuals right away, revise and try again.

Accommodations for Everyone. Remember that visuals and accompanying media tools can help make your presentation accessible but that some members of your audience may not be able to see your presentation or may have trouble seeing or hearing them. Here are a few key rules to remember:

- Use words to describe projected images. Something as simple as "That's Eleanor Roosevelt in 1944" can help audience members who have impaired vision appreciate what's on a screen.

- Use large print on slides so that people in the last row will be able to read it.

- Try to determine whether anyone in your audience will need some accommodation, such as an interpreter who can sign for people who are hearing impaired or who can describe visuals to anyone who can't see them.

- If you use video, take the time to label sounds that might not be audible to audience members who are hearing impaired. (Be sure your equipment is caption capable and use the captions; they can be helpful to everyone when audio quality is poor.)

- For a lecture, consider providing a written handout that summarizes your argument or putting the text on an overhead projector—for those who learn better by reading *and* listening.

Deliver a Good Show

When asked to identify the most important part of rhetoric, the ancient Greek orator Demosthenes replied that there are *three* most important parts: "Delivery, delivery, and delivery." This insight is as appropriate today as it was in the fourth century BCE—perhaps even more so. Experienced speakers have strategies for making sure they deliver a good show, starting with very careful preparation and lots of practice. (They also note that a little nervousness can be a good thing by keeping you on your toes.)

The most effective strategy, however, seems to be simply knowing your topic and material thoroughly. The more confident you are in your own knowledge, the more easily and naturally you will speak. And eloquence can be developed, and practice can make perfect. In addition to being well prepared, you may want to try some of the following strategies:

- Practice a number of times, running through every part of the presentation. Leave nothing out, even audio or video clips. Work with the equipment you intend to use so that you are familiar with it. It also may help to visualize your presentation, imagining the scene in your mind as you go through your materials.

- Time your presentation to make sure you stay within your allotted slot.

- Tape yourself (video, if possible) at least once so that you can listen to your voice. Tone of voice and body language can dispose audiences for—or against—speakers. For most oral arguments, you want to develop a tone that conveys commitment to your position as well as respect for your audience.

- Think about how you'll dress for your presentation, remembering that audience members notice how a speaker looks. Dressing for a presentation depends on what's appropriate for your topic, audience, and setting, but experienced speakers choose clothes that are comfortable, allow easy movement, and aren't overly casual or overly dressy: moderation is the key here. Looking your best indicates that you take pride in your appearance, have confidence in your argument, and respect your audience.

- Get some rest before the presentation, and avoid consuming too much caffeine.

- Relax! Consider doing some deep-breathing exercises. Then pause just before you begin, concentrating on your opening lines.

- Maintain eye contact with members of your audience. Speak to them, not to your text or to the floor.

- Interact with the audience whenever possible; doing so will often help you relax and even have some fun.

- Most speakers make a stronger impression standing than sitting, so stand if you have that option. Moving around a bit may help you maintain good eye contact.

- Remember to allow time for audience responses and questions. Keep your answers brief so that others may join the conversation.

- Finally, at the very end of your presentation, thank the audience for its attention to your arguments.

A Note about Webcasts: Live Presentations over the Web

This discussion of live oral presentations has assumed that you'll be speaking before an audience in the same room with you. Increasingly, though—especially in business, industry, and science—the presentations you make will be live, but you won't occupy the same physical space as the audience. Instead, you might be in front of a camera that will capture your voice and image and relay them via the Web to attendees who might be anywhere in the world. In another type of Webcast, participants can see only your slides or the software that you're demonstrating, using a screen-capture relay without cameras: you're not visible but still speaking live.

In either case, most of the strategies that work well for oral presentations with an in-house audience will continue to serve in Webcast environments. But there are some significant differences:

- Practice is even more important in Webcasts, since you need to be able to access online any slides, documents, video clips, names, dates, and sources that you provide during the Webcast.

- Because you can't make eye contact with audience members, it's important to remember to look into the camera (if you are using one), at least from time to time. If you're using a stationary Webcam, perhaps one mounted on your computer, practice standing or sitting without moving out of the frame and yet without looking stiff.

- Even though your audience may not be visible to you, assume that if you're on camera, the Web-based audience can see you. If you slouch, they'll notice. Assume too that your microphone is always live. Don't mutter under your breath, for example, when someone else is speaking or asking a question.

RESPOND•

Attend a presentation on your campus, and observe the speaker's delivery. Note the strategies that the speaker uses to capture and hold your attention (or not). What signpost language and other guides to listening can you detect? How well are visuals integrated into the presentation? What aspects of the speaker's tone, dress, eye contact, and movement affect your understanding and your appreciation (or lack of it)? What's most memorable about the presentation, and why? Finally, write up an analysis of this presentation's effectiveness.

16
Multimodal Arguments

The very first paragraph in this edition of *Everything's an Argument* features a tweet by actor and activist Alyssa Milano focusing on sexual harassment and assault. And throughout this book we draw on examples from a wide range of media and genres, including online news sources, blog posts and comments, cartoons, ads, maps, memes, posters, comics, video games, infographics, bumper stickers, even a selfie—of the pope, no less. In one way or another, all of these items illustrate principles of persuasion. And while this book is also about more conventional forms of argument—essays, extended articles, and academic papers— the fact is that many arguments are now shaped, distributed, and connected in ways that no one imagined a generation ago. In fact, we know that many college-age students today prefer visual communication and are on their smartphones a great deal of the time: 82 percent of these writers use Facebook (Twitter, at about 32 percent, seems to be waning); Snapchat users view over 7 million videos every single day; and savvy college-age entrepreneurs are vlogging, starting their own YouTube channels—and making money in the process.

These social networks, and many others, have virtually redefined the nature of influence and persuasion. The cascade of information, the 24-hour news cycle, the incessant connectivity of screens—all are now the new normal. More to the point for the purposes of this book: all this online and onscreen activity is deeply rhetorical in both its aims and its methods. We want to spend a chapter exploring new media, teasing out some connections between traditional modes of persuasion and those currently reshaping our social and political lives.

Old Media Transformed by New Media

Civic arguments and opinions used to be delivered orally, typically in speeches, debates, and dialogues and often at public forums. Later, especially after the development of printing, they arrived via paper, and then through other media such as film and over-the-air broadcasting. Some of these traditional channels of communication were actual physical objects distributed one by one: books, journals, newspapers, fliers, photographs. Other "old media" such as movies, TV news, or radio shows were more like performances that could not be distributed or shared readily, at least not until audio- and videotape became cheap. Yet these media were all-powerful, handy, and relatively inexpensive shapers of opinion: books and serious magazines appealed to readers accustomed to intellectual challenges; well-staffed newspapers provided professional (if sometimes sensational) coverage of local and world affairs; nightly, the three national TV networks reached large and relatively undistracted audiences, establishing some degree of cultural consensus.

At least that's the romantic side of old media. We all recognize today the remarkable limitations of paper books and journals or celluloid film and print photographs. But we didn't appreciate quite how clumsy, hard to locate, hard to distribute, hard to search, and hard to archive analog objects could be until they went digital.

Fortunately, to one degree or another, electronic media have made peace with all these genres and formats and "remediated" them, to use a term coined by media scholars Jay Bolter and Richard Grusin—though almost always with some compromises. Books on e-readers have become like ancient scrolls again, handy for sequential reading, but not so great for moving back and forth or browsing. Magazine articles or newspaper editorials (when not blocked by paywalls) can be found instantly online (or in databases), complete with updates and corrections, links that help establish their context, and, usually, lots and lots of comments. The

When NBA star Kevin Durant decided to move from the Oklahoma Thunder to the Golden State Warriors in 2016, he published a brief personal essay titled "My Next Chapter" online and in print in the *Players' Tribune,* hoping to reach the widest possible audience as he explained his decision.

Beck Diefenbach/AP Images

downside? Lots and lots of inane, offensive, and bitter comments. And of course films and music are now accessible everywhere. You can experience *Lawrence of Arabia*—with its awesome horizons and desert landscapes—on your iPhone while in line at McDonald's.

The bigger point is that the serious, attentive, and carefully researched arguments that represent the best of old media are still in no danger of disappearing. Books, research articles, and serious pieces of journalism are still being ground out—and read attentively—in the new media world because they play an essential role there. They provide the logos (see Chapter 4) for innumerable Web sites, the full-bodied arguments, research studies, and no-nonsense science propping up all those links in tighter, punchier new media features. They give clout and credibility to the quick blog post, the Facebook status, even the trending Twitter hashtag.

READING IN PRINT VS. ONLINE

Studies on reading continue to confirm that when the stakes are high—when you really need to comprehend something difficult—reading in print is still the way to go. As researchers note, reading print text tends to help us slow down and take in what we are reading, and it's a snap to make notes, highlight, and use other techniques to reinforce our memories. Online readers are still very easily distracted ("oh, look at that irresistible link!"). Yet these same studies all acknowledge that readers are changing and adapting: perhaps in another decade we will be able to exercise more self-discipline and read as efficiently and effectively online as in print. But for now, if the information is very important to you, or if your grade depends on your thorough understanding of an argument, you may be wise to stick to print.

New Content in New Media

As you well know, new media represent a vast array of interconnected, electronic platforms where ideas and arguments (and a great deal else) can be introduced and shared. In these environments, the content is almost anything that can be delivered digitally—words, pictures, movement, and sounds. Perhaps the first Web capability that writers and thinkers appreciated was the distribution of traditional printed texts via online databases; it made possible huge advances in speed, accuracy, and efficiency. (Consider, for a moment, the professional databases in every field and discipline that are available through your school library.)

Online content quickly evolved once it became apparent that just about anyone could create a Web site—and they did. Soon valuable sites emerged, covering every imaginable topic, many of them focusing on serious social and political concerns. Today, such sites range from those that collect short items and links to promote a topic or point of view (*Instapundit, The Daily Kos*) to slick, full-featured magazines with original content and extensive commentary (*Salon, Jezebel*). Social, political, and cultural sites such as *Slate*, *Drudge*, and *Politico* have become powerful shapers of opinion by showcasing a wide variety of writers and arguments. Right from the beginning, blogs demonstrated that interactive online sites could create virtual communities and audiences, enabling people (sometimes acting as citizen journalists) to find allies for their causes and concerns.

Enter social media and the wildly diverse worlds they now represent. Consider the vast difference among platforms and environments such as Facebook, YouTube, Reddit, Tumblr, Instagram Stories, WhatsApp, Yelp, and Twitter. Reviews on Yelp are by nature evaluative arguments, and many Facebook postings have a persuasive bent, though they may not go much beyond observations, claims, or complaints supported by links or images. Indeed, the frameworks of these self-selected environments encourage posting and, to varying degrees, opinion making and sharing. And what gets posted in social media? Everything allowed—especially stuff already available in digital form on other online sites: cool pictures, funny people and pets, outrageous videos, trendy performers, and, yes, lots of links to serious talk about politics, culture, and social issues.

Re-tweeting and forwarding is easy, but ensuring the accuracy of what you are sending on is hard. You know that there are trolls out there harassing, bullying, and pouring out misinformation: it's one of the responsibilities of a critical user of media not only to acknowledge this fact but to actively work to delegitimize such harmful and dishonest actions and to support the truth.

"Like" is easy; contributing is hard. (See Chapter 1 on the difference between convincing and persuading.)

New Audiences in New Media

When it comes to making arguments, perhaps the most innovative aspect of new media is its ability to summon audiences. Since ancient times (see p. 26), rhetoricians have emphasized the need to frame arguments to influence people, but new media and social networks now create places for specific audiences to emerge and make the arguments themselves, assembling them in bits and pieces, one comment or supporting link at a time. Audiences gather around sites that represent their perspectives on politics or mirror their social conditions and interests.

It seems natural. Democrats engage with different Web sites than do Republicans or Libertarians; champions (and foes) of immigration or gun rights have their favored places too. Within social networks themselves, supporters of causes can join existing activist communities or create new alliances among people with compatible views. And then all those individuals contribute to the never-ending newsfeeds: links, favorite books and authors, preferred images or slogans, illustrative videos, and so on. They stir the pot and generate still more energy, concern, and emotion. All this talking and arguing can be generative and exciting—or begin to sound like an echo chamber. And today, this echo chamber effect seems particularly pronounced, as lots of people don't even want to talk with someone who disagrees with their points of view and instead band together in online niches—sometimes in secret groups not

Amanda Hess analyzes how the digital age has ushered in a loss of privacy—for all but the very wealthy.

LINK TO P. 724

Here's what Twitter's audience looked like when the government of Turkey tried to ban the service in 2014. ADEM ALTAN/Getty Images

visible to the public—where participants simply reinforce each other's biases. Doing so is not good for rhetorical argumentation, which depends on listening carefully to others, really hearing them, and then presenting alternate ideas in clear, logical, and respectful ways. Rhetorical argumentation and persuasion aren't about shouting and screaming and pushing, but about listening and reasoning and searching for common ground that can help move ideas forward.

Still, social media platforms like Twitter allow writers and speakers to reach enormous audiences. Celebrities and political figures alike, for a wide variety of reasons, attract "followers" cued into their 140- (or 280-) character musings (as of March 2018 President Trump's main Twitter handle listed 48.8 million followers; Pope Francis: 40 million; Taylor Swift: 85 million). In some respects, "following" is simply a popularity contest or a bandwagon (see p. 84) that pulls people in by the millions. And, as a 2018 *New York Times* investigation found, some of those "followers" are actually fake accounts, known as bots. But the number of followers can also be a measure of ethos, the trust and connection people have in the person offering a point of view (see Chapter 3). Sometimes that ethos is largely just about media fame, narcissism, and self-aggrandizement, one reason some pundits refer to President Trump as the "Tweeter-in-Chief," but in other cases it may measure genuine influence that public figures have earned by virtue of their serious ideas or opinions. Logos would seem to have little chance of emerging in a platform like Twitter: can you do much more than make a bare claim or two in the few words and symbols allowed? That's where hashtags (signaled by the prefix #) come in, allowing people to identify a topic and place around which an audience may gather. You're probably using hashtags to gather information and to post your own messages. The swift rise of the #metoo hashtag (see p. 3) shows how Hollywood actors, directors, and writers used their ethos to attract an even larger audience to the issue of sexual harassment. At the end of 2016, Twitter announced the most often used hashtags of that year: #Rio2016; #Election 2016; #Pokemongo; #Oscars; #Brexit; #BlackLivesMatter. In all these cases, the audience for these topics showed its power in the sheer number of people weighing in on the topic, expressing their sentiments succinctly, but also accumulating a sense of direction, solidarity, and gravity—or engaging in attacks and counterattacks. It's also why political journalists or

The ubiquitous hashtag is liable to turn up anywhere. knape/Getty Images

Do social media platforms help inform—or merely distract—us? © Andy Singer/Cagle Cartoons, Inc.

print publications now routinely identify trending hashtags in their reporting or even direct audiences to Twitter to track breaking stories or social movements as they unfold there.

Analyzing Multimodal Arguments

As the previous section suggests, a multimodal argument can be complex. But you can figure it out by giving careful attention to its key components: the creators and distributors; the medium it uses; the viewers and readers it hopes to reach; its content and purpose; its design. Following are some questions to ask when you want to understand the rhetorical strategies in arguments and interactions you encounter in social media or on blogs, vlogs, Web sites, podcasts, or other nontraditional media. It's worth noting that the questions here don't differ entirely from those you might ask about books, journal articles, news stories, or print ads when composing a rhetorical analysis (see Chapter 6).

Questions about Creators and Distributors

- Who is responsible for this multimodal text? Experts? Bots? Trolls? Did someone else distribute, repurpose, or retweet the item?
- What can you find out about these people and any other work they might have done?
- What does the creator's attitude seem to be toward the content: serious, ironic, emotionally charged, satiric, comic? What is the attitude of the distributor, if different from the creator?
- What do the creator and the distributor expect the effects of the text or posting to be? Do they share the same intentions? (Consider, for example, that someone might post an item in order to mock or criticize it.)

Questions about the Medium

- Which media are used by this text? Images only? Words and images? Sound, video, animation, graphs, charts? Does the site or environment where the text appears suggest a metaphor: photo album, pin-up board, message board, chat room?
- In what ways is this text or its online environment interactive? Who can contribute to or comment on it? Where can an item be sent or redirected? How did it get to where you encountered it?
- How do various texts work together on the site? Do they make arguments? Accumulate evidence? Provide readers with examples and illustrations?
- What effect does the medium have on messages or items within it? How would a message, text, or item be altered if different media were used?
- Do claims or arguments play an explicit role in the medium? How are they presented, clarified, reinforced, connected, constrained, or commented upon?

Questions about Audience and Viewers

- What are the likely audiences for the text or medium? How are people invited into the text or site? Who might avoid the experience?
- How does the audience participate in the site or platform? Does the audience respond to content, create it, or something else? What

audience interactions or connections occur there? Can participants interact with each other?

- How does the text or media site evoke or reward participation? Are audience members texted or emailed about events or interactions in the site?

Questions about Content and Purpose

- What purpose does the multimodal text achieve? What is it designed to convey?

- What social, cultural, or political values does the text or site support? Cultural interaction? Power? Resistance? Freedom?

- Does the text, alone or in reaction to others, reinforce these values or question them? Does the text constitute an argument in itself or contribute to another claim in some way—as an illustration, example, exception, metaphor, analogy?

- What emotions does the multimodal site or text evoke? Are these the emotions that it intends to raise? How does it do it?

Questions about Design

- How does the site present itself? What draws you to it? How easy is the environment to learn, use, or subscribe to?

- How is the multimodal text or environment structured? Does the structure enhance its purpose or functionality? If it presents data, is the information easy to understand? (See also Chapter 14, "Visual Rhetoric.")

- How are arguments, concepts, or ideas presented or framed within the multimodal text or environment? How are ideas identified? How are these ideas amplified or connected to other supporting texts and ideas?

- What details are emphasized in the text or media environment? What details are omitted or de-emphasized? To what effect? Is anything downplayed, ambiguous, confusing, distracting, or obviously omitted? Why?

- What, if anything, is surprising about the design of the text or environment? What do you think is the purpose of that surprise?

- How are you directed to move within the text or site? Are you encouraged to read further? Click on links? Contribute links and information?

RESPOND•

Using the discussion of multimodal arguments in this chapter and the questions about multimodal texts and platforms above, find a multimodal text that makes an intriguing argument or a social media platform where you sometimes encounter debates about political and social issues. Then read carefully and critically in order to write a brief rhetorical analysis of the text or the site, focusing more on the way the messages are conveyed than on the messages that are in play. (See Chapter 6 for more on rhetorical analysis.)

Jess Kapadia's Web article on cultural appropriation of food was first published on Medium.com, an online publishing platform. Had she chosen to create a video or podcast about this topic, how might the content of her essay differed?

LINK TO P. 615

This is the central image on the homepage of Wikipedia, a collaborative nonprofit encyclopedia project. Since its launch (as Nupedia) in 2000, Wikipedia has grown to include 42 million articles in 295 languages (5.5 million articles in English), all of them authored by volunteers around the world. This central image acts as a logo, a portal to access the site's content, and, in a way, a mission statement for the organization. How does your eye construct this logo? What do you notice first, and how do your eyes move around the page? Do the parts make sense when you put them together?

Making Multimodal Arguments

Though it may feel like you have been active in new media platforms forever—browsing Web sites, checking Facebook, sending text messages, following "Texas Humor" on Twitter—you may not have thought of these activities as rhetorical. But they certainly can be, especially those that might have classroom or extracurricular connections. Here we discuss just a few such situations. In other chapters in this section, we talk in more detail about visual rhetoric (often a component in new media) and oral presentations, which now almost always have a digital component.

Web Sites

It's likely you have already created Web sites for a class or for an organization to which you belong. In planning any Web site, pay careful attention to your rhetorical situation (see Chapter 1)—the purpose of your site, its intended audience, and the overall impression that you want to make. To get started, you may want to study several sites that you admire, looking for effective design ideas or ways of organizing navigation and information. Creating a map or storyboard for your site will help you to think through the links from page to page.

Experienced Web designers such as Robin Williams cite several important principles for Web-based presentations. The first of these is *contrast*, which is achieved through the use of color, icons, boldface, and so on; contrast helps guide readers through the site (see also Chapter 14). The second principle, *proximity*, calls on you to keep together the parts of a page that are closely related, again for ease of reading. *Repetition* means using a consistent design throughout the site for the elements (such as headings and links) that help readers move smoothly through the environment. Finally, designers concentrate on an *overall impression* or mood for the site, which means that the colors and visuals on the pages should help to create that impression rather than challenge or undermine it.

The homepage for Vermont's Middlebury College Web site appears on the facing page. Designed by White Whale Web Services, it features a line of colorful vertical bars: when you hover the mouse over a bar, you can see where it will take you—to "faculty stories," for example, or "service learning in Japan," or "homecoming highlights"—an intuitive and efficient navigation system. The page also highlights a photo you can click on to see various stories about current events and programs at the college. And below the bars and photo are key links: to admissions,

An interactive and appealing design encourages users to explore a Web site.

academics, student life, and so forth. Finally, note the simple, uncluttered, clean design, which is easy on the eyes and welcoming.

Here are some additional tips that may help you design your site:

- The homepage should be informative, eye-catching, and inviting (see Chapter 14)—especially when making an argument. Use titles and illustrations to make clear what the site is about.

- Think carefully about two parts of every page—the navigation menus or links and the content areas. You want to make these two areas distinct from one another. And make sure you *have* a navigation area for every page, including links to the key sections of the site and to the homepage. Easy navigation is one key to a successful Web site.

- Either choose a design template that is provided by Web-building tools (such as SquareSpace or Wix) or create a template of your own that ensures that the elements of each page are consistent.

- Consider how to balance claims and evidence on a page. Claims might be connected to supporting links, or they can be enhanced by images or videos that dramatize a position you want to champion.

- Remember to include Web contact information on every page, but not your personal address or phone number.

Videos and Video Essays

Given the ease with which competent digital films can be produced, a video may be the best medium for delivering your message. Videos are ubiquitous, for example, on college and university sites, showcasing

The articles by Lauren Salm and Deanna Hartley on employers' use of social media are featured on the job searching site Careerbuilder, making it easy for them to reach their intended audience.

LINK TO PP. 708, 709

distinguished students and faculty or explaining programs. It is an effective way to enhance the ethos of a group or institution. Videos can also document public events or show how to do practical things such as registering to vote or navigating an unfamiliar campus. So whenever a video fits well with the purpose of the message, consider creating one.

You can, of course, shoot a video with your smartphone. But more sophisticated software might be needed to edit your film and get it ready for prime time: iMovie, Final Cut Pro, Movie Maker, Blender (for animation), or Animoto, Camtasia, and Soundslides (for combining media such as digital video, photos, music, and text).

A video essay analyzing a Beatles' album cover

The Nerdwriter, aka Evan Puschak, is very well known for his remarkable video essays, including one tracing the evolution of music album covers. Entitled *How the Beatles Changed Album Covers,* it includes several images from what Puschak calls "the holy grail of album covers"—*Sergeant Pepper's Lonely Hearts Club Band*—and discusses its power. After surveying the evolution of Beatles album covers, the essay focuses on how this particular cover invites viewers to ask questions, to try to figure out who all these people are, and to highlight the mixing of high culture (Marx, Dylan Thomas) with low (Marilyn Monroe, Johnny Weissmueller [Tarzan]), something the Beatles perfected in their own art. For the full video essay, see https://www.youtube.com/watch?v=_st4diqjpis.

If you decide on a video or video essay for your argument, these tips may be of help:

- Present most of the evidence in support of your argument visually, using voiceover to link the images together.

- Choose color palettes carefully to match the tone you want to create.

- Make a scratch outline or storyboard to map out your video essay.

- Draft a script for words that are spoken or used as voiceover.

- Experiment with camera angles and camera movement—and get feedback from your classmates or friends.

- List credits at the end, just as you would add a bibliography to a written text or a list of sources to a final slide in an oral presentation.

Wikis

To make working on group projects easier, many classes use wikis—Web-based sites that enable writers to collaborate in the creation of a single project or database. The most famous group effort of this kind is, of course, Wikipedia, but software such as DokuWiki, MediaWiki, or Tiki helps people to manage similar, if less ambitious, efforts of their own, whether it be exploring questions raised in academic courses or examining and supporting needs within a community. Wiki projects can be argumentative in themselves, or they might furnish raw data and evidence for subsequent projects.

If asked to participate in a wiki, make sure you know how to use the assigned software and follow course or project guidelines for entering and documenting the material you contribute. Just as you will expect your colleagues to use reliable sources or make accurate observations, they will depend on you to do your part in shaping the project. Within the wiki, participants will be able to draw upon each other's strengths and, ideally, to compensate for any weaknesses. So take your responsibilities seriously:

- Make sure that your contributions are based on reliable and credible sources: no fake news here, please!

- Listen to (or read) what others contribute very carefully, making sure you understand them and that you are being fair and respectful at all times, especially when editing what others have contributed.

- Think about how your contributions can move the project forward: suggest links, references, and sources you think will be helpful and credible.

- Remember to explain any technical terms that might be unfamiliar or confusing to a broad audience.

Blogs

Perhaps no Web texts have been more instrumental in advancing political, social, and cultural issues than blogs, which are now too numerous to count. Blogs open an ideal space for building interactive communities, engaging in arguments, and giving voice to views and opinions of ordinary citizens. Today, just about all major news media, including the most prestigious newspapers and journals, feature the functionality of blogs or sponsor blogs themselves as part of their electronic versions.

Like everything else, blogs have downsides: they are idiosyncratic, can be self-indulgent and egoistic, and can distort issues by spreading misinformation *very* quickly. If you're a fan of blogs, be sure to keep your critical reading hat on at all times, remembering that information on blogs hasn't been critically reviewed in the way that traditional print sources edit their stories. But also remember that blogs have reported many instances of the mainstream news sources failing to live up to their own standards.

Activist blogs of all kinds get plenty of attention, and you can easily join in on the conversation there, sharing your arguments in the comments section. If you do blog yourself, or comment on others' postings, remember to follow commonsense good manners: be respectful and think carefully about what you are saying and about the impression you want to leave with those who read you. The following tips may be of help as you get started:

- Aim for an eye-catching title for your blog post, one that includes key words that will help readers find you. And keep the title brief. In an article on *Hubspot*, writer Corey Wainwright gives an example of a blog post in its original and revised state:

  Before: Think Social Media Is Just for Kids? Here Are 10 Statistics Guaranteed to Prove You Wrong

  After: 10 Stats That Prove Social Media Isn't Just for Kids

- Choose easy-to-use blogging software, such as Blogger, Tumblr, and WordPress.

- Keep your posts fairly brief and to the point since most readers come to blogs looking for information, not long-winded musings. Keep the point you want to make (your argument!) in the front of your mind as you write.

- Consider using headings and subheadings or other elements to help orient and guide your readers.

- Embed audio and video clips and visual images that will help make your point clear and compelling for all kinds of learners.

Social Media

You are no doubt already a practiced user of social media and understand the strengths and weaknesses, the pros and cons, of platforms like Facebook, Twitter, Instagram, Snapchat, Tumblr, and more. Many arguments mounted on social media today come in the form of memes, a term coined by evolutionary biologist Richard Dawkins. Once thought of as a source of jokes and cute cats (Nyan cat was around forever!), memes can offer serious commentary via an image and short text. With a Twitter account and a hashtag, they seem to circle the globe in an instant. According to journalists Angela Watercutter and Emma Grey Ellis, memes today are used to declare and argue for political positions, cultural identities, and so on:

> The success of memes like the alt-right's Pepe the Frog . . . points to political memes' probable future function: spreading propaganda. . . . That space between truth and truthiness is where both memes and propaganda live. (If you're thinking that you'd never share propaganda, remember this: thanks to Russia, you probably already have.)
> —"The *Wired* Guide to Memes," April 1, 2018

Creating and responding to memes, not to mention the networks that distribute them, takes up a lot of metaphorical and literal space and time. As a result, many people benefit from "unplugging" every once in a while to make sure they are still in touch with real people in the real world. But everyone needs to be especially aware of how these networks influence our views on everything from what to eat to where (or if) to worship to who to vote for. That's because the Internet is pulsing with arguments being presented to us twenty-four hours a day, yet many of these arguments have nothing more than an uninformed opinion to back them up. So take a break from the social media scene and think carefully and critically about how the arguments we encounter online are supported—or not. Think about how these arguments draw us in and shape our thinking, even our beliefs. And make sure you are a critical as well as an ethical user of social media and that the causes you follow or champion are worthy of you.

And remember that in with the trash and the junk on social media, you can find serious and credible information, information you may well use in your academic work. Social media can lead you, for instance, to experts across a range of fields, who can help you gather reliable information on almost any topic or in any field. So social media provide powerful tools for expanding your knowledge base and your experience, if you approach information on such networks very carefully.

Posters

Perhaps you've been asked to make a poster presentation in one of your classes, or maybe you have created a poster for an organization you belong to. Poster sessions are increasingly popular at conferences, and

A well-designed poster presentation can pack an awful lot of information into a limited space.

a number of universities award prizes for the best and most informative poster presentations.

Above, you can see an award-winning poster made for a public policy class. It was created by Anna Shickele and demonstrates how much useful information can be conveyed in this format. Note the simple, uncluttered arrangement of this poster, from the title that runs in a banner across the top; to the three text columns that provide background information, state the research question, and describe methods; to the maps and photographs, including the photo of the author at the research site.

If you are making a poster, remember this example that is easy to look at and to take in at a glance. In addition:

- Do some brainstorming about how best to grab and hold your audience's attention: A central photo? A jaw-dropping question in bold font? Try these ideas out on classmates or friends.

- Make sure you understand the requirements for the poster: Is it to be of a certain size? Using certain materials? How will it be displayed?

- Lay out your poster either in a word processing document or with pencil and paper. Allot the most space to the most important information and do not crowd text or images.

- Choose colors that will be easy to see: dark colors with text in them won't be readable, for example, so choose white or light colors as background for text and primary colors for images.

- Finally, if you will be speaking to people who are looking at your poster, write out and practice a brief introduction to the project, telling viewers what your assignment was and what argument you are making in the poster. And be prepared to answer questions! (See Chapter 15 for more on giving presentations.)

Comics

Judging by the immense popularity of Comic Cons (in 2017, scores of them were scheduled from Seattle, Portland, San Francisco, and Los Angeles to all points east—Minneapolis, Salt Lake City, Santa Fe, Austin, Dallas, Nashville, Durham, Atlanta, Baltimore, and New York— and lots of spots in between), comics are experiencing a renaissance. Besides appearing in print, comics have found new life on television, on the big screen, even on the Broadway stage. Comics artist and speaker Lynda Barry believes that there is an artist lurking in every single one of us, as her standing-room-only workshops attest. On college campuses, comics are also finding a place in the curriculum: at Stanford University, for instance, the Graphic Novel Project is a twenty-week course in which undergraduate students do research in order to propose real-life stories that might be told in graphic form. The goal of the course is to "teach nonfiction research, visual story-telling, and long-form narrative structure . . . through the collaborative production of a graphic novel." Students direct every part of the project, from choosing the topic to conducting all of the research, and carrying out the storyboarding and drawing, the lettering and inking, and the full preparation of the text for the printer. In 2017, the student group published their seventh collaborative graphic novel, *Luisa,* about early twentieth-century Puerto Rican feminist and labor organizer Luisa Capetillo, known for her toughness, her perseverance—and her wearing of suits and ties.

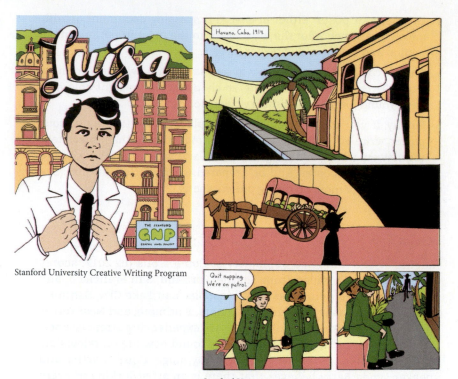

Stanford University Creative Writing Program

Stanford University Creative Writing Program

Here's the cover of the comic and its first page. Note the simple, clean design and bright colors of the cover, which draws our eyes to the central figure of Luisa (in one of her signature white suits) standing in front of Spanish-style buildings, with mountains in the background. The lower right box announces the authorship of the book. The panels on the first page are likewise simple: two page-wide rectangles stacked one above the other, with a smaller rectangle and a square at the bottom of the page. The words in a small banner at the top left (where a reader would first look) set the scene: Havana, Cuba, 1914. We see Luisa walking toward a building in the top panel, passing by a horse and vegetable/fruit cart in the second, and then approaching two officers of some kind in the third and fourth panels. These four panels plunge us into the story and invite us to read further. These artists and writers could have written a research essay about Luisa Capetillo, but their decision to render her story in graphic form makes for a much more memorable presentation.

Luisa is a major research project, one that took a whole group twenty weeks to put together. But you don't have to take a full course to use comics in your academic writing. Henry Tsai did just that in a history research project he conducted about a group of Vietnamese Americans who were triply displaced—first from their homeland after the Vietnam War, then from their arrival cities in the U.S. to New Orleans, and then from there to Houston during the Hurricane Katrina disaster. Based on extensive interviews with a dozen people, Tsai used their stories to illustrate his history project, drawing panels that brought them and their experiences to life. You can do the same kind of thing in your own academic writing.

If you do, a few tips may come in handy in getting started.

- Choose the topic of your comic or panels carefully, making sure it lends itself to visual depiction. The more action-filled and concrete the better.

- Decide what layout you will use: square panels, rectangular, triangular? Simpler will be better, especially for an early attempt. Pay attention to where the space between panels (the gutters) will be: they guide readers and give them a visual pause as they move from panel to panel. Remember that English speakers will expect to read these panels left to right, top to bottom.

- Check out free software for creating comics (such as EasyComic for PCs or ComicLife for Macs).

- Remember that comics panels could help you illustrate a research essay, such as one focusing on the events of Hurricane Harvey: in this case a picture you draw might be worth more than a thousand words.

- Don't forget to check out comics that you find particularly compelling: put your critical reading and viewing skills to work in analyzing what makes the panels in these comics so effective. See if you can learn how to emulate them.

- Create a series of actions you want to include—a verbal script for your panel(s).

- Rough out a storyboard, turning words into pictures—stick figures at this point will be fine.

- Put in the speech bubbles and work to make them succinct and to the point.

- For a final product, you'll have to carry out many additional steps, including the final drawing, lettering, and inking. But the steps in this list can help you get started.

A Final Note on Time

The projects illustrated in this chapter—from blog posts and Web sites to presentation posters and comics—are all time-consuming endeavors. Keep this in mind when you take on a multimodal project and manage your time and effort and resources accordingly.

RESPOND•

Go to a blog or a video essay that you admire and read/view it carefully and critically, taking note of what makes it especially effective and what appeals it uses to engage you. Then answer the following questions:

Why is the blog—a digital presentation—or the video essay the best way to present this material?

What advantages over a print text or a live oral and multimodal presentation does the blog or video essay have?

How could you "translate" the argument(s) of this blog or video essay into print format, oral format, or social media platform? What might be gained or lost in the process?

PART 4

RESEARCH AND
arguments

17
Academic Arguments

LEFT TO RIGHT: 06photo/Shutterstock; Rogelio V. Solis/AP Images; Macmillan Learning

Much of the writing you will do in college (and some of what you will no doubt do later in your professional work) is generally referred to as *academic discourse* or *academic argument*. Although this kind of writing has many distinctive features, in general it shares these characteristics:

- It is based on research and uses evidence that can be documented.
- It is written for a professional, academic, or school audience likely to know something about its topic.
- It makes a clear and compelling point in a fairly formal, clear, and sometimes technical style.
- It follows agreed-upon conventions of format, usage, and punctuation.
- It is documented, using some professional citation style.

Academic writing is serious work, the kind you are expected to do whenever you are assigned an essay, research paper, or capstone project. You will find two examples of such work at the end of this chapter.

Understanding What Academic Argument Is

Academic argument covers a wide range of writing, but its hallmarks are an appeal to reason and a reliance on research. As a consequence, such arguments cannot be composed quickly, casually, or off the top of one's head. They require careful reading, accurate reporting, and a conscientious commitment to truth. But academic pieces do not tune out all appeals to ethos or emotion: today, we know that these arguments often convey power and authority through their impressive lists of sources and their immediacy. But an academic argument crumbles if its facts are skewed or its content proves to be unreliable.

Look, for example, how systematically Susannah Fox and Lee Rainie, director and codirector of the Pew Internet Project, present facts and evidence in arguing (in 2014) that the Internet has been, overall, a big plus for society and individuals alike.

> [Today,] 87% of American adults now use the Internet, with near-saturation usage among those living in households earning $75,000 or more (99%), young adults ages 18–29 (97%), and those with college degrees (97%). Fully 68% of adults connect to the Internet with mobile devices like smartphones or tablet computers.
>
> The adoption of related technologies has also been extraordinary: Over the course of Pew Research Center polling, adult ownership of cell phones has risen from 53% in our first survey in 2000 to 90% now. Ownership of smartphones has grown from 35% when we first asked in 2011 to 58% now.
>
> Impact: Asked for their overall judgment about the impact of the Internet, toting up all the pluses and minuses of connected life, the public's verdict is overwhelmingly positive: 90% of Internet users say the Internet has been a good thing for them personally and only 6% say it has been a bad thing, while 3% volunteer that it has been some of both. 76% of Internet users say the Internet has been a good thing for society, while 15% say it has been a bad thing and 8% say it has been equally good and bad.
>
> —Susannah Fox and Lee Rainie, "The Web at 25 in the U.S."

Note, too, that these writers draw their material from research and polls conducted by the Pew Research Center, a well-known and respected organization. Chances are you immediately recognize that this paragraph is an example of a research-based academic argument.

You can also identify academic argument by the way it addresses its audiences. Some academic writing is clearly aimed at specialists in a field who are familiar with both the subject and the terminology that surrounds it. As a result, the researchers make few concessions to general readers unlikely to encounter or appreciate their work. You see that single-mindedness in this abstract of an article about migraine headaches in a scientific journal: it quickly becomes unreadable to nonspecialists.

Abstract

Migraine is a complex, disabling disorder of the brain that manifests itself as attacks of often severe, throbbing head pain with sensory sensitivity to light, sound and head movement. There is a clear familial tendency to migraine, which has been well defined in a rare autosomal dominant form of familial hemiplegic migraine (FHM). FHM mutations so far identified include those in CACNA1A (P/Q voltage-gated Ca(2+) channel), ATP1A2 (N(+)-K(+)-ATPase) and SCN1A (Na(+) channel) genes. Physiological studies in humans and studies of the experimental correlate—cortical spreading depression (CSD)—provide understanding of aura, and have explored in recent years the effect of migraine preventives in CSD. . . .

   —Peter J. Goadsby, "Recent Advances in Understanding
   Migraine Mechanisms, Molecules, and Therapeutics,"
   Trends in Molecular Medicine (January 2007)

Yet this very article might later provide data for a more accessible argument in a magazine such as *Scientific American*, which addresses a broader (though no less serious) readership. Here's a selection from an article on migraine headaches from that more widely read journal (see also the infographic on p. 408):

At the moment, only a few drugs can prevent migraine. All of them were developed for other diseases, including hypertension, depression and epilepsy. Because they are not specific to migraine, it will come as no surprise that they work in only 50 percent of patients—and, in them, only 50 percent of the time—and induce a range of side effects, some potentially serious.

 Recent research on the mechanism of these antihypertensive, antiepileptic and antidepressant drugs has demonstrated that one of their effects is to inhibit cortical spreading depression. The drugs' ability to prevent migraine with and without aura therefore supports the school of thought that cortical spreading depression contributes to

"Playing with Prejudice: The Prevalence and Consequences of Racial Prejudice in Video Games" meets the criteria described here for academic argument. It begins with an abstract that summarizes the research performed and its findings.

LINK TO P. 567

both kinds of attacks. Using this observation as a starting point, investigators have come up with novel drugs that specifically inhibit cortical spreading depression. Those drugs are now being tested in migraine sufferers with and without aura. They work by preventing gap junctions, a form of ion channel, from opening, thereby halting the flow of calcium between brain cells.

—David W. Dodick and J. Jay Gargus,
"Why Migraines Strike," *Scientific American* (August 2008)

Such writing still requires attention, but it delivers important and comprehensible information to any reader seriously interested in the subject and the latest research on it.

Infographic: The Root of Migraine Pain © Tolpa Studios, Inc.

Even when academic writing is less technical and demanding, its style will retain a degree of formality. In academic arguments, the focus is on the subject or topic rather than the authors, the tone is straightforward, the language is largely unadorned, and all the i's are dotted and t's crossed. Here's an abstract for an academic paper written by a scholar of communications on the Burning Man phenomenon, demonstrating those qualities:

Every August for more than a decade, thousands of information technologists and other knowledge workers have trekked out into a barren stretch of alkali desert and built a temporary city devoted to art, technology, and communal living: Burning Man. Drawing on extensive archival research, participant observation, and interviews, this paper explores the ways that Burning Man's bohemian ethos supports new forms of production emerging in Silicon Valley and especially at Google. It shows how elements of the Burning Man world—including the building of a socio-technical commons, participation in project-based artistic labor, and the fusion of social and professional interaction—help shape and legitimate the collaborative manufacturing processes driving the growth of Google and other firms. The paper thus develops the notion that Burning Man serves as a key cultural infrastructure for the Bay Area's new media industries.

—Fred Turner, "Burning Man at Google:
A Cultural Infrastructure for New Media Production"

You might imagine a different and far livelier way to tell a story about the annual Burning Man gathering in Nevada, but this piece respects the conventions of its academic field.

A scene from Burning Man MIKE NELSON/AFP/Getty Images

Another way you likely identify academic writing—especially in term papers or research projects—is by the way it draws upon sources and builds arguments from research done by experts and reported in journal articles and books. Using an evenhanded tone and dealing with all points of view fairly, such writing brings together multiple voices and intriguing ideas. You can see these moves in just one paragraph from a heavily documented student essay examining the comedy of Chris Rock:

> The breadth of passionate debate that [Chris] Rock's comedy elicits from intellectuals is evidence enough that he is advancing discussion of the foibles of black America, but Rock continually insists that he has no political aims: "Really, really at the end of the day, the only important thing is being funny. I don't go out of my way to be political" (qtd. in Bogosian 58). His unwillingness to view himself as a black leader triggers Justin Driver to say, "[Rock] wants to be caustic and he wants to be loved" (32). Even supporters wistfully sigh, "One wishes Rock would own up to the fact that he's a damned astute social critic" (Kamp 7).
>
> —Jack Chung, "The Burden of Laughter: Chris Rock Fights Ignorance His Way"

Readers can quickly tell that author Jack Chung has read widely and thought carefully about how to support his argument.

As you can see even from these brief examples, academic arguments cover a broad range of topics and appear in a variety of media—as a brief note in a journal like *Nature*, for example, a poster session at a conference on linguistics, a short paper in *Physical Review Letters*, a full research report in microbiology, or an undergraduate honors thesis in history. What do all these projects have in common? One professor we know defines academic argument as "carefully structured research," and that seems to us to be a pretty good definition.

Conventions in Academic Argument Are Not Static

Far from it. In fact, the rise of new technologies and the role that blogs, wikis, social media, and other digital discourses play in all our lives are affecting academic writing as well. Thus, scholars today are pushing the envelope of traditional academic writing in some fields. Physicians, for example, are using narrative (rather than charts) more often in medicine to communicate effectively with other medical personnel. Professional journals now sometimes feature serious scholarly work in new formats—such as comics (as in legal scholar Jamie Boyle's work on intellectual property, or Nick Sousanis's Columbia University PhD dissertation, which is entirely in comic form). And student writers are increasingly producing serious academic arguments using a wide variety of modalities, including sound, still and moving images, and more. Obviously, the "research paper" need not be a paper at all: most academic research these days is available online—though, because of pay walls, not everyone can access it.

Developing an Academic Argument

In your first years of college, the academic arguments you make will probably include the features and qualities we've discussed above—and which you see demonstrated in the sample academic arguments at the end of this chapter. In addition, you can make a strong academic argument by following some time-tested techniques.

Choose a topic you want to explore in depth. Even if you are assigned a topic, look for an issue that intrigues you—one you *want* to learn more about. One of the hardest parts of producing an academic argument is finding a topic narrow enough to be manageable in the time you have to work on it but also rich enough to sustain your interest over the same period. Talk with friends about possible topics and explain to them why you'd like to pursue research on this issue. Look through your Twitter feeds and social media postings to identify themes or topics that leap out as compelling. Browse through books and articles that interest you, make a list of potential subjects, and then zero in on one or two top choices.

Get to know the conversation surrounding your topic. Once you've chosen a topic, expect to do even more reading and browsing—a lot more. Familiarize yourself with what's been said about your subject and especially with the controversies that currently surround it. Where do scholars agree, and where do they disagree? What key issues seem to be at stake? You can start by exploring online, using key terms that are associated with your topic. But you may be better off searching the more specialized databases at your library with the assistance of a librarian who can help you narrow your search and make it more efficient. Library databases will also give you access to materials not available via Google or other online search engines—including, for example, full-text versions of journal articles. For much more on identifying appropriate sources, see Chapter 18, "Finding Evidence."

Assess what you know and what you need to know. As you read about your topic and discuss it with others, take notes on what you have learned, including what you already know about it. Such notes should soon reveal where the gaps are in your knowledge. For instance, you may discover a need to learn about legal issues and thus end up doing research in a law school library. Or perhaps talking with experts about your topic might be helpful. Instructors on your campus may have the knowledge you need or be able to point you in the right direction, so explore your school's Web site to find faculty or staff to talk with. Make an appointment to visit them during office hours and bring the sorts of questions to your meeting that show you've done basic work on the subject. And remember that experts are now only a click away: a student we know, working on Internet privacy concerns, wrote a brief message to one of the top scholars in the field asking for help with two particular questions—and got a response within two days!

Come up with a claim about your topic. The chapters in Part 2, "Writing Arguments," offer instruction in formulating thesis statements, which most academic arguments must have. Chapters 8–12, in particular, explain how to craft claims tailored to individual projects ranging from arguments of fact to proposals. Remember here, though, that good claims are controversial. After all, you don't want to debate something that everyone already agrees upon or accepts.

In addition, your claim needs to say something consequential about that important or controversial topic and be supported with strong evidence and good reasons (see Chapter 20). Here, for example, is the claim that student Charlotte Geaghan-Breiner makes after observing the alienation of today's children from the natural world and arguing for the redesign of schoolyards that invite children to interact with nature: "As a formative geography of childhood, the schoolyard serves as the perfect place to address nature deficit disorder." Charlotte develops her claim and supports it with evidence about the physical, psychological, academic, and social benefits of interacting with the natural world. She includes images illustrating the contrast between traditional schoolyards and "biophilic" (nature-oriented) schoolyards and establishes guidelines for creating natural play landscapes. (See Charlotte's complete essay, reprinted at the end of this chapter.)

Consider your rhetorical stance and purpose. Once you have a claim, ask yourself where you stand with respect to your topic and how you want to represent yourself to those reading your argument:

- You may take the stance of a reporter: you review what has been said about the topic; analyze and evaluate contributions to the conversation surrounding it; synthesize the most important strands of that conversation; and finally draw conclusions based on them.

- You may see yourself primarily as a critic: you intend to point out the problems and mistakes associated with some view of your topic.

- You may prefer the role of an advocate: you present research that strongly supports a particular view on your topic.

Whatever your perspective, remember that in academic arguments you want to come across as fair and evenhanded, especially when you play the advocate. For instance, in her essay about the effects of the phrase "thank you for your service" (or TYFYS) on veterans, sociology doctoral student Sidra Montgomery takes care to consider the feelings of both the civilians expressing gratitude and the veterans who receive it (see p. 432 later in this chapter). Your stance, of course, will always be closely tied to your purpose, which in most of your college writing will be at least twofold: to do the best job in fulfilling an assignment for a course and to support the claim you are making to the fullest extent possible. Luckily, these two purposes work well together.

Think about your audience(s). Here again, you will often find that you have at least two audiences—and maybe more. First, you will be writing to your instructor, so pay close attention to the assignment and, if possible, set up a conference to nail down your teacher's expectations: what will it take to convince this audience that you have done a terrific job of writing an academic argument? Beyond your instructor, you should also think of your classmates as an audience—informed, intelligent peers who will be interested in what you have to say. Again, what do you know about these readers, and what will they expect from your project?

Finally, consider yet another important audience—people who are already discussing your topic. These will include the authors whose work you have read and the larger academic community of which they are now a part. If your work appears online or in some other medium, you will reach more people than you initially expect, and most if not all of them will be unknown to you. As a result, you need to think carefully about the various ways your argument could be read—or misread—and plan accordingly.

Concentrate on the material you are gathering. Any academic argument is only as good as the evidence it presents to support its claims. Give each major piece of evidence (say, a lengthy article that addresses your subject directly) careful scrutiny:

- Summarize its main points.
- Analyze how those points are pertinent.
- Evaluate the quality of the supporting evidence.
- Synthesize the results of your analysis and evaluation.
- Summarize what you think about the article.

In other words, test each piece of evidence and then decide which to keep—and which to throw out. But do not gather only materials that favor your take on the topic. You want, instead, to look at all legitimate perspectives on your claim, and in doing so, you may even change your mind. That's what good research for an academic argument can do: remember the "conscientious commitment to truth" we mentioned earlier? Keep yourself open to discovery and change. (See Chapter 19, "Evaluating Sources," and Chapter 20, "Using Sources.")

Give visual materials and other media the same scrutiny you would to print sources, since you will likely be gathering or creating such materials in many academic disciplines. Remember that representing data visually always involves interpreting that material: numbers can lie and pictures distort. (For more information on evaluating and creating visuals, see Chapter 14.) In addition, infographics today often make complex academic arguments in a visual form. (See p. 179 for one such example.)

Take special care with documentation. As you gather materials for your academic argument, record where you found each source so that you can cite it accurately. For all sources, whether print or digital, develop a working bibliography either on your computer or in a notebook you can carry with you. For each book, write the name of the author, the title of the book, the publisher, the date of publication, and the place that you found it (the section of the library, for example, and the call number for the book). For an e-book, note the format (Nook, Kindle, etc.) or the URL where you accessed it. For each newspaper, magazine, or journal article, write the name of the author, the title of the article, the title of the periodical, and the volume, issue, publication date, and exact page numbers. If you accessed the article online, include the name of the Web site or database where you found the source, the full URL, the date it was published on the Web or most recently updated, and the date you accessed and examined it. Include any other information you may later need in preparing a works cited list or references list. The simplest way to ensure that you have this information is to print a copy of the source, highlight source information, and write down any other pertinent information.

Remember, too, that different academic fields use different systems of documentation, so if your instructor has not recommended a style of documentation to you, ask in class about it. Scholars have developed these systems over long periods of time to make research in an area reliable and routine. Using documentation responsibly shows that you understand and respect the conventions of your field or major, thereby establishing your position as a member of the academic community. (For more detailed information, see Chapter 22, "Documenting Sources.")

Think about organization. As you review the research materials you have gathered, you are actually beginning the work of drafting and designing your project. Study the way those materials are organized, especially any from professional journals, whether print or digital. You may need to include in your own argument some of the sections or features you find in professional research:

- Does the article open with an abstract, summarizing its content?
- Does the article give any information about the author or authors and their credentials?
- Is there a formal introduction to the subject or a clear statement of a thesis or hypothesis?
- Does the article begin with a "review of literature," summarizing recent research on its topic?
- Does the piece describe its methods of research?
- How does the article report its results and findings?
- Does the article use charts and graphs or other visuals to report data?
- Does the piece use headings and subheadings?
- How does the work summarize its findings or how does it make recommendations?
- Does the essay offer a list of works cited or references?

Anticipate some variance in the way materials are presented from one academic field to another.

As you organize your own project, check with your instructor to see if there is a recommended pattern for you to follow. If not, create a scratch outline or storyboard to describe how your essay will proceed. In reviewing your evidence, decide which pieces support specific points in the argument. Then try to position your strongest pieces of evidence in key places—near the beginning of paragraphs, at the end of the introduction, or toward a powerful conclusion. In addition, strive to achieve a balance between, on the one hand, your own words and argument and, on the other hand, the sources that you use or quote in support of the argument. The sources of evidence are important supports, but they shouldn't overpower the structure of your argument itself. Finally, remember that your organization needs to take into account the placement of visuals—charts, tables, photographs, and so on. (For specific advice on structuring arguments, review the "Thinking about Organization" sections in the "Guides to Writing" for Chapters 8–12.)

Consider style and tone. Most academic argument adopts the voice of a reasonable, fair-minded, and careful thinker who is interested in coming as close to the truth about a topic as possible. An essay that achieves that tone may have some of the following features:

- It strives for clarity and directness, though it may use jargon appropriate to a particular field.
- It favors denotative rather than connotative language.
- It is usually impersonal, using first person (*I*) sparingly.
- In some fields, such as the sciences, it may use the passive voice routinely.
- It uses technical language, symbols, and abbreviations for efficiency.
- It avoids colloquialisms, slang, and sometimes even contractions.

The examples at the end of this chapter demonstrate traditional academic style, though there is, as always, a range of possibilities in its manner of expression.

Consider genre, design, and visuals. Most college academic arguments look more like articles in professional journals than like those one might find in a glossier periodical like *Scientific American*—that is, they are still usually black on white, use a traditional font size and type (like 11-point Times New Roman), and lack any conscious design other than inserted tables or figures. But such conventions are changing.

Indeed, student writers today can go well beyond print, creating digital documents that integrate a variety of media and array data in strikingly original ways. But always consider what genres best suit your topic, purpose, and audience and then act accordingly. As you think about the design possibilities for your academic argument, you may want to consult your instructor—and to test your ideas and innovations on friends or classmates.

In choosing visuals to include in your argument, be sure each one makes a strong contribution to your message and is appropriate and fair to your topic and your audience. Treat visuals as you would any other sources and integrate them into your text. Like quotations, paraphrases, and summaries, visuals need to be introduced and commented on in

Safe Spaces, Brave Spaces by John Palfrey exemplifies a clear and direct academic style. Even though the author makes a complex argument, addressing a broad and difficult set of issues, his writing remains straightforward and readable.

LINK TO P. 731

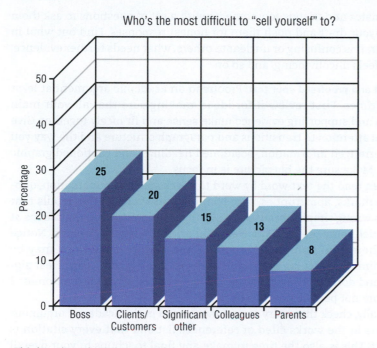

Who's the most difficult to "sell yourself" to?

This bar chart, based on data from a Sandler Training survey of 1,053 adults, would be listed in your works cited or references under the authors' names.

some way. In addition, label and number ("Figure 1," "Table 2," and so on) each visual, provide a caption that includes source information and describes the visual, and cite the source in your references page or works cited list. Even if you create a visual (such as a bar graph) by using information from a source (the results, say, of a Gallup poll), you must cite the source of the data. If you use a photograph you took yourself, cite it as a personal photograph.

Reflect on your draft and get responses. As with any important piece of writing, an academic argument calls for careful reflection on your draft. You may want to do a "reverse outline" to test whether a reader can pull a logical and consistent pattern out of the paragraphs or sections you have written. In addition, you can also judge the effectiveness of your overall argument, assessing what each paragraph contributes and what may be missing. Turning a critical eye to your own work at the draft stage can save much grief in the long run. Be sure to get some response from classmates and friends too: come up with a set of questions to ask them about your draft and push them for honest responses. Find out what in your draft is confusing or unclear to others, what needs further evidence, what feels unconvincing, and so on.

Edit and proofread your text. Proofread an academic argument at least three times. First review it for ideas, making sure that all your main points and supporting evidence make sense and fit nicely together. Give special attention to transitions and paragraph structure and the way you have arranged information, positioned headings, and captioned graphic items. Make sure the big picture is in focus.

Then read the text word by word to check spelling, punctuation, quotation marks, apostrophes, abbreviations—in short, all the details that can go wrong simply because of a slip in attention. To keep their focus at this level, some readers will even read an entire text backwards. Notice too where your computer's spelling and grammar checkers may be underlining particular words and phrases. Don't ignore these clear signals (and don't rely solely on them to spot errors, since such automated tools are not perfectly accurate).

Finally, check that every source mentioned in the academic argument appears in the works cited or references list and that every citation is correct. This is also the time to make any final touchups to your overall design. Remember that how the document looks is part of what establishes its credibility.

RESPOND●

1. Look closely at the following five passages, each of which is from an opening of a published work, and decide which ones provide examples of academic argument. How would you describe each one, and what are its key features? Which is the most formal and academic? Which is the least? How might you revise them to make them more—or less—academic?

> During the Old Stone Age, between thirty-seven thousand and eleven thousand years ago, some of the most remarkable art ever conceived was etched or painted on the walls of caves in southern France and northern Spain. After a visit to Lascaux, in the Dordogne, which was discovered in 1940, Picasso reportedly said to his guide, "They've invented everything." What those first artists invented was a language of signs for which there will never be a Rosetta stone; perspective, a technique that was not rediscovered until the Athenian Golden Age;

and a bestiary of such vitality and finesse that, by the flicker of torch-light, the animals seem to surge from the walls, and move across them like figures in a magic-lantern show (in that sense, the artists invented animation). They also thought up the grease lamp—a lump of fat, with a plant wick, placed in a hollow stone—to light their work-place; scaffolds to reach high places; the principles of stenciling and Pointillism; powdered colors, brushes, and stumping cloths; and, more to the point of Picasso's insight, the very concept of an image. A true artist reimagines that concept with every blank canvas—but not from a void.

—Judith Thurman, "First Impressions," *New Yorker*

I stepped over the curb and into the street to hitchhike. At the age of ten I'd put some pretty serious mileage on my thumb. And I knew how it was done. Hold your thumb up, not down by your hip as though you didn't much give a damn whether you got a ride or not. Always hitch at a place where a driver could pull out of traffic and give you time to get in without risking somebody tailgating him.

—Harry Crews, "On Hitchhiking," *Harper's*

Coral reef ecosystems are essential marine environments around the world. Host to thousands (and perhaps millions) of diverse organisms, they are also vital to the economic well-being of an estimated 0.5 billion people, or 8% of the world's population who live on tropical coasts (Hoegh-Guldberg 1999). Income from tourism and fishing industries, for instance, is essential to the economic prosperity of many countries, and the various plant and animal species present in reef ecosystems are sources for different natural products and medicines. The degrada-tion of coral reefs can therefore have a devastating impact on coastal populations, and it is estimated that between 50% and 70% of all reefs around the world are currently threatened (Hoegh-Guldberg). Anthro-pogenic influences are cited as the major cause of this degradation, including sewage, sedimentation, direct trampling of reefs, over-fishing of herbivorous fish, and even global warming (Umezawa et al. 2002; Jones et al. 2001; Smith et al. 2001).

—Elizabeth Derse, "Identifying the Sources of Nitrogen to Hanalei Bay, Kauai, Utilizing the Nitrogen Isotope Signature of Macroalgae," *Stanford Undergraduate Research Journal*

While there's a good deal known about invertebrate neurobiology, these facts alone haven't settled questions of their sentience. On the one hand, invertebrates lack a cortex, amygdala, as well as many of the other major brain structures routinely implicated in human emo-tion. And unsurprisingly, their nervous systems are quite minimalist compared to ours: we have roughly a hundred thousand bee brains worth of neurons in our heads. On the other hand, some invertebrates, including insects, do possess the rudiments of our stress response system. So the question is still on the table: do they experience emotion in a way that we would recognize, or just react to the world with a set of glorified reflexes?

—Jason Castro, "Do Bees Have Feelings?" *Scientific American*

Bambi's mother, shot. Nemo's mother, eaten by a barracuda. Lilo's mother, killed in a car crash. Koda's mother in *Brother Bear*, speared. Po's mother in *Kung Fu Panda 2*, done in by a power-crazed peacock. Ariel's mother in the third *Little Mermaid*, crushed by a pirate ship. Human baby's mother in *Ice Age*, chased by a saber-toothed tiger over a waterfall. . . . The mothers in these movies are either gone or useless. And the father figures? To die for!

—Sarah Boxer, "Why Are All the Cartoon Mothers Dead?" *Atlantic*

2. Working with another student in your class, find examples from two or three different fields of academic arguments that strike you as being well written and effective. If possible, examine at least one from an online academic database so you can see what features periodical articles tend to offer. Then spend time looking at them closely. Do they exemplify the key features of academic arguments discussed in this chapter? What other features do they use? How are they organized? What kind of tone do the writers use? What use do they make of visuals? Draw up a brief report on your findings (a list will do), and bring it to class for discussion.

3. Read the following paragraphs about one writer's experience with anorexia, taken from a recent memoir, and then list changes that the writer might make to convert them into an argument for an academic journal, considering everything from tone and style to paragraphing and format.

It began when I was at the start of my sophomore year in college, sleeping on my lofted bed and rising before dawn. Initially I was not focused on losing weight; I simply became . . . obsessed with asceticism and determined to get by on less. I mused on the phonetic similarity between "ascetic" and "aesthetic," believing that through self-denial I could achieve a sort of delicate beauty. Even words like "svelte" and "petite" began to assume, in my mind, a positive valence. Soon I would begin to think of anorexia in this way as well, conjuring a snow-white princess who glided along in a winter fairyland, leaving no footprints.

Although I never stopped eating three meals a day, I severely restricted my diet and the range of foods I would eat. As the number of calories I consumed decreased with each passing week, food assumed more and more a central role in my life. I drove myself to extremes of hunger so that during class I'd be fantasizing about a green apple in my backpack, counting down the minutes until the lecture would end and I would savor that first juicy bite.

—Ilana Kurshan, *If All the Seas Were Ink: A Memoir*

4. Choose two pieces of your college writing, and examine them closely. Are they examples of strong academic writing? How do they use the key features that this chapter identifies as characteristic of academic arguments? How do they use and document sources? What kind of tone do you establish in each? After studying the examples in this chapter, what might you change about these pieces of writing, and why?

5. Go to a blog that you follow, or check out one on the *Huffington Post* or *Ricochet*. Spend some time reading the articles or postings on the blog, and look for ones that you think are the best written and the most interesting. What features or characteristics of academic argument do they use, and which ones do they avoid?

Where the Wild Things Should Be: Healing Nature Deficit Disorder through the Schoolyard

CHARLOTTE GEAGHAN-BREINER

Title begins with a reference many readers will recognize (Sendak) and then points to the direction the argument will take.

The developed world deprives children of a basic and inalienable right: unstructured outdoor play. Children today have substantially less access to nature, less free range, and less time for independent play than previous generations had. Experts in a wide variety of fields cite the rise of technology, urbanization, parental over-scheduling, fears of stranger-danger, and increased traffic as culprits. In 2005 journalist Richard Louv articulated the causes and consequences of children's alienation from nature, dubbing it "nature deficit disorder." Louv is not alone in claiming that the widening divide between children and nature has distressing health repercussions, from obesity and attention disorders to depression and decreased cognitive functioning. The dialogue surrounding nature deficit disorder deserves the attention and action of educators, health professionals, parents, developers, environmentalists, and conservationists alike.

Background information introduces a claim that states an effect and traces it back to its various causes.

Considerable evidence supports the claim.

The most practical solution to this staggering rift between children and nature involves the schoolyard. The schoolyard habitat movement, which promotes the "greening" of school grounds, is quickly gaining international recognition and legitimacy. A host of organizations, including the National Wildlife Federation, the American Forest Foundation, and the Council for Environmental Education, as well as their international counterparts, have committed themselves to this cause. However, while many recognize the need for "greened school grounds," not many describe such landscapes beyond using

Presents a solution to the problem and foreshadows full thesis

---

Charlotte Geaghan-Breiner wrote this academic argument for her first-year writing class at Stanford University.

adjectives such as "lush," "green," and "natural." The literature thus lacks a coherent research-based proposal that both asserts the power of "natural" school grounds *and* delineates what such grounds might look like.

My research strives to fill in this gap. I advocate for the schoolyard as the perfect place to address nature deficit disorder, demonstrate the benefits of greened schoolyards, and establish the tenets of natural schoolyard design in order to further the movement and inspire future action.

Asphalt Deserts: The State of the Schoolyard Today

As a formative geography of childhood, the schoolyard serves as the perfect place to address nature deficit disorder. Historian Peter Stearns argues that modern childhood was transformed when schooling replaced work as the child's main social function (1041). In this contemporary context, the schoolyard emerges as a critical setting for children's learning and play. Furthermore, as parental traffic and safety concerns increasingly constrain children's free range outside of school, the schoolyard remains a safe haven, a protected outdoor space just for children.

Despite the schoolyard's major significance in children's lives, the vast majority of schoolyards fail to meet children's needs. An outdated theoretical framework is partially to blame. In his 1890 *Principles of Psychology*, psychologist Herbert Spencer championed the "surplus energy theory": play's primary function, according to Spencer, was to burn off extra energy (White). Play, however, contributes to the social, cognitive, emotional, and physical growth of the child (Hart 136); "[l]etting off steam" is only one of play's myriad functions. Spencer's theory thus constitutes a serious oversimplification, but it still continues to inform the design of children's play areas.

Most U.S. playgrounds conform to an equipment-based model constructed implicitly on Spencer's surplus

The author identifies a weakness in the proposed solution.

Ending paragraph of the introduction presents the full thesis and outlines the entire essay.

Author uses subheads to help guide readers through the argument.

Explains why it's valuable to focus on the schoolyard

energy theory (Frost and Klein 2). The sports fields, asphalt courts, swing sets, and jungle gyms common to schoolyards relegate nature to the sidelines and prioritize gross motor play at the expense of dramatic play or exploration. An eight-year-old in England says it best: "The space outside feels boring. There's nothing to do. You get bored with just a square of tarmac" (Titman 42). Such an environment does not afford children the chance to graduate to new, more complex challenges as they develop. While play equipment still deserves a spot in the schoolyard, equipment-*dominated* playscapes leave the growing child bereft of stimulating interactions with the environment.

Also to blame for the failure of school grounds to meet children's needs are educators' and developers' adult-centric aims. Most urban schoolyards are sterile environments with low biodiversity (see fig. 1). While concrete, asphalt, and synthetic turf may be easier to maintain and supervise, they exacerbate the "extinction of experience," a term that Pyle has used to describe the disappearance of children's embodied, intuitive

Fig. 1: Addison Elementary in Palo Alto, CA, conforms to the traditional playground model, dominated by synthetic landcover and equipment. Photo by Charlotte Geaghan-Breiner

Quotations by children provide evidence to support the claim and bring in a personal touch. Citations follow MLA style.

Presents reasons why schoolyards continue to be poorly designed

The figure is introduced in the text and has a caption.

experiences in nature. Asphalt deserts are major instigators of this "cycle of impoverishment" (Pyle 312). Loss of biodiversity begets environmental apathy, which in turn allows the process of extinction to persist. Furthermore, adults' preference for manicured, landscaped grounds does little to enhance children's creative outdoor play. Instead of rich, stimulating play environments for children, such highly ordered schoolyards are constructed with adults' convenience in mind.

THE GREENER, THE BETTER: THE BENEFITS OF GREENED SCHOOL GROUNDS

A great body of research documents the physiological, cognitive, psychological, and social benefits of contact with nature. Health experts champion outdoor play as an antidote to two major trends in children of the developed world: the Attention Deficit Disorder and obesity epidemics. A 2001 study by Taylor, Kuo, and Sullivan indicates that green play settings decrease the severity of symptoms in children with ADD. They also combat inactivity in children by diversifying the "play repertoire" and providing for a wider range of physical activity than traditional playgrounds. In the war against childhood obesity, health advocates must add the natural schoolyard to their arsenal.

Author cites research that discusses the health benefits of interacting with nature.

The schoolyard also has the ability to influence the way children play. Instead of being prescribed a play structure with a clear purpose (e.g., a swing set), children in natural schoolyards must discover the affordances of their environment—they must imagine what could be. In general, children exhibit more prosocial behavior and higher levels of inclusion in the natural schoolyard (Dyment 31). A 2006 questionnaire-based study of a greening initiative in Toronto found that the naturalization of the school grounds yielded a decrease in aggressive actions and disciplinary problems and a corresponding increase in civility and cooperation (Dyment 28). The greened schoolyard offers benefits

Social benefits of interacting with nature

beyond physical and mental health; it shapes the character and quality of children's play interactions.

The schoolyard also has the potential to shape the relationship between children and the natural world. In the essay "Eden in a Vacant Lot," Pyle laments the loss of vacant lots and undeveloped spaces in which children can play and develop intimacy with the land. However, Pyle overlooks the geography of schoolyards, which can serve as enclaves of nature in an increasingly urbanized and developed world. Research has shown that school ground naturalization fosters nature literacy and intimacy just as Pyle's vacant lots do. For instance, a school ground greening program in Toronto dramatically enhanced children's environmental awareness, sense of stewardship, and curiosity about their local ecosystem (Dyment 37). When integrated with nature, the schoolyard can mitigate the effects of nature deficit disorder and reawaken children's innate biophilia, or love of nature.

BIOPHILIC DESIGN: ESTABLISHING THE TENETS OF NATURAL SCHOOLYARD DESIGN

The need for naturalized schoolyards is urgent. But how might theory actually translate into reality? Here I will propose four principles of biophilic schoolyard design, or landscaping that aims to integrate nature and natural systems into the man-made geography of the schoolyard.

The author establishes four guidelines for redesigning schoolyards.

The first is biodiversity. Schools should strive to incorporate a wide range of greenery and wildlife on their grounds (see fig. 2). Native plants should figure prominently so as to inspire children's interest in their local habitats. Inclusion of wildlife in school grounds can foster meaningful interactions with other species. Certain plants and flowers, for example, attract birds, butterflies, and other insects; aquatic areas can house fish, frogs, tadpoles, and pond bugs. School pets and small-scale farms also serve to teach children important lessons about responsibility, respect, and compassion for animals. Biodiversity, the most vital feature of biophilic

Fig. 2: A seating area at Ohlone School in Palo Alto, CA, features a healthy range of plant species. Photo by Charlotte Geaghan-Breiner

design, transforms former "asphalt deserts" into realms teeming with life.

The second principle that schoolyard designers should keep in mind is sensory stimulation. The greater the degree of sensory richness in an environment, the more opportunities it affords the child to imagine, learn, and discover. School grounds should feature a range of colors, textures, sounds, fragrances, and in the case of the garden, tastes. Such sensory diversity almost always accompanies natural environments, unlike concrete, which affords comparatively little sensory stimulation.

Diversity of topography constitutes another dimension of a greened schoolyard (Fjortoft and Sageie 83). The best school grounds afford children a range of places to climb, tunnel, frolic, and sit. Natural elements function as "play equipment": children can sit on stumps, jump over logs, swing on trees, roll down grassy mounds, and climb on boulders. The playscape should also offer nooks and crannies for children to seek shelter and refuge. While asphalt lots and play structures are still fun for children, they should not dominate the school grounds (see fig. 3).

A figure illustrates a specific point about play structures.

Last but not least, naturalized schoolyards must embody the theory of loose parts proposed by architect Simon Nicholson. "In any environment," he writes, "both the degree of inventiveness and the possibility of discovery are directly proportional to the number and kinds of variables in it" (qtd. in Louv 87). Loose parts—sand, water, leaves, nuts, seeds, rocks, and sticks—are abundant in the natural world. The detachability of loose parts makes them ideal for children's construction projects. While some might worry about the possible hazards of loose parts, conventional play equipment is far from safe: more than 200,000 of children's emergency room visits every year in

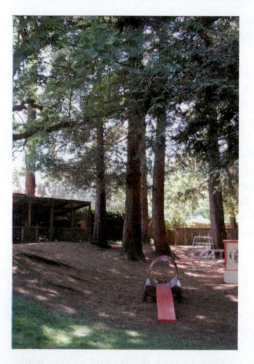

Fig. 3: Peninsula School in Menlo Park, CA, has integrated traditional equipment, such as a playhouse and slide, into the natural setting. Photo by Charlotte Geaghan-Breiner

the United States are linked to these built structures (Frost 217). When integrated into the schoolyard through naturalization, loose parts offer the child the chance to gain ever-increasing mastery of the environment.

The four tenets proposed provide a concrete basis for the application of biophilic design to the schoolyard. Such design also requires a frame-shift away from adult preferences for well-manicured grounds and towards children's needs for wilder spaces that can be constructed, manipulated, and changed through play (Lester and Maudsley 67; White and Stoecklin). Schoolyards designed according to the precepts of biodiversity, sensory stimulation, diversity of topography, and loose parts will go a long way in healing the rift between children and nature, a rift that adult-centric design only widens.

GROUNDS FOR CHANGE

In conclusion, I have shown that natural schoolyard design can heal nature deficit disorder by restoring free outdoor play to children's lives in the developed world. Successful biophilic schoolyards challenge the conventional notion that natural and man-made landscapes are mutually exclusive. Human-designed environments, and especially those for children, should strive to integrate nature into the landscape. All schools should be designed with the four tenets of natural schoolyard design in mind.

Author restates her claim.

Though such sweeping change may seem impractical given limitations on school budgets, greening initiatives that use natural elements, minimal equipment, and volunteer work can be remarkably cost-effective. Peninsula School in Menlo Park, California, has minimized maintenance costs through the inclusion of hardy native species; it is essentially "designed for neglect" (Dyment 44). Gardens and small-scale school farms can also become their own source of funding, as they have for Ohlone Elementary School in Palo Alto, California. Ultimately, the cognitive, psychological, physiological, and social

Offers examples of successful biophilic school-yard design

benefits of natural school grounds are priceless. In the words of author Richard Louv, "School isn't supposed to be a polite form of incarceration, but a portal to the wider world" (Louv 226). With this in mind, let the schoolyard restore to children their exquisite intimacy with nature: their inheritance, their right.

WORKS CITED

The list of works cited follows MLA style.

Dyment, Janet. "Gaining Ground: The Power and Potential of School Ground Greening in the Toronto District School Board." *Evergreen*, 2006. www.evergreen.ca/downloads/pdfs/Gaining-Ground.pdf.

Fjortoft, Ingunn, and Jostein Sageie. "The Natural Environment as a Playground for Children." *Landscape and Urban Planning*, vol. 48, no. 2, Winter 2001, pp. 83-97.

Frost, Joe L. *Play and Playscapes*. Delmar, 1992.

Frost, Joe L., and Barry L. Klein. *Children's Play and Playgrounds*. Allyn and Bacon, 1979.

Hart, Roger. "Containing Children: Some Lessons on Planning for Play from New York City." *Environment and Urbanization*, vol. 14, no. 2, October 2002, pp. 135-48, doi.org/10.1177/0995624780201400211.

Lester, Stuart, and Martin Maudsley. *Play, Naturally: A Review of Children's Natural Play*. Play England, National Children's Bureau, 2007.

Louv, Richard. *Last Child in the Woods: Saving Our Children from Nature-Deficit Disorder*. Algonquin of Chapel Hill, 2005.

Nicholson, Simon. "How Not to Cheat Children: The Theory of Loose Parts." *Landscape Architecture*, vol. 62, October 1971, pp. 30-35.

Pyle, Robert M. "Eden in a Vacant Lot: Special Places, Species, and Kids in the Neighborhood of Life." *Children and Nature: Psychological, Sociocultural, and Evolutionary Investigations*, edited by Peter H. Kahn and Stephen R. Kellert, MIT Press, 2002, pp. 305-27.

Stearns, Peter N. "Conclusion: Change, Globalization, and Childhood." *Journal of Social History*, vol. 38, no. 4, 2005, pp. 1041-46.

Taylor, Andrea F., et al. "Coping with ADD: The Surprising Connection to Green Play Settings." *Environment and Behavior*, vol. 33, no. 1, 2001, pp. 54-77.

Titman, Wendy. *Special Places; Special People: The Hidden Curriculum of Schoolgrounds*. World Wide Fund for Nature, 1994, files.eric.ed.gov/fulltext/ED430384.pdf.

White, Randy. "Young Children's Relationship with Nature: Its Importance to Children's Development and the Earth's Future." *Taproot*, vol. 16, no. 2, 2006. *White Hutchinson Leisure and Learning Group*, www.whitehutchinson.com/children/articles/childrennature.shtml.

White, Randy, and Vicki Stoecklin. "Children's Outdoor Play and Learning Environments: Returning to Nature." *Early Childhood News*, Mar. 1998. *White Hutchinson Leisure and Learning Group*, https://www.whitehutchinson.com/children/articles/outdoor.shtml.

The Emotion Work of "Thank You for Your Service"

SIDRA MONTGOMERY

In the post-9/11 era, "thank you for your service" (TYFYS) has become the new mantra of public support bestowed upon the veteran community. In the early 2000s, as the wars in Afghanistan and Iraq began escalating, "Support Our Troops" car magnets increasingly appeared on the trunks of cars across America. After well over 15 years of war, public gratitude is now most commonly expressed in small interactions between veterans and the public they've served—with strangers saying TYFYS or offering to pay for a coffee or meal. If you ask any recent servicemember or veteran how they feel when someone says TYFYS, you'll probably hear them express a strong opinion about the phrase. While some view it positively and enjoy these interactions, most find it awkward, uncomfortable or irritating. The message of support and gratitude that well-meaning Americans are attempting to express is often lost in translation with veterans.

A collection of op-ed pieces have addressed why servicemembers find TYFYS to be a point of disconnection rather than connection. James Kelly, an active-duty Marine, says that he hears the phrase so often it has become an "empty platitude," something people say only because it is "politically correct." Matt Richtel, a *New York Times* reporter, highlights how veterans feel the phrase can be self-serving; civilians get to pat themselves on the back because they are doing something for veterans, alleviating any sense of guilt in the era of an all-volunteer service. Another common complaint is that TYFYS doesn't start the conversation between veterans and civilians—it stunts it—leaving veterans feeling more isolated and less connected to the America they served. Veterans commonly remark that civilians don't even know what they are saying "thank you" for. Elizabeth Samet, a professor at West Point, argues that we've come to the other "unthinking extreme" with TYFYS as an attempt for atonement after the poor treatment of Vietnam veterans.

_____

Sidra Montgomery received her PhD in sociology in 2017 from the University of Maryland–College Park. Her work focuses specifically on the military and veterans. The piece appeared on March 21, 2017, on the Veterans Scholars Web site.

While many have tried to explain *why* veterans find TYFYS to be lacking, few have examined *how these interactions affect veterans.* Having interviewed servicemembers and veterans for the past 3 years in my professional life, and being a military spouse for the past 5 years, I have always been intrigued by how veterans handle these moments and interactions. I watch the discomfort when strangers approach my interview subjects or friends and say TYFYS—it becomes an awkward stumble for the veteran to find a way to muster their appreciation for a gesture that doesn't necessarily square with its intent.

EMOTION WORK

As I analyzed the data I collected for my dissertation, a total of 39 interviews with wounded, injured, and ill post–9/11 veterans, I realized these interactions require veterans to engage in *emotion work,* a sociological concept defined by Arlie Hochschild. Emotion work is defined by Hochschild as "trying to change, in degree or quality, an emotion or feeling" (1979:561). It is an active attempt to shape and direct one's feelings to match the appropriate emotions for a given situation. For example, when someone thanks you for something you've done, you're supposed to feel good, right? Gratitude should give you that warm, fuzzy feeling inside. This is called "feeling rules"; it's how we know what we should be feeling in any given moment. . . .

For veterans who genuinely appreciate and enjoy hearing TYFYS and other acts of gratitude, there is no "work" necessary because their feelings are appropriate given the situation. For Alex, a wounded Marine veteran, TYFYS makes him feel as though he is "seen" and that his service is validated:

> I like it. I really like it when people acknowledge my service. I'm not out there trying to get someone to do it, but when someone takes time out of their day to shake my hand and say, "Thank you for your service." It's like, "Wow. You know this country—it was worth it. You know it's—proud of your service to the country". . . That's something special.

Alex's emotions are in line with what we expect to feel when someone says thank you and acknowledges something that we have done. He doesn't have to control or wrangle his emotions because they already align with the socially prescribed "feeling rules" and expectations.

My dissertation data suggests that 15 to 20% of veterans share Alex's feelings; they enjoy and appreciate when people thank them for their service or demonstrate their gratitude through other acts and gestures. Personally and anecdotally, I've found about the same split: 10–20% find TYFYS gratifying and associate it with positive feelings, and 80–90% of servicemembers and veterans feel uncomfortable or upset about the phrase.

For the majority of wounded veterans I interviewed, who don't have positive associations with TYFYS, these interactions necessitate emotion work. As they go about their day-to-day life, they are thrust into situations where they must acknowledge and negotiate the gratitude of total strangers through their own emotional response: emotions that do not match their true feelings in the situation. Luis, a young Marine Corps veteran with visible injuries, describes how he wrestles with having to do emotion work in these interactions:

> When people say thank you for your service, thank you for what you did . . . it's kind of lost its shock value or something. I've heard it so much that I'm embarrassed that I can't give them . . . like that first time when someone said thank you for your service . . . I feel like I don't give them enough sincerity, I feel bad . . . I feel embarrassed for myself because I can't do that, you know? . . . I just hear it sooooo much.

Luis wants to give others a genuine emotional reaction each time they thank him for his service, but he feels he can't because of the overwhelming number of times this happens to him. From this quote it's clear he is blaming himself for even having to perform emotion work in the first place. Connor, an Army veteran with invisible injuries, discusses how he handles TYFYS:

> I give the standard, thanks, appreciate it or happy to do it. Or I don't get into it. Even if I know it's totally fake I'm like, yeah, appreciate it. And I'll give just a fake answer. As fake as I got [from them], that's how much I'll give back . . . It'll be like . . . "oh, thanks" with the plastic smile. You know what I mean?

Connor attempts to mirror the level of sincerity in the interaction, aligning his own response with it. His comment about how he puts on a "plastic smile" describes how he engages in surface acting: a way to present the necessary emotion to others even though his own feelings haven't changed.

Another common strategy for veterans, especially wounded veterans who are frequently thanked for their service, is the use of predetermined responses. Having a rolodex of appropriate responses minimizes impromptu emotion work. Jackson, a Marine Corps veteran who has visible injuries, says that hearing TYFYS "*just gets old*" because he hears it so much. When I asked him how he usually responds, he said:

> [I will say] ". . . no, *thank you*." Another one is like some people [say] "thank *you guys* for what *you do* . . . you guys made coming home so much easier and so much more worth it." So make them feel just as adequate in a way.

Jackson reveals the set of responses that he (and others) normally give. These prepackaged responses increase the efficiency of Jackson's emotion work by creating sentiments that acknowledge and reciprocate the gratitude—an intentional move on Jackson's part.

Several years after her Marine Corps service, Susan, an invisibly injured veteran, has gained a new perspective on the TYFYS issue. She is now able to see it from another point of view:

> You get to finally a point—I finally went, you know, these people are very sincere, and you've got to let them just say the thing. Because they generally want to thank you. And this is so not your experience. You don't have to have it with them. And then it became okay going, you know what, they're really caring, lovely people most of the time . . .

Susan describes taking away her own investment in these interactions as a way to distance herself from constantly engaging in emotion work whenever someone says "thank you." She understands the moment to be more about the other person than herself. She also describes her engagement with deep acting: working to change the way she truly feels about these interactions; trying to bring her own emotions in line with what's expected.

The Cumulative Effect for Visibly Injured Veterans

For current servicemembers, veterans, and invisibly injured veterans, these moments of invited gratitude from strangers happen occasionally or in concentrated environments where they know they may be thanked or approached. For visibly injured veterans, these interactions happen every day. Visibly injured veterans are disproportionately burdened with doing the emotional work surrounding public gratitude because their status as wounded veterans can't be hidden or "taken off" like a uniform. And their visible injury only amplifies feelings of gratitude among the public, causing them to experience more of these moments and interactions.

Thomas, an Army veteran with visible injuries, describes:

> [Civilians] . . . they just all want to do the right things. And I mean, to that person they have one chance to make a difference to one person. But if it's you, they're the 100th person today to say "thank you for your service."

The cumulative effect of these interactions wears on Thomas and other visibly injured veterans:

> And what if everybody did that to me? Like, everywhere I went, what if every single person thought they were doing me a favor and said "thank you for your service." I would spend my whole life giving to other people. I could literally go every five feet and just be doling out good feelings to everybody. And I'm sorry, I'm an emotional bank account, we're all just emotional bank accounts.

Thomas's comments clearly reveal how visibly injured veterans can quickly become exhausted from the emotion work of receiving TYFYS and other gestures of gratitude. What seems like a small interaction in the moment is continually repeated for wounded veterans like Thomas.

The treatment of U.S. veterans has significantly changed over time, from the prosperous return of World War II veterans to the protests and mistreatment of Vietnam veterans to the new era of the all-volunteer force. It is important that as a nation, we engage in a constant reflection process of how we treat our veterans, from the largest of government programs to the smallest interpersonal interactions. The well-meaning intent behind TYFYS isn't always received by post–9/11 veterans in the same way.

Practical Suggestions: What Should We Be Doing to Show Our Gratitude and Appreciation?

Inevitably, after presenting these issues with TYFYS I get asked: *"well, what **should** we be doing?"* This is both a prudent and complicated question, and there is no one-size-fits-all answer. We all have our own personal preferences of what is meaningful to us based on our personality, life experiences, and our thoughts. I'm not here to say that I have *the* answer, but I have a couple suggestions based on my work with veterans:

1. **Judge whether the military member or veteran seems open to conversation with a stranger.** You know how you can tell whether the person next to you on a plane wants to talk or wants to be left alone? The same should go for your interactions with veterans, servicemembers, and wounded veterans. Do they appear willing to engage with others (i.e., making eye contact or already engaging in a friendly conversation with you), or do they look like they just want to grab their coffee and go about their day? If the latter—let them go about their day and reflect privately on your gratitude for their willingness to lay their life on the line for our freedom.

2. **If you want to show your support for veterans, find a local organization that helps veterans in your community.** Do your research, find out what organizations are doing to serve veterans and improve their lives. Give your financial support or your time (through volunteering).

3. **Go beyond "thank you for your service."** Ask them why they served, ask them when and where they served, ask them what they most enjoyed about their service. Dig deeper; cultivate gratitude for their service by learning more about it.

18
Finding Evidence

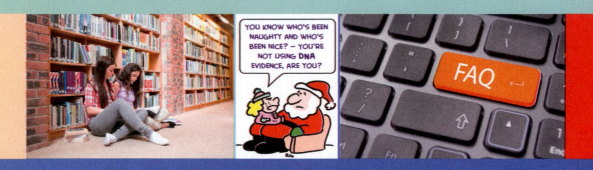

LEFT TO RIGHT: Wavebreakmedia Ltd/AGE Fotostock; Baloo-Rex May/CartoonStock.com; Zoonar/M KANG/AGE Fotostock

In making and supporting claims for academic arguments, writers use all kinds of evidence: data from journal articles; scholarly books; historical records from archives; blogs, wikis, social media sites, and other digital sources; personal observations and fieldwork; surveys; and even DNA. But such evidence doesn't exist in a vacuum. Instead, the quality of evidence—how and when it was collected, by whom, and for what purposes—may become part of the argument itself. Evidence may be persuasive in one time and place but not in another; it may convince one kind of audience but not another; it may work with one type of argument but not with the kind you are writing. The point is that finding "good" evidence for a research project is rarely a simple matter.

Considering the Rhetorical Situation

To be most persuasive, evidence should match the time and place in which you make your argument—that is to say, your rhetorical situation. For example, arguing that government officials in the twenty-first century should use the same policies to deal with economic troubles that were employed in the middle of the twentieth might not be convincing on its own. After all, almost every aspect of the world economy has changed in the past fifty years. In the same way, a writer may achieve excellent results by citing a detailed survey of local teenagers as evidence for education reform in her small rural hometown, but she may have less success using the same evidence to argue for similar reforms in a large urban community.

College writers also need to consider the fields that they're working in. In disciplines such as experimental psychology or economics, **quantitative data**—the sort that can be observed, collected and counted—may be the best evidence. In many historical, literary, or philosophical studies, however, the same kind of data may be less appropriate or persuasive, or even impossible to come by. As you become more familiar with a discipline, you'll gain a sense of what it takes to support a claim. The following questions will help you understand the rhetorical situation of a particular field:

- What kinds of data are preferred as evidence? How are such data gathered, tabulated, and verified?

- How are definitions, causal analyses, evaluations, analogies, and examples used as evidence?

- How are statistics or other numerical information used and presented as evidence? Are tables, charts, or graphs commonly used? How much weight do they carry?

- What or who counts as an authority in this field? How are the credentials of authorities established? How are research publications reviewed and research journals refereed?

- What weight do writers in the field give to **precedence**—that is, to examples of similar actions or decisions made in the past?

- Is personal experience allowed as evidence? When?

- How are quotations used as part of evidence?

- How are still or moving images or sound(s) used as part of evidence, and how closely are they related to the verbal parts of the argument being presented? Are other kinds of media commonly used to present evidence?

In "Getting Personal about Cybersecurity," Lindsay McKenzie cites research from surveys as well as quotations by experts to establish the difficulties of cybersecurity education on campus.

LINK TO P. 698

As these questions suggest, evidence may not always travel well from one field to another. Nor does it always travel easily from culture to culture. Differing notions of evidence can lead to arguments that go nowhere fast. For instance, when Italian journalist Oriana Fallaci interviewed Ayatollah Khomeini, Iran's supreme leader, in 1979, she argued in a way that's common in North American and Western European cultures: she presented claims that she considered to be adequately backed up with facts ("Iran denies freedom to people. . . . Many people have been put in prison and even executed, just for speaking out in opposition"). In response, Khomeini relied on very different kinds of evidence— analogies ("Just as a finger with gangrene should be cut off so that it will not destroy the whole body, so should people who corrupt others be pulled out like weeds so they will not infect the whole field") and, above all, the authority of the Qur'an. Partly because of these differing beliefs about what counts as evidence, the interview ended unsuccessfully.

The need for evidence depends a lot on the rhetorical situation. Mick Stevens/The New Yorker Collection/The Cartoon Bank

CULTURAL CONTEXTS FOR ARGUMENT

The Rhetorical Situation

To take another example, a *Harvard Business Review* blog post from December 4, 2013, on "How to Argue across Cultures" recounts the story of a Western businessperson who was selling bicycles produced in China to a buyer in Germany. When the business owner went to pick up the bicycles, he noticed that they rattled. In considering how to bring up this defect with the Chinese supplier, the businessperson could have confronted him directly, relying on physical evidence to support his claim. He rejected this form of evidence, however, because he knew that such a confrontation would result in loss of face for the supplier and very likely lead to an undesirable outcome. So instead, he suggested that he and the Chinese supplier take a couple of bikes out for a ride, during which the bikes rattled away. At the end of the ride, the Western businessperson quietly mentioned that he "thought his bike had rattled" and then departed, leaving the Chinese supplier to consider his subtle presentation of evidence. And it worked: when the Germans received the bicycle delivery, the rattle had been repaired.

It's always good to remember, then, that when arguing across cultural divides, whether international or more local, you need to think carefully about how you're accustomed to using evidence—and about what counts as evidence to other people (without surrendering your own intellectual principles).

Searching Effectively

The evidence you will use in most academic arguments—books, articles, videos, documents, photographs and other images—will likely come from sources you locate in libraries, in databases, or online. How well you can navigate these complex territories will determine the success of many of your academic and professional projects. Research suggests that most students overestimate their ability to manage these tools and, perhaps more important, don't seek the help they need to find the best materials for their projects. In this chapter, we aim to point you in the right direction for successful academic research.

Explore library resources: printed works and databases. Your college library has printed materials (books, periodicals, reference works) as well as computers that provide access to its electronic catalogs, other libraries' catalogs, and numerous proprietary databases (such as Academic Search Complete, Academic OneFile, JSTOR) not available publicly on the Web. Crucially, libraries also have librarians whose job it is to guide you through these resources, help you identify reputable materials, and show you how to search for materials efficiently. The best way to begin a serious academic argument then is often with a trip to the library or a discussion with your professor or a research librarian.

Also be certain that you know your way around the library. If not, ask the staff there to help you locate the following tools: general and specialized encyclopedias; biographical resources; almanacs, yearbooks, and atlases; book and periodical indexes; specialized indexes and abstracts; the circulation computer or library catalog; special collections; audio, video, and art collections; and the interlibrary loan office, for requesting materials not available at your own library.

At the outset of a project, determine what kinds of sources you will need to support your project. (You might also review your assignment to see whether you're required to consult particular types or a specific number of sources.) If you'll use print sources, find out whether they're readily available in your library or whether you must make special arrangements (such as an interlibrary loan) to acquire them. For example, your argument for a senior thesis might benefit from material available mostly in old newspapers and magazines: access to them might require time and ingenuity. If you need to locate other nonprint sources (such as audiotapes, videotapes, artwork, or photos), find out where those are kept and whether you need special permission to examine them.

Most academic resources, however, will be on the shelves or available electronically through databases. Here's when it's important to understand the distinction between library databases and the Web. Your library's computers hold important resources that aren't on the Web or aren't available to you except through the library's system. The most important of these resources may be your library's catalog of its own holdings (mostly books). But college libraries also pay to subscribe to *scholarly databases* that you can use for free by logging in through your school library—for example, guides to journal and magazine articles, the Academic Search Complete database (which holds the largest collection of multidisciplinary journals), the LexisNexis database of news stories and legal cases, and various compilations of statistics.

Though many of these Web and database resources may be searchable through your own computer, consider exploring them initially at your college library. That's because these professional databases aren't always easy to use or intuitive: you may need to learn to focus and narrow your searches (by date, field, types of material, and so on) so that your results are manageable and full of relevant items. That's when librarians or your instructor can help, so ask them for assistance. They expect your questions.

Librarians may, for example, draw your attention to the distinction between subject headings and keywords. The Library of Congress Subject Headings (LCSH) are standardized words and phrases that are used to classify the subject matter of books and articles. Library catalogs and databases routinely use these subject headings to index their contents by author, title, publication date, and subject headings. When you do a subject search of the library's catalog, you need to use the exact wording of the subject headings. On the other hand, searches with *keywords* use the computer's ability to look for any term in any field of the electronic record. So keyword searching is less restrictive, but you'll still have to think hard about your search terms to get usable results and to learn how to limit or expand your search.

Determine, too, early on, how current your sources need to be. If you must investigate the latest findings about, say, a new treatment for malaria, check very recent periodicals, medical journals, and the Web. If you want broader coverage with more context and background information, look for reference materials or scholarly books. If your argument deals with a specific time period, newspapers, magazines, and books written during that period may be your best assets.

How many sources should you consult for an academic argument? Expect to examine many more sources than you'll end up using, and be sure to cover all major perspectives on your subject. Read enough sources to feel comfortable discussing it with someone with more knowledge than you. You don't have to be an expert, but your readers should sense that you are well informed.

Explore online resources. Chances are your first instinct when you need to find information is to do a quick keyword search on the Web, which in many instances will take you to a site such as Wikipedia, the free encyclopedia launched by Jimmy Wales in 2001. For years, many teachers and institutions argued that the information on Wikipedia was suspect and could not be used as a reliable source, particularly since anyone can edit and change the content on a Wikipedia page. Times have changed, however, and many serious research efforts now include a stop at Wikipedia. As always, however, let the buyer beware: you need to verify the credibility of all of your sources! If you intend to support a serious academic argument, remember to approach the Web carefully and professionally.

Web search engines such as Google or Bing make searching for material seem very easy—perhaps *too* easy. For an argument about the fate of the antihero in contemporary films, for example, typing in *film* and *antihero* produces far too many possible matches, or hits. Some of those hits might be generic and geared to current moviegoers rather than someone thinking about an analytical essay. You could further narrow the search by adding a third or fourth keyword—say, *French* or *current*—or you could simply type in a specific question. Google will always offer pages of links. But you need to be a critical user too, pushing yourself well beyond any initial items you turn up or using those sources to find more authoritative, diverse, or academic materials.

Google does have resources to help you refine your results or direct you to works better suited to academic research. When you search for any term, you can click "Help" at the bottom of the results page, which takes you to the Google Help Center. Click on "Filter and refine your results" and then "Advanced search," which will bring more options to narrow your focus in important ways.

But that's not the end of your choices. With an *academic* argument, you might want to explore your topic in either Google Books or Google Scholar. Both resources direct you to the type and quality of materials (scholarly journal articles, academic books) that you probably need for a term paper or professional project. And Google offers multimodal options as well: it can help you find images, photographs, videos, blogs, and so on. The lesson is simple. If your current Web searches typically don't go much beyond the first items a search engine offers, you aren't close to using all the power available to you. Explore the search tools you routinely use and learn what they can really do.

You should work just as deliberately with the academic databases you may have access to in a library or online—such as Academic Search Complete or Business Source Complete, among many others. As noted earlier, searching these professional tools often requires more deliberate choices and specific combinations of search terms and keywords. In doing such searches, you'll need to observe the search logic followed by the particular database—usually explained on a search page. For

Most search engines offer many kinds of research tools like this "Advanced Search" page from Google.

example, using Boolean operators such as *and* between keywords (*movies and heroes*) may indicate that both terms must appear in a file for it to be called up. Using *or* between keywords usually instructs the computer to locate every file in which either one word or the other shows up, and using *not* tells the computer to exclude files containing a particular word from the search results (*movies not heroes*).

SEARCHING ONLINE OR IN DATABASES

- Don't rely on simple Web searches only.
- Find library databases targeted to your subject.
- Use advanced search techniques to focus your search.
- Learn the difference between *subject heading* and *keyword* searches.
- Understand the differences between academic and popular sources.
- Admit when you don't know how to find material—you won't be alone!
- *Routinely* ask for help from librarians and instructors.

Collecting Data on Your Own

Not all your supporting materials for an academic argument must come from print or online sources. You can present research that you have carried out yourself or been closely involved with, often called *field research*; such research usually requires that you collect and examine data. Here, we discuss the kinds of firsthand research that student writers do most often.

Perform experiments. Academic arguments can be supported by evidence you gather through experiments. In the sciences, data from experiments conducted under rigorously controlled conditions is highly valued. In other fields, more informal experiments may be acceptable, especially if they're intended to provide only part of the support for an argument.

If you want to argue, for instance, that the recipes in *Bon Appétit* magazine are impossibly tedious to follow and take far more time than the average person wishes to spend preparing food, you might ask five or six people to conduct an experiment—following two recipes from a recent issue and recording and timing every step. The evidence that you gather from this informal experiment could provide some concrete support—by way of specific examples—for your contention.

But such experiments should be taken with a grain of salt (maybe organic in this case). They may not convince or impress certain audiences. And if your experiments can easily be attacked as skewed or sloppily done ("The people you asked to make these recipes couldn't cook a Pop-Tart"), then they may do more harm than good.

Make observations. "What," you may wonder, "could be easier than observing something?" You just choose a subject, look at it closely, and record what you see and hear. But trained observers say that recording an observation accurately requires intense concentration and mental agility. If observing were easy, all eyewitnesses would provide reliable stories. Yet experience shows that when several people observe the same phenomenon, they generally offer different, sometimes even contradictory, accounts of those observations.

Before you begin an observation yourself, decide exactly what you want to find out, and anticipate what you're likely to see. Do you want to observe an action that is repeated by many people—perhaps how people behave at the checkout line in a grocery store? Or maybe you want to study a sequence of actions—for instance, the stages involved in student registration, which you expect to argue is far too complicated. Or maybe

you are motivated to examine the interactions of a notoriously contentious political group. Once you have a clear sense of what you'll analyze
and what questions you'll try to answer through the observation, use the
following guidelines to achieve the best results:

- Make sure that the observation relates directly to your claim.

- Brainstorm about what you're looking for, but don't be rigidly bound
  to your expectations.

- Develop an appropriate system for collecting data. Consider using a
  split notebook page or screen: on one side, record the minute details of
  your observations; on the other, record your thoughts or impressions.

- Be aware that how you record data will affect the outcome, if only in
  respect to what you decide to include in your observational notes and
  what you leave out.

- Record the precise date, time, and place of the observation(s).

- If the location you want to focus on is not a public one (for instance,
  an elementary school playground), ask for permission to conduct
  your observation.

You may be asked to prepare systematic observations in various science
courses, including anthropology or psychology, where you would follow
a methodology and receive precise directions. But observation can play
a role in other kinds of arguments and use various media: a photo essay
or audio/video clips, for example, might serve as academic arguments in
some situations.

Conduct interviews. Some evidence is best obtained through direct
interviews. If you can talk with an expert—in person, on the phone, or
online—you might obtain information you couldn't have gotten through
any other type of research. In addition to an expert opinion, you might
ask for firsthand accounts, biographical information, or suggestions of
other places to look or other people to consult. The following guidelines
will help you conduct effective interviews:

- Determine the exact purpose of the interview, and be sure it's directly
  related to your claim.

- Set up the interview well in advance—preferably by a written communication. (An email is more polite than a text message.) Explain
  who you are, the purpose of the interview, and what you expect to
  cover. Specify, too, how much time it will take, and if you wish to
  record the session, ask permission to do so.

- Prepare a written list of both factual and open-ended questions. (Brainstorming with friends can help you come up with good questions.) Leave plenty of space for notes after each question. If the interview proceeds in a direction that you hadn't expected but that seems promising, don't feel that you have to cover every one of your questions.

- Record the subject's full name and title, as well as the date, time, and place of the interview.

- Be sure to thank those people whom you interview, either in person or with a follow-up letter or email message.

A serious interview can be eye-opening when the questions get a subject to reveal important experiences or demonstrate his or her knowledge or wisdom.

Use questionnaires to conduct surveys. Surveys usually require the use of questionnaires distributed to a number of people. Questions should be clear, easy to understand, and designed so that respondents' answers can be easily analyzed. Questions that ask respondents to say "yes" or "no" or to rank items on a scale (1 to 5, for example, or "most helpful" to "least helpful") are particularly easy to tabulate. Because tabulation can take time and effort, limit the number of questions you ask. Note also that people often resent being asked to answer more than about twenty questions, especially online.

Here are some other guidelines to help you prepare for and carry out a survey:

- Ask your instructor if your college or university requires that you get approval from the local Institutional Review Board (IRB) to conduct survey research. Many schools waive this requirement if students are doing such research as part of a required course, but you should check to make sure. Securing IRB permission usually requires filling out a series of online forms, submitting all of your questions for approval, and asking those you are surveying to sign a consent form saying they agree to participate in the research.

- Write out your purpose in conducting the survey, and make sure that its results will be directly related to your purpose.

- Brainstorm potential questions to include in the survey, and ask how each relates to your purpose and claim.

- Figure out how many people you want to contact, what the demographics of your sample should be (for example, men in their twenties or an equal number of men and women), and how you plan to reach these people.

- Draft questions that are as free of bias as possible, making sure that each calls for a short, specific answer. Avoid open-ended questions, whose responses will be harder to tabulate.

- Think about possible ways that respondents could misunderstand you or your questions, and revise with these points in mind.

"Next question: I believe that life is a constant striving for balance, requiring frequent tradeoffs between morality and necessity, within a cyclic pattern of joy and sadness, forging a trail of bittersweet memories until one slips, inevitably, into the jaws of death. Agree or disagree?"

A key requirement of survey questions is that they be easy to understand. George Price/The New Yorker Collection/The Cartoon Bank

- Test the questions in advance on several people, and revise those questions that are ambiguous, hard to answer, or too time-consuming to answer.

- If your questionnaire is to be sent by mail or email or posted on the Web, draft a cover letter explaining your purpose and giving a clear deadline. For mail, provide an addressed, stamped return envelope.

- On the final draft of the questionnaire, leave plenty of space for answers.

- Proofread the final draft carefully. Typos will make a bad impression on those whose help you're seeking.

- After you've done your tabulations, set out your findings in clear and easily readable form, using a chart or spreadsheet if possible.

Draw upon personal experience. Personal experience can serve as powerful evidence when it's appropriate to the subject, to your purpose, and to the audience. If it's your only evidence, however, personal experience usually won't suffice to carry the argument. Your experiences may be regarded as merely "anecdotal," which is to say possibly exceptional, unrepresentative, or even unreliable. Nevertheless, personal experience can be effective for drawing in listeners or readers, as James Parker does in the following example. His full article goes on to argue that—in spite of his personal experience with it—the "Twee revolution" has some good things going for it, including an "actual moral application":

> Eight years ago or so, the alternative paper I was working for sent me out to review a couple of folk-noise-psych-indie-beardie-weirdie bands. I had a dreadful night. The bands were bad enough—"fumbling," I scratched in my notebook, "infantile"—but what really did me in was the audience. Instead of baying for the blood of these lightweights . . . the gathered young people—behatted, bebearded, besmiling—obliged them with patters of validating applause. I had seen it before, this fond curiosity, this acclamation of the undercooked, but never so much of it in one place: the whole event seemed to exult in its own half-bakedness. *Be as crap as you like* was the message to the performers. *The crapper, the better. We're here for you.* I tottered home, wrote a homicidally nasty nervous breakdown of a review, and decided I should take myself out of circulation for a while. No more live reviews until I calmed down. A wave of Twee—as I now realize—had just broken over my head.
>
> —James Parker, *Atlantic*, July/August 2014, p. 36

Moonrise Kingdom, directed by Wes Anderson, film's primary advocate of Twee
Indian Paintbrush/Kobal/REX/Shutterstock

RESPOND●

1. The following general topic ideas once appeared on Yahoo! Groups's
   "Issues and Causes" page. Narrow one or two of the items down
   to a more specific subject by using research tools in the library or
   online such as scholarly books, journal articles, encyclopedias,
   magazine pieces, and/or informational Web sites. Be prepared to
   explain how the particular research resources influenced your choice
   of a more specific subject within the general subject area.
   Also consider what you might have to do to turn your specific
   subject into a full-blown topic proposal for a research paper
   assignment.

Abortion debate	Human rights
Affirmative action	Immigration reform
Civil rights	Media ethics and accountability
Community service and volunteerism	Multiculturalism
	Overpopulation
Confederate flag debate	Peace and nonviolence
Current events	Poverty
Drunk driving	Race relations
Environment	Ranting
Food safety	Road rage
Gender wars	Voluntary simplicity
Housing	

2. Go to your school or local library's online catalog page and locate its list of research databases. You may find them presented in various ways: by subject, by field, by academic major, by type—even alphabetically. Try to identify three or four databases that might be helpful to you either generally in college or when working on a specific project, perhaps one you identified in the previous exercise. Then explore the library catalog to see how much you can learn about each of these resources: What fields do they report on? What kinds of data do they offer (newspaper articles, journal articles, historical records)? How do they present the content of their materials (by abstract, by full text)? What years do they cover? What search strategies do they support (keyword, advanced search)? To find such information, you might look for a help menu or an "About" link on the catalog or database homepages. Write a one-paragraph description of each database you explore and, if possible, share your findings via a class discussion board or wiki.

3. What counts as evidence depends in large part on the rhetorical situation. One audience might find personal testimony compelling in a given case, whereas another might require data that only experimental studies can provide. Imagine that you want to argue that advertisements should not include demeaning representations of chimpanzees and that the use of primates in advertising should be banned. You're encouraged to find out that a number of companies such as Honda and Puma have already agreed to such a ban, so you decide to present your argument to other companies' CEOs and advertising officials. What kind of evidence would be most compelling to this group? How

would you rethink your use of evidence if you were writing for the campus newspaper, for middle-schoolers, or for animal-rights group members? What can you learn about what sort of evidence each of these groups might value—and why?

4. Finding evidence for an argument is often a discovery process. Sometimes you're concerned not only with digging up support for an already established claim but also with creating and revising tentative claims. Surveys and interviews can help you figure out what to argue, as well as provide evidence for a claim.

Interview a classmate with the goal of writing a brief proposal argument about the career that he/she should pursue. The claim should be something like *My classmate should be doing X five years from now.* Limit yourself to ten questions. Write them ahead of time, and don't deviate from them. Record the results of the interview (written notes are fine; you don't need to tape the interview). Then interview another classmate with the same goal in mind. Ask the same first question, but this time let the answer dictate the next nine questions. You still get only ten questions.

Which interview gave you more information? Which one helped you learn more about your classmate's goals? Which one better helped you develop claims about his/her future?

19
Evaluating Sources

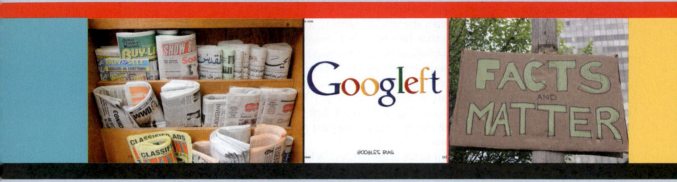

LEFT TO RIGHT: Bartomeu Amengual/AGE Fotostock; Michael P. Ramirez/Creators Syndicate, Inc.; J. Bicking/Shutterstock.com

All the attention paid to "fake news" in our current political culture only underscores the point of this chapter: the effectiveness of an argument often depends on the quality of the sources that support or prove it. It goes without saying then, that you'll need to carefully evaluate and assess all the sources you use in your academic or professional work, including those that you gather in libraries, from other print sources, in online searches, or in your own field research.

Remember that different sources can contribute in different ways to your work. In most cases, you'll be looking for reliable sources that provide accurate information or that clearly and persuasively express opinions that might serve as evidence for a case you're making. At other times, you may be seeking material that expresses ideas or attitudes—how people are thinking and feeling at a given time. You might need to use a graphic image, a sample of avant-garde music, or a controversial YouTube clip that doesn't fit neatly into categories such as "reliable" or "accurate" yet is central to your argument. With any and all such sources and evidence, your goals are to be as knowledgeable about them and as

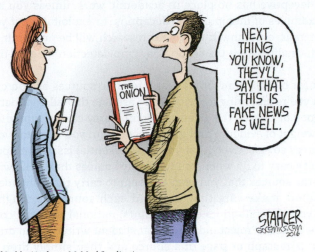

Jeff Stahler/Andrews McMeel Syndication

responsible in their use as you can be and to share honestly what you learn about them with readers.

No writer wants to be naïve in the use of source material, especially since most of the evidence that is used in arguments on public issues— even material from influential and well-known sources—comes with considerable baggage. Scientists and humanists alike have axes to grind, corporations have products to sell, politicians have issues to promote, journalists have reputations to make, publishers and media companies have readers, listeners, viewers, and advertisers to attract and to avoid offending. All of these groups produce and use information to their own benefit, and it's not (usually) a bad thing that they do so. You just have to be aware that when you take information from a given source, it will almost inevitably carry with it at least some of the preferences, assumptions, and biases—conscious or not—of the people who produce and disseminate it. Teachers and librarians are not exempted from this caution: even when we make every effort to be clear and comprehensive in reporting information, we cannot possibly see that information from every angle. So even the most honest and open observer can deliver only a partial account of an event.

It's worth noting, however, that some sources—especially those you might encounter on social media—have no other motive but to deceive readers or to garner clicks that generate revenue. Material this deliberately deceptive has no place in academic work, unless you are looking for examples of manipulation, deception, or exploitation. If you cite such materials, even unwittingly, your research will be undermined and may be discredited. (See the section on "crap detection" later in this chapter.)

To correct for biases, draw on as many reliable sources as you can handle when you're preparing to write. Don't assume that all arguments are equally good or that all the sides in a controversy can be supported by the same weight of evidence and good reasons. But you want to avoid choosing sources so selectively that you miss essential issues and perspectives. That's easy to do when you read only sources that agree with you or when the sources that you read all seem to carry the same message. In addition, make sure that you read each source thoroughly enough that you understand its overall points: national research conducted for the Citation Project indicates that student writers often draw from the first paragraph or page of a source and then simply drop it, without seeing what the rest of the source has to say about the topic at hand. Doing so could leave you with an incomplete or inaccurate sense of what the source is saying.

Consider that sources may sometimes have motives for slanting or selecting the news. John Cole/Cagle Cartoons, Inc.

Assessing Print Sources

Since you want information to be reliable and persuasive, it pays to evaluate each potential source thoroughly. The following principles can help you evaluate print materials:

- **Relevance.** Begin by asking what a particular source will add to your argument and how closely the source is related to your argumentative claim. For a book, the table of contents and the index may help you decide. For an article, look for an abstract that summarizes its content. If you can't identify what the source will add to your research, set it aside. You can almost certainly find something better.

- **Credentials of the author.** Sometimes the author's credentials are set forth in an article, in a book, or on a Web site, so be sure to look for them. Is the author an expert on the topic? To find out, you can gather information about the person on the Web easily enough—although you should check and cross-check what you discover. Another way to learn about the credibility of an author is to search Google Groups for postings that mention the author or to check a Citation Index to find out how other writers refer to this author. (If necessary, ask a librarian for assistance.) If you see your source mentioned by other sources you're using, look at how they cite it and what they say about it, which could provide clues to the author's credibility.

- **Stance of the author.** What's the author's position on the issue(s) involved, and how does this stance influence the information in the source? Does the author's stance support or challenge your own views?

- **Credentials of the publisher or sponsor.** If your source is from a newspaper, is it a major one (such as the *Wall Street Journal* or the *Washington Post*) that has historical credentials in reporting, or is it a tabloid? Is it a popular magazine like *O: The Oprah Magazine* or a journal sponsored by a professional group, such as the *Journal of the American Medical Association*? If your source is a book, is the publisher one you recognize or that has its own Web site? When you don't know the reputation of a source, ask several people with more expertise: a librarian, an instructor, or a professional in the field.

- **Stance of the publisher or sponsor.** Sometimes this stance will be obvious: a magazine called *Save the Planet!* will take a pro-environmental position, whereas one called *America First!* will

What stance does the Japanese American Citizens League take on the issue of what terminology to use in describing the experiences of Japanese Americans during World War II?

LINK TO P. 667

probably take a populist stance. But other times, you need to read carefully between the lines to identify particular positions and see how the stance affects the message the source presents. Start by asking what the source's goals are: what does the publisher or sponsoring group want to make happen?

- **Currency.** Check the date of publication of every book and article. Recent sources are often more useful than older ones, particularly in the sciences. However, in some fields (such as history and literature), the most authoritative works may well be the older ones.

- **Accuracy.** Check to see whether the author cites any sources for the information or opinions in the article and, if so, how credible and current they are.

- **Level of specialization.** General sources can be helpful as you begin your research, but later in the project you may need the authority or currency of more focused sources. Keep in mind that highly specialized works on your topic may be difficult for your audience to understand.

Note the differences between the covers of the *Journal of Abnormal Psychology*, an academic journal, and *The How of Happiness*, a book about psychology. (*Left*) Reproduced with permission. Copyright © 2013 by the American Psychological Association. No further reproduction or distribution is permitted without written permission from the American Psychological Association.

- **Documentation.** Purely academic sources, such as scholarly journal articles, will contain thorough citations, but you should also check that more popular sources you use routinely identify their sources or provide verifiable evidence for claims they make. In many Web sources, documentation takes the form of links to the evidence cited.
- **Audience.** Was the source written for a general readership? For specialists? For advocates or opponents?
- **Length.** Is the source long enough to provide adequate details in support of your claim?
- **Availability.** Do you have access to the source? If it isn't readily accessible, your time might be better spent looking elsewhere.
- **Omissions.** What's missing or omitted from the source? Might such exclusions affect whether or how you can use the source as evidence?

Assessing Electronic Sources

You'll probably find working with digital sources both exciting and frustrating, for even though these tools (the Web, social networks, Twitter, and so on) are enormously useful, they offer information of widely varying quality—and mountains and mountains of it. Yet there is no question that, for example, Twitter feeds from our era will be the subject of future scholarly analysis. Because Web sources are mostly open and unregulated, careful researchers look for corroboration before accepting factual claims they find online, especially if it comes from a site whose sponsor's identity is unclear.

simplified blogging

post
content
follower
shares
comments

© John Atkinson, Wrong Hands • gocomics.com/wrong-hands • wronghands1.com

© John Atkinson/Wrong Hands

Practicing Crap Detection

In online environments, you must be the judge of the accuracy and trustworthiness of the electronic sources you encounter. This is a problem all researchers face, and one that led media critic Howard

Every man [and woman] should have a built-in automatic crap detector operating inside him. —Ernest Hemingway, during a 1954 interview with Robert Manning Alfred Eisenstadt/ The Life Picture Collection/Getty Images

Rheingold to develop a system for detecting "crap," that is, "information tainted by ignorance, inept communication, or deliberate deception." To avoid such "crap," Rheingold recommends a method of triangulation, which means finding three separate credible online sources that corroborate the point you want to make. But how do you ensure that these sources are credible? One tip Rheingold gives is to use sites like FactCheck.org to verify information, or to use the search term "whois" to find out about the author or sponsor of a site.

In making judgments about online sources, then, you need to be especially mindful and to rely on the same criteria and careful thinking that you use to assess print sources. You may find the following additional questions helpful in evaluating online sources:

- Who has posted the document or message or created the site/ medium? An individual? An interest group? A company? A government agency? For Web sites, does the URL offer any clues? Note especially the final suffix in a domain name—*.com* (commercial), *.org* (nonprofit organization), *.edu* (educational institution), *.gov* (government agency), *.mil* (military), or *.net* (network). Also note the geographical domains that indicate country of origin—as in *.ca* (Canada), *.ar* (Argentina), or *.ru* (Russia). Click on some links of a Web site to see if they lead to legitimate and helpful sources or organizations.

- What can you determine about the credibility of the author or sponsor? Can the information in the document or site be verified in other sources? How accurate and complete is it? On a blog, for example, look for a link that identifies the creator of the site (some blogs are managed by multiple authors).

Consider the publisher's credentials by comparing Deanna Hartley's article about employers looking at social media profiles, published on Careerbuilder.com, with Scott O. Lilienfeld's article on the shortcomings of microaggressions, published in Aeon.com, a not-for-profit registered charity.

LINK TO PP. 709, 756

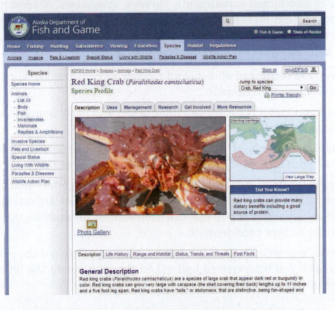

What are the kinds and levels of information available on these Web sites—a commercial site about the TV show *The Deadliest Catch* (top) and an Alaska Department of Fish and Game site on king crab (bottom)?

- Who is accountable for the information in the document or site? How thoroughly does it credit its sources? On a wiki, for example, check its editorial policies: who can add to or edit its materials?

- How current is the document or site? Be especially cautious of undated materials. Most reliable sites are refreshed or edited regularly and should list the date.
- What perspectives are represented? If only one perspective is represented, how can you balance or expand this point of view? Is it a straightforward presentation, or could it be a parody or satire?

Assessing Field Research

If you've conducted experiments, surveys, interviews, observations, or any other field research in developing and supporting an argument, make sure to review your results with a critical eye. The following questions can help you evaluate your own field research:

- Have you rechecked all data and all conclusions to make sure they're accurate and warranted?
- Have you identified the exact time, place, and participants in all your field research?
- Have you made clear what part you played in the research and how, if at all, your role could have influenced the results or findings?
- If your research involved other people, have you gotten their permission to use their words or other materials in your argument? Have you asked whether you can use their names or whether the names should be kept confidential?
- If your research involved interviews, have you thanked the person or persons you interviewed and asked them to verify the words you have attributed to them?

RESPOND•

1. The chapter claims that "most of the evidence that is used in arguments on public issues . . . comes with considerable baggage" (p. 455). Find an article in a journal, newspaper, or magazine that uses evidence to support a claim of some public interest. It might be a piece about new treatments for malaria, Internet privacy, dietary recommendations for schoolchildren, proposals for air-quality regulation, the rise in numbers of campus sexual assaults, and so on. Identify

several specific pieces of evidence, information, or data presented in the article and then evaluate the degree to which you would accept, trust, or believe those statements. Be prepared to explain specifically why you would be inclined to trust or mistrust any claims based on the data.

2. Check out Goodreads (you can set up an account for free) and see what people there are recommending—or search for "common reading programs" or "common reading lists." Then choose one of the recommended books, preferably a work of nonfiction, and analyze it by using as many of the principles of evaluation for printed books listed in this chapter as you can without actually reading the book: Who is the author, and what are his/her credentials? Who is the publisher, and what is its reputation? What can you find out about the book's relevance and popularity: Why might the book be on the list? Who is the primary audience for the book? How lengthy is it? How difficult? Finally, consider how likely it is that the book you have selected would be used in an academic paper. If you do choose a work of fiction, might the work be studied in a literature course?

3. Choose a news or information Web site that you visit routinely. Then, using the guidelines discussed in this chapter, spend some time evaluating its credibility. You might begin by comparing it with Google News or Arts & Letters Daily, two sites that have a reputation for being reliable—though not necessarily unbiased.

4. On Web sites or social media, find several items that purport to offer information or news, but lead readers into a tangle of ads, photos, commentary, and other clickbait. You've seen the teases: Most Unfriendly Cities in the US! The video Hillary Clinton doesn't want you to watch! Is this the smartest kitten ever? Analyze the strategies items like these use to attract readers and the quality of information they offer. Are such items merely irksome or do they seriously diminish online communication and social media?

20
Using Sources

LEFT TO RIGHT: pixal/imageBROKER/AGE Fotostock; kstudija/Shutterstock; Paul Faith/PA Wire URN:9724483 (Press Association via AP Images)

You may gather an impressive amount of evidence on your topic—from firsthand interviews, from careful observations, and from intensive library and online research. But until that evidence is thoroughly understood and then woven into the fabric of your own argument, it's just a stack of details. You still have to turn that data into credible information that will be persuasive to your intended audiences.

Practicing Infotention

Today it's a truism to say that we are all drowning in information, that it is dousing us like water from a fire hose. Such a situation has advantages: it's never been easier to locate information on any imaginable topic. But it also has distinct disadvantages: how do you identify useful and credible sources among the millions available to you, and how do you use them well once you've found them? We addressed the first of these questions in Chapter 18, "Finding Evidence." But finding trustworthy sources is only the first step. Experts on technology and information like professors Richard Lanham and Howard Rheingold point to the next challenge: managing *attention*. Lanham points out that our age of information calls on us to resist the allure of every single thing vying for our attention and to discriminate among what deserves notice and what doesn't. Building on this insight, Rheingold has coined the term "**infotention**," which he says "is a word I came up with to describe a mind-machine combination of brain-powered attention skills and computer-powered information filters" (Howard Rheingold, "Infotention," http://www.rheingold.com).

Practicing infotention calls for synthesizing and thinking critically about the enormous amount of information available to us from the "collective intelligence" of the Web. And while some of us can learn to be mindful while multitasking (a fighter pilot is an example Rheingold gives of those who must learn to do so), most of us are not good at it and need to train ourselves, literally, to pay attention to attention (and intention as well), to be aware of what we are doing and thinking, to take a deep breath and notice where we are directing our focus. In short, writers today need to learn to focus their attention, especially online, and learn to avoid distractions. So just how do you put all these skills together to practice infotention?

Building a Critical Mass

Throughout the chapters in Part 4, "Research and Arguments," we've stressed the need to discover as much evidence as possible in support of your claim and to read and understand it as thoroughly as you can. If you can find only one or two pieces of evidence—only one or two reasons or illustrations to back up your thesis—then you may be on unsteady ground. Although there's no definite way of saying just how much evidence is enough, you should build toward a critical mass by having several pieces of evidence all pulling in the direction of your claim. Begin by putting Rheingold's triangulation into practice: find at least three credible sources that support your point.

And remember that **circumstantial evidence** (that is, indirect evidence that *suggests* that something occurred but doesn't prove it directly) may not be enough if it is the only evidence that you have. In the infamous case of Jack the Ripper, the murderer who plagued London's East End in

© Cog Design Ltd.

1888, nothing but circumstantial evidence ever surfaced and hence no one was charged with or convicted of the crimes. In 2007, however, amateur detective Russell Edwards bought a shawl at auction—a shawl found at one of the murder sites. After consulting with a number of scientific experts and using DNA evidence, Edwards identified Jack the Ripper as Aaron Kosminski, who eventually died in an asylum.

If your support for a claim relies solely on circumstantial evidence, on personal experience, or on one major example, you should extend your search for additional sources and good reasons to back up your claim—or modify the argument. Your initial position may simply have been wrong.

Synthesizing Information

As you gather information, you must find a way to make all the facts, ideas, points of view, and quotations you have encountered work with and for you. The process involves not only reading information and recording data carefully (paying "infotention"), but also pondering and synthesizing it—that is, figuring out how the sources you've examined come together to support your specific claims. **Synthesis**, a form of critical thinking highly valued by academia, business, industry, and other institutions—especially those that reward innovation and creative thinking—is hard work. It almost always involves immersing yourself in your information or data until it feels familiar and natural to you.

At that point, you can begin to look for patterns, themes, and commonalities or striking differences among your sources. Many students use highlighters to help with this process: mark in blue all the parts of sources that mention point A; mark in green those that have to do with issue B; and so on. You are looking for connections among your sources, bringing together what they have to say about your topic in ways you can organize to help support the claim you are making.

You typically begin this process by paraphrasing or summarizing sources so that you understand exactly what they offer and which ideas are essential to your project. You also decide which, if any, sources offer materials you want to quote directly or reproduce (such as an important graph or table). Then you work to introduce such borrowed materials so that readers grasp their significance, and organize them to highlight important relationships. Throughout this review process, use "infotention" strategies by asking questions such as the following:

- Which sources help to set the context for your argument? In particular, which items present new information or give audiences an incentive for reading your work?

- Which items provide background information that is essential for anyone trying to understand your argument?

- Which items help to define, clarify, or explain key concepts of your case? How can these sources be presented or sequenced so that readers appreciate your claims as valid or, at a minimum, reasonable?

- Which of your sources might be used to illustrate technical or difficult aspects of your subject? Would it be best to summarize such technical information to make it more accessible, or would direct quotations be more authoritative and convincing?

- Which sources (or passages within sources) furnish the best support or evidence for each claim or sub-claim within your argument? Now is the time to group these together so you can decide how to arrange them most effectively.

- Which materials do the best job outlining conflicts or offering counterarguments to claims within a project? Which sources might help you address any important objections or rebuttals?

Remember that *yours* should be the dominant and controlling voice in an argument. You are like the conductor of an orchestra, calling upon separate instruments to work together to create a rich and coherent sound. The least effective academic papers are those that mechanically walk through a string of sources—often just one item per paragraph—without ever getting all these authorities to talk to each other or with the author. Such papers go through the motions but don't get anywhere. You can do better.

Paraphrasing Sources You Will Use Extensively

In a **paraphrase**, you put an author's ideas—including major and minor points—into your own words and sentence structures, following the order the author has given them in the original piece. You usually

D.K., the author of "Shooting Guns: It's Rather Fun, Actually," presents a strong narrative explaining the appeal of shooting, while at the same time synthesizing information on gun fatalities and the financial influence of the National Rifle Association.

LINK TO P. 544

Backing up your claims with well-chosen sources makes almost any argument more credible. Ed Fisher/The New Yorker Collection/The Cartoon Bank

"Who is the fairest one of all, and state your sources!"

paraphrase sources that you expect to use heavily in a project. But if you compose your notes well, you may be able to use much of the paraphrased material directly in your paper (with proper citation) because all of the language is your own. A competent paraphrase proves you have read material or data carefully: you demonstrate not only that you know what a source contains but also that you appreciate what it means. There's an important difference.

Here are guidelines to help you paraphrase accurately and effectively in an academic argument:

- Identify the source of the paraphrase, and comment on its significance or the authority of its author.

- Respect your sources. When paraphrasing an entire work or any lengthy section of it, cover all its main points and any essential details, following the same order the author uses. If you distort the shape of the material, your notes will be less valuable, especially if you return to them later, and you may end up misconstruing what the source is saying.

- If you're paraphrasing material that extends over more than one page in the original source, note the placement of page breaks since it is highly likely that you will use only part of the paraphrase in your argument. For a print source, you will need the page number to cite the specific page of material you want to use.

- Make sure that the paraphrase is in your own words and sentence structures. If you want to include especially memorable or powerful language from the original source, enclose it in quotation marks. (See "Using Quotations Selectively and Strategically" on p. 471.)

- Keep your own comments, elaborations, or reactions separate from the paraphrase itself. Your report on the source should be clear, objective, and free of connotative language.

- Collect all the information necessary to create an in-text citation as well as an item in your works cited list or references list. For online materials, be sure to record the URL so you know how to recover the source later.

- Label the paraphrase with a note suggesting where and how you intend to use it in your argument.

- Recheck to make sure that the words and sentence structures are your own and that they express the author's meaning accurately.

Here is a passage from linguist David Crystal's book *Language Play*, followed by a student's paraphrase of the passage.

> Language play, the arguments suggest, will help the development of pronunciation ability through its focus on the properties of sounds and sound contrasts, such as rhyming. Playing with word endings and decoding the syntax of riddles will help the acquisition of grammar. Readiness to play with words and names, to exchange puns and to engage in nonsense talk, promotes links with semantic development. The kinds of dialogue interaction illustrated above are likely to have consequences for the development of conversational skills. And language play, by its nature, also contributes greatly to what in recent years has been called metalinguistic awareness, which is turning out to be of critical importance to the development of language skills in general and literacy skills in particular (180).

Paraphrase of the Passage from Crystal's Book

In *Language Play*, David Crystal argues that playing with language—creating rhymes, figuring out riddles, making puns, playing with names, using inverted words, and so on—helps children figure out a great deal, from the basics of pronunciation and grammar to how to carry on a conversation. This kind of play allows children to understand the overall concept of how language works, a concept that is key to learning to use—and read—language effectively (180).

Note how the student clearly identifies the title and author of the source in the opening line of her paraphrase, and how she restates the passage's main ideas without copying the exact words or phrasing of the original passage.

Summarizing Sources

Unlike a paraphrase, a **summary** records just the gist of a source or a key idea—that is, only enough information to identify a point you want to emphasize. Once again, this much-shortened version of a source puts any borrowed ideas into your own words. At the research stage, summaries help you identify key points you want to make or key points your sources are making that you want to refute and, just as important, provide a record of what you have read. In a project itself, a summary helps readers understand the sources you are using.

Here are some guidelines to help you prepare accurate and helpful summaries:

- Identify the thesis or main point in a source and make it the heart of your summary. In a few detailed phrases or sentences, explain to yourself (and readers) what the source accomplishes.

- When using a summary in an argument, identify the source, state its point, and add your own comments about why the material is significant for the argument that you're making.

- Include just enough information to recount the main points you want to cite. A summary is usually much shorter than the original. When you need more information or specific details, you can return to the source itself or prepare a paraphrase.

- Use your own words in a summary and keep the language objective and denotative. If you include any language from the original source, enclose it in quotation marks.

In her article about how one evangelical church is embracing gay rights, Nicole Pasulka summarizes the recent evolution of legal, political, and social perspectives on gay marriage.

LINK TO P. 547

- Collect all the information necessary to create an in-text citation as well as an item in your works cited list or references list. For online sources without page numbers, record the paragraph, screen, or section number(s) if available.

- Label the summary with a note that suggests where and how you intend to use it in your argument. If your summary includes a comment on the source (as it might in the summaries used for annotated bibliographies), be sure that you won't later confuse your comments with what the source itself asserts.

- Recheck the summary to make sure that you've captured the author's meaning accurately and that the wording is entirely your own.

Following is a summary of the David Crystal passage on page 469:

> In *Language Play*, David Crystal argues that playing with language helps children figure out how language works, a concept that is key to learning to use—and read—language effectively (180).

Notice that the summary is shorter and—relatedly—less detailed than the paraphrase shown on page 470. The paraphrase gives several examples to explain what "language play" is, while the summary sticks to the main point of the passage.

Using Quotations Selectively and Strategically

To support your argumentative claims, you'll want to quote (that is, to reproduce an author's precise words) in at least three kinds of situations:

1. when the wording expresses a point so well that you cannot improve it or shorten it without weakening it,

2. when the author is a respected authority whose opinion supports your own ideas powerfully, and/or

3. when an author or authority challenges or seriously disagrees with others in the field.

Consider, too, that charts, graphs, and images may also function like direct quotations, providing convincing visual evidence for your academic argument.

In an argument, quotations from respected authorities will establish your ethos as someone who has sought out experts in the field. Just as important sometimes, direct quotations (such as a memorable phrase in your introduction or a detailed eyewitness account) may capture your

A tragedy, not a sport? AFP/Getty Images

readers' attention. Finally, carefully chosen quotations can broaden the appeal of your argument by drawing on emotion as well as logic, appealing to the reader's mind and heart. A student who is writing on the ethical issues of bullfighting, for example, might introduce an argument that bullfighting is not a sport by quoting Ernest Hemingway's comment that "the formal bull-fight is a tragedy, not a sport, and the bull is certain to be killed" and then accompany the quotation with an image such as the one above.

The following guidelines can help you quote sources accurately and effectively:

- Quote or reproduce materials that readers will find especially convincing, purposeful, and interesting. You should have a specific reason for every quotation.

- Don't forget the double quotation marks [" "] that must surround a direct quotation in American usage. If there's a quote within a quote, it is surrounded by a pair of single quotation marks [' ']. British usage does just the opposite, and foreign languages often handle direct quotations much differently.

- When using a quotation in your argument, introduce its author(s) and follow the quotation with commentary of your own that points out its significance.

- Keep quoted material relatively brief. Quote only as much of a passage as is necessary to make your point while still accurately representing what the source actually said.

- If the quotation extends over more than one page in the original source, note the placement of page breaks in case you decide to use only part of the quotation in your argument.

- In your notes, label a quotation you intend to use with a note that tells you where you think you'll use it.

- Make sure you have all the information necessary to create an in-text citation as well as an item in your works cited list or references list.

- Copy quotations carefully, reproducing the punctuation, capitalization, and spelling exactly as they are in the original. If possible, copy the quotation from a reliable text and paste it directly into your project.

- Make sure that quoted phrases, sentences, or passages fit smoothly into your own language. Consider where to begin the quotation to make it work effectively within its surroundings or modify the words you write to work with the quoted material.

- Use square brackets if you introduce words of your own into the quotation or make changes to it ("And [more] brain research isn't going to define further the matter of 'mind'").

- Use ellipsis marks if you omit material ("And brain research isn't going to define . . . the matter of 'mind'").

- If you're quoting a short passage (four lines or fewer in MLA style; forty words or fewer in APA style), it should be worked into your text, enclosed by quotation marks. Longer quotations should be set off from the regular text. Begin such a quotation on a new line, indenting every line a half inch or five to seven spaces. Set-off quotations do not need to be enclosed in quotation marks.

- Never distort your sources or present them out of context when you quote from them. Misusing sources is a major offense in academic arguments.

"Some irresponsible gossip mongers around the office have misquoted me as calling you a 'silly goose'."

Cartoon Resource/Shutterstock

Framing Materials You Borrow with Signal Words and Introductions

Because source materials are crucial to the success of arguments, you need to introduce borrowed words and ideas carefully to your readers. Doing so usually calls for using a signal phrase of some kind in the sentence to introduce or frame the source. Often, a signal phrase will precede a quotation. But you need such a marker whenever you introduce borrowed material, as in the following examples:

> According to noted primatologist Jane Goodall, the more we learn about the nature of nonhuman animals, the more ethical questions we face about their use in the service of humans.

> The more we learn about the nature of nonhuman animals, the more ethical questions we face about their use in the service of humans, according to noted primatologist Jane Goodall.

> The more we learn about the nature of nonhuman animals, according to noted primatologist Jane Goodall, the more ethical questions we face about their use in the service of humans.

In each of these sentences, the signal phrase tells readers that you're drawing on the work of a person named Jane Goodall and that this person is a "noted primatologist."

Now look at an example that uses a quotation from a source in more than one sentence:

> In *Job Shift*, consultant William Bridges worries about "dejobbing and about what a future shaped by it is going to be like." Even more worrisome, Bridges argues, is the possibility that "the sense of craft and of professional vocation . . . will break down under the need to earn a fee" (228).

The signal verbs *worries* and *argues* add a sense of urgency to the message Bridges offers. They also suggest that the writer either agrees with—or is neutral about—Bridges's points. Other signal verbs can have a more negative slant, indicating that the point being introduced by the quotation is open to debate and that others (including the writer) might disagree with it. If the writer of the passage above had said, for instance, that Bridges *unreasonably contends* or that he *fantasizes,* these signal verbs would carry quite different connotations from those associated with *argues*.

In some cases, a signal verb may require more complex phrasing to get the writer's full meaning across:

> Bridges recognizes the dangers of changes in work yet refuses to be overcome by them: "The real issue is not how to stop the change but how to provide the necessary knowledge and skills to equip people to operate successfully in this New World" (229).

As these examples illustrate, the signal verb is important because it allows you to characterize the author's or source's viewpoint as well as your own—so choose these verbs with care.

Some Frequently Used Signal Verbs

acknowledges	claims	emphasizes	remarks
admits	concludes	expresses	replies
advises	concurs	hypothesizes	reports
agrees	confirms	interprets	responds
allows	criticizes	lists	reveals
argues	declares	objects	states
asserts	disagrees	observes	suggests
believes	discusses	offers	thinks
charges	disputes	opposes	writes

Note that in APA style, these signal verbs should be in a past tense: *Blau (1992) claimed; Clark (2018) has concluded.*

Using Sources to Clarify and Support Your Own Argument

The best academic arguments often have the flavor of a hearty but focused intellectual conversation. Scholars and scientists create this impression by handling research materials strategically and selectively. Here's how some college writers use sources to achieve their own specific goals within an academic argument.

Establish context. Michael Hiltzik, whose article "Don't Believe Facebook: The Demise of the Written Word Is Very Far Off" appears in Chapter 8, sets the context for his argument when, at the end of his first paragraph, he paraphrases the claim of Facebook executive Nicola Mendelsohn: "In five years, she told a Fortune conference in London, her platform will probably be 'all video,' and the written word will be essentially dead." Then he uses a second paragraph to go into greater detail because Mendelsohn's view represents precisely the notion he intends to contest:

> "I just think if we look already, we're seeing a year-on-year decline on text," she said. "If I was having a bet, I would say: video, video, video." That's because "the best way to tell stories in this world, where so much information is coming at us, actually is video. It conveys so much more information in a much quicker period. So actually the trend helps us to digest much more information."

Only then does Hiltzik present his thesis—and it is short and sweet: "This is, of course, exactly wrong." As they say, *game on*. Readers clearly know what's at stake in the article and perhaps what evidence to expect from the paragraphs to follow (see pp. 193–96).

Review the literature on a subject. You will often need to tell readers what authorities have already written about your topic, thus connecting them to your own argument. So, in a paper on the effectiveness of peer editing, Susan Wilcox does a very brief "review of the literature" on her subject, pointing to three authorities who support using the method in writing courses. She quotes from the authors and also puts some of their ideas in her own words:

> Bostock cites one advantage of peer review as "giving a sense of ownership of the assessment process" (1). Topping expands this view, stating that "peer assessment also involves increased time on task: thinking, comparing, contrasting, and communicating" (254). The extra time spent thinking over the assignment, especially in terms of helping someone else, can draw in the reviewer and lend greater importance to taking the process seriously, especially since the reviewer knows that the classmate is relying on his advice. This also

When using Web sources such as blogs, take special care to check authors' backgrounds and credentials. Roz Chast/The New Yorker Collection/The Cartoon Bank

adds an extra layer of accountability for the student; his hard work—or lack thereof—will be seen by peers, not just the instructor. Cassidy notes, "[S]tudents work harder with the knowledge that they will be assessed by their peers" (509): perhaps the knowledge that peer review is coming leads to a better-quality draft to begin with.

The paragraph is straightforward and useful, giving readers an efficient overview of the subject. If they want more information, they can find it by consulting Wilcox's works cited page.

Introduce a term or define a concept. Quite often in an academic argument, you may need to define a term or explain a concept. Relying on a source may make your job easier *and* enhance your credibility. That is what Laura Pena achieves in the following paragraph, drawing upon two authorities to explain what teachers mean by a "rubric" when it comes to grading student work:

To understand the controversy surrounding rubrics, it is best to know what a rubric is. According to Heidi Andrade, a professor at SUNY-Albany, a rubric can be defined as "a document that lists criteria and describes varying levels of quality, from excellent to poor, for a specific assignment" ("Self-Assessment" 61). Traditionally, rubrics have been used primarily as grading and evaluation tools (Kohn 12), meaning that a rubric was not used until after students handed their papers in to their teacher. The teacher would then use a rubric to evaluate the students' papers according to the criteria listed on the rubric.

Note that the first source provides the core definition while information from the second offers a detail important to understanding when and how rubrics are used—a major issue in Pena's paper. Her selection of sources here serves her thesis while also providing readers with necessary information.

Present technical material. Sources can be especially helpful, too, when material becomes technical or difficult to understand. Writing on your own, you might lack the confidence to handle the complexities of some subjects. While you should challenge yourself to learn a subject well enough to explain it in your own words, there will be times when a quotation from an expert serves both you and your readers. Here is Natalie San Luis dealing with some of the technical differences between mainstream and Black English:

> The grammatical rules of mainstream English are more concrete than those of Black English; high school students can't check out an MLA handbook on Ebonics from their school library. As with all dialects, though, there are certain characteristics of the language that most Black English scholars agree upon. According to Samy Alim, author of *Roc the Mic Right,* these characteristics are the "[h]abitual *be* [which] indicates actions that are continuing or ongoing. . . . Copula absence. . . . Stressed *been.* . . . *Gon* [indicating] the future tense. . . . *They* for possessive. . . . Postvocalic *r.* . . . [and] *Ank* and *ang* for 'ink' and 'ing'" (115). Other scholars have identified "[a]bsence of third-person singular present-tense *s.* . . . Absence of possessive *'s,*" repetition of pronouns, and double negatives (Rickford 111-24).

Note that using ellipses enables San Luis to cover a great deal of ground. Readers not familiar with linguistic terms may have trouble following the quotation, but remember that academic arguments often address audiences comfortable with some degree of complexity.

Develop or support a claim. Even academic audiences expect to be convinced, and one of the most important strategies for a writer is to use sources to amplify or support a claim.

Here is Manasi Deshpande in a student essay making a specific claim about disability accommodations on her campus: "Although the

University has made a concerted and continuing effort to improve access, students and faculty with physical disabilities still suffer from discriminatory hardship, unequal opportunity to succeed, and lack of independence." Now watch how she weaves sources together in the following paragraph to help support that claim:

> The current state of campus accessibility leaves substantial room for improvement. There are approximately 150 academic and administrative buildings on campus (Grant). Eduardo Gardea, intern architect at the Physical Plant, estimates that only about nineteen buildings comply fully with the Americans with Disabilities Act (ADA). According to Penny Seay, PhD, director of the Center for Disability Studies at UT Austin, the ADA in theory "requires every building on campus to be accessible."

Highlight differences or counterarguments. The sources you encounter in developing a project won't always agree with each other or you. In academic arguments, you don't want to hide such differences, but instead point them out honestly and let readers make judgments based upon actual claims. Here is a paragraph in which Laura Pena again presents two views on the use of rubrics as grading tools:

> Some naysayers, such as Alfie Kohn, assert that "any form of assessment that encourages students to keep asking, 'How am I doing?' is likely to change how they look at themselves and what they're learning, usually for the worse." Kohn cites a study that found that students who pay too much attention to the quality of their performance are more likely to chalk up the outcome of an assignment to factors beyond their control, such as innate ability, and are also more likely to give up quickly in the face of a difficult task (14). However, Ross and Rolheiser have found that when students are taught how to properly implement self-assessment tools in the writing process, they are more likely to put more effort and persistence into completing a difficult assignment and may develop higher self-confidence in their writing ability (sec. 2). Building self-confidence in elementary-age writers can be extremely helpful when they tackle more complicated writing endeavors in the future.

In describing Kohn as a "naysayer," Pena may tip her hand and lose some degree of objectivity. But her thesis has already signaled her support for rubrics as a grading tool, so academic readers will probably not find the connotations of the term inappropriate.

These examples suggest only a few of the ways that sources, either summarized or quoted directly, can be incorporated into an academic argument to support or enhance a writer's goals. Like these writers, you should think of sources as your partners in developing and expressing ideas. But you are still in charge.

Avoiding "Patchwriting"

When using sources in an argument, writers—and especially those new to research-based writing—may be tempted to do what Professor Rebecca Moore Howard terms "**patchwriting**": stitching together material from Web or other sources without properly paraphrasing or summarizing and with little or no documentation. Here, for example, is a patchwork paragraph about the dangers wind turbines pose to wildlife:

> Scientists are discovering that technology with low carbon impact does not mean low environmental or social impacts. That is the case especially with wind turbines, whose long, massive fiberglass blades have been chopping up tens of thousands of birds that fly into them, including golden eagles, red-tailed hawks, burrowing owls, and other raptors in California. Turbines are also killing bats in great numbers. The 420 wind turbines now in use across Pennsylvania killed more than 10,000 bats last year—mostly in the late summer months, according to the State Game Commission. That's an average of 25 bats per turbine per year, and the Nature Conservancy predicts as many as 2,900 turbines will be set up across the state by 2030. It's not the spinning blades that kill the bats; instead, their lungs effectively blow up from the rapid pressure drop that occurs as air flows over the turbine blades. But there's hope we may figure out solutions to these problems because, since we haven't had too many wind turbines heretofore in the country, we are learning how to manage this new technology as we go.

The paragraph reads well and is full of details. But it would be considered plagiarized (see Chapter 21) because it fails to identify its sources and because most of the material has simply been lifted directly from the Web. How much is actually copied? We've highlighted the borrowed material:

> Scientists are discovering that technology with low carbon impact does not mean low environmental or social impacts. That is the case especially with wind turbines, whose long, massive fiberglass blades have been chopping up tens of thousands of birds that fly into them, including golden eagles, red-tailed hawks, burrowing owls, and other raptors in California. Turbines are also killing

bats in great numbers. The 420 wind turbines now in use across Pennsylvania killed more than 10,000 bats last year—mostly in the late summer months, according to the State Game Commission. That's an average of 25 bats per turbine per year, and the Nature Conservancy predicts as many as 2,900 turbines will be set up across the state by 2030. It's not the spinning blades that kill the bats; instead, their lungs effectively blow up from the rapid pressure drop that occurs as air flows over the turbine blades. But there's hope we may figure out solutions to these problems because, since we haven't had too many wind turbines heretofore in the country, we are learning how to manage this new technology as we go.

But here's the point: an academic writer who has gone to the trouble of finding so much information will gain more credit and credibility just by properly identifying, paraphrasing, and quoting the sources used. The resulting paragraph is actually more impressive because it demonstrates how much reading and synthesizing the writer has actually done:

Scientists like George Ledec of the World Bank are discovering that technology with low carbon impact "does not mean low environmental or social impacts" (Tracy). That is the case especially with wind turbines. Their massive blades spinning to create pollution-free electricity are also killing thousands of valuable birds of prey, including eagles, hawks, and owls in California (Rittier). Turbines are also killing bats in great numbers (Thibodeaux). The *Pittsburgh Post-Gazette* reports that 10,000 bats a year are killed by the 420 turbines currently in Pennsylvania. According to the state game commissioner, "That's an average of 25 bats per turbine per year, and the Nature Conservancy predicts as many as 2,900 turbines will be set up across the state by 2030" (Schwartzel). It's not the spinning blades that kill the animals; instead, *Discovery News* explains, "the bats' lungs effectively blow up from the rapid pressure drop that occurs as air flows over the turbine blades" (Marshall). But there's hope that scientists can develop turbines less dangerous to animals of all kinds. "We haven't had too many wind turbines heretofore in the country," David Cottingham of the Fish and Wildlife Service points out, "so we are learning about it as we go" (Tracy).

Works Cited

Marshall, Jessica. "Wind Turbines Kill Bats without Impact." *Discovery News,* 25 Aug. 2008, dsc.discovery.com/news/2008/08/25/wind-turbine-bats.html.

Rittier, John. "Wind Turbines Taking Toll on Birds of Prey." *USA Today,* 4 Jan. 2005, usatoday30.usatoday.com/news/nation/2005-01-04-windmills-usat_x.htm.

Schwartzel, Erich. "Pa. Wind Turbines Deadly to Bats, Costly to Farmers."
    Pittsburgh Post-Gazette, 17 July 2011, www.post-gazette.com/business/
    businessnews/2011/07/17/Pa-wind-turbines-deadly-to-bats-costly-to
    -farmers/stories/201107170197.

Thibodeaux, Julie. "Collateral Damage: Bats Getting Caught in Texas Wind
    Turbines." *GreenSourceDFW*, 31 Oct. 2011, www.greensourcedfw.org/articles/
    collateral-damage-bats-getting-caught-texas-wind-turbines.

Tracy, Ryan. "Wildlife Slows Wind Power." *The Wall Street Journal,* 10 Dec. 2011,
    www.wsj.com/articles/SB10001424052970203501304577088593307132850.

RESPOND.

1. Select one of the essays from Chapters 8–12 or 17. Following the guidelines in this chapter, write a paraphrase of the essay that you might
   use subsequently in an academic argument. Be careful to describe the
   essay accurately and to note on what pages specific ideas or claims
   are located. The language of the paraphrase should be entirely your
   own—though you may include direct quotations of phrases, sentences, or longer passages you would likely use in a paper. Be sure
   these quotations are introduced and cited in your paraphrase: *Hiltzik
   leaves no doubt that he rejects Mendelsohn's claim: "This is, of course, exactly
   wrong" (193).* When you are done, trade your paraphrase with a partner to get feedback on its clarity and accuracy.

2. Summarize three readings or fairly lengthy passages from Parts 1–3 of
   this book, following the guidelines in this chapter. Open the item with
   a correct MLA or APA citation for the piece (see Chapter 22). Then provide the summary itself. Follow up with a one- or two-sentence evaluation of the work describing its potential value as a source in an
   academic argument. In effect, you will be preparing three items that
   might appear in an annotated bibliography. Here's an example:

   > Hiltzik, Michael. "Don't Believe Facebook: The Demise of the Written Word
   >   Is Very Far Off." *Everything's an Argument*, by Andrea A. Lunsford and
   >   John J. Ruszkiewicz, 8th ed., Bedford, 2019, pp. 193–96. Argues that
   >   those who believe that video will soon supplant print as the primary
   >   vehicle for news are primarily marketers who underestimate the
   >   efficiency and precision of print. The journalistic piece cites studies
   >   and provides arguments that suggest print is far from dead.

3. Working with a partner, agree upon an essay that you will both read from Chapters 8–12 or 17, examining it as a potential source for a research argument. As you read it, choose about a half-dozen words, phrases, or short passages that you would likely quote if you used the essay in a paper and attach a frame or signal phrase to each quotation. Then compare the passages you selected to quote with those your partner culled from the same essay. How do your choices of quoted material create an image or ethos for the original author that differs from the one your partner has created? How do the signal phrases shape a reader's sense of the author's position? Which set of quotations best represents the author's argument? Why?

4. Select one of the essays from Chapters 8–12 or 17 to examine the different ways an author uses source materials to support claims. Begin by highlighting the signal phrases you find attached to borrowed ideas or direct quotations. How well do they introduce or frame this material? Then categorize the various ways the author actually uses particular sources. For example, look for sources that provide context for the topic, review the scholarly literature, define key concepts or terms, explain technical details, furnish evidence, or lay out contrary opinions. When you are done, write a paragraph assessing the author's handling of sources in the piece. Are the borrowed materials integrated well with the author's own thoughts? Do the sources represent an effective synthesis of ideas?

21

Plagiarism and Academic Integrity

In many ways, "nothing new under the sun" is more than just a cliché. Most of what you think or write is built on what you've previously read or experienced or learned from others. Luckily, you'll seldom be called on to list every influence on your life. But you do have responsibilities in school and professional situations to acknowledge any intellectual property you've made use of when you create arguments of your own. If you don't, you may be accused of **plagiarism**—claiming as your own the words, research, or creative work of others.

What is intellectual property? It's complicated. But, for academic arguments in Western culture, it is the *expression* of ideas you find in works produced by others that you then use to advance and support your own claims. You have to document not only when you use or reproduce someone's exact words, images, music, or other creations (in whole or in part), but also when you borrow the framework others use to put ideas together in original or creative ways. Needless to say, intellectual property rights have always been contentious, but never more so than today, when digital media make it remarkably easy to duplicate and distribute all sorts of materials. Accustomed to uploading and downloading files, cutting and pasting passages, you may be comfortable working with texts day-to-day in ways that are considered inappropriate, or even dishonest, in school. You may, for example, have patched together sources without putting them in your own words or documenting them fully, practices that will often be seen as plagiarism (see p. 480).

"It's not cheating, it's crowdsourcing."

Mark Anderson/Andertoons.com

So it is essential that you read and understand any policies on academic integrity that your school has set down. In particular, pay attention to how those policies define, prosecute, and punish cheating, plagiarism, and collusion. Some institutions recognize a difference between intentional and unintentional plagiarism, but you don't want the honesty of anything you write to be questioned. You need to learn the rules and understand that the penalties for plagiarism are severe not only for students but for professional writers as well.

But don't panic! Many student writers today are so confused or worried about plagiarism that they shy away from using sources—or end up with a citation for almost every sentence in an essay. There's no reason to go to such extremes. As a conscientious researcher and writer, you simply need to give your best effort in letting readers know what sources you have used. Being careful in such matters will have a big payoff: when you give full credit to your sources, you enhance your ethos in academic arguments—which is why "Academic Integrity" appears in this chapter's title. Audiences will applaud you for saying thanks to those who've helped you. Crediting your sources also proves that you have done your homework: you demonstrate that you understand what others have written about the topic and encourage others to join the intellectual conversation. Finally, citing sources reminds you to think critically about how to use the evidence you've collected. Is it timely and reliable? Have you referenced authorities in a biased or overly selective way? Have you double-checked all quotations and paraphrases? Thinking through such questions helps to guarantee the integrity of your academic work.

Giving Credit

Proper acknowledgment of sources is crucial in academic writing. Check out C. Richard King's extensive references for an example of how to do it right.

LINK TO P. 554

The basic principles for documenting materials are relatively simple. Give credit to all source materials you borrow by following these three steps: (1) placing quotation marks around any words you quote directly, (2) citing your sources according to the documentation style you're using, and (3) identifying all the sources you have cited in a list of references or works cited. Materials to be cited in an academic argument include all of the following:

- direct quotations
- facts that are not widely known
- arguable statements
- judgments, opinions, and claims that have been made by others
- images, statistics, charts, tables, graphs, or other illustrations that appear in any source
- collaboration—that is, the help provided by friends, colleagues, instructors, supervisors, or others

However, three important types of evidence or source material do not need to be acknowledged or documented. They are the following:

1. Common knowledge, which is a specific piece of information most readers in your intended audience will know (that Donald Trump won the 2016 presidential election in the Electoral College, for instance).

2. Facts available from a wide variety of sources (that humans walked on the Moon for the first time on July 20, 1969, for example). If, for instance, you search for a piece of information and find the same information on dozens of different reputable Web sites, you can be pretty sure it is common knowledge.

3. Your own findings from field research (observations, interviews, experiments, or surveys you have conducted), which should be clearly presented as your own

For the actual forms to use when documenting sources, see Chapter 22.

Of course, the devil is in the details. For instance, you may be accused of plagiarism in situations like the following:

- if you don't indicate clearly the source of an idea you obviously didn't come up with on your own

- if you use a paraphrase that's too close to the original wording or sentence structure of your source material (*even* if you cite the source)

- if you leave out the parenthetical in-text reference for a quotation (*even* if you include the quotation marks themselves)

And the accusation can be made even if you didn't intend to plagiarize.

But what about all the sampling and mashups you see all the time in popular culture and social media? And don't some artistic and scholarly works come close to being "mashups"? Yes and no. It's certainly fair to say, for example, that Shakespeare's plays "mash up" a lot of material from *Holinshed's Chronicles*, which he used without acknowledgment. But it's also true that Shakespeare's works are "transformative"—that is, they are made new by Shakespeare's art. Current copyright law protects such

An infographic from groups supporting "Fair Use Week" defends the importance of the fair use principle.

The "Fair Use Week" infographic, continued.

works that qualify as transformative and exempts them from copyright violations. But the issues swirling around sampling, mashups, and other creative uses of prior materials (print and online) are far from clear, and far from over. Perhaps Jeff Shaw (in a posting that asks, "Is Mashup Music Protected by Fair Use?") sums up the current situation best:

> Lest we forget, the purpose of copyright law is to help content creators and to enhance creative expression. Fair use is an important step toward those ends, and further legislative work could solidify the step forward that fair use represents.
>
> —Jeff Shaw, "Is Mashup Music Protected by Fair Use?"

Getting Permission for and Using Copyrighted Internet Sources

When you gather information from Internet sources and use it in your own work, it's subject to the same rules that govern information gathered from other types of sources.

A growing number of online works, including books, photographs, music, and video, are published under the Creative Commons license, which often eliminates the need to request permission. These works—marked with a

Creative Commons license—are made available to the public under this alternative to copyright, which grants permission to reuse or remix work under certain terms if credit is given to the work's creator.

Even if the material does not include a copyright notice or symbol ("© 2019 by Andrea A. Lunsford and John J. Ruszkiewicz," for example), it's likely to be protected by copyright laws, and you may need to request permission to use part or all of it. "Fair use" legal precedents allow writers to quote brief passages from published works without permission from the copyright holder if the use is for educational or personal, noncommercial reasons and if full credit is given to the source. For blog postings or any serious professional uses (especially online), however, you should ask permission of the copyright holder before you include any of his/her ideas, text, or images in your own argument.

If you do need to make a request for permission, here is an example:

From: sanchez.32@stanford.edu
To: litman@mindspring.com
CC: lunsford.2@stanford.edu
Subject: Request for permission

Dear Professor Litman:

I am writing to request permission to quote from your essay "Copyright, Owners' Rights and Users' Privileges on the Internet: Implied Licenses, Caching, Linking, Fair Use, and Sign-on Licenses." I want to quote some of your work as part of an article I am writing for the *Stanford Daily* to explain the complex debates over ownership on the Internet and to argue that students at my school should be participating in these debates. I will give full credit to you and will cite the URL where I first found your work (msen.com/~litman/dayton.htm).

Thank you very much for considering my request.

Raul Sanchez

Acknowledging Your Sources Accurately and Appropriately

While artists, lawyers, and institutions like the film and music industries sort out fair use laws, the bottom line in your academic work is clear: document sources accurately and fully and do not be careless about this very important procedure.

Here, for example, is the first paragraph from a print essay by Russell Platt published in the *Nation*:

> Classical music in America, we are frequently told, is in its death throes: its orchestras bled dry by expensive guest soloists and greedy musicians' unions, its media presence shrinking, its prestige diminished, its educational role ignored, its big record labels dying out or merging into faceless corporate entities. We seem to have too many well-trained musicians in need of work, too many good composers going without commissions, too many concerts to offer an already satiated public.
>
> —Russell Platt, "New World Symphony"

To cite this passage correctly in MLA documentation style, you could quote directly from it, using both quotation marks and some form of note identifying the author or source. Either of the following versions would be acceptable:

> Russell Platt has doubts about claims that classical music is "in its death throes: its orchestras bled dry by expensive guest soloists and greedy musicians unions" ("New World").

> But is classical music in the United States really "in its death throes," as some critics of the music scene suggest (Platt)?

You might also paraphrase Platt's paragraph, putting his ideas entirely in your own words but still giving him due credit by ending your remarks with a simple in-text note:

> A familiar story told by critics is that classical music faces a bleak future in the United States, with grasping soloists and unions bankrupting orchestras and classical works vanishing from radio and television, school curricula, and the labels of recording conglomerates. The public may not be willing to support all the talented musicians and composers we have today (Platt).

All of these sentences with citations would be keyed to a works cited entry at the end of the paper that would look like the following in MLA style:

> Platt, Russell. "New World Symphony." *The Nation*, 15 Sept. 2005, www.thenation .com/article/new-world-symphony/.

How might a citation go wrong? As we indicated, omitting either the quotation marks around a borrowed passage or an acknowledgment of the source is grounds for complaint. Neither of the following sentences provides enough information for a correct citation:

> But is classical music in the United States really in its death throes, as some critics of the music scene suggest, with its prestige diminished, its educational role ignored, and its big record labels dying (Platt)?

> But is classical music in the United States really in "its death throes," as some critics of the music scene suggest, with "its prestige diminished, its educational role ignored, [and] its big record labels dying"?

Just as faulty is a paraphrase such as the following, which borrows the words or ideas of the source too closely. It represents plagiarism, despite the fact that it identifies the source from which almost all the ideas—and a good many words—are borrowed:

> In "New World Symphony," Russell Platt observes that classical music is thought by many to be in bad shape in America. Its orchestras are being sucked dry by costly guest artists and insatiable unionized musicians, while its place on TV and radio is shrinking. The problem may be that we have too many well-trained musicians who need employment, too many good composers going without jobs, too many concerts for a public that prefers *The Real Housewives of Atlanta*.

Even the fresh idea not taken from Platt at the end of the paragraph doesn't alter the fact that the paraphrase is mostly a mix of Platt's original words, lightly stirred.

Acknowledging Collaboration

Writers generally acknowledge all participants in collaborative projects at the beginning of the presentation, report, or essay. In print texts, the acknowledgment is often placed in a footnote or brief prefatory note.

The eighth edition of the *MLA Handbook* (2016) calls attention to the shifting landscape of collaborative work, noting that

> Today academic work can take many forms other than the research paper. Scholars produce presentations, videos, and interactive Web projects, among other kinds of work . . . but the aims will remain the same: providing the information that enables a curious reader, viewer, or other user to track down your sources and giving credit to those whose work influenced yours.

RESPOND•

1. Define *plagiarism* in your own terms, making your definition as clear and explicit as possible. Then compare your definition with those of two or three other classmates, and write a brief report on the similarities and differences you noted in the definitions. You might research terms such as *plagiarism*, *academic honesty*, and *academic integrity* on the Web. Also be certain to check how your own school defines the words.

2. Spend fifteen or twenty minutes jotting down your ideas about intellectual property and plagiarism. File sharing of music and illegally downloading movies used to be a big deal. Is it simpler/better now just to subscribe to Netflix and Apple Music? Do you agree that forms of intellectual property—like music and films—need to be protected under copyright law? How do you define your own intellectual property, and in what ways and under what conditions are you willing to share it?

3. Come up with your own definition of *academic integrity*, based on what you have observed yourself and other students doing in high school, in college, and, perhaps, on the job. Think about the consequences, for example, of borrowing materials and ideas from each other in a study group or while working on a collaborative project.

4. Not everyone agrees that intellectual material is property that should be protected. The slogan "information wants to be free" has been showing up in popular magazines and on the Internet for a long time, often with a call to readers to take action against protection such as data encryption and further extension of copyright.

   Using a Web search engine, look for pages where the phrase "information wants to be free" or "free information" appears. Find several sites that make arguments in favor of free information, and analyze them in terms of their rhetorical appeals. What claims do the authors make? How do they appeal to their audience? What's the site's ethos, and how is it created? After you've read some arguments in favor of free information, return to this chapter's arguments about intellectual property. Which arguments do you find most persuasive? Why?

5. Although this book is concerned principally with ideas and their written expression, other forms of intellectual property are also legally protected. For example, scientific and technological developments are protectable under patent law, which differs in some significant ways from copyright law (see the "Fair Use Fundamentals" infographic in this chapter on pp. 487–88).

Find the standards for protection under U.S. copyright law and U.S. patent law. You might begin by visiting the U.S. copyright Web site (copyright.gov). Then imagine that you're the president of a small high-tech corporation and are trying to inform your employees of the legal protections available to them and their work. Write a paragraph or two explaining the differences between copyright and patent, and suggest a policy that balances employees' rights to intellectual property with the business's needs to develop new products.

22

Documenting Sources

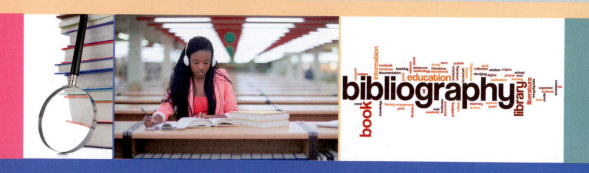

LEFT TO RIGHT: Seregam/Shutterstock; Zero Creatives/Image/AGE Fotostock; ibreakstock/Shutterstock

What does documenting sources have to do with argument? First, the sources that a writer chooses become part of any argument, showing that he/she has done some research, knows what others have said about the topic, and understands how to use these items as support for a claim. Similarly, the list of works cited or references makes a statement, saying, "Look at how thoroughly this essay has been researched" or "Note how up-to-date I am!"

Writers working in digital spaces sometimes simply add hotlinks so that their readers can find their sources. If you are writing a multimodal essay that will appear on the Web, such links will be appreciated. But for now, college assignments generally call for full documentation rather than simply a link. You'll find the information you need to create in-text citations and works cited/references lists in this chapter.

Documentation styles vary from discipline to discipline, with one format favored in the social sciences and another in the natural sciences, for example. Your instructor will probably assign a documentation style for you to follow. If not, you can use one of the two covered in this chapter. But note that even the choice of documentation style makes an argument in a subtle way. You'll note in the instructions that follow, for example, that the Modern Language Association (MLA) style requires putting the date of publication of a print source at or near the end of a works cited list entry, whereas the American Psychological Association (APA) style places that date near the beginning of a references list citation. Such positioning suggests that in MLA style, the author and title are of greater importance than the date for humanities scholars, while APA puts a priority on the date—and timeliness—of sources. Pay attention to such fine points of documentation style, always asking what these choices suggest about the values of scholars and researchers who use a particular system of documentation.

MLA Style

Widely used in the humanities, the latest version of MLA style—described in the *MLA Handbook* (8th edition, 2016)—has been revised significantly "for the digital age." If you have used MLA style in the past, you'll want to check the models here closely and note the differences. Below, we provide guidelines drawn from the *MLA Handbook* for in-text citations, notes, and entries in the list of works cited.

In-Text Citations

MLA style calls for in-text citations in the body of an argument to document sources of quotations, paraphrases, summaries, and so on. For in-text citations, use a signal phrase to introduce the material, often with the author's name (*As Geneva Smitherman explains, . . .*). Keep an in-text citation short, but include enough information for readers to locate the source in the list of works cited. Place the parenthetical citation as near to the relevant material as possible without disrupting the flow of the sentence, as in the following examples.

1. Author Named in a Signal Phrase

Ordinarily, use the author's name in a signal phrase to introduce the material, and cite the page number(s) in parentheses.

> Ravitch chronicles how the focus in education reform has shifted toward privatizing school management rather than toward improving curriculum, teacher training, or funding (36).

2. Author Named in Parentheses

When you don't mention the author in a signal phrase, include the author's last name before the page number(s) in the parentheses. The name and page number are *not* separated by a comma.

> Oil from shale in the western states, if it could be extracted, would be equivalent to six hundred billion barrels, more than all the crude so far produced in the world (McPhee 413).

3. Two Authors

Use both authors' last names.

> Gortner and Nicolson maintain that "opinion leaders" influence other people in an organization because they are respected, not because they hold high positions (175).

4. Three or More Authors

When there are three or more authors, brevity (and the MLA) suggests you use the first author's name with *et al.* (in regular type, not italicized).

Similarly, as Goldberger et al. note, their new book builds on their collaborative experiences to inform their description of how women develop cognitively (xii).

5. Organization as Author

Give the full name of a corporate author if it's brief or a shortened form if it's long.

Many global economists assert that the term "developing countries" is no longer a useful designation, as it ignores such countries' rapid economic growth (Gates Foundation 112).

6. Unknown Author

Use the complete title of the work if it's brief or a shortened form if it's long.

"Hype," by one analysis, is "an artificially engendered atmosphere of hysteria" ("Today's Marketplace" 51).

7. Author of Two or More Works

When you use two or more works by the same author, include the title of the work or a shortened version of it in the citation.

Gardner presents readers with their own silliness through his description of a "pointless, ridiculous monster, crouched in the shadows, stinking of dead men, murdered children, and martyred cows" (*Grendel* 2).

8. Authors with the Same Last Name

When you use works by two or more authors with the same last name, include each author's first initial in the in-text citation.

Public health officials agree that the potential environmental risk caused by indoor residual spraying is far lower than the potential risk of death caused by malaria-carrying mosquitoes (S. Dillon 76).

9. Multivolume Work

Note the volume number first and then the page number(s), with a colon and one space between them.

Aristotle's "On Plants" is now available in a new translation edited by Barnes (2: 1252).

10. Literary Work

Because literary works are often available in many different editions, you need to include enough information for readers to locate the passage in any edition. For a prose work such as a novel or play, first cite the page number from the edition you used, followed by a semicolon; then indicate the part or chapter number (114; ch. 3) or act or scene in a play (42; sc. 2).

In Ben Jonson's *Volpone*, the miserly title character addresses his treasure as "dear saint" and "the best of things" (1447; act 1).

For a poem, cite the stanza and line numbers. If the poem has only line numbers, use the word *line(s)* in the first reference (lines 33–34) and the number(s) alone in subsequent references.

On dying, Whitman speculates, "All that goes onward and outward, nothing collapses, / And to die is different from what any one supposed, and luckier" (6.129-30).

For a verse play, omit the page number, and give only the act, scene, and line numbers, separated by periods.

Before he takes his own life, Othello says he is "one that loved not wisely but too well" (5.2.348).

As *Macbeth* begins, the witches greet Banquo as "Lesser than Macbeth, and greater" (1.3.65).

11. Works in an Anthology

For an essay, short story, or other short work within an anthology, use the name of the author of the work, not the editor of the anthology; but use the page number(s) from the anthology.

In the end, if the black artist accepts any duties at all, that duty is to express the beauty of blackness (Hughes 1271).

12. Sacred Text

To cite a sacred text, such as the Qur'an or the Bible, give the title of the edition you used, the book, and the chapter and verse (or their equivalent), separated by a period. In your text, spell out the names of books. In a parenthetical reference, use an abbreviation for books with names of five or more letters (for example, *Gen.* for Genesis).

> He ignored the admonition "Pride goes before destruction, and a haughty spirit before a fall" (*New Oxford Annotated Bible,* Prov. 16.18).

13. Indirect Source

Use the abbreviation *qtd. in* to indicate that what you're quoting or paraphrasing is quoted (as part of a conversation, interview, letter, or excerpt) in the source you're using.

> As Catherine Belsey states, "to speak is to have access to the language which defines, delimits and locates power" (qtd. in Bartels 453).

14. Two or More Sources in the Same Citation

Separate the information for each source with a semicolon.

> Adefunmi was able to patch up the subsequent holes left in worship by substituting various Yoruba, Dahomean, or Fon customs made available to him through research (Brandon 115-17; Hunt 27).

15. Entire Work or One-Page Article

Include the citation in the text without any page numbers or parentheses.

> Kazuo Ishiguro's dystopian novel *Never Let Me Go* explores questions of identity and authenticity.

16. Nonprint or Electronic Source

Give enough information in a signal phrase or parenthetical citation for readers to locate the source in the list of works cited. Usually give the author or title under which you list the source. If the work isn't numbered by page but has numbered sections, parts, or paragraphs, include the name and number(s) of the section(s) you're citing. (For paragraphs, use the abbreviation *par.* or *pars.*; for section, use *sec.*; for part, use *pt.*)

> In his film version of *Hamlet,* Zeffirelli highlights the sexual tension between the prince and his mother.

> Zora Neale Hurston is one of the great anthropologists of the twentieth century, according to Kip Hinton (par. 2).

> Describing children's language acquisition, Pinker explains that "what's innate about language is just a way of paying attention to parental speech" (qtd. in Johnson, sec. 1).

17. Visual Included in the Text

Number all figures (photos, drawings, cartoons, maps, graphs, and charts) and tables separately.

> This trend is illustrated in a chart distributed by the College Board as part of its 2014 analysis of aggregate SAT data (see fig. 1).

Include a caption with enough information about the source to direct readers to the works cited entry. (For an example of an image that a student created, see the sample page from an MLA-style essay on p. 514 in this chapter.)

Explanatory and Bibliographic Notes

We recommend using explanatory notes for information or commentary that doesn't readily fit into your text but is needed for clarification, further explanation, or justification. In addition, bibliographic notes will allow you to cite several sources for one point and to offer thanks to, information about, or evaluation of a source. Use a superscript number in your text at the end of a sentence to refer readers to the notes, which usually appear as endnotes (with the heading *Notes*, not underlined or italicized) on a separate page before the list of works cited. Indent the first line of each note five spaces, and double-space all entries.

Text with Superscript Indicating a Note

> Stewart emphasizes the existence of social contacts in Hawthorne's life so that the audience will accept a different Hawthorne, one more attuned to modern times than the figure in Woodberry.[3]

Note

³Woodberry does, however, show that Hawthorne was often unsociable. He emphasizes the seclusion of Hawthorne's mother, who separated herself from her family after the death of her husband, often even taking meals alone (28). Woodberry seems to imply that Mrs. Hawthorne's isolation rubbed off on her son.

List of Works Cited

A list of works cited is an alphabetical listing of the sources you cite in your essay. The list appears on a separate page at the end of your argument, after any notes, with the heading *Works Cited* centered an inch from the top of the page; don't underline or italicize it or enclose it in quotation marks. Double-space between the heading and the first entry, and double-space the entire list. (If you're asked to list everything you've read as background—not just the sources you cite—call the list *Works Consulted.*) The first line of each entry should align on the left; subsequent lines indent one-half inch or five spaces. See page 515 for a sample works cited page.

Print Books

The basic information for a book includes three elements, each followed by a period:

- the author's name, last name first (for a book with multiple authors, only the first author's name is inverted)
- the title and subtitle, italicized
- the publication information, including the publisher's name (such as Harvard UP) followed by a comma, and the publication date

1. One Author

Larsen, Erik. *Dead Wake: The Last Crossing of the Lusitania*. Crown
     Publishers, 2015.

2. Two or More Authors

Jacobson, Sid, and Ernie Colón. *The 9/11 Report: A Graphic Adaptation*. Farrar,
     Straus, and Giroux, 2006.

3. Organization as Author

American Horticultural Society. *The Fully Illustrated Plant-by-Plant Manual of Practical Techniques*. DK, 1999.

4. Unknown Author

National Geographic Atlas of the World. National Geographic, 2004.

5. Two or More Books by the Same Author

List the works alphabetically by title. Use three hyphens for the author's name for the second and subsequent works by that author.

Lorde, Audre. *A Burst of Light*. Firebrand Books, 1988.

---. *Sister Outsider*. Crossings Press, 1984.

6. Editor

Rorty, Amelie Oksenberg, editor. *Essays on Aristotle's Poetics*. Princeton UP, 1992.

7. Author and Editor

Shakespeare, William. *The Tempest*. Edited by Frank Kermode, Routledge, 1994.

8. Selection in an Anthology or Chapter in an Edited Book

List the author(s) of the selection or chapter; its title; the title of the book in which the selection or chapter appears; *edited by* and the name(s) of the editor(s); the publication information; and the inclusive page numbers of the selection or chapter.

Brown, Paul. "'This thing of darkness I acknowledge mine': *The Tempest* and the Discourse of Colonialism." *Political Shakespeare: Essays in Cultural Materialism*, edited by Jonathan Dollimore and Alan Sinfield, Cornell UP, 1985, pp. 48-71.

9. Two or More Works from the Same Anthology

Include the anthology itself in the list of works cited.

Gates, Henry Louis, Jr., and Nellie McKay, editors. *The Norton Anthology of African American Literature*. Norton, 1997.

Then list each selection separately by its author and title, followed by a cross-reference to the anthology.

Karenga, Maulana. "Black Art: Mute Matter Given Force and Function." Gates and McKay, pp. 1973-77.

Neal, Larry. "The Black Arts Movement." Gates and McKay, pp. 1960-72.

10. Translation

Ferrante, Elena. *The Story of the Lost Child*. Translated by Ann Goldstein, Europa Editions, 2015.

11. Edition Other Than the First

Lunsford, Andrea A., et al. *Everything's an Argument with Readings*. 8th ed., Bedford/St. Martin's, 2019.

12. Graphic Narrative

If the words and images are created by the same person, cite a graphic narrative just as you would a book (see item 1 on p. 501).

Bechdel, Alison. *Are You My Mother?* Houghton Mifflin Harcourt, 2012.

If the work is a collaboration, indicate the author or illustrator who is most important to your research before the title. Then list other contributors in order of their appearance on the title page. Label each person's contribution to the work.

Stavans, Ilan, writer. *Latino USA: A Cartoon History*. Illustrated by Lalo Arcaraz, Basic Books, 2000.

13. One Volume of a Multivolume Work

Byron, Lord George. *Byron's Letters and Journals*. Edited by Leslie A. Marchand, vol. 2, John Murray, 1973. 12 vols.

14. Two or More Volumes of a Multivolume Work

Byron, Lord George. *Byron's Letters and Journals*. Edited by Leslie A. Marchand, John Murray, 1973-82. 12 vols.

15. Preface, Foreword, Introduction, or Afterword

Dunham, Lena. Foreword. *The Liars' Club*, by Mary Karr, Penguin Classics, 2015,
pp. xi-xiii.

16. Article in a Reference Work

Robinson, Lisa Clayton. "Harlem Writers Guild." *Africana: The Encyclopedia of the
African and African American Experience*, 2nd ed., Oxford UP, 2005.

17. Book That Is Part of a Series

Include the title and number of the series after the publication
information.

Moss, Beverly J. *A Community Text Arises*. Hampton, 2003. Language and Social
Processes Series 8.

18. Republication

Trilling, Lionel. *The Liberal Imagination*. 1950. Introduction by Louis Menand,
New York Review of Books, 2008.

19. Government Document

Canada, Minister of Aboriginal Affairs and Northern Development. *2015-16 Report
on Plans and Priorities*. Minister of Public Works and Government Services
Canada, 2015.

20. Pamphlet

The Legendary Sleepy Hollow Cemetery. Friends of Sleepy Hollow Cemetery, 2008.

21. Published Proceedings of a Conference

Meisner, Marx S., et al., editors. *Communication for the Commons: Revisiting
Participation and Environment*. Proceedings of Twelfth Biennial Conference
on Communication and the Environment, 6-11 June 2015, Swedish U
of Agricultural Sciences, International Environmental Communication
Association, 2015.

22. Title within a Title

Shanahan, Timothy. *Philosophy and* Blade Runner. Palgrave Macmillan, 2014.

Print Periodicals

The basic entry for a periodical includes three elements:

- the author's name, last name first, followed by a period
- the article title, in quotation marks, followed by a period
- the publication information, including the periodical title (italicized), the volume and issue numbers (if any, not italicized), the date of publication, and the page number(s), all followed by commas, with a period at the end of the page numbers

For works with multiple authors, only the first author's name is inverted. Note that the period following the article title goes inside the closing quotation mark.

23. Article in a Print Journal

Give the issue number, if available.

Matchie, Thomas. "Law versus Love in *The Round House*." *Midwest Quarterly,* vol. 56, no. 4, Summer 2015, pp. 353-64.

Fuqua, Amy. "'The Furrow of His Brow': Providence and Pragmatism in Toni Morrison's *Paradise*." *Midwest Quarterly*, vol. 54, no. 1, Autumn 2012, pp. 38-52.

24. Article That Skips Pages

Seabrook, John. "Renaissance Pears." *The New Yorker*, 5 Sept. 2005, pp. 102+.

25. Article in a Print Monthly Magazine

Nijhuis, Michelle. "When Cooking Kills." *National Geographic*, Sept. 2017, pp. 76-81.

26. Article in a Print Weekly Magazine

Grossman, Lev. "A Star Is Born." *Time*, 2 Nov. 2015, pp. 30-39.

27. Article in a Print Newspaper

Bray, Hiawatha. "As Toys Get Smarter, Privacy Issues Emerge." *The Boston Globe,* 10 Dec. 2015, p. C1.

28. Editorial or Letter to the Editor

Posner, Alan. "Colin Powell's Regret." *The New York Times*, 9 Sept. 2005, p. A20.

29. Unsigned Article

"Court Rejects the Sale of Medical Marijuana." *The New York Times*, 26 Feb. 1998, late ed., p. A21.

30. Review

Harris, Brandon. "Black Saints and Sinners." Review of *Five-Carat Soul*, by James McBride. *The New York Review of Books*, 7 Dec. 2017, pp. 50-51.

Digital Sources

Most of the following models are based on the MLA's guidelines for citing electronic sources in the *MLA Handbook* (8th edition, 2016), as well as on up-to-date information available at its Web site (mla.org). The MLA advocates the use of URLs but prefers a Digital Object Indicator (DOI) where available. A DOI is a unique number assigned to a selection, and does not change regardless of where the item is located online. The basic MLA entry for most electronic sources should include the following elements:

- name of the author, editor, or compiler
- title of the work, document, or posting
- publication information (volume, issue, year or date). List page numbers or paragraph numbers only if they are included in the source.
- name of database, italicized
- DOI or URL

31. Document from a Web Site

Begin with the author, if known, followed by the title of the work, title of the Web site, publisher or sponsor (if it is notably different from the title of the Web site), date of publication or last update, and the Digital Object Identifier or URL. If no publication or update date is available, include a date of access at the end.

"Social and Historical Context: Vitality." *Arapesh Grammar and Digital Language Archive Project*, Institute for Advanced Technology in the Humanities, www.arapesh.org/socio_historical_context_vitality.php. Accessed 22 Mar. 2017.

32. Entire Web Site

Include the name of the person or group who created the site, if relevant; the title of the site, italicized; the publisher or sponsor of the site; the date of publication or last update; and the URL.

> Barcus, Jane. *What Jane Saw*. Liberals Arts Development Studio/University of Texas at Austin, 2013, whatjanesaw.org.

> Halsall, Paul, editor. *Internet Modern History Sourcebook*. Fordham U, 4 Nov. 2011, legacy.fordham.edu/halsall/index.asp.

33. Course, Department, or Personal Web Site

For a course Web site, include the instructor's name; the title of the site, italicized; a description of the site (such as *Course home page*, *Department home page*, or *Home page*—not italicized); the sponsor of the site (academic department and institution); dates of the course or last update to the page; and the URL. Note that the MLA spells *home page* as two separate words. For an academic department, list the name of the department; a description; the academic institution; the date the page was last updated; and the URL.

> Film Studies. Department home page. *Wayne State University, College of Liberal Arts and Sciences*, 2016, clas.wayne.edu/FilmStudies/.

> Masiello, Regina. 355:101: Expository Writing. *Rutgers School of Arts and Sciences*, 2017, wp.rutgers.edu/courses/55-355101.

34. Online Book

Cite an online book as you would a print book. After the print publication information (if any), give the title of the Web site or database in which the book appears, italicized; and the DOI or URL.

> Riis, Jacob A. *How the Other Half Lives: Studies among the Tenements of New York*. Edited by David Phillips, Scribner's, 1890. *The Authentic History Center*, www.authentichistory.com/1898-1913/2-progressivism/2-riis/.

Treat a poem, essay, or other short work within an online book as you would a part of a print book. After the print publication information (if any), give the title of the Web site or database, italicized; and the DOI or URL.

> Milton, John. *Paradise Lost: Book I. Poetry Foundation*, 2014, www
.poetryfoundation.org/poem/174987.

35. Article in a Journal on the Web

For an article in an online journal, cite the same information that you would for a print journal. Then add the DOI or URL.

Wells, Julia. "The 'Terrible Loneliness': Loneliness and Worry in Settler Women's Memoirs from East and South-Central Africa, 1890–1939." *African Studies Quarterly*, vol. 17, no. 2, June 2017, pp. 47-64, africa.ufl.edu/asq/v17/v17i2a3.pdf.

36. Article in a Magazine or Newspaper on the Web

For an article in an online magazine or newspaper, cite the author; the title of the article, in quotation marks; the name of the magazine or newspaper, italicized; the date of publication; and the URL of the page you accessed.

Leonard, Andrew. "The Surveillance State High School." *Salon*, 27 Nov. 2012, www.salon.com/2012/11/27/the_surveillance_state_high_school/.

Crowell, Maddy. "How Computers Are Getting Better at Detecting Liars." *The Christian Science Monitor*, 12 Dec. 2015, www.csmonitor.com/Science/Science-Notebook/2015/1212/How-computers-are-getting-better-at detecting-liars.

37. Entry in a Web Reference Work

Cite the entry as you would an entry from a print reference work (see item 16). Follow with the name of the Web site, the date of publication, and the URL of the site you accessed.

Durante, Amy M. "Finn Mac Cumhail." *Encyclopedia Mythica*, 17 Apr. 2011, www.pantheon.org/articles/f/finn_mac_cumhail.html.

38. Post or Comment on a Web Site

Begin with the author's name; the title of the posting, in quotation marks; the name of the blog, italicized; the sponsor of the blog; the date of the most recent update; and the URL of the page you accessed.

mitchellfreedman. Comment on *"Cloud Atlas*'s Theory of Everything," by Emily Eakin. *NYR Daily*, NYREV, 3 Nov. 2012, www.nybooks.com/daily/2012/11/02/ken-wilber-cloud-atlas/.

39. Entry in a Wiki

Since wikis are collectively edited, do not include an author. Treat a wiki as you would a work from a Web site (see item 31). Include the title of the entry; the name of the wiki, italicized; the date of the latest update; and the URL of the page you accessed.

"House Music." *Wikipedia,* 16 Nov. 2017, en.wikipedia.org/wiki/House_music.

40. Post on Social Media

To cite a post on Facebook or another social media site, include the writer's name, a description of the posting, the date of the posting, and the URL of the page you accessed.

Bedford English. "Stacey Cochran Explores Reflective Writing in the Classroom and
     as a Writer: http://ow.ly/YkjVB." *Facebook,* 15 Feb. 2016, www.facebook.com/
     BedfordEnglish/posts/10153415001259607.

41. Email or Message on Social Media

Include the writer's name; the subject line, in quotation marks (for email); *Received by* (not italicized or in quotation marks) followed by the recipient's name; and the date of the message. You do not need to include the medium, but may if you are concerned there will be confusion.

Thornbrugh, Caitlin. "Coates Lecture." Received by Rita Anderson, 20 Oct.
     2015.

42. Tweet

Include the writer's real name, if known, with the user name (if different) in parentheses. If you don't know the real name, give just the user name. Include the entire tweet, in quotation marks. Include the publisher (Twitter) in italics, follow by the date and time of the message and the URL.

Curiosity Rover. "Can you see me waving? How to spot #Mars in the night sky:
     https://youtu.be/hv8hVvJlcJQ." *Twitter,* 5 Nov. 2015, 11:00 a.m., twitter
     .com/marscuriosity/status/672859022911889408.

43. Work from an Online Database or a Subscription Service

For a work from an online database, list the author's name; the title of the work; any print publication information; the name of the database, italicized; and the DOI or URL.

Goldsmith, Oliver. *The Vicar of Wakefield: A Tale*. Philadelphia, 1801. *America's Historical Imprints*, infoweb.newsbank.com.ezproxy.bpl.org/.

Coles, Kimberly Anne. "The Matter of Belief in John Donne's Holy Sonnets." *Renaissance Quarterly*, vol. 68, no. 3, Fall 2015, pp. 899-931. *JSTOR*, doi:10.1086/683855.

44. Computer Software or Video Game

Include the title, italicized; the version number (if given); and publication information. If you are citing material downloaded from a Web site, include the title and version number (if given), but instead of publication information, add the publisher or sponsor of the Web site; the date of publication; and the URL.

Edgeworld. Atom Entertainment, 1 May 2012, www.kabam.com/games/edgeworld.

Words with Friends. Version 5.84, Zynga, 2013.

Other Sources (Including Online Versions)

45. Unpublished Dissertation

Abbas, Megan Brankley. "Knowing Islam: The Entangled History of Western Academia and Modern Islamic Thought." Dissertation, Princeton U, 2015.

46. Published Dissertation

Kidd, Celeste. *Rational Approaches to Learning and Development*. Dissertation, U of Rochester, 2013.

47. Article from a Microform

Sharpe, Lora. "A Quilter's Tribute." *The Boston Globe*, 25 Mar. 1989, p. 13. Microform. *NewsBank*: Social Relations 12, 1989, fiche 6, grids B4-6.

48. Personal, Published, or Broadcast Interview

For a personal interview, list the name of the person interviewed, the label *Personal interview* (not italicized), and the date of the interview.

Cooper, Rebecca. Personal interview. 1 Jan. 2018.

For a published interview, list the name of the person interviewed, the title (if any), along with the label *Interview by [interviewer's name]* (not italicized); then add the publication information, including the URL if there is one.

Weddington, Sarah. "Sarah Weddington: Still Arguing for *Roe*." Interview by
    Michele Kort. *Ms.,* Winter 2013, pp. 32-35.

Jaffrey, Madhur. "Madhur Jaffrey on How Indian Cuisine Won Western Taste Buds."
    Interview by Shadrach Kabango. *Q,* CBC Radio, 29 Oct. 2015, www.cbc
    .ca/1.3292918.

For a broadcast interview, list the name of the person interviewed; the title, if any; the label *Interview by* (not italicized); and the name of the interviewer (if relevant). Then list information about the program, the date of the interview, and the URL, if applicable.

Fairey, Shepard. "Spreading the Hope: Street Artist Shepard Fairey." Interview
    by Terry Gross. *Fresh Air,* National Public Radio, WBUR, Boston,
    20 Jan. 2009.

Putin, Vladimir. Interview by Charlie Rose. *Charlie Rose: The Week,* PBS,
    19 June 2015.

49. Letter

Treat a published letter like a work in an anthology, but include the date of the letter.

Jacobs, Harriet. "To Amy Post." 4 Apr. 1853. *Incidents in the Life of a Slave Girl,*
    edited by Jean Fagan Yellin, Harvard UP, 1987, pp. 234-35.

50. Film

For films, ordinarily begin with the title, followed by the director and major performers. If your essay or project focuses on a major person related to the film, such as the director, you can begin with that name or names, followed by the title and performers.

> *Birdman or (The Unexpected Virtue of Ignorance)*. Directed by Alejandro González Iñárritu, performances by Michael Keaton, Emma Stone, Zach Galifianakis, Edward Norton, and Naomi Watts, Fox Searchlight, 2014.

> Jenkins, Patty, director. *Wonder Woman*. Performances by Gal Gadot, Chris Pine, and Robin Wright, Warner Bros., 2017.

51. Television or Radio Program

> "Free Speech on College Campuses." *Washington Journal*, narrated by Peter Slen, C-SPAN, 27 Nov. 2015.

> "Take a Giant Step." *Prairie Home Companion*, narrated by Garrison Keillor, American Public Media, 27 Feb. 2016, prairiehome.publicradio.org/listen/full/?name=phc/2016/02/27/phc_20160227_128.

52. Online Video Clip

Cite a short online video as you would a work from a Web site (see item 31).

> Nayar, Vineet. "Employees First, Customers Second." *YouTube*, 9 June 2015, www.youtube.com/watch?v=cCdu67s_C5E.

53. Sound Recording

> Blige, Mary J. "Don't Mind." *Life II: The Journey Continues (Act 1)*, Geffen, 2011.

54. Work of Art or Photograph

List the artist or photographer; the work's title, italicized; and the date of composition. Then cite the name of the museum or other location and the city.

> Bradford, Mark. *Let's Walk to the Middle of the Ocean*. 2015, Museum of Modern Art, New York.

> Feinstein, Harold. *Hangin' Out, Sharing a Public Bench, NYC*. 1948, Panopticon Gallery, Boston.

To cite a reproduction in a book, add the publication information.

O'Keeffe, Georgia. *Black and Purple Petunias*. 1925, private collection. *Two Lives: A Conversation in Paintings and Photographs*, edited by Alexandra Arrowsmith and Thomas West, HarperCollins, 1992, p. 67.

To cite artwork found online, add the title of the database or Web site, italicized; and the URL of the site you accessed.

Clough, Charles. *January Twenty-First*. 1988-89, Joslyn Art Museum, Omaha, www.joslyn.org/collections-and-exhibitions/permanent-collections/ modern-and-contemporary/charles-clough-january-twenty-first/.

55. Lecture or Speech

Smith, Anna Deavere. "On the Road: A Search for American Character." National Endowment for the Humanities, John F. Kennedy Center for the Performing Arts, Washington, 6 Apr. 2015. Address.

56. Performance

The Draft. By Peter Snoad, directed by Diego Arciniegas, Hibernian Hall, Boston, 10 Sept. 2015.

57. Map or Chart

"Map of Sudan." *Global Citizen*, Citizens for Global Solutions, 2011, globalsolutions .org/blog/bashir#.VthzNMfi_FI.

58. Cartoon

Ramirez, Michael P. "Eagle and Loon." *Michael P. Ramirez*, 31 Aug. 2017, http://www.michaelpramirez.com/loon-and-eagle.html. Cartoon.

59. Advertisement

Louis Vuitton. *Vanity Fair,* Aug. 2017, p. 35. Advertisement.

On p. 514, note the formatting of the first page of a sample essay written in MLA style. On p. 515, you'll find a sample works cited page written for the same student essay.

Sample First Page for an Essay in MLA Style

Lesk 1

Name, instructor, course, date aligned at left

Emily Lesk

Professor Arraéz

Electric Rhetoric

15 November 2014

Title centered

Red, White, and Everywhere

America, I have a confession to make: I don't drink Coke. But don't call me a hypocrite just because I am still the proud owner of a bright red shirt that advertises it. Just call me an American. Even before setting foot in Israel three years ago, I knew exactly where I could find one. The tiny T-shirt shop in the central block of Jerusalem's Ben Yehuda Street did offer other designs, but the one with a bright white "Drink Coca-Cola Classic" written in Hebrew cursive across the chest was what drew in most of the dollar-carrying tourists. While waiting almost twenty minutes for my shirt (depicted in fig. 1), I watched nearly every customer ahead of me ask for "the Coke shirt, *todah rabah* [thank you very much]."

Figure number and caption noting the source of the photo

Fig. 1. Hebrew Coca-Cola T-shirt. Personal photograph. Despite my dislike for the beverage, I bought this Coca-Cola T-shirt in Israel. Emily Lesk

At the time, I never thought it strange that I wanted one, too. After having absorbed sixteen years of Coca-Cola propaganda through everything from NBC's Saturday morning cartoon lineup to the concession stand at Camden Yards (the Baltimore Orioles' ballpark), I associated the shirt with singing along to the "Just for the Taste of It" jingle and with America's favorite pastime, not with a brown fizzy beverage I refused to consume.

Sample List of Works Cited for an Essay in MLA Style

Lesk 7

Heading centered

Works Cited

Coca-Cola Santa pin. Personal photograph by the author, 9 Nov. 2008.

"The Fabulous Fifties." *Beverage Industry,* vol. 87, no. 6,

Subsequent lines of each entry indented

1996, p. 16. *General OneFile,* go.galegroup.com/.

"Fifty Years of Coca-Cola Television Advertisements." *American Memory*. Motion Picture, Broadcasting and Recorded Sound Division, Library of Congress, memory .loc.gov/ammem/ccmphtml/colahome.html. Accessed 5 Nov. 2014.

"Haddon Sundblom and Coca-Cola." *The History of Christmas,* 10 Holidays, 2004, www.thehistoryofchristmas .com/sc/coca_cola.htm.

Hebrew Coca-Cola T-shirt. Personal photograph by the author, 8 Nov. 2014.

List is alphabetized by authors' last names (or by title when there is no author)

Ikuta, Yasutoshi, editor. *'50s American Magazine Ads*. Graphic-Sha, 1987.

Pendergrast, Mark. *For God, Country, and Coca-Cola: The Definitive History of the Great American Soft Drink and the Company That Makes It*. 2nd ed., Basic Books, 2000.

APA Style

The Publication Manual of the American Psychological Association (7th edition, 2020) provides comprehensive advice to student and professional writers in the social sciences. Here we draw on the *Publication Manual's* guidelines to provide an overview of APA style for in-text citations, content notes, and entries in the list of references.

In-Text Citations

APA style calls for in-text citations in the body of an argument to document sources of quotations, paraphrases, summaries, and so on. These in-text citations correspond to full bibliographic entries in the list of references at the end of the text.

1. Author Named in a Signal Phrase

Generally, give the author's name in a signal phrase to introduce the cited material, using the past tense for the signal verb. Place the date, in parentheses, immediately after the author's name. For a quotation, the page number, preceded by *p.* (not italicized), appears in parentheses after the quotation. For electronic texts or other works without page numbers, paragraph numbers, preceded by the abbreviation *para.*, section headings, figure or table numbers, slide numbers, or time-stamps may be used. For a long, set-off quotation, position the page reference in parentheses one space after the punctuation at the end of the quotation. The location of cited material is optional for paraphrases and summaries, but they can be helpful for long or complex works.

> Zhang (2019) showed that "when academics are strongly motivated to teach . . . , they tend to develop positive feelings toward their . . . jobs and their . . . universities in general" (p. 1325).

> According to Brandon (1993), Adefunmi opposed all forms of racism and believed that black nationalism should not be a destructive force (p. 29).

> Myers (2019) extolled the benefits of humility (para. 5).

2. Author Named in Parentheses

When you don't mention the author in a signal phrase, give the name and the date, separated by a comma, in parentheses at the end of the cited material.

> *The Sopranos* has achieved a much wider viewing audience than ever expected, spawning a cookbook and several serious scholarly studies (Franklin, 2002).

3. Two Authors

Use both names in all citations. Use *and* in a signal phrase, but use an ampersand (&) in parentheses.

> Associated with purity and wisdom, Obatala is the creator of human beings, whom he is said to have formed out of clay (Edwards & Mason, 1985).

4. Three or More Authors

List just the first author's last name followed by *et al.* (in regular type, not underlined or italicized).

> Lenhoff et al. (1997) cited tests that indicate that segments of the left brain hemisphere are not affected by Williams syndrome, whereas the right hemisphere is significantly affected (p. 1641).

> Examining the lives of women expands our understanding of human development (Belenky et al., 1986).

5. Organization as Author

If the name of an organization or a corporation is long, spell it out the first time, followed by an abbreviation in brackets. In later citations, use the abbreviation only.

First Citation   (Federal Bureau of Investigation [FBI], 2002)

Subsequent Citations   (FBI, 2002)

6. Unknown Author

Use the title or its first few words in a signal phrase or in parentheses. (In the example below, a book's title is italicized.)

> The school profiles for the county substantiate this trend (*Guide to secondary schools*, 2003).

7. Authors with the Same Last Name

If your list of references includes works by different authors with the same last name, include the authors' initials in each citation.

> G. Jones (1998) conducted the groundbreaking study of retroviruses, whereas P. Jones (2000) replicated the initial trials two years later.

8. Two or More Sources in the Same Citation

List sources by the same author chronologically by publication year. List sources by different authors in alphabetical order by the authors' last names, separated by semicolons.

> While traditional forms of argument are warlike and agonistic, alternative models do exist (Foss & Foss, 1997; Makau, 1999).

9. Two or More Works by the Same Author in the Same Year

Use lowercase letters (*a*, *b*, etc.) before the year to differentiate between the works.

> Soot-free flames can be produced by stripping the air of nitrogen and then adding that nitrogen to the fuel (Conover, 2019b).

10. Specific Parts of a Source

Identify the part (chapter, section, paragraph, figure, footnote, etc.) in your sentence.

> In his foreword to Anthony Ray Hinton's moving book (2018), Bryan Stevenson wrote . . . (p. iv).

11. Online Document

To cite a source found on the Internet, use the author's name and date as you would for a print source, and indicate the chapter or figure of the document, as appropriate. If the source's publication date is unknown, use *n.d.* ("no date"). To document a quotation, include the paragraph number, section heading, slide number, or time-stamp to indicate the location of the cited material.

> In her TED talk on vulnerability, Brown (2014) noted that shame is "highly, highly correlated with addiction, depression, violence, aggression, bullying, suicide, eating disorders" (14:16).

12. Email and Other Personal Communication

Cite any personal letters, emails, text messages, electronic postings, telephone conversations, or personal interviews by giving the person's initial(s) and last name, the identification, and the date. Do not include an entry in the references list.

> E. Ashdown (personal communication, March 9, 2015) supported these claims.

Content Notes

The APA recommends using content notes for material that will expand or supplement your argument but otherwise would interrupt the text. Indicate such notes in your text by inserting superscript numerals. Type the notes themselves either at the bottom of the page or on a separate page headed *Footnotes* (not italicized or in quotation marks), centered at the top of the page. Double-space all entries. Indent the first line of each note one-half inch or five spaces, and begin subsequent lines at the left margin.

Text with Superscript Indicating a Note

Data related to children's preferences in books were instrumental in designing the questionnaire.[1]

Note

[1]Rudine Sims Bishop and members of the Reading Readiness Research Group provided helpful data.

List of References

The alphabetical list of sources cited in your text is called *References*. (If your instructor asks you to list everything you've read as background—not just the sources you cite—call the list *Bibliography*.) The list of references appears on a separate page or pages at the end of your paper, with the heading *References* in boldface type (not underlined, italicized, or in quotation marks) centered on the first line, with no space above or below. Double-space the entire list. For print sources, APA style specifies the treatment and placement of four basic elements: author, publication date, title, and source information. Each element is followed by a period.

- **Author:** List all authors up to and including 20 with last name first, and use only initials for first and middle names. Separate the names of multiple authors with commas, and use an ampersand (&) before the last author's name.
- **Publication date:** Enclose the publication date in parentheses. Use only the year for books and journals; use the year, a comma, and the month or month and day for magazines and newspapers. Do not abbreviate the month. If a date is not given, put *n.d.* ("no date," not italicized) in the parentheses. Put a period after the parentheses.

- **Title:** Italicize titles and subtitles of books and periodicals. Do not enclose titles of articles in quotation marks. For books and articles, capitalize only the first word of the title and subtitle and any proper nouns or proper adjectives; also capitalize the first word following a colon. Capitalize all major words in the title of a periodical.

- **Source information:** For a book, provide the publisher's full name, dropping business terms such as *Ltd.* and *Inc.* For a periodical, follow the periodical title with a comma, the volume number (italicized), the issue number (if provided) in parentheses and followed by a comma, and the inclusive page numbers of the article. For chapters in edited books, include the abbreviation *p.* ("page") or *pp.* ("pages"). End with the digital object identifier (DOI) or URL, if there is one.

The following APA style examples appear in a "hanging indent" format, in which the first line aligns on the left and the subsequent lines indent one-half inch or five spaces.

Print Books

1. One Author

Isenberg, N. (2016). *White trash: The 400-year untold history of class in America.* Viking.

2. Two or More Authors

Include up to 20 authors' names in the entry, separating them with commas and using an ampersand (&) before the final author's name.

Steininger, M., Newell, J. D., & Garcia, L. (1984). *Ethical issues in psychology.* Dow Jones-Irwin.

3. Organization as Author

Omit the publisher when the organization is both the author and the publisher.

Linguistics Society of America. (2002). *Guidelines for using sign language interpreters.*

4. Unknown Author

National Geographic atlas of the world. (2010). National Geographic Society.

5. Edited Book

Hardy, H. H. (Ed.). (1998). *The proper study of mankind*. Farrar, Straus and Giroux.

6. Selection in an Anthology or an Edited Book

Villanueva, V. (1999). An introduction to social scientific discussions on class. In A. Shepard, J. McMillan, & G. Tate (Eds.), *Coming to class: Pedagogy and the social class of teachers* (pp. 262–277). Heinemann.

7. Translation

Pérez-Reverte, A. (2002). *The nautical chart* (M. S. Peden, Trans.). Harvest. (Original work published 2000)

8. Edition Other Than the First

Bok, D. (2015). *Higher education in America* (Rev. ed.). Princeton University Press.

9. One Volume of a Multivolume Work

Will, J. S. (1921). *Protestantism in France* (Vol. 2). University of Toronto Press.

10. Article in a Reference Work

Chernow, B., & Vattasi, G. (Eds.). (1993). Psychomimetic drug. In *The Columbia encyclopedia* (5th ed., p. 2238). Columbia University Press.

If no author is listed, begin with the article title, followed by the year, and the rest of the citation as shown here.

11. Republication

Sharp, C. (1978). *History of Hartlepool*. Hartlepool Borough Council. (Original work published 1816)

12. Graphic Narrative

If the words and images are created by the same person, cite a graphic narrative just as you would a book with one author (see item 1 on p. 520).

Bechdel, A. (2012). *Are you my mother?* Houghton Mifflin Harcourt.

If the work is a collaboration, indicate the author or illustrator who is most important to your research, followed by other contributors in order of their appearance on the title page. Label each person's contribution to the work.

> Stavans, I. (Writer), & Arcaraz, L. (Illustrator). (2000). *Latino USA: A cartoon history.* Basic.

13. Government Document

If no author is given, list the department that produced the document.

> U.S. Bureau of the Census. (2001). *Survey of women-owned business enterprises.* Government Printing Office.

14. Two or More Works by the Same Author

List the works in chronological order of publication. Repeat the author's name in each entry.

> Lowin, S. (2006). *The making of a forefather: Abraham in Islamic and Jewish exegetical narratives.* Brill.

> Lowin, S. (2013). *Arabic and Hebrew love poems in Al-Andalus.* Routledge.

Print Periodicals

15. Article in a Journal Paginated by Volume

> Bowen, L. M. (2011). Resisting age bias in digital literacy research. *College Composition and Communication, 62,* 586–607.

16. Article in a Journal Paginated by Issue

> Carr, S. (2002). The circulation of Blair's Lectures. *Rhetoric Society Quarterly, 32*(4), 75–104.

17. Article in a Monthly Magazine

> Considine, A. (2017, December). From stage to page and back again. *American Theatre 34*(10), 32–35.

18. Article in a Newspaper

> Finucane, M. (2019, September 25). Americans still eating too many low-quality carbs. *The Boston Globe*, B2.

19. Letter to the Editor or Editorial

Insert the appropriate label in brackets after the title.

Erbeta, R. (2008, December). Swiftboating George [Letter to the editor].
    Smithsonian, 39(9), 10.

20. Unsigned Article

Guidelines issued on assisted suicide. (1998, March 4). *The New York Times*, A15.

21. Review

Avalona, A. (2008, August). [Review of the book *Weaving women's lives: Three
    generations in a Navajo family*, by L. Lamphere]. *New Mexico, 86*(8), 40.

22. Published Interview

Shor, I. (1997). [Interview with A. Greenbaum]. *Writing on the Edge, 8*(2), 7–20.

23. Two or More Works by the Same Author in the Same Year

List two or more works by the same author published in the same
year alphabetically by title (excluding *A*, *An*, or *The*), and place lowercase
letters (*a*, *b*, etc.) after the dates.

Murray, F. B. (1983a). Equilibration as cognitive conflict. *Developmental Review, 3*,
    54–61.

Murray, F. B. (1983b). Learning and development through social interaction. In L.
    Liben (Ed.), *Piaget and the foundations of knowledge* (pp. 176–201). Erlbaum.

Digital Sources

The following models are based on the *Publication Manual of the American
Psychological Association* (7th edition). When one is available, use a digital
object identifier (DOI) instead of a URL to locate an electronic source. The
DOI is a unique number assigned to an electronic text (article, book, or
other item) and intended to give reliable access to it. List the retrieval

date with the URL only if a source changes very frequently. The basic APA entry for most electronic sources should include the following elements:

- name of the author, editor, or compiler
- date of electronic publication or most recent update
- title of the work, document, or posting
- publication information, including the title, volume or issue number, and page numbers, paragraph numbers, headings, time-stamps, or other ways of locating the cited information
- the DOI, if available
- a direct-link URL, only if a DOI is not available, with no angle brackets and no closing punctuation

24. Document from a Web Site

To cite a whole site, give the URL in parentheses in the text. To cite a document from a Web site, include information as you would for a print document, followed by the DOI or direct-link URL. Provide a date of retrieval only if the information is likely to change frequently.

American Psychological Association. (2013). *Making stepfamilies work.* http://www.apa.org/helpcenter/stepfamily.aspx

Mullins, B. (1995). Introduction to Robert Hass. In *Readings in contemporary poetry at Dia Center for the Arts.* Retrieved from http://awp.diaart.org /poetry/95_96/intrhass.html

25. Article from a Periodical on the Web

If no DOI is available, provide the direct-link URL. You may shorten a lengthy URL via shortdoi.org or bitly.com. Do not include the name of the database you used, if any.

Le Texier, T. (2019). Debunking the Stanford Prison Experiment. *American Psychologist, 74*(7), 823–839. https://doi.org/10.1037/amp0000401

Vlahos, J. (2019, March). Alexa, I want answers. *Wired,* 58–65. https://www.wired.com/story/amazon-alexa-search-for-the-one-perfect-answer/

Daly, J. (2019, August 2). Duquesne's med school plan part of national trend to train more doctors. *Pittsburgh Post-Gazette.* https://bit.ly/2Vzrm2l

26. Dissertation

Include the DOI if one has been assigned. If the dissertation was posted online by the granting university, include the university archive, department, or library in the source position and a direct-link URL.

Degli-Esposti, M. (2019). *Child maltreatment and antisocial behaviour in the United Kingdom: Changing risks over time* [Doctoral dissertation, University of Oxford]. Oxford University Research Archive. https://ora.ox.ac.uk/objects/ uuid:6d5a8e55-bd19-41a1-8ef5-ef485642af89

27. Mobile Application Software (App)

Google LLC. (2019). *Google earth* (Version 9.3.3) [Mobile app]. App Store. https:// apps.apple.com/us/app/google-earth/id293622097

28. Online Government Document

Cite an online government document as you would a printed government work, adding the direct-link URL.

National Park Service. (2019, April 11). *Travel where women made history: Ordinary and extraordinary places of American women.* U.S. Department of the Interior. https://www.nps.gov/subjects/travelwomenshistory/index.htm

29. Entry in an Online Reference Work

Cite the entry as you would an entry from a print reference work (see item 10), ending with the direct-link URL. If a source is intended to be updated regularly, include a retrieval date. Since Wikipedia makes archived versions available, you need not include a retrieval date. Instead, include the URL for the version you used, which you can find by clicking on the "View history" tab on the site.

Tour de France. (2019, November 7). In *Encyclopaedia Britannica.* https://www .britannica.com/sports/Tour-de-France

Behaviorism. (2019, October 11). In *Wikipedia.* https://en.wikipedia.org/w/index. php?title=Behaviorism&oldid=915544724

30. Comment on an Online Article

Provide a direct-link URL to the comment, if available, or to the article, if not.

lollyl2. (2019, September 25). My husband works in IT in a major city down South. He is a permanent employee now, but for years [Comment on the article "The Google workers who voted to unionize in Pittsburgh are part of tech's huge contractor workforce"]. *Slate.* https://fyre.it/0RT8HmeL.4

31. Blog Post

After the author's name, include the title of the post; the publication date; the title of the blog, italicized; and the direct-link URL.

Fister, B. (2019, February 14). Information literacy's third wave. *Library Babel Fish*. https://www.insidehighered.com/blogs/library-babel-fish/information-literacy%E2%80%99s-third-wave

32. Post on Social Media

To cite a post on a public Facebook page or other social media, include the writer's name, the date of the post, the title or caption of the post or its first 20 words, a label in brackets, the website on which it was posted, and the URL with no end punctuation. Describe any images or attachments in brackets after the title. Include an access date only if the content is likely to change (for example, a profile page).

Georgia Aquarium. (n.d.). *Home* [Facebook page]. Facebook. Retrieved October 15, 2019, from https://www.facebook.com/GeorgiaAquarium/

Georgia Aquarium. (2019, June 25). *True love ♥ ♥ Charlie and Lizzy are a bonded pair of African penguins who have been together for more than* [Image attached] [Status update]. Facebook. https://www.facebook.com/GeorgiaAquarium/photos/a.163898398123/10156900637543124/?type=3&theater

Smithsonian [@smithsonian]. (n.d.). *#Apollo50* [Highlight]. Instagram. Retrieved October 15, 2019, from https://www.instagram.com/stories/highlights/17902787752343364/

33. Tweet

Include the entire text of the tweet with no end punctuation, followed by a label in brackets; the name of the website, and the URL with no end punctuation.

Schiller, C. [@caitlinschiller]. (2019, September 26). *Season 6 of Simplify is here! Today we launch with the one and only @susancain, author of* Quiet [Thumbnail with link attached] [Tweet]. Twitter. http://twitter.com/caitlinschiller/status/1177214094191026176

34. Online Forum Post

Include in the list of references only if the post is archived.

ScienceModerator. (2018, November 16). *Science discussion: We are researchers working with some of the largest and most innovative companies using DNA to help people* [Online forum post]. Reddit. https://www.reddit.com/r/science/comments/9xlnm2/science_discussion_we_are_researchers_working/

35. Email, Text Message, or Synchronous Communication

Because the APA stresses that any sources cited in your list of references must be retrievable by your readers, omit entries for email, text messages, or synchronous communications (MOOs, MUDs); instead, cite these sources in your text as forms of personal communication (see item 12 on p. 518). And remember that you shouldn't quote from other people's email without asking their permission to do so.

Other Sources

36. Technical or Research Reports and Working Papers

Kinley-Horn and Associates. (2011). *ADOT bicycle safety action plan* (Working Paper No. 3). Arizona Department of Transportation.

37. Unpublished Paper Presented at a Meeting or Symposium

Welch, K. (2002, March 20–23). *Electric rhetoric and screen literacy* [Paper presentation]. Conference on College Composition and Communication, Chicago, IL, United States.

38. Unpublished Dissertation

Bacaksizlar, N. G. (2019). *Understanding social movements through simulations of anger contagion in social media* (Publication No. 13805848) [Doctoral dissertation, University of North Carolina at Charlotte]. ProQuest Dissertations & Theses.

39. Poster Session

Wood, M. (2019, January 3–6). *The effects of an adult development course on students' perceptions of aging* [Poster session]. Forty-First Annual National Institute on the Teaching of Psychology, St. Pete Beach, FL, United States. https://nitop.org/resources/Documents/2019%20Poster%20Session%20II.pdf

40. Film

Peele, J. (Director). (2017). *Get out* [Film]. Universal Pictures.

41. Television or Radio Program

Waller-Bridge, P. (Writer), & Bradbeer, H. (Director). (2019, March 18). The provocative request (Season 2, Episode 3) [TV series episode]. In P. Waller-Bridge, H. Williams, & J. Williams (Executive Producers), *Fleabag*. Two Brothers Pictures; BBC.

Young, R. (Host). (2018, March 1). How "Black Panther" is inspiring black cosplayers [Radio series episode]. In K. McKenna (Senior producer), *Here and now*. https://www.wbur.org/hereandnow/2018/03/01/black-panther-black-cosplayers

42. Online Video or Audio

List as the publisher the source through which you accessed the video or audio file (for example, YouTube).

Wray, B. (2019, May). *How climate change affects your mental health* [Video]. TED Conferences. https://www.ted.com/talks/britt_wray_how_climate_change_affects_your_mental_health

TED. (2019, September 20). *Britt Wray: How climate change affects your mental health* [Video]. YouTube. https://www.youtube.com/watch?v=-IlDkCEvsYw

BBC. (2018, November 19). *Why do bad managers flourish?* [Audio]. In Business Matters. https://www.bbc.co.uk/programmes/p06s8752

43. Sound Recording

Nielsen, C. (2014). *Carl Nielsen: Symphonies 1 & 4* [Album recorded by the New York Philharmonic Orchestra]. Dacapo Records. (Original work published 1892–1916)

Carlile, B. (2018). *By the way, I forgive you* [Album]. Low Country Sound; Elektra.

Carlile, B. (2018). The mother [Song]. On *By the way, I forgive you*. Low Country Sound; Elektra.

44. Podcast or Episode from a Podcast

Boilen, B. (Host). (2008–present). *Tiny desk concerts* [Video podcast]. NPR. https://www.npr.org/series/tiny-desk-concerts/

Boilen, B. (Host). (2019, September 11). Come from away [Video podcast episode]. In *Tiny desk concerts*. NPR. https://www.npr.org/2019/09/11/758080813/come-from-away-tiny-desk-concert

45. Advertisement

America's Biopharmaceutical Companies [Advertisement]. (2018, September). *The Atlantic, 322*(2), 2.

Sample Title Page for an Essay in APA Style

Page number
appears flush
right on first
line of every
page

1

Title is
centered in
boldface type,
3 to 4 double
line spaces
from the top

**Mood Music: Music Preference and the Risk for
Depression and Suicide in Adolescents**

Tawnya Redding

Department of Psychology, Oregon State University

PSY 480, Clinical Methods in Psychology

Professor Samuel Ede

November 15, 2019

Name,
department
and school,
course
number and
course title,
instructor's
name, and
due date, all
centered and
double-spaced

Sample First Text Page for an Essay in APA Style

2

Full title, centered in boldface type

Mood Music: Music Preference and the Risk for Depression and Suicide in Adolescents

Paragraphs indented

Music is a significant part of American culture. Since the explosion of rock and roll in the 1950s, there has been a concern for the effects that music may have on listeners, and especially on people ages 13 to 19. The genres most likely to come under suspicion in recent decades have included heavy metal, country, and blues. These genres have been suspected of having adverse effects on the mood and behavior of young listeners. But can music really alter the disposition and create self-destructive behaviors in listeners? And if so, which genres and aspects of those genres are responsible? The following review of the literature will establish the correlation between potentially problematic genres of music such as heavy metal and country and depression and suicide risk. First, correlational studies concerning music preference and suicide risk will be discussed, followed by a discussion of the literature concerning the possible reasons for this link. Finally, studies concerning the effects of music on mood will be discussed. Despite the link between genres such as heavy metal and country and suicide risk, previous research has been unable to establish the causal nature of this link.

Boldface headings help organize review

The Correlation Between Music and Depression and Suicide Risk

Parenthetical references follow APA style

A large portion of studies over the past two decades have focused on heavy metal and country music as the main genre culprits associated with youth suicidality and depression (Lacourse et al., 2001; Scheel & Westefeld, 1999; Stack & Gundlach, 1992). Stack and Gundlach (1992) examined the radio airtime devoted to country music in 49 metropolitan areas and found that the

Sample References List for an Essay in APA Style

References begin on new page

9

References

Heading is centered in boldface type

Baker, F., & Bor, W. (2008). Can music preference indicate mental health status in young people? *Australasian Psychiatry, 16*(4), 284–288. https://doi .org/10.1080/10398560701879589

George, D., Stickle, K., Rachid, F., & Wopnford, A. (2007). The association between types of music enjoyed and cognitive, behavioral, and personality factors of those who listen. *Psychomusicology, 19*(2), 32–56.

Lacourse, E., Claes, M., & Villeneuve, M. (2001). Heavy metal music and adolescent suicidal risk. *Journal of Youth and Adolescence, 30*(3), 321–332.

Lai, Y. (1999). Effects of music listening on depressed women in Taiwan. *Issues in Mental Health Nursing, 20,* 229–246. doi:10.1080/016128499248637

DOI is provided for an electronic source

Martin, G., Clark, M., & Pearce, C. (1993). Adolescent suicide: Music preference as an indicator of vulnerability. *Journal of the American Academy of Child and Adolescent Psychiatry, 32,* 530–535.

Scheel, K., & Westefeld, J. (1999). Heavy metal music and adolescent suicidality: An empirical investigation. *Adolescence, 34*(134), 253–273.

Siedliecki, S., & Good, M. (2006). Effect of music on power, pain, depression and disability. *Journal of Advanced Nursing, 54*(5), 553–562. doi:10.1111 /j.1365-2648.2006.03860

Smith, J. L., & Noon, J. (1998). Objective measurement of mood change induced by contemporary music. *Journal of Psychiatric & Mental Health Nursing, 5,* 403–408.

RESPOND•

1. The MLA and APA styles differ in several important ways, both for in-text citations and for lists of sources. You've probably noticed a few: the APA uses lowercase letters for most words in titles and lists the publication date right after the author's name, whereas the MLA capitalizes most words and puts the publication date at the end of the works cited entry. More interesting than the details, though, is the reasoning behind the differences. Placing the publication date near the front of a citation, for instance, reveals a special concern for that information in the APA style. Similarly, the MLA's decision to capitalize titles isn't arbitrary: that style is preferred in the humanities for a reason. Working in a group, find as many consistent differences between the MLA and APA styles as you can. Then, for each difference, speculate about the reasons these groups organize or present information in that way. The MLA and APA style manuals themselves may be of help. You might also begin by determining which academic disciplines subscribe to the APA style and which to the MLA.

2. Working with another person in your class, look for examples of the following sources: an article in a journal, a book, a film, a song, and a TV show. Then make a references page or works cited list (five entries in all), using either MLA or APA style.

arguments

23
How Does Popular Culture Stereotype *You?*

LEFT TO RIGHT: Walt Disney Studios Motion Pictures/Photofest; Sunpix Travel/Alamy; Sarah L. Voisin/The Washington Post/Getty Images

Check the dictionary, and you'll learn that the term *stereotype* originally referred to a printing plate cast in metal from the mold of a page of set type. Although English borrowed the word from French, its parts are ultimately of Greek origin: *stereo* means "solid" or "three-dimensional" and *type* means "model." By extension, the word has come to mean a widely held image that is fixed, allowing for little individuality among a group's members. Ironic, isn't it, that a term originally referring to a three-dimensional printing plate has come to mean a one-dimensional representation of an entire group?

The selections in this chapter focus on stereotyping in popular culture, challenging you to analyze what many consider to be unsavory stereotypes of various groups often found there. At the same time, the chapter challenges you to think about whether it is possible to undo stereotypes, to move from one-dimensional representations of groups to representations that acknowledge the groups' complexities.

The chapter opens with a selection by Alli Joseph that considers how the 2016 blockbuster film *Moana* was initially received among Native Americans and Pacific Islanders, groups who contend that they have not been fairly represented in American culture. Because it focuses on a Disney film, the article understandably raises questions about how well Disney succeeded in doing a better job with *Moana* than it had done in the past with other films, even as the article also seeks to explain why making films about marginalized groups is difficult—period.

The second reading is a 2015 selection by a writer identified only as D.K., which discusses the ways in which people who enjoy shooting guns are often misrepresented by Americans wanting stronger gun-control regulations. Its two audiences—readers in the U.S. and those around the world—make for an interesting rhetorical situation as the writer seeks to explain U.S. culture to the rest of the world and also to his intended American readers.

In the third selection, Nicole Pasulka presents a case study that may encourage readers to examine stereotypes about fundamentalist Christians and LGBTQ individuals. This 2015 selection also documents generational changes taking place in many fundamentalist communities, reminding us of a limitation of stereotypes—both stereotypes and those who subscribe to them get stuck in time.

Next is an excerpt from C. Richard King's 2016 book, *Redskins: Insult and Brand*. It historicizes the controversy over the name of the Washington, D.C., professional football team, seeking to encourage readers to examine their own assumptions (and stereotypes) about what these debates are and aren't about.

The fifth selection, an excerpt from a 2011 research article by five psychologists led by Melinda C. R. Burgess, investigates the prevalence and consequences of racial stereotypes in video games, calling attention to the way such stereotypes show up in unexpected places.

The visual argument for this chapter is three cereal boxes by Canadian artist Sonny Assu from his 2006 *Breakfast Series*. Assu uses illustrations and text on the boxes to mock stereotypes of the First Nations people of Canada.

The chapter closes with Sara Morrison's 2016 report on how journalists are learning to do a better job covering the transgender community, moving beyond "coming out" stories to examine issues important to that community.

Originally, stereotypes were part of a printer's trade, enabling the printer to disseminate information quickly and cheaply. No less a part of popular culture today, stereotypes of different sorts continue disseminating information, much of which we increasingly find problematic. These readings may help you examine your experience with stereotypes, offering ways to think about undoing those you've decided it's time to discard.

With Disney's *Moana*, Hollywood Almost Gets It Right: Indigenous People Weigh In

ALLI JOSEPH

This Thanksgiving the receipts for the opening weekend of the new Disney film *Moana* rocketed to $82 million domestically and $99 million globally. At this rate the new film is poised to crush *Frozen* and *Big Hero 6*.

What's more, after only a week in business, it is already winning critical acclaim and beginning to rack up award nominations. Maybe most encouraging of all, Native Americans and other indigenous people are loving *Moana*, which means "ocean" and tells the story of a young Pacific Islander chief's daughter, a bold, strong and independent teen who sets sail to save her people.

Walt Disney Studios Motion Pictures/Photofest

I took my children, who are of mixed ethnicity—part Native American, African American and white—to see *Moana* last weekend, and I lamented that they would never understand how much progress this represents for the portrayal of **indigenous** people in mass media. True, they're little kids, and they should be expected to watch an animated film only with the limited scope and wonder of all children. But the experience impelled me to write about the swelling pride I felt during this film and how my late mother would have felt about it.

◀ *Alli Joseph wears many media hats as a writer and producer who works in print, broadcast journalism, and online. Joseph is also president of Seventh Generation Stories, a company that helps groups and individuals preserve their family's stories. A member of the Shinnecock Indian Nation, Joseph refers to herself as a "Native [sic] New Yorker." In this essay, which appeared in December 2016, a week after Disney released* Moana, *Joseph examines the responses of Americans of indigenous heritage to the movie. This piece first appeared at Salon .com, where Joseph is a contributing editor. As you read, consider why members of some groups have frequently found Disney films, so popular in the U.S. and worldwide, problematic and how Disney's recent efforts to change that script are being received.*

indigenous: native to a place; increasingly, this term is used in reference to the groups that lived in the Americas and the Pacific before the arrival of Europeans.

Auli'i Cravalho Tinseltown/Shutterstock

Shinnecock Indian Nation: a federally recognized Native tribe, part of the Algonquian peoples, located on the eastern end of Long Island, New York.

Lin-Manuel Miranda (1980–): award-winning American composer, lyricist, playwright, and actor of Puerto Rican descent. He is best known for his work on the 2015 Broadway musical, *Hamilton: An American Musical,* for which he wrote the book, lyrics, and music and in which he acted.

Tinseltown/Shutterstock

She passed away nine years ago today and was a fierce advocate for equal and civil rights and outspoken about the horrible racist stereotypes of Native Americans, black people and other brown folks specifically in Disney films. She might have actually tipped her hat to this one, as I did. Here's why.

It's easy to see why most are loving on the film. This is the first time that a female 5 Pacific Islander is the principal character of a major Disney animation film. She doesn't need a man. She sails her own boat. The ocean, which is a character in the film, loves and propels her.

Many Pacific Islanders have praised *Moana* across social media, with tweets expressing joy and optimism about the character and the film. The young indigenous Hawaiian actress who voiced the character, Auli'i Cravalho, knows she has added responsibility portraying the first Disney person of color from the Pacific.

"I carry, of course, such a big responsibility with the Polynesian community and I love it. I really do," 16-year-old Cravalho told *People* magazine recently. "It warms my heart every time I think about it."

Closer to home, Natahne Dennis, a member of the **Shinnecock Indian Nation**, took her young daughter to see the film last weekend. She wrote on Facebook, "I was watery-eyed through half of it. . . . It's all about not forgetting who you are and where you come from . . . keeping with your traditions, listening to your elders and respecting the power of all our elements . . . very relative to what's happening right now."

Though it's a film made for children, *Moana* has a cultural and social relevance for adults as well. I cried, too, at the soaring songs, and their lyrics by **Lin-Manuel Miranda**, which rang out about freedom and the import of knowing where you come from.

What Disney got right was its portrayal of a strong, teenage female character of 10 color—again, an indigenous person—without a love interest. It is the first Disney film in which the heroine, a bona fide Disney princess though she is, has no male suitor and she's not interested in finding one. Moana is bright, resourceful, strong and adventurous, making decisions from the heart and based on her heritage that she feels will benefit her people and save their homeland from destruction at the hands of a folkloric demon.

Disney didn't get it all right, however. Critics observe the corporate animation house stole brown peoples' cultural **mores** and identity to make a buck, and didn't fully consult them on content all the way through. The critics aren't wrong, but what they expect is not realistic: Making big studio features is a business proposition; crafting a documentary that explores true culture and origins typically is not.

Cultural appropriation is a common complaint about the media and not surprising here—and disappointing, as *Moana* is overall an uplifting, beautiful film. But the film's achievements are not enough for some to cite progress toward more accurate, less-stereotypical portrayal of other cultures in film. In **Indian Country Today**, Vicente Diaz wrote, "A small but growing movement of Pacific Islanders . . . are expressing outcry, mostly in social media." Diaz said protesters decry the "company's trafficking on indigenous cultural heritage."

As a Native American and a member of the media who has worked in advertising, broadcasting and Web content creation over the past 20 years, I understand the **confluence** of imagery, cost and influence that goes into making a successful brand. Those who are angry at Disney managers' trading on cultures not their own fail to acknowledge or accept the way business is done. We may not like it, but understanding it gives perspective.

That said, it is a valid argument to demand consistent and responsible input from respected elders and historians from the culture being portrayed. And if you want change, sometimes you have to accept progress when it comes, endorse it but ask for more—and then observe.

Native American scholars including **Kelsey Leonard**, a Harvard and Oxford   15 educated Shinnecock tribal member, have urged caution when labeling a film an "accurate portrayal" of indigenous people "especially if we are not from, as in the case of *Moana*," a Pacific Island nation, as Leonard put it.

"If you do not know the oral history, are not from those islands, have never visited those places, do not understand the vast diversity of languages and peoples, then extreme caution should be used in making sweeping claims about this movie," Leonard said. "If they made a movie about Shinnecocks, I wouldn't want a Navajo telling me if it was an accurate portrayal."

Disney has maintained that everybody involved in the production of the picture did their level best to make a responsible film that honors Pacific Island culture, traditions and history. Early reports that director and New Zealander **Taika Waititi** was consulted through the entire film, were not accurate.

---

mores (pronounced *mo-rayz*): a community's customs, traditions, and ways of behaving shaped by its social norms.

cultural appropriation (sometimes *cultural misappropriation*): the use of elements of a minority culture—clothing, foodways, music, etc.—by the majority culture, often to the benefit of members of the majority culture and denigration of the source culture. *To appropriate* something is to borrow and use it without permission.

Indian Country Today: from 2011 to 2017, Indian Country Today was first a weekly online newsletter and later a Web site and multimedia news platform about the Native peoples of North America.

confluence: a merging or coming together, as of two rivers.

Kelsey Leonard (1980–): first Native American woman to earn a degree from Oxford University in England, where she received her MSc in Water Science, Policy and Management. She was also the first member of the Shinnecock Indian Nation to graduate from Harvard University, where she studied sociology, anthropology, and ethnic studies.

Taika Waititi (1975–): also known as Taika Cohen, is among the most successful New Zealand film directors. His father is Māori, the indigenous people of New Zealand, while his mother is of Russian Jewish heritage.

colonial: having been colonized by a foreign power. The colonial powers involved in colonizing various Pacific islands have included the Portuguese, the Spanish, the Dutch, the British, the Germans, the Americans, and the Japanese.

neoliberal: a late twentieth-century political movement that places strong faith in markets, privatization of what had been public (or government) programs, deregulation, and free trade. Here, the focus is the mass marketing of often inaccurate replicas of things related to specific cultural groups (e.g., as Halloween costumes, toys, etc.).

postcolonial: the state of having once been colonized. Once people become independent, legacies of the colonial period often play a major role in how they see themselves and how their societies are organized, and economic relationships with the former colonizer often shape the society.

gaffes: unintentional blunders.

Variety: a Web site that publishes information on the entertainment industry. Founded as a weekly newspaper in 1905 reporting on New York City theater and vaudeville, a daily edition focusing on the movie industry was added in Los Angeles in 1933. Since 2013, it has existed only online as variety.com.

Indeed the voice cast is almost fully comprised of actors with Pacific Island heritage and Waititi apparently did write an early draft of the script for *Moana*. But the script was ultimately rewritten by Jared Bush, a non-Pacific Islander. "It continues to be disappointing that when people are called as advisory cultural and artistic consultants on projects that their work is not respected all the way through," Courtney Leonard, another Shinnecock woman and sister of Kelsey Leonard, wrote. "It's also a lot of responsibility when you come from that culture to please everyone under the auspices and pretenses that are what Disney is."

Diaz wrote in Indian Country Today, "Any altruism associated with this latest commercial ad-venture will always be trumped by the proverbial bottom line, but more depressingly, by an enduring **colonial** legacy in the Pacific islands that is further animated in the 21st century by **neoliberal** and **postcolonial** desires for selling and consuming native culture of a very specific type."

As Disney often does, the script is populated by characters that are a mash-up of   20 Pacific Island cultures, and therefore are not as accurate in their representation as they could be. Disney made some early **gaffes** in the associated merchandise, like a tattooed skin suit of the Polynesian demigod Maui featured in the film (oh no!) and plastic toy figures that turn Pele, the Hawaiian fire goddess responsible for volcanoes, lightening and wind respectfully referred by those in the culture as Madame Pele, into the lava witch seen in the film (ugh!).

Both products have been pulled from stores. Copy on the tattoo skin suit packaging, according to *Variety*, had cheerily read, "Your little one will set off on adventures in this Maui costume featuring the demigod's signature tattoos, rope necklace, and island-style skirt. Plus, padded arms and legs for mighty stature!"

So, yeah, Disney thought it would be fun for your kid to wear a replica suit of a person's skin. I would have liked to have joined the marketing meeting where that was approved.

Disney briefly hung its head, telling *Variety* in September when the toys and costumes were released, "The team behind *Moana* has taken great care to respect the cultures of the Pacific Islands that inspired the film, and we regret that the Maui costume has offended some. We sincerely apologize and are pulling the costume from our website and stores."

The crows from *Dumbo* AF archive/Alamy Stock Photo

The animation, music and storyline, in Disney fashion, are largely airtight in quality—almost magical. And in spite of any controversy, the film represents progress in the way indigenous people are portrayed by big media. *Moana* represents huge strides from 1989's crab Sebastian in *The Little Mermaid*, who sounded Jamaican and sang to the princess Ariel that life "under the sea" is better because no one has to have a job underwater. And from the way-back machine, there were the 1941 crows in *Dumbo*, who **step 'n' fetched** it, talked jive and were unintelligent. The list goes on, from "**Uncle Remus**" to the racist and slutty Native American portrayals in *Peter Pan* and *Aladdin*.

Stepin Fetchit 20th Century Fox/Getty Images

Still, wrote my cousin Adrienne Silva, "It's nice to have characters and toys that   25
look more like us. I saw a crispy white dad and his daughter excitedly looking for
a **Tiana** doll when *The Princess and the Frog* came out. It's not perfect, but it's a start.
As a parent, I purchase my kids all brown when possible . . . and unfortunately,
the fact that it's even a possibility is 'progress' in this country."

The Little Mermaid: a highly successful 1989 animated Disney film based on a Danish folktale by Hans Christian Anderson and much appreciated for its sophisticated animation.

Dumbo: a very successful 1941 animated film about an elephant, Dumbo, that can use his very large ears to fly. The movie included a group of crows, all but one of which was voiced by African Americans. Some film critics have argued that the crows represented African Americans in terms of negative stereotypes circulating in American culture at the time.

step 'n' fetched: a reference to the American comedian and film star Stepin Fetchit (1902–1985), born Lincoln Thomas Monroe Andrew Perry. Fetchit's stage name was a play on "step and fetch it." In the 1930s and 1940s, he portrayed a character claiming to be "the laziest man in the world." He was the first African American actor to receive credit for a film he appeared in and the first to earn a million dollars in the industry. By the 1950s, his popularity declined as many came to see the character he portrayed as one that perpetuated false and harmful stereotypes of African Americans.

Uncle Remus: the narrator in seven books of African American folk tales by white southern author Joel Chandler Harris, the first published in 1881. In 1946, Disney released a live action/animated musical, *Song of the South*, based on Harris's books. Controversy relating to the books and the film stems from their representation of African American language and their patronizing portrayal of African Americans.

Peter Pan: an animated 1953 Disney film based on J. M. Barrie's 1904 play, *Peter Pan, or The Boy Who Wouldn't Grow Up*. It has been criticized for its negative portrayal of Native Americans.

Aladdin: an animated 1992 Disney film based on a folktale from *A Thousand and One Nights,* an important collection of tales in Arabic literature. It was the source of great controversy because of its portrayal of Arabs, among other issues.

Tiana: the main character in the 2009 Disney film *The Princess and the Frog*. Tiana was the ninth Disney Princess and the first of African American descent.

Said Natahne Dennis: "I'm sure there were inaccurate portrayals, there's always something wrong to critics," adding, "I know my child left feeling empowered as she quoted lines from the movie. If nothing else, it was an indigenous woman determined to bring healing back to her people."

And this universal theme, of knowing where you come from and honoring that, may have to be enough for now.

RESPOND•

1. Joseph has in many ways offered a critical evaluation of *Moana*. What criteria has she used in offering her evaluation? (See Chapter 10 on evaluative arguments.) If you have seen the film, what was your response to Joseph's observations? Had you considered these issues before? Why or why not, do you think?

2. Joseph assumes many readers will accept the claim that, despite their best current efforts, Disney films do not manage to avoid misrepresenting cultures around the world. What specific evidence does she cite to support the claim with regard to *Moana*? (See the discussion of kinds of evidence in logical arguments in Chapter 4.)

3. Joseph offers what is ultimately a very interesting evaluation of the Disney film *Moana*. On the one hand, she is jubilant about many aspects of it and its possible value to children, especially girls, of indigenous heritage. At the same time, she is quick to acknowledge that Disney didn't get everything right. Yet, she is also, in many regards, an apologist—that is a defender—of Disney's efforts, despite what she and others see as the film's problems. How does Joseph establish her ethos as someone qualified to represent Native perspectives? As someone who understands how the media operate in the U.S. and internationally? (See Chapter 3 for information on arguments based on ethos.)

4. **THINKING CRITICALLY**   As Joseph notes, she is a member of the Shinnecock Nation and not a Pacific Islander, yet she clearly feels a strong connection to *Moana* and links it in important ways to her own experience as someone of Native heritage. And in paragraph 15 of the article, Joseph quotes another Shinnecock who "urged caution when labeling a film an 'accurate portrayal'" of an indigenous group one has no direct familiarity with. First, what set of circumstances might lead Native Americans to feel they have a stake in the representations of Pacific Islanders in popular culture, a stake not shared by white Americans, for example? Second, what challenges do groups like

Native Americans and Pacific Islanders, both of which have been historically marginalized in the larger society, face in finding common ground?

5. Paragraph 24 of the article catalogs several Disney films that have been criticized for their representations of various groups; the earlier of these films were made at a time when fewer people were concerned with such issues. That situation has changed—a change many Americans have been happy to see. Choose one of these films and **write an evaluative essay** about it. Watch the movie, and evaluate it with regard to the question of whether any groups are represented in negatively stereotypical ways. (This would be a good assignment to engage in with one or two classmates, ideally of different backgrounds, so that you would have several perspectives on the film as you wrote. Consult Chapter 10 on writing evaluations.)

▼ *"Shooting Guns: It's Rather Fun, Actually" was published in February 2015 on the economist.com, the Web site of the Economist, a widely read weekly magazine published in London; half its readers are in the United States. The Economist's target audience is "highly educated, cultured readers," especially those in business and policy. D.K., the author, identifies as "a liberal European reporter" and uses spellings we'd expect from a European writer and a British publication: centre, realise, neighbourhoods, organisation, and Mr without a period. The piece appeared in a regular feature of the Economist, "Democracy in America," which seeks to describe aspects of American democracy that differ in crucial ways from, say, democracies in Europe. As you read, consider the stereotypes D.K. is calling into question and those he or she is perpetuating. Likewise, try to assess whether you believe D.K. is male or female and why you draw that conclusion; doing so may give you insight into how stereotypes work.*

Shooting Guns: It's Rather Fun, Actually

D.K.

Shooting a handgun at a target is a thrill; don't let anyone tell you otherwise. You load bullets into a clip, push it up into the gun, turn off the safety catch, take careful hold of the gun with two hands, aim and shoot. The thing jumps in your hand and you see the bullet knock a hole in the target and spark off the floor at the back of the range. There is an extraordinary rush and then you do it again. Another spark; perhaps this time the hole in the target is a little closer to the centre. Soon you have fired the whole clip and you're loading the deadly weapon in your hand again.

That is just to preface a more obvious point. To a liberal European reporter, from afar, American gun culture appears utterly insane. Americans are far more likely to murder someone or to kill themselves than people in almost all Western European countries, largely because guns make it easier. That almost 33,000 people are killed with firearms each year in America (including three Muslims in Chapel Hill, North Carolina, earlier this week) is a colossal and largely unnecessary waste of life. That people celebrate these deadly devices and carry them around while shopping, picking up their children from school or working, seems monstrous.

Yet shooting is fun. And what Europeans—and liberal Americans—often don't realise is that these deadly weapons are also an accessible, affordable and interesting hobby for millions of people. My experience of firing a pistol took place at a shooting range in the Maryland suburbs, about half an hour's drive outside of Washington, DC. I had until then never visited a shooting range and I had no idea of what to expect. But the experience was actually oddly familiar. This place was not a temple to violence. Rather, it mostly closely resembled the golf driving range that my father would occasionally take me to as a child.

Most of the building's space was given over to sales. **Punters** could buy all manner of guns, from something that resembled a sniper rifle to a pink pistol around the size of a mobile phone. But they could also buy clothes: camouflage hunting jackets; bright high-vis jackets; Smith and Wesson baseball caps and T-shirts. Much of the gear was police-themed, since police officers are

punter: in British English, an informal term for a client or customer.

apparently loyal customers (which is also true of driving ranges). T-shirts commemorating dead cops, bullet-proof jackets and leather badge holders sat a little awkwardly alongside more conventional sporting gear.

In the range people fired 5 guns gleefully at targets. Some were white, male, middle-aged and so fit the stereotype. But not all. Across from where I fired my

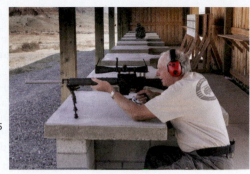

Sunpix Travel/Alamy

pistol, two black women, one with a small son, were taking turns (the child heavily supervised). Shooting targets was a fine family day out. At a practice target outside of the range, plenty of people were learning how to hold a weapon for the first time, without pointing it at anyone, dropping it or injuring themselves as it recoiled. Again, it resembled a driving range: people hitting targets for fun.

And the truth is that in the range, the violence that guns inflict on America felt extremely remote. A few stickers here and there made political points ("My right to own a gun is what protects your right to tell me I can't," said one). But mostly, the idea of guns as a means to kill somebody was absent. And so it is for most people who fire guns. The most dangerous neighbourhoods for gun violence in America are in poor cities, not in the suburban areas where most gun owners live. Most of the 21,000 or so suicides in which guns are used take place behind closed doors. And the numbers, while devastatingly high, are not so high that most Americans will know someone who was killed with a gun.

For the majority of gun owners, being told that their harmless hobby is somehow responsible for the deaths of other people must be deeply unpleasant. Worse still is when they are told it by **metropolitan** types with more money than them. Michael Bloomberg, for example, New York's billionaire

ex-mayor. Or possibly me. And it makes me wonder whether one of the problems—certainly not the main problem, but one of them—with attempts to control guns is precisely that the people making the loudest case for reform are people like Mr Bloomberg and me.

My evidence for this is this advert, put together by the NRA, in which the viewer is warned that Mr Bloomberg, guarded by armed men (a hypocrite as well as a snob!), wants to take away your safety. The NRA is an extremely nasty organisation. Supported by the money of gun manufacturers, it has created a machine whereby politicians must take stances on gun control that are more extreme than most of their voters believe, because otherwise they will be punished with attack adverts.

But the NRA is not the voice of most gun owners. Poll after poll shows that solid majorities of gun owners would prefer stricter background checks. The NRA, however, gets its support by convincing gun owners that their hobby is under threat from metropolitan liberal elitists.

But keeping guns out of the hands of criminals 10 and the mentally ill is not incompatible with widespread gun ownership. And bringing about the changes that will make America safer means convincing people who routinely use guns safely that they are not the enemy. Perhaps what gun control needs is a few advocates who are a little more visibly familiar with the sheer fun of holding a pistol and pulling the trigger.

metropolitan: referring to urban areas.

<u>**RESPOND**</u>●

1. How well has D.K. made his or her case? Where and how does D.K. provide evidence that shooting guns is or can be fun? What is your response to those descriptions?

2. Where and how does D.K. call into question stereotypes some Americans, especially those who want far stronger gun control regulations, have of those who use guns at shooting ranges or in certain other contexts? In what ways does D.K. seek to create a sympathetic view of such individuals? How successful do you believe the author is?

3. Although D.K. apparently comes to see some gun owners and users in a (more) sympathetic light based on his or her experience at the shooting range, s/he has no kind words for the National Rifle Association. How does s/he use polling data to level a criticism at the NRA? Might the claim hold with respect to other organizations or other hot-button political issues? How would this situation contribute to stereotypes and political polarization?

4. **THINKING CRITICALLY**   As noted, the *Economist* is a British-based publication, although a large percentage of its readership is located in the U.S. In what ways do we see D.K. writing for an audience of both Americans and non-Americans, a complex intended/ideal audience? Who is likely D.K.'s invoked audience, that is, the audience whose values are reflected in the text? And who is now among D.K.'s real audience? (See Chapter 1 on the complex question of audiences.)

5. The *Guardian*, another British-based publication, produces an online version for U.S. audiences. In 2013, it ran a feature, "13 Misconceptions about Gun Owners," based on responses to a query to readers who owned guns about such misconceptions (bit.ly/2njgPYB). The feature is in the form of a listicle, a relatively recent genre consisting of a list of items. **Choose two of the misconceptions submitted by readers who said they owned guns and use them as the basis of short arguments of fact.** In other words, for each misconception, write a healthy paragraph of four or five sentences in which you begin with the misconception as stated and then explain what the stereotype is and how the comment submitted calls it into question. To help you with this assignment, imagine your audience to be a group of international students who have recently arrived in the U.S. and who have limited knowledge of American culture. Consider the information you'll need to provide so that your newly arrived classmates can understand this complicated and contentious part of American culture. (See Chapter 8 on arguments of fact.)

How a Bible-Belt Evangelical Church Embraced Gay Rights

NICOLE PASULKA

When Dale Wigden went to services at Grace Pointe **Evangelical** Church in Franklin, Tennessee, for the first time around two years ago, he wasn't expecting much. Since coming out as gay in his 20s, he'd had a complicated relationship with organized religion.

Skyhobo/Getty Images

Wigden, who is now 40, grew up in a very religious **Independent Baptist** family just outside Rochester, New York. His mother and much of his family still go to the same church they always have—a community Wigden says he finds "insular and closed-minded." After he told his family he was gay, they tried to stage **interventions**, and he rebuffed their efforts outright. By the time he moved to Nashville in 2012, all the rejection meant Wigden was "not in the religious frame of mind."

◀ *New York–based Nicole Pasulka is an award-winning researcher, reporter, and writer who covers topics related to the criminal justice system, gender and sexuality, social justice, and business. She has written for National Public Radio, the Believer, Mother Jones, BuzzFeed, Hazlitt, and the New York Observer. This essay appeared in January 2015 on TakePart, which was a digital news and lifestyle magazine focusing on issues relating to culture and social justice. In 2016, TakePart was merged with its parent company's operations as part of Participant Media, a motion picture studio. As you read, consider the many levels at which stereotypes are at play within and across the groups described here.*

evangelical: referring to a form of Protestant Christianity that focuses on individual salvation by grace through faith in Jesus Christ in the form of a conversion experience ("being saved"), the authority of the Christian Bible as the word of God, and the need to convert those who have not been saved.

Independent Baptist: Baptist churches that are not affiliated with larger hierarchical groups of Baptists; thus, each church is independent. Such churches are generally quite conservative theologically and politically.

intervention: here, an effort by a group of family members or friends to confront someone who has a serious problem (e.g., an addiction or behavioral issue) in an effort convince the person to address the problem, often by seeking some sort of professional help or participation in some sort of recovery program.

interdenominational: celebrating the strengths of many denominations, here, Protestant ones.

Bible Belt: a term often applied to the southeastern and south-central U.S., where conservative Protestantism has long played a key role in daily life and in politics; church attendance is much higher in this region of the country than in others.

World Christian Broadcasting Company: a nonprofit organization that operates a Christian short-wave radio station currently broadcasting around the world in Mandarin, Russian, and English. While the content includes discussions of the Bible, it is largely geared toward secular listeners as a form of evangelism.

The uncommon spelling of the word "pointe" in Grace Pointe's name made him think it was probably some sort of "boutique church," so he was skeptical. He'd attended a gay-friendly church while living in Chicago, but "it just seemed like anything goes." Even though he knew his own lifestyle wasn't considered moral by many people's standards, the style of worship there "bugged me," Wigden says.

"Where is the place where I can be gay and Christian?" he wondered.

That first day at Grace Pointe, an **interdenominational** church with a membership   5
of about 1,500, the pastors were leading an old-fashioned hymn sing. When they got to "Amazing Grace," Pastor Melissa Greene said something that "hit me right square between the eyes," Wigden says. Speaking about the line "that saved a wretch like me," Greene said the church didn't agree with the word "wretch."

"It doesn't matter what you've done or who you are, you were born beloved by God," Wigden says she told the congregation. According these pastors, God didn't want to punish him. From that moment on, he says, he was "hooked on Grace Pointe."

While the Grace Pointe leadership, staff, and congregation emphasize love and encourage people to ask questions and voice doubts, this is no hotbed of progressive activism. The town of Franklin is in what Greene calls "the buckle of the **Bible Belt**." Half an hour outside Nashville, Franklin is affluent, overwhelmingly conservative, and about 85 percent white. With a population of around 68,000 people, it's also the home of the **World Christian Broadcasting Company**.

There are strong lines drawn between right and wrong at Grace Pointe Church. "Everyone has sin in their lives," Greene told TakePart. However, not everyone at Grace Pointe agrees on what actions are sinful. Despite some opposition from within the congregation, this Bible Belt church is now making a religious argument for gay rights.

More than 70 percent of Americans know a gay or lesbian person. Following stunning legal victories for gay marriage over the past four years, gay rights have moved from the fringe to the mainstream. Antigay attitudes haven't disappeared, but even some of the most conservative corners of the country have started to advocate for a tempered version of gay rights. On Tuesday, the Mormon Church leadership issued a statement in support of an LGBT anti-discrimination law in

Utah. Though the state law includes a wide exemption for religious freedom, the Mormon Church's statement suggests that conservative circles can no longer ignore the presence of out gay people.

Many deeply religious Christian communities are often assumed to condemn same-sex relations. But the truth is, evangelical churches are diverse and evolving quickly on the question of how to include LGBT members. In a 2014 poll by Public Religion Research Institute, a nonprofit, nonpartisan group, 42 percent of **millennial** evangelical Christians surveyed said they support same-sex marriage.

Just outside Seattle earlier this month, Eastlake Community Church—a **megachurch** that holds 13 services a week across six locations—announced it would become LGBT-inclusive. Last year in Los Angeles, a pastor named Danny Cortez was dismissed from the Southern Baptist Convention after he began speaking out in support of same-sex marriage.

Behind the scenes for Cortez's decision was Brandan Robertson, the spokesperson for Evangelicals for Marriage Equality, a Washington, D.C.–based group that will bring a petition with more than 1,179 signatures of faithful evangelicals who support same-sex marriage rights to the Ethics and Religious Liberty conference in October. The ERLC has been adamant that marriage is a "union between one man and one woman."

A **counterculture** within evangelical Christianity seems determined to challenge this idea. At this year's **Gay Christian Network** Conference, Robertson spoke to a room of 150 evangelicals who support LGBT rights. He told them it's "vital" that they stay in their evangelical communities and "not join **liberal churches** or **LGBT churches**."

Change begins "in the pews," Robertson says. Though he believes the movement for LGBT acceptance in more conservative churches is gaining momentum, he acknowledges that LGBT evangelicals "have a long way to go."

Wigden was always open about the fact that he's gay. When he first started attending services at Grace Pointe in 2012, LGBT people were part of the congregation but weren't allowed to hold leadership roles or have weddings in the church.

The leaders were telling the congregation everyone was welcome, but "we weren't a place where everyone is welcome here and has equal benefits," says Greene.

millennial: referring to those who became adults early in the twenty-first century.

megachurch: a large church with over 2,000 weekly attendees; the term is generally used to refer to large evangelical or conservative Protestant churches.

counterculture: opposing the dominant social norms.

Gay Christian Network: Christian interdenominational ministry representing a range of theological positions that was formed in 2001 to serve as an LGBTQ ally by working to change the attitudes of Christians on LGBTQ issues, especially within churches.

liberal churches: mainline Protestant denominations that have affirmed a commitment to welcoming and including LGBTQ individuals; they are termed *liberal* because they do not rely on literalist readings of the Christian scriptures but seek to understand them in terms of the historical contexts out of which they grew.

LGBT churches: churches established to serve specifically the LGBTQ community (though all are welcomed); an example would be Metropolitan Community Church, founded in 1968.

Greene is the pastor of worship and arts at Grace Pointe, and for the past six years she's led the music every Sunday and curated the services from top to bottom. She knows most of the people who come to church on Sunday and believes that around 15 percent of them identify as LGBT. In June 2012, close to the time Wigden moved to Nashville and started attending services, country singer and Grace Pointe member Carrie Underwood came out in support of gay marriage and told a U.K. newspaper that the church was "gay friendly."

In many ways, it was. Everyone knew out members like Wigden. He felt accepted and had plenty of friends in the congregation, even though he didn't have equal rights there. But the virulently antigay **Westboro Baptist Church** heard Underwood's comments and called to ask about the church's stance on gay inclusion. When Westboro announced it was going to picket Grace Pointe, "we felt like this is a good pitch for us to bring this dialogue to the forefront," Greene says.

In order to broach the subject more openly, in August 2012 Pastor Stan Mitchell devoted five services to a detailed interrogation of the biblical arguments against homosexuality—the passages that are often called "clobber texts" and cited as proof that same-sex desires are against God.

Westboro Baptist Church: an independent Baptist church known for its fiery language about a number of groups including LGBTQ individuals, Jews, Muslims, Mormons, Catholics, and Orthodox Christians. It came to public attention for its picketing at funerals, including those of Matthew Shephard and of U.S. soldiers killed in various Middle East conflicts. Member of the church contend that the soldiers' deaths are God's punishment of the country for its moral laxity, in particular, its growing acceptance of LGBTQ individuals.

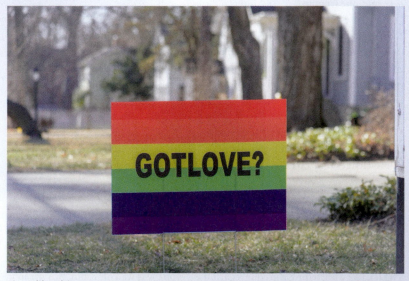

Signs like this one supporting marriage equality can be seen in front of LGBTQ-friendly churches. Kristen Prahl/Shutterstock

Dressed in jeans and a striped polo shirt, Mitchell told the congregation that   20
though the church needs to deal with the question of same-sex marriage, the
Bible does not explicitly prohibit loving, consensual same-sex relationships. "The
evil desires of those men in **Sodom and Gomorrah** had nothing to do with the
problem of whether genuine love can be expressed between consenting adults of
the same sex—zero," he said.

Though Mitchell wasn't changing policies, just digging into scripture, Greene
estimates that Grace Pointe lost about 20 percent of its membership as a result of
the service.

Still, the church kept inching toward wider acceptance, always with the question
of whether the Bible condemns same-sex desire. After this meticulous analysis
of the "clobber texts," Greene says the leadership was more convinced than ever:
"LGBT inclusion is the beautiful byproduct of what we believe the **Gospel** says."

Then, on Jan. 11, after more than two years of deliberation, Mitchell announced
that Grace Pointe would allow LGBT people to take leadership roles, have baby
dedications, and, yes, get married.

Some jumped to their feet at the news and began applauding. Wigden says he was
"thrilled." He'd known the conversations were taking place but didn't expect the
announcement to happen that day. Others were less than enthusiastic and sat
quietly, absorbing the news. "I understand why the people who cheered, cheered,"
says one congregant, who wanted to remain anonymous because he still isn't sure
how he feels about the decision. "I just wish the victory they felt could have been
amongst themselves, somewhere else."

Though Greene says the recent decision to fully accept LGBT members represents   25
"God's heart, as far as we can tell," she thinks the church will lose hundreds of
members and take a financial hit as a result. Sunday attendance declined from
an average 800 to 1,000 to 482 two weeks after the sermon, and January giving
dropped by almost 50 percent.

The congregant who is struggling to accept the new policies but is still a member
of the church tells TakePart that the applause after Mitchell's announcement
made Grace Pointe "seem divided."

"Of course, it is divided," he continues. "But I didn't want to see a victory lap
from anybody. I wanted them to be reverent and respectful."

Sodom and Gomorrah: cities mentioned in the Hebrew Bible (Genesis 18–19) as sinful. Two angels in the form of men had visited Lot, the nephew of Abraham. The men of the city of Sodom insisted that Lot turn the visitors over to the crowd, which Lot refused to do. As part of a larger narrative, the cities were destroyed by brimstone and fire. Theological debates about the sin of Sodom focus on how to interpret the passage. Did the text imply that the visiting men would be gang-raped? Was the sin homosexual behavior? Rape? A failure to offer hospitality to the strangers, a recurring command the Deity gave to the Hebrew people?

Gospel: here, the teachings of Jesus.

Many of the congregants at Grace Pointe were raised in more conservative religious communities that were uncompromising in their condemnation of homosexuality. A spirit of inclusion is in conflict with the history of exclusion both at Grace Pointe and in evangelical churches across the region.

Right now, congregants are paying close attention to the way church leaders address such politically charged differences among the congregation. Wigden's reaction to the church's validation of LGBT people reveals a great deal about the narrow line that many walk when trying to live as evangelical and gay.

Before he moved to Nashville in 2012, Wigden and a man he was in a relationship 30 with lived in Chattanooga. They had friends in the city's gay neighborhood, but the couple chose to live in a largely heterosexual, conservative suburb. "The focus, in my mind," Wigden says, "is integration." He says he and his partner lived there mainly to prove to straight, suburban people that "we were just like them."

Eventually the couple broke up, and Wigden moved to Nashville for work, but he still keeps in touch with many of his old neighbors on Facebook. "That, to me, is changing people's minds about being gay. It's not always about the pride parade or drag show."

Wigden is excited about the new church policy. He feels bad that other congregants are leaving the church over the decision after investing "their blood sweat and tears" in the congregation. But he's also scared about the potential influx of more politically vocal LGBT congregants.

"The last thing you want is for a church to do something like this and then other gay people come in being very militant about stuff and demanding things," he says. Though he cried with happiness when Mitchell announced Grace Pointe would marry gay couples, he's nervous that these changes will make it seem like "gay church."

"I don't want Grace Pointe to have a booth at the [gay] pride festival," Wigden says. "That's not the way this church is."

RESPOND●

1. In what ways does Pasulka's article challenge common stereotypes of evangelical Christians held by those outside this group? Of LGBTQ individuals by those outside this group? How does it demonstrate diversity within each group?

2. Even though Dale Wigden is quite happy that Grace Pointe came to publicly and fully accept LGBTQ individuals as part of the congregation, he is, at the same time, quite clear that he believes acceptance should come with limits. What are his limits, and what might motivate them? Do you agree with them? Why or why not? To what extend does Wigden rely on stereotypes in describing the experience of LGBTQ individuals?

3. Although Pasulka uses several kinds of evidence to support her claims in this selection, her major organizational strategy is to use the story of Dale Wigden as a way of unifying the essay. Look carefully at the points in the essay where he is mentioned and those where he is not. How does Pasulka rely on Wigden's story as a frame for structuring her essay?

4. **THINKING CRITICALLY**   Chapter 1 (pp. 28–29) discusses the important notion of *kairos*, or the right, critical, or opportune moment for action, as key to understanding the rhetorical situation, that is, the moment when it may be possible to persuade the audience of one's perspective. Where do we see kairotic moments described in this article? What changes, and what brought about those changes? What do these situations demonstrate about the power of argument?

5. Using your responses to Questions 1 through 4, **write a rhetorical analysis of Pasulka's essay**, focusing in particular on the sorts of arguments and evidence she uses as well as how she arranges those arguments and that evidence. (Building on Chapters 2–4, which discuss arguments based on emotion, character, and facts and reason, respectively, Chapter 6 describes how to compose a rhetorical analysis.)

▼ *"Redskins: Insult and Brand" is the opening chapter of C. Richard King's 2016 book of the same name. Professor King, who teaches at Washington State University, writes on topics related to the racial politics of culture, predominantly in the U.S. but recently in Austria as well. The book from which this selection comes treats the continuing debate over the name of the Washington, D.C., professional football team. On the one hand, it represents a very recognizable and lucrative brand; on the other, the term is now considered an insult by nearly all Americans and certainly by Native Americans. King's goal is to ask questions about how mainstream understandings of Native Americans and their cultures work against fully including them in American culture. Particularly because this selection focuses on the power of language, we include the "Author's Note on Language" at the beginning so that you can see the decisions Professor King has made about his own linguistic choices. As you read, consider the power that labels and labeling play in constructing and perpetuating stereotypes of any kind.*

Redskins: Insult and Brand

C. RICHARD KING

AUTHOR'S NOTE ON LANGUAGE

Names and naming, as this book details, always carry a charge in the study of indigenous people, precisely because they articulate power, identity, and representation so succinctly, forcefully, and often invisibly. Thus, one must take great care in the interpretation and application of language. Colonial histories, national narratives, and cultural practices do not make this easy. In what follows, I make two conscious language choices. First, I will use American Indians, Native Americans, indigenous peoples, *and* native nations *interchangeably in this text. Second, I endeavor to avoid the r-word. I understand it to be a racial slur, on par with the n-word. While the former enjoys wider acceptance and use than the latter, this is not a defensible rationale for relying on it. In fact, persistent reiteration makes it appear reasonable and even appropriate, a pattern that I think important to disrupt and undermine. To this end, I will substitute phrases like* the Washington professional football team *and* the DC NFL franchise, *as well as* the team *and* the franchise. *When unavoidable, I employ an altered version of the word,* R*dskin(s), *to underscore its unspeakable, problematic nature. I have not edited the usage of others in direct quotations, in part to remain faithful to my sources and in part to draw attention to the slur.*

Redskin is a problem. It is an outdated reference to an American Indian. It is best regarded as a racial slur on par with other denigrating terms. In fact, while similar terms have been crossed out of our collective vocabulary as inappropriate and offensive, . . . it still finds use. Most visibly, it remains the **moniker** of the Washington professional football team, long anchoring its brand and traditions. This should unsettle us. The word has deep connections to the history of anti-Indian violence, marked by ethnic cleansing, dispossession, and displacement. It is a term of contempt and derision that targets indigenous people. As much a weapon as a word, then, it injures and excludes, denying history and humanity. Its lingering presence undermines the pursuit of equality, inclusion, and empowerment by American Indians. Indeed, this continued use of a racial slur as the name of a professional sports team, the ongoing defense of it, and the willingness of the franchise, the National Football League (NFL), and their media partners to profit from it pose an even more troubling set of problems.

Sportscaster Bob Costas seemed to recognize as much when in October 2013, during halftime of the Sunday Night Football game between Dallas and Washington, he offered a sharply worded critique of the latter's team name, describing it as a "slur" and an "insult."[1] In denouncing the continued use of the moniker, he followed a growing number of high-profile journalists, from Peter King and Bill Simmons to Christine Brennan and Dave Zirin. At the same time, he joined media figures, including Howard Stern, Matthew Berry, and John Oliver, and athletes, like Billy Mills, Mike Tyson, and Martina Navratilova, who have all publicly spoken out against the name.[2] And in the subsequent NFL season, use of the team name declined by 27 percent, as sportscasters "deferred to 'Washington' more often."[3] Costas's comments, moreover, echoed the long-standing position of the National Congress of American Indians (NCAI) and nearly a dozen tribes. And they found support in positions taken by a number of professional organizations, including the American Studies Association, the American Sociological Association, and the Organization of American Historians; religious groups; and news outlets, like *Mother Jones*, the *Seattle Times*, and the *Washington City Paper*.[4] Even Larry Dolan, owner of the Cleveland Indians, infamous for its continued use of the caricature Chief Wahoo, has remarked, "If we were the Redskins, the day after I owned the team, the name would have been changed."[5]

These changing attitudes coincide with a recent ruling in *Blackhorse et al. v. Pro Football, Inc.*, which stripped the team of several of its trademarks (and was upheld by a federal court in the first round of appeals). They unfold alongside, if not in direct response to, Change the Mascot, a well-orchestrated campaign spearheaded by the National Congress of

moniker: informal term for a name.

Blackhorse et al. v. Pro Football, Inc.: a 2013 case, the second dealing with the issue, in which a group of American Indians petitioned the U.S. Patents and Trademarks Office to cancel the trademark registrations of the Washington pro football team, an action which would have forced the team to change its name and logo. After a series of rulings and appeals involving arcane aspects of trademark law and whether the First Amendment is applicable to trademarks, the case went to the Supreme Court. Before it could be decided there, the Court ruled in 2017 in *Matal v. Tam*, a case in which the Asian American rock band The Slants was suing for the right to trademark its name (see p. 158), that part of the relevant law under which *Blackhorse* was being argued was unconstitutional and that trademarks are protected as private speech under the First Amendment. Therefore, the *Blackhorse* case was moot, meaning that the laws on which the legal arguments were based were no longer valid. In light of the ruling, both sides in the *Blackhorse* case withdrew their complaints.

Oneida Nation: federally recognized tribe of the Oneida people located in New York state.

epiphany: a sudden insight or realization into the nature or meaning of a situation.

Indian Country: legally, the term refers to several categories of self-governing Native communities in the U.S. (It is important to remember here that over the years, the U.S. government has signed over 600 treaties and contracts with Native communities, giving them certain rights in return for land or other concessions.) Colloquially, it often refers to any place that indigenous Americans live.

logo: a graphic or symbol to encourage brand recognition; Apple's logo is a stylized apple with a bite taken out, while Nike's logo is a swoosh.

Rose Carson/Shutterstock

self-determination: a principle of international law that people have or should have the right to determine for themselves what sort of political system they will have and to pursue the group's cultural, social, and economic goals.

American Indians and the **Oneida Nation**, and a growing grassroots movement, armed with social media. The shifts in public opinion, moreover, find resonance in recent calls for action from members of the U.S. Congress, including fifty U.S. senators who demanded change in a letter to the organization, in President Obama's statement that he would think about changing the team name, and in efforts by the Obama administration to block the building of new stadium in the District of Columbia so long as the franchise has its current moniker. Some seventy years after its inception, the name makes many people uncomfortable. Some, in fact, are so uneasy, they have resolved not to use it. These individual **epiphanies**, actions, and condemnations together direct attention to a shift around popular understandings of racial images, ideas, and identities. While all of these actions were undoubtedly fomented by a broader movement within **Indian Country** intent on reclaiming dignity, sovereignty, and humanity, in part by bringing stereotypes like mascots to an end, Costas did not highlight these unsettling politics. Instead, he anchored his critique in the seemingly settled truths found in dictionaries, where the word is defined as an offensive, antiquated, and insulting reference to an American Indian.

As a scholar who has written about the history and significance of Native 5 American mascots for more than two decades, I have long known the franchise to exemplify the practices associated with playing Indian in athletics, offering some of the most vivid and troubling examples of popular uses and understandings of American Indians.[6] Among the most prominent and profitable in sport, the organization since its inception has offered insights into the privileges and pleasures associated with taking and remaking Indianness. This alone would merit study and reflection, but in recent years, something even more significant has begun to unfold. Recent events suggest to me that we have reached something of a critical juncture, which makes this an especially opportune moment to reflect on the past, present, and possible futures of the Washington professional football team.

Perhaps most obviously, a dynamic, multifaceted opposition has converged around the moniker and **logo**. While far from united, this critical mass has its roots in Indian Country and has important connections to broader struggles for **self-determination** and **decolonization**. Unprecedented in size, scope, and diversity, it has made the once-unremarkable, and often-celebrated, team and its traditions the subject of debate, rendering them increasingly indefensible. In doing so, it has actively challenged anti-Indian racism, while pushing to restore dignity and humanity to indigenous people.

The ongoing debate, moreover, has fostered a shifting defense of the organization and its use of American Indians, which has appealed to and exposed the complex contours of racial politics and cultural identity today. Much of the defense casts the franchise and fans in a positive light, stressing that they have good intentions and mean to convey honor with the moniker, logo, and associated practices. And more, it has stressed indigenous support, highlighting the importance of public opinion polls as well as endorsements of the team by prominent individuals and reservation communities. Importantly, the defense is about more than Indianness. In particular, it turns in spoken and unspoken ways on whiteness. On the one hand, it invokes the attachments and sentimentality of white fans to legitimate the team and its traditions. On the other hand, it derives from and defends a series of entitlements or prerogatives anchoring a long history of owning Indians and Indianness in U.S. settler society.

Current events also focus our understanding of the past. They provide much-needed critical distance to assess the creation of the brand and its broader significance. That the team would have settled on its name unselfconsciously underscores how deep the entitlement and attachment to things "Indian" were at the time and how deeply embedded anti-Indian racism was in American public culture. It was, not to overstate things, a paradoxical love of imagined Indians and a loathing of actual, embodied Indians that continues to this day. Not surprisingly, the franchise, in common with other sports teams, Hollywood films, and commercial culture generally, traded in stereotypical renderings of Native Americans that, like the moniker, distorted and dehumanized them. To fans, journalists, and owners alike, the logo, fight song, and marching band all were in good fun. And while they meant no harm, a point many make today, these traditions create hostile environments that do in fact harm. Then, as now, such images and attitudes encouraged a kind of thoughtlessness. Such thoughtlessness allowed people to take the team and its traditions for granted without the burdens of history or introspection.

Finally, the critical juncture produced by recent events may be the beginning of the end. It is certainly a moment of change, a moment when

decolonization: efforts to undo colonization, including efforts to reject seeing one's people in the way the colonizer saw them. In this case, an effort to reject the negative views of Indians promulgated by the dominant culture as well as to establish a viable way of life for contemporary indigenous Americans.

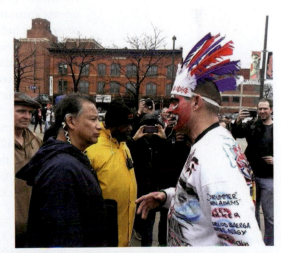

A Native American confronts a Cleveland Indians fan dressed as Chief Wahoo, the team's mascot.
© Cleveland Frowns/Peter Pattakos

countless people call for the team to change, when individuals create new team names and logos, and when many others imagine a time after the current moniker and mascot have been changed. Of course, this moment of change and what it has brought into being are about much more than the brand, its use of a slur, or even the **intransigence** of the current owner. The issue is about dignity and respect, combating anti-Indian racism while furthering self-determination and decolonization. As such, when the name changes, for that action to be of lasting and meaningful importance, it must be paired with deeper transformations, including education, coming to terms with the past, and expressing honor for indigenous people by honoring treaties made with native nations.

intransigence: refusal to change one's opinion or stance on some issue.

The critical juncture explored in this book has been marked by public condemnations of the team and calls for change, which have heightened public awareness of the word and its origins. Recent events likely played a key role in the increase in online searches. In 2014 Dictionary.com dubbed the team name, along with *caliphate, Ebola*, and *sociopath*, one of its eleven trending words.[7] Growing interest and increased attention, moreover, may explain why Americans generally remain supportive of the franchise but have growing unease about the word. A recent survey, for instance, found that 83 percent of Americans indicated they would not use the word in a conversation with a Native American.[8] One pizza restaurant in Washington DC learned how profoundly attitudes have shifted around the term. In fall 2014, when it ran a promotion, "Redskins score, You score," the reaction from its customers was so negative that it felt compelled to issue an apology less than six hours later. It read in part, "We are listening to all of your feedback. . . . We agree that the use of the name is wrong, offensive, and hurtful to all. In our future promotions and emails, we will make sure not to make the same mistake."[9]

10

Whatever the precise cause, the conservative columnist Charles Krauthammer rightly concludes that words and public usage of and attitudes toward them change:

Fifty years ago the preferred, most respectful term for African Americans was Negro. The word appears 15 times in Martin Luther King's "I have a dream" speech. . . . The preferred term is now black or African American. With a rare few legacy exceptions, Negro carries an unmistakably patronizing and demeaning tone.

invidious: unfair or unjust.

connotations: the feelings or attitudes associated with a word or set phrase, in contrast to its dictionary definition or denotation. *Nasal mucus* and *snot* have identical denotations, but very different connotations.

If you were detailing the racial composition of Congress, you wouldn't say: "Well, to start with, there are 44 Negroes." . . . Similarly, regarding the further racial breakdown of Congress, you wouldn't say: "And by my count, there are two redskins." It's inconceivable, because no matter how the word was used 80 years ago, it carries **invidious connotations** today.[10]

For Krauthammer, like Costas and growing numbers of people, these changing sensibilities do not simply argue against use of the slur to describe an American Indian, they also argue against its continued use as name for a professional football team.

Even as the past few years have witnessed an unparalleled push toward and increasing momentum for change, it would be wrong to conclude that concern with the team and its traditions is of recent origin or driven by forces outside of Indian Country. For more than four decades, American Indians and their allies have voiced their opposition. They have appealed to the ownership, held rallies and demonstrations at NFL games, and filed lawsuits to strip the team of its trademarks. They have created art, produced public service announcements, and formed organizations devoted to change. They have funded studies, launched protests on social media, and lodged complaints with governmental bodies, like the Federal Communications Commission. Through it all, they have worked to develop a diverse coalition within and beyond Indian Country and across cultural and racial lines in the nation's capital. These efforts have had noticeable impacts on public opinion. They have also prompted the franchise and the league to repeatedly respond to questions and criticism, secure support among indigenous people—often through questionable, if not fraudulent, means—and wage a series of public relations campaigns.

Even as Costas, Congress, and myriad others have called the team and its name into question, it has remained one of the most valuable franchises in professional sports. It has an easily recognizable and familiar brand, which is at once hugely popular and highly profitable. It is, according to *Forbes*, the third most valuable NFL franchise.[11] By way of comparison, in 2014 the Bureau of Indian Affairs had a total operating budget of $2.6 billion, while the team had a total value of $2.4 billion and total revenues of $395 million.[12] The franchise's ownership has bristled at the ongoing critique, suggesting that the team name is in fact quite positive, enjoying support from the majority of Americans and American Indians. Far from being an ethnic slur, the team has long asserted, its moniker conveys respect and honor. The franchise, moreover, has sought to reframe the controversy through a sophisticated promotional campaign rooted in focus groups, polls, and philanthropic initiatives. The National Football League, for its part, has actively defended the team, endorsed its interpretation of the name and its origins, and supported it in court. And even as more journalists and news outlets have spoken out against the team name, according to the *Washington Business Journal*, in an editorial ending its use of the moniker, "The vast majority of media outlets continue to use it. Our sister paper, the *Sports Business Journal*, reported last week that 44 of 48 major newspapers—those in cities with NFL teams along with the *Wall Street Journal, L.A. Times* and *USA Today*—still use the name."[13] Finally, fans largely have continued to support the team. Disappointing play has not diminished pride or attendance appreciably. And many are quite vocal in defense of the team and its traditions on social media. Nevertheless, merchandise sales, in a possible sign of things to come, were down 35 percent in 2014.[14] Despite this and in keeping with the general support of the organization, according to *Forbes*, the valuation and revenues for the team rose during the same period.[15]

The ongoing struggle lends itself to binary thinking, moral declarations, and public denunciations. To many, either the moniker is respectful or it is racist. It is a stereotype or not. Such arguments, whatever their merits, simplify the conflict and its cultural import. They discourage full understanding of the significance of the debate, competing claims, and key words. Indeed, the struggle over the team name, what it means, and why it matters raises important questions about popular perceptions of American Indians, the cultural life of brands, and existing obstacles to inclusion and equality. It also encourages deeper reflection on race and racism, the shifting contours of American attitudes and identities, and the possibilities and limitations of change in consumer society.

Some of these complexities find expression in the city that has long cele-   15
brated the franchise. Washington DC exemplifies racial politics in the United States. Built in part by slave labor, on land taken from native nations, the seat of American democracy was long marked by pronounced segregation and black-white racial tensions. For much of its first three decades in DC, the team played off these tensions, endeavoring to cast itself as the team of the South. Even as the city has changed, the centrality of race has not, and a rising Latino population has introduced a new dynamic that has complicated established assumptions. Economic and demographic shifts, moreover, have fostered a whitening of the urban core, increasingly pushing the poor and people of color to the margins. For all of this, on any given Sunday, residents of the metropolitan area form an imagined community united in shared identification with a team and becoming cultural citizens by exalting imaginary Indians. Even as they dress in feathers and sing the praises of their braves on the warpath, fans erase indigenous people. They make claims on and through images of them but disclaim their histories or continued relevance. In the process, they forget the past and its legacies. They forget about dispossession, displacement, and death. Few will remember that the team currently plays on the ancestral territory of the Piscataway Tribe or that the

capital is built on the homelands of the Patawomeck Tribe. And even as they don its colors or sing its fight song, fewer still will acknowledge the ways in which a professional football team continues to profit from anti-Indian stereotypes and stories.

The creation, consumption, and **contestation** of the brand, then, have emerged and evolved in a context marked by the interplay of racisms. What the team means and how individuals and institutions make sense of it can be understood only in light of overlapping identities, ideologies, and exclusions. Perhaps most obviously, the moniker and logo reflect the force of anti-Indian racism to dehumanize and deny. As such, they underscore the importance and invisibility of U.S. settler society, particularly the ingrained prerogatives of taking and remaking land, culture, and identity, which actively contribute to the erasure and exclusion of indigenous people. At the same time, arguments around the team and its traditions also reveal the centrality of a model of black-white race relations for assessing the shape and significance of racism generally.

contestation: the act of disputing.

Of course, one cannot speak of **settler colonialism**, prevailing understandings of race and racism, or the team and its traditions without talking about the construction of whiteness. The assumptions, aspirations, and anxieties of Euro-Americans not only introduce Indianness into athletics in the form of mascots and monikers but anchor the ongoing defense of them as well. At root, this cultural complex, as embodied by the Washington professional football team, turns on owning Indians. The franchise has long regarded Indianness as a resource or raw material to exploit for pleasure and profit. The establishment of its brand depended on embellishments of pseudo-Indian motifs. In fact, over its first three decades, the organization elaborated on popular stereotypes and romantic images of American Indians to create a logo, rituals, marching band, cheer squad, and identity. Fans and the franchise alike have felt entitled to use Indians and Indianness as they have seen fit. Even as the franchise ownership has become uneasy with outside criticism of its name, the organization has fought to prop up the brand through philanthropy that some interpret as little more than bribery and fake instances of indigenous support for its racist image. Anxiety, along with entitlement, has shaped the origin, elaboration, and defense of the brand. Jennifer Guiliano has identified the historic anxieties that prompted the emergence of American Indian mascots. She has argued in particular that the changing shape and significance of white masculinities in the wake of modernity, urbanization, and industrialization gave rise to American Indian mascots and monikers like those associated with the Washington

settler colonialism: a form of colonization whereby the newly arrived settlers work to occupy the land and displace the indigenous people. The settlement of what are today the U.S. and Canada was a process of settler colonialism.

postindustrialization: the era after the industrial era, that is, the current era in which heavy industry is in great decline as a result of globalization and technological advances that permit industry to need fewer employees to do the same amount of work—or even more—because of increased efficiency and automation.

professional football team.[16] Today a new set of anxieties paces the defense of the team and its traditions; specifically, it reflects the shape and significance of white masculinities in the wake of multiculturalism, feminism, and **postindustrialization**. Arguments for the team and its traditions, then, often hinge on other issues, circle around whites and whiteness, and display deep-seated resentments about a changing world as much as they purport to pay homage and convey respect. Thus, while it may be easy to see the team name as a slur, it is difficult, even for many critics, to recognize and respond to the ways that attachment, entitlement, identity, and anxiety shape the debate and stymie change.

Ultimately, the name, the team, and the brand matter not just because they reference an offensive racial slur or profit on hurtful stereotypes. They have pressing significance because of how they encourage anti-Indian racism, reinforce white privilege, and perpetuate distorted understandings of people and the past. As Amanda Blackhorse, lead plaintiff in a current legal challenge, notes, "Native American people have been targeted for their race, their land, and their resources. So when the dominant culture believes they are superior to the indigenous population they will dehumanize and dominate us for their own good. This includes the dehumanization of our entire being, especially our identity."[17] Clearly part of a deeper history and larger struggle, the prerogative to imagine and exploit popular ideas about American Indians for pleasure and profit, as the franchise has long done, negatively affects indigenous people, belittling, disempowering, and marginalizing them on any given Sunday. For Blackhorse, this pattern raises two questions seldom asked: "Why have we not achieved true self-determination as indigenous people?" and "Why is it that in this day and age are we still fighting for common decency to be respected by our nonnative counterparts?"[18] Tracing the history of the team and studying the defense of its use of a racial slur may be a first and necessarily partial step toward addressing these big questions. Such efforts offer an important opportunity to better comprehend the problem posed by *R*dskin* today, creating an important means of combating the ongoing dehumanization of indigenous people in the United States. Echoing Blackhorse, for the franchise and its fans, for the league and its media partners, for politicians and the public, the key challenge posed by the critique of the team and its traditions might be phrased as two overlapping questions: How do we stop the dehumanization of indigenous peoples? And how do we create new stories and spaces, reimagine self and society, and otherwise transform traditions to rehumanize them?

NOTES

1. Kogod, "Bob Costas on Redskins Name."
2. Anderson, "How Media Organizations Are Handling the Redskins Name"; Beaujon, "Here's a List"; Keene, "Who Has Spoken Out?"
3. Burke, "'Redskins' Mentions Down 27%"; Bene, "Broadcasters Really Are Saying 'Redskins' a Lot Less."
4. Anderson, "How Media Organizations Are Handling the Redskins Name"; Beaujon, "Here's a List"; Keene, "Who Has Spoken Out?" On the ethics of using the name in news coverage, see Jensen, "Banning 'Redskins'"; Lindsay, "Representing Redskins."
5. Wulf, "Why Use of Native American Nicknames."
6. On the team, see Coombe, "Sports Trademarks and Somatic Politics"; Goddard, "I Am a Red-Skin"; Harjo, "Fighting Name-Calling"; Sigelman, "Hail to the Redskins?"; Strong, "Trademarking Racism"; Waggoner, "On Trial."
7. "11 Trending Words of 2014."
8. Brady, "Poll."
9. Steinberg, "Pizza Chain Apologizes."
10. Krauthammer, "Redskins and Reason."
11. "Washington Redskins Valuation."
12. Odle, "What's in a Name?"
13. Fruehling, "We Won't Use Redskins Anymore."
14. Ley, "Washington Merchandise Sales Are Down."
15. "Washington Redskins Valuation."
16. Guiliano, *Indian Spectacle*.
17. Blackhorse, "This Is What Dehumanization Looks Like."
18. Blackhorse, "This Is What Dehumanization Looks Like."

BIBLIOGRAPHY

Anderson, Monica. "How Media Organizations Are Handling the Redskins Name." Pew Research Center, October 30, 2013. http://www.pewresearch.org/2013/10/30/how-media-organizations-are-handling-the-redskins-name/.

Beaujon, Andrew. "Here's a List of Outlets and Journalists That Won't Use the Name 'Redskins.'" Poynter Mediawire, June 19, 2014. http://www.poynter.org/news/mediawire/256258/heres-a-list-of-outlets-and-journalists-who-wont-use-the-name-redskins/.

Bene, Ross. "Broadcasters Really Are Saying 'Redskins' a Lot Less This Year." Deadspin, September 17, 2014. http://regressing.deadspin.com/broadcasters-really-are-saying-redskins-a-lot-less-th-1635806862.

Blackhorse, Amanda. "This Is What Dehumanization Looks Like." *Indian Country Today*, March 20, 2015. http://indiancountrytodaymedianetwork.com/2015/03/20/blackhorse-what-dehumanization-looks-159694.

Brady, Erik. "Poll: 83% Would Not Call Native American a 'Redskin.'" *USA Today*, November 20, 2014. http://www.usatoday.com/story/sports/nfl/redskins/2014/11/20/washington-redskins-poll-name-controversy-daniel-snyder/19297429/.

Burke, Timothy. "'Redskins' Mentions Down 27% on NFL Game Broadcasts in 2014." Deadspin, December 30, 2014. http://regressing.deadspin.com/redskins-mentions-down-27-on-nfl-game-broadcasts-in-1676147358.

Coombe, Rosemary J. "Sports Trademarks and Somatic Politics: Locating the Law in Critical Cultural Studies." In *SportCult*, edited by R. Martin and T. Miller, 262–88. Minneapolis: University of Minnesota Press, 1999.

"11 Trending Words of 2014." Dictionary.com, December 18, 2014. http://blog.dictionary.com/trending-words-2014/.

Fruehling, Douglas. "We Won't Use Redskins Anymore." *Washington Business Journal*, August 1, 2014. http://www.bizjournals.com/washington/print-edition/2014/08/01/we-won-t-use-redskins-anymore.html.

Goddard, Yves. "'I Am a Red-Skin': The Adoption of a Native-American Expression (1769–1826)." *European Review of Native American Studies* 19, no. 2 (2005). http://anthropology.si.edu/goddard/redskin.pdf.

Guiliano, Jennifer. *Indian Spectacle: College Mascots and the Anxiety of Modern America.* New Brunswick, NJ: Rutgers University Press, 2015.

Harjo, Suzan Shown. "Fighting Name-Calling: Challenging 'Redskins' in Court." In *Team Spirits: Essays on the History and Significance of Native American Mascots*, edited by C. Richard King and Charles Fruehling Springwood, 189–207. Lincoln: University of Nebraska Press, 2001.

Jensen, Robert. "Banning 'Redskins' from the Sports Page: The Ethics and Politics of Native American Nicknames." *Journal of Mass Media Ethics* 9 (1994): 16–25.

Keene, Adrienne. "Who Has Spoken Out against the Redskins?" *Native Appropriations* (blog), June 23, 2014. http://nativeappropriations.com/2014/06/who-has-spoken-out-against-the-redskns.html.

Kogod, Sarah. "Bob Costas on Redskins Name: 'It's an Insult, a Slur.'" *Washington Post*, October 13, 2013. http://www.washingtonpost.com/blogs/dc-sports-bog/wp/2013/10/13/bob-costas-on-redskins-name-its-an-insult-a-slur/.

Krauthammer, Charles. "Redskins and Reason." *Washington Post*, October 17, 2013. http://www.washingtonpost.com/opinions/charles-krauthammer-redskins-and-reason/2013/10/17/cbb11eee-374f-11e3-ae46-e4248e75c8ea_story.html.

Ley, Tom. "Washington Merchandise Sales Are Down 35 Percent," Deadspin, September 5, 2014. http://deadspin.com/washingtons-merchandise-sales-are-down-35-percent-1631023843.

Lindsay, Peter. "Representing Redskins: The Ethics of Native American Team Names." *Journal of the Philosophy of Sport* 35 (2008): 208–24.

Odle, Mairin. "What's in a Name? On Sports Teams and Scalp Bounties." *Junto* (blog), December 22, 2014. http://earlyamericanists.com/2014/12/22/guest-post-whats-in-a-name-on-sports-teams-and-scalp-bounties/.

Sigelman, Lee. "Hail to the Redskins? Public Reactions to a Racially Insensitive Team Name." *Sociology of Sport Journal* 15 (1998): 317–25.

Steinberg, Dan. "Pizza Chain Apologizes for Using 'Wrong, Offensive, and Hurtful' Redskins Name." *Washington Post*, September 19, 2014. http://www.washingtonpost

.com/blogs/dc-sports-bog/wp/2014/09/19/pizza-chain-apologizes-for-using
-wrong-offensive-and-hurtful-redskins-name/.

Strong, Pauline Turner. "Trademarking Racism: Pseudo-Indian Symbols and the
Business of Professional Sports." *Anthropology Now*, September 2014. http://
anthronow.com/print/trademarking-racism-pseudo-indian-symbols-and
-the-business-of-professional-sports.

Waggoner, Linda M. "On Trial—The Washington R*dskins' Wily Mascot: Coach William Lone Star Dietz." *Montana: The Magazine of Western History* 63, no. 1 (Spring
2013): 24–47. http://nmai.si.edu/sites/1/files/pdf/seminars-symposia/
WaggonerWEBSpr2013.pdf.

"Washington Redskins Valuation." *Forbes*, August 2014. http://www.forbes.com/
teams/washington-redskins/.

Wulf, Steve. "Why Use of Native American Nicknames Is an Obvious Affront."
ESPN, September 3, 2014. http://espn.go.com/espn/otl/story/_/id/11426021/
why-native-american-nicknames-stir-controversy-sports.

RESPOND.

1. What argument(s) is King making about the use of the term *redskin*? In what ways it is an invitational argument, that is, one that invites readers to explore a complex set of issues they may not have previously considered? (See Chapter 1 on invitational arguments.)

2. Where in King's argument can we find logical appeals? pathetic appeals? ethical appeals? (See Chapters 1–4 on these categories of appeals and arguments.)

3. What various sorts of logical evidence, in particular, does King use to support his claims as he writes? Why is logical evidence useful and important when constructing arguments about topics as controversial as this one? (See Chapter 4 on evidence for arguments based on fact and reason.)

4. **THINKING CRITICALLY** King clearly hopes that the Washington football team's owners will one day change the team's name and its logo. What forces—historical and contemporary—have led to the current situation, both the use of this name and logo and the refusal of the owners and supporters to want to change the team's name and logo?

5. In paragraph 8, writing about the representations of American Indians created at earlier and even in recent times in the U.S., King notes:

   And while they meant no harm, a point many make today, these traditions create hostile environments that do in fact harm. Then, as now,
   such images and attitudes encourage a kind of thoughtlessness. Such
   thoughtlessness allowed people to take the team and its traditions for
   granted without the burden of history or introspection.

Obviously, King believes that all of us have a responsibility to consider the burden of history and to engage in introspection when we create images or express attitudes about groups of which we are not a member. **Write an argument of definition** in which you explore the meaning of the notions of "the burden of history" or "introspection" as it relates to how we represent cultures of which we are not a part, whether through images (e.g., Halloween costumes or cartoons) or language (the use of specific terms or the making of remarks that assume all members of a group are the same). If, on the other hand, you would contend that we have no obligation to consider the burden of history or to engage in introspection with respect to these matters, **write an evaluative argument** in which you evaluate and reject King's assumption, being careful to present and justify your evaluative criteria. (See Chapter 9 on arguments of definition and Chapter 10 on evaluative arguments.)

▼ *This selection is an excerpt from a 2011 research article that appeared in* Media Psychology. *As the abstract notes, the study uses content analysis of video game magazines to make claims about the perpetuation of racial stereotypes in the world of video gaming and about the possible consequences of such stereotypes.*

In excerpting this article, we have retained the abstract, the introduction (including the literature review), and part of Study 1, specifically, the discussion of the method used, the content variables analyzed, the first part of the results section, the discussion section, and the conclusion. We have omitted the technical part of the results section, which reports the statistical analyses of the data presented in Table 1; we also omitted Studies 2 and 3. We found the authors' discussion of the theoretical importance of stereotyped portrayals—part of the literature review—especially relevant for this chapter.

At the time of the article's publication, its authors were teaching or conducting research at Southwestern Oklahoma State University (Burgess and Burgess), UC–Santa Barbara (Dill), Oklahoma State University (Stermer), and UNC–Wilmington (Brown).

In their general discussion at the end of the study, the authors wrote, "Whereas schools are teaching children to tolerate and even celebrate diversity, this research demonstrates that some forms of popular media are sending opposing signals with troubling effects" (pp. 308–9). As you read, consider how these researchers provide evidence to back up this claim and give serious thought to the ways other kinds of popular media perpetuate, rather than challenge, stereotypes of various sorts.

Playing with Prejudice: The Prevalence and Consequences of Racial Stereotypes in Video Games

MELINDA C. R. BURGESS, KAREN E. DILL, S. PAUL STERMER, STEPHEN R. BURGESS, AND BRIAN P. BROWN

ABSTRACT

A content analysis of top-selling video game magazines (Study 1) and of 149 video game covers (Study 2) demonstrated the commonality of overt racial stereotyping. Both studies revealed that minority females are virtually absent in game representations. Study 1 revealed that, in video game magazines, minority males, underrepresented generally, were more likely to be portrayed as athletes or as aggressive, and less likely to be depicted in military combat or using technology, than White males. Study 2 also showed evidence of the "dangerous" minority male stereotype in video game covers. Again, underrepresented overall, minority males were overrepresented as thugs, using extreme guns, and also as athletes. Study 3, an experiment, exposed players to both violent and nonviolent games with both White and Black characters. Participants were faster at classifying violent stimuli following games with Black characters

and at classifying nonviolent stimuli following games with White characters, indicating that images of popular video game characters evoke racial stereotypes.

INTRODUCTION

Emerging in recent years as one of the most **ubiquitous** forms of entertainment, video games have become a media giant with U.S. sales recently reaching a record high of over $21 billion (Ortutay, 2009). Children between 8 and 17 years old make up the group that plays the most video games (Gentile et al., 2007), with approximately 90% of this age group being regular players (Walsh et al., 2005). There is a sizeable **effects literature** demonstrating that games influence behaviors, thoughts, feelings, and attitudes (Anderson, Berkowitz, et al., 2003; Anderson, Gentile, et al., 2007; Dill, Brown, & Collins, 2008; Konijn et al., 2007). Recent brain research even demonstrates differences in the brain's **empathic** responding based on differential video game exposure (Bartholow et al., 2006).

Only recently has gaming research begun to concern itself with the portrayals of game characters, and this research has often focused on the portrayal of women in games (e.g., Burgess et al., 2007; Dill & Thill, 2007). Two initial investigations of race in video games (Dill, Gentile, et al., 2005; Glaube et al., 2001) revealed a pattern of infrequent appearance for minority characters and stereotyped depictions when minorities were present. Glaube et al.'s (2001) examination of 70 console games (such as PlayStation) found that some minorities (e.g., Latina women and

Portland Press Herald/Getty Images

Native American men) were never present, and that children's games included only White and nonhuman characters. This pattern was echoed in a sample of 20 computer games examined by Dill, Gentile, et al. (2005), which revealed only a few Black and Latino men in the role of main characters and not a single Latino or Latina secondary character. Beyond this, both investigations found frequent stereotyping of minority characters. Glaube et al. (2001) found that Latino characters were only present in sports games, that Asian characters were largely consigned to a wrestling or fighting role, and that Black characters were typically depicted as unaffected by violence through a lack of pain or physical suffering. Interestingly, even in games created before the terror attacks of 9/11, targets of violence were disproportionately likely to be portrayed as Middle Eastern (Dill, Gentile, et al., 2005).

---

ubiquitous: present everywhere.

effects literature: a body of research in a particular discipline focusing on the effects of some phenomenon (e.g., stereotypes in the media, eating too much sugar, exercising, praying).

empathic: showing evidence of understanding others' feelings or life situations.

Other content analyses have focused specifically on portrayals of aggression related to gender and race. Smith et al. (2003) found that, across all game types, 71% of perpetrators of violence and 65% of targets were White, and that 79% of perpetrators and 77% of targets were male. In a further investigation, these same authors classified the ethnicity of violent characters as White, Black, Hispanic, Native American, Asian/Pacific Islander, Middle Eastern, or undefined. Results showed that the majority of characters were White (40.5%) with the next largest group being Asian/Pacific Islander, at only 8%. Interestingly, whereas mild violence was the most common form of violence, Asian/Pacific Islanders was the ethnicity most likely to engage in extreme violence, defined in part by large scale bloodshed and disfiguring injuries.

Whereas the portrayal of game characters has been a concern, there is also a growing body of research examining the social effects of media images, from video game as well as other outlets, on young adults (Dill, Brown, et al., 2008; Johnson et al., 2008). Dill, Brown, et al. (2008) exposed participants to images of women and men that were either stereotypical sex-typed images from video games or professional images from press photographs. Then participants gave their reactions to a real-life account of the sexual harassment of a female college student by her male professor. Results demonstrated that men who were exposed to the video game images (female sex objects and powerful males) were more tolerant of sexual harassment. This research suggests that exposure to stereotypical imagery in the media can alter social judgments, such as deciding that a case of sexual harassment is less serious or requires less action against the perpetrator. The larger meaning is that stories we glean from mass media can change how we behave in the real world.

In one study dealing with racial stereotypes (Dill & 5 Burgess, 2011), White students saw either video game images of Black men who fit the aggressive criminal or "dangerous minority" stereotype or media images of esteemed Black leaders such as Barack Obama alongside analogous White images. Next, in a purportedly unrelated study, participants evaluated the Web site of a political candidate named Peter Smith who was either Black or White. Results revealed **interactive effects of the exemplar prime** (negative or positive) on favorability and capability ratings of this candidate. Those who saw the negative (Black video game) exemplars rated the Black candidate as less favorable and capable than the White candidate. In a reversal, those who saw the positive (Black leader) exemplars rated the Black candidate as more favorable and capable than the White candidate.

Whereas there is a sufficient body of literature to appreciate the damage inherent in repeated negative and stereotyped portrayals of minorities and women, there has been a **paucity** of research on racial portrayals in video games. At the same time, there has been public interest in these portrayals, centering on a sample of blatantly stereotypical portrayals. Perhaps most notably, *Grand Theft Auto: Vice City* was criticized for depicting Haitians and

---

interactive effects of the exemplar prime: the priming image here was the initial video game image—"Black men who fit the aggressive criminal or 'dangerous minority' stereotype or

media images of esteemed Black leaders"—while the interactive effects refer to the consequences of the first images seen on the evaluation of the candidate, Peter Smith, when presented as Black or White. In other

words, the researchers were examining whether there is an interaction between the image research subjects were first exposed to and their subsequent evaluations of the fictitious character, Peter Smith.

paucity: only a limited amount.

Cubans as criminals and for potentially inciting hate crimes (NBC News, 2003). The game's producer, Rockstar, responded to public protest about game content by removing the lines "Kill the Haitians" and "Kill the Cubans" from the game.

Theoretical Importance of Stereotyped Portrayals

Stereotypes have both **cognitive** (e.g., generalizations) and **affective** (e.g., fear) components (Amodio & Devine, 2006). Repeated exposure to a particular portrayal of a group teaches that this cultural view is a relevant **schema** for processing members of that particular group. For example, exposure to the schema of the violent Black man teaches that it is appropriate to experience **apprehension** when approached by a Black male. Further, exposure to these stereotypical images triggers access to thoughts, preferences, and evaluations, ultimately predicting discriminatory behavior (Amodio & Devine, 2006).

Stereotypes may sometimes be consciously processed, but stereotypes can also provoke thoughtless, non-conscious, impulsive reactions. In an update of his **cognitive neoassociation theory** of aggression, Berkowitz (2008) underlined the theoretical importance of these automatic processes, and the role of classical conditioning in inciting hostility and aggression. Negative ideas and feelings associated with a group are applied to other group members. These negative associations can trigger negative affect which, in turn, prompts impulsive aggressive reactions that preempt more conscious reasoning. "My cognitive-neoassociationistic analysis . . . suggests what kinds of external stimuli have this relatively compelling capacity to elicit aggressive reactions: primarily situational features that are associated with aggression and those that are linked to decidedly negative experiences" (Berkowitz, 2008, p. 120).

Berkowitz (2008) noted that African Americans are commonly stereotyped as aggressive, hostile, and criminal (see also Devine, 1989), and that these are devalued social identities. He wrote, ". . . those people who are associated with aggression generally and/or with **gratifications** for aggression in particular or who are associated with negative affect are especially likely to be the victims of aggression" (p. 128). Again, for aggression to be evoked, the perpetrator need not engage in a conscious cognitive appraisal (of the stereotype or situation) because aggression can be provoked through an automatic, impulsive route. Berkowitz cited research—particularly that of Devine (1989) and of Bargh et al. (1996)—as examples of how even unconscious exposure to images of Blacks and words associated with Black stereotypes evoke hostility and aggression. He noted that aggressive portrayals activate hostility toward African Americans, which in turn makes aggression toward them more likely. ". . . [N]on-conscious activation of the African American stereotype can promote hostile-aggressive behavior towards others" (Berkowitz, 2008, p. 122).

---

cognitive: relating to thought.

affective: relating to feelings or emotions.

schema: pattern of thought that influences how we process new information.

apprehension: fear or anxiety.

cognitive neoassociation theory: psychological theory developed by Berkowitz to explain the link between negative feelings and anger or hostile behavior toward some group or situation.

gratifications: sources of pleasure.

Relating this explicitly to mass media, imagery that associates African American men with the negative stereotypes of aggression, hostility, and criminality conditions viewers to associate this constellation of negativity with African American men in general. Subsequently, unrelated Black men will trigger this association, which can, in turn, provoke increased aggression and hostility.

It is important to note that the stereotypical images of Black video game characters are not even real people, but they can still provide fodder for negative social judgments and negative reactions to real Black men. Support for this notion comes from Slusher and Anderson (1987), who found that even when people are simply asked to imagine stereotypes such as a rich lawyer, they do not distinguish between what they have imagined and what they have seen in reality. Slusher and Anderson call this a failure of reality monitoring. People treat their imaginary vision as they would a real-life image and it supports their stereotypes. If this is true, then it follows logically that seeing another type of imaginary or fantasy image—a picture of a video game character—might also be treated as confirmation of a stereotype. There will be little difference from seeing a Black thug in a video game and seeing a real Black criminal—both will be taken as evidence confirming the culturally held stereotype of the Black male criminal.

Given the large body of violent video game research (see Anderson, Berkowitz, et al., 2003), we expected portrayals of aggression. We were also aware of the racially charged discussions surrounding games like *Grand Theft Auto* (Leonard, 2009) and wanted to explore whether or not the portrayal of aggression differed as a function of the race of characters. A theoretically relevant way of characterizing this portrayal of violence is whether or not it is socially sanctioned (Lachlan, Tamborini, et al., 2009). We were interested in whether Whites would be more likely to be portrayed as engaged in socially sanctioned violence compared to minorities.

STUDY 1

METHOD

Study 1 is an **exploratory content analysis** designed to investigate how Black males are portrayed in imagery from top-selling video game magazines. The variables, described below (and the percent agreement between the two raters), are: race (.98), hypermasculinity (.99), aggression (.99), war/military aggression (.96), fighting (1.00), athletics (.91), and use of technology (.94). The sample used in the present study included images taken from the six top-selling game magazines on sale in January 2006. One issue from each magazine was selected, and the largest male and female images on every page from each issue were included. This produced a sample of 482 images (362 male images and 120 female images), which were then coded by one White male and one White female undergraduate research assistant. For details about magazine and image selection, and for rating procedures, see Dill and Thill (2007).

CONTENT VARIABLES

For each image, the following races were coded following Dill and Thill (2007): White, Black, Hispanic,

---

exploratory (study): a study that seeks to explore some topic in a new way rather than directly continuing an existing research tradition.

content analysis: in the social sciences, a method of analyzing texts with a focus on their content.

Asian, other, and humanoid. The other category was reserved for characters who appeared to be human and who appeared to be of a non-White race that was not always determinable. Only three races (Native American, Egyptian, and undeterminable) were listed by coders under the other category.

Hypermasculinity was defined as exaggerated male characteristics such as unnaturally large muscles or expressions of dominance. Hypermasculinity relates to features of extreme dominance, power, and aggression (Dill & Thill, 2007; Scharrer, 2004, 2005).

Aggression was defined as being engaged in behavior intended to harm another living being (Aronson et al., 2007). Of the violence categories used in Study 1, we categorized war and military aggression as socially sanctioned and fighting as not socially sanctioned. We argue that military violence should be considered relatively more socially sanctioned than fighting because military aggression is legal and, thus, sanctioned by governments and often respected by citizens. In contrast, violence in the form of non-sports fighting is most often considered criminal activity and thus, by definition, is not socially sanctioned. Therefore, aggressive images were further coded as war/military aggression or fighting (no identifiable military rationale). Some images did not fit either category, such as a violent athlete. These images were simply coded as aggressive and not included in the subcategorical analysis.

In the initial stages of this exploratory investigation, we remarked that computer and technology use were regularly portrayed in gaming magazines. We were also aware that sports games have ranked consistently among the top sellers. We, therefore, coded computer and technology use and athletics by race of character.

15

RESULTS

The data were coded using the variables described above. Frequency data were calculated for each race on the variables described above (see Table 1).

DISCUSSION

The results of this content analysis illustrate that, although by no means were all minorities portrayed stereotypically, portrayals of race in video game magazines did differ across racial lines in a manner that was consistent with stereotypes. First, from a simple perspective of frequency, minority characters were underrepresented as compared to U.S. Census statistics, even when using the comparison group of gamers. It is interesting to note that humanoid (alien) characters were depicted more often than minority humans. Minority females were particularly underrepresented.

From the perspective of **pedagogy** it is useful to consider actual frequency of nonviolent character portrayals, as opposed to relative frequency. Minority male characters were generally infrequent (constituting only 23.6% of the total male images), and nonviolent minorities were even more infrequent (only 5.5% of the total male images). In fact, nonviolent White males (25.6% of the total male images) were as common as all minority males.

20

Finally, results of exploratory analysis revealed that minority males were more than twice as likely as White males to be portrayed as athletic. Computer and technology use was almost exclusively limited to White males with White males being more than twice as likely as Black males to be depicted using technology. These data are possibly consistent with stereotypes about minorities, for example, that Black males are more athletic and less intelligent than Whites (Berkowitz, 2008). However, because these are

pedagogy: teaching.

Table 1. Character portrayals as a function of race in video game magazines (%)

	White	Black	Asian	Hispanic	Other
Frequency (*N*) of males	223	37	6	5	21
Frequency (%) of males	76.4	12.7	2.1	1.7	7.2
U.S. population (%)	66.9	12.8	4.3	14.4	2.7
Gamers (%)	59	15	3	18	5
Frequency (*N*) of females	91	3	5	2	5
Frequency (%) of females	85.8	2.8	4.7	1.9	4.7
U.S. population (%) — whites vs. all minorities	66.9	12.8	4.3	14.4	2.7
Gamers (%) — whites vs. all minorities	59	15	3	18	5
Hypermasculine — males	21.2	29.8	0	20	38.1
Aggressive (males) — yes	66.4	73	66.6	80	85.7
Socially sanctioned (military) (out of aggressive)	8.1	0	0	0	0
Fighting (out of aggressive)	37.8	48.1	25	75	55.5
Aggressive (males) — no	33.6	27	33	20	14.3
Armor (males) (out of aggressive)	48	22.2	0	0	77.7
Posing with weapons (males) — (out of aggressive)	39.2	18.5	0	25	66.6
Athlete (males)	8.1	29.7	0	0	9.5
Violent and/or athletic	74.4	100	75	80	95
Technology use (males)	13.9	2.7	33.3	20	0

exploratory data, we will be conservative when speculating on reasons for these patterns.

Conclusions

Research has shown that those exposed to false information in fictional stories are persuaded by it and that persuasion persists over time (Appel & Richter, 2007). Furthermore, Slusher and Anderson (1987) demonstrated that people fail to distinguish between stereotyped associations they imagine and those they have actually seen. The results of this content analysis of gaming magazines illustrates that there are consistent racial stereotypes in video game magazines and that representations of race do not match with reality. The problem with this is that the magazines may shape reality by being a source of social information to those who are exposed to them. In other words, after seeing negative racial stereotypes in video game magazines, players may experience failures in reality monitoring and may believe that they have had actual stereotype-confirming experiences. Furthermore, given what we know about the persuasive power of false information in fiction (Appel & Richter, 2007), it is likely that this information could alter gamers' thoughts, feelings, and behaviors.

REFERENCES

Amodio, D. M., & Devine, P. G. (2006). Stereotyping and evaluation in implicit race bias: Evidence for independent constructs and unique effects on behavior. *Journal of Personality and Social Psychology, 91*(4), 652–661.

Anderson, C. A., Berkowitz, L., Donnerstein, E., Huesmann, R. L., Johnson, J., Linz, D., . . . Wartella, E. (2003). The influence of media violence on youth. *Psychological Science in the Public Interest, 4*, 81–110.

Anderson, C. A., Gentile, D. A., & Buckley, K. E. (2007). *Violent video game effects on children and adolescents: Theory, research, and public policy.* Oxford University Press.

Appel, M., & Richter, T. (2007). Persuasive effects of fictional narratives increase over time. *Media Psychology, 10*, 113–134.

Aronson, E., Wilson, T. D., & Akert, R. M. (2007). *Social psychology* (6th ed.). Pearson Prentice Hall.

Bargh, J. A., Chen, M., & Burrows, L. (1996). Automaticity of social behavior: Direct effects of trait construct and stereotype activation on action. *Journal of Personality and Social Psychology, 71*, 230–244.

Bartholow, B. D., Bushman, B. J., & Sestir, M. A. (2006). Chronic violent video game exposure and desensitization to violence: Behavioral and event-related brain potential data. *Journal of Experimental Social Psychology, 42*, 532–539.

Berkowitz, L. (2008). On the consideration of automatic as well as controlled psychological processes in aggression. *Aggressive Behavior, 34*, 117–129.

Burgess, M. C. R., Stermer, S. P., & Burgess, S. R. (2007). Sex, lies, and video games: The portrayal of male and female characters on video game covers. *Sex Roles, 57*, 419–433.

Department of Defense. (2002). *Population representation in the military services.* http://www.defense link.mil/prhome/poprep2002/summary/summary.htm

Devine, P. G. (1989). Stereotyping and prejudice: Their automatic and controlled components. *Journal of Personality and Social Psychology, 56*, 5–18.

Dill, K. E., Brown, B. P., & Collins, M. A. (2008). Effects of exposure to sex-stereotyped video game characters on tolerance of sexual harassment. *Journal of Experimental Social Psychology, 44*, 1402–1408.

Dill, K. E., & Burgess, M. C. R. (2011). *Media images as positive and negative exemplars of race: Evoking Obama or video game characters changes outcomes for black men.* [Paper presentation]. Thirtieth Annual Conference of the Society for Southeastern Social Psychologists, Greenville, SC, United States.

Dill, K. E., Gentile, D. A., Richter, W. A., & Dill, J. C. (2005). Violence, sex, age and race in popular video games: A content analysis. In E. Cole & J. Henderson-Daniel (Eds.), *Featuring females: Feminist analyses of media* (pp. 115–130). American Psychological Association.

Dill, K. E., & Thill, K. P. (2007). Video game characters and the socialization of gender roles: Young people's perceptions mirror sexist media depictions. *Sex Roles, 57*, 851–864.

Funk, J. B. (2005). Children's exposure to violent video games and desensitization to violence. *Child and Adolescent Psychiatric Clinics of North America, 14*, 387–403.

Gentile, D. A., Saleem, M., & Anderson, C. A. (2007). Public policy and the effects of media violence on children. *Social Issues and Policy Review, 1*, 15–61.

Glaube, C. R., Miller, P., Parker, M. A., & Espejo, E. (2001). *Fair play? Violence, gender, and race in video games.* http://publications.childrennow.org/publications/media/fairplay_2001b.cfm

Johnson, J. D., Bushman, B. J., & Dovidio, J. F. (2008). Support for harmful treatment and reduction of empathy toward Blacks: Remnants of stereotype activation involving Hurricane Katrina and L'il Kim. *Journal of Experimental Social Psychology, 44*, 1506–1513.

Lachlan, K., Tamborini, R., Weber, R., Westerman, D., Skalski, P., & Davis, J. (2009). The spiral of violence: Equity of violent reprisal in professional wrestling and its dispositional and motivational features. *Journal of Broadcasting & Electronic Media, 53*, 56–75.

Leonard, D. (2009). Young, black (& brown) and don't give a fuck: Virtual gangstas in the era of state violence. *Cultural Studies/Critical Methodologies, 9*, 248–272. https://doi.org/10.1177/1532708608325938

NBC News. (2003, December). *Haitian, Cuban leaders denounce GTA.* http://www.nbc6.net/entertainment/2706043/detail.html

Ortutay, B. (2009). *Video game sales top $21 billion in 2008.* http://www.msnbc.msn.com/id/28682836/ns/technology_and_science-games/t/video-game-sales-top-billion/

Scharrer, E. (2004). Virtual violence: Gender and aggression in video game advertisements. *Mass Communication & Society, 7*, 393–412.

Scharrer, E. (2005). Hypermasculinity, aggression, and television violence: An experiment. *Media Psychology, 7,* 353.

Slusher, M. P., & Anderson, C. A. (1987). When reality monitoring fails: The role of imagination in stereotype maintenance. *Journal of Personality and Social Psychology, 52,* 653–662.

Smith, S. L., Lachlan, K., & Tamborini, R. (2003). Popular video games: Quantifying the presentation of violence and its context. *Journal of Broadcasting & Electronic Media, 47,* 58–76.

State and County Quick Facts. (2008). http://quickfacts.census.gov/qfd/states.00000.html

Stermer, P., Burgess, S., Burgess, M., Davis, C., McCarter, Jones, K., et al. (2006, April). *Video game playing experience and preferences in males and females* [Paper presentation]. Southwestern Psychological Society, Austin, TX., United States.

Walsh, D., & Gentile, D. (2007). *12th annual MediaWise video game report card.* National Institute on Media and the Family with results from the 2007 MediaWise-Harris Interactive Poll. http://www.mediafamily.org/research/2007_Video_Game_Report_Card.pdf

Walsh, D., Gentile, D., Walsh, E., Bennett, N., Robideau, B., Walsh, M., et al. (2005). *MediaWise video and computer game report card.* http://www.mediafamily.org/research/report_vgrc_2005.shtml

RESPOND•

1. How do Burgess and her coauthors use data to support their claims **(a)** that the representations of minorities found in gaming magazines correspond to stereotypes, rather than reality, and **(b)** that such stereotyping is far from innocent in its consequences? In other words, what sorts of evidence do Burgess et al. provide for their claims?

2. What are the benefits of using the careful and clearly stated methods of analyzing quantifiable data that are associated with a field like psychology when dealing with a topic as complex and controversial as the one Burgess et al. are tackling?

3. As you no doubt noted, Burgess et al. define the variables in their study—race, hypermasculinity, aggression (both socially sanctioned and unsanctioned), and the use of technology—in the section "Content Variables." What kind of definition do they provide for each of these variables? (See Chapter 9 on kinds of definitions.) Do you think you could code data from a gaming magazine appropriately and consistently based on these definitions? Why or why not? (The answer to this question illustrates something important about this kind of definition.) How do these variables and the definitions of them map onto the categories used in Table 1 of the article? Why might the list of portrayals be more detailed than the list of variables that are defined?

4. **THINKING CRITICALLY** Research studies in fields like psychology and in the social, natural, and applied sciences all have a similar format, often referred to as IMRAD (introduction, methods, results, analysis,

and discussion), and the sections are often labeled by their function. What are the advantages of having such a standardized format for writers? For readers?

5. Carefully reread the discussion and conclusions sections of this study to be sure you understand the logic of the authors' claims in the conclusion, including the ways the researchers qualify their claims. (It may also be useful to review the section on the theoretical importance of stereotyped portrayals.) **Write an essay** in which you evaluate these claims by describing the stereotyped portrayal of some group in a specific example of popular culture—a movie, a television series, or a video game. (For a discussion of evaluative arguments, see Chapter 10.) To complete this assignment, you'll obviously need to study the example you are analyzing with some care, and you may well wish to code instances of certain stereotyped portrayals, as the authors of this research study did. At the end of your essay, be sure to speculate about how the stereotyped portrayal may, in light of the study excerpted here, be harmful for the individuals who consume it and for society at large.

▼ Sonny Assu (1975–) is an award-winning contemporary Canadian artist from British Columbia who works in a range of media. He is also a member of the Ligwilda'xw of the Kwakwaka'wakw Nations. Raised in the suburbs, only at age eight did he learn of his First Nations heritage. Assu's art combines Kwakwaka'wakw and Western traditions in an effort to understand what it means to be an indigenous person living in "the colonial state of Canada," as he and other indigenous Canadians refer to the country. Assu received his BFA at Emily Carr University in Vancouver, BC, and his MFA at Concordia University in Montreal, QC.

   At first, Breakfast Series (2006) appears to be nothing more than popular cereal boxes, three of which are reproduced here: Treaty Flakes, Salmon Loops, and Lucky Beads. On closer inspection, however, the viewer realizes that Assu has taken popular brands of breakfast cereal as a starting point for raising hot-button issues in indigenous communities across North America, including Native land rights, treaties, and cultural foodways. As you study these visual arguments, note the complex ways in which Assu appropriates the components of cereal boxes to critique the way the dominant culture sees and has treated Native peoples. (To appropriate something is to use it, generally without permission, for one's own purposes.)

Breakfast Series

SONNY ASSU (Gwa'gwa'da'ka)

Sonny Assu

Treaty Flakes

(Front) Kwakwaka'wakw
Frosted Treaty Flakes
(Side) Kwakwaka'wakw
Frosted Treaty Flakes
Nutritional Facts
per ¾ cup (30g or 200ml)
Amount 30g Cereal With Milk*
Calories 120 180

Member Nations:
Camp Mudge 100%
Campbell River 100%
Kwiakah 100%
Comox 100%

Total Land
14,000 Hectares

Government BS 100%

DOES NOT CONTAIN A
GOVERNMENT REFERENDUM
Ingredients: Sugar-coated lies,
government bureaucracy, self-
governance, land resources,
broken promises, acknowl-
edging the past, securing the
future

Kwakwaka'wakw
Kitchens
Satisfaction Guaranteed!
A/P [signature] '06

A/P: artist's proof.

577

Sonny Assu

Salmon Loops

(Front) Kwakwaka'wakw
Salmon Loops
Now BURSTING with even
more delicious Salmon Flavor!
(Side) Kwakwaka'wakw
Salmon Loops
Contains 100% Pacific Salmon
Sea-Lice Free!
Nutritional Facts
per ¾ cup (30g or 200ml)
Amount 30g Cereal With Milk*
Calories 120 180

% Daily Value
Fat* 100%
Fibre None
Protein 30g

Salmon
Coho 10%
Pink 50%
Chinook 7%
Chum 30%
Sockeye 3%

*It's good fat, don't worry.
Makes you smart.

Ingredients:
Pacific Salmon (Coho, Chum,
Pink, Sockeye, Chinook),
Honey, Salt, Eulachon Oil,
Smoke.
May contain traces of kelp.

Kwakwaka'wakw
Kitchens
Satisfaction Guaranteed!
A/P [signature] '06

Sonny Assu

Lucky Beads

(Front) General Custer (with
logo)
Good source of
trickery—12 essential
lies & deceptions
Lucky Beads
Free plot of land in every box!
(Side) General Custer (with
logo)
Nutritional facts
per ¾ cup (30g or 200ml)
Amount 30g Cereal With Milk*
Calories 120 180

Lies 100%
Deception 100%
Shiny Beads: A handful
Pompous, stuck up, greedy,
laughing white rich men
rubbing their hands together
saying "stupid Indians" 100%

Ingredients:
Sugar, lies, deception, wheat,
corn, bullshit, beads, giggling
white men, broken trust,
North American, Manhattan

Kwakwaka'wakw
Kitchens
Satisfaction Guaranteed!
A/P [signature] '06

RESPOND.

1. Parody involves imitation with humorous exaggeration, often as a form of critique, a kind of evaluative argument. (See Chapter 10 on evaluative arguments.) In what ways does each of these cereal boxes represent a parody of an actual breakfast cereal box? Why are breakfast cereal boxes an especially interesting resource to employ in critiquing the majority culture's perspectives on indigenous Americans?

2. As the headnote explains, Assu's art focuses on the situation of Native Canadians and their complex and troubled history with Canadians of European descent. How do we see those conflicts represented in *Breakfast Series?*

3. Of these three pieces from *Breakfast Series* (the complete series includes five cereal boxes), which do you find to offer the strongest critique of the treatment of Native Americans in Canada? Which do you see as most positive in its representation of Native culture? Why?

4. **THINKING CRITICALLY**   *Breakfast Series* is currently on display in the Seattle Art Museum in Seattle, Washington. The museum's blog posting on the cereal boxes characterizes them as displaying a "lighthearted presentation . . . of serious social issues" (bit.ly/2FrNtyt). Do you find this to be an accurate portrayal of Assu's method? Why or why not? If not, how would you describe Assu's method? Why?

5. As Chapter 8 explains, arguments of fact are generally the basis of all other kinds of arguments, and they frequently include detailed descriptions of some object or phenomenon under consideration. **Write a robust description** of one of the three cereal boxes in Assu's *Breakfast Series.* Your goal is to describe as thoroughly and dispassionately as possible the box you have chosen, being sure to include any visual imagery that carries meaning. (For example, because of the font and color used, the Kwakwaka'wakw logo on two of the boxes, *Treaty Flakes* and *Salmon Loops*, is reminiscent of the Kellogg's logo while the logo "General Custer" on the *Lucky Beads* box recalls the logo of General Mills because of the shape of the letter G.) As part of your description, be sure to explain to the reader each of the design aspects you have chosen to include. (Information in Chapter 14 on visual rhetoric will likely prove useful here.)

▼ *Sara Morrison is a New York journalist who has been a contributor to the Atlantic Wire, senior writer/associate editor at Boston.com, and staff writer for Vocativ; she is currently deputy editor at CAFE. As a freelancer, her work has appeared in the Guardian, Hitfix, Death and Taxes, and Pacific Standard, among others. This 2016 selection was part of a Nieman Report on journalistic coverage of minority communities that won an Eddie Award for journalistic excellence. Morrison's original article included the glossary at the end, and we have retained it as a useful reference. As you read, notice the spots where Morrison is seeking to educate other journalists on how to avoid reinforcing stereotypes as they write.*

Covering the Transgender Community: How Newsrooms Are Moving Beyond the "Coming Out" Story to Report Crucial Transgender Issues

SARA MORRISON

In March of 2014, Jorge Rivas, Fusion's national affairs correspondent, was working on a story about undocumented immigrants when he heard about a transgender woman being held in a men's detention center. "She was stuck in a detention center surrounded by men, often experiencing the same type of harassment she was fleeing in the first place," Rivas says.

Rivas told investigative reporter Cristina Costantini, his co-writer on the story, what he'd heard. It sounded familiar. Their colleague, Kristofer Ríos, recently told Costantini he had heard similar things about transgender detainees during his own immigration reporting. The three teamed up for a six-month investigation into the treatment of transgender people in Immigration and Customs Enforcement (ICE) detention centers. "Why Did the U.S. Lock Up These Women With Men?" was the headline. The story received an award for outstanding digital journalism from GLAAD (formerly the Gay & Lesbian Alliance Against Defamation), and, in June of 2015, ICE announced it would implement new guidelines for transgender detainees.

This past year has been a watershed for media coverage of transgender issues. In 2014, ESPN's Grantland [a blog] was sharply criticized for a piece that outed a transgender woman and may have contributed to her suicide, while talk show hosts Katie Couric and Piers Morgan were derided for insensitivity toward transgender guests on their respective programs.

In 2015, in contrast, ABC News produced a deeply researched, widely praised educational special in which Caitlyn Jenner came out as transgender. The

Washington Post profiled a transgender woman who until recently had been out of work and homeless. In a story focused on a transgender man who is Muslim, the *Los Angeles Times* looked at conflicts between an individual's religion and gender identity. And in a series of editorials the *New York Times* called for changes in the treatment of transgender people and invited the transgender community to tell its own stories on the *Times* website. In May, VIDA: Women in Literary Arts announced that it would include statistics on the number of articles written by LBTQI (lesbian, bisexual, transgender, queer, and intersex) writers and writers with disabilities in its next annual VIDA Count of bylines in literary publications.

Transgender people—models, actors, musicians, 5 authors, athletes, a former Army soldier serving time for espionage—have increasingly entered the public consciousness. With this increased visibility has come increased media coverage. Kris Hayashi, executive director of the Transgender Law Center in the San Francisco Bay Area, remembers how when he came out as transgender in the late 1990s there was very little to be found in the mainstream media about people like him. Now, he says, the transgender community is covered with a frequency that was "unimaginable" even three years ago.

Says Meredith Talusan, who in 2015 became Buzz-Feed's first openly transgender staff writer and covers transgender issues for the website, "Now, it's actually possible to gain knowledge about trans issues from mainstream media sources. More of those sources have been willing to respect the ways in which trans people want to be addressed and portrayed, though there's still a lot to be done."

Despite this progress, the general population still knows relatively little about the transgender community. In a recent survey by the Human Rights Campaign (HRC), the largest LGBT civil rights organization in the U.S., only 22 percent of respondents said they knew a transgender person. This lack of knowledge, combined with the rapid rise in visibility for transgender people, has created unique challenges for newsrooms. Very few newsrooms have any openly transgender staffers.

How do journalists cover a community, which has been for so long maligned and voiceless, in ways that are considerate of that community's needs as well as those of readers, some of whom need basic concepts explained? Most coverage to date has tended to focus on one transgender person's pre-transition life and gender reassignment surgery, while rarely reporting on the wider transgender community. Stories have also often used terminology and pronouns that were objectionable to the transgender person. Reporters writing about the transgender community, for which violence and discrimination are major concerns, have to educate themselves about terminology and spend extra time building the rapport that can lead to nuanced coverage.

That was certainly the case with the Fusion investigation of transgender detainees in federal immigration facilities. Rivas and his Fusion colleagues needed to talk to transgender people, some of whom were victims of sexual assault, whose shaky immigration statuses landed them in ICE detention centers. Any of these three factors on its own could make a source wary of going public. In addition, the Fusion reporters needed people who were willing to tell their stories on camera. Apart from the reporting challenges, Rivas says, the team wondered how much readers who weren't transgender would care about their subjects, members of a long-stigmatized community.

Before Rivas could meet with Barbra Perez, a 10 transgender detainee featured in his Fusion piece, he met with Olga Tomchin, whose work at the Transgender Law Center focused on advocating for transgender people in immigration detention. The process of developing a relationship with a source or a source's representative wasn't different from any other story except for one thing: Tomchin asked if Rivas was going to film any of the transgender sources putting on makeup. Tomchin explained that this **trope** in coverage of transgender women is widely considered a superficial demonstration of femaleness to which **cisgender** women are rarely subjected. Rivas hadn't intended to shoot that kind of footage, but learning that it was considered a cliché was "a lesson" for him. "We do try very hard to avoid putting our clients in situations where they feel exploited by media or that their story was manipulated," says Jill Marcellus, senior communications manager at the Transgender Law Center.

More and more reporters are educating themselves on how to adequately cover transgender people. Couric and Morgan drew criticism for lines of questioning perceived as insensitive. Both Couric, who interviewed actress **Laverne Cox** and model **Carmen Carrera**, and Morgan, who interviewed writer **Janet Mock**, asked about their guests' genitals, questions many transgender individuals and advocates regard as an invasion of privacy. "People ask trans people all the time, 'So, have you had the surgery?'" says Dawn Ennis, a news editor at the *Advocate*, the oldest LGBT-interest magazine in the U.S., who is transgender. "People are curious about it because it's so unusual, but it really is a violation of people's privacy to ask those questions."

Couric responded to the subsequent backlash by inviting Cox back on her ABC show to discuss what she had done wrong, saying she'd now have to hold up her show as an example of how not to report on transgender people. Morgan invited Mock back on his show for a contentious interview in which he demanded to know why he'd been "viciously abused" on social media by the transgender community after he said he had shown support for transgender people by promoting Mock's book and calling her a woman.

After the Fusion reporters won the trust of Tomchin, the Transgender Law Center representative, they had to win the trust of the women they wanted to profile. Johanna Vasquez's story was probably the hardest to tell. After being brutally sexually assaulted in her native El Salvador, she fled to America. But she was beaten by her male cellmate in an ICE detention center and then locked in solitary confinement for seven months because guards didn't know where else to put her. Rivas and Costantini say they met with her several times without a camera or even a notebook so they could establish the level of trust Vasquez needed to tell her story.

---

trope: here, a recurring theme. In discussions of rhetoric, the term often refers to a figurative or metaphorical use of language. (See the discussion of tropes in Chapter 13 on style.)

cisgender: relating to someone whose sense of gender identity corresponds to the sex they were assigned at birth (Latin *cis-* "same side as" + *gender*); the complement of *transgender*.

Laverne Cox: American actress best known for her role as Sophia Burset in the Netflix series *Orange Is the New Black*, for which she received a Primetime Emmy Award nomination. She later received a Daytime Emmy Award for *Laverne Cox Presents: The T Word*.

Carmen Carrera (1965–): American media personality who has appeared on *RuPaul's Drag Race* and, on occasion, called him out on what she considers to be transphobic remarks or behaviors.

Janet Mock (1983–): American writer, TV host, and transgender activist. Her first book, *Redefining Realness*, became a bestseller.

The Fusion team also needed data to show the scope of the problem. While a Government Accountability Office report stated that from October 2009 to May 2013, three of the 15 victims in cases of "substantiated allegation of sexual abuse" in ICE detention were transgender, ICE told the journalists it didn't have a count of the total transgender detainee population.

Costantini consulted with the Williams Institute at the UCLA School of Law, a think tank that researches LGBT law, public policy, and demographics, and has produced transgender population estimates. The Williams Institute's oft-cited number puts America's transgender population at nearly 700,000, but this is largely based on surveys from two states: Massachusetts and California. Gender identity is rarely included on official forms from which this kind of data is usually drawn.

Determining statistics on violence perpetrated against transgender people—a very real concern in the community, especially for women of color—is similarly difficult. Most states don't require that crimes based on gender identity be reported as hate crimes, and the police may simply report victims as whatever sex and the gender identity that traditionally accompanies it is on their legal IDs, which may not be accurate. This is also a problem when it comes to reporting on violence against transgender people; journalists may rely on police reports that refer to the pre-transition gender expression of the victim. "There's still a ton of misgendering, often of victims of violence, which is particularly awful," says BuzzFeed's Talusan.

GLAAD has recommendations for how the media should cover transgender victims of violence, including referring to them by the name and pronouns consistent with how they identified at the time of the incident, and refraining from **salacious** and unnecessary details about the victim's appearance or gender identity. "In major cities, we've seen a lot of growth in terms of media understanding and ability to think beyond just what the plain old police report says," according to the *Advocate*'s Ennis.

A big uptick in stories about transgender people occurred after April 2015, when **Caitlyn Jenner** came out as transgender in a two-hour special on ABC's "20/20." ABC News producer Sean Dooley says the show was a unique opportunity not just to tell Jenner's story, but also to educate a largely uninformed television audience, some of whom wouldn't normally watch a special about a transgender person but watched this one because of Jenner's fame as an Olympic athlete or reality show star.

Dooley says ABC News spoke with several advocacy groups and experts, including GLAAD and the National Center for Transgender Equality, to prepare for the special. Susan Stryker, an associate professor of gender and women's studies at the University of Arizona and director of the school's Institute for LGBT Studies, says she was on the phone with producers three times a week for about a month.

That effort was evident when the special aired. Host Diane Sawyer didn't just use Jenner's chosen pronoun, she also noted that she was doing so and explained why. Allowing transgender people to decide which pronouns should be used in referring to them is an important issue for the transgender community. This was especially important as, at the time, Jenner's pronoun preference was male, which could potentially lead people to think it's acceptable to refer to all

15

20

Caitlyn Jenner (1949–): a retired gold-medal Olympic decathlete who later became an American television and film personality.

salacious: exhibiting irrelevant or inappropriate interest in matters related to sex.

transgender women with male pronouns. And Sawyer didn't just ask which surgical steps Jenner might take in her transition, she also noted that it was Jenner's choice to discuss this, and that, generally, asking a transgender person about their genitals is inappropriate.

The special was largely well received—and watched by about 17 million people that night, more than twice as many people as usually watch the network in that time slot. Many transgender advocates, worried that a profile of a reality show star on mainstream television would be sensationalist and exploitative, applauded the program.

A couple months later, *Vanity Fair* ran a cover story about Jenner. While the release of the cover broke *Vanity Fair*'s single-day online traffic record with 9 million unique visitors, Buzz Bissinger's accompanying profile was criticized for his use of male pronouns when referring to her pre-transition, which GLAAD's media guide says should be avoided. Transgender advocacy groups recommend referring to a transgender person by their post-transition name and pronoun, even when describing the person pre-transition. Stryker compares it to writing about **Malcolm X**; though he was born Malcolm Little, journalists rarely call him that when writing about him as a child.

Sara Simone hugs a friend who provided shelter when she was homeless. Sarah L. Voisin/The Washington Post/Getty Images

As a contrast to Jenner's story, *Washington Post* feature writer Monica Hesse profiled Sara Simone, a transgender woman in her 50s a few years into her

---

Malcolm X (1925–1965): African American Muslim and human rights activist who was highly critical of white racism in American society. He converted to the Nation of Islam and took the family name X while in prison in the late 1940s, noting of his birth name, Little, that "the white slavemaster . . . had imposed [it] upon [his] paternal forebears." After his travels to the Arab world in 1964, including making the hajj, or Muslim pilgrimage to Saudi Arabia, he took the name el-Hajj Malik el-Shabbaz, forsaking the Nation of Islam for Sunni Islam and emphasized black self-determination and pan-Africanism.

transition who was, until very recently, unemployed and homeless.

According to the National Transgender Discrimination survey, carried out in 2011 by the National Center for Transgender Equality and the National Gay and Lesbian Task Force (now known as the National LGBTQ Task Force), 15 percent of transgender people and gender-nonconforming people surveyed said they earned less than $10,000 annually, compared with just 4 percent of the general population. Transgender people are also twice as likely as the general population to be unemployed, and one in five said they had experienced homelessness at some point in their lives because of their gender identity.

Simone was willing to share details about her 25 financial troubles for the profile. She was not willing to share her birth name, however.

While Hesse and her editor, *Post* senior editor at large Ann Gerhart, needed to know Simone's birth name for fact-checking purposes—verifying that she served in the armed forces, for instance—they saw no need to include it in the story. "One of the ways we looked at it was, this is her legal name now," Hesse says. "When we write about women who have taken on their husband's names and those are their legal names, do we then make sure to include their maiden names? No, we don't do that."

Similarly, they didn't see a need to dwell on Simone's life before her transition. This was a story about Simone's life now. At the same time, Gerhart says, Simone had lived as a man for five decades: "Journalistically, I had questions about how she dealt with that. What are the ways you can reconcile the person who you had been and who you are relieved you aren't anymore, and integrate that into your experience now?" A chance encounter at Simone's workplace gave the story insight into those questions.

Simone worked at a nonprofit that helped homeless veterans. While meeting with one of those veterans, she noticed that he'd been stationed in the same place as Simone around the same time. Simone faced a decision. She could tell him about her own service, possibly helping her bond with the client. But that would mean revealing that she served under another name, opening her up to harassment for being transgender. Fear of harassment and violence from people who discover Simone is transgender is a recurring theme in the story. In the end, Simone didn't reveal her military service to the veteran.

Simone's fears are well grounded. Transgender women, especially women of color, are often targets of violence. A 2015 report from the HRC and the Trans People of Color Coalition, which advocates for transgender people of color, estimates that transgender women are 4.3 times more likely than cisgender women to be the victim of a homicide, and half of all transgender people will be sexually assaulted in their lifetimes. As of this past November, at least 21 transgender people—a majority of whom were transgender women of color—had been murdered in 2015.

"It's a real clear crisis that's happening, but it's not a 30 new crisis," says the Transgender Law Center's Kris Hayashi. While some outlets have covered this issue, he says, it hasn't gotten anywhere near the attention that Jenner has. Stryker, the University of Arizona professor, says it's important for the media to remember that the transgender community is diverse, and not everyone in it will have the same experience. The progress that has been made may be beneficial to some, mostly white people of means, but not necessarily all, especially transgender women of color or people living in poverty.

Simone's comments on social media are also quoted throughout the *Post* story, something Hesse and Gerhart say was crucial since it allowed them to let Simone talk about herself and her experience unprompted. In a video post in which she describes an abusive past relationship, Simone says, "This man tried to destroy me, but he didn't destroy me." "I am very, very lovable," she writes in another update. "I am not a loser. I am lovable."

Simone friended Hesse on Facebook, which gave Hesse unexpected insight into her own reporting process. In the beginning, Simone would often say things on Facebook that she apparently didn't yet feel comfortable saying to Hesse. "Every time I would go home, she would post on Facebook an analysis of how she thought I had done that day," Hesse recalls. "What questions I had asked that she thought were stupid, or what she was afraid I wasn't getting. It was really interesting to see your reporting reviewed in real time that way."

It also gave Hesse a measure of how much her subject grew to trust her over the week they spent together. As time went on, the things Simone said on Facebook began to match what she told Hesse. To help foster a trusting relationship with Simone, Hesse had sent her a few articles she had written, including a profile of an agender (someone who doesn't identify as male or female) teenager. She didn't take any notes on the first day. By the end of the week Hesse spent following Simone to work, to her home, and even going out with friends, Simone trusted Hesse enough that she let Hesse meet her brother, someone she'd initially been reluctant to include in the story. Hesse thought the brother was necessary to the story because she felt she needed another scene of Simone interacting with someone who knew her well, and who was the closest family member Simone had at the time.

Unlike Hesse, *Los Angeles Times* reporter Garrett Therolf wasn't looking to write a story about a transgender person when he covered the Los Angeles Pride parade in June 2015. But then he met Alex Bergeron, who was there as one of three winners of the Colin Higgins Youth Courage Award, given out by the Colin Higgins Foundation to LGBTQ people under 21 who advocate for their community. Therolf and Bergeron got to talking, and Bergeron mentioned struggling to reconcile being transgender with being Muslim, a subject Therolf had not seen covered before. Therolf had never written about transgender issues, but he had spent time reporting in Iraq and Egypt and was familiar with that region's conservative views toward LGBT people.

Therolf found an expert on transgender issues and 35 Islam in Emory University professor Scott Siraj al-Haqq Kugle, who has written multiple books about the subject of LGBT issues and Islam. "He helped me to realize how lonely it can be for folks trying to find their way and just how very nascent this movement [of LGBT Muslims] still is," Therolf says. "And he helped me understand the theological underpinnings for the work that is just beginning."

Therolf wrote in his story that in America "mosques tend to be conservative, and visits to the local imam or mosque committee chairman usually draw stern **rebukes** for LGBTQ Muslims."

Therolf was unsure whether he made the right call when it came to the pronouns he used for Bergeron. Bergeron's preferred pronoun is "they," because, as Therolf's article explains, Bergeron sees gender identity as a spectrum, rather than a binary. People who prefer gender-neutral singular pronouns, then, must either use invented terms like "ze" or the plural pronoun "they" as a singular. Both options are potentially

---

rebuke: sharp criticism or disapproval.

Alex Bergeron struggles to reconcile being transgender and Muslim, an issue explored in a Los Angeles Times *story.*
Don Bartletti/Los Angeles Times

confusing to reporters and readers who aren't used to seeing them.

Therolf got permission from the copy desk to use "they" and wrote a draft of the story, but ultimately he found it was too confusing to use a plural pronoun for an individual. "It is technically ungrammatical and it can be quite cumbersome and distracting for readers in a news story," Therolf says. "I don't know if we made the right call by reverting back to 'he,' but I will point out that Alex himself uses 'he' pronouns most of his day and so do the people around him." The Transgender Law Center, in its "Trans Youth" guide to reporting on transgender and gender-nonconforming young people, notes that many in that community use "they" as a pronoun.

Henry Fuhrmann, an assistant managing editor who oversees the *Los Angeles Times* copy desk, says Therolf's decision to use "he" instead of "they" this time should not indicate that's what the paper will do if the issue comes up again. "We'll consider then what we think will work best for the story and its intended audience," Fuhrmann says. "We'll need to balance sensitivity to a subject against the risk of confusing readers." Therolf says he thinks that as the concept of using "they" as a singular gender-neutral pronoun becomes more prevalent, it'll be less confusing to readers.

In just the few months since Therolf's story was 40 published, both the *New York Times* and the *Washington Post* have used new gender-neutral terms. At the beginning of December, *Post* copy editor Bill Walsh sent out a memo stating that "they" could be used as a pronoun for people who did not identify as male or female. In late November, the *New York Times* used "Mx." as an honorific—to much notice.

In the spring of 2015, the *New York Times* ramped up its coverage of the transgender community, launching a series of editorials, "Transgender Today," focusing on relevant policy issues. "A lot of people were paying attention to transgender people in a way that we hadn't really seen in the past," says editorial board member Ernesto Londoño. "We thought that we would do a public service by outlining some of the policy issues, some of the unresolved issues that are hugely important for this community—that, for a lot of people, are a matter of life and death."

More than 20 people—from developers to designers to photographers to editorial writers—helped get the series off the ground. Londoño had written about a transgender person before, but some members of the team had not. "It was an education for a lot of us," Londoño says. Much of that education took place in the early stages of the project, when the team spent a lot of time discussing what was sensitive and what wasn't, not just in the writing, but also in photography and design choices. This, says Transgender Law Center's Marcellus, is an important but often overlooked component in coverage. A reporter can be extremely knowledgeable about the correct

Kristin Beck, a transgender former Navy SEAL, shares images from her past during a talk at an FBI office in Clarksburg, West Virginia. FBI

terminology, but an article can be completely undermined if it's accompanied by an insensitive photo caption or headline.

For the series, Londoño says advocacy groups were helpful in identifying issues the transgender community faced and providing necessary historical context and case law. There's also a significant contribution from transgender people, in their own words and images. "We thought it would be very important to find a way to let transgender people tell their own stories and be their own advocates," Londoño says.

To do this, the paper created a "storywall" for the series, allowing readers to submit their own experiences in text, photo, or video form, or a combination of all three. Brynn Tannehill's video starts with the former Navy pilot describing when she realized she wanted to fly planes, and how she ultimately had to make a choice between her military

career and coming out as transgender. Jesse writes about how he came out as transgender and began his transition while working as an educator in Louisiana—and how his students and co-workers have been largely supportive. Scott writes about being fired from his job at a software company in the San Francisco Bay Area after co-workers found out he was a transgender man. Katherine Bradford writes about being transgender and a parent, and sometimes explaining this to her children's new friends or their parents.

Londoño wasn't sure how eager transgender peo- 45 ple would be to share their stories so publicly. He says the paper hoped for 50 stories by the end of the year. It got 40 by the end of the first day.

"One of the things that struck me when we started getting submissions was a lot of them were from veterans and people who talked about how hard it had been to wrestle with their gender identity and their career in the military," Londoño says. "A lot of those people were discharged or saw no option but to leave the service. Those voices, I think, were very valuable for me and for us as we set out to make the case for a new policy in the military that allowed open transgender service."

That editorial was published in June, and Londoño, who worked on the article with the LBGT organization Service Members, Partners, Allies for Respect and Tolerance for All, which specializes in military issues, says it's the one of which he's most proud. In July, the U.S. Department of Defense announced that it was working on new policies that would allow transgender people to serve openly in the military.

Reporting on the transgender community has come a long way in a very short time, but transgender individuals and advocates say there is still much work to be done. Among other things, BuzzFeed's Talusan would like to see more stories about transgender people that aren't just about their gender identity, stories where being transgender is not a subject's defining characteristic.

"I would just like to see stories about what trans people are doing with their lives and in many ways not focusing on their transgender-ness unless it's relevant somehow," says the University of Arizona's Stryker. "I think we're just getting to that point."

Transgender Terminology

Covering the transgender community involves a specific vocabulary, from pronoun usage to medical descriptions. A glossary:

Cisgender Used by some to describe people who are not transgender. *Cis-* is a Latin prefix meaning "on the same side as," and is therefore an antonym of *trans-*.

Gender dysphoria The American Psychiatric Association's description of the condition in which the sex someone is assigned at birth does not match their gender identity. Some transgender advocates believe a medical diagnosis is necessary for health insurance that covers treatments recommended for transgender people.

Gender expression External manifestations of gender, expressed through names, pronouns, clothing, haircut, behavior, voice, or body characteristics. Typically, transgender people seek to make their gender expression align with their gender identity, rather than the sex they were assigned at birth.

Gender identity The internal, deeply held sense of one's gender. For transgender people, their own internal gender identity does not match the sex they were assigned at birth.

Gender-nonconforming Used to describe those whose gender expression is different from conventional expectations of masculinity and femininity.

Genderqueer Used by some who experience their gender identity and/or gender expression as falling outside the categories of male and female.

Pronouns The Associated Press style guide says to refer to an individual by their preferred gendered pronoun, or, if it's not possible to ask for a preference, the pronoun that is most consistent with an individual's gender expression. Many major publications follow this rule, but the usage of gender-neutral pronouns—the singular "they" or new

(continued)

terms such as "ze" or "xe"—varies and is changing rapidly. The *Washington Post* recently announced that it would allow the singular "they," while the *New York Times* recently allowed the honorific "Mx.," although standards editor Philip Corbett wrote that the paper doesn't have a set rule on gender-neutral terms and has avoided using "nontraditional" pronouns. BuzzFeed, on the other hand, says it will use any preferred pronoun, possibly accompanied by a short explainer if the term is less familiar.

Sex reassignment surgery (SRS) Refers to doctor-supervised surgical interventions, which not all transgender people choose, or can afford, to undergo. Also known as gender reassignment surgery or gender affirming surgery.

Transgender An umbrella term, often abbreviated as "trans," for people whose gender identity and/or gender expression differs from what is typically associated with the sex they were assigned at birth. A transgender man is someone whose assigned sex at birth was female but identifies and lives as a man. A transgender woman is someone whose assigned sex at birth was male but identifies and lives as a female.

Transition Altering one's birth sex is a complex process that occurs over a long period of time and may include medical and legal steps, using a different name and new pronouns, dressing differently, hormone therapy, and surgery.

—GLAAD's "Media Guide on Transgender Terminology"

RESPOND●

1. As this selection makes clear, the last few years have seen a great deal of public discussion about transgender issues, and part of this discussion has included a focus on language and on various forms of negative stereotyping. What specific observations related to language and various forms of stereotyping does Morrison make? How many of these were new to you? Why, do you think?

2. As explained in the headnote, Morrison clearly positions competent journalists as learners, that is, they understand and appreciate that throughout their careers, as they cover various communities, they will need to learn about those communities in order to avoid representing them in terms of inaccurate and offensive stereotypes. Where do you see evidence of Morrison's positioning? In short, where do we see

journalists learning specific information about the transgender community, how to interact with transgender individuals, and how to avoid stereotyping?

3. Chapter 14 discusses visual rhetoric and the roles that images can play in supporting an argument. How do the images that are part of this selection contribute to the selection's overall argument? Do they pass the test of avoiding negative stereotyping? Why or why not?

4. **THINKING CRITICALLY**   In a profound sense, this selection focuses on undoing stereotypes, that is, in finding ways to fight against stereotypes of a group by avoiding one-dimensional representations of them, a topic touched on in the introduction to this chapter. How does Morrison achieve this goal without directly criticizing or blaming her colleagues? In your opinion, is this a more effective strategy than other options Morrison might have had? Why or why not?

5. Choose a group that you are part of that you believe is unfairly stereotyped on at least some occasions or in some contexts. **Write an essay** in which you explain to outgroup members (those who do not belong to the group) how you understand your group to be negatively stereotyped and how they might avoid repeating such stereotypes when commenting on your group. While your essay could take many forms, it will likely have aspects of definitional, evaluative, and proposal arguments, treated in Chapters 9, 10, and 12, respectively.

24

How Does What We Eat Define Who We Are?

According to many commentators, the United States is in the midst of a food revolution. Americans are concerned—and some would argue obsessed—with what we eat and where it comes from in ways we have not been in the past, at least not the recent past. We eat and eat out more than we ever have before. We consume a wider variety of foods and flavors associated with a broader range of cultures than we ever have before. We choose, often dogmatically, among a wider range of diets—vegan, vegetarian, pescatarian, carnivorous, paleo, gluten-free, and the list goes on. We can watch cooking shows on TV 24/7. And at the same time, a considerable number of Americans, including college students, live with the reality of food insecurity, not certain if there will be enough to eat or if what we have to eat is sufficiently nutritious. The selections in this chapter encourage you to think about how what we eat reflects and ultimately defines who we are—and aren't.

In the chapter's opening selection, Sophie Egan reminds readers how intimately linked food and foodways are with culture. A major focus of this selection is the way that American culture has long adopted and adapted the foods of its immigrant communities, which, in turn, respond to American food culture in various ways. She likewise examines some of the factors encouraging the Americanization of what some continue to refer to as "ethnic" foods, which are, in fact, well on their way to becoming as American as apple pie—if they are not purely American creations.

The second selection relies on visual arguments to carry most of the load in examining how Americans' dietary habits have changed over the past several decades. Given the format in which the data are presented, you'll see that it also provides an opportunity to consider how constraints like medium and context influence what makes for an effective visual argument.

Rob Greenfield's arguments against veganism, the third selection, are especially interesting because he is a committed vegan. What advantages might there be to admitting the potential limitations of one's own position and acknowledging the validity of alternative positions? Greenfield's argument, it turns out, may have a lot to teach us all about topics other than veganism, especially at this moment in our very polarized society.

The chapter's fourth and fifth selections take on a topic that has received a lot of recent press, especially with Americans' growing hunger for novel tastes from around the world. The question is that of cultural appropriation, particularly with regard to food. Can foodways rightly be said to belong to any culture or any one? In what sense of *belong*? Does it matter if the question is preparing "somebody else's" food in your own kitchen or doing so for commercial purposes? Is it fine for just anyone to open a food cart or restaurant selling West African chicken with peanut sauce or Tunisian tajine (not to be confused with the very different Moroccan dish of the same name)? Why or why not? Jess Kapadia can't understand what the fight is about. At first glance, she contends anyone can "own" and even sell any food; a careful study of her comments, however, indicates that she may impose limits on her own claims. Briahna Joy Gray sees things quite differently; for her, we always need to consider issues of exploitation and cultural disrespect. You'll get to evaluate these authors' positions on this knotty set of issues.

The chapter closes with a research report by James Dubick and two coauthors on food insecurity on college campuses. For some readers, the results of this survey may be shocking; for others, it may be daily reality. Does your campus have a food bank, as a growing number do? Should it? After reading this report, perhaps you'll be challenged to learn more about these issues on your own campus and act on what you learn. If so, that's persuasion in action.

In this selection from her 2016 book Devoured: How What We Eat Defines Who We Are, *Sophie Egan explores American foodways, particularly the way that American cuisine has long incorporated and adapted foods from around the world and continues to do so. (It should, of course, be obvious that when foods travel, they will change at least minimally because different varieties of vegetables will be grown in different places, and even the same variety will taste different because of the soil and climate. Lovers of wine are obsessed with the notion of the terroir, the French term meaning literally soil or earth and, by extension, the environment in which the grapes are grown and the wine bottled.) To achieve her goal, Egan focuses in particular on Italian American cuisine and ways that it differs from, say, Chinese American cuisine in terms of how the respective immigrant communities responded to their new American environment. Egan also considers the recent rise of fusion cuisine and its contribution to our country's foodways. As you read, consider how your own ways of eating are like and not like those of your parents and grandparents and what influences have shaped them.*

The American Food Psyche

SOPHIE EGAN

American *food culture* is the set of customs, values, and behaviors related to eating and drinking. These form the scaffolding of daily life.

Here are some examples of American food culture:

- Fast food. This is arguably the best-known feature of our food culture, and the one we've exported most widely around the globe. Not just the food but the way it's consumed, at drive-thrus or taking it to go.

- When we watch movies, we eat popcorn.

- At state fairs, food is fried. Foods you didn't even know could be fried are fried.

- In the summer, we invite friends over for barbecues.

- Unlike in Britain, Canada, or Ireland, in the United States, bacon is supposed to be crispy.

- Don't eat anything when riding the subway.

- Eat pizza. All kinds. Any time.

  - When eating pizza, adhere to some very important rules regarding the delivery of the slice into your mouth: New York style = fold it. Chicago deep dish = fork and knife. Otherwise, no utensils involved. Unless, of course, you want to look like an Italian, in which case: Pinkies up. . . .

Michael Pollan, author of *The Omnivore's Dilemma: A Natural History of Four Meals* and many other books about food, has said that, given Americans' multiethnic makeup and our relatively new status as a nation, we have never had a stable food culture—as in passing on customs of eating from one generation to the next. This leaves us vulnerable to marketing and the latest nutrition study, "willing to throw it all out every few years," as he once said in an interview.

In other words, without an enduring set of social norms around eating, we are constantly reinventing them. The support for this idea is in strong supply, but there is an untapped layer that deserves inspecting: how this unstable food culture is shaped by our core values as a country. . . . They help explain why we eat the things we eat and the ways we eat them—and they equip us to understand how we might eat in the future. . . .

A melting pot is defined as "a place where a variety of races, cultures, or individuals assimilate into a cohesive whole." Americans take immense pride in this notion. How this concept influences our eating relates to the term's second definition: "a process of blending that often results in invigoration or novelty." This means that the hope for the future of food in America sits on the positive side of the coin of reinvention. It's why we are willing to embrace new norms around dining, like wine for the masses, food trucks, Tex-Mex, and Italian food that is really a distinct Italian *American* genre, without which there would be no "American" food to speak of. . . .

When Americans order takeout and delivery, Chinese, Mexican, and Italian 5 top the list; when we eat at a restaurant, the most popular types of international cuisines are sushi, Thai, Vietnamese, Brazilian/Argentinian, Greek, and Southeast Asian. That's according to a 2015 study conducted on behalf of the National Restaurant Association, entitled "Global Palates: Ethnic Cuisines and Flavors in America."

But historians and food studies experts point to Italian food as the original symbol of a broader phenomenon: the gradual incorporation of foreign cuisines into traditionally bland American palates. Two-thirds of Americans now eat a greater variety of cuisines from around the world than they did just five years ago. The vast majority of us enjoy eating these types of food both at restaurants that serve only that type of food—what you might consider the more authentic experiences—*and* as part of "mainstream menus," as the study called them, at other types of restaurants.

Spaghetti and meatballs: standard Italian-American fare
Clynt Garnham Food & Drink/Alamy Stock Photo

fusion: joining two or more things to create something new and different; with respect to food, the term refers to the blending of the elements of two or more culinary traditions to create a way of cooking that previously didn't exist—for example, kimchi grilled-cheese sandwiches, which are available at a Portland, Oregon, food cart.

chop suey, chow mein: two popular dishes of American Chinese cuisine consisting generally of stir-fried meat, celery, perhaps other vegetables, and a cornstarch-based sauce; the dishes are served over rice or noodles.

WASP (White Anglo-Saxon Protestant): an acronym originally used to refer to those well-to-do white Protestant Americans descended from the country's founders who shaped the country and its political culture, the term is now often used to refer broadly, and often pejoratively, to the elements of American culture associated with the dominant ethnic group, composed of European Americans.

frijoles refritos: a dish associated with Mexican and Tex-Mex cuisine made of pinto beans that have been cooked and mashed. Sometimes—not generally, though—the beans are fried or baked. Thus, the name (a literal translation from Spanish of *refried beans*; that is, beans that have been thoroughly fried) is, in fact, not an accurate representation of the dish itself.

Spaghetti and meatballs is a great case study of our ever-more-daring tastes, and the quests for culinary adventure, that *today* define American appetites. The dish reveals the making of a true **fusion** cuisine in American culture.

In the culinary community, "fusion" gets a bad rap. It tends to be taken as meaning the food has no identity. But this is misguided. I'm referring to our cuisine at large.

And when I ask the question, What does our food show about who we are?, the story of spaghetti and meatballs suddenly isn't just about Italian American food. It's the story of the melting pot, and the novel, distinctly American cuisine that bubbles up out of it. Spaghetti and meatballs is merely one of countless dishes and ways of eating that never existed anywhere else. And collectively, these comprise a national food culture. One you might call Immigrant American.

Chinese immigrants also found certain dishes that could appeal to American tastes—General Tso's chicken not least among them. This adaptation, the mixing and compromising to create entirely new foods, was much the same. One difference between Italian food and other immigrant cuisines in America, though, is the way Italian Americans responded to its Americanization. Chinese Americans, as Harvey Levenstein writes in *Food in the USA*, "generally found the concoctions served in '**chop suey**' houses and made-in-Minnesota canned '**chow mein**' to be abominations," while "Italian-Americans generally shared the native-born **WASP**'s enthusiasm for the Americanized version of their cuisine." They were proud that non-Italian Americans gave their food recognition.

Not long ago, Harvey Levenstein points out, many Americans "equated tacos and **frijoles refritos** with stomach cramps and diarrhea." Consider, for a moment, that by 1991 salsa outsold ketchup in retail stores. By $40 million. Now, Chipotle is the envy of every restaurateur in the land.

"In 2009, the dollar share of 'ethnic' frozen meals (Asian, Mexican, etc.) surpassed the dollar share of traditional American recipes (e.g., **beef Stroganoff, Salisbury steak**, mac and cheese, etc.)," reads a presentation slide by the Hartman Group. . . . Hartman also notes that a little fewer than one in

beef Stroganoff, Salisbury steak: respectively, a dish of Russian origin composed of narrow strips of beef often sautéed with mushrooms and onions and served in a sour-cream sauce over egg noodles; an American dish, generally sold fully cooked, in which the "steak" is composed of ground beef (which can include pork), egg, seasonings, vegetables, and mushrooms. Many baby boomers associate these dishes with frozen TV dinners from the 1960s.

eight adult meals eaten at home involves an "emerging global food," while at a restaurant it's more than one of every five meals.

What's driving the *accelerated* integration of global cuisines into mainstream culture, then, is the increased number of meals we eat outside the home. The greater percentage of the total bites we eat in a given day or week that are made by someone else. Why *not* give lamb **adobo** a try on your Munchery app? **Chicken tikka masala** from the Trader Joe's prepared food section looks whirl-worthy. What these and other new food-service models have done from an innovation standpoint, from an industry disruption standpoint, is make foreign dishes more accessible to the masses.

It's the silver lining, if you will, that comes from our not cooking as much anymore.

Two novel business models have dramatically heightened the pace at 15 which—and the fervor with which—American consumers embrace the exotic: food trucks and the Chipotle format of fast-casual dining. Some people are happy committing a whole Saturday night to trying a family-run Himalayan restaurant, or driving to a retail district where they don't recognize the letters on the signs. But some people are not. It's far easier to shift, say, one turkey sandwich you'd normally have for lunch on Tuesday to a **kati roll** if the food truck is parked right outside your office. The same thinking goes for everything from Indian "**nanini**" and Filipino pork **sisig** rice bowls to Vietnamese **banh mi** and Austrian **schnitzel**. The speed and price point of food truck food—you'll be on your way for under ten dollars in under ten minutes—further reduces barriers to consumption.

Fast-casual restaurants with the create-your-own format—also offering that ten-dollar, ten-minute mark—have a similar effect: You start with a base, pick a protein, and add sauces and toppings as you like. Importantly, that **cheffing** includes tailoring the spiciness and complexity of flavors to your comfort level.

As the author John Hooper notes, there is a crucial distinction between diversity and disunity. We are a country of political, cultural, and

adobo: Spanish, meaning "marinade," "seasoning," or "sauce"; a method of preserving meat and fish and enhancing their flavor by marinating them in a sauce of paprika, garlic, salt, oregano, vinegar, and soy sauce. The tradition arose in Spain and Portugal and spread during the colonial period to what is today Latin America and the Philippines, developing regional variants in various locations.

chicken tikka masala: a South-Asian-inspired dish composed of chicken that has been marinated in a spicy yogurt sauce, cooked in a tandoori oven, and flavored with tomatoes and the spice mixture masala. Cooks or chefs in several countries—India, Britain, and Scotland—claim to have invented it. It is particularly popular in Great Britain.

kati roll: originally street food in Kolkata, a kebab (chunks of meat, often chicken, roasted on a skewer) wrapped in a flatbread such as Indian roti along with coriander chutney, egg, and bits of vegetable.

nanini: a combination of the words *naan*, an Indian flatbread, and *panini*, a grilled Italian sandwich. (It's worth noting that the Italian term for the sandwich is *panino*; *panini* is the plural in Italian. English has borrowed the plural form and uses it as the singular. Thus, an American might ask for a panini.)

sisig: a dish of Filipino origin made from pig's head and liver, seasoned with a local citrus fruit and peppers.

cheffing: working as a chef.

banh mi: a sandwich of Vietnamese origin consisting of a small baguette (or loaf of bread) filled, traditionally, with pork sausage, coriander leaves, and pickled carrots, radishes, and cucumbers, as well as mayonnaise and pâté, a paste made of cooked ground meat and fat. The latter two ingredients, like baguettes, have their origin in French cuisine. The French directly colonized Vietnam from 1887 until 1954. Hence banh mi serves as a clear example of fusion cuisine.

schnitzel: originally from Austria, a main dish of veal tenderized by pounding and coated with egg, flour, and bread crumbs, before being fried. As it has traveled around the globe, the term has come to refer to any piece of pounded meat that is breaded and fried.

Banh mi Myung J. Chun/Getty Images

mutant: a deviation, often with the very negative connotation of monstrosity.

truffle: a highly valued and expensive fungus that grows underground.

sullied: stained, damaged, polluted, spoiled.

commendable: praiseworthy.

ideological diversity, spread across many far-reaching geographic subsections. But there are features that reveal themselves in the foods we eat that characterize us broadly as a people.

Various arguments try to explain why Americans like "foreign" food, such as increased international travel, shifts in immigration policies that have altered our country's demographics, and so on. But it comes down to one uniquely American value: As a people, we are curious, open to the new—the unknown or lesser known. We care about discovery.

All within certain limits of course, because don't forget, all this "**mutant** mash-up food," as Anthony Bourdain has called it, is happening *alongside* an only deepened popularity of our old standbys: the Five Guys and Shake Shacks selling burgers and milkshakes, except better (apparently), or the craft beer boom with brewpubs selling Reubens and grilled cheese and fries, except with, you know, **truffle** seasoning. All at a time when the average American still eats three hamburgers a week.

American fare is far from a thing of the past. It's just a matter of how 20 American fare is defined. So it's not as if we've hopped on another bandwagon entirely—we've welcomed a whole caravan of new wagons into our fleet.

In 2014, *Bon Appetit's* Andrew Knowlton featured a restaurant in San Antonio, Texas, called Hot Joy, an Asian fusion joint he called "rule-breaking" and "trendsetting." Knowlton writes: "Chef Quealy Watson has never been to Asia. Everything he knows about Chinese, Japanese, Indian, or the rest of that vast region's cuisine he picked up from cookbooks and the Internet. But who cares anymore? Authenticity and rigid adherence to tradition are overrated. Deliciousness is king."

So it turns out that one of our biggest problems as eaters, our unstable food culture, is also one of our greatest strengths: The idea that anything goes—that in throwing it all into the mix something wonderful emerges—is why we have culinary gems you can't find anywhere else.

Korean tacos and naan pizza and California rolls. Some might consider these horrors. **Sullied** versions of the *true* cultural entities. But not us. In America, collisions are **commendable**.

RESPOND ●

1. How effectively do you think Egan has described American food culture? In short, do her characterization and examples of American food culture in the opening paragraphs capture your understanding of the food-related practices Americans engage in? Can you add additional items to the list of examples she gives?

2. A major concern of Egan's is the changing nature of Americans' tastes—literally, the foods we prefer to eat, the ingredients that make them up, the ways we prefer our foods to be seasoned, and even the methods of preparation. Can you find evidence in your own life of the changing nature of America's preferences with regard to food? Are there foods you eat now that you didn't eat as a child? Are there foods you enjoy that your parents or grandparents do not? What might account for these differences?

3. One reviewer characterized Egan's writing style as "breezy." Based on this selection and specifically the passages below, what might the reviewer have meant? What adjectives might you use to describe her style? (The discussion of style in arguments in Chapter 13 should prove helpful in responding to this question.)

   > In the culinary community, "fusion" gets a bad rap. It tends to be taken as meaning the food has no identity. But this is misguided. I'm referring to our cuisine at large.

   > And when I ask the question, What does our food show about who we are?, the story of spaghetti and meatballs suddenly isn't just about Italian American food. It's the story of the melting pot and the novel, distinctly American cuisine that bubbles up out of it.

   > It's the silver lining, if you will, that comes from our not cooking as much anymore.

4. **THINKING CRITICALLY**   Looking at the first quoted passage in the previous question, what changes would you need to make in order to paraphrase it for an academic paper? In other words, what changes in vocabulary and sentence structure would you need to make in order to convey Egan's content while avoiding plagiarism, on the one hand, and ensuring that the language you use would be appropriate for an academic context, on the other? In addition to paraphrasing the passage, write a healthy paragraph about which features of it you changed and why. (The information in Chapter 21 on plagiarism and academic integrity, Chapter 17 on academic arguments, and Chapter 13 on style in arguments will be useful here.)

5. Agreeing with Michael Pollan, Egan contends that Americans have "never had a stable food culture—as in passing on customs of eating from one generation to the next" (paragraph 11). In a sense, Egan is arguing that the only thing stable about American foodways is change. Reflect on your response to Question 2 above, and **write an argument of fact** in which you describe differences in the food culture between you or your generation, on the one hand, and your parents or grandparents, on the other. In planning this essay, you may want to conduct an interview to get useful information. You might, for example, interview older members of your family (if they are alive and available) or other older people you know about how they ate as children. From a different angle, you might interview someone who owns or works in a restaurant or in a food cart about what they have observed about generational differences in taste or how tastes have changed across time. Another possibility is to do some research on the growth of so-called "ethnic" grocery stores or restaurants in your area over time; you might, for instance, examine ads in print newspapers or telephone books for such establishments at five-year intervals for the past thirty years. (Chapter 8 provides information on arguments of fact, while Chapter 18 on finding evidence includes information on conducting interviews.)

▼ In seeking selections for this chapter, we were grateful to find the incredibly detailed data available on the United States Department of Agriculture (USDA) Web site. Among other topics, the USDA tracks food availability, food consumption, nutrient availability, diet quality, and food prices—factual information that is relevant to the tasks of government at various levels, to industry, and to the public. Out of the scores of specific foods tracked by the USDA, we have chosen almost thirty to illustrate how Americans' food habits have changed since 1970, when the data was first collected. While showing all foods on such a chart would be far too large for this book, we have provided all the data instead in the format of a table, with the goal of making apparent some basic aspects of the power of visual displays of information.

Of course, many sorts of factors have shaped the data. The increase in Americans' consumption of fresh vegetables and fruit in the past few decades isn't just about changing taste. It also reminds us that immigration, globalization, and trade deals like NAFTA have had consequence for the availability of these foods in particular, and Americans have gladly seized those opportunities. When data were first collected in the 1970s, high-fructose corn syrup was just being introduced, and its presence in foods and carbonated beverages, in particular, has increased exponentially because of its low cost and availability.

As with all statistical data, readers have to beware when interpreting them. A huge increase or decrease in the percentage of consumption of a particular item may not represent a large increase or decrease in actual consumption. If Americans weren't consuming much of a particular food in the early 1970s, even a modest increase in consumption would represent a great increase in terms of percentage.

As you study the chart and the table that we've created from a selection of the complete data, consider the power of visual arguments and the changing dietary habits of Americans over the past several decades.

How Do Your Eating Habits Differ from Your Grandparents'?

UNITED STATES DEPARTMENT OF AGRICULTURE

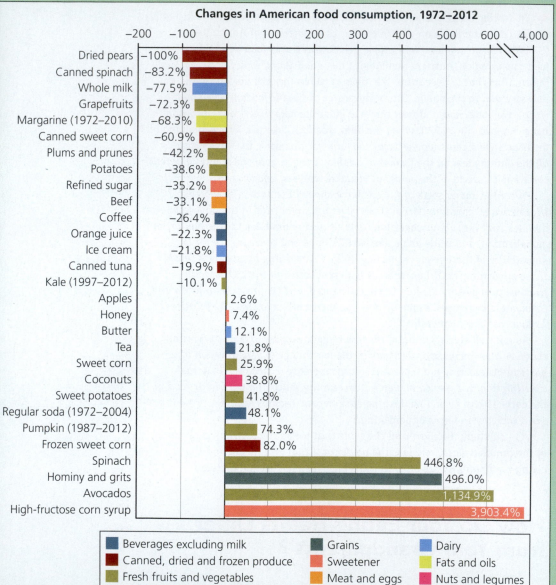

Changes in American food consumption, 1972–2012

Food	Change
Dried pears	−100%
Canned spinach	−83.2%
Whole milk	−77.5%
Grapefruits	−72.3%
Margarine (1972–2010)	−68.3%
Canned sweet corn	−60.9%
Plums and prunes	−42.2%
Potatoes	−38.6%
Refined sugar	−35.2%
Beef	−33.1%
Coffee	−26.4%
Orange juice	−22.3%
Ice cream	−21.8%
Canned tuna	−19.9%
Kale (1997–2012)	−10.1%
Apples	2.6%
Honey	7.4%
Butter	12.1%
Tea	21.8%
Sweet corn	25.9%
Coconuts	38.8%
Sweet potatoes	41.8%
Regular soda (1972–2004)	48.1%
Pumpkin (1987–2012)	74.3%
Frozen sweet corn	82.0%
Spinach	446.8%
Hominy and grits	496.0%
Avocados	1,134.9%
High-fructose corn syrup	3,903.4%

Legend:
- Beverages excluding milk
- Canned, dried and frozen produce
- Fresh fruits and vegetables
- Grains
- Sweetener
- Meat and eggs
- Dairy
- Fats and oils
- Nuts and legumes

United States Department of Agriculture

602

Food	% Change	Category
Dried pears	−100.0	Canned, dried, and frozen produce
Canned cherries	−97.0	Canned, dried, and frozen produce
Canned plums	−93.1	Canned, dried, and frozen produce
Canned apricots	−88.2	Canned, dried, and frozen produce
Frozen plums	−87.8	Canned, dried, and frozen produce
Canned spinach	−83.2	Canned, dried, and frozen produce
Veal	−83.0	Meat and eggs
Canned salmon	−79.7	Canned, dried, and frozen produce
Prune juice	−79.6	Beverages excluding milk
Canned asparagus	−78.3	Canned, dried, and frozen produce
Whole milk	−77.5	Dairy
Canned green beans	−74.5	Canned, dried, and frozen produce
Flavored whole milk	−72.8	Dairy
Grapefruits	−72.3	Fresh fruits and vegetables
Grapefruit juice	−72.0	Beverages excluding milk
Lamb	−71.2	Meat and eggs
Margarine (1972–2010)	−68.3	Fats and oils
Whole evap/condensed milk	−66.9	Dairy
Frozen asparagus	−62.1	Canned, dried, and frozen produce
Canned sweet corn	−60.9	Canned, dried, and frozen produce
Canned carrots	−60.8	Canned, dried, and frozen produce
Canned cabbage for kraut	−59.1	Canned, dried, and frozen produce
Canned potatoes	−58.1	Canned, dried, and frozen produce
Buttermilk	−58.0	Dairy
Canned peaches	−57.0	Canned, dried, and frozen produce
Cranberries	−56.5	Fresh fruits and vegetables
Lard (1972–2010)	−55.1	Fats and oils
Rye flour	−53.7	Grains
Cottage cheese	−51.5	Dairy
Escarole/endive	−48.0	Fresh fruits and vegetables
Canned sardines	−47.4	Canned, dried, and frozen produce
Canned pears	−44.3	Canned, dried, and frozen produce
Canned cucumbers for pickles	−43.4	Canned, dried, and frozen produce
Canned pineapple	−42.7	Canned, dried, and frozen produce
Plums and prunes	−42.2	Fresh fruits and vegetables
Frozen lima beans	−42.1	Canned, dried, and frozen produce
Corn dextrose	−42.0	Grains
Peanuts cleaned in-shell	−41.2	Nuts and legumes
Frozen apples	−40.3	Canned, dried, and frozen produce
Dried figs	−39.0	Canned, dried, and frozen produce
Potatoes	−38.6	Fresh fruits and vegetables
Sherbert	−38.6	Dairy

Food	% Change	Category
Frozen cauliflower	−37.2	Canned, dried, and frozen produce
Total milk	−36.7	Dairy
Head lettuce	−36.6	Fresh fruits and vegetables
Canned snap beans	−35.5	Canned, dried, and frozen produce
Refined sugar	−35.2	Sweetener
Mustard greens (1997–2012)	−34.4	Fresh fruits and vegetables
Beef	−33.1	Meat and eggs
Frozen yogurt (1989–2012)	−30.0	Dairy
Other edible fats and oils (1972–2010)	−27.3	Fats and oils
Coffee	−26.4	Beverages excluding milk
Oranges and temples	−26.1	Fresh fruits and vegetables
Frozen apricots	−25.2	Canned, dried, and frozen produce
Cured fish	−23.8	Meat and eggs
Barley products	−23.0	Grains
Turnip greens (1997–2012)	−22.5	Fresh fruits and vegetables
Orange juice	−22.3	Beverages excluding milk
Canned apples/applesauce	−22.1	Canned, dried, and frozen produce
Canned shellfish	−21.9	Canned, dried, and frozen produce
Ice cream	−21.8	Dairy
Nonfat dry milk	−21.0	Dairy
Frozen blackberries	−20.5	Canned, dried, and frozen produce
Other peanuts	−20.4	Nuts and legumes
Frozen carrots	−20.0	Canned, dried, and frozen produce
Canned tuna	−19.9	Meat and eggs
Cabbage	−19.6	Fresh fruits and vegetables
Prunes	−18.7	Fresh fruits and vegetables
Eggs (pounds)	−17.1	Meat and eggs
Pork	−17.1	Meat and eggs
Radishes	−16.5	Fresh fruits and vegetables
Celery	−16.5	Fresh fruits and vegetables
Pineapple juice	−14.8	Beverages excluding milk
Shortening (1972–2010)	−13.0	Fats and oils
Canned mushrooms	−12.2	Canned, dried, and frozen produce
Canned other	−11.7	Canned, dried, and frozen produce
Eggnog	−10.4	Dairy
Kale (1997–2012)	−10.1	Fresh fruits and vegetables
Frozen green peas	−9.2	Canned, dried, and frozen produce
Hazelnuts	−8.8	Nuts and legumes
Other frozen berries	−6.2	Canned, dried, and frozen produce
Dried apples	−3.3	Canned, dried, and frozen produce
Peanut candy	−2.0	Nuts and legumes
Frozen cherries	−0.1	Canned, dried, and frozen produce

Food	% Change	Category
Potatoes for chips	0.8	Fresh fruits and vegetables
Pecans	0.9	Nuts and legumes
Peaches and nectarines	1.0	Fresh fruits and vegetables
Selected fruit juices	1.4	Beverages excluding milk
Canned tomatoes	2.3	Canned, dried, and frozen produce
Dried whey	2.4	Canned, dried, and frozen produce
Apples	2.6	Fresh fruits and vegetables
Corn glucose	4.6	Sweetener
Snack peanuts	4.9	Nuts and legumes
Potatoes for dehydrating	5.3	Fresh fruits and vegetables
Honey	7.4	Sweetener
Oat products	10.2	Grains
Low-fat ice cream	11.0	Dairy
Butter	12.1	Dairy
Cantaloupe	12.1	Fresh fruits and vegetables
Dry edible beans	14.1	Nuts and legumes
Skim condensed milk	14.5	Dairy
Fresh/frozen fish	18.1	Meat and eggs
Canned vegetables, other	18.3	Canned, dried, and frozen produce
Frozen spinach	18.4	Canned, dried, and frozen produce
Melons	18.9	Fresh fruits and vegetables
Carrots	19.6	Fresh fruits and vegetables
Wheat flour (1972–2010)	19.6	Grains
Watermelon	20.2	Fresh fruits and vegetables
Walnuts	20.6	Fresh fruits and vegetables
Cocoa	20.7	Spices and cocoa
Collard greens (1997–2012)	21.0	Fresh fruits and vegetables
Tea	21.8	Beverages excluding milk
Pears	22.4	Fresh fruits and vegetables
Apricots	23.9	Fresh fruits and vegetables
Other nuts	25.6	Nuts and legumes
Sweet corn	25.9	Fresh fruits and vegetables
Snap beans	28.8	Fresh fruits and vegetables
Dried dates	32.2	Canned, dried, and frozen produce
Edible syrups	33.2	Sweetener
Brussels sprouts	35.0	Fresh fruits and vegetables
Peanut butter	35.7	Nuts and legumes
Raisins	37.3	Canned, dried, and frozen produce
Coconuts	38.8	Nuts and legumes
Frozen snap beans	39.4	Canned, dried, and frozen produce
Cauliflower	41.0	Fresh fruits and vegetables
Other frozen dairy products	41.4	Dairy
Bananas	41.7	Fresh fruits and vegetables

Food	% Change	Category
Sweet potatoes	41.8	Fresh fruits and vegetables
Dried peaches	41.9	Canned, dried, and frozen produce
Honeydew	47.8	Fresh fruits and vegetables
Regular soda (1972–2004)	48.1	Beverages excluding milk
Canned olives	49.0	Canned, dried, and frozen produce
Dry buttermilk	51.8	Dairy
Flavored milk	54.0	Dairy
Whole dry milk	55.8	Dairy
Lemon juice	55.9	Beverages excluding milk
Frozen strawberries	56.2	Canned, dried, and frozen produce
2 percent milk	59.3	Dairy
Onions for dehydrating	63.0	Fresh fruits and vegetables
Frozen peaches	66.2	Canned, dried, and frozen produce
Durum flour (1972–2010)	68.3	Grains
Tomatoes	68.7	Fresh fruits and vegetables
American cheese	71.2	Dairy
Pumpkin (1987–2012)	74.3	Fresh fruits and vegetables
Frozen potatoes	74.7	Canned, dried, and frozen produce
Grape juice	76.2	Beverages excluding milk
Turkey (carcass)	77.8	Meat and eggs
Total soda	77.8	Beverages excluding milk
Frozen sweet corn	82.0	Canned, dried, and frozen produce
Onions	85.3	Fresh fruits and vegetables
Spices	89.9	Spices and cocoa
Tangerines and tangelos	94.0	Fresh fruits and vegetables
Chicken	95.0	Meat and eggs
Cranberry juice (1989–2012)	95.9	Beverages excluding milk
Cream	100.9	Dairy
Macadamia nuts	100.9	Nuts and legumes
Skim milk	103.2	Dairy
Lemons	104.5	Fresh fruits and vegetables
Fresh/frozen shellfish	104.8	Meat and eggs
Other milk	105.7	Dairy
Frozen vegetable, misc.	111.7	Canned, dried, and frozen produce
Eggplant	126.7	Fresh fruits and vegetables
Dry peas and lentils	127.3	Nuts and legumes
Frozen blueberries	140.9	Canned, dried, and frozen produce
Canned chili peppers (1980–2012)	142.4	Canned, dried, and frozen produce
Cornstarch	142.9	Grains
Cucumbers	159.4	Fresh fruits and vegetables
Okra (1974–2012)	164.0	Fresh fruits and vegetables
Artichokes	164.2	Fresh fruits and vegetables
Dried apricots	175.3	Canned, dried, and frozen produce

Food	% Change	Category
Frozen broccoli	176.0	Canned, dried, and frozen produce
Rice (1972–2010)	191.6	Grains
Grapes	209.7	Fresh fruits and vegetables
Frozen raspberries	216.4	Canned, dried, and frozen produce
Salad and cooking oils (1972–2010)	218.5	Fats and oils
Corn flour and meal	219.2	Grains
Squash	221.0	Fresh fruits and vegetables
Sour cream	221.3	Dairy
Romaine and leaf lettuce (1985–2012)	253.4	Fresh fruits and vegetables
Asparagus	258.7	Fresh fruits and vegetables
Other cheese	283.1	Dairy
Cherries	296.0	Fresh fruits and vegetables
Apple juice	308.0	Beverages excluding milk
Lime juice	336.8	Beverages excluding milk
Strawberries	370.3	Fresh fruits and vegetables
Bell peppers	385.7	Fresh fruits and vegetables
Diet soda (1972–2004)	386.8	Beverages excluding milk
Flavored skim milk	406.9	Dairy
Spinach	446.8	Fresh fruits and vegetables
Kiwis (1982–2012)	449.9	Fresh fruits and vegetables
Almonds	454.8	Nuts and legumes
1 percent milk	483.6	Dairy
Garlic	494.8	Fresh fruits and vegetables
Hominy and grits	496.0	Grains
Mushrooms	652.2	Fresh fruits and vegetables
Blueberries (1980–2012)	663.7	Fresh fruits and vegetables
Raspberries (1992–2012)	674.5	Fresh fruits and vegetables
Pineapples	728.8	Fresh fruits and vegetables
Edible tallow (1979–2010)	746.8	Fats and oils
Pistachios	768.7	Nuts and legumes
Papayas	774.2	Fresh fruits and vegetables
Broccoli	797.6	Fresh fruits and vegetables
Yogurt	992.3	Dairy
Limes	1118.9	Fresh fruits and vegetables
Avocados	1134.9	Fresh fruits and vegetables
Lima beans (1989–2012)	1164.8	Fresh fruits and vegetables
Mangoes	2801.3	Fresh fruits and vegetables
High-fructose corn syrup	3903.4	Sweetener

RESPOND.

1. What was your response to the information presented in these visual displays of information? Did you find any of the information surprising? Encouraging? Distressing? Why?

2. Given the sort of data presented here, why is a bar chart a logical way of displaying the information? Why would these data not be a good candidate for, say, a pie chart?

3. As Chapter 14 on visual rhetoric explains, writers can use visuals to create pathos, support ethos, and/or support logos. Which of these functions could this chart serve and why?

4. **THINKING CRITICALLY** Study the chart that we have created, comparing it to the accompanying table, which contains all the data. Aside from the different amount of information presented, what other differences do you see in terms of the two visual displays of information? In short, which specific features of the chart make it much more effective than the table in terms of demonstrating aspects of the changes in Americans' diets? In what ways is it less effective? By the way, did you notice that there is a break in the vertical axis between 600 and 4000, as indicated by the two lines at an angle? Obviously, this was done because of space constraints. Indicating the scale from -200% to 4,000% would have required a foldout—visually impressive, but very expensive to produce. A common way that those creating bar charts misrepresent information is to use a break in the vertical axis. In what ways could such a break mislead those who are not reading carefully? (The information in Chapter 14 on visual rhetoric may prove helpful here.) Likewise, consider these questions: Would the table or the chart be effective on a PowerPoint slide? Why or why not? How does the use of color in the table make it easier for someone to find trends in the use of a particular food group?

5. A very common task in academic writing is describing visual arguments in the text. In other words, writers don't generally simply insert a chart or table with no comment. Instead, they refer to the table by name, explain to the reader what the chart or table shows, and then relate that information to the ongoing argument being made. **Write a description**, that is a factual argument, that might accompany the table that we have constructed from the USDA data. Be sure to refer to it by name, tell readers how it is formatted (how many columns? what information do they give readers?), and explain the information contained in the table, including generalizations we can draw from the data. Your description should be a healthy paragraph of several sentences.

▼ *Rob Greenfield (1986–) is an adventurer, environmental activist, humanist, and entrepreneur who often uses what one source terms "attention-grabbing tactics" to make his arguments. In his own words, he's gone from being a "drunk dude" to "a dude making a difference." Giving up an early focus on becoming a millionaire by 30, at age 24, Greenfield began to pursue a much simpler life as he came to realize the role his own behavior played in many of the world's problems. He is known for having 111 possessions, all of which fit in his backpack; for living off the grid in a 50-square-foot house as a Teeny Greeny (he auctioned off the house and raised $10,000 to build ten tiny houses for San Diego's homeless); and for projects like Food Waste Fiasco. For the latter, he "dove into more than two thousand dumpsters across the United States to demonstrate how nearly half of all food in the U.S. is wasted while 50 million (1 in 7) Americans are food insecure." This 2015 blog posting is from his Web site RobGreenfield.TV. As you read it, notice how carefully he, as a vegan, seeks to offer arguments for veganism while acknowledging its limits and admitting that certain carnivores (people who eat meat) may be living healthier and more environmentally friendly lives than some vegans.*

An Argument against Veganism . . . from a Vegan

ROB GREENFIELD

The topic of meat eating can be quite controversial and often becomes pretty heated. So whether you eat meat or not, please take a deep breath and chill out for a second.

To the vegans reading this, I want to be upfront that I utterly support veganism. It is my first recommendation to anyone who asks me how to live a more earth-friendly life. I eat an almost completely plant-based diet myself; about 95–99% of what I eat is plant-based.

To the meat eaters reading this, please read this fully before you quickly use this blog as an excuse to blindly eat food that is detrimental to the earth, to other species, and to you.

This is my argument against veganism by someone who strongly supports veganism.

We live on a planet that is home to seven billion people, and amongst that massive population there are many, many different cultures. Some are vegetarian by nature, some vegan by nature, and others eat a lot of meat and animal

5

609

products. I write this argument, in part because some people believe that veganism is the one and only way, no exceptions. That's totally understandable given many of the horrifying practices that are taking place in our current industrial agriculture system.

There's the factory farming with complete disregard to animals being living beings. Chickens are grown too big for them to walk. Female chicks are debeaked shortly after birth, and the male chicks are thrown into the trash. Pigs are grown in cages so small that they never get to stand up. Cows never get to graze in the field and barely see the light of day.

There's the fact that eating a vegan diet is the single largest thing that an American can do to decrease their environmental impact. Raising meat is the single largest contributor to our increasing droughts and our resource depletion. A hamburger takes over 600 gallons of water to produce.

palm oil: oil derived from the fruit of certain species of palm trees, especially those found in Africa. Palm oil is commonly used in commercial foods; however, environmentalists increasingly oppose its use because its production contributes to the deforestation of tropical areas. Likewise, the nutritional consequences of palm oil consumption are a subject of debate among scientists.

There's the rainforest deforestation that takes place to raise soy and grains to feed the animals that we eat.

There's the health risk of eating meat as well. We are pumping our animals full of dangerous hormones and antibiotics that are doing a huge injustice to the human race.

The list goes on and on as to why we should all give up meat and animal products. 10 We'd be doing a great service to the earth, to the other species we share the earth with, and to ourselves. But there is another side to the story that many vegans and vegetarians often leave out. There are cultures of people who eat meat and animal products in a manner that causes less harm to earth and animals than some vegan diets do.

All vegan diets are not created equal. I would argue that a person who lives off the land and includes meat in their diet can have a smaller environmental impact than a person who lives in the city and eats all vegan food that's been packaged and shipped in. Vegan diets often include food that is shipped from halfway around the world, food that is covered in packaging which is very resource-intensive (whether it's recycled or not), and food that contains harmful ingredients like **palm oil**. There's also the fact that increasing cropland to grow plant-based food displaces animal populations

Packaged vegan foods like these take a toll on the environment. Sean Gallup/Getty Images

and kills many of them. A vegan diet made up of industrially produced food is likely killing animals or harming animals one way or another. Of course, diets that contain meat can do all of the above as well; so below, I've included some examples of diets that incorporate meat that may actually have a smaller environmental impact than an urban vegan diet.

- I spent time in Louisiana and found it is a state with many self-sufficient people. For many of them, the **bayou** is their bloodline and they live off this land. Their diets include alligators, crayfish, fish, rabbit, deer and so much more. These swamps are absolutely teeming with life and I believe that when they hunt it responsibly, these folk can eat a more earth-friendly diet than an urban vegan that purchases everything in packages at the supermarket.

- There's the exploding wild boar population in Texas that is causing serious environmental problems. They are one of the most destructive invasive species in the US today displacing native species populations, devouring crops, and tearing up the land they roam. I think that hunting and eating these boars has a much smaller environmental impact (and likely even a positive impact) than just about any vegan food you can buy at the supermarket.

- Hunting deer in your own neck of the woods, like my friends in Wisconsin do, can also be far less destructive than being dependent on large-scale production of any food. These deer live wild, eating grasses their whole life, and no unsustainable resources must be used in their existence. Plus, by having to hunt their food themselves, these hunters can be much more connected to their food than the urban vegan.

- The **Inuit** people live primarily on animals that they hunt and trap locally. Imagine if they instead had all their food shipped in from warmer lands where it could be grown. That would be so much more detrimental than living off their land.

Those are just a few examples of why I would argue against a blanket statement for veganism. To say that everyone should be vegan I think would discredit many of the societies and cultures that are living in harmony with the earth to a far greater extent than many of today's urban vegans.

But after all that, many people would say that we've become an advanced enough society to know that it is inhumane to eat meat. **Gandhi** said, "The greatness of a nation can be judged by the way its animals are treated." I completely agree. We do have a moral obligation to cause no pain or suffering now that we've learned that we can live very healthy lives (seemingly healthier) without killing any animals. We absolutely must practice complete humanity

bayou: slow-moving stream, marshy outlet, or wetland; or a stream or creek containing brackish water whose direction reverses daily as the tides change. The bayou region in the Gulf Coast comprises areas of the Mississippi Delta, Louisiana, and eastern Texas.

Inuit: the indigenous peoples of the Arctic regions of the United States (Alaska), Canada, Greenland, Russia, and Denmark. In Canada and increasingly in the U.S., the term is used instead of *Eskimo*, which these groups do not use to refer to themselves and which some of them consider pejorative.

(Mahatma) Gandhi (1869–1948): leader of the struggle for Indian independence from Britain in the second quarter of the twentieth century. Gandhi employed the methods of nonviolent civil disobedience, inspiring movements for freedom around the world. (Dr. Martin Luther King Jr. was greatly affected by Gandhi's methods and employed them in the U.S. Civil Rights movement.) Like Hindus generally, Gandhi was vegetarian.

towards all species. However, some would follow that line of thought and say that we have become so elevated that even just the death of an animal by our hands is inhumane.

That thought has one huge flaw in my mind though. I believe that idea separates the human species from all other species on earth. It is saying that we are not a part of the circle of life like other species are. A wolf can kill a deer, and that is nature—but if we were to hunt a deer, many of us would not consider that nature. Humans are still animals and we are a part of nature, and a part of the natural cycle of life. Yes, we are unique, but so is every other species. We are not above all other species, or any species for that matter. I believe that it is this separation thinking that has gotten us into much of the trouble that we are in. We know that we have only one earth. We know that everything on earth is connected. Rather than think of us as separate creatures, above all others, I think we should remember that we are animals too and we are a part of the food chains on earth. We can be the predator and we can be the prey. But if we are to be predators, we must use the knowledge we've gained to be ethical predators.

Vegans should absolutely continue promoting vegan diets, and they should   15
pursue it with great passion. We are in dire times, and reducing meat consumption is something that we can all do today to lessen our burden on the earth and other species. I commend all activists and organizations out there campaigning for meat-free diets. I commend everyone out there who is reducing his or her meat consumption. I commend all vegans and vegetarians.

One recommendation I would make to vegans and vegetarians is to be compassionate to all humans too, not just all animals. We live in a messed up time and it's very challenging to make ethical decisions. It's not easy in this country to do the right thing. So much of mainstream society stacks the odds against us leading environmentally-friendly lifestyles. So campaign hard and lead by example, but remember that all people have feelings too and have their own challenging circumstances.

I'm going to continue eating a plant-based diet myself. There really are very few arguments against the evidence—across cultures, a diet high in plants and low in animals is the most beneficial to human health. I used to eat a lot of meat but since I stopped a few years ago, I've seen so many benefits. I'm absolutely healthier than ever before. My body naturally stays fit with little need for exercise. I feel great about myself knowing that I'm not supporting any unethical businesses or practices. I'm living in alignment with my morals and beliefs.

I live in San Diego now, and it seems to currently not be possible to support a meat-eating population ethically or sustainably in this city or any other densely populated area. So as long as I'm here, you probably won't find me eating meat—unless I'm down at the pier to catch and take home a small fish. If I move out of the city to live off the land, however, or if I am on a long trek through the wild, it could be a different story.

We all have a unique situation, so doing what is right for you, all creatures, and the earth is going to take some thinking and some resourcefulness. We can all make improvements no matter where we are today, but only you can decide to do this for yourself. To be of help to you, here are my top ten recommendations to make your diet more Planet Friendly in relation to meat.

1. Eat a plant-based diet, which means no meat or animal products.

2. If you do eat meat or animal products, do it in moderation. A few times per week is plenty. If you eat a lot of meat currently, start by eating one animal-free day per week (such as Meatless Monday) or one animal-free meal per day.

3. If you do eat meat or animal products, get to know your farmer or hunter and get it locally.

4. Be certain that the animal is ethically raised/harvested. Purchasing organic will help with this a lot, but not all organic is equal. Small organic farms typically trump large-scale organic production.

5. If you eat meat or animal products, try to raise it or hunt it yourself. Start with raising chickens for eggs, which can be done even in large cities.

6. Choose dairy and eggs over meat. It is far more environmentally friendly to choose these over meat.

7. Choose sustainably farmed chicken over beef and pork. Chicken has a far smaller environmental impact than beef or pork. Beef is the most environmentally taxing and often the unhealthiest, so choose this last.

8. Use every part of the animal and waste nothing. The liver and bone marrow are two of the most nourishing parts of the animal.

9. Make a list of goals and take it one step at a time. Don't be overwhelmed by all the things that you may want to change. Instead, make short-term and long-term goals and have fun checking them off the list.

10. Realize that this will not be more expensive. Although it may appear to be to the untrained eye, eating vegan and healthier food is not more expensive. Simple plant-based food, such as a meal of rice, beans, and veggies, is far less expensive than meat. My meals at home usually cost

me between $1 and $2. There's also the money saved in health costs, gym memberships, diet plans, and the many other ways we waste money to make ourselves look better which won't be needed when you take control of your diet.

RESPOND•

1. What is your response to Greenfield's argument? How convincing a case does he make that there are valid arguments against veganism even though he is a committed vegan?

2. How would you characterize Greenfield's audiences in this blog posting? In other words, which group(s) would constitute his intended or ideal readers, his invoked readers, and his real readers? Cite specific evidence from the text—anything from word choice to kinds of appeals to evidence offered—for the first two of these categories. (See Chapter 1 on kinds of audiences.)

3. As Chapter 1 explains, rather than being dogmatically oppositional, Rogerian argumentation seeks to build on common ground. How do we see Greenfield seeking to find common ground and build on it as he argues that veganism isn't necessarily the best option in all cases? As he seeks to argue that other options are indeed sometimes more healthy and environmentally friendly? How do these strategies relate to his ultimate goals and to his multiple audiences (see Question 2)?

4. **THINKING CRITICALLY**   One of the most interesting things about this selection is how rarely we see such arguments in contemporary American culture. When, for example, was the last time you heard someone acknowledge the limitations of their own position and concede that those taking a very different view might, at least in certain cases, be able to claim the higher moral ground? What does it say about our society at this moment that it is rare to find such arguments on any topic, if possible at all? How might our society be different if we, as individuals and as members of various groups, began creating such arguments? What, if anything, might motivate us to do so?

5. Choose a cause you are devoted to in much the same way that Greenfield is devoted to veganism, and **write a proposal argument** much like his in which you seek to convince those who share your commitment to that cause of the potential limitations of that position and the possible moral or ethical advantages that those you often see as "the other side" might ultimately hold. (See Chapter 12 on proposal arguments.)

I Still Don't Understand the Cultural Appropriation of Food

JESS KAPADIA

Last week, the *Washington Post* published a Portland, OR-centric story titled "Should White Chefs Sell Burritos?" The story explains the mounting accusations of appropriation against Portland chefs who become famous for and profit from the cuisine of cultures that are not their own. The *Post* asserts that these accused chefs aren't harming anyone's culture by **disseminating** facets of it—in fact, they're more ambassadors of the culture they've chosen to represent than anything else.

One of the white burrito makers accused of appropriation Thomas Teal

Like those chefs, the best part of my food career has only ever been sharing—sharing the labors of our Test Kitchen with colleagues and friends, the knowledge of the extraordinary chefs we work with and the little secrets that will help nervous home cooks become confident culinary enthusiasts. As a result, I'm having trouble even interpreting the term **"cultural appropriation"** with regards to food. Actually, that's an understatement: I don't understand the cultural appropriation of food at all. Case in point: I had a freaking sushi doughnut the other day and wasn't mad at it. Sushi. Doughnut. (Sushi McDoughnut?)

◀ Jess Kapadia is a New York–based digital content creator, currently serving as senior editor at Food Republic, a Web site that seeks to serve as "the global hub for news and information about the new culture of food across a multitude of media platforms." This selection first appeared there in June 2017 in response to debates about a pair of young women in Portland, OR, who had opened a food cart selling burritos. Like many online pieces, this one reminds us that digital texts today are parts of a chain of texts, each commenting on earlier texts and each paving the way for future responses. As you read this selection, consider how Kapadia uses ethical arguments as the basis for some of her claims.

disseminate: spread.

cultural appropriation (sometimes *cultural misappropriation*): the use of elements of a minority culture—clothing, foodways, music, etc.—by the majority culture, often to the benefit of members of the majority culture and denigration of the source culture. *To appropriate* something is to borrow and use it without permission.

It's easy to say "cultural appropriation" the same way it's easy to say "racist" or "ignorant." It feels good to say "cultural appropriation"—it rolls off the tongue nicely, sounds intellectual and all of a sudden you're on the road to moral superiority. The moment you get the opportunity, you need people to know that you've cultivated and discerned yourself, and you're not like those meat-and-potatoes people at all, so don't associate you with those people! . . . Except we're not, nobody is.

I'd venture to say that this many years into the age of pop food media and recipe-sharing, no food *belongs* to anyone anymore. I for one refuse to fight about food or believe anything edible belongs to me or either of my cultures (I'm bi-racial). Not when our school lunches are fashioned from ketchup and breadcrumbs, a few corporations pay millions to lobbyists to keep their monopolies legal and mass-produce the majority of our food, and one in six Americans is food-insecure. So in an earnest attempt to help unify the food media community and its consumers, I'd like to share some instances that could be conceivably viewed as cultural appropriation of food, but aren't.

Ahem!   5

My mother, a professional Indian chef and certified white blonde Jewish lady from Long Island, learned the endless complexities of South Asian food by immersing herself in residential kitchens around India, where my dad is from (often to the utter perplexity of the cooks, none of whom spoke English). She learned some of her best-loved dishes from my uncle's mother, who is Indian, via Pakistan, via Afghanistan.

Speaking of my mother, I ended up hanging out in-utero for more than a week longer than anticipated. To get things moving, my mom sought a fiery solution from a family friend who is a fifth-degree karate black belt of Jamaican and Chinese heritage. No, he didn't roundhouse kick me out of her; but he did promise that his extra-spicy goat curry recipe would shake me loose in no time flat. I was born later that evening. I told that story to a week-overdue pregnant friend who's been doggedly learning to make authentic **Yorkshire pudding** for her British husband.

Yorkshire pudding: a traditional English accompaniment to roast beef made of eggs, flour, milk or water, and often drippings from the meat. It much more resembles a popover, or puffy pastry, than anything Americans refer to as pudding.

Our lead recipe developer Paul Harrison makes phenomenal Mexican food, having worked as a prep cook for years in a small Michoacán restaurant in the Los Angeles area. Where's Michoacán, you ask? Ask him, he's done the research and grunt work, soaked the chilis, blended up the salsas and marinades, churned out thousands of tortillas, fed the staff and spoken the Spanish.

My fiancé was formerly married to a Japanese woman. As a result, he makes the **okonomiyaki** in our house, grating slippery mountain yams by hand (which any Japanese person will tell you is a labor of love and source of itchy red hand sores). I was formerly married to a Swedish guy, via Iraq. As a result, I make the biryani in our house. That's a win-win, right there, a house with killer okonomiyaki and **biryani**. Come over for dinner any time!

Okonomiyaki K Le/Shutterstock

The best Korean taco I've ever had was in Korea.

The best Chinese food I've ever had was not in China, but in India.

The best Indian food I've ever had was not in India, but Singapore.

The best Singapore **chow mei fun** I've ever had was not in Singapore, but in New York.

And the best street hot dog I ever had was not in New York, but in Amsterdam. There may have been some contributing factors involved, but it certainly speaks to the point that these assertions are all subjective and relative anyway.

None of these examples ever agitated feelings of theft, fraud or any of the sentiments behind public outcries of cultural appropriation, and all come back to my original idea of sharing as a kind of protective status. While profiting off the longstanding craft honed by another culture might sound like a convenient livelihood, it's not like most chefs are making enough money to leave their kitchens for cookbook tours. Working hard for the purpose of nourishing minds and bodies *has* to be exempt from negativity, doesn't it? We can't exactly share some white dude's Chinese tattoo that means "perseverance" (hopefully) or his sweaty, molting feather headdress at a music festival. We can only throw him **side-eye** and hope he gets with it at some point. But if he decided to devote his time to learning how to make killer **pao de queijo** from his Brazilian girlfriend's grandmother and start a food truck, called, I dunno, "Pao Pao Pao!" I'd have nothing but admiration.

That said, if we still need to decide whether this chef or that individual is guilty of what sounds more and more like the largely fabricated charge of cultural food appropriation, let's apply some more reasonable criteria than "Is it authentic?"

One: has this person learned the recipes and techniques from a primary source out of a passion for cooking? Two: is this person diluting the potency of the source itself or willfully diverting diners away from a primary source? And finally: what precisely would be accomplished by bringing up this facet of "call-out culture" after all is said and done and the dishes are washed? Of all the issues the greater food community has been tasked with solving, is a white chef's (delicious, mind you) ethnic food honestly worth a headline? Including this one?

10

15

okonomiyaki: savory Japanese pancake made of flour, grated yams, water or stock, shredded cabbage, and other ingredients.

biryani: South Asian main dish made of rice, spices, and meat.

chow mei fun: Southern Chinese dish made of pan-fried rice noodles, meat, vegetables, and spices, including curry powder.

side-eye: a glance out of the side of one's eyes, often expressing disapproval, scorn, or contempt.

pao de queijo: Brazilian "cheese bread" (literally, in Portuguese). This popular snack is less a traditional bread than a cheese puff made from tapioca or cassava flour, eggs, milk, oil, and grated cheese.

RESPOND.

1. What does Kapadia understand the term *cultural appropriation* to mean, specifically with regard to foods associated with particular ethnic or cultural groups? Why does she reject such a notion in this context? Do you agree or disagree with her stance? Why or why not?

2. Make a quick list of the arguments or evidence Kapadia makes to support her position. What sorts of evidence does she offer? How convincing do you find it? Kapadia relies largely on the trope of *copia* (Latin for *abundance*) in supporting her thesis—that is, she piles up many examples of a very similar kind. (For more on tropes, see Chapter 13.) What are the advantages and disadvantages of such a rhetorical strategy?

3. In what ways does Kapadia rely on ethical appeals as part of her argument, specifically in terms of the evidence she provides and which you listed in response to Question 2? For example, to what extent does she seek to boost the strength of her evidence by citing personal examples or those from people she knows? Is it relevant that Paul Harrison (paragraph 8) has "spoken the Spanish"? Why or why not? Should it be? What sorts of hypothetical examples does she cite? How convincing are they?

4. **THINKING CRITICALLY**   Kapadia obviously believes there are instances in which cultural appropriation is, in fact, inappropriate, as indicted when she writes, "We can't exactly share some white dude's Chinese tattoo that means 'perseverance' (hopefully) or his sweaty, molting feather headdress at a music festival. We can only throw him side-eye and hope he gets with it at some point" (paragraph 15). What distinction is Kapadia making between the examples of a "white dude" having certain tattoos from a language he (presumably) does not know or wearing a feather headdress from an indigenous group he (again, presumably) is not part of and claims made about the appropriation of foodways? Considering Kapadia's argument as an evaluative argument, what appears to be the criterion or criteria for claiming that the notion of cultural appropriation makes no sense with respect to foodways?

5. A careful reading of Kapadia's argument demonstrates, first, that she believes that cultural appropriation can occur and, second, that it doesn't make sense to apply that notion to foodways, even of cultures one is not a part of. At the same time, her examples fall into those categories that are limited to one's private life—who makes the biryani and who makes the okonomiyaki—and those involving commercial ventures, where someone is seeking to make a profit from

knowledge, however obtained, of a culture of which they are not a part. **Write an evaluative essay** in which you agree or disagree with Kapadia's stance, dealing explicitly with these two categories of examples. Are these two categories of situations the same—or should they be—or they clearly distinct? If they are the same in your eyes, on the basis of what criteria do make such a claim, or if they are distinct, where do you draw the line and why? (See Chapter 10 on evaluative arguments.)

▼ *Briahna Joy Gray is a contributing editor for the bimonthly magazine* Current Affairs: A Magazine of Politics and Culture, *where this selection first appeared in print in September 2017. Gray also co-hosts the podcast SWOTI (Someone's Wrong on the Internet). Here, Gray examines the current debate about the appropriation of foodways by contextualizing it as part of larger ongoing debates about cultural appropriation in areas like music and art. As you read this selection, consider how Gray is, in fact, seeking to construct a definitional argument that ultimately redefines how we think about cultural appropriation.*

The Question of Cultural Appropriation

BRIAHNA JOY GRAY

The trouble with **Elvis's** version of "Hound Dog" is not that it is bad. It's that it doesn't make any goddamn sense. **Big Mama Thornton's** original 1952 version of the song is sleazy

Big Mama Thornton Michael Ochs Archives/ Getty Images

and defiant. In a bluesy growl, she tells off the low-down guy who keeps "snooping round her door." It's a declaration of independence by a woman who is sick and tired of having a "hound dog" of a man take her for granted. The lyrics are full of dirty double-entendres: "You can wag your tail, but I ain't gonna feed you no more." In Elvis's version, sanitized for a pop audience, the line is changed to "You ain't never caught a rabbit, and you ain't no friend of mine." Drained of its original meaning, the song seemingly becomes about . . . an actual dog. Yet Elvis's version of "Hound Dog" sold 10 million copies and became his single best-selling song. It's ranked #19 on *Rolling Stone*'s list of the 500 Greatest Songs of All Time.

The term "cultural appropriation," a pejorative used to criticize certain types of ostensibly

---

Elvis Presley (1935–1977): American singer, actor, and sex symbol, often referred to as the "King of Rock and Roll," who sang in a range of genres, including rock and roll, country, blues, and gospel.

Willie Mae "Big Mama" Thornton (1926–1984): American rhythm-and-blues singer whose style was influenced by the African American gospel music she heard as a child.

Elvis Presley Bettmann/Getty Images

Open Casket, by Dana Schutz Johannes Schmitt-Tegge/AP Images

Emmett Till Everett Collection
Historical/Alamy

illegitimate borrowing from other people's cultures, gets a lot of people into a lot of arguments. That's especially true now that it is used to describe an ever-widening set of acts. What constituted "cultural appropriation" might once have been relatively clear: if you wore a ceremonial Native American headdress without actually being a Native American performing a ceremony, you were disrespectfully appropriating a culture that was not your own. But nowadays, the notion can be far more expansive in its scope. "Cultural appropriation" has been taken to mean that only blacks are entitled to create art about black historical figures: white artist Dana Schutz was boycotted and protested after displaying a painting of **Emmett Till's** body, on the theory that black suffering was not a fit

Emmett Till (1941–1955): Chicago-born African American teenager who was lynched by local white men while visiting relatives in Mississippi. When his body was returned home, his mother insisted on an open-casket funeral, permitting everyone to see the violence her son had endured. The widespread publication of images of Till in the coffin galvanized black communities across the country and helped convince many white Americans of the need to address African Americans' lack of civil rights nationwide.

subject matter for nonblack painters. It's also infamously been invoked to suggest there's something wrong with people making foods from cultures other than their own.

If the definition of "appropriation" had stayed narrow, it would be easy enough to defend. It's obvious why it's insulting and upsetting for a white person to casually sport a feathered headdress: they are items of deep symbolic meaning to the people who originated them, bestowed in recognition of great achievements. Treating them like party hats cheapens and dishonors them, and slights those people who have the same feelings about their tribal regalia that military members have about the sanctity of medals and uniforms. If "don't culturally appropriate" just means "don't treat things that are sacred to other people with ignorance and mockery," critics of the concept could easily be dismissed. The demand to be permitted to appropriate would simply be the demand to be able to act like a jackass without social consequence, and if there is one thing jackasses inarguably deserve, it is social consequences.

But as the "appropriation" concept has been used to object to many formerly innocuous forms of cultural mixing, certain criticisms of the term become increasingly credible. The more things are stuffed under the "cultural appropriation" tent, the more legitimate the concern that it may put limits on creativity, cultural exchange, and innovation. If taken to its logical extreme, critics of the concept delight in pointing out, the consequences would be outlandish: only Asians could use chopsticks and only Italians could play the violin. (And apparently, as one man

deeply ignorant in the history of science urged on Twitter, only whites could use "technology.")

It should be obvious that there is no such thing 5 as a "pure" culture. Any "technology" the oblivious tweeter might have had in mind relies on a numerical system invented by Arabs. We wear textiles from central Asia; we eat "Italian" pasta brought to Europe from China in the 13th century; and we developed our earliest legal framework from East Africans. (And that "Italian" violin is a Persian derivative.) So many of humankind's most exciting achievements result from centuries of cross-pollination, and if the term cultural appropriation is to have any meaning, it can't simply function to condemn the very exchange of ideas on which all progress depends.

"Appropriation" also suffers from an inherent theoretical difficulty: it depends on having a clear notion of cultural "ownership." The term tends to be defined as "the adoption or use of the elements of one culture by members of another culture"—often with the added proviso "without permission."

But how can a cultural group give "permission" to take or use a cultural product? It's not as if each ethnic group has a council or bureaucratic agency that processes requests for cultural exchange like **ASCAP** licenses music. Anyone claiming to give "permission" is adopting authority they do not have; after all, what happens if other members of the culture disagree? Do we put it to a majority vote? Once we accept the core idea of "cultural appropriation," that there is a coherent concept of cultural "ownership" that operates the

---

ASCAP: American Society of Composers, Authors and Publishers, an organization that protects members' copyrights by collecting licensing fees for performances that are then distributed as royalties to its members for their intellectual property.

Mardi Gras Indians Gerald Herbert/AP Images

way other forms of property rights do, all kinds of impossible questions are raised. These go beyond the usual "Can white men sing the blues?" (to which the answer remains, as always, "Yes, but usually not well.") What do we do, for example, about New Orleans' Mardi Gras Indians, who are black rather than Native American, but who wear elaborate feathered garb including—yes—headdresses and adopt tribal names? The Mardi Gras Indian tradition is meant to honor Native Americans, but it certainly never received "permission" from the U.S.'s indigenous population. If we accept the notions of ownership underlying "appropriation" analysis, we seem destined for either absurd logical extremes or arbitrary line-drawing.

And yet: discarding the concept entirely also seems like a mistake. Certain patterns of cultural exchange *do* seem to entail a kind of "theft," and in considering whether cultural appropriation is a helpful idea, we should be careful not to throw a useful analytical baby out with its muddy conceptual bathwater, so to speak. A **"property rights" framework** doesn't actually fit culture very well. Its boundaries are too amorphous,

property rights framework: here, a metaphor—that of the rights accruing to the owner of property of whatever kind—in contrast to other possible metaphors for thinking about questions that fall under the broad umbrella of questions of cultural appropriation.

its creation too much a collective enterprise, for us to be able to divide up rights of proprietorship like parcels of land. But if we abandon the "appropriation" idea altogether, it becomes hard to describe what feels wrong about the misuse of tribal artifacts or the commercialization of artistic works made by marginalized groups.

So I'd like to propose what I believe to be a better approach than "cultural appropriation" for understanding problems with using other people's culture. I think when we talk about appropriation, we're really talking about two separate issues: first, an issue of cultural exploitation, and second, an issue of cultural disrespect.

One core issue that the "appropriation" idea tries 10 to get at is economic exploitation. In an economic landscape where some groups get rewarded disproportionately to others, the people who make the culture are often not the ones who see the rewards from it; i.e., the problem is not that white men play the blues, it's that white men who have played the blues have gotten rich from it, while the black people who invented the blues stayed poor. (**Led Zeppelin**, for instance, notoriously didn't even give credit to the Delta bluesmen who had written their songs, thereby depriving them of both royalties and public recognition.) Non-white cultural products have often been repackaged for white audiences, reaping tremendous profits, none of which accrue to those who actually originated the culture.

That brings us back to Elvis, Big Mama Thornton, and "Hound Dog." The issue there isn't that Elvis

Led Zeppelin Granamour Weems Collection/Alamy Stock Photo

shouldn't sing "Hound Dog." It's that when Elvis sang Hound Dog, it made him rich and he became "The King," while when Thornton sang what is—let's be honest—an objectively better version of the song, she *didn't* become a world-famous megastar. Elvis's early records, the ones that made his name, are filled with covers of songs by black artists ("That's All Right," "Mystery Train," "Milkcow Blues," etc.), but the life stories of early 20th-century black musicians are stories of poverty and exploitation by a predatory music industry that lifted their sounds and left them with nothing. The trouble isn't that Elvis sang the songs but that he did so in a viciously racist economic landscape that didn't reward black cultural innovation with black economic success. Using cultural "ownership" doesn't help us here—after all, "Hound

---

Led Zeppelin: British band active from 1968 to 1980 (along with several reunion tours) and known for hard rock, blues rock, folk rock, and heavy metal.

Dog" was written by white songwriters, albeit specifically for Thornton, who added her own improvisations. But it's still obvious we're dealing with a racially unequal music industry.

Interestingly, it was the story of Elvis Presley that writer **Kenan Malik** recently used in order to argue that cultural appropriation is a good and necessary thing. Malik acknowledges that Elvis's success ended up overshadowing the contributions of black rock 'n' roll innovator Chuck Berry: *"In the 1950s, white radio stations refused to play [Berry's] songs, categorizing them as 'race music.' Then came Elvis Presley. A white boy playing the same tunes was cool. Elvis was feted, Mr. Berry and other black pioneers largely ignored. Racism defined who became the cultural icon."*

But, Malik says, "imagine that Elvis had been prevented from appropriating so-called black music. Would that have challenged racism, or eradicated Jim Crow laws? Clearly not. It took a social struggle—the civil rights movement—to bring about change." Now, let's for a moment set aside the irrelevant rhetorical question, which is oddly reminiscent of Hillary Clinton's similarly disingenuous "If we broke up the big banks tomorrow, would that end racism?" (The answer to both is the same: no, but the fact that something doesn't in and of itself "end racism" doesn't mean it shouldn't be done.) Malik believes that cultural appropriation is good because it gave us Elvis, even if that meant the eclipse of Chuck Berry, and even if that eclipse occurred for obviously racist reasons, i.e., because a white public wanted to have black songs performed by white artists.

Here we see why it's more helpful to look at things in terms of economic exploitation rather than ownership: it takes the focus off whether Elvis was entitled to *sing*, and instead looks at why Elvis had the *economic* success he did. Malik is right that strict notions of cultural ownership would stifle innovation, but he doesn't follow through the implications of the Presley/Berry problem: we're talking

Chuck Berry Michael Ochs Archives/Getty Images

Kenan Malik (1960–):
Indian-born British writer, trained as a scientist, who often writes on questions of race, religion, and multiculturalism.

A protest against Jim Crow laws Library of Congress/Getty Images

about a system of cultural production in which people of color produce certain sounds, which are then taken and imitated for profit. In some cases, this was even more blatant: in the '50s, white pop singer **Pat Boone** was hired to produce wholesome, advertiser-friendly versions of black R&B songs like **Little Richard's** "Tutti Frutti." As Richard said:

> *They didn't want me to be in the white guys' way. . . .* 15
> *I felt I was pushed into a rhythm and blues corner to keep out of rockers' way, because that's where the money is.*

Pat Boone (1934–):
American singer, composer, and TV personality popular in the 1950s and early 1960s; his success was second only to that of Elvis Presley during the time.

Pat Boone Hulton Deutsch/Getty Images

Little Richard (1932–):
the stage name of Richard Wayne Penniman, an American singer, songwriter, and actor, whose music and performance style profoundly influenced rhythm and blues, rock and roll, and soul music.

Little Richard Michael Ochs Archives/Getty Images

When 'Tutti Frutti' came out, . . . they needed a rock star to block me out of white homes because I was a hero to white kids. The white kids would have Pat Boone upon the dresser and me in the drawer 'cause they liked my version better, but the families didn't want me because of the image that I was projecting."

To frame the Elvis question as Malik does, then, is akin to asking "Well, shouldn't Pat Boone be *allowed* to cover Little Richard songs?" It misses the whole point: it's not that black songs should never be sung by white people, it is that there has been a long history of people pushing black creators to the margins while making millions of dollars off their work.

If the music business hadn't been riddled with racism, and if the measure of financial success was "whether a person (of any race) had created something original and good" rather than "whether a white person could copy and repackage an unknown black song for a white audience more concerned with color than content," there would be no injustice. Music is inherently appropriative. It thrives on creative allusions, sampling, and embellishing the groundwork laid by earlier artists. I embrace that: after all, I'm a woman who grew up with—and still prefers—**Aretha Franklin's** version of "Eleanor Rigby," and I didn't realize the song was a Beatles

---

Aretha Franklin (1942–): American singer and songwriter, often referred to as "The Queen of Soul."

Aretha Franklin Ron Galella/Getty Images

original until adulthood. However, "borrowing" becomes a problem when a piece of art is given preferential treatment *because of* preexisting racial hierarchies of value—causing the work of people of color to be devalued, and artists to be undercompensated for their innovation.

The "exploitation" instead of "appropriation" perspective also helps clear up some of the issues

surrounding food. **When two white women shut down their Portland burrito truck** after being accused of culturally appropriating Mexican food, the incident was used as an indictment of the absurdity of the appropriation concept. Once you have a racial test for whether someone can vend burritos, you might need to rethink your theory. Yet from an economic perspective, there *is* a problem with elite white yuppies opening an artisanal burrito truck: because there are massive racial wealth disparities in the United States, white people are disproportionately endowed with the capital that will allow them to open successful Mexican food restaurants; we can end up with a world full of Mexican restaurants where food is made by Mexican workers but the profits accrue to white owners. Just as with music, the problem is not that a TV chef like **Rick Bayless** makes Mexican food, it's that Rick Bayless makes *millions of dollars* making Mexican food while Mexican people bus tables in his restaurants. Public prejudice and an unequal economy make Bayless disproportionately *more able* to capitalize on Mexican cuisine than a working-class Mexican immigrant would be.

Across every cultural field, there are examples of white people receiving opportunities to benefit economically from a cultural product originating with people of color. Compare, for example, the fate of

"When two white women shut down their Portland burrito truck": Here is a quotation from one of the two women who opened the truck to the interviewer from the *Willamette Week* <http://bit.ly/2rfFSQ5>, which broke the story that became the basis for the debate:

"I picked the brains of every tortilla lady there in the worst broken Spanish ever, and they showed me a little of what they did," Connelly says. "They

told us the basic ingredients, and we saw them moving and stretching the dough similar to how pizza makers do before rolling it out with rolling pins. They wouldn't tell us too much about technique, but we were peeking into the windows of every kitchen, totally fascinated by how easy they made it look. We learned quickly it isn't quite that easy."

Thus, the original debate was not simply about who might "own"

foodways but how those with knowledge of foodways get it as well.

Rick Bayless (1953–): American chef, restaurateur, cookbook author, and media personality whose specialty is contemporary Mexican cuisine. As an undergraduate, he studied Spanish and Latin American culture and did doctoral work in linguistic anthropology. He lived in Mexico for six years in the 1980s while working on his first cookbook.

Rick Bayless Gustavo Caballero/Getty Images

Kayla Newman, the young black woman who coined the term "on fleek," with Danielle Bregoli, the young white woman who famously used urban slang on the Dr. Phil show ("**cash me outside howbow dah**"). Bregoli now commands appearance fees of $30,000 per event, while Newman is struggling to crowdfund a cosmetic line.

Not only is there a difference in remuneration, but non-white cultural products are often considered more valuable or esteemed when performed by whites. The "**race records**" made by black R&B musicians were considered "jungle music," while the white covers were innocuous "pop." We can even see it in hairstyles, too. Those associated with black Americans, like cornrows, are seen to reflect lower-class status, ugliness, and even criminality, until they are adopted by particular celebrities like Kim Kardashian or Katy Perry, at which point they are rebranded and called "new." Contrast the *New York Post*'s breathless treatment of the "new" style they termed "Boxer Braids"—e.g., cornrows or French plaits—with *Fashion Police*'s Giuliana Rancic's critique of young half-black actress Zendaya's **locs** as "probably" smelling "like patchouli or weed." That difference in perception can have real-world consequences: a black 12-year-old was recently threatened with expulsion for refusing to cut her natural afro-textured hair, and just this past May, two black students at a charter school in Malden, Massachusetts, faced detention and suspension for wearing their hair in braids. And until this year, the military prohibited locks, two-strand twists, and other natural (read black) hairstyles, essentially requiring that black women either shave our heads or chemically straighten our hair to serve our country. (It's also easier to dehumanize people when their cultural contributions are erased. When a people is depicted as "savage," their lives can be disregarded. When one conceives of the Middle East as tribal and backward—rather than as the wellspring of mathematics and the violin, it seems more natural to bomb its countries; Baghdad is simply a "war zone" where violent death is *normal* rather than a great centuries-old cultural center.)

Exploitation analysis may be more helpful than 20 appropriation in understanding why certain kinds of cultural lifting feel unjust. But it doesn't get at the entirety of the issue: we still have cases in which

---

cash me outside howbow dah: phrase the 13-year-old Bregoli used to challenge the show's audience to a fight, "Catch me outside, how about that?"

race records: 78 rpm records featuring black artists performing genres of music and comedy popular in the African American community, including jazz, gospel, and blues, and marketed to that community from the 1920s until the 1940s.

locs: shortened or clipped form of *dreadlocks,* which has negative connotations in some contexts.

Zendaya Jordan Strauss/AP Images

nobody is necessarily *profiting*, but where it feels as if a particular culture is being misused—e.g., the head-dress scenario. It may be best, then, to combine an objection to cultural exploitation with an objection to cultural *disrespect*, meaning acts which flatten or diminish the original meaning or value of the cultural product. If Native American objects hold particular spiritual and cultural meaning, using them purely for their aesthetic value implies a lack of interest in or empathy for the values of those who create the objects. That would apply equally well to those who intentionally used Christian religious objects without caring how Christians felt, but in the case of Native Americans, it is literally an insult added to an injury, given the country's viciously genocidal history.

"Cultural disrespect" also helps us appreciate *good* kinds of borrowing. When a person truly tries to study and pay tribute to a different culture, their use of it becomes less objectionable. The most cringeworthy white blues is played by those who least understand it, but when people have truly immersed themselves in another culture and done their research, the results can be moving. So Mardi Gras Indians are fine: they are honoring a culture rather than simply cheaply replicating it. And Rick Bayless can have a *serious* cultural exploitation problem without necessarily having a cultural disrespect problem, if his *understanding* of Mexican cuisines is deep and genuine.

Like Kenan Malik, I am uncomfortable with the possibility that a certain brand of cultural appropriation critique might inhibit artistic creativity. The idea that only black artists have the right to address Emmett Till's murder through art seems wrong. The question should never be: "Who is *allowed* to express their feelings about the racially motivated murder of a child?" After all, when Till's mother chose to keep his casket open to show his brutally beaten body to the press, she was doing so in order that white America could understand its own brutality. Blacks already knew what she was showing them, but she wanted to awaken whites' humanity and provoke a white response. Critics of Dana Schutz's Till painting said that "the subject matter is not Schutz's," but this seems wrong: the *subject* of Till's death is important to humanity writ large, and it should move us *all* to the point where we express our feelings, whether through art or otherwise. (There is, of course, a separate question about whether the work was in good taste or succeeded artistically.)

Yet there was another sense, the "exploitation" sense, in which the critics of Schutz have a point. Depicting Till is not a problem, but *using* Till to garner profit and acclaim would be. There are also serious questions about differing access to museum

Lionel Shriver GL Portrait/Alamy

exploring the perspectives of many different kinds of characters.

What Shriver ignored was the exploitation 25 question. Chris Cleave, if his portrayal is rich and well-researched, may produce a novel that isn't *disrespectful* toward Nigerians. Yet it's still bizarre and unfair that the people who write bestselling books about the lives of Nigerian girls aren't . . . Nigerian girls. An author is welcome to use whatever source material produces the best art. But when we talk about cultural exploitation we're not just talking about "writing" as a pastime. We're talking about the publishing industry, where people make *money* from writing, and in that context it's fair to raise the question of whether packaging and selling the richness of African life, without Africa receiving any benefit, is exploitative. The goal is not to stop white people from writing about black lives, but to stop a racist economy from remunerating the white people who write about the lives rather than the black people who live them.

Once we clearly understand what the actual problems are, it's easy to see how free cultural exchange can occur without creating injustice. The problems are largely those of economics and respect, and if we evaluate cultural borrowing by these measures, we can get rid of the racism without getting rid of the borrowing itself. A few simple questions can help us think about specific cases: (1) Is there a historic record of exploitation between the appropriator and the originating group? (2) Is the originating group and its culture being celebrated, appreciated, and respected, or are they being degraded, mocked, and accessorized? (There's a difference between Eminem's genuine relationship to the environment of 8 Mile Road and his immersion in Detroit hip hop and, say, a person wearing a tacky, cruelly stereotypical, and cartoonish Mexican Halloween costume.) (3) Is the appropriator actually *claiming* to be the owner or innovator, or

space and artistic recognition: it's both fair and important to point out the ways in which certain people are given a platform to tell black stories while others aren't.

It was this dimension that novelist Lionel Shriver missed in her infamous "sombrero speech" at the Brisbane Writers Festival. Shriver, indignant at criticisms faced by white authors who write from the perspective of non-white characters, said that fiction was about "trying on other people's hats" and writers should be allowed to depict lives different from their own. (She did not exactly help win over her critics by choosing to illustrate the point by wearing a colorful sombrero.) Shriver cited the example of Chris Cleave's *Little Bee*, which is written from the perspective of a 14-year-old Nigerian girl even though Cleave himself is white, male, and British. Shriver suggested that the "hypersensitive" left was cramping the authorial imagination, by prohibiting writers from allowing the media to create a **false origin narrative**? (E.g., Elvis as the "King" or Miley Cyrus's "invention" of twerking.) (4) Is differential economic enrichment occurring? Is the cultural product more valuable in the hands of the appropriator, and does that have wider financial or political consequences for certain groups?

Both the concept of cultural appropriation and the backlash to it are, to use a popular term, "problematic." Rigid ideas of cultural ownership would

lead us to absurdity, but profiteering and cultural disrespect are important to recognize. If we embrace a strict prohibition on borrowing, as Kenan Malik says, we wouldn't get Elvis Presley. But if we don't recognize how racial inequities structure the success of different cultural products, we might lapse into an even worse fate: listening to Elvis's version of "Hound Dog" rather than Big Mama Thornton's.

false origin narrative: a story that misrepresents the historical origin of a practice or object to the benefit of the one(s) creating the narrative and the detriment of the individual or group that created the practice or object.

RESPOND•

1. Gray obviously relies on a series of definitions, specifically of the terms *cultural exploitation, exploitation,* and *cultural disrespect.* How does she define each? What sort(s) of definition does she offer for each? How effective are these definitions in clarifying for readers her understanding of these concepts and distinguishing among them? How do they contribute to her argument? (See Chapter 9 for a discussion of kinds of definitions.)

2. Ultimately, Gray uses these definitions to offer a set of questions—criteria—that can be used as the basis of an evaluative argument about whether cultural exchange is occurring "without creating injustice." Do her criteria follow directly from her definitions of exploitation and cultural disrespect? Why or why not? Do you find her criteria useful in thinking about this set of issues? Why or why not? (See Chapter 10 on evaluative arguments, including criteria of evaluation.)

3. How do Gray's criteria for evaluation compare with those given by Jess Kapadia in the previous selection, "I Still Don't Understand the Cultural Appropriation of Food"? Given their criteria and examples, how do you think each might respond to the quotation given above in the gloss for "When two white women shut down their Portland burrito truck"? Why?

4. **THINKING CRITICALLY**   In what ways does Gray's argument complicate Kapadia's argument in the previous selection, "I Still Don't Understand the Cultural Appropriation of Food"? That is, how does Gray seek to demonstrate that the issues may be larger than food alone and the ability of prepare it, whether for one's own consumption or as a commercial venture? Which aspects of each argument do you find most compelling? Least compelling? Why?

5. As noted about this selection and the previous one by Kapadia, these Internet texts are part of ongoing conversations. Gray is, in some ways, in conversation with Kenan Malik, whose original comments <http://nyti.ms/2sB1OpJ> and response to Gray <http://bit.ly/2C0HfUk> are readily available. Read this trio of pieces—Malik's original observations, Grey's response, and Malik's response to Gray—and **write an evaluative argument** in which you evaluate the arguments supporting and criticizing what is generally referred to as cultural appropriation with a focus on foodways while acknowledging that examples from other cultural domains may be relevant. (See Chapter 10 on evaluative arguments, especially the section on developing an evaluative argument and the guide to writing an evaluation.)

▼ Hunger on Campus: The Challenge of Food Insecurity for College Students *is a 2016 research report written by James Dubick, Brandon Mathews, and Clare Cady. James Dubick is Director at the National Student Campaign Against Hunger and Homelessness (NSCAHH), while Brandon Mathews is the Associate Director of the College and University Food Bank Alliance (CUFBA). Clare Cady is codirector and cofounder of CUFBA. The report was a project of four organizations: CUFBA, NSCAHH, the Student Government Resource Center, and the Student Public Interest Research Groups. Gathering data from thirty-four campuses representing a range of colleges and universities across the nation, the study seeks to document the extent and consequences of food insecurity among students. Although, as explained, the results are not generalizable to the population of college and university students as a whole, they are indicative of sorts of problems many U.S. undergraduates face with respect to food insecurity. The original report also examined housing insecurity, but the excerpt presented here includes only those parts focusing on food insecurity. Likewise, we have not reprinted the appendices on methodology or resources for food-insecure students. The entire report is available at http://bit.ly/2jrwMJk. As you read the selection, consider how aware you are of issues related to food insecurity on your own campus or in the area where you live.*

Hunger on Campus: The Challenge of Food Insecurity for College Students

JAMES DUBICK, BRANDON MATHEWS, CLARE CADY

FOOD INSECURITY IS COMMON AMONG COLLEGE STUDENTS

The most recent data indicate that 14 percent of U.S. households experience some form of food insecurity each year.[1] No comprehensive national research has been conducted to firmly establish the prevalence of food insecurity among college students, but available literature suggests that the rate of food insecurity among college students is up to four times greater than the national average.[2]

Local studies performed at individual colleges and university systems in recent years have documented extensive food insecurity among college students at those institutions.

- The Wisconsin HOPE Lab, a leading research lab at the University of Wisconsin that aims to increase college attainment, studied Wisconsin **Pell Grant** recipients in 2008 and 2009 and found that 71 percent of Pell recipients reported

---

Pell Grant: a form of financial aid provided by the United States government for undergraduates with demonstrated financial need. Unlike loans, Pell Grants generally do not need to be repaid.

Melissa Phillip/AP Images

changing their eating habits due to lack of funds; 27 percent said that were eating less than they should or cutting meal sizes; and 7 percent of two-year college students reported going an entire day without food.[3]

- A 2011 study done at the City University of New York (CUNY) system found that 39 percent of respondents were food insecure.[4]

- A 2014 study found that 59 percent of students at Western Oregon University had experienced food insecurity at some point over the span of a year.[5]

- A 2015 study by the Wisconsin HOPE Lab surveyed students at 10 community colleges and found that 19 percent of students were experiencing low food security and 20 percent were experiencing very low food security.[6]

- A separate 2015 study by the Wisconsin HOPE Lab surveyed low- and moderate-income students at 10 Wisconsin colleges and universities and found that 61 percent were food insecure at some point during the school year.[7]

- In July 2016, the University of California published the results of a survey conducted across their 10-campus system. They found that 23 percent of students were experiencing low food security and another 19 percent were experiencing very low food security.[8]

- Also in 2016, a study at California State University, Long Beach found that 24 percent of students were in some way food insecure.[9]

Currently, one of the challenges in interpreting these studies is the variation in the way food insecurity was measured from study to study. While the literature does not provide a clear overall picture of the prevalence of student food insecurity, it plainly indicates that food insecurity affects many U.S. college students.

SURVEY OF FOOD INSECURITY ON THIRTY-FOUR CAMPUSES

To better understand the extent and consequences of food insecurity for college students, four organizations—the College and University Food Bank Alliance, the National Student Campaign Against Hunger and Homelessness, the Student Government Resource Center, and the Student Public Interest Research Groups—surveyed college students at 34 community colleges and four-year colleges in 12 states.

HOW FOOD INSECURITY WAS EVALUATED

Staff and volunteers of the organizations used face-to-face outreach to collect 3,765 surveys from March through May 2016. At most schools, this was done by setting up an information table and asking students to stop and fill out a survey on food issues. At schools where this approach was not an option, students handed out leaflets with the survey website in classrooms.

The participating schools included 8 community colleges and 26 four-year colleges. The collected surveys represent roughly 0.5 percent of the student population at the participating schools. The gender, racial, and ethnic breakdown of survey respondents closely aligns with students enrolled at these particular campuses. However, the sample is more heavily weighted toward younger students and students of color than the national student population.

The U.S. Department of Agriculture measures food security along a scale from "high food security" to "very low food security," with three categories to indicate levels of food insecurity.

- **"Moderate food security"** describes households with some level of concern or challenge in accessing quality food without significant decreases in quality, variety, or quantity.
- **"Low food security"** describes households where quality, variety, and desirability are negatively impacted, but quantity is not.
- **"Very low food security"** indicates decreases in all areas (quality, variety, desirability, quantity) as well as disrupted eating patterns due to inability to access adequate food.[10]

The survey assessed the food security level of the respondents using the questions provided in the U.S. Department of Agriculture's Adult Food Security Survey Module.[11] Based on their responses to these questions, respondents were given a score of zero through ten. Their food security status was then determined based on their score:

- Score of zero—High food security
- Score of 1–2—Marginal food security
- Score of 3–5—Low food security
- Score of 6–10—Very low food security

Students with a score of three or more were considered "food insecure." Students with a score of six or more were considered to be "very food insecure" and likely to be suffering from hunger.

STUDENT FOOD INSECURITY IS WIDESPREAD

Of the respondents, 48 percent qualified as food insecure in the previous 30 days. That figure includes 22 percent who qualified as hungry, meaning they experienced very low food security. [10]

When comparing these findings to existing research on student food insecurity, the rates of low and very low food security are in keeping with other studies. However, this report found a lower than normal percentage of respondents who qualify as highly food secure, which may suggest that the survey oversampled students with a tendency toward food insecurity.

In their answers to the survey questions, respondents expressed significant concern both about their

TABLE 1: Food Security Level of Survey Respondents in Last 30 Days

FOOD SECURITY SCORE	
Zero (High food security)	31%
1–2 (Marginal food security)	21%
3–5 (Low food security)	26%
6–10 (Very low food security)	22%

TABLE 2: Responses to Initial Food Security Questions, Last 30 Days

	SOMETIMES TRUE	*OFTEN TRUE*
I worried whether my food would run out before I got money to buy more.	38%	16%
The food that I bought just didn't last, and I didn't have money to get more.	35%	11%
I couldn't afford to eat balanced meals.	36%	18%

ability to afford food and their ability to afford nutritious food. . . .

Respondents who showed signs of food insecurity in these initial questions were then asked a series of follow-up questions. Forty-four percent said that they had been forced to cut back on the size of their meals or skip meals entirely in the last 30 days due to lack of money, and 35 percent said that they were hungry but didn't eat because there wasn't enough money for food (see Table 3).

In addition, a significant percentage reported more severe levels of food insecurity. Twenty percent of these survey-takers reported having skipped eating for an entire day due to lack of money in the last 30 days, and 15 percent said that they had lost weight in the last 30 days because they couldn't afford to eat.

When the study looked at responses by demo- 15 graphic groups, the results showed that food insecurity was more prevalent among the students of color who participated in the survey. Students who identified as "Hispanic or Latino" or "Black or African American" were more likely to be food insecure and much more likely to experience very low food security.

The study also found that 56 percent of **first-generation students** were food insecure, compared to 45 percent of students whose parents did attend college.

TABLE 3: Responses to Food Security Follow-Up Questions, Last 30 Days

	YES
Did you ever cut the size of your meals or skip meals because there wasn't enough money for food?	44%
Did you ever eat less than you felt you should because there wasn't enough money for food?	43%
Were you ever hungry but didn't eat because there wasn't enough money for food?	35%
Did you lose weight because there wasn't enough money for food?	15%
Did you ever not eat for a whole day because there wasn't enough money for food?	20%

Note: The sample for these questions was made up of respondents who answered "sometimes true" or "often true" to one of the initial food security questions listed in Table 2.

TABLE 4: Food Security Levels by Race/Ethnicity and Parental Education

	FOOD SECURITY LEVEL			
	High	Marginal	Low	Very Low
RACE/ETHNICITY				
White	38%	21%	23%	17%
Asian	34%	22%	28%	17%
Hispanic or Latino	22%	22%	31%	25%
Black or African American	22%	23%	29%	28%
PARENTAL EDUCATION				
Neither parent attended college	22%	21%	25%	31%
At least one parent attended some college	34%	22%	26%	19%

Percentages may not add to 100 due to rounding.

first-generation students: students whose parents or guardians did not attend or graduate from college.

TABLE 5: Food Insecurity among All Respondents at Community Colleges and Four-Year Schools

	COMMUNITY COLLEGE	FOUR-YEAR COLLEGE
Food insecure	50%	47%
Very food insecure	25%	20%

The food insecure category includes respondents who had low or very low food insecurity.

Food insecurity was moderately more prevalent among the community college students in the study. Twenty-five percent of community college students qualified as very food insecure, compared to 20 percent at four-year schools.

Community colleges serve a wider range of non-traditional students and are often seen as a more affordable pathway to higher education, so it's not surprising that community college students are more likely to be financially insecure and thus vulnerable to food insecurity. . . .

Food Insecurity Harms Students' Education

Food insecurity on college campuses has a negative impact on the educational experience. It's hard to concentrate in class or to focus on your studies when you're hungry or worrying about financial obstacles. Whether due to nutritional deficits or the stress and distraction of dealing with financial hardship,[12] food insecurity can compromise students' ability to perform well in their classes.[13] In extreme cases, food insecurity can force students to take time off from school or discontinue their education entirely.

In one recent survey of food insecure students at the University of Massachusetts, Boston, 80 percent of respondents reported that their food insecurity affected their class performance. More than 55 percent indicated that food insecurity 20

TABLE 6: Educational Impact of Food and Housing Insecurity on Food Insecure Students, Last 12 Months

	YES
Have hunger or housing problems had an impact on your education?	32%
HAVE HUNGER OR HOUSING PROBLEMS CAUSED YOU TO DO ANY OF THE FOLLOWING?*	
Done any of the following	86%
Miss a class	53%
Miss a study session	54%
Miss a club meeting	37%
Opt not to join an extracurricular activity	55%
Not buy a required textbook	55%
Drop a class	25%
Not perform as well in your academics as you otherwise could have	81%

*Asked only of students who responded "yes" to the previous question about educational impact.

compromised their ability to attend classes, and four percent stated that they had to forego college for one or more semesters due to food or housing insecurity.[14]

Of the food insecure students surveyed for this report, 32 percent believed that hunger or housing problems had an impact on their education. When asked about the impact caused by their hunger and housing problems, 55 percent reported that these problems caused them to not buy a required textbook, 53 percent reported missing a class, and 25 percent reported dropping a class.

Food Insecurity Persists Despite Students' Efforts

Food insecurity is a problem even for students who participate in a campus meal plan, are employed, or seek other financial or material help.

STUDENTS WITH CAMPUS MEAL PLANS ARE NOT IMMUNE TO FOOD INSECURITY

Ideally, participating in a meal plan with a campus dining hall would eliminate the threat of food insecurity. Responses from students at four-year universities (community colleges generally do not have dining programs) show that this is not necessarily the case. Forty-three percent of students who were enrolled in a campus meal plan were still food insecure.

To understand this finding, consider the way that campus meal plans are structured. At most universities, students have several options for the number of meals to buy as part of their meal plan. For example, many students choose to buy a plan with 7 or 14 meals per week and then find their remaining meals someplace else, either because they want to have more variety in their eating options, they don't want to pay for a larger meal plan, or they can't afford a larger meal plan.[15]

Fifty-six percent of meal plan enrollees reported eating nine meals or fewer per week in the dining hall. Not surprisingly, meal plan enrollees who were food insecure tended to eat less often in the dining hall— 69 percent reported eating nine meals or fewer there per week. In addition, 46 percent of food insecure students reported having run out of meal points before the end of the term at some time in the past, compared to 33 percent of all students on a meal plan.

It seems clear that access to a dining hall meal plan is not necessarily a cure for food insecurity.

THE MAJORITY OF FOOD INSECURE STUDENTS ARE EMPLOYED

Since financial problems are at the root of most food security issues, the survey asked food insecure students about their employment situation.

The study found that 56 percent of food insecure students were currently employed. Of those employed students, 38 percent worked 20 hours or more per week.

TABLE 7: Food Insecurity among Campus Meal Plan Enrollees at Four-Year Colleges

MEAL PLAN ENROLLEES AT FOUR-YEAR COLLEGES	YES	
Experiencing food insecurity	43%	
	ALL STUDENTS ON MEAL PLAN	FOOD INSECURE STUDENTS ON MEAL PLAN
Have you ever run out of meal points before the end of the term?	33%	46%
MEALS EATEN PER WEEK AT DINING HALL		
Less than 5 meals	24%	31%
5–9 meals	32%	38%
10–14 meals	30%	22%
15 or more meals	13%	9%

TABLE 8: Employment among Food Insecure Students

	YES
Currently employed	56%
HOURS WORKED PER WEEK*	
Less than 5 hours	9%
5–9 hours	17%
10–14 hours	20%
15–19 hours	17%
20–24 hours	14%
25–29 hours	10%
30–34 hours	6%
35–39 hours	3%
40 hours or more	5%

*This sample consisted of food insecure students who were currently employed. Percentages may not add to 100 due to rounding.

TABLE 9: Financial Aid Use among Food Insecure Students

	RECEIVED THIS ACADEMIC YEAR
Received any of the following	75%
Pell Grant	52%
Other government grant (FSEOG, TEACH, etc.)	15%
Private scholarship	18%
Stafford Loan	24%
Other government loan (Perkins Loan, etc.)	24%
Private (e.g., bank) loan	9%
Other aid	24%

TABLE 10: Student Loan Debt among Food Insecure Students

STUDENT LOANS TAKEN OUT TO DATE	
No Loans	45%
$1–$4,999	11%
$5,000–$9,999	12%
$10,000–$14,999	7%
$15,000–$19,999	4%
$20,000–$24,999	4%
$25,000–$29,999	2%
$30,000–$39,999	3%
$40,000–$49,000	2%
$50,000 or more	3%
Don't know	7%

Most Food Insecure Students Receive Financial Aid

Given the wide range of financial aid programs available to students, the study investigated whether food insecure students are utilizing these programs. The study found that 75 percent of food insecure students received some form of financial aid. Fifty-two percent reported receiving Pell Grants during the current academic year and 37 percent reported taking out student loans.

The study also asked food insecure students how much student debt they had accumulated during their academic career. Forty-eight percent reported having some level of student debt.

Utilizing Assistance Programs Does Not Eliminate Food Insecurity

There is a wide range of services available to assist students in need, ranging from local food banks and pantries to government programs like SNAP (food stamps). However, some students may not be taking advantage of these services, possibly because they are unaware of some programs, are intimidated by the enrollment process, or are avoiding these programs due to social stigma.[16]

The survey asked students about their use of more than a dozen available benefits and found that 61 percent of food insecure students reported that their household had taken advantage of at least one aid service in the past 12 months. The survey asked about a wide range of benefits, with the assumption that any benefits that address poverty might help to reduce food insecurity.

The most widely used services were public benefit programs like Medicaid, which was used by 28 percent, and the Supplemental Nutrition Assistance Program (SNAP), which was used by 25 percent. These usage rates are comparable with those found by other recent research on food insecure students.[17]

In terms of other food programs, seventeen percent of food insecure students reported utilizing a campus food pantry, while 14 percent reported going to an off-campus food pantry or food bank.

Given these low rates of usage, it's likely that many of the food insecure students in the study are missing out on benefits for which they would be eligible, including easily accessed services like local food banks.

TABLE 11: Use of Available Services by Food Insecure Students and Their Households, Last 12 Months

SERVICES USED	
Used any of the following	61%
SNAP (food stamps)	25%
WIC (nutritional assistance for pregnant women and children)	8%
Free or reduced-price school meals	20%
Campus food pantry	17%
Off-campus food pantry or food bank	14%
Home in a public housing project	5%
Public housing voucher	4%
Utility assistance	6%
TANF (welfare)	6%
SSI (social security)	11%
SSDI (disability)	7%
Medicaid or public health insurance	28%
Child care assistance	5%
Unemployment compensation/insurance	6%
Transportation assistance (discounted transit fares, dial-a-ride, etc.)	12%
Tax refunds based on low-income tax credits	18%
Tax refunds based on higher education tax credits	11%
Veteran's benefits	4%

It is also worth noting that use of these services was not exclusive to food insecure students. For example, nine percent of food secure respondents reported making use of SNAP in the past 12 months. This suggests that there may be some students who are at risk but have managed to avoid food insecurity by utilizing SNAP and other available services.

Conclusions

This study's findings paint a picture of campus food insecurity that raises deep concerns. The data suggests that a large segment of the student population—nearly 50 percent—may be food insecure, and that life

for these food insecure students is full of financial hardship and educational roadblocks.

There are many reasons for such a high percentage of students to experience food insecurity. Today's college students are expected to pay both their living expenses and the cost of their education, all at a time when their income is limited because their classes make it difficult to work full-time. The inevitable result of high expenses and low income is poverty. While financial aid is meant to cover the difference, it regularly falls short. For example, the Pell Grant—the premier aid program for low-income students—no longer provides the level of financial assistance necessary to meet most students' needs.[18]

Additionally, this study suggests that the majority of food insecure students are struggling to make ends meet despite working or reaching out for assistance. Seventy-five percent report receiving some form of financial aid, 56 percent report working while going to school, and 61 percent report taking advantage of benefit programs like SNAP.

When a student can receive financial aid and earn a part-time salary and still not be able to afford adequate, nutritious food, our educational system is failing to provide that student with a viable path to success in their higher education. Moreover, the students who often need support the most—first-generation college students and students of color—appear to be the most likely to be food and housing insecure.

Ultimately, the findings of this study highlight the need for additional research to explore a number of important questions in greater depth. A better understanding of this issue is needed in order to develop comprehensive solutions. The most compelling questions that demand scrutiny include:

- What percentage of U.S. students actually experience food insecurity?

- Which are the largest factors contributing to food insecurity among college students? What can be done to prevent these risks?

40

- How can we increase the number of food insecure students who utilize the existing safety net of services?

- Which services or combination of services are the most effective in meeting these students' needs?

- What is the impact of food insecurity on students' educational success?

- What is the combined impact of food and housing insecurity?

- How do we specifically reduce food insecurity among students of color and first-generation students?

- Do food insecure students continue to be food insecure after graduation?

RECOMMENDATIONS

The growing awareness of hunger and food insecurity on college campuses has triggered a national conversation in higher education over how to assist students in overcoming these challenges. Reducing the number of food insecure students will require action by colleges, universities, and policymakers.

RECOMMENDATIONS FOR COLLEGES AND UNIVERSITIES

For colleges and universities, the task of improving student retention and completion is only becoming more difficult. Fortunately, college and university administrations, student organizations, and nonprofit organizations are pioneering a wide range of programs designed to support food insecure students.

Schools are also becoming creative in finding ways to fund these new programs, with support coming variously from the universities themselves, student governments, alumni associations, local businesses, and charitable foundations.

Programs That Promote Food Security

Colleges and universities should support and develop 45 on-campus programs that directly address food insecurity. The following are examples of successful programs that schools should replicate.

- **Campus Food Pantries**   One of the fastest growing movements to combat hunger on college campuses is the development of campus food pantries. In 2009, fewer than ten campus food pantries existed; today there are more than 350.[19] Because of their flexibility in operating styles and limited need for physical infrastructure, campus food pantries can be easy to establish. On-campus pantries are easier for students to utilize, since they don't require students to travel off campus to receive food benefits. In addition, because the food pantry is a campus-run program, students seem more likely to utilize its services because they see it as a student resource rather than a community program.

- **Food Recovery Programs**   Programs like the Food Recovery Network[20] and the Campus Kitchens Project[21] collect unused food from campus dining halls and other sources, then utilize on-campus kitchen space to repurpose this food into ready-to-eat meals that can be donated to the campus food pantry or an off-campus food program. In addition to reducing food waste and stocking local food programs, one benefit of these food recovery programs is that they provide students with ready-made meals that just need warming.

- The MEANS mobile app offers a different model for food recovery. Their online system allows restaurants, dining halls, and other food donors to post a notice when they have excess food available. Local food pantries and food banks, including campus food pantries, can then claim the excess food, at which time they are given the contact information of the donor and can schedule a time to pick up the surplus food.[22]

- Another approach seeks to make use of excess food from catered events on campus. At California State University, Fresno, for example, the Catered

Cupboard mobile app notifies students when an on-campus catered event ends and there is leftover food available.[23]

- **Dining Center Meal Donations**   Many campus dining hall meal plans provide students with a set number of pre-paid meal dollars or points to spend. If students have unused points at the end of the term, those points are usually lost. At many schools, programs like Swipe Out Hunger have helped students and dining halls create systems where students can donate some of their extra meal points.[24] Depending on the agreement made with the dining hall, these donated points are converted to money that is then given to a local anti-hunger charity, converted to food that is given to local food programs, or used to fund dining hall vouchers for food insecure students.[25]

- **Improving Access to Benefits**   Students often do not know where or how to access benefit programs that could provide them with valuable assistance with needs like food, child care, rent, utilities, and medical care. Programs like Single Stop set up a campus location where students can stop in to learn about available benefits.[26] Trained staff or volunteers help students find out if they qualify for benefit programs, then assist them with the application process. At Oregon State University, the Human Services Resource Center was established to offer many of the services described in this section, including providing students with assistance in applying for benefits.[27]

- **SNAP Retailer on Campus**   A small number of colleges and universities have started the process to be able to accept SNAP dollars (food stamps) in their campus stores, but the regulatory requirements are extensive. Oregon State University and Humboldt State University are the only two schools that appear to have succeeded so far. At OSU, for example, students can now use their Oregon Trail Card (state-issued benefits card) to buy groceries at the on-campus Cascadia Market.[28]

- **Campus Community Gardens**   Campus community gardens provide a way to increase students' access to fresh produce while also giving students a hands-on way to address food insecurity, build community, and learn agricultural skills. Once established, campus gardens can easily be integrated into existing food programs by providing produce to the campus dining halls or food pantry. At the University of Arkansas, the campus community garden is hosted by Gro-Green, a student organization, and donates half of its yield to the Jane B. Gearhart Food Pantry on campus.[29]

- **Campus Farmers Markets**   On-campus farmers markets provide another way to increase students' access to fresh produce, providing them with an additional source for healthy, affordable food. For example, at Humboldt State University, the student-run Oh SNAP! program hosts a weekly farm stand on campus.[30] Campus farmers markets can do even more to support food insecure students by participating in the national "Double Bucks" program, through which farmers markets provide a $1-for-$1 match for SNAP recipients to buy fresh produce. The University of Utah Farmers Market, a mostly student-run operation that provides fresh produce for sale on campus and to the dining hall, is one of several on-campus farmers markets that already participate in Double Bucks.[31]

RECOMMENDATIONS FOR POLICYMAKERS

While colleges and universities should take immediate steps to support their students, some changes are beyond their reach. Federal policymakers should take the following steps to improve the situation for food insecure students.

- **Add Food Security Measurement to the NPSAS**
The National Center for Education Statistics implements the National Postsecondary Student Aid Study (NPSAS) each year to examine the characteristics of the nation's college students, with special focus on how they finance their education. Adding food security questions to the list of issues assessed by the NPSAS would provide policymakers and researchers with the data to determine the true prevalence of student food insecurity and assess potential solutions.[32]

- **Simplify the FAFSA** The Free Application for Federal Student Aid (FAFSA) is the form that determines a student's eligibility for federal financial aid programs. Completing the FAFSA can be an unnecessarily confusing and intimidating process for students. The FAFSA includes up to 136 questions, including detailed questions about income and assets that are difficult to document and often have little or no impact on a student's eligibility for aid. There are an estimated two million students currently enrolled in college who are eligible for a Pell Grant but never applied for aid, likely because they were intimidated by the process or did not know that aid was available.[33] In order to ensure that students receive the aid they deserve, the FAFSA should be simplified to remove unnecessary questions, particularly for the applicants with the greatest need.[34]

- **Expand the SNAP Eligibility Requirements for College Students** College students who are enrolled in school at least half-time are ineligible for SNAP unless they meet certain exceptions (for example, having a child under the age of six or working at least 20 hours per week).[35] These restrictions prevent many students from utilizing SNAP, even though they meet the program's income eligibility thresholds and could benefit from the program. SNAP eligibility requirements should be simplified for students and the rules should be adjusted to remove the work requirement for full-time students.[36]

- **Improve the Aid Process for Homeless Students**
The federal financial aid process provides particular obstacles for homeless students, which can cause them to miss out on aid entirely. These students often face a confusing system which bounces them between high school and college administrators. At both levels, administrators are often confused about their authority to verify a student's homeless status or what type of documentation to require. This bureaucratic nightmare can cause students to miss filing deadlines and be denied aid, preventing them from attending college. Clear guidelines should be provided to financial aid administrators and students to explain the process and students should be given easy access to government records that can help establish their homeless status.[37]

In addition, the process becomes more difficult with each subsequent year, as it typically becomes harder for students to provide documentation of their homeless status the longer they are in college. The process should be changed to eliminate the need for yearly redetermination of a student's homeless status.[38]

ENDNOTES

1. U.S. Department of Agriculture, "Food Security in the U.S.: Key Statistics & Graphics," September 8, 2015, http://www.ers.usda.gov/topics/food-nutrition-assistance/food-security-in-the-us/key-statistics-graphics.aspx.

2. Clare Cady, "Food Insecurity as a Student Issue," Journal of College and Character, no. 4 (2014), 265–271, doi:10.1515/jcc-2014-0031.

3. Katharine Broton et al., Wisconsin HOPE Lab, "Safety, Security, and College Attainment: An Investigation of Undergraduates' Basic Needs and Institutional Response," October 2014, http://www.wihopelab.com/publications/APPAM.Draft.10.28.2014.pdf.

4. Nicholas Freudenberg, Healthy CUNY Initiative, "Food Insecurity at CUNY: Results from a Survey of CUNY Undergraduate Students," April 2011, http://bit.ly/1MkQ2Vx.

5. Megan Patton-Lopez et al., Western Oregon University, "Prevalence and Correlates of Food Insecurity among Students Attending a Midsize Rural University in Oregon," http://ir.library.oregonstate.edu/xmlui/bitstream/handle/1957/45177/PattonLopez_JNEB_foodinsecurity_11414.pdf.

6. Sara Goldrick-Rab et al., Wisconsin HOPE Lab, "Hungry to Learn: Addressing Food & Housing Insecurity Among Undergraduates," December 2015, http://www.wihopelab.com/publications/Wisconsin_HOPE_Lab_Hungry_To_Learn.pdf.

7. Wisconsin HOPE Lab, "What We're Learning: Food and Housing Insecurity among College Students: A Data Update from the Wisconsin HOPE Lab," January 13, 2016, http://bit.ly/2dHI8L1.

8. Suzanna Martinez et al., University of California Global Food Initiative, "Student Food Access and Security Study," July 11, 2016, http://regents.universityofcalifornia.edu/regmeet/july16/e1attach.pdf.

9. Rashida Crutchfield, California State University, "Serving Displaced and Food Insecure Students in the CSU," January 2016, http://www.calstate.edu/AcadAff/documents/ServingDisplacedandFoodInsecureStudetnsintheCSUJanuary20163.8.16.pdf.

10. U.S. Department of Agriculture, "Definitions of Food Insecurity," September 8, 2015, http://www.ers.usda.gov/topics/food-nutrition-assistance/food-security-in-the-us/definitions-of-foodsecurity.aspx.

11. U.S. Department of Agriculture Economic Research Service, "U.S. Adult Food Security Survey Module: Three-Stage Design, With Screeners," September 2012, http://www.ers.usda.gov/datafiles/Food_Security_in_the_United_States/Food_Security_Survey_Modules/ad2012.pdf.

12. Roger Hughes et al., "Student Food Insecurity: The Skeleton in the University Closet," Nutrition and Dietetics 2001, 68: 27–32.

13. Maya E. Maroto, "Food Insecurity among Community College Students: Prevalence and Association with GPA, Energy, and Concentration," Community College Journal of Research and Practice, 39(6), 515–526.

14. Meghan R. Silva et al., "The Relationship Between Food Security, Housing Stability, and School Performance among College Students in an Urban University," Journal of College Student Retention: Research, Theory & Practice, 1521025115621918, December 14, 2015, doi:10.1177/1521025115621918.

15. Sara Goldrick-Rab et al., The Century Foundation, "The Real Price of College," March 3, 2016, https://tcf.org/content/report/the-real-price-of-college.

16. Tara Bahrampour, "More College Students Battle Hunger as Education and Living Costs Rise," Washington Post, April 9, 2014, http://www.washingtonpost.com/local/more-college-studentsbattle-hunger-as-education-and-living-costs-rise/2014/04/09/60208db6-bb63-11e3-9a05-c739f29ccb08_story.html.

17. Sara Goldrick-Rab et al., Wisconsin HOPE Lab, "Hungry to Learn: Addressing Food & Housing Insecurity Among Undergraduates," December 2015, http://www.wihopelab.com/publications/Wisconsin_HOPE_Lab_Hungry_To_Learn.pdf.

18. Sara Goldrick-Rab et al., Wisconsin HOPE Lab, "Hungry to Learn: Addressing Food & Housing Insecurity Among Undergraduates," December 2015, http://www.wihopelab.com/publications/Wisconsin_HOPE_Lab_Hungry_To_Learn.pdf.

19. College and University Food Bank Alliance, "Our Members," http://bit.ly/2dpDhhx.

20. Food Recovery Network, "About Us," http://bit.ly/2dpEA0c.

21. The Campus Kitchens Project, "How We Do It," http://bit.ly/1bziXNb.

22. MEANS, "About," http://www.meansdatabase.com/about.

23. Fresno State University Food Security Project, "Catered Cupboard," http://www.fresnostate.edu/studentaffairs/foodsecurity/mobile-app.html.

24. Swipe Out Hunger, "About," http://www.swipehunger.org/about.

25. Emma Miller, "Columbia University Unveils Plan to Feed Students Who Can't Afford to Eat," USA Today, September 22, 2015, http://usat.ly/1MHjDHN.

26. Single Stop, "Our Work," http://bit.ly/2dHUGC9.

27. Oregon State University Office of Student Life, "Human Services Resource Center," http://studentlife.oregonstate.edu/hsrc.

28. Oregon State University, "On-Campus Markets," http://bit.ly/2dpwrIV.

29. GroGreen, "GroGreen: UARK Community Garden," http://www.facebook.com/groups/151775711209/.

30. Humboldt State University Oh SNAP!, "HSU Farm Stand," http://www.hsuohsnap.org.

31. University of Utah Sustainability Resource Center, "U of U Farmers Market," http://sustainability.utah.edu/resource-center/get-involved/farmers-market.php.

32. Sara Goldrick-Rab and Christopher J. Nellum, Wisconsin HOPE Lab and American Council on Education, "Request to Add Measurement of Food Insecurity to the National Postsecondary Student Aid Study," http://bit.ly/2d15to9.

33. White House Office of the Press Secretary, "Fact Sheet: The President's Plan for Early Financial Aid: Improving College Choice and Helping More Americans Pay for College," September 13, 2015, http://bit.ly/2cR0Uta.

34. National Association of Student Financial Aid Administrators, "NASFAA FAFSA Working Group Report: FAFSA Simplification," July 2015, http://www.luminafoundation.org/files/resources/fafsa-simplification.pdf.

35. Elizabeth Lower-Basch and Helly Lee, Center for Law and Social Policy, "SNAP Policy Brief: College Student Eligibility," February 6, 2014, http://www.clasp.org/resources-and-publications/publication-1/SNAP_College-Student-Eligibility.pdf.

36. Sara Goldrick-Rab et al., Wisconsin HOPE Lab, "Hungry to Learn: Addressing Food & Housing Insecurity Among Undergraduates," December 2015, http://www.wihopelab.com/publications/Wisconsin_HOPE_Lab_Hungry_To_Learn.pdf.

37. U.S. Government Accountability Office, "Actions Needed to Improve Access to Federal Financial Assistance for Homeless and Foster Youth," May 2016, http://www.help.senate.gov/imo/media/doc/d16343.pdf.

38. National Association for the Education of Homeless Children and Youth, "Financial Aid for Unaccompanied Homeless Youth," 2014, http://www.naehcy.org/sites/default/files/dl/fafsasurvey-report.pdf.

RESPOND.

1. Research-based reports like this one are typically proposal arguments. They begin by stating a problem, offering definitions, presenting the data collected, analyzing and interpreting the data collected, and making representations. How does each of these steps relate to the kinds of argument we find in stasis theory? (See Chapter 1 for a discussion of stasis theory.)

2. How is the term *food insecurity* defined in this report? What sort of definition is given? Why is such a definition necessary for research? What are the advantages of such a definition over discussions framed in terms of hunger? (See Chapter 9 on kinds of definition.)

3. What was your response to the findings presented in this survey? Were they surprising at all? Do you think students, faculty, and administrators on your campus are aware of food insecurity as a challenge faced by many students nationwide? Why or why not? If they are, what has led to this awareness? If not, what might have led to this lack of awareness?

4. **THINKING CRITICALLY**   What is the purpose of the section entitled "Food Insecurity Persists Despite Students' Efforts"? How would the report have been different—and we might argue weaker—had this section not been included?

5. Investigate issues of food insecurity on your campus or in the area where you live. Is any recent information available about the current situation with regard to this challenge? Are there available resources to assist those who experience food insecurity? (Here, you may wish to consult the original report to get information about the sorts of resources they provide.) What might be done to deal with the situation? Depending on what you discover, you may wish to **write an argument of fact**, focusing on what you learn about the current situation; **an evaluative argument**, considering options for dealing with food insecurity; or **a proposal argument**, offering possible courses of action. (See Chapters 8, 10, and 12 on arguments of fact, evaluative arguments, and proposal arguments, respectively.)

25

How Does Language Influence Our World?

LEFT TO RIGHT: Michael Zagaris/Getty Images; The U.S. National Archives;
Alice Che/Shutterstock

Perhaps more than any other trait, language makes us human. Many animal species have complex systems of communication, but they don't have language—a system of communication that permits us to talk about the past, to imagine a future, and to create extremely complex individual and group identities for ourselves and others. Our language defines us in multiple ways. The way we speak or write comes to be part of our individual style. We don't expect someone who has lived their entire life in a small Ohio town to sound like someone who has grown up in Seattle—and usually, they don't. But as the selections in this chapter seek to demonstrate, the language we use and the language used about us define who we are and who we aren't, often in more subtle ways that generally go unnoticed.

In his blog posting, Ernie Smith weighs in on a currently heated debate about the English language, the shifting use of the pronoun *they*. Since speakers and writers of English have used it for centuries to refer to a single individual in certain cases—*If anyone needs a pencil, they can borrow mine*—can't and perhaps shouldn't that usage be extended to situations in which a known individual, for whatever reasons, does not wish to be referred to as *she* or *he*?

The well-known commentator and linguist John McWhorter tackles a different question, writing as an African American who doesn't "sound black." In addition to asking the basic question of what it might mean to "sound black" or "sound white" or sound anything, McWhorter wants readers to consider how we understand situations where individuals do not fit our stereotypes of how they should sound. How can thinking about these questions remind us that, indeed, we have stereotypes and we use them as a way of making sense of the world, sometimes in ways that ignore the complexity of reality before us?

Focusing on the power of labeling, a handbook produced by the Japanese American Citizens League challenges us to rethink what we've likely been taught about the experiences of Japanese Americans during World War II. From our history classes and popular culture, we may have learned that during the war, Japanese Americans were evacuated to relocation centers. How does our understanding of that narrative change if we use more direct and accurate language, stating that they were forcibly removed from their homes to American concentration camps? The chapter's visual argument uses maps showing the distribution of languages other than English in the United States to encourage us to think about linguistic diversity in this country and about maps as visual arguments.

Noted essayist, novelist, and comic-book writer Roxanne Gay challenges the press and readers to consider the ways in which the language generally used to characterize sexual violence fails to represent the reality of the situation, particularly for those who suffer such violence.

Finally, Jorge Encinas explains how the growing number of Latinos who are welcomed to the U.S. to play professional baseball—as well as the growing popularity of the game across Latin America—demonstrates the ways that major league baseball has traditionally not provided sufficient language support for these players, the forces at work to change that situation, and their consequences.

These selections provide evidence for the claim of rhetorician and philosopher Kenneth Burke that the words we choose select, reflect, and deflect particular views of reality, being arguments in themselves. The selections also invite you to consider the ways you likely take language for granted as you use it to construct identities and realities—yours and those of others.

▼ Ernie Smith is a social media journalist based in Washington, D.C. He is also the creator of the twice-weekly blog Tedium: The Dull Side of the Internet, which he founded in 2015. Like many online blog postings, this text is a sort of mash-up, combining not only Smith's words but information from other sources that work to complement and in some ways complete the argument. In this posting from August 2016, Smith takes on what in fact is a much-debated question about language these days, the use of they as a gender-neutral replacement for he and he or she in formal writing, such as the writing you do for college classes. While this argument has raged for decades, some basic facts are clear. Despite the grammatical problem of a plural pronoun being used for a singular subject, they has been used with indefinite pronouns like everyone, someone, and anyone in spoken English for centuries—for example, Has everyone got their homework? As Smith notes, such usage has shown up in writing as far back as Chaucer, in the fourteenth century. Smith explains how in different political and social climates, the use of they came to be considered wrong. While the use of they was much discussed during the 1970s with the rise of feminism, what has brought the debate to life again in this century is the desire of some transgender individuals (and their allies) to be referred to as they to avoid being gendered (or misgendered). Thus, rather than Eleanor forgot her book, many prefer to say Eleanor forgot their book in reference to a book that belongs to Eleanor, or Zach has lost their car keys in speaking about the keys of Zach's car. Such usage enables speakers to identify a subject (Eleanor, Zach) without forcing a gender upon that subject (she, he). As you read, you'll want to be thinking about both sets of situations—the campaign of earlier feminists and the current push by transgender individuals—and the reactions you have to them. Smith's piece also considers the role that copy editors ultimately have in determining what is acceptable in various written contexts. So, as you read, you'll also want to be thinking about how and why copy editors came to have such authority.

They Should Stop: In Defense of the Singular *They*

ERNIE SMITH

The "Cultural Contexts" box in Chapter 13 discusses the range of personal pronouns that are in use now.

LINK TO P. 326

"In the past year, new expressions of gender identity have generated a deal of discussion, and singular *they* has become a particularly significant element of that conversation. While many novel gender-neutral pronouns have been proposed, *they* has the advantage of already being part of the language."

—Ben Zimmer, the chairman of the New Words Committee of the American Dialect Society, discussing the group's decision to make the singular *they* its word of the year. The vote favored *they* in part because of *they*'s increasing importance as a way to make room for people who don't fit a predefined gender binary. (It helps that the word drops the added complication of *he or she*.)

IS THE SINGULAR *THEY* A PROBLEM THAT LINGUISTS CREATED FOR THEMSELVES?

For some word **purists**, the singular *they* is the linguistic equivalent of an ingrown hair, but for others, the solutions for getting around the problem are way messier.

For centuries, the singular *they* was not only accepted by the public but by some of our most famous authors—Geoffrey Chaucer, Jane Austen, and Shakespeare, just to name three.

But around the late 18th and early 19th century, something happened: Critics of the specific usage appeared. The reason for this critical reassessment came about partly out of **prescriptive** vibes around the English language at the time. Long story short: We wanted English to be more like Latin, and that meant rethinking the use of plural nouns in singular contexts.

In 1975, researcher Ann Bodine broke this down in a landmark paper, "**Androcentrism** in Prescriptive Grammar: Singular 'They,' Sex-Indefinite 'He,' and 'He or She.'" The text, republished in the 1999 book *The Feminist Critique of Language*, notes that the influence of Latin grammar played an important role in the increase of rules around modern grammar—and specifically gave the world the "**generic** *he*," a term that followed Latin form but didn't mesh with modern concerns about gender equality. She added that the then-recent attempts to ditch the generic *he* were really attempts to *roll back* a controversial change.

"Intentionally or not, the movement against **sex-indefinite** '***he***' is actually a **counter-** 5 **reaction** to an attempt by prescriptive grammarians to alter the language," she wrote.

And many of those grammarians who tried to remedy the problem caused by this attempt to make English more like Latin have tried to patch things up. For hundreds of years, English-speakers have tried to invent words that fill the English language's most unsightly gap. Nearly all of them have failed.

University of Illinois professor Dennis Baron, a longtime supporter of the singular *they*, has long maintained a list of gender-neutral pronouns that people have attempted to add to the English language, the most recent example from 2015, but most of the interesting ones from the 19th century. Terms like "thon," "e," and "um" were among the most prominent attempts to improve the language. Additionally, Baron notes, complaints about the common use of the singular *they* were fairly common during the 19th century.

---

purists: those who are committed to keeping a language pure from what they consider contamination of any kind, which would include changes in the language (although languages that are being spoken and written will always demonstrate evidence of change).

prescriptive: with respect to language, giving rules for how the language ought to be used. Purists are prescriptivists, who focus on rule giving, in contrast to *descriptivists*, who focus on describing how the language is, in fact, used. From a descriptivist point of view, the use of *they* with indefinite pronouns like *everyone* and *someone* is acceptable in all but the most formal of contexts because that is what most people do anyway.

androcentrism: being male-centered.

generic he: the use of *he* as the third-person singular pronoun when the apparent sex or gender of an individual is not clear. For example, *Every student must bring his book to class,* meaning that all students must bring their books to class, would be an example of using *he* generically.

sex-indefinite he: the same as generic *he* in contrast to *he* used to refer to specifically to a male or males.

counter-reaction: an effort to reverse something, frequently a move in a politically conservative direction; a reaction in response to another's reaction to an original stimulus.

interpose: to place oneself between.

"If only occasionally found in the best writings, it is because the proofreader **interposes** his correction before the sentence reaches the public, for every editor [knows] how often even careful writers make the mistake," a writer for the Findlay, Ohio, *Jeffersonian* wrote in 1877.

Baron, in introducing the concept in an essay, is quick to stick a knife in its heart before it even had a chance to fly:

> These pronouns fill a need, but none has been widely adopted, hence they are the words that failed. What has succeeded is singular *they*, which arose naturally in English hundreds of years ago, and is used both by speakers and writers concerned that their pronouns be inclusive, and also by many who don't give the matter much thought at all.

Over at the dearly departed site *The Toast*, linguist Gretchen McCulloch calls the root cause "a series of historical accidents," but suggests that the issues raised by grammarians are practical in nature, even if the solutions are in many ways worse than the problems in the first place.

It's an empty space for a broken term, but who broke it?

Identifying one's preferred pronouns is becoming more common. Alice Che/Shutterstock

unmarked: in linguistics, what is expected, usual, or regular. The unmarked word order in English is SUBJECT + VERB + OBJECT, for example, *The child ran into the room.*

Tunica: indigenous language of the United States spoken by the Tunica Indians of the Mississippi Valley. The last native speaker died in 1948.

FIVE LANGUAGE-WORLD STANCES ON THE SINGULAR *THEY*

1. *"The fact that the masculine is the **unmarked** gender in English (or that the feminine is unmarked in the language of the **Tunica** Indians) is simply a feature of grammar."* —A 1971 open letter in the *Harvard Crimson*, signed by 17 professors and teaching fellows, attempting to defend the use of gendered pronouns in the classroom, using history as a precedent for the thought process

2. *"From long habit, in any case,* **epicene** *he is comfortably read as 'he or she' without much extra thought: 'If a customer has a coupon, he can get a free ice cream cone' would not be interpreted by any literate person as limiting the deal to males."* —Iohannes Helonapë, a.k.a. "The Ozarks Latinist," making the case for the "generic *he*" from the perspective of a Latin teacher

3. *"Using 'their' for singular* **antecedents** *is one that I think people need to [just give into]. As I've argued, it only occurs in a very limited set of circumstances, and those circumstances very unlikely to produce confusion about what is meant."* —blogger and academic Freddie deBoer, discussing the limited use cases of the singular *their*

4. *"Saying that singular* they *has been used for centuries by respected writers, that it appears to follow fairly well-defined rules, and that the* **proscription** *against it is not based in linguistic fact is descriptive; saying that people need to get over their dislike and accept it is not."* —Linguist Jonathan Owen, who attempts to straddle the line between prescriptivism and descriptivism in a 2015 blog post <www.arrantpedantry.com/2015/03/04/why-descriptivists-are-usage-liberals> offering both sides of the singular *they* debate

5. *"Many* **ACES** *stalwarts—copy editors, journalists, grammarians, lexicographers, and linguists—stand ready to embrace the singular 'their.' But not us. We avoid it whenever we can."* —Mary Norris, the "comma queen" at *The New Yorker*, emphasizing the magazine's hardline stance against the singular *they*. Linguistics blogs had a field day with this comment.

254: The number of languages tracked by the World Atlas of Language Structures Online that do not make gender distinctions in their pronouns. Of the 378 examples listed on the atlas's website, roughly two-thirds, or 67 percent, have no gender distinctions at all for their pronouns, and those that do, like English, are most likely to use third-person singular pronouns along gender lines.

epicene: of indeterminate sex. An epicene pronoun would not indicate the sex of the person being referred to. In English, our first-person singular pronoun (*I*) and our second-person singular pronoun (*you*) are epicene; that is, they do not indicate the sex or gender of individuals about whom they are used. Some languages, however, have different first- and/or second-person pronouns for females and males to use.

antecedent: in grammar, the noun that a pronoun refers to. For example, in *Pierre brought his pet to class*, *Pierre* is the antecedent for the pronoun *his*.

proscription: a statement or rule stating what *not* to do. For example, *Don't say "ain't"* is a proscription. Proscriptions contrast with *prescriptions*, which are statements or rules stating what to do; for example, *Be sure that the subject and verb of a sentence agree in number* is a prescription.

ACES: the American Copy Editors Society, a professional organization for copy editors.

THE REAL SOLUTION TO THE SINGULAR *THEY* PROBLEM LIES IN THE HANDS OF COPY EDITORS

Last year, prominent *Washington Post* copy editor Bill Walsh (who was not a football coach for the San Francisco 49ers) drew a line in the sand in favor of the singular *they*, revealing in a deeply nerve-wracking blog post that he had been wanting to make the big change for years, despite how divisive it was for some.

"What finally pushed me from acceptance to action on gender-neutral pronouns was the increasing visibility of gender-neutral people," he wrote.

visceral: from the gut; related to deep feelings rather than the intellect.

Associated Press Stylebook: the manual of grammar and style used by journalists working with the Associated Press, a U.S.-based international news organization. Style manuals explain and illustrate various rules of grammar and usage that are to be used by writers and editors. Insofar as they tell writers and editors how to use the language, they are prescriptive.

more than *vs.* over: although most speakers of American English, even highly educated ones, often use these two interchangeably, until 2014, the *AP Stylebook* and purists claimed we should not—a prescriptivist stance. The *Stylebook* contended that *over* should be used only in references to relative size—for example, *She towered* over *her brother*—not in reference to numbers or quantities.

Oxford comma: so called because it is mandated by the Oxford University Press in Oxford, England; a comma used after the next-to-last element of a list and before the conjunction, as in this sentence: *Frankie brought the cake, the balloon, and the napkins.* A sentence without the Oxford comma would have no comma after *balloon.* Generally, in the United States, the Oxford comma is preferred.

Walsh, the author of some popular books read by copy editors, is seen as something of a trailblazer on this issue, even though he pledges his desk will use the term sparingly.

Problem is, it won't be easy to win over everyone else in the journalism world. The 15
issue is that many copy editors simply struggle with the conundrum that the word creates, some treating it as a pet peeve even though it's common in regular speech.

In a blog post last year, the *Baltimore Sun*'s John E. McIntyre noted the lingering controversy, citing one Facebook feed that called the singular *they* an "idiot epicene."

"I know any number of editors who share this **visceral** dislike of the singular *they*," McIntyre wrote. "It cuts no ice with them that linguists have demonstrated widespread use by reputable writers for centuries . . . or that we somehow contrive to use *you* in both singular and plural senses without growing red-faced and shouting."

Copy editors may never find peace on this issue, even though the American Copy Editors Society has been laying the groundwork for such a change, last January noting with positivity the American Dialect Society's move to make the singular *they* its word of the year.

Eventually, the **Associated Press Stylebook** will make a call on this grammatical controversy, like they did when it decided to allow **"more than" and "over"** to be used interchangeably. But I wonder to myself if they'll be the last ones to figure out that most non-journalists are pro-*they*.

(Hey, at least this piece isn't about the **Oxford comma**.)   20

Perhaps the most interesting comment on this whole issue, among the many items and eras I've quoted in this piece, comes not from a vintage study or an old academic paper, but from a *Christian Science Monitor* columnist who literally wrote about this very issue last week.

Ruth Walker, the writer of the publication's Verbal Energy feature, makes an astute comparison between grammar and "desire lines"—the pathways that people create on their own when the sidewalks prove inefficient paths.

Walker isn't exactly psyched about the singular *they* right now, but she sees the case for it going forward.

"Whatever the motivation, and however we feel about it, singular *they* is a kind of shortcut through the traditional grammar rules that is coming to be more accepted all the time," she wrote. "It's like that shortcut at the library—which rejoins the main path and may someday get paved."

The tide is turning on this terminology. Whoever is getting in the way of its progress, they should stop.   25

RESPOND.

1. Smith provides five "language-world stances" on the use of singular *they*. Which do you find most comfortable for you? Why is this stance more appealing than the others offered? Which is least appealing? Why? Given your preferred stance, how would you acknowledge the concerns of others while supporting your own position?

2. As noted, Smith's blog post exemplifies a mash-up, a genre in which an author pulls together bits of information—quotations or even visual elements from other texts, often adding commentary of their own. (By the way, did you notice that we used singular *they* in the previous sentence: **an author** . . . **their** own? We'll bet you didn't, although your instructor may have. In earlier editions of this textbook, we likely wouldn't have used *they* but *his or her* instead. Our practice reflects how the language is changing.) How do the various parts of Smith's post work together to create an argument? What does each contribute? What, if anything, would be missing if any of the pieces of the posting had not been included?

3. Of course, the current support for singular *they* is not the first time that efforts have been made to alter how English is used. As Smith notes, grammarians during the eighteenth century, in particular, sought to shape the language in certain ways (and were highly successful with regard to standardized written English in a number of ways). Likewise, supporters of feminism and gender equality in the 1970s began using *he and she* and finding other alternatives permitting them to avoid generic *he*. They also introduced the use of *Ms.*, which has led to the almost total disappearance of *Miss* and the greatly reduced use of *Mrs.* Today, most users of English understand the use of *he* not to be a generic and assume those who use it that way are sexist, and many women, married or single, use *Ms.* These facts are evidence that language can and does change and that users can intervene to seek to alter how a language is used and understood. How do these

facts challenge prescriptivist views of language that dictate the "correct" way of using language?

4. **THINKING CRITICALLY** Smith's post does not acknowledge a very real challenge with extending the use of *they* from referring to indefinite pronouns that could be male or female, like *everybody*, to referring to specific individuals, as in *Eleanor forgot their book*. In such an example, the book in question is Eleanor's alone, so the plural *they* introduces new kinds of ambiguity. How easy will it be for speakers to understand the intent during this transitional phrase of our language? How might they do so?

5. Return to your answer to Question 1, and use it as the basis for **writing a proposal argument** for dealing with the current situation, one where you seek to use Rogerian argumentation as discussed in Chapters 1 and 7. Thus, rather than focusing on how other perspectives are wrong (and certainly rather than belittling them), seek to build as much common ground as possible and acknowledge the validity of other perspectives even as you argue for why you prefer the alternative you do.

Thick of Tongue

JOHN McWHORTER

Given that I am the kind of black person who is often termed "articulate," it may seem surprising that I spend much of my life feeling quite **thick of tongue**. I am one of those unfortunate black people who sound white. It is, of all things, a social handicap.

John McWhorter James Leynse/ Getty Images

"So *white* . . . !", then, I seemed, years ago, to a black administrative assistant. I was told of the assessment some time later by an acquaintance of hers, but I could sense that this lady couldn't stand me as soon as we met. This was long before I had any public notoriety for **unconventional views about race issues**; I was an utterly anonymous new professor of linguistics. That she found me so disagreeable must have had something to do with me as a person. I arrived into the situation with good intentions and was interested in ingratiating myself as much as possible with everyone there, so I have reason to assume that what repelled her is the way I talk, which does indeed sound "so white."

Some will say that this woman was especially narrow-minded or ignorant, but she wasn't—that's just the thing. I could tell countless similar stories, about the couple of black listeners who liked my recorded linguistic courses in the **Great Courses** series but complained about the way I speak, one of them adding that a friend heard me and thought I lacked "swagger." When I was twelve, a cousin of mine, not yet three, remarked that my sister and I didn't sound like everybody else he knew. This kind of thing, for me, is and has always been just part of living.

I hardly consider myself significantly oppressed on this score. It is well documented that sounding black on the phone makes you less likely to be shown an apartment or house or to get a job interview. A black kid who uses Black English in school is often criticized by teachers and thought less intelligent. Classic experiments have shown that people's evaluation of someone reading a passage changes according to whether it's read by a white or black person.

◀ John McWhorter (1965–), whose primary training is in linguistics, teaches at Columbia University, where he offers courses in that field, philosophy, and music history. He is also author of numerous books about language and race/ethnicity and continues to publish in a number of popular venues in a way that few academics do. This March 2016 selection is from Guernica: A Magazine of Global Art and Politics, an online volunteer-run nonprofit magazine now in its second decade. As you read, consider how McWhorter problematizes the link between race or ethnicity and language that is a defining feature of American culture.

thick of tongue: here, McWhorter is using an expression that sometimes means "having impaired or unclear speech." He is likely also mocking a persistent racist ideology among whites that African Americans speak as they do because they have thicker tongues than white Americans. Such a claim is obviously false because, first, as McWhorter notes, African Americans do not all speak in the same way and, second, there is no such physiological difference among racial or ethnic groups in the United States or elsewhere.

unconventional views about race issues: McWhorter, who was at one time employed by a conservative think tank, has characterized himself as "as cranky liberal Democrat . . . [who] disagrees sustainedly with many of the tenets of the Civil Rights orthodoxy" in ways that few African Americans do.

Great Courses: a commercially produced college-level audio and video lecture series for "life-long learners." McWhorter has been featured in several Great Course series about language.

a cross to bear: a burden; the metaphor is Christian in origin.

cachet: a mark of value, prestige, or distinction.

O.J. Simpson (1947–): former award-winning pro-football running back, actor, and broadcaster. In the mid-1990s, he was accused of the murder of his former wife and her then-boyfriend. In the widely covered criminal trial, he was acquitted of the crime by a jury, but a civil court later issued a $33.5 million judgment against him for the death of the two victims.

The black voice is rated less favorably—considered less bright, less friendly. My burden, in comparison, is a mere personal **cross to bear**, worse than having a hard-to-spell name but hardly on the order of being denied services and thought dim. Yet to an extent that few would have reason to know, I suffer.

When you're black and you sound just like a white person, it puts a lot of black 5 people off. The vast majority of black Americans, including educated ones, are identifiable as black from their speech; the "black sound" is a subconscious but near-universal hallmark of black American culture. This means that if you are black, upon meeting you, a great many black people will tacitly expect that the two of you will speak more similarly to one another—at the very least in terms of that certain "sound"—than either of you do to white people. That similarity is an index of acceptance and warmth in a society that looks askance on black people in so many ways. Then it turns out that you don't sound similar, despite your black face. The wrong voice is coming out of you.

Although the expectation that you were going to sound black was not conscious, the fact that you don't is processed quite consciously: it's the discrepancy that elicits attention. You are heard as talking "like that," though you know no other way to talk. It seems, perhaps, that you purposefully distanced yourself from the normal black way of talking in a quest to join whites. More certainly, you sound snooty, chilly, not like the type anyone would want to have a beer (or anything else!) with. To a black person who knows only other black people who speak with the same sound, your different sound is not just peculiar but, because it is a "white sound," snobbish. The matter is not one of perplexity or discomfort, but irritation, even contempt.

Plus, these days, the "black sound" has acquired a certain **cachet** in mainstream society through the popularity of hip hop, so increasingly someone like me finds that even whites below a certain age process him as "square." Call it stereotyping or call it progress, but a lot of white people happily anticipate a certain hipness, "realness," from a black person. We're so "down," so approachable, so "the shit," apparently. In talking to these people, just as to so many black people, I disappoint. I offend.

One of the hardest things about this is that so many people would be inclined to say that the problem—being read as not sounding black—doesn't exist.

During the **O.J. Simpson** trial, in response to one witness who claimed to have heard a "black voice" at the scene of the murder of Simpson's wife and her friend, lawyer **Johnnie Cochran** objected: "What's a black voice?" The mostly black jury assented. Cochran was implying that the very idea that black speech has a particular sound is racist; often, people making the claim insist that black people simply talk like Southerners.

Most any American knows that a white Southerner is unlikely to sound like **Chris Rock** while a black person is unlikely to sound like **Paula Deen**. Black and Southern English overlap, but just that. Did the Reverend Martin Luther King and the white police officers beating and arresting him speak the same dialect? Yet the notion of a "black sound" smells like it could bring on accusations of stereotyping, so one is inclined to just step around the issue.

Black people's own ticklish orientation when it comes to acknowledging a black way of speech is understandable for two reasons. The first is the racist past (and present) of this country—so often, that which is black is trashed as deficient; one becomes permanently wary. Then also, Black English is primarily associated with what are considered errors—*ain't*, *he be*, *aks*, and so on. Naturally, one worries that any characterization of black people's speech will be a critique rather than a neutral description. To many, the idea that even educated black people have this sound will seem like a prelude to the claim that even educated black people are incapable of mastering "proper language."

But the same people who hotly deny that there is such a thing as a black sound will notice immediately when a black person "sounds white," as countless black people teased about this as children can attest to. Logic dictates that if a black person can sound white—and this accusation is uncontroversial in black America—then the norm must be for black people to sound something else.

So what exactly is this "black sound" I am insisting exists?

I am not referring to black **slang**. Plenty of black people use little street slang and yet still have a black *sound*. The question is why you could tell most black people were black if they read you a shopping list over the phone.

Scholarship has confirmed what most of us sense intuitively: whites and blacks are very good at identifying black voices, even from an isolated word. The black sound is, though we don't usually use the term this way, an accent. It differs from standard English's sound in the same way that other dialects do, in certain shadings of vowels, aspects of intonation, and also that elusive thing known as timbre, most familiar to singers—degrees of breathiness, grain, huskiness, "space."

10

15

Johnnie Cochran (1937–2005): attorney best known for his role in the defense and acquittal of Simpson, among other media personalities.

Chris Rock (1965–): among the most popular stand-up comedians of all time, Rock is also known for his work as an actor in TV and film, as a producer, and as a director.

Paula Deen (1947–): celebrity chef, cookbook author, and restaurateur from Georgia; Deen was at the center of a controversy in 2013, having been accused of speaking in disparaging ways about African Americans.

slang: informal words or phrases often associated with social groups defined by age, region, race/ethnicity, class, etc.

Contrary to how some may read me here, I am not bragging about how "well" I speak. I'm not. The black sound has nothing whatsoever to do with whether one is capable of expressing their feelings elegantly, convincing others to their point of view, weaving an engaging story. It's just a matter of some vowels—it's like the difference between one carpet color and another, nothing more.

But *why* is there a black sound? Well, in actuality, there is nothing inherently "black" about it. It isn't genetic, of course, and it isn't a degradation or departure from standard English. When English came to America, it developed in many directions, of which today's standard and black varieties are but two. Black and standard English share the relationship of two sisters, not that of a mother and her wayward daughter. Sisters begin as different people, and over time become even more different. Dialects of a common language behave the same way. This is why actors in old movies sound increasingly weird to us; people who learned to speak in 1900 picked up sounds at a different stage of drift than they're at now. Fred Astaire proclaims "This is revo-LYEW-tion!" where we would say "revo-LOO-tion." William Powell as The Thin Man prepares to round up what he calls the "sus-PECTS" instead of the "SUS-pects."

Sounds change. An *ah* might become an *aw* or an *ay*. A *t* might become a *d* or a *ch*. The way a sound progresses is no more meaningful in itself than changing hemlines, the fact that the fade-out on pop recordings went out of fashion, or that avocado was such a popular color in home décor for a while. But when these random changes happen at the same time to two different dialects, over long periods, they'll seem more and more distinct. This is why black people have a different sound than whites.

The differences between the white sound and the black sound that tip an American listener off to a speaker's race are subtle. I am not talking here about obvious, bluesy things, like saying *thang* for *thing* or *mo* for *more*, which are patterns less likely of educated people. One difference is that the *eh* sound before *m* or *n* sounds a little more like *ih*, so that, for example, *mention* sounds not exactly but to a whisper of an extent like *mintion*. Or, the *er* sound is slightly distinct: *bird* will sound a touch like *buh-urd*—not in a drawly way, but enough to alert the American brain. Then there is the timbre, fine-grained differences in vocal placement and texture that analysts have yet to characterize in detail, though the ear and mind can pick them up easily enough.

As dry as such details are in isolation, together they are why you might sometimes 20 have heard a voice on National Public Radio and known the person was black, no matter whether they were talking about the latest doings in Congress or tomorrow's weather. If you have ever had that impression, you may well have felt guilty about it, especially if you're white.

The dominant conception is that only racism could create the impression that black people have a particular way of speaking. The assumption, roughly, is that educated black people talk just like educated white people, while less educated black people usually (but not always) speak a combination of Southern English and bad grammar. There is little room in our public discourse for the reality, which is that 1) almost all black people code-switch between standard and Black (not Southern) English to varying degrees, 2) even the most educated black people typically talk with vowel colorings and a general cadence that most Americans readily hear as "black" (and not "Southern") after a few sentences, and 3) there isn't a thing wrong with that.

The result of all of this, for me, is an ongoing **cognitive dissonance** in my relations with other people. Yet I stopped bringing it up long ago. You just hit a wall trying.

Though I often wish I did, I don't have the vowels and cadence of the "blaccent." I have lost count of how many times callers-in to radio shows I appeared on have assumed I was white (including plenty of black ones) or asked whether I was. Radio hosts often gently advise me to, when commenting on racial issues, mention my race on air—which indicates that it's not evident from my voice that I'm black. Several listeners to my Great Courses lectures have written to me and mentioned that they didn't know I was black until they saw my photograph. Once, answering the phone for a white roommate, I listened as an old man drifted, when a news event came up, into a diatribe about "niggers" coming over the horizon; clearly, he did not hear blackness in my voice. I barely code-switch—after drinks, awakened in the middle of the night, talking to my daughters, amused or angry, I sound pretty much the same: boring Mid-Atlantic American. I have written here and there about the fact that black Americans have a larger English than most white Americans. Alas, my English isn't large at all.

My noting that I don't have a black-sounding voice has, on a couple of occasions, seemed to peeve the black person I was talking to. I think they were wondering whether I was claiming that, unlike other black people, I speak "properly." I mean no such thing—though much of what made it seem like I did was surely my "white" voice and the subconscious associations it brings up.

cognitive dissonance: mental stress resulting from holding contradictory sets of beliefs or values; here, the disjuncture between the things McWhorter knows as a linguist and his experience of being in the world as an African American whose language doesn't match the stereotype held by many of how black Americans sound or should sound.

Ebonic: an adjective derived from *Ebonics,* a term popularized in the press in the late 1990s to refer to what linguists more often term African American English, the variety of English that McWhorter is contrasting with "sounding white" and standard English.

Rosetta Stone: a software company that sells well-known language-learning materials for a variety of languages.

Idrissa Akuna "Idris" Elba (1972–): award-winning British-born actor, DJ, and hip-hop musician who played Nelson Mandela in *Mandela: Long Walk to Freedom* (2013).

Thandie Newton (1972–): award-winning English actress who has starred in British and American films.

There has also been the occasional white person who has sincerely suggested that I just take on a black sound if I feel so uncomfortable. But they were unclear as to what I meant when I referred to "sounding black." One white woman said, while making vaguely vernacular street gestures, "Can't you just, like, 'Heyyy . . . '?" Well, I suppose I could "Heyyy"—but, for one thing, it would be stepping outside of my natural self. The fluently "**Ebonic**" guy expected to speak standard English does not need to adopt a foreign code to do so—any black person can speak standard as well as Black English, even if they would rather dwell in the latter. I didn't grow up saying "Heyyy," and **Rosetta Stone** offers no materials that might instruct me in the art.

Accent is the hardest thing to pick up in a new way of speaking after the age of about fourteen. The colorings that constitute a blaccent are subtle, deeply ingrained, and even *harder* to master for someone whose home base is standard English, precisely because Black English and standard English are so similar. And no, my being a linguist doesn't help: we have neither the training nor the inherent talent that would make us better at this than other people. It's professional actors who wangle it—**Idris Elba** and **Thandie Newton** have, dazzlingly, managed to learn a light blaccent for their roles despite growing up outside of the United States. I could no more master a subtle blaccent than I could learn to blink, lift a fork, or laugh differently. Your accent is your you.

Why do I sound so white when I talk? It's a good question. Both of my parents were black (some people ask, and they must be spurred on by my voice, as I'm not that light-skinned). I grew up around plenty of black people—in an integrated Philadelphia neighborhood where my friends were all black kids, and then all-black Lawnside, New Jersey. Most of my friends were black until adolescence; my best friend had a working-class black Philadelphian accent himself. Neither of my parents were given to code-switching to full-blown Black English—but both of them used a somewhat more Black English-inflected way of speaking when talking comfortably with black people.

Yet somehow I came out sounding like an announcer in a 1940s newsreel. I'm tempted to say that as an inveterate nerd I identified more with the teachers and students at the private schools I attended, who were mostly white. But plenty of middle-class black kids—of whom, by the 1970s, there were more every year—went to school with whites and played at home with blacks and emerged sounding like home, not school.

I'm not a joiner, and people around me are more likely to pick up speech habits from me than I am to pick up speech habits from them. But then, my sister is more of a joiner than I am, and also had a richness of black experience at all-black **Spelman College** that I never had. She had an extremely light blaccent that she developed in those years to identify with her friends, but that was just a phase; on the whole, she has always spoken exactly like me. Truth to tell, I'm not quite sure why I sound like this. But I do.

It is more my curse than it is my sister's. I know that, especially in school, black   30
girls get teased for "talking white" as much as black boys do. But I submit that, particularly in adulthood, not having a black voice is less of a social stain for a black woman than a black man. Linguists have discovered that with almost eerie consistency, across societies, women tend to speak more "properly" than men. Certainly women use slang and profanity and say *singin'* instead of *singing*—but less than men do. For this reason, the black woman's "white" speech can be processed, for better or worse, as "ladylike," sophisticated. However, sounding white is not associated with masculinity—if anything, when it pertains to a man it can be heard as suggesting effeminacy.

I thwart expectations in glum little ways. It comes down to the idea that black equals funky. A white woman I dated in the nineties watched me play a semi-classical piece on the piano and then smiled, "I'm waiting to see you really get into it." "Into it"? It turned out she was waiting for me to play some blues. Of course, a black man isn't "really" playing the piano until he "jams." In the same way, another woman I dated said, about my lack of a blaccent, "I've been waiting for you to do it." To her, my actual voice was preliminary, public, stiff. She assumed that once comfortable I would glide from *Word!* into "Wuh-urd!"—from *no* into "naw," from *hold on* into a little "hode on." I already was comfortable—and was talking the way I am comfortable talking. But to her, my vocal comfort zone constituted "not really getting into it."

One of the strangest things about being a white-sounding black person is that, in one regard and only in that regard, I would have felt more comfortable in the past. Until the 1960s, the linguistic landscape in America was prissier than it is now. In public, language was to be presented in its Sunday best, and casual speech was only for off-time with intimates. Even grade school inculcated hardcore spelling and grammar rules, such that modestly educated soldiers during the Civil War wrote letters that sound practically Shakespearian (and sometimes quote the man). This divide between "high" and "low" was maintained as strictly

Spelman College: the country's oldest private liberal-arts historically black college for women, located in Atlanta, Georgia.

Booker T. Washington (1856–1915): educator, orator, author of *Up from Slavery* (1901), and founder of what is today Tuskegee University, a historically black institution in Tuskegee, Alabama. Born into slavery, Washington was in many regards the most influential African American of the late nineteenth and early twentieth centuries.

Mary McLeod Bethune (1875–1955): educator, philanthropist, civil rights activist, and advisor to President Franklin Roosevelt. The descendent of slaves, she founded what later became Bethune-Cookman University, a private historically black university in Daytona Beach, Florida.

A. Phillip Randolph (1889–1979): activist in civil rights, labor rights, and socialist politics. He organized the Brotherhood of Sleeping Car Porters, the first predominantly African American labor union. His lobbying of the White House during WWII resulted in an executive order banning racial discrimination in all defense industries. He later served as the head of the 1963 March on Washington.

in the black community as anywhere else, and what it meant was that it was not considered odd for an educated black person to not "sound black" at all.

One of the oddest things about listening to recordings of **Booker T. Washington**, educator **Mary McLeod Bethune**, civil rights titan **A. Phillip Randolph**, or operatic contralto **Marian Anderson** is that, in their public speech, at least, they did not have, or barely had, blaccents, where their equivalents today would. This is true of countless educated black people of the time, who surprise the modern ear listening to oral histories and other late-in-life interviews in that they sound so utterly white.

The social boundaries of Black English, which has existed since at least the early 1700s, expanded starting in the late sixties, when the counterculture encouraged a new informality and black activists and intellectuals taught black America to be proud of its **vernacular** heritage. A friend of mine, who was young at the time and has no blaccent, recalls a party in 1968 during which she sensed the change in the black linguistic landscape. Two black men of modest education teased her for not being able to enunciate "motherfucker" as they thought she should; she wasn't speaking "blackly" enough. That scene would have been much less likely ten years earlier, and just about impossible twenty years before that. Newly, this woman was heard as sounding white rather than just well-spoken.

I certainly do not yearn for a return to the time when one had to work so hard   35
on one's speech patterns to be heard by wider society. Or to the time when black people were subject to such decisive segregation there was no question as to whether any black person "knew they were black" or not, no matter how they spoke. But I do envy that black people did not have a tacit expectation that all people of their color, regardless of education level, temperament, or socioeconomic background, would share a way of speaking. I would like to be able to have a conversation with a black person of whatever social position without worrying that he thinks I don't sound black or that I think I'm better than him. I don't think I'm better than anybody and am quite aware that I am not white.

Am I oversimplifying the problem? Maybe—I suspect many would say that the issue isn't only that I sound white, but that I am reserved. That's true; I know black men without blaccents who are heartier types than I am and who probably put black people off less than I do vocally. But: a reserved black man who does have the black vowels and cadence is read as contained, as keeping his own counsel, not as cold, unfriendly, classist, uptight.

Though my speaking voice often feels like a club foot, I do not hate myself. I also have black friends who do not hear **froideur** in the way I talk, sometimes because they themselves lack blaccents, and sometimes because they are just wired differently than that administrative assistant. And, as I am rounding fifty, my voice will increasingly come off as the fussiness of an "older" gent, quaint rather than offensive. I'm already sensing this with people younger than twenty-five. It's the sole facet of aging I'm enjoying.

Still, when I read that Jewish immigrants at the turn of the twentieth century learning English felt like they might open their mouths to speak only for shards of glass to fall out, I identify. I all but stopped doing live talks on race years ago despite the money I could earn, out of a sense that using my "white" voice to have such discussions was ineffective and makes me sound disconnected from the issues. I mainly write on race instead; on paper my vowels and cadence don't distort my message.

Sounding black? What's *that* all about? Well, that. A minor problem in the grand scheme, I know. But I'm just saying. (Luckily, in print.)

RESPOND.

1. What is your response to McWhorter's argument? What is your visceral response, that is, how does it make you feel? (As his essay illustrates, our responses to others' language—or even discussions about it—is often visceral in nature: we have a gut response to how others sound or what is said about how others sound.) And what is your intellectual response to it? That is, what do you understand his main claims to be, and how well has he provided support for them?

2. In many regards, McWhorter's analysis rests on definitional arguments, including the definition of "sounding black" as well as characterizations of the attitudes held by African Americans and by white Americans toward not only sounding black but also individuals who are black but who do not sound black. Make three columns, listing all the features McWhorter gives of each of these three phenomena: sounding black; African American attitudes toward those who sound black and those who do not sound black; and white attitudes toward those who sound black and those who do not sound black. (See Chapter 9 on definitional arguments.)

Marian Anderson (1897–1993): one of the most celebrated vocal artists of the twentieth century, known for her performances and recordings of art songs, operatic arias, and spirituals. A key event in Anderson's career and in the civil rights movement was the refusal of the Daughters of the American Revolution to permit her to sing to an integrated audience at Independence Hall in Philadelphia early in 1939. Eleanor Roosevelt arranged for Anderson to offer an open-air concert on the steps of the Lincoln Memorial on Easter Sunday of that year; the concert began with Anderson singing "My Country 'Tis of Thee." Over 75,000 people heard the concert, and it was broadcast to millions. In 1955, she became the first African American—indeed, the first black person—to perform at the Metropolitan Opera in New York City.

vernacular: here, relating to a culture or subculture, ordinary or popular (in the sense of "of the people") in contrast to elite.

froideur: standoffishness, coolness with respect to other people.

3. As the discussion of stasis theory in Chapter 1 explains, arguments of definition rely on arguments of fact. What factual information about language, language varieties, and language attitudes does McWhorter present in this chapter? How much, if any, of this information was new to you?

4. **THINKING CRITICALLY**   Chapter 1 and Chapter 7 discuss invitational arguments, that is, arguments that invite us into a space where we can consider a complex issue from numerous perspectives. What specific issues—and there are many—is McWhorter asking us to consider and even to confront about ourselves and our society?

5. Some Americans increasingly argue that they do not see color, that is, that they are "color blind" when it comes to matters of race or ethnicity. McWhorter's text reminds us that, whatever we may believe about color-blind societies as a goal or as reality, we, as Americans, hear color along with other social categories; that is, on hearing individuals (even on the phone) we cannot help but attribute features to them. In short, we place people as belonging (or not) to specific social groups based on sex or gender, sexual identity, race or ethnicity, class, place of origin, and educational level as well as personality traits like likeability, competence, and trustworthiness. (Although McWhorter does not cite the research to support this claim, he is well aware of it, and be assured that the research on this topic is plentiful and robust. Furthermore, it is not only Americans who engage in these behaviors; all humans do.) With this background and your responses to the earlier questions, **write a rhetorical analysis** of McWhorter's argument, focusing on how McWhorter seeks to prod readers to examine some of the consequences of not sounding black; that is, not conforming to the linguistic stereotypes of those we might encounter in daily life. Be sure to consider this situation from the perspective of both the person who is stereotyped and the one who does the stereotyping. (See Chapter 6 on rhetorical analyses.)

The Japanese American Citizens League (Nikkei Amerikajin Shimin Dōmei), founded on the West Coast in 1929, has focused primarily on civil rights issues that affect not just Japanese Americans or even Asian Pacific Americans but all groups that are the targets of bigotry. These issues include interracial marriage, race-based restrictions on immigration, and segregation. The League is also concerned with documenting and preserving the history of the Japanese American experience. This selection is an excerpt from a 2012 handbook published by the organization in its efforts to help those outside the Japanese American community correct misconceptions about what Japanese Americans endured during the Second World War. As you read, consider how and why word choices ultimately help construct reality as we perceive it by thinking about the very different images that are represented by the terms traditionally used (e.g., relocation) and those being suggested by the Japanese American Citizens League (forced removal).

from The Power of Words

JAPANESE AMERICAN CITIZENS LEAGUE

"History is written by the victors" is an old saying. Is it true? What about for those who suffered "**collateral damage**" as with Japanese Americans during World War II—because they looked like the enemy? As the Nikkei (persons of Japanese ancestry outside Japan) culturally Americanized over the 20th century, were they to be forever burdened with historical accounts of their WWII experience written in euphemistic and misleading vocabulary? It is now time to acknowledge and correct this misleading language of the past and focus on truth and accuracy for the future. The objective here is to suggest vocabulary that facilitates a more accurate understanding of events and actions experienced by the Nikkei during this tragic time.

Much of the U.S. government activity was shrouded in secrecy during the war. This was implemented in the popular press and media accounts of that time by the use of euphemistic terms by government agencies to make these actions more acceptable to the public. In the decades following the war, as scholars, analysts, and historians began to probe the realities of the WWII Nikkei experience, what emerged was that the familiar vocabulary of the war era did not adequately describe what actually happened. The widespread use of euphemistic terms, such as *evacuation* and *assembly centers*, made the government actions seem **benign** and acceptable in the context of wartime (Daniels, 2005; Kashima, 2003). Their concerns about euphemisms were underscored in the 1980's with the release of previously classified documents (via the Freedom of Information Act), which revealed the scope and breadth of this misleading practice (Civil Liberties Public Education Fund, 1997).

collateral damage: according to the U.S. military, "unintentional or incidental damage to non-combatant [that is, civilian] casualties and non-combatant property." (The term *collateral* usually means "parallel" or "additional.") The term dates from 1961 and began to be widely used during the Vietnam War. Many people consider it to be a euphemism for death and injury inflicted by the military.

benign: not harmful, gentle.

667

Benjamin Lee Whorf (1897–1941): American linguist who argued that the structure of a language influences how its users conceptualize the world.

Ralph Waldo Emerson (1803–1882): American essayist, lecturer, and poet most often associated with the Transcendentalist movement. Emerson praised the value of the individual, often criticizing social pressures that kept individuals from expressing their true selves.

William Safire (1929–2006): American journalist, author, and presidential speech writer; he characterized himself as a "libertarian conservative." He is best known to many older Americans for his column for the *New York Times Magazine* entitled "On Language."

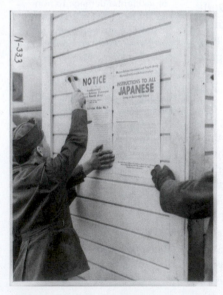

Notice for Japanese Americans Library of Congress, Prints & Photographs Division, [LC-USZ62-95986]

Language shapes the way we think.
——**Benjamin Lee Whorf,** American linguist (1897–1941)

Language is the archive of history.
——**Ralph Waldo Emerson,** American poet (1803–1882)

In looking to the future, we are guided by the words of Whorf and Emerson. Like any other history, that of Japanese Americans during WWII needs to be told accurately and fairly, especially because the Constitutional issues that were involved then have been revisited anew in the United States since September 11, 2001. In compiling relevant documentation and references, it is the hope that this document will encourage more accurate discourse on the history of Nikkei in American concentration camps during WWII and its relevance to contemporary events. Moreover, it is the hope that what took place against Americans of Japanese ancestry during WWII never happens again.

DICTIONARY DEFINITIONS AND EUPHEMISTIC TERMS

A euphemism is "a mild word or expression substituted for one considered blunt and embarrassing" (Chantrell, 2002, p. 186). It comes from the Greek *euphemismos*, from *euphemizein* "use auspicious words." The formative elements are *eu* "well" and *pheme* "speaking." The term has been used in English since the late 16th century (Chantrell, 2002). In more modern times, author **William Safire** (1981) writes: "To some degree, euphemism is a strategic misrepresentation" (p. 82).

Typically in everyday polite discourse, speakers of English do not 5 like to talk about death. So instead of saying "he died," we say, "he passed away" or "he departed." A similar example comes from Japanese, where the word for death *shi* has the same pronunciation as the number *four*. In conversations about prices or numbers, speakers of Japanese generally avoid *shi*, using *yon*, a word of a different origin having no connection with death, instead (Hayakawa, 1964).

However, euphemisms can be used for other purposes and are often purposeful alternatives with hidden motives. During WWII, the U.S. government used euphemistic language to control public perceptions about the forced removal of Japanese American citizens from their West Coast homes to desolate American concentration camps further inland. The public was told that Nisei and Issei [non-citizens] were being "evacuated" to "relocation centers" and "internment camps." Terms like "evacuation" of people sounded like they were being rescued from some kind of disaster (like an earthquake). To obscure the unconstitutional nature of these forced removals, the government referred to the Nisei victims as "non-aliens" instead of "citizens," which might provoke public inquiries like: "Why is the U.S. imprisoning citizens without due process of law?" Once in camp, Nisei could earn back their citizenship by embracing their "right" to defend their country and to serve on the "same basis" as other Americans in the military (but in the segregated U.S. Army 442nd Regimental Combat Team) (Lyon, 2012).

Over time, researchers and scholars, studying historical artifacts, documents, and accounts of the period, have increasingly pointed out the euphemistic nature of the language employed by the U.S. government during WWII in relation to the concentration camps in which Japanese American citizens were incarcerated (Daniels, 2005; Kashima, 2003; Okamura, 1982). After the national trauma of the Vietnam War era, the consciousness-raising civil rights movement, and the passage of the Civil Liberties Act of 1988, which provided redress to Japanese Americans incarcerated during WWII, it is compelling to have the historical record reflect reality. While history per se cannot be rewritten, scholars, the media, and analysts of the future should be guided by more accurate vocabulary and appropriate descriptors that relate to the events experienced by Japanese Americans during this period.

Japanese American children with identification tags The U.S. National Archives

Bringing attention to the connotation of words and calling for change, the Japanese American Citizens League offers a proposal argument that has consequences for the way we describe the incarceration of Japanese Americans during World War II.

LINK TO P. 286

Vocabulary Related to WWII Incarceration of Japanese Americans

We now focus in more detail on a list of words, which over time have elicited concerns about accuracy and authenticity to the events, actions, or reality to which they were applied—or not. While the published record cannot be changed, current and future analyses and assessments of historical facts will be better served for accuracy by using the recommended word or phrase, or explaining why they do not. In some cases, citing the word placed in quotation marks may be appropriate.

EVACUATE/EVACUATION

The dictionary defines this verb/noun as "the process of temporarily moving people away from an immediate and real danger, such as a fire, flood, shoot-out, or bomb threat" (*Merriam-Webster Dictionary*, 2011, para. 1). Its usage to describe the forced removal by the federal government of over 110,000

Japanese and Japanese Americans from their homes on the West Coast and Arizona is not accurate. They were not "evacuated" to protect them from a disastrous environment. By using these words, the government only made it seem that these individuals were being "helped."

Recommendation: The words *forced removal* should be used instead. This phrase more accurately describes the lack of choice provided to Japanese Americans who were ordered to leave their homes. 10

RELOCATE/RELOCATION

These terms suggest that people voluntarily moved from one location (private homes) to another (War Relocation Authority camp). Their usage obscures the fact that the U.S. military forced "all Japanese persons, both alien and non-alien," to leave their homes and many of their belongings behind, often with less than a week's notice.

Recommendation: The phrase *forced removal,* as above, should be used instead. This phrase more accurately describes the lack of choice provided to Japanese Americans who were ordered to leave their homes.

INTERNMENT

This word has a legal definition that refers to the confinement or impounding of enemy aliens in a time of war (*Merriam-Webster Dictionary*, 2011). Most of the several tens of thousands of people of Japanese ancestry that were incarcerated in War Relocation Authority (WRA) camps during World War II were American citizens; thus, the term does not apply. A few thousand mostly Issei [non-citizen] men were held in the Army and Department of Justice internment camps, but with the family reunification program and Nikkei from Latin American countries, the total exceeded 17,000 men, women, and children.

Recommendation: The word *incarceration* more accurately describes those held in WRA camps. *Incarcerate* is generally defined as "to confine or imprison, typically as punishment for a crime." This term reflects the prison-like conditions faced by Japanese Americans as well as the view that they were treated as if they were guilty of sabotage, espionage, and/or suspect loyalty.

ASSEMBLY CENTER

When many Japanese and Japanese Americans were initially forced to leave 15 their homes, they were directed to live temporarily in "assembly centers," officially "Wartime Civil Control Administration" camps. (The WCCA was essentially a branch of the U.S. Army.) These makeshift detention facilities

Japanese Americans behind barbed wire Library of Congress, Prints & Photographs Division, [LC-USZ62-59860]

were often crudely fashioned from animal stalls at racetracks and fair grounds, still emitting the stench of animal waste but surrounded by barbed wire and search lights with armed soldiers to contain the people of Japanese descent. The euphemistic nature of this term hid the degrading lack of amenities and very crude living spaces in these facilities. For example, on December 18, 1944, Supreme Court Justice Owen J. Roberts stated that "an 'Assembly Center' was a euphemism for a prison . . . so-called 'Relocation Centers,' a euphemism for concentration camps" (Ishizuka, 2006, p. 72).

Recommendation: The more accurate term is *temporary detention center.* A detention center is generally a place where prisoners are temporarily held pending some further disposition, which in the case of Nikkei civilians was being shipped to WRA concentration camps. In certain discussions of historical context, the phrase *assembly center* may be appropriate only as part of a proper name such as the Fresno Assembly Center. Otherwise, it is not recommended for general usage, even with quotation marks.

RELOCATION CENTER

This term, like "assembly center," was used by the government to give an impression to the general public that the forcibly moved Japanese and Japanese Americans were placed in pleasant "summer camp-like" facilities. This somewhat innocuous imagery was in stark contrast to the reality which was crude tar-papered wood barracks located in harsh, desolate climates in compounds surrounded by barbed wire fences with guard towers where the sentries pointed their weapons toward those inside the barbed wire fences.

Recommendation: The recommended more accurate term is *American concentration camp* (see discussion below). Alternatively, *incarceration camp* may be used as well as *illegal detention center*. In certain discussions of historical context, the term "relocation" may be appropriate only as part of a proper name such as War Relocation Authority (WRA). Otherwise, it is not recommended for general usage, even with quotation marks.

CONCENTRATION CAMP

This term was not generally used in public discourse by the U.S. government in relation to Nikkei incarceration, even though it has been found in non-public documents and transcriptions by high government officials including President Roosevelt (Civil Liberties Public Education Fund, 1997). One dictionary simply defines *concentration camp* as "a facility where persons (as prisoners of war, political prisoners, or refugees) are detained or confined" (*Merriam-Webster*, 2011, para. 1). The *Encyclopedia Britannica* (1977) describes a concentration camp as an internment center for political prisoners and members of national or minority groups who are confined for reasons of state security, exploitation, or punishment, usually by executive decree or military order. Persons are placed in such camps often on the basis of identification with a particular ethnic or political group rather than as individuals and without benefit either of indictment or fair trial.

These are different from prisons for convicted criminals, prisoner of war 20 camps, or refugee camps.

As the *Encyclopedia* notes, among the earliest examples of the use of the term occurred during the 1901–02 South African War, in which the British confined non-combatants of the republics of Transvaal and Cape Colony in concentration camps. The incarceration of Japanese and Japanese Americans during WWII is cited as another example of non-combatant civilians in concentration camps. German concentration camps were first established in 1933 to confine opponents of the Nazi party. During WWII, the target shifted to minority groups, mainly Jews, and also became extermination centers. Most notorious were Auschwitz, Majdanek and Treblinka in Poland and Buchenwald in Germany. When these horrors became known to the world, these concentration camps became synonymous with death camps—the Holocaust.

In 1994, the Japanese American National Museum (JANM) in Los Angeles curated a new exhibit entitled "America's Concentration Camps: Remembering the Japanese American Experience," which ran from November 11 to October 15 of the following year. A traveling version was exhibited at the Ellis Island Immigration Museum in New York in 1998–1999. But in the preparation of moving the exhibit from Los Angeles to Ellis Island, a controversy over the term "concentration camps" emerged in New York where a large Jewish population lives. A number of Holocaust survivors and relatives expressed sensitivity towards public confusion over "death camps" with "concentration camps." A meeting of representatives from JANM and seven American Jewish organizations resulted in the following text, which was placed at the beginning of the exhibition and which distinguished the Nazi death camps from the American concentration camps (Ishizuka, 2006, pp. 166–167):

> A concentration camp is a place where people are imprisoned not because of any crimes they committed, but simply because of who they are. Although many groups have been singled out for such persecution throughout history, the term "concentration camp" was first used at the turn of the century in the Spanish American and Boer Wars.
>
> During World War II, America's concentration camps were clearly distinguishable from Nazi Germany's. Nazi camps were places of torture, barbarous medical experiments, and summary executions; some were extermination centers with gas chambers. Six million Jews and many others including Gypsies, Poles, homosexuals, and political dissidents were slaughtered in the Holocaust.
>
> In recent years, concentration camps have existed in the former Soviet Union, Cambodia, and Bosnia. Despite the difference, all had one thing in common: the people in power removed a minority group from the general population and the rest of society let it happen.

Recommendation: Instead of *relocation center*, the phrase *American concentration camp* is recommended. Depending on the context, the phrase in quotation marks *"American concentration camp"* may be used. Alternatives are *incarceration camp* or *illegal detention center*. Ten types of U.S. imprisonment centers during WWII have been described by Kashima, 2003, p. 11.

SUMMARY TABLE OF ACCURATE TERMS

The table below, based on Ishizuka, 2006, p. 72, summarizes the various euphemistic terms and their more accurate counterparts.

EUPHEMISM	ACCURATE TERM
evacuation	exclusion, or forced removal
relocation	incarceration in camps; also used after release from camp
non-aliens	U.S. citizens of Japanese ancestry
civilian exclusion orders	detention orders
any or all persons	primarily persons of Japanese ancestry
may be excluded	evicted from one's home
native American aliens	renunciants (citizens who, under pressure, renounced U.S. citizenship)
assembly center	temporary detention facility
relocation center	American concentration camp, incarceration camp, illegal detention center; inmates held here are "incarcerees"
internment center	reserve for DOJ or Army camp holding alien enemies under Alien Enemies Act 1798

REFERENCES

Chantrell, G. (2002). *The Oxford dictionary of word histories*. Oxford University Press.

Civil Liberties Public Education Fund. (1997). *Personal justice denied: Report of the Commission on Wartime Relocation and Internment of Civilians 1982–83*. University of Washington Press.

Daniels, R. (2005). Words do matter: A note on inappropriate terminology and the incarceration of the Japanese Americans. In L. Fiset & G. Nomura (Eds.), *Nikkei in the Pacific Northwest: Japanese Americans and Japanese Canadians in the twentieth century* (pp. 183–207). University of Washington Press.

Encyclopedia Britannica. (1977). *Micropedia* (Vol 3.), pp. 60–61. Encyclopedia Britannica.

Hayakawa, S. I. (1964). *Language in thought and action* (2nd ed). Harcourt, Brace & World.

Ishizuka, K. L. (2006). *Lost and found: Reclaiming the Japanese American incarceration.* University of Illinois Press.

Kashima, T. (2003). *Judgment without trial: Japanese American imprisonment during World War II.* University of Washington Press.

Lyon, C. M. (2012). *Prisons and patriots: Japanese American wartime citizenship: Civil disobedience, and historical memory.* Temple University Press.

Merriam-Webster Dictionary. (2011). Concentration camp. Retrieved from http://www.merriam-webster.com/dictionary/concentration%20

Merriam-Webster Dictionary. (2011). Euphemism. Retrieved from http://www.merriam-webster.com/dictionary/euphemism

Okamura, R. Y. (1982). The American concentration camps: A cover-up through euphemistic terminology. *Journal of Ethnic Studies,* 10, 95–109.

Safire, W. (1981). *On language.* Times Books.

RESPOND.

1. What was your response to this selection? How familiar were you with the events described in it? To the extent that you were aware of them, what terms did you use to characterize these events? Did you, for example, think in terms of *evacuation* or *forced removal*? Why, do you imagine?

2. Chapter 13 on style discusses connotation, the feeling a word evokes, in contrast to its dictionary meaning, or denotation. To what extent does this selection focus primarily on denotation? On connotation? How does it illustrate the ways that denotation and connotation can be tools for euphemism, as defined in this selection?

3. Like strong proposal arguments generally, this selection includes arguments based on fact, arguments based on definition, arguments of evaluation, and causal arguments, as well as the actual proposal. Mark the sections of the selection that represent each of these kinds of argument.

4. **THINKING CRITICALLY**   Read about the treatment of Japanese Americans during World War II. (Quick references here would include the Wikipedia entries on "Internment of Japanese Americans" and "Japanese American Service in World War II.") With this information, evaluate whether the terms traditionally used or those proposed in this selection more accurately reflect what, in fact, happened during the war.

5. This selection is a good example of the twentieth-century philosopher and rhetorician Kenneth Burke's claim that once we choose the terms for describing a situation, arguments in some sense complete themselves. In short, the conclusions of many arguments are little more than working out the consequences of the labels chosen for things out in the world. (If this claim is not clear to you, consider the difference between the labels *fetus* and *unborn child* in terms of how they shape individuals' understanding of abortion.) **Write a causal essay** in which you examine several of the terms discussed in this selection and the ways in which they, once chosen, lead readers toward certain conclusions while leading them away from others. In preparing for this assignment, study Chapter 11 carefully because effective causal arguments are quite complex to construct.

English and Languages Other Than English in the United States

CENSUS DATA

▶ What is today the United States has been home to multiple languages since the first indigenous peoples arrived here from Asia. Along with other immigrant languages, English represents a later addition to what we might term the linguistic landscape of the United States. Despite the presence of other languages, however, there is no question that English has become and will remain this country's national language—that is, it is the most widely used language and the one generally expected in most government bureaucracies and in other contexts, especially official ones.

This selection, comprising maps and a table showing the presence of languages other than English and the reported ability of speakers of those languages to speak English, encourages you to consider the country's linguistic diversity at the state or territory level. (Obviously, the maps would look different if the level of analysis were the country as a whole or the counties making up each state.) The data on which these maps are based come from the American Community Survey, 2009–2013, and represent the most recent data available from the U.S. Census Bureau. Census data are self-report data; that is, individuals report information about themselves. In this case, an adult in the family reports the language(s) other than English spoken by members of the household who are five years or older and assesses their proficiency in English, that is, stating that they speak English "very well," "well," "not well," or "not at all." Understandably, self-report data are problematic. Your "very well" might be my "not well," and for many reasons, individuals may under- or over-report knowledge of languages other than English. Despite their shortcomings, they are the best data we have about languages in this country.

Of course, the presence and absence of other languages tells us important things about our country's history. The sub-Saharan languages spoken by African slaves brought to the United States in earlier centuries played key roles in the development of the creoles Gullah (spoken along the South Carolina and Georgia coasts) and Afro-Seminole (spoken in Brackettville, Texas) and influenced the development of African American English as well as varieties of Southern English and American English more broadly. (Gumbo and okra are both of sub-Saharan origin.) Despite their legacies, those languages quickly disappeared. The diminishing number of speakers of Native American languages reflects a history of residential schools that Indian children were forced to attend from the mid-nineteenth century until the mid-twentieth century. These children were prohibited from speaking their tribal languages and were severely punished for doing so; furthermore, children from different tribes were put into the same classroom to minimize the use of any language other than English. Not surprisingly, the indigenous languages began to disappear. And the existence of Hawai'ian Creole English stands as evidence of the intermixing of cultures in what is today Hawai'i.

As the table on p. 679 shows, we find speakers of Italian or German or Spanish or Arabic or other languages in areas of the United States where immigrants from corresponding regions of the world ultimately settled. (Particularly in the Southwest, Spanish was spoken in the area long before English arrived.) There is strong evidence that immigrants to the United States become speakers of English fairly quickly, and by the third generation, the grandchildren of immigrants often do not speak their heritage language at all. At the same time, some communities find ways to preserve a language other than English that is important to them for religious or cultural reasons, and a growing number of language groups continue to seek ways to maintain or revitalize their heritage language.

By the way, the census does not ask about the use of American Sign Language (ASL), which is a completely distinct language from English. (In other words, its grammatical system and word order are not those of English.) There is strong evidence that ASL is the third-most frequently used language in the United States after English and Spanish.

Here are three visual arguments that present state-by-state information on three topics; data are also included for Washington, D.C., and the Commonwealth of Puerto Rico. The first presents information on the number of individuals who report speaking a language other than English at home. The second is a chart listing the three most spoken languages other than English. The final visual presents the percentage of individuals who report speaking a language other than English at home and who also report speaking English "very well." (Here, you'll need to compare the information in this map to that in the first map. As will become clear, only a small part of the total population reports speaking English less than "very well.") As you study these visuals, consider what they say about the complex nature of our nation and how they function as arguments of fact.

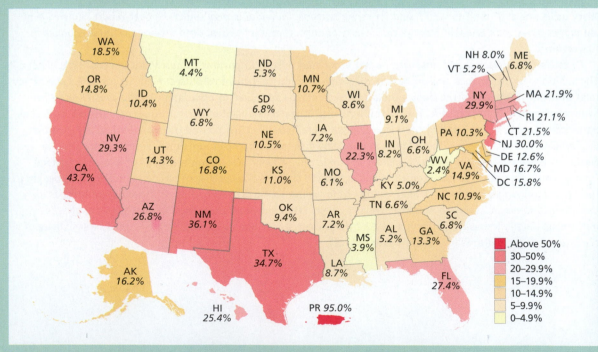

Percentage of Population Who Report Speaking a Language Other Than English at Home

Top Three Languages Other Than English Spoken, by State/Territory

Figures represent percentage of state population who speak each language; top 11 languages highlighted in color

State	1st		2nd		3rd	
Alabama (AL)	Spanish	3.37%	German	0.22%	Korean	0.17%
Alaska (AK)	Spanish	3.37%	Yupik	2.91%	Tagalog	2.13%
Arizona (AZ)	Spanish	20.40%	Navajo	1.39%	German	0.38%
Arkansas (AR)	Spanish	5.24%	German	0.20%	Vietnamese	0.17%
California (CA)	Spanish	28.76%	Tagalog	2.18%	Chinese	1.63%
Colorado (CO)	Spanish	11.82%	German	0.54%	Vietnamese	0.42%
Connecticut (CT)	Spanish	10.96%	Polish	1.11%	Portuguese	1.09%
Delaware (DE)	Spanish	6.72%	Chinese	0.59%	French	0.39%
District of Columbia (DC)	Spanish	7.63%	French	1.43%	Amharic	0.90%
Florida (FL)	Spanish	20.21%	French Creole	2.00%	French	0.60%
Georgia (GA)	Spanish	7.77%	Korean	0.49%	Vietnamese	0.45%
Hawaii (HI)	Tagalog	4.53%	Ilocano	4.20%	Japanese	3.55%
Idaho (ID)	Spanish	7.82%	German	0.31%	French	0.22%
Illinois (IL)	Spanish	13.06%	Polish	1.54%	Tagalog	0.67%
Indiana (IN)	Spanish	4.56%	German	0.58%	Chinese	0.30%
Iowa (IA)	Spanish	5.24%	German	0.20%	Vietnamese	0.17%
Kansas (KS)	Spanish	7.32%	German	0.49%	Vietnamese	0.47%
Kentucky (KY)	Spanish	2.56%	German	0.32%	French	0.20%
Louisiana (LA)	Spanish	3.53%	French	2.38%	Vietnamese	0.62%
Maine (ME)	French	3.60%	Spanish	0.92%	German	0.27%
Maryland (MD)	Spanish	6.91%	French	0.93%	Chinese	0.86%
Massachusetts (MA)	Spanish	8.06%	Portuguese	2.91%	Chinese	1.13%
Michigan (MI)	Spanish	2.91%	Arabic	1.20%	German	0.42%
Minnesota (MN)	Spanish	3.85%	Hmong	1.10%	Cushite	0.76%
Mississippi (MS)	Spanish	2.36%	Vietnamese	0.24%	French	0.16%
Missouri (MO)	Spanish	2.63%	German	0.41%	Chinese	0.26%
Montana (MT)	Spanish	1.49%	German	0.76%	Crow	0.41%
Nebraska (NE)	Spanish	6.98%	Vietnamese	0.45%	German	0.33%
Nevada (NV)	Spanish	20.34%	Tagalog	2.72%	Chinese	0.69%
New Hampshire (NH)	Spanish	2.14%	French	1.92%	German	0.31%
New Jersey (NJ)	Spanish	15.40%	Portuguese	1.01%	Tagalog	0.98%
New Mexico (NM)	Spanish	28.68%	Navajo	3.32%	Keres	0.62%
New York (NY)	Spanish	14.76%	Chinese	1.84%	Russian	1.24%
North Carolina (NC)	Spanish	7.30%	French	0.29%	Chinese	0.26%
North Dakota (ND)	Spanish	1.43%	German	1.33%	Norwegian	0.22%
Ohio (OH)	Spanish	2.23%	German	0.50%	Arabic	0.32%
Oklahoma (OK)	Spanish	6.37%	Vietnamese	0.43%	German	0.30%
Oregon (OR)	Spanish	8.78%	Vietnamese	0.71%	Russian	0.60%
Pennsylvania (PA)	Spanish	4.37%	Chinese	0.46%	Pennsylvania Dutch	0.43%
Puerto Rico (PR)	Spanish	94.90%	Chinese	0.03%	French	0.03%
Rhode Island (RI)	Spanish	10.99%	Portuguese	3.22%	French	1.07%
South Carolina (SC)	Spanish	4.47%	German	0.29%	French	0.25%
South Dakota (SD)	Spanish	2.12%	Dakota	1.44%	German	1.00%
Tennessee (TN)	Spanish	3.87%	Arabic	0.28%	German	0.23%
Texas (TX)	Spanish	29.46%	Vietnamese	0.82%	Chinese	0.43%
Utah (UT)	Spanish	9.63%	German	0.35%	Navajo	0.32%
Vermont (VT)	French	1.57%	Spanish	1.04%	German	0.37%
Virginia (VA)	Spanish	6.67%	Korean	0.74%	Vietnamese	0.63%
Washington (WA)	Spanish	8.18%	Vietnamese	0.94%	Russian	0.89%
West Virginia (WV)	Spanish	1.05%	German	0.17%	Chinese	0.12%
Wisconsin (WI)	Spanish	4.55%	Hmong	0.77%	German	0.68%
Wyoming (WY)	Spanish	4.81%	German	0.31%	French	0.19%

United States Census Bureau

679

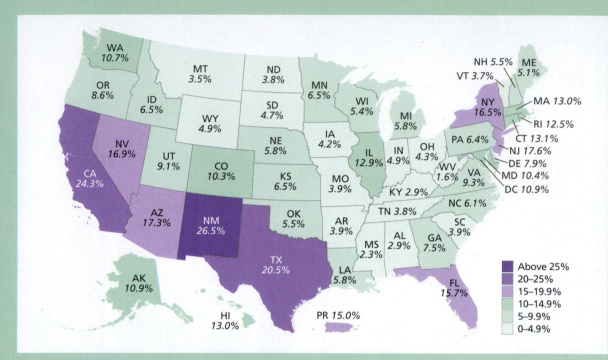

Percentage of Population Who Report Speaking a Language Other Than English at Home and Also Report Speaking English "Very Well"

RESPOND•

1. Had you ever thought about the topic of languages other than English in the United States as an aspect of American history? Why or why not, do you think? Would you expect others to have the same response to this question? Why or why not? Why might many Americans not be aware of the presence of other languages across U.S. history?

2. Which of these visuals contains the most new information for you? Which aspects of the map or table, in particular, do you find most effective?

3. In what sense can each of these visuals be said to be making an argument? What argument(s) might it be making, or which argument(s) might it play a role in supporting?

4. **THINKING CRITICALLY**   Review the discussion in Chapter 14 of the ways that visual arguments can be used to support logical, pathetic, and ethical arguments. Categorize the answers you gave to Question 3 according to these criteria. Likewise, use these criteria as ways of thinking about additional arguments each of the maps could be used to support.

5. An increasingly necessary (and generally challenging) skill for success in academic writing is writing effectively about visual displays of information, including maps and tables. Choose the visual you find most interesting in terms of content or design, and write a healthy paragraph about it that might be included in an essay. Be sure to refer to the visual by name, describe what it shows, and explain what the map tells readers. (Here, you may find it useful to refer to your responses to Questions 3 and 4.)

▼ *Roxane Gay teaches fiction and nonfiction creative writing at Purdue University. Gay is the author of several books, most recently Hunger: A Memoir of (My) Body (2017), as well as one of the writers of the comic book World of Wakanda, which helped inspire the 2018 film, Black Panther. Her writing frequently examines topics related to race and ethnicity, gender, sexuality, and identity. As the daughter of Haitian immigrants to the United States, she is also concerned with the immigrant experience and the ways Americans do and don't understand other cultures and societies. She served as the founding Essays Editor for The Rumpus, an online literary magazine, where this essay first appeared in 2011; it was later anthologized in her best-selling 2016 collection, Bad Feminist. In the essays in that volume, she writes about her own experience of being gang-raped at age twelve, although she does not mention that episode here. As you read this selection, consider Gay's language—the tone she chooses—as well as her claims: that the language we often use about sexual violence is misdirected, encouraging us to ignore what is really going on.*

The Careless Language of Sexual Violence

ROXANE GAY

Roxane Gay Sthanlee Mirador/Sipa USA/Newscom

The unspeakable will be televised: an ironic allusion to a 1970 poem and song by Gil Scott-Heron, "The Revolution Will Not Be Televised" and the earlier use of the slogan among the U.S. Black Power movement of the 1960s.

There are crimes and then there are crimes and then there are atrocities. These are, I suppose, matters of scale. I read an article in the *New York Times* about an eleven-year-old girl who was gang raped by eighteen men in Cleveland, Texas.

The levels of horror to this story are many, from the victim's age to what is known about what happened to her, to the number of attackers, to the public response in that town, to how it is being reported. There is video of the attack too, because this is the future. **The unspeakable will be televised**.

The *Times* article was entitled, "Vicious Assault Shakes Texas Town," as if the victim in question was the town itself. James McKinley Jr., the article's author, focused on how the men's lives would be changed forever, how the town was being ripped apart, how those poor boys might never be able to return to school. There was discussion of how the eleven-year-old girl, the child, dressed like a twenty-year-old, implying that there is a realm of possibility where a woman can "ask for it" and that it's somehow understandable that eighteen men would rape a child. There were even questions about the whereabouts of the mother, given, as we all know, that a mother must be with her child at all times or whatever ill may befall the child is clearly the mother's fault. Strangely, there were no questions about the whereabouts of the father while this rape was taking place.

The overall tone of the article was what a shame it all was, how so many lives were affected by this one terrible event. Little addressed the girl, the child. It was an eleven-year-old girl whose body was ripped apart, not a town. It was an eleven-year-old girl whose life was ripped apart, not the lives of the men who raped her. It is difficult for me to make sense of how anyone could lose sight of that and yet it isn't.

We live in a culture that is very permissive where rape is concerned.   5 While there are certainly many people who understand rape and the damage of rape, we also live in a time that necessitates the phrase "rape culture." This phrase denotes a culture where we are inundated, in different ways, by the idea that male aggression and violence toward women is acceptable and often inevitable. As Lynn Higgins and Brenda Silver ask in their book *Rape and Representation*, "How is it that in spite (or perhaps because) of their erasure, rape and sexual violence have been so ingrained and so rationalized through their representations as to appear 'natural' and inevitable, to women as men?" It is such an important question, trying to understand how we have come to this. We have also, perhaps, become immune to the horror of rape because we see it so often and discuss it so often, many times without acknowledging or considering the gravity of rape and its effects. We jokingly say things like, "I just took a rape shower," or "My boss totally just raped me over my request for a raise." We have appropriated the language of rape for all manner of violations, great and small. It is not a stretch to imagine why James McKinley Jr. is more concerned about the eighteen men than one girl.

The casual way in which we deal with rape may begin and end with television and movies where we are inundated with images of sexual and domestic violence. Can you think of a dramatic television series that has not incorporated some kind of rape storyline? There was a time when these storylines had a certain educational element to them, *à la A Very Special Episode*. I remember, for example, the episode of *Beverly Hills, 90210* where Kelly Taylor discussed being date raped at a slumber party, surrounded, tearfully, by her closest friends. For many young women that episode created a space where they could have a conversation about rape as something that did not only happen with strangers. Later in the series, when the show was on its last legs, Kelly would be raped again, this time by a stranger. We watched the familiar trajectory of violation, trauma, disillusion, and finally vindication, seemingly forgetting we had sort of seen this story before.

Every other movie aired on Lifetime or Lifetime Movie Network features some kind of violence against women. The violence is graphic and gratuitous while still being strangely antiseptic where more is implied about the actual act than shown. We consume these representations of violence and do so eagerly. There is a comfort, I suppose, to consuming violence contained in 90-minute segments and muted by commercials for household goods and communicated to us by former television stars with feathered bangs.

didactic: teaching a moral lesson.

sweeps: the period during which networks are vying for viewers in highly calculated ways in order to up their ratings (and hence their ability to attract advertisers).

While once rape as entertainment fodder may have also included an element of the **didactic**, such is no longer the case. Rape, these days, is good for ratings. *Private Practice*, on ABC, recently aired a story arc where Charlotte King, the iron-willed, independent, and sexually adventurous doctor, was brutally raped. This happened, of course, just as February **sweeps** were beginning. The depiction of the assault was as graphic as you might expect from prime time network television. For several episodes we saw the attack and its aftermath, how the once vibrant Charlotte became a shell of herself, how she became sexually frigid, how her body bore witness to the physical damage of rape. Another character on the show, Violet, bravely confessed she too had been raped. The show was widely applauded for its sensitive treatment of a difficult subject.

The soap opera *General Hospital* is currently airing a rape storyline, and the height of that story arc occurred, yes, during sweeps. *General Hospital*, like most soap operas, incorporates a rape storyline every five years or so when they need an uptick in viewers. Before the current storyline, Emily Quartermaine was raped, and before Emily, Elizabeth Webber was raped, and long before Elizabeth Webber, Laura, of Luke and Laura, was raped by Luke, but that rape was okay because Laura ended up marrying Luke, so her rape doesn't really count. Every woman, *General Hospital* wanted us to believe, loves her rapist. The current rape storyline has a twist. This time the victim is a man, Michael Corinthos Jr., son of Port Charles mob boss Sonny Corinthos, himself no stranger to violence against women. While it is commendable to see the show's producers trying to address the issue of male rape and prison rape, the subject matter is still handled carelessly, is still a source of **titillation**, and is still packaged neatly between commercials for cleaning products and baby diapers.

titillation: excitement of pleasure or interest, often by means of sexually suggestive language or images.

Law & Order: SVU: here, *SVU* stands for "Special Victims Unit."

Of course, if we are going to talk about rape and how we are inundated by 10 representations of rape and how, perhaps, we've become numb to rape, we have to discuss ***Law & Order: SVU***, which deals, primarily, in all manner of sexual assault against women, children, and once in a great while, men.

Each week the violation is more elaborate, more lurid, more unspeakable. When the show first aired, **Rosie O'Donnell**, I believe, objected quite vocally when one of the stars appeared on her show. O'Donnell said she didn't understand why such a show was needed. People dismissed her objections and the incident was quickly forgotten. The series is in its twelfth season and shows no signs of ending anytime soon. When O'Donnell objected to SVU's premise, when she dared to suggest that perhaps a show dealing so explicitly with sexual assault was unnecessary, was too much, people treated her like she was the crazy one, the prude censor. I watch SVU religiously, have actually seen every single episode. I am not sure what that says about me.

I am trying to connect my ideas here. Bear with me.

It is rather ironic that only a couple of weeks ago, the *Times* ran an editorial about the War on Women. This topic is, obviously, one that matters to me. I recently wrote an essay about how, as a writer who is also a woman, I increasingly feel that to write is a political act whether I intend it to be or not because we live in a culture where McKinley's article is permissible and publishable. I am troubled by how we have allowed intellectual distance between violence and the representation of violence. We talk about rape but we don't talk about rape, not carefully.

We live in a strange and terrible time for women. There are days, like today, where I think it has always been a strange and terrible time to be a woman. It is nothing less than horrifying to realize we live in a culture where the "**paper of record**" can write an article that comes off as sympathetic to eighteen rapists while encouraging victim blaming. Have we forgotten who an eleven-year-old is? An eleven-year-old is very, very young, and somehow, that amplifies the atrocity, at least for me. I also think, perhaps, people do not understand the trauma of gang rape. While there's no benefit to creating a hierarchy of rape where one kind of rape is worse than another because rape is, at the end of day, rape, there is something particularly insidious about gang rape, about the idea that a pack of men feed on each other's frenzy and both individually and collectively believe it is their right to violate a woman's body in such an unspeakable manner.

Gang rape is a difficult experience to survive physically and emotionally. There is the exposure to unwanted pregnancy and sexually transmitted diseases, vaginal and anal tearing, **fistula** and vaginal scar tissue. The reproductive system is often irreparably damaged. Victims of gang rape, in particular, have a higher chance of miscarrying a pregnancy. Psychologically, there are any number of effects including **PTSD**, anxiety, fear, coping with the social stigma, and coping with shame, and on and on. The actual rape ends but the

Rosie O'Donnell (1962–): American television personality, actress, author, and comedian known for her willingness to express strong opinions and for her activism for lesbian rights.

(news)paper of record: a major newspaper that is regarded as having high professional standards and whose accounts are taken as authoritative.

fistula: an abnormal hole that can develop between the vagina and the rectum, ureter, or bladder. Consequences include incontinence of urine or feces, infertility, and depression, among others.

PTSD (Post-Traumatic Stress Disorder): a psychiatric disorder that can occur after a person is exposed to some horrific event or series of events such as serving or living in a war zone, surviving sexual assault, living through natural disaster, or surviving major accidents. Individuals with PTSD suffer from mental distress, including disturbing feelings or thoughts, which can be triggered by situations that in some way parallel the source of the original trauma.

aftermath can be very far reaching and even more devastating than the rape itself. We rarely discuss these things, though. Instead, we are careless. We delude ourselves that rape can be washed away as neatly as it is on TV and in the movies where the trajectory of victimhood is neatly defined.

I cannot speak universally but given what I know about gang rape, the 15 experience is wholly consuming and a never-ending nightmare. There is little point in pretending otherwise. Perhaps McKinley Jr. is, like so many people today, anesthetized or somehow willfully distanced from such brutal realities. Perhaps it is that despite this inundation of rape imagery, where we are immersed in a rape culture, that not enough victims of gang rape speak out about the toll the experience exacts. Perhaps the right stories are not being told or we're not writing enough about the topic of rape. Perhaps we are writing too many stories about rape. It is hard to know how such things come to pass.

I am approaching this topic somewhat selfishly. I write about sexual violence a great deal in my fiction. The why of this writerly obsession doesn't matter but I often wonder why I come back to the same stories over and over. Perhaps it is simply that writing is cheaper than therapy or drugs. When I read articles such as McKinley's, I start to wonder about my responsibility as a writer. I'm finishing my novel right now. It's the story of a brutal kidnapping in Haiti and part of the story involves gang rape. Having to write that kind of story requires going to a dark place. At times, I have made myself nauseous with what I'm writing and what I am capable of writing and imagining, my ability to *go there*.

As I write any of these stories, I wonder if I am being gratuitous. I want to *get it right*. How do you get this sort of thing right? How do you write violence authentically without making it exploitative? There are times when I worry I am contributing to the kind of cultural numbness that would allow an article like the one in the *Times* to be written and published, that allows rape to be such rich fodder for popular culture and entertainment. We cannot separate violence in fiction from violence in the world no matter how hard we try. As Laura Tanner notes in her book *Intimate Violence*, "the act of reading a representation of violence is defined by the reader's suspension between the **semiotic** and the real, between a representation and the material dynamics of violence which it evokes, reflects, or transforms." She also goes on to say that, "The distance and detachment of a reader who must leave his or her body behind in order to enter imaginatively into the scene of violence make it possible for representations of violence to obscure the material dynamics of bodily violation, erasing not only the victim's body but his or her pain." The way we currently represent rape, in books, in newspapers, on television, on

semiotic: relating to representation systems, rather than reality itself. Thus, language, music, and visual arts—painting and photography, for example—can all be seen as semiotic systems, which, as Gay notes, are distinct from the reality of lived experience (although they can, in important ways, become part of lived experience).

the silver screen, often allows us to ignore the material realities of rape, the impact of rape, the meaning of rape.

While I have these concerns, I also feel committed to telling the truth, to saying these violences happen even if bearing such witness contributes to a spectacle of sexual violence. When we're talking about race or religion or politics, it is often said we need to speak carefully. These are difficult topics where we need to be vigilant not only in what we say but how we express ourselves. That same care, I would suggest, has to be extended to how we write about violence, and sexual violence in particular.

In the *Times* article, the phrase "sexual assault" is used, as is the phrase "the girl had been forced to have sex with several men." The word "rape" is only used twice and not really in connection with the victim. That is not the careful use of language. Language, in this instance, and far more often than makes sense, is used to buffer our sensibilities from the brutality of rape, from the extraordinary nature of such a crime. Feminist scholars have long called for a rereading of rape. Higgins and Silver note that "the act of rereading rape involves more than listening to silences; it requires restoring rape to the literal, to the body: restoring, that is, the violence—the physical, sexual violation." I would suggest we need to find new ways, whether in fiction or creative nonfiction or journalism, for not only rereading rape but rewriting rape as well, ways of rewriting that restore the actual violence to these crimes and that make it impossible for men to be excused for committing atrocities and that make it impossible for articles like McKinley's to be written, to be published, to be considered acceptable.

An eleven-year-old girl was raped by eighteen men. The suspects ranged 20 in age from middle-schoolers to a 27-year-old. There are pictures and videos. Her life will never be the same. The *New York Times,* however, would like you to worry about those boys, who will have to live with this for the rest of their lives. That is not simply the careless language of violence. It is the criminal language of violence.

RESPOND●

1. Gay is angry, very angry, and she is, of course, angry at two levels: she is outraged about sexual violence against women in this society, but she is also outraged about how we minimize that violence through the language we use to discuss it. What evidence does Gay offer for her claims with regard to how such misdirected language deflects attention from the more basic problem of sexual violence against women?

2. How would you characterize Gay's tone? Given that she is a professor, do you find the piece to be academic? Formal? Stuffy? Conversational? Committed? What adjectives come to mind for you? As noted in Question 1, Gay is angry, but, we contend, her tone is not characterized by the ranting or raving we often associate with anger. How and where does Gay's anger come out? Consider also the fact that this essay was written for an online context. In what ways might that fact influence the tone of the essay? In responding to this question, be sure to point to specific points in the text as evidence. (Chapter 13 on style may give you helpful ideas to use in responding to this question.)

3. Since Gay wrote this essay, a number of events have enabled freer talk among Americans about sexual violence toward women. These events would include a number of high profile and highly disputed incidents on campuses involving alcohol and sex; the trial of the male university doctor who sexually assaulted well over 200 female athletes, including Olympic athletes, for decades; and the #MeToo movement, which encouraged women to share their stories of sexual violence and harassment. How would you evaluate the extent to which American culture is willing to talk frankly about sexual violence against women or men at this time? What sort of language gets used to discuss these topics? What evidence would you give?

4. **THINKING CRITICALLY**   As the headnote explains, Gay has written quite publicly of her own gang rape as a young adolescent, yet she refers to this aspect of her past only indirectly in this text. How, specifically, does she allude to it? What might have been her motivation for treating her life history as she did when writing about this subject? How would the essay have been different had she not acknowledged that history in any way? If she had focused the essay on her own past? How do all these questions relate to issues of ethos? (See Chapter 3 on the creation of ethos.)

5. Find one or two articles on a topic that matters to you for whatever reason and examine critically the language used in them. Then **write an evaluative essay** in which you assess how language is used about this topic. Much like Gay, you may wish to focus on an article or articles that anger you because of the way the topic is treated. Like Gay, you will also have to consider carefully how you will construct your ethos and how you will provide support for your claims. (See Chapter 10 on writing evaluative arguments and Chapter 3 on constructing ethos.)

▼ *Jorge Encinas is a freelance journalist living in Tucson, Arizona. Follow-ing two tours of duty in Iraq with the U.S. Army, Encinas completed his BA and MA at the University of Arizona School of Journalism. After graduation, he served as an intern at Code Switch: Race and Identity Remixed, an award-winning production of National Public Radio. Code Switch began as a blog in 2013 and added weekly podcasts in 2016. It seeks to present stories about aspects of race and ethnicity that offer insight into American culture in ways that daily news programs often do not. Its name comes from the linguistic phenomenon of code-switching—the way speakers of multiple languages or dialects generally move effortlessly between them as they negotiate the social realities of everyday life, creating complex identities for themselves in the process of doing so. In this selection, we read about the situation of a growing number of baseball players who are immigrants and whose first language is not English as they seek to create a professional image for themselves. As you read this blog posting from 2017, consider the ways not being comfortable speaking a language can have consequences of many kinds.*

How Latino Players Are Helping Major League Baseball Learn Spanish

JORGE ENCINAS

With the start of baseball season in sight, millions of Latino fans in the U.S., the Caribbean, and Latin America will be rooting for their favorite players, many of whom are transplants from places like Venezuela, Dominican Republic, and Cuba. But Spanish-speaking fans, millions of whom watch Spanish-language broadcasts of baseball games, will have little idea of the lingering challenge some Latino players in the States have long faced: inadequate language support from the minor and major leagues.

Much of the issues surround the inability of the Latino players to meaningfully communicate with the press. This can be the result of simply not speaking each other's language, a barrier in how cultural norms affect the use of language, or from poor reporting on Latino players. One such incident of lackluster coverage happened last year when Brian T. Smith from the *Houston Chronicle* wrote an article on the struggling performance of Carlos Gómez during his season with the Houston Astros. Gómez, born in the Dominican Republic, speaks English, but not with native proficiency. When Smith quoted Gómez as saying, "For the last year and this year, I not really do much for this team. The fans be angry. They be disappointed," the mangled language sparked a backlash about how the media can sometimes cover players in a way that demeans their intelligence or leaves them embarrassed.

Adrian Burgos Jr., a professor at the University of Illinois who specializes in Latino and sports history, says there is a history of English-language media being insensitive in the coverage Latino players have received in the past. "The practice of poking fun at the accents that Latino players used has been a traditional exercise of the English-language press," Burgos said. He says they tend to highlight the accents and fail to adequately convey the ideas that Latino players are trying to express.

When the backlash against Gómez quotes began, freelance writer Britni De La Cretaz wrote an article pointing to the lack of diversity in newsrooms as contributing to the lack of sensitivity from both Smith and the editors who did not address the grammatically-poor quotes before publishing the article. De La Cretaz pointed to The 2014 Associated Press Sports Editors Racial and Gender Report Card which concluded that more than 91 percent of sports editors and 85 percent of reporters are white.

"For me, what's important is talking to journalists in the community and trying   5
to make sure that I am respectfully representing people," De La Cretaz, who does not speak Spanish, said about covering these players. "I think the responsibility there lies with newsrooms and that's kind of part of the problem, too," she said. "Since I'm a white writer who is writing and my editor is a white editor there's a huge blind spot there."

According to the 2014 AP report, there has been an increase in people of color in sports newsrooms, but most of the progress can be attributed to the diversity found at ESPN. For instance, if the male columnists of color employed by ESPN were removed from the total number of sports staffers at the over 100 newspapers and websites AP reviewed, the percentage of columnists of color would drop from more than 17 percent to three percent.

Significantly, ESPN has dedicated major resources to its Spanish-language viewers and, by extension, to the coverage it gives Spanish-speaking athletes in general.

Freddy Rolón, vice president and general manager at **ESPN Deportes**, oversees the network's business and television's more than 4,500 live hours of Spanish-language content every year. "When we look at the marketplace for the Hispanic audience, we see actually growth in both the English side and the Spanish-language side. And we're seeing a big growth in the overlap as well with the bilingual audience," he said.

Rolón points out that while the bilingual market is growing, Latinos tend to gravitate towards the Spanish ESPN Deportes network for sports like fútbol, soccer, and English ESPN for American football despite the complex overlap in the bilingual audience. That, Rolón says, is the result of each English or Spanish side of the network having cultivated more expertise through a longer history of covering the two different sports.

But covering baseball is complicated, in large part because of its astronomical   10
popularity in and equally important fan bases in the U.S. and Latin America. "When you speak about baseball, it speaks to Latinos on both sides of their being," Rolón said. "There's a question of identity and how that is mixed between your country of origin and the country that you are part of and you live in. That is very much a fabric of baseball."

Rolón says when ESPN Deportes launched in 2004, they found a "huge void" at the intersection of Spanish and baseball that was not being filled. This gap in Spanish coverage led ESPN to realize there was an opportunity to get that coverage from the reporters to bleed into the English programming. "By getting more candid conversations with the players, by letting them open up a little bit more because we're talking to them in their native languages, we got better stories and we were better at serving fans because we could tell them things they might not have heard if they were just looking at it from an English-language lens," Rolón said.

ESPN's Pedro Gomez, a bilingual journalist who has covered baseball for more than 20 years, says covering the players in two languages has improved the reporting and how the players express themselves. "I remember when I started back in the late '80s, early '90s, I can't think of another bilingual reporter that existed on the baseball beat," Gomez said. "And now you walk into a club house, and there are more and more bilingual reporters covering Major League Baseball." While there are more bilingual reporters, Gomez says he would not go as far as agreeing that Spanish-speaking players are not comfortable enough to approach the press more readily today than in the past.

ESPN Deportes (Spanish, "ESPN Sports"): U.S. Spanish-language sports television broadcaster whose target audience is Hispanic viewers. It broadcasts to some 5.5 million Hispanic households in the United States. In addition to broadcasting from the U.S., it also broadcasts from Mexico City.

ESPN's Pedro Gomez interviews American League All-Stars David Ortiz and Miguel Cabrera during the 2010 State Farm Home Run Derby at Angel Stadium of Anaheim on July 12, 2010. Michael Zagaris/Getty Images

MLB (Major League Baseball): the oldest professional sports organization in the U.S. and Canada composed of 30 teams. In 2017, MLB revenues exceeded $10 billion.

For the 2016 season, **MLB** mandated that all teams provide interpreters for players with limited or no English proficiency. Foreign-born Latinos made up a quarter of the players on opening day of the 2016 season and come from countries where English proficiency may be limited and Spanish is the primary language. Gomez believes interpreters are a step in the right direction. "Players used to have to grab a coach, a teammate who spoke both languages and kind of use them as a translator and of course these people weren't trained as professional translators," Gomez said.

Paul Mifsud, an MLB vice president and deputy general counsel, says the interpreters the teams are required to hire, which are subsidized by the league and included in negotiations with the players union, will be in place for the next five years. "There was initial skepticism about the value of it, but at this point all teams, I think, have really bitten into it and find it extremely useful," Mifsud said. "It's really started to improve the communication dynamic in the clubhouse and the ability of the players who may have felt uncomfortable talking to the media."

Ozzie Guillén, former White Sox shortstop and manager, said there has been improvement, but there is much still needed to help Latinos when it comes to language. "Baseball [has] improved a lot, but it's hard right now to speak the language because you don't need to," Guillén said. "Some players think, 'If I produce, I don't need to speak English, and they have to figure [it] out to understand what I'm saying.'"

15

Guillén also joked that when you're good you don't need to learn English, but if you're not, you had better learn English. However, he did say it was important that players learn English. But he added that a language barrier is accompanied by a cultural barrier in how that language is used: what is being said and how it is interpreted by the public. Guillén says that gap in cultural translation landed him in trouble because what is appropriate in Spanish and his culture might not be perceived the same way in the U.S.

In one instance Guillén received backlash while managing the White Sox for saying it was unfair for Asian players to be given interpreters while Latinos were left without them. In 2010, *USA Today* reported him as saying:

Chicago White Sox manager Ozzie Guillén, left, talks with first base coach Harold Baines in the dugout during a game in 2011.
Nam Y. Huh/AP Images

"Very bad. I say, why do we have Japanese interpreters, and we don't have a Spanish one. I always say that. Why do they have that privilege and we don't?" Guillén said Sunday before Chicago played the Oakland Athletics. "Don't take this wrong, but they take advantage of us. We bring a Japanese player, and they are very good, and they bring all these privileges to them. We bring a Dominican kid . . . go to the minor leagues, good luck. Good luck. And it's always going to be like that. It's never going to change. But that's the way it is."

There was a divide in the media over what Guillén said and how it was interpreted, leading to friction between him and the MLB.

While there were some interpreters before the 2016 requirement was put in place, 20 they were not mandated by MLB and were hired at the discretion of the teams. With just a handful of Asian players in the league and on different teams around the country, coaching staff and fellow players were not readily available to translate.

This generalized "lost in translation" effect is being addressed by MLB with acculturation and language lessons to Latino players while in minor league teams. "Players who are going to be successful major leaguers for many years, there's obvious advantages to having those players be bilingual and not just speak Spanish," Mifsud said.

Guillén agrees that there are missed opportunities for Latino players to take up leadership roles because they cannot be outspoken about what they feel and think. That, he says, is a reason some great Latino players never become managers or join a team's leadership ranks. Guillén says learning English and acclimating to U.S. culture are most important for young players in the minors who have less money and support, both on and off the field. During the 2016 Minor League Baseball season, Latinos accounted for more than 41 percent of the players.

While long overdue, MLB's plan to improve language services and cultural acclimation and the press's continued efforts to more accurately cover Spanish-speaking players should result in players feeling more at ease with the press and their fans, and fans gaining more access to and insights into their favorites.

RESPOND.

1. Encinas would likely claim that he has written an argument based on fact. What claim or thesis has he used these facts to support? (See Chapter 8 for information on arguments based on fact.)

2. What sorts of "hard evidence" does Encinas use to support these claims? (Here, you might make a two-column chart, with the categories of hard evidence in one column—facts, statistics, surveys and polls, and testimonies and narratives—and all the examples of hard evidence you find in the other.) How appropriate is this evidence in terms of kind and amount, given the argument Encinas is making? By the way, is there relevance to the fact that MLB profits in 2017 exceeded $10 billion? Why or why not? Why might Encinas not have mentioned this fact? (See Chapter 4 on kinds of hard evidence.)

3. What are the short- and long-term consequences of the language challenges faced by some baseball players who are immigrants to the United States? (We have framed the question as we have because some players from other countries arrive speaking English well.) How easy do you think it would be for you to master a new language well enough to feel confident being interviewed on television? How can this situation help us appreciate some of the challenges immigrants might face more broadly?

4. **THINKING CRITICALLY**   Study the comment in paragraph 3 by Professor Burgos. Do you agree with his claim that the press has traditionally "poked fun" at the accents of Latino players? What are the consequences of such a practice? Is it limited to Latino players? What might the consequences be of mocking and belittling the accents of

those who do not speak American English natively, particularly given how few Americans can speak a language other than English with any degree of fluency or with a native-like accent? How is such mocking related to issues of power?

5. Do some research on the resources available in your area to help immigrants to the United States learn English. Here, rather than focusing on intensive English programs that prepare international students to study at U.S. colleges and universities, look for information about programs that teach English to immigrants, refugees, and asylees. How many such programs are there? Where are they located? How does this line up with where the immigrant populations live? What are the fees, if any? How large are the programs? Are there waiting lists for admission? Are the programs adequate to meet both the community's and the newcomers' needs? Why or why not? Some of this information you may be able to find online, but you may also need or want to interview individuals associated with the programs—administrators, teachers, or students. When you've concluded your research, present it in an essay. Depending on what you discover, you may wish to **write an argument of fact or evaluation or offer a proposal**. (Chapter 18 on finding evidence will prove useful here, particularly the section on collecting data on your own. Chapters 8, 10, and 12 treat factual, evaluative, and proposal arguments, respectively.)

26

Has the Internet Destroyed Privacy?

Over the past three decades, the Internet has changed many aspects of daily life in the United States and around the world. If you don't access it from your cell phone, there's always a laptop, tablet, or campus computer. Who can get access to your accounts? How easily? For what purposes? Every Web page you visit potentially leaves a trace of where you've been and the device you used to get there. Who has or should have access to this information? What might they be doing with it? Are individuals, companies, or governments profiting from that information? The selections in this chapter encourage you to consider these issues and perhaps to reflect on your own online behavior.

In a blog post, Lindsay McKenzie reports on the ways that UMass Amherst developed a campaign to remind students about the need to avoid weak passwords. Weak passwords are, of course, a threat to an individual's account—and hence their private information—and to the school's entire computer system. Although such a fact is obvious, McKenzie observes that students at UMass (and perhaps your campus, too) still often choose weak passwords like the name of their pet.

The second selection, visual arguments, presents a series of cartoons, all of which focus on aspects of privacy online. The third selection is composed of two short blog postings by Lauren Salm and by Deanna Hartley from Careerbuilder.com. Both focus on how employers use information about individuals available online to screen applicants, whether screening them out because of information on social media or screening them in because of how they've presented their online selves to relevant employers. The privacy issues here relate ultimately to questions of ethos—the self-image you create for yourself (and that others create of you) on social media and online more broadly: based on what employers can find online, what sort of potential employee do you appear to be?

The fourth selection, by Lauren Carroll of PolitiFact, evaluates a claim from the nonprofit Fight for the Future (FFTF) when it tweeted, "215 members of Congress just voted to let your ISP spy on what type of underwear you buy and sell that data to advertisers." As you'll see, PolitiFact concludes that advertisers can now find out private information about you that you might never have expected, and they can use that information to their benefit. The stark example Carroll uses—what kind of underwear you buy or even look at—makes clear the sorts of things that are at stake when we debate issues of privacy on the Internet.

In an excerpt from his 2017 book, *World without Mind: The Existential Threat of Big Tech*, Franklin Foer explains why he thinks the Internet—and Big Tech, in particular—are well on their way to killing our privacy. He, however, has a proposal for what Americans can do based on a precedent, an action we've taken in a similar situation in the past.

Amanda Hess, who writes for the *New York Times*, contends that privacy is now a commodity—and luxury—that only the rich and powerful can manage to afford. She supports her claims with an interesting discussion of the changing nature of privacy—the word and the concept—from Ancient Greece to the present.

As we write these words, the latest online privacy scandal involves Cambridge Analytica, which has been accused of scraping Facebook users' data without permission in an effort to sway U.S. elections, creating "Facebook's worst crisis" and causing many users to try to delete their accounts. Of this situation, Mark Zuckerberg commented that when he started Facebook in his dorm room in 2004, he would never have imagined that fourteen years later, his biggest worry would be stopping governments from seeking to influence one another's elections. This scandal will likely be history by the time you read these selections, but challenges raised by privacy online will no doubt continue to emerge.

This November 2017 selection was written by Lindsay McKenzie, a technology writer for InsideHigherEd.com, an online publication devoted to issues in higher education in the United States and worldwide. It reports on one university's efforts to get its students to be vigilant about a persistent problem: the use of weak passwords that compromise their own personal accounts and the security of the campus network as a whole. McKenzie highlights the challenge to campus technology professionals: figuring out a creative way to make a compelling argument to a well-defined audience. As you read, take note of not only the aims of argument at play but also the additional benefits that the campaign described here reaped. Consider as well why we chose to begin this chapter on privacy with a discussion of passwords on campus.

IT: information technology.

Educause: a U.S. nonprofit organization seeking "to advance higher education through the use of information technology."

Getting Personal about Cybersecurity

LINDSAY McKENZIE

Today's students may be digital natives, but that doesn't mean institutions can count on them to protect themselves from cyberattacks.

A recent survey by the technology firm CDW-G found that the No. 1 cybersecurity challenge facing **IT** professionals on campus is educating users about security policies and practices. Among students surveyed, just 25 percent dubbed the cybersecurity training or education efforts on their campus as very effective.

One institution, however, may have found a way to reach students—by making them, and their pets, the stars of a cybersecurity-awareness campaign.

Speaking at the annual meeting of **Educause** in Philadelphia this month, representatives from the University of Massachusetts at Amherst shared how they leveraged students' love of social media and personalized content to encourage them to up their cybersecurity game.

"There was a recognition that we needed to do something different, something fun," said Iris Chelaru, web communications manager at UMass. While previous awareness campaigns had been informative, they failed to connect with students on a personal level, said Chelaru. Cybersecurity awareness is a bit like public health awareness, she said—"things that we have to do but that we don't want to." 5

As students are both creators and curators of content online, who better than them to advise and help design an awareness campaign, Chelaru said. She and her team worked with the student government and other campus organizations to design an approach that was both informative and "warm and fuzzy," said Chelaru.

Rather than presenting information on multiple security risks, as the university had previously, UMass officials decided to pick just one issue—weak passwords—as the center of their campaign. Pet names emerged as something that students regularly use as passwords, but that can be easily guessed, said Chelaru. With this in mind, the team created a website where students can create posters with pictures of their pets, underneath the tagline "My name is not a good password."

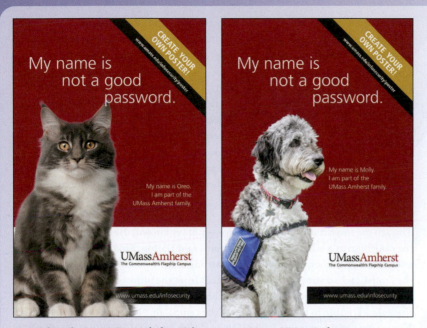

Posters from the Getting Personal About Cyberspace campaign at UMass Amherst University of Massachusetts, Amherst

"We were thinking about things that are familiar to students and that they know, maybe something from home that they miss," said Chelaru. The posters, which could be easily shared on social media, saw much more engagement from students than previous campaigns did, said Matthew Dalton, chief information security officer at UMass Amherst.

Though the campaign started with posters of student pets, it quickly broadened, said Dalton. To make the campaign even more interactive, the team created giant photo frames that students could pose with in real life, under the same "My name is not a good password" banner. The team set up tables in areas with high student traffic at lunchtimes in October as part of National Cyber Security Awareness Month and offered prizes to encourage engagement. Soon the football team's mascot, Sam the Minuteman, and the university administration were in on the campaign.

While Dalton and colleagues hailed the campaign as a success, evaluating its impact has been tricky, he acknowledged. They have seen a decrease in student account breaches, but Dalton said he can't be sure this campaign is responsible, as opposed to other security work the team has done. It would be difficult to

10

The campus Internet security professionals found that their campaigns were more effective when they connected to their audience—students—on a personal level.

LINK TO P. 24

track whether the campaign had actually resulted in behavior change without cracking student passwords to check if they contain pet names, said Dalton. But he is planning to look at whether password change activity has risen, he said.

Dalton said that the password campaign, now entering its third year, continues to have an impact because it doesn't overload students with information. Where previously students might have been referred to the National Institute of Standards and Technology's guidelines on how to create a good password (make them complicated, change them regularly, include numbers and special characters, etc.), now students are just being made to think about what makes a bad password. The details come later, when the students actually log in to change their passwords, said Dalton.

Though the impact on student behavior is not yet known, the institution views the campaign as a success for other reasons, said Dalton. First, all the posters and photos shared on social media had strong institutional branding. Second, the campaign had support and engagement from the university administration, including backing from the vice chancellor for information services. Third, students were able to take ownership of the campaign. "People were willing to become part of the message," said Dalton. "With any participation event, that's key—especially with security awareness."

RESPOND•

1. What problem gave rise to the arguments made by the UMass Amherst cybersecurity campaign described in this selection? How did the IT professionals define the rhetorical situation? How did their understanding of the rhetorical situation shape their response? What sorts of research did they do? Whose help did they enlist? Why? (Reviewing Chapter 1's discussion of the rhetorical situation may be helpful in thinking about this question.)

2. What is your response to the solution that the students at UMass Amherst came up with? Do you think you would likely find it convincing enough to move you to action, that is, to pay attention to the security on your own computer account—to make passwords complicated and not likely predictable, to change them regularly, and to include numbers and special characters? Why or why not?

3. How would you characterize the argument made by this selection: is it an argument of fact, one of definition, an evaluative argument, a causal argument, or a proposal? Why? (The discussion of stasis theory in Chapter 1 may prove useful here.)

4. **THINKING CRITICALLY**   What were the unforeseen consequences of the campaign described here? Why are they important? What does a situation like this one teach us about the nature of argument and its potential consequences or benefits?

5. Imagine you were given the task of creating a proposal to address the problem of cybersecurity on your campus by raising student awareness of the issue. Is there a solution that you believe might be more effective than the one used on the UMass Amherst campus? Working individually or in small groups, **construct a proposal argument** containing a plan for addressing this challenge. (Chapter 12 offers a discussion of proposal arguments.)

▼ Although you've likely never considered it, producing an effective cartoon requires an interesting and complex set of rhetorical skills. Cartoonists have a limited amount of space to convey their messages. The five cartoons included here range from a single panel to four panels, the latter representing a widely syndicated cartoon strip. A cartoon's message has to be pithy—much like a tweet—and it has to combine one or more images with words. The words, of course, may take the form of a caption, or they may be part of the image. The images have multiple functions: they have to capture the reader's attention, but they must also thrust the reader into a narrative, a story, one that unfolds almost instantaneously.

Cartoons likewise have to rely on the two-edged sword of humor—always risky—to make their point. In this regard, even simple cartoons represent sophisticated visual rhetoric—multimodal arguments—that merit careful attention. Furthermore, cartoons must be timely, speaking to a current topic of interest or debate; in short, they must seize the kairotic moment, as discussed in Chapter 1. As you consider the five cartoons in this selection, all of which consider aspects of privacy, use your rhetorical skills to analyze how each of the cartoonists manages to pack what is often an implied but powerful argument into such a small package.

Making a Visual Argument: The Issue of Privacy

Pickles is an award-winning Sunday comic by Brian Crane that has been syndicated since 1990. The main characters, Opal and Earl Pickles, shown in this strip, are in their seventies and were originally based loosely on Crane's retired in-laws. In this cartoon strip from September 2016, Opal notices that Facebook is capable of what she terms "mind infiltration"—a noteworthy word choice! And yet very quickly Opal goes from being offended by the alleged privacy violation to being susceptible to the targeted advertising. . . . As you read, consider your own responses to the way social media feeds on and reinforces our interests, our values, our desires, and our fears. *Pickles* used with the permission of Brian Crane, the Washington Post Writers Group and the Cartoonist Group. All rights reserved.

Chris Slane is an award-winning New Zealand cartoonist, illustrator, puppeteer, and author who has been publishing cartoons since 1991. He specializes in the topics of privacy, security, and freedom of information, and he claims that his database on these subjects is likely the largest in the world. His cartoons on these topics have appears in at least nine countries and been translated into four languages, reminding us that these subjects present challenges worldwide. As you study this cartoon, consider how it complements and contrasts with the message of the previous one by Brian Crane. © Chris Slane

Chris Wildt's cartoons appear in the *Cape Gazette* (Delaware). As you study this cartoon, consider how it builds on and expands the arguments made by Lauren Salm's and Deanna Hartley's blog postings, in the third selection in the chapter, about the growing role that social media play in the hiring process. © Chris Wildt/ CartoonStock Ltd.

Mike Smith's syndicated cartoon, "Smith's World," appears daily on the editorial page of the *Las Vegas Sun*. In his work as a "geeky artist," he seeks to be "an equal opportunity offender," poking fun across the political spectrum. He reports that he is grateful for his liberal arts degree from a Jesuit school because it taught him to "question authority and be a person who practices critical thinking." He has likewise stated that "editorial cartooning is really about reading. It's about absorbing as much information as you can, because the spark to the creative process is information." This cartoon, from 2016, comments on a specific legal question—whether a cellular phone manufacturer should be able to hack the phones they sell in order to provide information to a government. Since Smith's original cartoon, the questions have become broader—stretching to all social media—and more urgent. Notice how deftly Smith is able to pack all that controversy into a single cartoon.

J. D. Crowe is statewide cartoonist for the Alabama Media Group, which includes several newspapers, magazines, and Web sites, all related to Alabama life. He has stated that he believes it is "[his] duty to weed out numbskull politicians on the homefront before they can grow in the national spotlight." He likewise "generously spreads his tough love to international and national issues based on the news of the day." This 2017 cartoon comments on the same Congressional decision that is discussed in a later selection, Lauren Carroll's "Congress Let Internet Providers 'Spy' on Your Underwear Purchases, Advocacy Group Says." As you study this cartoon, consider how its effectiveness compares with the tweet Carroll's group evaluates. © J.D. Crowe, Cagle Cartoons

RESPOND.

1. Which of these five cartoons do you find most effective at communicating the argument it is making? How does it encourage readers to think about issues of privacy in an electronic environment? Why? (The discussion of evaluative criteria in Chapter 10 may be useful here.)

2. Analyze how each of these cartoons works as a visual argument, as discussed in Chapter 14. Consider the visual design, including the images and colors used, the style of drawing, and the relationship between the images and text of each.

3. Choose one of the cartoons, and analyze it in terms of its appeals to emotions, of the character of its creator, and of the facts or reasoning the cartoon represents. These appeals are discussed in Chapter 1 and again in Chapters 2, 3, and 4, respectively.

4. **THINKING CRITICALLY**   Someone searching databases for cartoons generally uses a keyword search, as discussed in Chapter 18. Here, we've listed the keywords for three of the cartoons:

Brian Crane, "Oh, My Gosh! When Did Facebook Start with Mind Infiltration?"

> *advertisement, advertising, bag, by hand, comic strip, Facebook, generous, gosh, hand, handbag, internet, internet privacy, Italian, manipulate, manipulation, marketing, marketing advertising, media, mind, network, online, online advertising, online privacy, ooh, privacy, private, purse, screen, social, social media, social network, soft, start*

Chris Wildt, "Impressive Résumé . . ."

> *verification, verifications, resume, resumes, social media, social medias, social network, social networks, social networking, cv, cvs, businessmen, businessman, profile, profiles, online, avatar, website, websites, hr, human resources, verifying, personnel*

Mike Smith, "I Agree with Apple . . ."

> *agree, apple, Apple Computer, cell, cell phone, cell phone privacy, cellular, computer, computer privacy, computer software, computer technology, data, editorial, editorial cartoon, encrypt, encryption, Facebook, government, government computer, hack, information, internet, internet privacy, iPhone, media, Mike, mobile, online, online privacy, personal, personal data, personal information, phone, political media, poster, privacy, private, private information, Smith, social, social media, software, tech, technology, user*

What might account for both overlap and differences in the lists, given the content of each cartoon? Can you think of other terms that someone might have used to search for these cartoons? Can you imagine why they weren't included in the list of keywords? How can studying lists of keywords like these help you improve your own keyword searches?

5. Many writers struggle with incorporating a visual of any kind—a cartoon, a figure, a table—into a text they are writing in a way that helps readers understand the meaning and significance of the visual argument with regard to the ongoing argument. Imagine that you are writing an essay about the nature of privacy in electronic environments and that you decide to use one of these cartoons to illustrate a point you wish to make. Specify the point you wish to make (in other words, what argument could the cartoon be used to illustrate or

support), and then write a healthy paragraph that could be used to incorporate the cartoon into the text. You will need both to describe the cartoon to some degree and to explain its message or significance. Using a phrase like "the cartoon shows . . ." or "in the cartoon, the reader sees . . ." will help you as you describe the cartoon. This will be a **factual argument** of the sort discussed in Chapter 8 because your task will be to describe as accurately as possible the information contained in the cartoon. The discussion of using visuals in your own arguments in Chapter 14 should help you with this task.

▶ This selection includes two short 2017 blog postings from Careerbuilder.com, an employment Web site providing not only job listings from around the world but also practical advice to help those seeking jobs. These articles fall into the latter category. Lauren Salm explains how employers scrutinize job candidates' social media profiles, while Deanna Hartley offers ways to maximize the potential of social media when preparing for the job market. Their advice certainly relates to Aristotle's claim that rhetoric is "finding the available means of persuasion." For job seekers, that means carefully doing certain things online while studiously avoiding others. As you read, consider how the advice both women offer relates to the rhetorical notion of kairos, as discussed in the opening chapter of this book.

70 Percent of Employers Are Snooping Candidates' Social Media Profiles

LAUREN SALM

Scrolling through your photos from this past weekend and laughing at the debauchery of your *Hangover*-esque charades? Ranting about your current job or co-workers because you think you're just among "friends?" Think again. According to a new CareerBuilder survey, 70 percent of employers use social media to screen candidates before hiring, which is up significantly from 60 percent in 2016. So pause before you post—if you think it could be questionable or inappropriate, you should go with your gut.

SO, WHAT TO FLAUNT VS. FLOP?

Social recruiting is now a "thing" when it comes to hiring candidates—3 in 10 employers have someone dedicated to solely getting the scoop on your online persona.

Employers are searching for a few key items when researching candidates via social networking sites as good signs to hire:

- Information that supports their qualifications for the job (61 percent)
- If the candidate has a professional online persona at all (50 percent)
- What other people are posting about the candidates (37 percent)
- For any reason at all not to hire a candidate (24 percent)

And they aren't stopping there either—69 percent are using online search engines such as Google, Yahoo and Bing to research candidates as well, compared to 59 percent last year.

THE NO-NOS WHEN USING SOCIAL NETWORKS

With more than half of employers (54 percent) finding content on social media that caused them not to hire a candidate, why take your chances? Pause before you post and remember these key reasons that employers were turned off by a candidate's online presence:

- Candidate posted provocative or inappropriate photographs, videos or information: 39 percent
- Candidate posted information about them drinking or using drugs: 38 percent
- Candidate had discriminatory comments related to race, gender or religion: 32 percent

5

- Candidate bad-mouthed their previous company or fellow employee: 30 percent
- Candidate lied about qualifications: 27 percent
- Candidate had poor communication skills: 27 percent
- Candidate was linked to criminal behavior: 26 percent
- Candidate shared confidential information from previous employers: 23 percent
- Candidate's screen name was unprofessional: 22 percent
- Candidate lied about an absence: 17 percent
- Candidate posted too frequently: 17 percent

USING SOCIAL MEDIA TO YOUR ADVANTAGE

You don't have to look at your online persona as problem. There are things you can do on Twitter or Facebook that can actually up your chances of employment. Use it as an opportunity to stand out in a positive way and showcase your personality. In fact, more than 44 percent of employers have found content on a social networking site that caused them to hire the candidate.

Among the primary reasons employers hired a candidate based on their social networking site were: candidate's background information supported their professional qualifications (38 percent), great communication skills (37 percent), a professional image (36 percent), and creativity (35 percent). But don't avoid the stress all together by deleting or hiding your profiles. Believe it or not, this can be even more detrimental to your brand. Fifty-seven percent of employers are less likely to call someone in if the candidate is a ghost online.

The bottom line? Think before you post, because there's always someone watching. Don't put anything online that you wouldn't want your mom, grandma, dad, uncle, best friend's mom or cat to see or read.

Creative Ways to Get Noticed by Employers on Social Media

DEANNA HARTLEY

From making flippant racial remarks to posting unhygienic pictures on the job at a fast food restaurant, there are larger-than-life instances of what NOT to do on social media. On the flip side, social media could work in your favor if you're looking for a job—if you do it right.

Some savvy job seekers are leveraging it to their benefit to catch the attention of potential employers, and you can follow suit with these tips.

Update your social media profile. Whether you like it or not, social media is an extension of your personal brand. Did you know that 70 percent of employers are peeking into candidates' social media profiles? So clean up your Facebook profile or make it private. Add skills and/or recommendations to your professional social media profiles, and make sure to use keywords wherever you can so your profile is easily searchable.

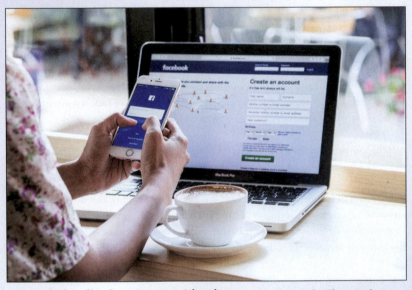

Your Facebook profile is fair game to potential employers tongcom photographer/Shutterstock

Use multimedia to supplement your resume. While some job seekers have actually gone to extremes by advertising themselves using social ads on Facebook or Google AdWords, being over-the-top dramatic is not always necessary to catch an employer's attention. Consider creating an online portfolio of your work, creating videos that show off your skills, producing a Snapchat channel that highlights your creativity or using other non-traditional avenues that would give employers a sense of your professional prowess.

Make strategic connections. While it's great to connect with Ron from the last networking event you went to, be proactive and seek out professionals in your field. Don't be afraid to ask for advice—many professionals, as busy as they are,

5

will be happy to help. Establish connections with individuals who work at the company you're applying to and reach out to them for tips on how to get your foot in the door.

Follow your dream employer's social media accounts. Not only will it help you connect with the company, but you can also follow the social media feeds to do some more research about the company and determine if it's a good cultural fit. Oftentimes, brands tend to be more authentic and engaging on social media than other corporate channels, so look for personality and fit.

Start interacting with corporate social accounts. The recruiter or hiring manager at your dream company may not return your calls or queries in a timely fashion, but chances are you'll have a better shot at a two-way communication using social media. Retweet and share relevant posts. You don't need to be a subject-matter expert or thought leader to reply to their tweets or comment on LinkedIn posts or Facebook posts—but do so only if you have legitimate feedback/opinions or something constructive to add to the conversation.

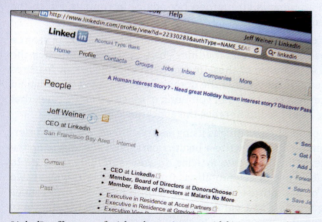

LinkedIn offers a way for job-seekers to interact with hiring companies
Bloomberg/Getty Images

Personalize conversations. What you find out about a company or hiring manager online can help you find topics that sit well with the hiring manager so you can personalize conversations or even thank-you notes. Keep in mind there's a line between being diligent (scouring for professional insights) and creepy (looking to see how many children they have), so don't cross it.

RESPOND.

1. Were you surprised to learn about the findings of the surveys mentioned in these two articles? Why or why not? If someone scrutinized your social media accounts, might they find things that could lead to your not getting (or even losing) a job? Do you see such things on the social media accounts of others? Why, in your opinion, does the situation discussed in this article persist; that is, why do people continue to post compromising information, including photos and videos, online for all the world to see?

2. How do these two articles ultimately treat issues of privacy on- and offline? Do you believe that employers should be able to scrutinize the social media accounts of employees and job candidates? Why or why not? Do you believe that anything online can truly be private? Why or why not?

3. Like many arguments that offer advice (a subgenre of proposal arguments, in fact), these two arguments use facts to create the context for and support the advice they offer. Salm, in particular, relies heavily on fact-based arguments. In your opinion, does such a reliance on fact-based arguments strengthen her advice in comparison to the advice offered by Hartley? Why or why not?

4. **THINKING CRITICALLY** How do the audience—job seekers from a range of backgrounds—and medium—blog postings—influence the shape and appearance of these texts? What specific layout features can you identify? Why would the authors have assumed these would be useful to their readers? Can you think of other layout features that might have been used to improve the appearance of these texts?

5. A key part of research writing is using sources effectively. Using information from Chapter 20, **write a healthy paragraph summarizing the advice offered in these two articles.** In your summary, be sure to include at least two direct quotations from each article as well as two instances of paraphrase. Pay special attention to the differences between quotation and paraphrase, the correct way to punctuate each, and the appropriate ways to credit sources.

▼ *This selection, from PolitiFact, presents an argument within an argument from March 2017. First, we have a tweet posted by Fight for the Future (FFTF), another nonprofit organization, which advocates on issues related to digital rights, including online privacy. The tweet presents itself as an argument of fact. Then, we have what is obviously an evaluative argument by PolitiFact, a Pulitzer Prize–winning Web site operated by the Tampa Bay Times and the Poyner Institute that investigates and evaluates claims made by politicians, lobbyists, and interest groups. As you can see, PolitiFact ultimately rates the FFTF's tweet as "mostly true" on its Truth-O-Meter. The author of this evaluative argument was Lauren Carroll, who was a staff writer at PolitiFact; the author of the FFTF tweet was not identified. As you read, pay attention to the research process that Carroll used as well as to PolitiFact's process for documenting the research it conducts and the criteria it uses in arriving at its evaluative ranking.*

Congress Let Internet Providers "Spy On" Your Underwear Purchases, Advocacy Group Says

LAUREN CARROLL

Your Internet service provider has intimate knowledge about your intimates, and a bill headed to President Donald Trump's desk allows them to sell that information, says Internet privacy advocacy group Fight for the Future.

Voting along party lines, Republicans in Congress recently passed a joint resolution that reverses a landmark Federal Communications Commission rule requiring Internet service providers (ISPs), like Comcast or Verizon, to ask customers for their explicit permission before handing user data over to advertisers and other third parties. President Donald Trump is expected to sign it into law.

"215 members of Congress just voted to let your ISP spy on what type of underwear you buy and sell that data to advertisers," Fight for the Future tweeted March 28, after the bill passed the House.

Fight for the Future has the vote count right; 215 members of the House of Representatives voted for the measure. We decided to dig into whether the group is right about what the bill means for online shopping.

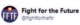

Fight for the Future
@fightfortheftr

215 members of Congress just voted to let your ISP spy on what type of underwear you buy and sell that data to advertisers #BroadbandPrivacy

BREAKING:

The House of Representatives just voted to let ISPs like Comcast and Verizon sell your data without your permission.

The companies you pay for Internet can now spy on you and sell information about what you do online to the highest bidder.

FIGHT FOR THE FUTURE ●

3:24 PM - 28 Mar 2017

A Fight for the Future tweet Twitter

713

ISPs AND THE BILL

Fight for the Future's tweet might give the misleading impression that ISPs can't   5
already see their customers' online purchases and sell that information. They can.
Congress's action just makes this explicitly legal.

An ISP's function is to connect its users to websites or online apps, and so it
can see nearly everything its users do on the Internet, including what kind
of underwear they buy. An advertiser might be interested in purchasing that
information from an ISP because then it can predict whether a given user is more
likely to respond to an ad for boxers, briefs or tighty-whities.

Beyond shopping habits, ISPs and advertisers can glean more significant personal
information about their customers from Internet browsing patterns—like that a
spouse is contemplating divorce because he looked up "best divorce lawyers in my
area," or that a person has a chronic medical condition because she spent a long
time reading certain pages on WebMD.

In October 2016, the FCC established rules intended to give consumers more
control over how ISPs used their data. The rules required ISPs to obtain explicit
information from their customers before using and sharing their web browsing
history, which would include underwear purchases.

The rule also required the ISPs to get consent before sharing other "sensitive
information," like Social Security numbers, precise geolocation data and
financial or health information. Many Internet companies and trade associations
had already committed to requiring consumers to opt-in before they can share
that sort of information, per guidance from the Federal Trade Commission.

But these opt-in rules never went into effect; Congress killed them in March 2017,   10
months before the December 2017 start date. So ISPs can see and use customers'
web browsing data as they always have.

"Practically speaking, I expect consumers will see no change in how their data is
collected and marketed," said Brent Skorup, a technology policy research fellow
at George Mason University's Mercatus Center.

Fight for the Future Campaign Director Evan Greer said Congress's vote was
significant because it gives ISP companies explicit permission to engage in
practices that some privacy advocates consider "abusive," and it gives ISPs an
incentive to invest in systems to further these practices.

ISPs have been expanding the scope of their operations, merging with other varieties of service providers, such as Verizon purchasing AOL, or AT&T's planned deal to purchase Time Warner, Inc. This, combined with Congress's reversal of the FCC rules, might encourage ISPs to expand their role in online advertising, said Peter Swire, a professor at Georgia Tech and the chief counselor for privacy during President Bill Clinton's administration.

"There's a lot of online advertising today," Swire said. "Now the big broadband companies will play more actively in that space."

Those who supported gutting the FCC rules argue that the regulations put ISPs   15
at a disadvantage compared to other Internet companies, like search engines or social media sites, that already sell users' data without first getting permission. They also say the rules stifle technology innovation.

Privacy advocates, however, say that ISPs have an especially large window into its users Internet habits, and this rule could have opened up the possibility of beginning to enact privacy regulations on other web-based companies.

"This is troublesome because of the larger question: Is privacy opt in or opt out?" said Jamie Winterton, director of strategy for Arizona State University's Global Security Initiative. "Can your browser behaviors be bought and sold?"

PRIVACY PROTECTIONS

Though they can see a lot, there are limitations to what ISPs can see.

Some websites use encryption, so the ISP can see the domain name but not the exact page on that website the user is browsing. A website is encrypted if the address starts with "https" not "http." For example, if a web user visit the Macy's website, which is encrypted, their ISP will know they're browsing the Macy's website, but it won't know if they're shopping for underwear, a prom dress or bedding. (The article you're currently reading is not encrypted.)

However, if someone visits MeUndies.com right after visiting VictoriasSecret.   20
com—both encrypted—an advertiser can probably make an educated guess that the person is in the market for some underwear. There are many more sophisticated ways an ISP or third party can glean information about a user even when the data is encrypted.

Regardless, most ecommerce sites remain unencrypted, Swire said.

As a fact-checking organization, PolitiFact's Truth-O-Meter evaluates statements by politicians on a scale of six degrees of truthfulness, ranging from "True" to "Pants on Fire." Politifact.com

By evaluating statements from politicians, lobbyists, and interest groups, PolitiFact takes the work of "crap detection" seriously.

LINK TO P. 459

An Internet user who really does not want an ISP tracking any of their data can use a Virtual Private Network, which, put simply, is a way to scramble all Internet traffic so the ISP and potential hackers can't get at it. But this might not completely eliminate privacy concerns because some VPNs themselves don't fully protect users' data.

"If you don't want any of your information out there, you'd have to do all sorts of things," Winterton said. "It's a lot to ask of people."

OUR RULING

Fight for the Future said, "215 members of Congress just voted to let your ISP spy on what type of underwear you buy and sell that data to advertisers."

ISPs can see most of the websites their customers visit. Congress, with 215 votes   25 from the House, sent a bill to Trump's desk that codified ISPs' ability to sell their customers' web browsing data, including any online underwear purchases that aren't encrypted.

Regulations enacted in 2016 would have required ISPs to ask customers for explicit permission to share this data with advertisers or other third parties. But Congress acted before the regulations went into effect.

Fight for the Future's phrasing—and use of the loaded term "spy"—might lead people to think that Congress's action gave ISPs new freedoms, but they could always view and sell users' web browsing information. Now they have Congress's stamp of approval to do so without getting users' permission first.

That context is important, so we rate Fight for the Future's claim Mostly True.

ABOUT THIS STATEMENT

Published: Thursday, March 30th, 2017 at 5:27 p.m.
Researched by: Lauren Carroll
Edited by: Angie Drobnic Holan
Subjects: Congress, Privacy, Technology

SOURCES

Competitive Enterprise Institute, "Six Reasons FCC Rules Aren't Needed to Protect Privacy," March 27, 2017
Congress.gov, S.J.Res.34, accessed March 30, 2017

CTIA, "Internet Companies Reaffirm Consumer Privacy Principles as FCC Reviews Flawed Wheeler Era Broadband Rules," Jan. 27, 2017

Email interview, Fight for the Future campaign director Evan Greer, March 30, 2017

Email interview, George Mason research fellow Brent Skorup, March 30, 2017

Email interview, Upturn principal Aaron Rieke, March 29, 2017

FCC, "FCC Adopts Privacy Rules to Give Broadband Consumers Increased Choice, Transparency and Security for Their Personal Data," Oct. 27, 2016

Georgia Tech, "Online Privacy and ISPs: ISP Access to Consumer Data Is Limited and Often Less Than Access by Others," Feb. 29, 2016

New York Times, "How the Republicans Sold Your Privacy to Internet Providers," March 29, 2017

NPR, "As Congress Repeals Internet Privacy Rules, Putting Your Options in Perspective," March 28, 2017

Phone interview, Georgia Tech professor Peter Swire, March 29, 2017

Phone interview, Jamie Winterton, strategy director at ASU's Global Security Initiative, March 29, 2017

Proskauer, "The Clock Has Started: What ISPs Need to Do and When to Comply with the FCC's Broadband Privacy Rules," Dec. 7, 2016

Upturn, "What ISPs Can See," March 2016

RESPOND.

1. Prior to reading this selection, how much thought had you given to the specific issues of Internet privacy discussed here—the sale of data about the sites you visit and the purposes for which such data might be used? What advantages and disadvantages do you see of making user information available? What do you think someone might assume about you if they had access to your Internet viewing history? (You may not wish to share your response to this last question, but we'd contend that it bears reflecting on.)

2. Should there be limits to who can or cannot purchase or have access to the information discussed in this selection or the purposes for which it could or should be used? Why or why not? What criteria would you propose for deciding these questions?

3. The actual bill being discussed by the FFTF tweet and PolitiFact's evaluation of it is "S.J.Res.34-A joint resolution providing for congressional disapproval under chapter 8 of title 5, United States Code, of the rule submitted by the Federal Communications Commission relating to 'Protecting the Privacy of Customers of Broadband and Other Telecommunications Services.'" Obviously, the FFTF could not have used the complete name in a tweet because it is far longer than 140 (or even 280)

characters—a question of the medium, a tweet, influencing the form the message or argument takes. Why might FFTF have constructed the tweet as it did, with its use of #BroadbandPrivacy and the example of underwear? In other words, how does the tweet show clear evidence that its creators at FFTF had audience and rhetorical purpose in mind? (See Chapter 1 for a discussion of audience and rhetorical purpose.)

4. **THINKING CRITICALLY**   Consider how carefully PolitiFact has constructed its evaluative argument. Don't rely simply on the information presented here, but also investigate the procedures PolitiFact uses by visiting the methodology page on its Web site: http://bit.ly/2CiIJcI. What specific steps does it take to demonstrate the credibility of its claims? How trustworthy do you find its procedures? What criteria do you find yourself using in arriving at your evaluation? (Check out Chapter 10 on the nature of evaluative arguments.)

5. **Write an evaluative essay** in which you use a research process similar to the one that PolitiFact uses when checking claims made by politicians, lobbyists, and interest groups. Choose a claim—and a tweet would be an ideal choice—made in the past few weeks by a politician, lobbyist, or interest group you're familiar with, and investigate its likely veracity. You probably won't be able to conduct interviews as PolitiFact does, but you can certainly seek credible sources of information to support your evaluation. As you've learned in responding to Question 3, the process PolitiFact uses is a multistep procedure involving the author, a reviewing editor, and two additional editors. First, a staff writer researches the claim, keeping what researchers would generally term an "audit trail," a list or "map" of where the various bits of information came from. Then, once the research is completed and written up, an editor reviews it with the writer. Once the document has been revised, the editor shares it with two other editors, and all three vote on the veracity of the statement. Only then is the "Our Ruling" section of the evaluation created. We'd encourage you to try this process with classmates as part of writing your evaluative essay. (Chapters 18–20 on finding sources, evaluating them, and using them appropriately will be especially useful for this assignment, as will Chapter 21 on plagiarism and academic integrity.)

from World without Mind: The Existential Threat of Big Tech

FRANKLIN FOER

The big tech companies believe we're fundamentally social beings, born to collective existence. They invest their faith in the network, the wisdom of crowds, collaboration. They harbor a deep desire for the **atomistic** world to be made whole. By stitching the world together, they can cure its ills. Rhetorically, the tech companies gesture toward individuality—to the empowerment of the "user"—but their worldview rolls over it. Even the **ubiquitous invocation** of users is telling, a passive, bureaucratic description of us.

The big tech companies—the Europeans have charmingly, and correctly, lumped them together as GAFA (Google, Apple, Facebook, Amazon)—are shredding the principles that protect individuality. Their devices and sites have collapsed privacy; they disrespect the value of authorship, with their hostility to intellectual property. In the realm of economics, they justify **monopoly** with their well-articulated belief that competition undermines our pursuit of the common good and ambitious goals. When it comes to the most central tenet of individualism—free will—the tech companies have a different way. They hope to automate the choices, both large and small, that we make as we float through the day. It's their **algorithms** that suggest the news we read, the goods we buy, the path we travel, the friends we invite into our circle.

It's hard not to marvel at these companies and their inventions, which often make life infinitely easier. But we've spent too long marveling. The time has arrived to consider the consequences of these monopolies, to reassert our own role in determining the human path. Once we cross certain thresholds—once we transform the values of institutions, once we abandon privacy—there's no turning back, no restoring our lost individuality. . . .

One of the clichés of our time: *Data is the new oil*. This felt like hyperbole when first articulated, but now feels perfectly apt. "Data" is a bloodless word, but what it represents is hardly bloodless. It's the record of our actions: what we read, what we watch, where we travel over the course of a day, what we purchase, our correspondence, our search inquiries, the thoughts we begin to type and then delete. With enough data, it is possible to see correlations and find patterns. The computer security guru Bruce Schneier has written, "The accumulated data can probably paint a better picture of how you spend your

---

◀ This selection comes from Franklin Foer's 2017 book, World Without Mind: The Existential Threat of Big Tech. Foer, a fellow at the New American Institute and a correspondent for the Atlantic, is former editor of the New Republic and author of How Soccer Explains the World.

An existential threat is, of course, one that threatens our very existence. Foer is convinced that the big technology companies that control much of the Internet represent such a threat to humans and especially to our privacy, among other things Americans cherish. At the same time, Foer has a proposal for how we can meet that threat head on and defeat it. As you read this selection, consider how Foer examines a common metaphor in an especially telling way and uses that critique as the basis for his proposal.

atomistic: here, unconnected or fragmented into many parts.

ubiquitous: found everywhere.

invocation: mentioning or calling upon; the word often has religious connotations (a prayer to the deity asking for help) or connotations of magic (an incantation or spell).

monopoly: a corporation that has exclusive control of providing a good or service; the opposite situation would be a market where there is competition among providers.

algorithms: an unambiguous procedure for solving a problem; used here to refer to the computer programs online companies use to make recommendations to you about information, goods, services, and people that might appeal to you.

psyche: the human spirit, soul, or mind.

proliferation: rapid growth or increase.

convergence: the coming together of distinct or disparate things.

time, because it doesn't have to rely on human memory." Data amounts to an understanding of users, a portrait of our **psyche**. Eric Schmidt once bragged, "We know where you are. We know where you've been. We can more or less know what you're thinking about."

A portrait of a psyche is a powerful thing. It allows companies to predict 5 our behavior and anticipate our wants. With data, it is possible to know where you will be tomorrow within twenty meters and to predict, with reasonable accuracy, whether your romantic relationship will last. Capitalism has always dreamed of activating the desire to consume, the ability to tap the human brain to stimulate its desire for products that it never contemplated needing. Data helps achieve this old dream. It makes us more malleable, easier to addict, prone to nudging. It's the reason that Amazon recommendations for your next purchase so often result in sales, or why Google ads result in clicks.

The dominant firms are the ones that have amassed the most complete portraits of us. They have tracked us most extensively as we travel across the Internet, and they have the computing power required to interpret our travels. This advantage becomes everything, and it compounds over time. Bottomless pools of data are required to create machines that effectively learn—and only these megacorporations have those pools of data. In all likelihood, no rival to Google will ever be able to match its search results, because no challenger will ever be able to match its historical record of searches or the compilation of patterns it has uncovered.

In this way, data is unlike oil. Oil is a finite resource; data is infinitely renewable. It continuously allows the new monopolists to conduct experiments to master the anticipation of trends, to better understand customers, to build superior algorithms. Before he went to Google, as the company's chief economist, Hal Varian cowrote an essential handbook called *Information Rules*. Varian predicted that data would exaggerate the workings of the market. "Positive feedback makes the strong get stronger and the weak get weaker, leading to extreme outcomes." One of these extreme outcomes is the **proliferation** of data-driven monopolies.

It's a disturbing **convergence**: These companies have become dominant on the basis of their extensive surveillance of users, the total monitoring of activities, their ever-growing dossiers—what Maurice Stucke and Ariel Ezrachi call "a God-like view of the marketplace." Put bluntly, they have built their empires by pulverizing privacy; they will further ensconce themselves by continuing to push boundaries, by taking even more invasive steps that build toward an even more complete portrait of us. Indeed, the threats to privacy and the competitive marketplace are now one and the same. The problem of monopoly has changed shape. . . .

What we need is a Data Protection Authority to protect privacy as the government protects the environment. Both the environment and privacy are goods that the market would destroy if left to its own devices. We let business degrade the environment within limits—and we should tolerate the same with privacy. The point isn't to prevent the collection or exploitation of data. What are needed, however, are constraints, about what can be collected and what can be exploited. Citizens should have the right to **purge** data that sits on servers. Rules should require companies to set default options so that citizens have to opt for surveillance, rather than passively accept the loss of privacy, a far more robust option than the incomprehensible take-it-or-leave-it terms of service agreements.

This is a matter of **autonomy**; The intimate details embedded in our data 10 can be used to undermine us; data provides the basis for invisible discrimination; it is used to influence our choices, both our habits of consumption and our intellectual habits. Data provides an X-ray of the soul. Companies turn that photograph of the inner self into a commodity to be traded on a market, bought and sold without our knowledge.

It's a basic, intuitive right, worthy of **enshrinement**: Citizens, not the corporations that **stealthily** track them, should own their own data. The law should demand that these companies treat this data with the greatest care, because it doesn't belong to them. Possessing our data is a heavy responsibility that must come with ethical obligations. The American government has a special category for corporations that profit from goods that they don't truly own: We call them trustees. This is how the government treats radio and television broadcasters. Those companies make money from their use of the public airwaves, so the government requires that these broadcasters adhere to a raft of standards. At times, they were asked to broadcast civil defense warnings and public service announcements; they were asked to adhere to decency standards and were required to provide equal airtime to candidates of both political parties. The government, in the form of the Federal Communications Commission, supervises the broadcasters to guarantee that they don't shirk these obligations. . . .

A Data Protection Authority would be the heir to this tradition. Unlike the Federal Trade Commission, which evaluates mergers to preserve low prices and economic efficiency, the authority would review them to protect privacy and the free flow of information. It would constrain monopolies as they attempt to carry their power into the next era, creating the opening through which challengers can ultimately emerge. . . . The health of our democracy demands that we consider treating Facebook, Google, and Amazon with the

purge: here, remove or have removed.

autonomy: independence or freedom outside control.

enshrinement: the act of treating something as sacred and, thus, protecting it, in this case, by making laws or government policies about it.

stealthily: in a secret, hidden manner.

same firm hand that led government to wage war on AT&T, IBM, and Microsoft—even dismembering them into smaller companies if circumstances (and the law) demand a forceful response. While it has been several generations since we wielded **antitrust** laws with such vigor, we should remember that these cases created the conditions that nurtured the invention of an open, gloriously innovative Internet in the first place. . . .

***antitrust:* encouraging competition rather than monopolies.**

The long history of regulation also shows that the project is not nearly as futile as its critics claim. When government tries to remodel the economy for the sake of efficiency, it has amassed a mixed record. When government uses its power to achieve clear moral ends, it has a strong record. There are notable failures, for sure. But our automobiles are safer, our environment is cleaner, our food doesn't poison us, our financial system is fairer and less prone to catastrophic collapse, even though those protective provisions have imposed meaningful costs on the private sector. . . . The Internet is amazing, but we shouldn't treat it as if it exists outside history or is exempt from our moral structures, especially when the stakes are nothing less than the fate of individuality and the fitness of democracy.

RESPOND●

1. Foer clearly believes the Internet is killing privacy. How does he see the Internet as doing so? In other words, what, for Foer, are the specific threats associated with the Internet, and why should they be considered threats?

2. What is your response to Foer's analysis of how the Internet is killing privacy? Do you agree or disagree with Foer? Why or why not? And what is your response to his proposal for dealing with the threat? Do you believe it is necessary? sufficient? possible? Why or why not?

3. As explained in the headnote, a major section of Foer's argument is built around his careful examination and critique of a metaphor, that is, a comparison between two things. In Foer's discussion, what two things are equated? In what ways are the two things in fact similar? Where, for Foer, does the metaphor fall apart, that is, what are its limits? Why do these limits matter for him and the argument he is making? What can we, as writers, learn from considering such careful considerations of the limits of metaphor? (See Chapter 13 on style in argument for a discussion of metaphor.)

4. **THINKING CRITICALLY**   As also mentioned in the headnote, Foer proposes a way of addressing the threat he contends the Internet poses. What specific evidence or criteria for evaluating evidence does he use

in establishing the existence of an actual threat? What specific evidence or criteria for evaluating evidence does he offer in support of his proposal? Evaluate both these sets of evidence and criteria. (Chapter 10 provides information about evaluative arguments; that information will help you appreciate Foer's argument and evaluate the criteria he uses in it.)

5. **Write a proposal argument** in which you support or rebut Foer's proposal for dealing with the threat he defines. (As Chapter 12 on proposals points out, you may well need to draw on earlier chapters about factual, definitional, evaluative, and causal arguments.) You may wish to support Foer's proposal fully or to argue for a modified version of it. If you oppose his proposal, you may wish to offer a counterproposal in addition to demonstrating the shortcomings of the proposal he makes.

▶ Amanda Hess is a David Carr fellow at the New York Times, where this selection appeared in the "First Words" column of the Times's Sunday magazine in May 2017. She writes regularly about Internet culture, and her work has appeared in Slate, Elle, Marie Claire, and WIRED, among other publications. In this selection, Hess examines, first, the extent to which privacy in American society is commodified—that is, bought and sold—and, second (and understandably), the ways in which it then becomes the privilege of the wealthy alone. As you read, consider how Hess comments on a number of issues raised by the selections in this chapter as well as what the consequences might be of the situation Hess describes for you.

How Privacy Became a Commodity for the Rich and Powerful

AMANDA HESS

Recently I handed over the keys to my email account to a service that promised to turn my spam-bloated inbox into a sparkling model of efficiency in just a few clicks. Unroll.me's method of instant unsubscribing from newsletters and junk mail was "trusted by millions of happy users," the site said, among them the "Scandal" actor Joshua Malina, who tweeted in 2014: "Your inbox will sing!" Plus, it was free. When a privacy policy popped up, I swatted away the legalese and tapped "continue."

Last month, the true cost of Unroll.me was revealed: The service is owned by the market-research firm Slice Intelligence, and according to a report in *The Times*, while Unroll.me is cleaning up users' inboxes, it's also rifling through their trash. When Slice found digital ride receipts from Lyft in some users' accounts, it sold the anonymized data off to Lyft's ride-hailing rival, Uber.

Suddenly, some of Unroll.me's trusting users were no longer so happy. One user filed a class-action lawsuit. In a blog post, Unroll.me's chief executive, Jojo Hedaya, wrote that it was "heartbreaking to see that some of our users were upset to learn about how we monetize our free service." He stressed "the importance of your privacy" and pledged to "do better." But one of Unroll.me's founders, Perri Chase, who is no longer with the company, took a different approach in her own post on the controversy. "Do you really care?" she wrote. "How exactly is this shocking?"

This Silicon Valley "good cop, bad cop" routine is familiar, and we spend our time surfing between these two modes of thought. Chase is right: We've come to understand that privacy is the currency of our online lives, paying for petty conveniences with bits of personal information. But we are blissfully ignorant of what that means. We don't know what data is being bought and sold, because, well, that's private. The evidence that flashes in front of our own eyes looks harmless enough: We search Google for a new pair of shoes, and for a time, sneakers follow us across the web, tempting us from every sidebar. But our information can also be used for matters of great public significance, in ways we're barely capable of imagining.

> *Privacy costs often become clear only after they've already been paid.*

When I signed up for Unroll.me, I couldn't predict that my emails might be   5
strategic documents for a power-hungry company in its quest for total road
domination. Such privacy costs often become clear only after they've already
been paid. Sometimes a private citizen is caught up in a viral moment and learns
that a great deal of information about him or her exists online, just waiting to
be splashed across the news—like the guy in the **red sweater** who, after asking a
question in a presidential debate, had his Reddit porn comments revealed.

But our digital dossiers extend well beyond the individual pieces of information
we know are online somewhere; they now include stuff about us that can be
surmised only through studying our patterns of behavior. The psychologist and
data scientist Michal Kosinski has found that seemingly mundane activity—like
the brands and celebrities people "like" on Facebook—can be leveraged to reliably
predict, among other things, intelligence, personality traits and politics. After
our most recent presidential election, the company Cambridge Analytica boasted
that its techniques were "instrumental in identifying supporters, persuading
undecided voters and driving turnout to the polls" on Donald Trump's behalf. All
these little actions we think of as our "private" business are actually data points
that can be aggregated and wielded to manipulate our world.

Years ago, in 2009, the law professor Paul Ohm warned that the growing
dominance of **Big Data** could create a "database of ruin" that would someday
connect all people to compromising information about their lives. "In the
absence of intervention," he later wrote, "soon companies will know things about
us that we do not even know about ourselves." Or as the social scientist and
Times contributor Zeynep Tufekci said in a recent talk: "People can't think like
this: I didn't disclose it, but it can be inferred about me." When a peeping Tom
looks between the blinds, it's clear what has been revealed. But when a data firm
cracks open our inboxes, we may never find out what it has learned.

Privacy has not always been seen as an asset. The ancient Greeks, for instance,
distinguished between the public realm ("*koinon*") and the private realm ("*idion*").
In contrast to those public citizens engaged
in political life, humble private citizens were
known as "*idiotai*," a word that later evolved
into "idiots." Something similar is true of the
English word "privacy." As **Hannah Arendt** wrote
in "The Human Condition," privacy was once closely associated with "a state of
being deprived of something, and even of the highest and most human of man's
capacities." In the 17th century, the word "private" arose as a more politically
correct replacement for "common," which had taken on condescending overtones.

> Privacy is increasingly seen not as a right but as a luxury good.

---

red sweater guy: a reference to Kenneth Bone, who, after asking a televised question as part of a panel of undecided voters during the 2016 presidential campaign while wearing a red sweater, became an Internet meme. He was initially characterized as "all that's right about America." However, his image quickly became tarnished when comments he'd made on a range of topics, from sex to the killing of Trayvon Martin, came to light.

Big Data: here, not merely electronic data sets that are so massive that they cannot be processed by traditional software applications, but additionally predictive analytics, methods of extracting data and analyzing patterns in them from these large data sets. Most of the discussions of privacy in this chapter focus on issues related to predictive analytics applied to big data.

Hannah Arendt (1906–1971): American political theorist who immigrated to the United States after fleeing Nazi Germany and living in several other European countries. One of the most important political philosophers of the last century, Arendt frequently wrote on the nature of totalitarianism, direct democracy, and authority.

George Orwell's **1984:** a novel published in 1949 by Orwell, an English novelist (1903–1950). The book recounted a country (clearly what had been Great Britain) where everyone was directly or indirectly under government control. The elites were under constant surveillance via telescreens, constantly reminding them, "Big Brother is watching you." In contrast, the *proles*, a shortened form of *proletariat*, or working class, were left to work and breed though their lives were under indirect control of the government as well. The term *Orwellian* has come to mean unwarranted government control and intrusion into the lives of individuals, often through mass surveillance of varying sorts.

Samuel Warren (1852–1910) and Louis Brandeis (1856–1941): Harvard-trained attorneys—second and first in their graduating class, respectively—whose 1890 essay "The Right to Privacy" in the *Harvard Law Review* is credited with creating the notion of a right to privacy in American legal theory and popular culture. They defined privacy as "the right to be let alone." After practicing law, Warren managed the family paper mill while Brandeis, known as the "people's lawyer," became the first Jewish Supreme Court justice. Brandeis's opinions stand as some of the finest arguments for freedom of speech and the right of privacy penned by any justice or legal theorist.

And yet somewhere along the way, privacy was recast as a necessity for cultivating the life of the mind. In **George Orwell's "1984,"** the proles are spared a life of constant surveillance, while higher-ranking members of society are exposed to Big Brother's watchful eye. The novel's protagonist, Winston, begins to suspect that real freedom lies in those unwatched slums: "If there is hope," he writes in his secret diary, "it lies in the proles." In the influential 1967 book "Privacy and Freedom," Alan Westin described privacy as having four functions: personal autonomy, emotional release, self-evaluation and intimate communication. This modern understanding of privacy as an intimate good grew up right alongside the technology that threatened to violate it. At the end of the 18th century, the Fourth Amendment to the United States Constitution protected Americans from physical searches of their bodies and homes. One hundred years later, technological advancements had legal minds thinking about a kind of mental privacy too: In an 1890 paper called "The Right to Privacy," **Samuel Warren and Louis Brandeis** cited "recent inventions and business methods"—including instant photography and tabloid gossip—that they claimed had "invaded the sacred precincts of private and domestic life." They argued for what they called the right "to be let alone," but also what they called "the right to one's personality."

Now that our privacy is worth something, every side of it is being monetized. 10
We can either trade it for cheap services or shell out cash to protect it. It is increasingly seen not as a right but as a luxury good. When Congress recently voted to allow internet service providers to sell user data without users' explicit consent, talk emerged of premium products that people could pay for to protect their browsing habits from sale. And if they couldn't afford it? As one congressman told a concerned constituent, "Nobody's got to use the internet." Practically, though, everybody's got to. Tech companies have laid claim to the public square: All of a sudden, we use Facebook to support candidates, organize protests and pose questions in debates. We're essentially paying a data tax for participating in democracy.

The smartphone is an intimate device; we stare rapt into its bright light and stroke its smooth glass to coax out information and connect with others. It seems designed to help us achieve Westin's functions of privacy, to enable emotional release and moments of passive reflection. We cradle it in bed, at dinner, on the toilet. Its pop-up privacy policies are annoying speed bumps in the otherwise instantaneous conjuring of desires. It feels like a private experience, when really it is everything but. How often have you shielded the contents of your screen from a stranger on the subway, or the partner next to you in bed, only to offer up your secrets to the data firm tracking everything you do?

The surveillance economy works on such information **asymmetry**: Data-mining companies know everything about us, but we know very little about what they know. And just as "privacy" has grown into an anxious buzzword, the powerful have co-opted it in order to maintain control over others and **evade** accountability. As we bargain away the amount of privacy that an ordinary person expects, we've also watched businesses and government figures grow ever more indignant about their own need to be left alone. Companies mandate **nondisclosure agreements** and demand out-of-court **arbitration** to better conceal their business practices. In 2013, Facebook revoked users' ability to remain unsearchable on the site; meanwhile, its chief executive, Mark Zuckerberg, was buying up four houses surrounding his Palo Alto home to preserve his own privacy. Sean Spicer, the White House press secretary, has defended President Trump's secretive meetings at his personal golf clubs, saying he is "entitled to a bit of privacy," and the administration has cut off public access to White House visitor logs, citing security risks and "privacy concerns." When The New York Times reported that the president takes counsel from the Fox News host Sean Hannity, Hannity indignantly tweeted that his conversations were "PRIVATE."

We've arrived at a place where public institutions and figures can be precious about their privacy in ways we're continually deciding individual people can't. Stepping into the White House is now considered more private than that weird rash you Googled. It's a cynical inversion of the old association between private life and the lower class: These days, only the powerful can demand privacy.

asymmetry: here, inequality because knowledge flows in only one direction rather than bidirectionally.

evade: avoid.

nondisclosure agreement: a binding legal agreement, usually between two parties, detailing information that is known or can be shared among those parties but cannot be disclosed to anyone else. Such agreements are sometimes referred to as "confidentiality agreements."

arbitration: a method of resolving disputes out of court in which the parties agree to permit a trained third party or parties, known as arbitrators, to decide the matter after being presented with the facts of the case. The results of such arbitration are often required to remain confidential, and, as noted, arbitration is frequently imposed by one party—often a corporation—on another—often an individual.

RESPOND.

1. Do you agree with Hess's claim that privacy has become a privilege, one that only the rich and powerful can afford or demand? Why or why not?

2. Hess's argument is composed of three sections: paragraphs 1–7, 8–10, and 11–13. Summarize the argument made in each section, noting how it contribute to Hess's overall claim.

3. An interesting aspect of this selection is its use of logical appeals of several types: testimonies in the form of statements made by various parties and references to specific individuals that stand as facts as well as arguments based on etymology (the history of a word's meaning) or the history of a concept, among others. Make a list of all the logical appeals you can find in this selection, categorizing them by type. How and why do they support Hess's claims? (Chapter 4 on logical arguments will be useful in completing this assignment.)

4. **THINKING CRITICALLY**   Hess frequently uses what Chapter 13 refers to as "special effects" in terms of choosing words or constructing phrases both to advance her argument and to create her own personal style. One example would be "Years ago, in 2009, . . ." (para. 7), another would be the phrase "petty conveniences" (4), and a third would be her observation that the ancient Greek term *idiotai* is the source of the English word *idiots* (8). Make a list of all the special effects you can find in the selection, and discuss how they contribute to Hess's argument.

5. **Construct an academic argument** about issues relating to privacy and the Internet. Rather than treating a broad question like "Has the Internet Killed Privacy?," you will likely want to focus on a narrower aspect of this topic, either one treated in these readings or a different one that you have become aware of. As with most academic arguments, you will almost assuredly need to conduct research to understand the issues and support your claims. (Chapter 17 provides information on academic arguments while Chapters 18–20 will help you find, evaluate, and use sources. Be sure to consult Chapter 21 on academic integrity and avoiding plagiarism.)

27

How Free Should Campus Speech Be?

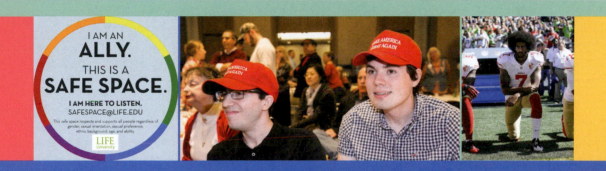

LEFT TO RIGHT: Life University; LAURA BUCKMAN/Getty Images; Ted S. Warren/AP Images

In 1994, the well-known literary critic and legal scholar Stanley Fish published a controversial book, *There's No Such Thing as Free Speech . . . And It's a Good Thing Too*. Fish argued that the notion that Americans could or should be able to say anything they like anytime and anyplace was, in fact, deeply flawed—even on college campuses, where the idea of free and open debate has long been held as close to sacred. The selections in this chapter provide strong evidence that the issues that concerned Fish still dominate campus discussions today even though the terms in which those debates are framed have shifted.

The chapter opens with introduction to John Palfrey's 2017 *Safe Spaces, Brave Spaces: Diversity and Free Expression in Education*, in which Palfrey makes an impassioned plea for the value of living in and learning from the tensions between supporting free speech and finding ways to create campus communities where people from all sorts of backgrounds and of all sorts of perspectives can feel they are heard. The second selection, from a 2018 Knight Foundation survey of over 3,000 college students about issues related to free expression on campus, provides strong evidence that a stance such as Palfrey's represents the views of most

U.S. college and university students. This fact-based argument demonstrates that the overwhelming majority of students are committed to findings ways to support free speech while promoting an inclusive society welcoming of diverse groups. The challenge, of course, is figuring out how to achieve such a goal.

In the third selection, comedian and actor Ben Schwartz examines questions of free speech in light of the decision of some well-known comedians to stop performing on college campuses because of concerns about what one critic has termed a "humor crisis." This selection reminds us of both the potential value and the danger of humor as a rhetorical tool.

The next three selections treat the topic of microaggressions. The first visual argument is a poster designed by a consulting firm to help students and employees in businesses appreciate what microaggressions are and why they are harmful. The second is a cartoon demonstrating the way that speakers' assumptions and presuppositions can result in questions or comments that listeners may find offensive. Next, psychologist Scott Lilienfeld contends that although there should be no denying the reality of prejudice in American society, he has grave concerns about the social science research used in support of the campus programs seeking to contain microaggressions.

Sarah Brown considers the roles that athletes increasingly play as activists for social causes on campus, from taking a knee to making politically charged comments to threatening to boycott playoff games. Such actions by individuals, groups of athletes, or entire teams raise complex questions about the possible limits of free speech, especially for students who, as athletes, are often seen as representing the institution.

The chapter's final selection by professor Catherine Nolan-Ferrell narrates how the issues raised in selections in this chapter played out in her classroom during and after the presidential election of 2016 at the University of Texas at San Antonio, where nearly half the students identify as Latino. Writing for an audience of professors, Nolan-Ferrell describes how she and her students sought to live in and learn from the tensions described by Palfrey in the chapter's opening selection. She demonstrates the complex ways in which teaching and learning in classrooms are highly contextualized rhetorical acts, providing multiple opportunities for examining and applying the concepts taught throughout *Everything's an Argument*.

Safe Spaces, Brave Spaces

JOHN PALFREY

Free expression and diversity are essential components of democracy in the twenty-first century. In the United States, our shared commitment to both principles, especially as they developed in the late twentieth century, ensures that a democracy and the world at large benefit from heterogeneity. These two concepts rely on and reinforce one another.

The arguments in favor of diversity and free expression are not exactly the same, but neither are they unrelated. There are reasons for diversity that have little or nothing to do with free expression; and there are reasons for free expression that have little or nothing to do with diversity. The areas of overlap, though, are plentiful—and they are essential to finding the best path forward. At their essence, both of these ideals support democracy because they mean that societies are educating informed, engaged citizens and seeking to establish a sense of fair play and justice in political systems. While diversity and free expression are too often pitted against one another as competing values, they are more compatible than they are opposing.

The American experiment at its best calls for diversity and free expression to coexist. That coexistence has not been easy, nor has it been all that successful, especially for those who have had less power. The American experience has been a lot easier for whites, males, Christians, heterosexuals, the able-bodied, and the wealthy in particular. And free expression has been interpreted in ways that have tended to support those in authority rather than all people **equitably**. These critiques of the American experiment are all grounded in historical truth. But it is also true that free expression can serve all of us. Diversity is about self-expression, learning from one another, working together in productive ways across differences, and in turn strengthening our democracy. Diversity that also encompasses and supports intellectual and academic freedom—without condoning hate speech—has enormous force, promise, and importance.

WHY DIVERSITY MATTERS

Our commitment to seeking the truth and making sound decisions, in intellectual communities and in the public sphere, relies on the coexistence of diversity and free expression. One of the reasons to have a diverse

◀ *John Palfrey (1972–) is an educator, currently serving as Head of School at Andover Academy, and legal scholar, having served as executive director of Harvard University's Berkman Center for Internet & Society from 2002 to 2008. An authority on law and new media, he is a strong advocate for Internet freedom. This selection comes from the introduction to Palfrey's 2017 book,* Safe Spaces, Brave Spaces: Diversity and Free Expression in Education. *Here, Palfrey is arguing that "free expression and diversity are essential components of democracy in the twenty-first century" and that that two are ultimately compatible despite frequently being set in opposition to one another. As you read this academic argument, pay careful attention to how Palfrey structures it, particularly the ways he anticipates alternative positions and seeks to respond to them respectfully.*

The American experiment: a description that reminds readers that America—and indeed, every country—is an experiment, one that can succeed or fail, depending on the actions of individuals.

equitably: fairly, which may well not mean treating everyone the same.

731

community—one in which we truly welcome adults and young people with a broad range of racial, class, ethnic, religious, cultural, and political backgrounds, as well as people with a range of gender and sexual orientations—is that they bring various viewpoints that can help a community reach good, moral, and truthful decisions. This range of viewpoints also helps communities reach just decisions that a broad range of people will believe to be legitimate.

As one example, consider the field of journalism and the need for a 5 diverse corps of reporters to serve a multicultural democracy well. Among other things, a democracy depends on a strong, independent field of journalism to function effectively. Journalism enables the public to stay informed about crucial issues in such a way that the people may determine their own best interests. Journalism offers plentiful examples of this concurrent need for diversity and free expression in support of democracy. A well-trained, professional team of journalists—even if they all come from one racial background, say all Latino/Latina—may be able to cover the stories of a large and complex city with a reasonable degree of accuracy. But getting to the truth of what is really going on in, say, that city's Chinatown section will be enhanced by someone on the staff coming from that neighborhood or from a Chinese-speaking background. At a minimum, that team of reporters would need to rely on sources and informants from Chinatown in order to tell that story with a fidelity to what actually occurred and what it meant. In either event, a diverse set of voices—whether as authors or sources—can lead to a deeper understanding of the truth in a complex environment than a homogeneous group of voices can. In turn, those who rely on this journalism have a greater likelihood of discerning their own true interests and acting accordingly as citizens.[1]

Or consider the discipline of writing and studying U.S. history, which I teach to high school juniors and seniors at Andover. If virtually all the authorities writing prominent history books are white men (as they were for a long time), the likelihood is high that their narratives would extol the great male military and political leaders, not the women and many of the people of color who lived then. The idea behind diversifying the ranks of our history teachers and scholars is that a more diverse group of authors will tell a more complete—and correspondingly more truthful—version of what happened. The point is not to eliminate political and military history or the lives of "great men" from our narratives but rather to include social and cultural history—for instance, as it is told by women or people of color, unwelcome in political and military leadership for much of our history. The point is also not that only African Americans can write about the lives of those enslaved or what it was like to be subject to Jim Crow laws, but rather that having a more diverse group of teachers and authors results in a broader range of perspectives. As the **professoriate** continues to become more diverse, the narratives that we teach in history are becoming more diverse and richer.

professoriate: the group of people who teach at colleges and universities.

WHY FREE EXPRESSION MATTERS

Free expression, likewise, enables us to find the truth. If certain views are unwelcome or barred, then the likelihood that societies will find or embrace the truth diminishes. The extreme case is an authoritarian regime—for instance, in North Korea—where dissent is nearly impossible and the free flow of ideas is nonexistent. If criticism of political figures, whether accurate or not, is disallowed or strongly discouraged—as it is, for instance, in present-day Turkey, Russia, or Thailand—then the likelihood that the truth about their activities will emerge is much lower. When Saddam Hussein received 100 percent of the votes cast in the election of 2002—all 11,445,638 of them—one can reasonably infer that the Iraqi people were not free to discuss the potential shortcomings of the next Hussein administration.[2] In the case of the urban journalists, free expression supports understanding of the real dynamics at play in Chinatown. In the case of the historians, free expression enables broader consideration of events and patterns that had previously lain uncovered—and that may have been inconvenient to unearth, discuss, and publish. Without commitment to free expression, the truth is much less likely to emerge. Without a route to the truth, the likelihood of good policy decisions, fair dealing with communities, and just outcomes of disputes is much lower.

ADDITIONAL LINKS BETWEEN DIVERSITY AND FREE EXPRESSION

Diversity and free expression are linked, too, as principles that lead to higher levels of equity and fairness. The success of these ideals provides legitimacy for a democratic system. One reason to pursue a diverse environment, especially in a school or university setting, is to ensure that every young person has a roughly equal chance at the positive gains possible through education. If a school admits only young people of a single race, gender, ethnicity, faith, sexuality, or type of ability, then the opportunities at that school are not equitably afforded to those with other characteristics. In a knowledge-dominated economy, access to the benefits of education is of fundamental importance. Diversity initiatives—including but not limited to affirmative action policies—aim to ensure that the inequities of the past are not paid for in the future. These commitments ensure that every member of an academic environment feels and is valued for what they offer to the community and can accomplish while in school and afterward. The benefits of addressing inequity on campus connect directly to the degree of equality in the polity at large.

Free expression, in its purest form, is also a driver of equity and justice. Free expression means that no voice is categorically entitled to greater freedom than any other. At the level of principle, freedom of expression is even-handed: it means that the color of one's skin, or faith, or sexuality should not be a bar to expressing one's point of view, participating in civic life through speech, and so forth. In practice, in most societies, this form of equity has rarely existed: some people are able to speak louder and more freely than others.

Free expression is linked to a series of other freedoms with similar connections to equity. In the context of the United States, these freedoms are enshrined in the First Amendment to the Constitution: the right to free speech and a free press, the right to assemble peaceably, and the right to religious beliefs. Alongside the right to free expression, these other rights also protect those who might otherwise suffer persecution: the unpopular minority group has the right to come together peaceably in a community, or to pursue their faith, or to publish their views through a specialized press, or to seek redress from the government. Taken together, these rights have great force on behalf of an equitable society. 10

SOME ARGUMENTS TO THE CONTRARY

The matter, of course, is not as simple as saying that diversity and free expression are mutually supportive concepts, on campus and in society at large. There are serious theoretical arguments to the contrary. There are hard cases that make these principles difficult to reconcile. The hardest cases, customarily involving hate speech, require balancing of competing interests that can leave no one happy.

The most forceful argument, expressed from the political left, against my view that these two principles should coexist comes with the (truthful) claim that the right to free expression arose in the context of inequality. The First Amendment to the U.S. Constitution, for instance, was drafted by white, powerful men of European descent—many of whom enslaved their fellow Americans. Moreover, the interpretation of the right of free expression in the United States has been historically carried out by and large by male judges, often white and well off. Given this history, the right to free expression has been a tool of empowered people, not those who have been marginalized.

As such, this counterargument goes, the right to free expression is flawed and less worthy of support than diversity, equity, and inclusion, especially where these two values conflict. While I acknowledge the force of this argument, I think it is less compelling than the claim that the two principles, in a more equitable historical moment, can and should be upheld in common.

Other counterarguments take issue with either the specific application of free expression or diversity or both. It is one thing to make a broad claim about the importance of diversity and free expression coexisting; it is quite another to determine how best to apply them in an actual society.

Free expression, for instance, evokes a range of possible policies, from one in which truly "anything goes" to the constrained version of free expression (which I favor) that is enshrined in the U.S. Constitution. This latter vision of free expression calls for limits to free expression in certain circumstances, known as **"time, place, and manner" restrictions.** Gender and racial harassment, fighting words, obscenity, and libel, for instance, are not protected speech even under the First Amendment. In the context of a campus, the limits to free expression often take another form: disallowing students from using hate speech targeted at another student, for instance. None of these types of restrictions on free expression would bar citizens or students from expressing a political opinion, however unpopular, as long as it does not target or put at risk another person. While some disagree with the idea of any restrictions on free expression, others wish for speech restrictions to further limit or ban certain additional forms of speech.

A similar counterargument might take issue with the forms of diversity 15 that I favor in this book. As in the case of free expression, the views fall along a broad spectrum. On the one end, diversity extends to a strong form of equality and inclusion, brought about by affirmative policies intended to accomplish what proponents refer to as "social justice." On the other end of the spectrum falls extreme **xenophobia**—whether expressed by white supremacists or by those who express hatred toward others from a religious viewpoint. For the purposes of this argument, I favor a form of diversity that makes good on the promises of the American ideal: a nation that invites those from all over the world to form a community together, representing a range of backgrounds and viewpoints. On campuses, this ideal means seeking young people from all over the country and the world, from all races, ethnicities, faith backgrounds, sexual orientations, with a range of abilities, and from families with different political viewpoints. Here, too, there are, and must be, restrictions of various sorts. A nation must limit those who can immigrate in certain ways in order to avoid systems being overwhelmed by the sheer number of residents; similarly, enrollment on a campus ought to be

"time, place, and manner" restrictions: the categories of restrictions that can, under current federal law, be placed on free speech provided they are content neutral. They are narrowly tailored, and they leave open alternative means of expression. Thus, assuming these conditions are met, a school could likely legally limit free speech (or certain kinds of free speech) to certain times (e.g., not on Sunday), certain places (e.g., a free speech zone), or certain manners (e.g., no PA systems), although it would need to be able to justify the need for doing so. The restrictions are from the ruling *Linmark Associates, Inc. v. Township of Willingboro*, 431 U.S. 85 (1977).

xenophobia: irrational fear or hatred of strangers and, by extension, those from other countries or ethnic groups (Greek, *xenos* [stranger] + *phobos* [fear]).

limited to a number of students who can in fact thrive in that particular learning environment. Some might agree that this definition of diversity is too generous; others might oppose the limits I suggest or favor more radical policies to accomplish the goals of diversity, equity, and inclusion.

Life University

THE CHALLENGING PARADOX

The hardest theoretical problem in holding these two ideals together is not one of definition, as thorny as that can be—it has to do with a **paradox** at the heart of this combination. One goal of diversity, equity, and inclusion—taken together—is tolerance. These ideals call for a community to enable all members to enjoy equal privileges. This notion of equity is especially hard to accomplish in environments that have been the least equal in the past—for instance, campuses that have only recently been opened to those of a certain gender or race, where intolerance has been the norm for a long time. The paradox becomes evident when someone does not believe in tolerance. The belief they hold—or the expression they wish to convey freely—is that the very idea of tolerance is wrong.

Must a community tolerate intolerance? It is this hard problem that presented itself on so many campuses in the fall of 2015 and again in the presidential election of 2016, and that will remain with us for the foreseeable future. Some campus activists argue for no as an answer to that question. From my perspective, the answer is yes, at least to some extent. Tolerance must extend not only to those who believe in tolerance but also to those who do not. In a democratic system at large, we give votes regardless of a person's viewpoint. As humans and communities, we learn when we are presented with viewpoints different from our own.

The difficulty with this idea—and the primary shortcoming of the view that we must tolerate some degree of intolerant speech—is that the costs of such tolerance will be borne disproportionately by those who are the targets of the intolerance. In America, those people are likely the same people whose forebears have been the targets of intolerance in the past: people of color, women, those who identify as **LGBTQIA+**, those who do not identify squarely on the **cis-gendered** binary (female or male), and those with different abilities. This argument—that we ought to hold diversity and free expression as mutually reinforcing principles—is at its most vulnerable when we consider the disproportionality of the costs of extreme tolerance.

LGBTQIA+: umbrella term including lesbian, gay, bisexual, transgender, queer, intersex, asexual, and others who do not identify with the heterosexual and cis-gendered majority.

cis-gendered: having a gender identity that corresponds with the sex one was assigned at birth.

There are ways to mitigate this problem, though it may be a long time (or a rare place) before the problem is fully addressed. The roots of discrimination are long and run deep; they are not easily pulled out of any soil, without trace or likelihood of regrowth.

One form of mitigation is to limit free expression in specific ways. There must be a point at which the tolerant should not have to tolerate the intolerant. One limitation, sensibly included in campus policies, is to disallow hate speech personally directed at an individual. If a member of the community directs hate speech at another individual (rather than at a group), the speech can be subject to restriction and the speaker to disciplinary measures or other recourse. Specific campuses or communities might have narrowly tailored rules along these lines to protect those most vulnerable. It is easy to imagine that rules at a school for young children would be even more protective in this respect than the rules at a high school or those at a university, given the different educational aims of these types of institutions and different maturity levels of their students.

Where a speaker expresses a general political viewpoint, communities must seek to tolerate these expressions, even if she or he preaches something inconsistent with the majority viewpoint on campus. If this political speech is intolerant toward some community members, the response should be to address this intolerant viewpoint with more speech. An affirmative obligation to speak up falls on those who oppose the position. In a civic context, it is imperative that citizens and political leaders speak up to defend the rights of all people in the community. This burden must not fall just on those threatened by the speech; those who already feel the most marginalized, undervalued, or invisible in communities may find it hard to voice their concerns. The burden ought to fall less on those directly affected and more on those who are in the favored position. In the campus context, those representing the institution itself—a college president, a university board chair, or a school principal—ought to establish a point of view that favors tolerance, diversity, equity, and inclusion over hate and intolerance. The best approach for the long run is for the truthful, positive, values-driven viewpoint to be given the chance to win out. The stronger argument should prove more sustainable and more broadly embraced over time if it is contested than if it is merely insisted on without interrogation. To impose a rule against the less tolerant political viewpoint, or to ban that viewpoint from the commons, would have high costs in the long run, but so too does tolerating certain hateful speech on campuses.

NOTES

1. Alex Garcia, "Why Diversity in Media Matters in Making Free Speech Really Free," *Medium*, https://medium.com/@Alex_Garcia/why-diversity-in-media-matters-in-making-free-speech-really-free-a25cb760bd80#.zay4kev7j.
2. "Saddam Wins '100% of Vote,'" *BBC News*, October 16, 2002, http://news.bbc.co.uk/2/hi/2331951.stm.

RESPOND

1. What is your response to Palfrey's claim that "[f]ree expression and diversity are essential components of democracy"? Of a successful learning environment in higher education? If you do not agree with his claims, which parts of his argument do you have trouble accepting or agreeing with? Why do you think you and Palfrey might disagree?

2. A major component of this selection is the extended definitional argument focusing on the meaning and nature of free expression and on diversity. Working in pairs or small groups, list all the ways Palfrey defines, describes, or characterizes one of these two concepts, including the paragraph number where that comment occurs. (Your instructor may wish to divide the work among the pairs or groups in the class

so that more than one group considers each concept.) Once you have completed your list, analyze the elements of the list in terms of the kinds of definitions discussed in "Kinds of Definitions" in Chapter 9. If there are items that do not fit neatly into these categories, try to label the functions those items serve in helping clarify Palfrey's understanding of the concept. Once your group has completed its task, compare your findings with those of other groups in the class, working to clarify the class's understanding of these concepts as Palfrey defines them.

3. Likely because of his training as a lawyer and legal scholar, Palfrey constructs arguments in ways that closely resemble Toulmin argumentation, discussed in Chapter 7. While there are several ways to frame Palfrey's argument, let us assume the following statement encapsulates his claim: "Our commitment to seeking the truth and making sound decisions, in intellectual communities and in public spaces, relies on the coexistence of diversity and free expression" (para. 4). Using the information given in Chapter 7 and beginning with this claim, construct an outline of Palfrey's argument (cf. p. 150), providing any explicit qualifications to the claim, the reason(s) for the claim, the warrant(s) for the claim, the forms of backing provided for the warrant, evidence for the backing, the authority or authorities cited in support of this evidence, the conditions of rebuttal, and possible responses these conditions might engender. If you find that Palfrey's argument is not a perfect Toulmin argument, note the elements that are lacking and speculate about why they might be absent. (You will find your response to Question 2 helpful in responding to this question. You may wish to work in small groups on this question as well.)

4. **THINKING CRITICALLY** A key feature of academic arguments is making explicit the logical connections between ideas or sentences. Examine paragraph 12, reproduced below, and explain the function(s) of each of the italicized words or phrases with regard to making explicit the logical connections between ideas. (One way to think about the question is to read the passage without these elements, making minor changes so that the text would still make sense, and then to put them back in.)

> The most forceful argument, expressed from the political left, against my view that these two principles [of free expression and diversity] should coexist comes with the *(truthful)* claim that the right to free expression arose in the context of inequality. The First Amendment to the U.S. Constitution, *for instance*, was drafted by white, powerful men of European descent—many of whom enslaved their fellow Americans. *Moreover*, the interpretation of the right of free expression in the United

States has been historically carried out by and large by male judges, often white and well off. *Given this history,* the right to free expression has been a tool of empowered people, not those who have been marginalized. *As such, the counterargument goes,* the right to free expression is flawed and less worthy of support than diversity, equity, and inclusion, especially where these two values conflict. *While I acknowledge the force of this argument, I think* it is less compelling than the claim that the two principles, in a more equitable historical moment, can and should be upheld in common.

5. As noted, Palfrey's argument is very much an academic argument in the sense discussed in Chapter 17. **Write an academic argument** in response to the position Palfrey takes in this selection, seeking to be as systematic and respectful of other positions as he is. We assume that you will likely not agree with all of the assumptions or claims made by Palfrey. If you don't agree completely with Palfrey, your argument will focus on those areas of disagreement, and you will make explicit the differences between your perspective and Palfrey's, giving support for your assumptions or claims. Should you agree completely with Palfrey's claims, your argument will explain why you contend that Palfrey's analysis is the correct one, again providing evidence for your assumptions or claims.

▼ *This selection presents excerpts from a March 2018 Knight Foundation Report on free speech issues on campus. The survey, conducted in November–December 2017, polled over three thousand students across the country at various kinds of institutions of higher education on their ideas about First Amendment issues. Here, we reproduce the report's summary conclusion as a background to the report's detailed analysis of responses to two specific questions:*

1. *Do you think each of the following rights is very secure, secure, threatened, or very threatened in the country today: Freedom of speech, freedom of religion, freedom of the press, freedom for people to assemble peaceably, and freedom to petition the government? and*

2. *How important do you consider each of the following to be in our democracy: Protecting citizens' free speech rights and promoting an inclusive society that is welcoming of diverse groups?*

Building on a 2016 survey, this project was supported by five organizations with different value orientations but with a common commitment to First Amendment issues: Gallup, a U.S.-based international consulting company highly respected for its sophisticated opinion polls; the John S. and James L. Knight Foundation, a nonprofit foundation one of whose goals is to support high quality journalism; the American Council on Education, a nonprofit organization of over 1,800 accredited member institutions of higher education; the Charles Koch Foundation, a foundation supporting libertarian and conservative causes in higher education; and the Stanton Foundation, which supports a free press and an informed citizenry. (The entire report is available at http://kng .ht/2G9huqZ. We encourage you to check it out to get additional information about the questions included here and about other questions related to the topic of free speech on campus.)

As you study this selection, consider the value of trustworthy polling data on complex and controversial issues like the ones reported on here and the ways in which they can be used to support a range of arguments.

Free Speech on Campus: What Students Think about First Amendment Issues

GALLUP/KNIGHT FOUNDATION

College students generally endorse First Amendment ideals in the abstract. The vast majority say free speech is important to democracy and favor an open learning environment that promotes the airing of a wide variety of ideas. However, the actions of some students in recent years—from milder actions such as claiming to be threatened by messages written in chalk promoting Trump's candidacy to the most extreme acts of engaging in violence to stop attempted speeches—raise issues of just how committed college students are to upholding First Amendment ideals.

As discussed in Chapter 18, survey data, such as the data featured in this report, can provide important information that may not have been collected before.

LINK TO P. 446

Most college students do not condone more aggressive actions to squelch speech, like violence and shouting down speakers, although there are some who do. However, students do support many policies or actions that place limits on speech, including free speech zones, speech codes and campus prohibitions on hate speech, suggesting that their commitment to free speech has limits. As one example, barely a majority think handing out literature on controversial issues is "always acceptable."

Further, college students acknowledge that campus norms can act to deter speech—a larger majority than a year ago perceive that their campus climate prevents some people from expressing their ideas for fear of offending others. Also, students perceive that some groups on campus have a lesser ability to voice their opinions than other groups do.

Issues surrounding the First Amendment can present dilemmas for college officials, as they attempt to address student concerns about campus matters in a way that does not infringe on other students' First Amendment rights. Some actions colleges have taken have been perceived by students, opinion leaders, public officials and the courts as going too far in restricting those rights.

Every year new controversies arise, driven by technological advances in 5 communication, evolving social mores and new cohorts of students entering college who may have different understandings of what the Constitution guarantees its citizens. As such, colleges will need to continue to keep First Amendment considerations in mind when deciding on policies to meet these new challenges.

COLLEGE STUDENTS ARE LESS LIKELY TO SEE FIRST AMENDMENT RIGHTS AS SECURE

As colleges across the country continue to grapple with the issue of free speech on campus, majorities of U.S. college students still feel the five freedoms guaranteed by the First Amendment to the U.S. Constitution are secure in this country. However, they are less likely now than they were in 2016 to say each right is secure.

Compared with the 2016 survey, students now perceive the five freedoms as significantly less secure. This includes a 21-percentage-point decline in perceptions that freedom of the press is secure and nine-point declines for free speech, freedom of assembly and freedom to petition the government. Freedom of the press was viewed as the most secure right in 2016, but now it ranks only above freedom of assembly.

Students Believe All Five First Amendment Rights Are Less Secure

Do you think each of the following rights is very secure, secure, threatened, or very threatened in the country today?

■ % Very secure/Secure

	2016	2017
FREEDOM OF SPEECH	73	64
FREEDOM OF RELIGION	68	64
FREEDOM OF THE PRESS	81	60
FREEDOM FOR PEOPLE TO ASSEMBLE PEACEFULLY	66	57
FREEDOM TO PETITION THE GOVERNMENT	76	67

MAJORITIES OF STUDENTS CONSIDER BOTH SPEECH AND INCLUSION TO BE IMPORTANT TO DEMOCRACY

For a democracy to thrive, citizens must be able to express their views on important issues to inform their elected leaders about what they want them to do. But all citizens, regardless of their background, should have the same opportunity to express their views—something that has not always been the reality in democratic societies, including the U.S. Students place a high value on protecting free speech rights in a democracy: 56% say it is "extremely important" to do so, and 33% say it is "very important." Nearly as many say promoting an inclusive society that welcomes diverse groups is extremely (52%) or very (31%) important to democracy.

College Students Say Both Free Speech Rights, Inclusive Society Are Highly Important to Democracy

How important do you consider each of the following to be in our democracy?

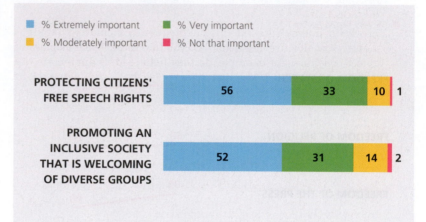

While Democratic and Republican students are about equally likely to regard protecting free speech rights as important, Democrats are much more likely than Republicans are to say promoting an inclusive society is important. Only modest racial and gender differences exist for the perceived importance of an inclusive society that welcomes diverse groups.

RESPOND.

1. What is your response to this selection? Were the findings at the time of the survey or the changes since 2016 surprising in any way, or do they reflect your experience?

2. Research-based reports like this survey represent a particular category of argument of fact. Rather than searching for evidence to support a claim, as discussed in Chapter 8, the researchers analyze the data collected, seek to interpret them, and then work to draw conclusions based on the data. At the same time, the trustworthiness of such reports is a matter of ethos. Consider how the authors of this report seek to create an ethos that encourages readers to believe the information presented. Likewise, consider matters of word choice (both the

language used and language that might have been used but was not), the formulation and inclusion of the questions asked, and the interpretation of the data presented. (The discussion of surveys and polls in Chapter 4, which treats appeals to logos, will help you respond to this question.)

3. Reports of survey data like this one frequently include visual arguments. How effective and helpful do you find these visual displays of data to be? How, for example, do they help readers appreciate the meaning of the data being analyzed in ways that words alone might not? (Chapter 14 on visual rhetoric and the discussion of design and visuals in Chapter 8 on arguments of fact may prove useful in responding to this question.)

4. **THINKING CRITICALLY** How do the data and analysis presented in this selection call into question or provide support for claims made by John Palfrey in the previous selection, the introduction to his recent book *Safe Spaces, Brave Spaces: Diversity and Free Expression in Education*? How do they call into question or provide support for your own opinions about freedom of speech on campus?

5. A challenge for all but the most experienced writers is summarizing sources for use as part of a longer text they are creating. Using information presented in Chapter 20 on synthesizing information, **write a healthy paragraph** summarizing the response to each of the two survey questions included in this excerpt of the Gallup/Knight Report. In each paragraph, be sure to include direct quotations, using them strategically; paraphrases; and appropriate signal words. The best responses will construct paragraphs that, in fact, support a claim or argument of fact, as discussed in Chapter 8.

▼ Ben Schwartz (1981–) is an actor, comedian, and author who is especially interested in the history of humor in America between WWI and WWII. This selection appeared in June 2015 in the "Word Factory" column of the *Baffler,* a print and digital magazine that analyzes culture, business, and politics. In it, Schwartz is ultimately asking questions about permissible and impermissible comedy: an issue of the possible limits of free speech. As you read, consider where you draw a line about which subjects, if any, can't be treated humorously. Likewise, consider whether and how context matters. Does the identity of the performer matter? The identity or identities of the audience? Should they? Do you draw the line differently for comedians and for class members whose casual efforts at humor may offend? And what about location—are things permitted in a comedy club on campus that wouldn't be permissible for you in an academic setting? In short, give serious thought to the criteria you use in evaluating the appropriate and inappropriate uses of humor, a two-edged rhetorical sword.

Shutting Up

BEN SCHWARTZ

This weekend, I used up one of my ten free monthly views of *The New York Times* to find film critic A. O. Scott declaring a national "humor crisis." No, he wasn't referring to any of his colleague Maureen Dowd's perennial struggles with political humor; rather, he described a culture-wide danger zone in which comedians actually get criticized—and worse, not *nicely.* "The world is full of jokes and also of people who can't take them," Scott wrote. "We love jokes that find the far edge of the permissible, but we also love to turn against the joker who violates our own closely held taboos."

So much to unpack here—are you really humorless because you don't like a joke? Are comedians violating edgy taboos? Or more often than not, reinforcing tired old ideas, and flogging views the audience has left behind?

Then, Monday, in a widely circulated clip from the **Colin Cowherd** show, a cranky senior from Long Island, **Jerry Seinfeld,** called in to chat with Cowherd about how "PC" complaints on college campuses are why comics like he and **Chris Rock** quit doing campus shows. In the kind of hushed tones

Colin Cowherd (1964–): sports radio and TV personality whose comments about particular racial and ethnic groups have been the subject of controversy and have cost him at least one job.

Jerry Seinfeld (1954–): actor, writer, director, producer, and stand-up comedian best known for playing a character based on himself in the highly syndicated, eponymously named *Seinfeld.*

Chris Rock (1965–): actor, writer, director, producer, and stand-up comedian best known for his work in film, appearances on *Saturday Night Live,* and the TV series, *Everybody Hates Chris,* which he created.

Jerry Seinfeld Tasos Katopodis/Getty Images

that most sports radio personalities reserve for wringing their hands about "the good of baseball," or losing a beloved NFL player to a wife-beating charge just before a play-off game, Cowherd asks, "Does it . . . does it hurt comedy?"

Poor comedy, that needy **waif** of pop culture, is getting bullied. "Laughter is supposed to be a unifying force," A. O. Scott wrote, "a leveler of distinctions and a healer of divisions. But it often seems to be just as divisive as anything else in our angry and polarized climate. Can't we just all have a good time together?"

Chris Rock Kathy Hutchins/ Shutterstock

If you see comedy as a progressive kindergarten, or a family outing to the zoo, uh, sure. But that leveling process? It's not about healing, really. It often reflects some vicious and ugly divisions in our country that many comedians and audience members don't see as anywhere close to level—or even agree among themselves, for that matter, that leveling is the needful social remedy in question. Comedy isn't *supposed* to be anything, except what the comedian tries to make it—harmless, mean, political, dirty, dumb. You wouldn't say that music or fiction are "supposed" to be anything; so why do we saddle all comedy with a curative democratic mission? Too often we view comedy as a craft, a service brought to us by cheerful comfort-workers, more than the work of serious artists. Thus, when they don't comfort us, we want to complain to the manager.

Have Twitter and noisy college kids put comedy (whatever that abstract term is supposed to mean) on the ropes? The thing I find most tiresome about this "too PC" argument is that so many people talking about it today think it's new, like something suddenly went wrong all at once with the nation's millions of millennial PC liberal kids as they logged themselves onto the Internet. **Bill Maher** named his first talk show *Politically Incorrect* back in 1993. You can find Southern civic groups in the 1850s banning abolitionist comedians in the lead-up to the Civil War. Those comedians were **minstrels**. Today they would be attacked for that style of comedy, no matter how vitally progressive their views in the 1850s.

This isn't a problem, nor is it a crisis. The redefining of "funny" for each generation is a constant of our humor. And it's not censorship. Local **vaudeville** theater managers once had the authority to censor and **blacklist** comics at every

5

waif: a helpless person, often a child.

Bill Maher (1956–): comedian, television host, and commentator known for his political satire and sarcastic tone.

minstrels: white performers in blackface and black performers under the direction of whites who, during the nineteenth and twentieth centuries, were part of comic shows representing people of African descent in negative ways.

vaudeville: variety entertainment performances popular in the U.S. and Canada during the late nineteenth and early twentieth centuries.

blacklist: create a list of individuals or groups to be censored or not employed, generally because of their identities or their politics.

David Letterman (1947–): comedian, television host, and film and TV producer; he remains the longest-serving late night talk-show host in U.S. history.

Bill Hicks (1961–1994): comedian, musician, and social critic who died of pancreatic cancer at 32. He was known for his dark humor on controversial topics. Although Hicks had appeared on *Late Night with David Letterman* eleven times, in 1993 Letterman decided not to air a segment taped earlier that evening before a live audience because of the controversial jokes Hicks had told. Years later, in 2009, Letterman aired the segment and stated he had been wrong not to do so in the first place.

Bob Hope (1903–2003): comedian, vaudevillian, actor, dancer, singer, and author. Hope is among the most famous comedians and actors of the twentieth century. Between 1941 and 1994, he made 57 tours with United Service Organizations (USO), which provides live entertainment to active-duty military abroad. During one of his tours in Vietnam, he was booed when he made a statement that President Nixon had a clear plan for winning the war. In 1997, Congress named him an honorary veteran of the U.S. military, the only time such an award has been bestowed.

Amy Schumer (1981–): stand-up comedian, film and Broadway actor, and author; known for *Inside Amy Schumer* on Comedy Central.

level from the 1870s through the 1930s, on the basis of nothing more than purely whimsical local tastes. Movie studios, TV networks, magazine editors, newspaper critics (when they had weight), and even other comedians (see **David Letterman** versus **Bill Hicks**)—have all done far more to censor comedy and damage careers than anyone on Twitter or college campuses can today. Comedy has never had more venues, more outlets, more diversity than this moment, right now.

Americans have always told comedians to shut up, and American comedians, to their credit, have rarely done it. They've *been* shut up at times, yes: fired from shows, shouted down, banned from clubs, etc. But that's not what's happening today. No one banned Seinfeld and Rock from doing campus shows; instead, they opted out, because that's not their audience anymore. That's just show business. Last year, students uninvited Maher from a commencement speech appearance, and he was then re-invited by the chancellor, hours later. He continues to offend people weekly, and often daily, on Twitter. No one was more surprised to be booed during Vietnam than **Bob Hope**. It shouldn't surprise anyone if one day, and maybe one day soon, the same thing happens to **Amy Schumer** or **John Oliver**.

Amy Schumer Splash News/Alamy

"It's no good longing for a simpler age," Scott wrote of the current humor crisis, "though it is possible to imagine that once upon a time things were clearer." In the clearer time he imagines, Scott describes an America where Jewish comics weren't part of the mainstream culture and remained on the "**borscht belt**." That flies in the face of our most common understanding of how American humor evolved ever since Jews first arrived on these shores.

No, times weren't any more clear back then, ever. If the past seems more clear to   10
anyone now, that's perhaps because large segments of the audience were silenced, or never asked what they thought—be they people of color, women, or LGBT people.

Long ago, *Times* writers who held Scott's job could shut down a movie they disliked with a single review. One famous instance of this was Warren Beatty's 1967 film ***Bonnie and Clyde***, declared dead on arrival by *Times* critic Bosley Crowther, who was appalled by the rude new culture it represented. **Pauline Kael** had to save it with a *New Yorker* review. That was nearly fifty years ago. Today,

Poster advertising the film Bonnie and Clyde Movie Poster Image Art/Getty Images

Scott is equally uncomfortable with the rude new culture of diversity on the Internet. "A crisis of authority is not for the faint of heart," Scott wrote in an essay last year, where he worried over the death of adult culture in America. No, not if it threatens you. For some of us, it's exhilarating.

Comedy is more often than not a **populist** business, so why are we surprised when the response it engenders in its audience is equally populist? What we could use is a better vocabulary to criticize and answer comedians. Is every comment about race, gender, or sexuality we don't agree with a sure sign the comedian is a racist or bigot whose career needs to end? While watching a comedian in a club, do we really need to shout them down in the middle of a set because we fear that it's heading somewhere that we won't like? In short, a little patience, a little of the tolerance we insist that our comedians demonstrate, would be welcome from the audience, too.

RESPOND•

1. What, specifically, is Schwartz's argument in this selection? To what extent does he agree with A. O. Scott and Jerry Seinfeld, both of whom he cites, and to what extent is he seeking to reframe the issues in a different way?

2. As Schwartz notes, there is "so much to unpack here" (para. 2). Although he is referring specifically to Scott's comments, in fact, his observation applies to uses of humor more broadly. Why is the use of

John Oliver (1997–): British-born comedian, actor, producer, and political commentator known for his work on *The Daily Show with John Stewart*, the podcast *The Bugle,* and *Last Week Tonight with John Oliver*. His commentary on political issues has helped influence legislation, giving rise to the "John Oliver Effect," the ability of Oliver (and other entertainers) to turn often arcane legislative issues into viral phenomena.

borscht belt: now-defunct summer resorts in the Catskill Mountains of New York that were popular with Jews of Eastern European heritage from New York City from the 1920s until the 1970s. (Borscht is a beet-based soup popular among Eastern Europeans.) Many famous American comedians of Jewish heritage got their start performing on the borscht belt circuit.

Bonnie and Clyde: highly popular and influential biographical film about Depression-era bank robbers Bonnie Parker and Clyde Barrow starring Faye Dunaway and Warren Beatty. It broke a number of taboos with regard to the depiction of violence and sex in particular.

Pauline Kael (1919–2001): especially influential film critic during the second half of the twentieth century. She wrote for the *New Yorker* magazine; frequently, her opinions differed from those of other powerful critics.

populist: literally, of the people; the word's connotations, however, most often imply the common people, in contrast to the elite.

humor always complex, and why and how do users of humor open themselves up to criticism? Is it helpful or necessary to distinguish between humor used by comedians during performances and humor used in other contexts? Why or why not?

3. Schwartz presents a considerable number of specific examples of comedians and humorous entertainment in American history. What sorts of appeals do these examples represent? Why? For what purposes is Schwartz using them?

4. **THINKING CRITICALLY**   What is the relationship between comedy and free speech for you, and what experiences have led you to this position? Here are four possible options, though there are surely others in addition to combinations of these four. One common position is that any topic should be fair game for a comedian. If patrons choose to pay to watch a comedian perform or show up at a free performance on campus, for example, they shouldn't be surprised if something they find offensive gets said—in fact, they should perhaps expect to be offended. A second position argues that humor is or at least can be a tool for combatting various kinds of social and societal problems by naming them publicly and mocking them. Related to this position is the acknowledgment that such humor often is truly funny, even when it comes at the expense of members of groups we do or don't belong to. A third position contends that context is crucial—the identity of the person using the humor, the homogeneity or values of the particular audience, and the specific location where the humor is used all matter. A fourth position claims that there can be no humor about certain topics; in short, these topics are to be treated as taboos when it comes to humor.

5. In his closing paragraph, Schwartz issues challenges both through a series of rhetorical questions and in his comment that "What we could use is a better vocabulary to criticize and answer comedians." **Write a proposal argument** in which you respond to this challenge or to one of the questions Schwartz poses about how comedians get labeled or how audience members sometimes react when anticipating what a comedian is about to do. Focus your argument on the specific context of college and university campuses, which, as the selections in this chapter are quick to remind us, are different in important ways from other public venues. (Chapter 11 will guide you in writing a proposal argument.)

▼ Over the past several years, microaggressions have been the subject of great debate in several English-speaking countries, particularly on college campuses and in the workplace. The term microaggression is heavily contested, as you'll discover in the next selection by Scott Lilienfeld. However, it generally refers to "under the radar," everyday comments, phrases, and labels that seem innocent, innocuous, or even complimentary to the speaker but that feel offensive to the recipient. While the person making the comment may think nothing of what is said, the recipient is reminded that, in some sense, they don't belong or they are doing something wrong (even if whoever they are or whatever they are or are not doing is out of their control). Such comments are directly or indirectly linked to putting people into boxes, often boxes based on race or ethnicity, gender, sexuality, social class, ability, body type, or some other aspect of identity. While we might expect microaggressions always to be small or minor, it is clear that frequently the comments that get labeled "microaggressions" should more properly be termed "macroaggressions," a fact that a New York Times video referenced in Question 4 in the following selection invites you to explore.

There are two visual arguments for this chapter, a poster about racial microaggressions produced by the Turner Consulting Group in Toronto, Canada, and a cartoon by illustrator Alexandra Dal. The Turner Group serves workplaces and schools in their efforts to respond to diversity within their organizations. The company's goal is not merely helping organizations comply with local or national laws but, more importantly, helping them flourish as they create more inclusive environments for all—employees, clients, students. (A commonly made observation is that diversity is something people see while inclusion is something they feel.) Alexandra Dal is a Native American cartoonist and illustrator who lives and works in San Antonio, Texas. Both of these visual arguments focus on the sorts of specific questions ethnic or racial minorities frequently encounter—and some would argue have to endure—in North American society.

From a rhetorical point of view, microaggressions are interesting because they remind us that what speakers or writers intend is often less important than the effect on the audience of what is said or written. The creators of both selections make this effect visual in the frustrated, sad, or angry expressions of their minority characters.

Microaggressions are likewise interesting because they immediately reveal assumptions the speaker is making, not merely about the person to whom the question is addressed but also about what the world is like or should be like, as the questions in Dal's cartoon make undeniably clear. As Dal notes on her Web site in reference to this comic, the questioners in the frames on the right likely do not imagine that they are engaging in behaviors that could be termed offensive, "inappropriate," or "racist." In fact, when they ask a person of color if she is the first member of her family to attend college, they may even assume their question functions as a compliment or display of support: Dal observes that even before the young person can reply, the questioner often adds, "Your parents must be so proud!"

[The questioners] think they're giving you the opportunity to . . . trot out your inspirational horror story of clawing your way out of the hood and avoiding teen pregnancy and gangs while simultaneously helping your single mother raise your 5 younger siblings.

While such a story is, indeed, the story of some college students' lives—and that is a fine thing—the problem is the questioners' insidious assumption that students of color are likely to be first-generation college students. Dal further points out that those asking such questions often see themselves as "progressive and unprejudiced," but it is most unlikely that they would make similar remarks to white people, as illustrated by the frames of the comic on the left.

751

Efforts to encourage discussion of microaggressions in places like classrooms or the workplace generally have several related goals. Certainly, they seek to help those involved in these discussions find ways of talking about the power of language and, more particularly, the ways that comments—often the most casual remarks, even ones that can be well intentioned—can sting. They work more broadly to remind everyone that they likely make faulty assumptions about those they encounter based on the boxes into which they have put those individuals.

In so doing, these discussions encourage individuals to reflect on things they may have said without thinking, on the categories of social difference they so easily fall back on, and on the nature and limits of what some would term "free speech." Such discussions also work to remind those who have been on the receiving end of microaggressions—likely everyone at some point because of some aspect of their identity—that they are not alone. However, the fact that everyone may at some point be the recipient of such remarks does not justify their recurring use. Rather, it can—and many would argue should—lead everyone to consider why members of some groups are much more likely to be repeated recipients of them or why the versions of them they receive are far more painful than a momentary sting. As you study the Turner Group's poster and Dal's cartoon, consider why the comments and questions they contain could seem innocuous to the speaker but exhausting, if not offensive, to the hearer. Microaggressions are often compared to wasp stings. A rare or occasional one might not be too irritating, but being stung repeatedly or constantly has significant consequences for a person's well-being.

Racial Microaggressions Poster

TURNER CONSULTING GROUP

Questions

ALEXANDRA DAL

RESPOND●

1. How would you describe the argument being made by the poster from the Turner Consulting Group? The cartoon by Alexandra Dal? What assumptions or presuppositions are behind each of the questions asked in the poster and the cartoon? How effective is each as a visual argument? Which of the two is more effective? Why? (Chapter 14, on visual rhetoric, will help you respond to this question.)

2. This poster and the cartoon focus on microaggressions grounded in race. What other types of microaggressions might be successfully tackled in this medium? Draft a poster like this one to call out microaggressions of other types (class, sexual orientation, ability, gender, and more) on campus, at your workplace, or in your community.

3. As the headnote points out, microaggressions have become a topic of discussion—and debate—on college campuses and in the workplace. Watch this YouTube video on "White Fragility Training" in the workplace: <https://www.youtube.com/watch?v=ZPDpcYEdiOg> or <https://bit.ly/2gXd5Hx>. (By the way, *white fragility* is defined by the Oxford dictionaries as "discomfort and defensiveness on the part of a white person when confronted by information about racial inequality or injustice.") As you watch the video, consider how it recognizes microaggressions and at the same time mocks programs in cultural sensitivity and diversity training. What do you think the goals of this video are, and how effective do you find it? What are the advantages and disadvantages of using humor as the means to try to educate viewers about microaggressions? Does the video, for example, let certain groups off the hook? (Chapter 2 offers a discussion of the challenges of using humor effectively.)

4. **THINKING CRITICALLY**   Efforts to document microaggressions have given rise to Facebook and Instagram pages as well as more than one photography project. An especially interesting photographic response to microaggressions is the *I'm Tired Project* <https://theimtiredproject .com/>, begun in 2015 by Paula Apkan and Harriet Evans, then twenty-one-year-old college graduates. While begun in Britain, this photojournalism project has expanded and now includes photos from the United States and other countries. Each black-and-white photograph shows the naked back of an individual with a sentence beginning with the words "I'm tired…" painted on it. Here are some examples of the things they are tired of:

   • I'm tired of being told I sound "white"
   • I'm tired of being the angry Black woman

- I'm tired of being told I'm not real
- I'm tired of being "pretty for an Indian girl"
- I'm tired of my intelligence being associated with my ethnicity
- I'm tired of assumptions being made about my eating habits because of my size
- I'm tired of people using the word *crazy*
- I'm tired of people saying racism is over

What might you surmise about the identity of the individual based on their comment? For example, the person who stated "I'm tired of being told I sound 'white'" is an African American male. If this seems strange to you, read John McWhorter's essay "Thick of Tongue" in Chapter 25 (p. 657). Consider the ease with which we put individuals into boxes. What sort of comments might have been made to lead these individuals to be "tired"?

5. Return to the comments listed in Question 4, and choose the one you find makes the most effective argument for taking the notion of microaggressions seriously. Then, analyze that argument in the way that Toulmin might. As Chapter 7 explains, the British philosopher Stephen Toulmin offers an especially useful method for analyzing arguments. In this case, the statements in Question 4 represent the claim of the argument. Working backward from the claim, try to put into words the reason(s), warrant(s), backing, and evidence for such a conclusion. In short, detail the chain of reasoning leading to the claim. (Note that you do not need to agree with the claim; your task is to analyze it and, as best as possible, to explain why the individual making the statement assumes the claim is valid.) When you have completed your analysis, present it by **writing it up as an argument of fact**. (Again, your task is not to evaluate the argument, but to present it in its best light—that is, to support it as strongly as possible.) As noted, you will find information on Toulmin's method of analysis in Chapter 7, while Chapter 8 discusses arguments of fact.

▼ Scott O. Lilienfeld (1960–) is a professor of psychology at Emory University in Atlanta, Georgia. Throughout his career, he has been a strong supporter of evidence-based methods and treatment practices in his field. With colleagues, he has often sought to call into question claims about psychological phenomena that have not been rigorously tested, which is something we see in this selection. Aeon, a British online magazine, published a longer version of this essay, which was in turn adapted from Lilienfeld's academic journal article, "Microaggressions: Strong Claims, Inadequate Evidence." As you read, pay careful attention to the ways in which Lilienfeld repeatedly seeks to make clear the limits of the claims he is making, focusing on the challenges of rigorously investigating microaggressions from the perspective of social psychology.

Why a Moratorium on Microaggressions Is Needed

SCOTT O. LILIENFELD

Prejudice remains a huge social evil but evidence for harm caused by microaggression is incoherent, unscientific, and weak.

Across college campuses, a big idea has taken hold: the notion that microaggressions—subtle but offensive comments or actions directed at minorities or other powerless people—can lower performance, lead to ostracism, increase anxiety, and sometimes cause so much psychological pain that the recipient might even commit suicide. Yet despite the good intentions and passionate embrace of this idea, there is scant real-world evidence that microaggression is a legitimate psychological concept, that it represents unconscious (or **implicit) prejudice**, that intervention for it works, or even that alleged victims are seriously damaged by these under-the-radar acts. It is entirely possible that future research will alter some of these verdicts. Until the evidence is in, though, I recommend abandoning the term microaggression, which is potentially misleading. In addition, I call for a **moratorium** on microaggression training programs and publicly distributed microaggression lists now widespread in the college world.

Context is all-important here. Despite impressive societal strides, racial prejudice remains an inescapable and deeply troubling reality of modern life. As recently as 2008, 4 to 6 percent of Americans acknowledged in a national poll that they would be unwilling to vote for any African-American candidate as president. And this deeply troubling figure might be an underestimate given the **social undesirability**

---

implicit prejudice: prejudice—that is, negative beliefs or feelings about a group—that individuals are not aware that they have.

moratorium: pause, freeze.

social desirability: a form of bias that sometimes occurs in social science research when participants respond in ways they believe will be viewed positively by others, especially the researchers. Social desirability bias leads subjects to overreport "positive" behaviors and underreport "negative" ones.

attached to admissions of racism. Indeed, a growing number of scholars contend that prejudice often manifests in subtler forms than it did decades ago. From this perspective, prejudice has not genuinely declined—it has merely become more indirect and **insidious**.

Enter the concept of microaggressions, those subtle snubs, slights and insults directed at minorities, as well as women and other historically stigmatized groups. Compared with overtly prejudicial comments and acts, they are commonly understood to reflect less direct, although no less **pernicious**, forms of racial bias. Last year, Shaun R. Harper, founder of the Center for the Study of Race and Equity in Education at the University of Pennsylvania, told an Intelligence Squared debate about meeting an African-American student whose engineering professor had expressed incredulity that he'd received a perfect score on an exam. Few would dispute that such remarks, even if not **malicious**, are almost certainly **callous**. Prejudice undoubtedly manifests itself in subtle and indirect ways that have until recently received **short shrift** in psychological research.

Over the past few years, the concept of microaggression has made its way into public discussions at dozens, if not hundreds, of colleges and universities, with many institutions offering workshops to faculty members on identifying and avoiding microaggressions and disseminating lists of microaggressions to caution faculty and students against expressing statements that might cause offense.

All of these applications hinge on one overarching 5 assumption: that the microaggression research program aimed at documenting the phenomenon is sound and that the concept itself has withstood rigorous scientific scrutiny. This is not the case. Microaggressions have not been defined with nearly enough clarity to allow rigorous scientific investigation. No one has shown that they are interpreted negatively by all or even most minority groups. No one has demonstrated that they reflect implicit prejudice or aggression. And no one has shown that microaggressions exert an **adverse** impact on mental health.

I am hardly the first to raise questions regarding this body of research. Over the past few years in particular, the microaggression concept has been the target of withering attacks from social critics, especially—although not exclusively—on the right side of the political spectrum. These writers have raised legitimate concerns that concepts such as microaggression can at times discourage controversial speech and inadvertently perpetuate a victim culture among aggrieved individuals.

My major concern is the rigor of the psychological science itself. In no way do I deny that subtle forms of prejudice exist and are becoming more prevalent in some sectors of society. Nor do I wish to discourage, let alone reject, research into implicit prejudice. Nor do I contend that microaggressions don't exist. Instead, I contend only that microaggressions must be studied properly before we can claim to know their impact or the best ways of reducing the pain that they might cause. Good intentions are a start but are not sufficient.

The term *microaggression* was coined by psychiatrist Chester Pierce at Harvard in 1970 to describe seemingly minor but damaging put-downs and indignities experienced by African Americans. Pierce wrote: "Every Black must recognize the offensive

---

insidious: deceptive, sneaky.
pernicious: damaging, harmful.

malicious: spiteful, nasty, cruel.
callous: unfeeling, insensitive, uncaring.

short shrift: little consideration.   *adverse:* hostile.

mechanisms used by the collective White society, usually by means of cumulative proracist micro-aggressions, which keep him [sic] psychologically accepting of the **disenfranchised** state."

But it was not until 2007 that the microaggression concept began to filter into the academic mainstream. In an influential article in *American Psychologist*, the psychologist Derald Wing Sue defined microaggressions as "brief and commonplace daily verbal, behavioral, or environmental indignities, whether intentional or unintentional, that communicate hostile, derogatory, or negative racial slights and insults toward people of color." Microaggressions can be verbal comments, for instance subtle racial slights; behaviors, such as ignoring minority individuals; or environmental decisions, including naming all buildings on a college campus after white individuals, or even former slave owners. Sue and his team have called microaggressors "perpetrators," but I prefer the somewhat ungainly term "deliverers" to avoid any connotation of intentionality or malevolence.

To Sue and his colleagues, microaggressions are 10 pernicious precisely because they are usually ambiguous. Victims are typically trapped in a **catch-22**. Because they are uncertain of whether prejudice has actually been expressed, recipients frequently find themselves in a no-win situation. If they say nothing, they risk becoming resentful. Furthermore, they might inadvertently encourage further microaggressions from the same person. In contrast, if they say something, the deliverer might deny having engaged in prejudice and accuse minority-group members of being hypersensitive or paranoid.

Sue and his team differentiated among three subtypes of microaggressions, based on observation. *Microassaults*, which are the most blatant of the three, are explicit racial derogations "characterized primarily by a verbal or nonverbal attack meant to hurt the intended victim through name-calling, avoidant behavior, or purposeful discriminatory actions." They might include using racial slurs, drawing a swastika on someone's door, or referring to an African American as "colored." In contrast to other microaggressions, microassaults are often intentional.

Microinsults are barbs and put-downs that impart negative or even humiliating messages to victims; they "convey rudeness and insensitivity and demean a person's racial heritage or identity." For example, an employer who says: "I believe that the most qualified person should get the job, regardless of race" is delivering a microinsult.

Finally, *microinvalidations* "exclude, negate, or nullify the psychological thoughts, feelings, or experiential reality of a person of color." According to Sue, a microinvalidation could be a white person informing an African American that "I don't see color"; it might also be an African-American couple receiving poor restaurant service and being told by white friends that they were oversensitive in interpreting this poor service as race-related.

Scott O. Lilienfeld builds his argument around operational definitions of *microaggressions* and its three subcategories, *microassaults*, *microinsults*, and *microinvalidations*. See Chapter 9 for more on definitional arguments.

LINK TO P. 200 ·

disenfranchised: literally, deprived of being able to vote; more often, as here, used in the broader sense of marginalized.

catch-22: a dilemma or double bind; a situation in which any possible solutions cancel each other out.

Intriguing as they are, Sue's conclusions are really just theoretical conjectures based on information gleaned largely from **focus groups** and are in no way backed up by rigorous data or experimental techniques. Despite this limitation, the past decade has witnessed the extension of the microaggression concept to other groups who historically have been the targets of prejudice and discrimination, including women; gay, lesbian, and transgender individuals; Asian Americans; Latinos; Muslim Americans; and the obese. Virtually all of these extensions presume that the microaggression concept has already been validated and is well-established in African Americans—despite the fact that, by any standard of psychological science, this concept does not pass scientific scrutiny.

In the case of the microaggression concept, it is 15 dubious whether its definition is sufficiently clear to permit adequate scientific progress. For example, it is not evident which kinds of actions constitute a verbal, behavioral or environmental indignity, nor what severity of indignity is necessary for an action to constitute a microaggression.

All this vagueness and ambiguity can lead to outright contradictions in what is or is not a slight. For example, both ignoring and attending to minority students in classrooms have been deemed to be microaggressions by some authors: one researcher called out "teachers ignoring the raised hands of Asian-American students in classrooms" as a microaggression. Another regarded complimenting the student with a remark such as "That was a most articulate, intelligent, and insightful analysis" as a microaggression. In still other cases, they have regarded both praising and criticizing minority individuals as microaggressions.

Compounding this problem, microaggressions necessarily lie in the eye of the beholder. It is doubtful whether an action that is largely or exclusively subjective can legitimately be deemed "aggressive." The "eye of the beholder" assumption generates other logical quandaries. In particular, it is unclear whether any verbal or nonverbal action that a certain proportion of minority individuals perceives as offensive would constitute a microaggression. Would a discussion of race differences in personality, intelligence or mental illness in an undergraduate psychology course count? What about news coverage of higher crime rates among certain minority populations than among majority populations? It is likely that some or all of these admittedly uncomfortable topics would elicit pronounced negative emotional reactions among at least some minority group members.

The boundaries of the microaggression concept appear so indistinct as to invite misuse or abuse. One major scholar in the field even regarded the statement "I don't usually do this, but I can waive your fees if you can't afford to pay for counselling" as a microaggression. At least one research team has even classified saying "God bless you" following another person's sneeze as a microaggression, presumably because it could offend nonreligious individuals. According to

focus group: a small group of people, often diverse in nature, interviewed to get their beliefs, opinions, or attitudes about a specific topic, issue, or possible product as a way of understanding and predicting how the larger population might respond. This qualitative technique is widely used in market research, political analysis, and certain kinds of social psychological research.

some expansive definitions of microaggressions, this article itself could presumably constitute a microaggression, as it challenges the subjective experience of certain minority-group individuals. Given the fluid boundaries of the concept, in hindsight even statements that might appear to be explicitly anti-prejudiced have been interpreted as microaggressions. Sue's team, for instance, analyzed what the Arizona senator and then-presidential candidate John McCain said in response to an elderly white woman during a 2008 campaign stop. The woman said: "I can't trust Obama. . . . He's an Arab," and McCain immediately grabbed the microphone to correct her. "No ma'am," McCain retorted, "he's a decent family man [and] citizen that I just happen to have disagreements with. . . . He's not [an Arab]!"

While acknowledging that McCain's defense of Obama was "well-intentioned," the researchers dubbed it a "major microaggression." According to Sue, McCain's assertion that Obama is "a decent family man" implicitly communicated the message that most Arab or Muslim males are not decent family men, as well as the message that were Obama in fact a Muslim (which he is not), it would have implied that he was somehow dangerous or at least unworthy of admiration.

Although these post-hoc interpretations of   20 McCain's comments might be defensible, they are concerning. In particular, they raise the possibility that a vast number of statements can be retrospectively labelled microaggressions. For example, had McCain responded: "No ma'am, he's not an Arab—but what would be wrong if he were?"—which is the response that Sue said McCain should have

given—some advocates could have contended that McCain was subtly intending to insinuate that Obama might indeed be a Muslim. Furthermore, Sue's interpretation overlooks the possibility that McCain was merely responding to the affective gist of the woman's comment—namely, that Obama is a bad and untrustworthy person—rather than to its literal content. In doing so, he effectively communicated his central point—namely, that although he disagreed with Obama on many things, he did not believe that Obama was trying to conceal or lie about his ancestry or that Obama was a bad person.

The microaggression field, like much of psychology, lacks diversity of thought, and it shows. For instance, "Attaining a racially color-blind society is unattainable and only reinforces racism and societal inequality," wrote Sue in his book *Race Talk and the Conspiracy of Silence* (2015). Although this position might be defensible, it is hardly the only legitimate perspective on racial color-blindness. For example, many non-prejudiced participants might view the goal of a racially color-blind society as achievable in principle, if not fully in practice. Ironically, conceptualizing such statements as microaggressions runs counter to the crux of Reverend Martin Luther King Jr.'s eloquent affirmation: "I have a dream that my four little children will one day live in a nation where they will not be judged by the color of their skin, but by the content of their character." A compelling argument could be advanced that many **putative** microaggressions, especially micro-invalidations, lend themselves to a **myriad** of potential interpretations, some of them largely malignant, others largely benign. . . .

---

putative: presumed but not (fully) demonstrated to be the case.

myriad (of): numerous or even innumerable.

Some microaggression researchers—and the people reporting so much pain from these comments and acts—might be themselves committing a similar error. For example, Sue regarded the question "Where were you born?" directed at Asian Americans as a microaggression because it reflects the assumption that recipients are "different, less than, and could not possibly be, 'real' Americans." Yet most **cognitive-behavioral therapists** would maintain that leaping to this inference without attempting to check it out constitutes mind-reading. Instead of prejudice, it might in many cases reflect genuine and sincere curiosity regarding an individual's culture of origin.

Even the word "microaggression" can lead us astray. It implies that statements are aggressive in nature. Yet, confusingly, microaggression advocates posit that such behaviors are typically unintentional. As a result, the root word "aggression" in "microaggression" is conceptually confusing and misleading. Essentially, all contemporary definitions of aggression in the social-psychological and personality literatures propose or at least strongly imply that the actions comprising this construct are intentional. From this perspective, the concept of an unintentional microaggression is an **oxymoron**.

Does it matter? Research suggests that it might, because the perception of intent is a critical correlate of, and perhaps contributor to, aggression. Specifically, **social-cognitive research** on *hostile attribution of intent* suggests that if individuals perceive aggressive intent, they are more likely to respond aggressively in turn. Hence, labelling ambiguous statements or actions as "aggressive" might inadvertently foster aggression in recipients. And labelling certain statements or acts as "microaggressions" could fuel anger and even overt aggression in recipients: this possibility should be examined in the lab.

Even the prefix "micro" sometimes gets things 25 wrong—implying that these transgressions are barely visible or at least challenging to detect. Yet for a number of purported microaggressions, especially microassaults, this assumption is dubious. In particular, many or most microassaults appear to be emblematic of traditional, "old-fashioned" racism. Sue and his team include in their list of microassaults the act of using racial epithets—but, really, is that kind of verbal attack "micro" in the least? Such statements and behaviors are grossly offensive, and subsuming them under the broad microaggression umbrella could inadvertently trivialize patently racist acts. Moreover, if investigators find that total scores on microaggression are associated

---

cognitive-behavioral therapy: a form of psychosocial therapy whose goal is helping individuals develop coping strategies for overcoming unhealthy patterns of emotional self-regulation or unhealthy thoughts, beliefs, attitudes, and behaviors.

oxymoron: a phrase or concept made up of contradictory elements or ideas, often with the connotation, as here, of self-contradiction. Some examples of oxymorons could include *deafening silence, alone together,* and *the living dead,* all of which are used figuratively but would present logical contradictions if taken literally.

social-cognitive research: psychological research on how individuals process and apply information about social situations and other people. The research begins with the claim that how we think about other people has important consequences for how we construct our understanding of the social world, including interacting with others.

hostile attribution of intent: the tendency to assume the behavior of others is, in fact, hostile even though it may be ambiguous or even positive.

with minority psychopathology, might this not merely reflect already-established statistical associations between overt racism and mental health?

The terrain is **fraught**. Numerous items identified as microaggressive in the literature appear fairly common in everyday life, and not necessarily driven by hostile intent. For example, being passed over by a taxi driver for a white person has been listed as a microaggression. In a study of microaggressions experienced by African-American faculty members in counselling and psychology programs, the researchers identified a student calling a professor by his or her first name as a microaggression.

Yet it is likely that virtually all individuals who have lived in a major city, regardless of their race, have at least once been passed over by a taxi driver for a white person, and that virtually all faculty members, regardless of their race, have at least once had a student address them by their first name. Without at least some information concerning the frequency of the events, it's difficult to exclude the possibility that many microaggressions merely reflect everyday occurrences in the lives of both majority and minority individuals.

All this requires a hard and careful look. Numerous studies have revealed robust correlations between microaggressions and adverse mental-health outcomes, such as psychological distress, anxiety and depression, among minorities. Researchers have argued that the cumulative effects of microaggressions shorten life expectancy and even foster suicidal ideation, but where is the solid proof?

Let's be clear: prejudice and discrimination remain part and parcel of the daily landscape of many minority individuals. In a recent survey by the American Psychological Association, more than three-fourths of African Americans reported encountering at least some instances of discrimination on a day-to-day basis, and almost two in five African-American males said that they had been mistreated by the police. Given these sobering statistics, it is essential that psychological science continues to elucidate the sources and consequences of acts of prejudice and discrimination, both subtle and overt.

The study of microaggressions is a potentially fruit- 30 ful step in this direction, but it leaves a daunting number of critical scientific questions, both conceptual and methodological, unaddressed and unanswered. In this regard, the microaggression research program (MRP) might be little different from other **nascent** psychological constructs that await refinement in light of additional scientific knowledge. Given the numerous unresolved questions surrounding microaggression, MRP scholars must be circumspect in advocating for the application of this **fledgling** concept to colleges until more science has been conducted. In the interim, humility should be the watchword.

So, what to do? Although the MRP is presently highly problematic, we should not throw the baby out with the bathwater. Subtle prejudice undeniably exists, and a certain proportion of what are now misleadingly termed "microaggressions" probably reflect such prejudice. If we could reconceptualize most microaggressions as inadvertent cultural and racial slights, we'd all be better off. The microaggression culture prevalent on many campuses makes just about everyone feel threatened, and could **amp up** already **simmering** racial tensions. Distributing lists of

---

fraught: burdened and, here, politically charged in numerous ways.

nascent: emerging, often with the connotation of promising.

fledgling: fairly new, untried.

amp up: amplify, increase, or magnify.

simmering: on the verge of boiling over.

"forbidden" phrases to campus administrators or faculty members or mandating microaggression training for employees are unlikely to be helpful. A time-out on these ill-advised programs is long overdue.

Yes, many majority individuals say unintentionally offensive things to minority individuals from time to time, often because they are careless or oblivious or because they are simply unaware of these individuals' past racial and cultural experiences. Microaggressions should be the start of an open dialogue, not the end. Telling someone: "What you just said is a microaggression. You offended me and you have to stop" is unlikely to be conducive to a productive two-way conversation. In contrast, it could be a fruitful entry point into a difficult but mutually enlightening discussion to say: "You probably didn't mean this, but what you said bothered me. Maybe we're both misunderstanding each other. I realize that we're coming from different places. Let's talk."

RESPOND●

1. In this selection, what specifically is Lilienfeld critiquing? Why? How does he seek to limit the scope of his critique? In other words, what does he do as a writer to help readers understand what he is and is not claiming? Consider specific statements he makes as well as where and how often he makes them.

2. How does Lilienfeld use the three categories of microaggressions as grounds for critique of the general concept? (The simplest way to answer this question will be to read carefully the relevant paragraphs, making a list of Lilienfeld's claims so that you can see the progression of his argument as well as the distinctions made among the categories.) As a psychologist, Lilienfeld is understandably concerned with operational definitions—definitions that are explicit enough to permit us, first, to determine clearly whether or not some phenomenon is present and, second, to count it so that we may analyze it quantitatively. What does Lilienfeld's critique teach about the need for appropriately detailed definitions of terms, especially in research contexts? (See Chapter 9 on definitional arguments.)

3. Lilienfeld is obviously concerned with precision in language use. How does each of the following passages illustrate his concern with precise language?

   a. "Every Black must recognize the offensive mechanisms used by the collective White society, usually by means of cumulative proracist microaggressions, which keep him [sic] psychologically accepting of the disenfranchised state" [when quoting a text from 1970, before writers commonly used inclusive language].

   b. Sue and his team have called microaggressors "perpetrators," but I prefer the somewhat ungainly term "deliverers" to avoid any connotation of intentionality or malevolence.

c. Even the word "microaggression" can lead us astray. It implies that statements are aggressive in nature. Yet, confusingly, microaggression advocates posit that such behaviors are typically unintentional. As a result, the root word "aggression" in "microaggression" is conceptually confusing and misleading. Essentially, all contemporary definitions of aggression in the social-psychological and personality literatures propose or at least strongly imply that the actions comprising this construct are intentional. From this perspective, the concept of an unintentional microaggression is an oxymoron.

How do these statements contribute to Lilienfeld's ethos for social science readers who link precision in language with careful analysis? How do they serve to call into question at least some claims about microaggressions? (Chapter 13 discusses word choice and precision.)

4. **THINKING CRITICALLY**   To what extent can Lilienfeld's critique be seen as minimizing or undermining his own acknowledgment of the fact that racism and other sorts of harmful or malicious comments in fact exist and are part of the daily life of members of certain groups? Consider, for example, the comments reported in this video from 2016 about the sorts of comments made to Asian Americans: <https://www.nytimes.com/video/us/100000004706646/thisis2016-asian-americans-respond.html> OR <http://nyti.ms/2iTViTr>. (Please be aware that this video from the *New York Times* contains explicit language and that watching it may prove challenging for some individuals.) Should these comments be considered microaggressions? If so, of which type? (See Question 2 above.) Do any of them rise to a category that we might want or need to term *macroaggressions*? And how does Lilienfeld's suggestion in the final paragraph of the selection shift the burden of responsibility for the situation from the person who made the comment to the person who was the target? Does such a suggestion seem fair in contexts like those represented in the video? Why or why not?

5. Building on your responses to Questions 2 and 4, **write a three-part evaluative essay**. First, seek to use the evaluative distinctions given for microinsults, microassaults, and microinvalidations in paragraphs 11–13 of the selection. Categorize three of the comments made in the video discussed in Question 4. Second, use what you learn in trying to use these categories as the basis for evaluating Lilienfeld's critiques of the concept of microaggressions. Finally, address what is likely the important question to be considered: how might arguing about terminology—or even using the term *microaggression* as a label for the comments reported in the video—deflect attention from the real issues that many would argue need to be dealt with?

Activist Athletes

SARAH BROWN

Ariyana Smith, a women's basketball player at Knox College, lay down on the court before a game—and stayed there for four and a half minutes. Eric Striker, a University of Oklahoma football player, filmed a Snapchat video on his phone that went viral. The University of Missouri's football team staged a full-on boycott, refusing to practice or play altogether.

These demonstrations, protesting racial injustice, reflect the many ways that college athletes have taken public stands in recent years to send a message or bring about change.

Collegiate athletes—particularly in revenue-generating sports like football and men's basketball—have a national platform that many of their fellow students do not. They can also **leverage** the massive amounts of money that pour into college sports each year.

Ariyana Smith WCS Photography

◀ *This selection first appeared in February 2017 in the Chronicle of Higher Education, a newspaper and Web site focusing on news related to colleges and universities; its primary audience is professors, administrators, and staff at such institutions. It was one of a series of trend reports, which examined hot-button issues on college campuses that would likely continue to shape campus life. Sarah Brown, who has written for the Chronicle since 2015, frequently writes on topics such as diversity, sexual assault, and state policies toward higher education. As you read this selection, consider our society's changing understanding of college and professional athletes, the power they potentially wield, and the ways these issues intersect with understandings of freedom of speech and expression.*

leverage: using something—here, the visibility, profit, and importance a school may place on athletics—to its maximum advantage, in this case so as to lobby for social change.

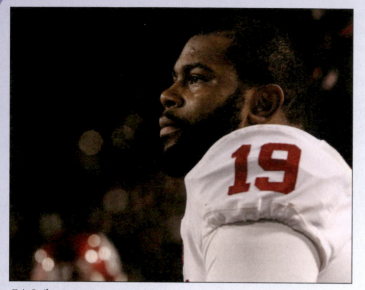

Eric Striker Brett Deering/Getty Images

The most recent uptick in athlete activism on campuses began in 2014, in the aftermath of Michael Brown's death at the hands of a police officer in Ferguson, Missouri. That incident inspired some players to call attention to what they saw as systemic racial bias in law enforcement. Later that year, players on a number of basketball teams wore shirts saying "I can't breathe" before games, a reference to what Eric Garner, another black man, had said when he was put in a chokehold by a New York City police officer. He later died.

In 2015, 32 players on Missouri's football team 5 wanted to call attention to what they saw as poor institutional responses to racial incidents on the campus. So they refused to play until Timothy Wolfe, then the president of the

Members of the University of Missouri football team in 2016 Gary McCullough/AP Images

university system, resigned. The boycott began a few days before a scheduled game against Brigham Young University, and if Missouri had canceled the game, it would have owed BYU $1 million. Mr. Wolfe was also facing growing pressure from student protesters, including one who vowed not to eat until the president resigned. He stepped down two days after the football boycott began.

In 2016, with political polarization and racial tensions running high, athletes' activism increased. They were inspired largely by Colin Kaepernick, the quarterback of the San Francisco 49ers, who in August started refusing to stand during the national anthem as a means of protesting injustices against black people. Since then, many college football and basketball players, as well as marching-band members, have demonstrated in some way during the anthem.

While many such protests are about race, they touch on other issues as well. The University of Minnesota's football team decided to boycott its bowl game in December because the university had suspended 10 players for an alleged sexual assault. Team members said they wanted to call attention to what they considered a lack of due process for students accused of misconduct. Players ended the boycott two days later, after Minnesota's investigation report into the incident was made public. It contained many lurid allegations about the case, in which the alleged victim claimed that she was pressured to have sex with multiple men, including several football players.

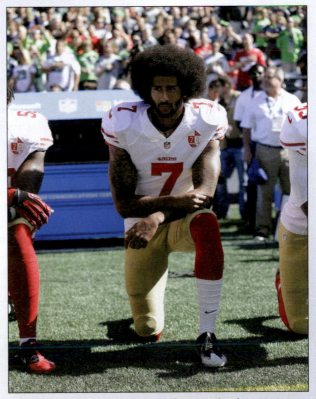

Given the widespread opposition to President Trump, experts on sports and social movements say they expect even more athletes to join the fray.

When college officials see such activism and aren't sure how to handle it, their first call is often to Harry Edwards, a prominent sports sociologist and emeritus professor at the University of California at Berkeley. Lately his phone has been ringing off the hook. "Oftentimes I'll get a call or query or be invited to a university, and what they want to know is, How we can avoid this?" he says. "They cannot avoid it."

Colin Kaepernick taking a knee during the national anthem, 2016
Ted S. Warren/AP Images

Mr. Edwards tells college presidents, athletics directors, and coaches that "they 10 should be aware of where their locker rooms are." Many athletic administrators seem surprised, he said, that their players are talking and tweeting about broader societal issues.

Given their potential influence, it may seem surprising that more college athletes don't engage in protests. But even as their activism has gained more traction, these students continue to face pressures that might have given some of their peers pause before speaking out.

One factor is simply the way athletics teams operate. "The sports structure in and of itself is not designed to cultivate activism," says Joseph N. Cooper, an assistant professor at the University of Connecticut who studies sports, race, and culture. "It's really designed to cultivate conformity." He likens it to the military: "You have leaders who provide orders, you don't question them, and you're not thinking critically about what you're doing." College players also have a lot on the line—namely, dreams of a professional career. If their activism rubs people the wrong way, that could put their futures at risk.

Athletics officials and coaches stand to lose, too, if angry alumni or fans stop donating or buying tickets for games, or if politicians try to punish their campuses. After six female basketball players at the University of Arkansas knelt during the anthem in November, in protest of police violence against black people, a state lawmaker placed a temporary hold on the institution's budget request. Then there's the possibility of reputational damage, which could affect recruiting. So campus officials have tended to be wary of such activism.

Since athletes are at the mercy of their coaches in terms of playing time and scholarships, coaches and team managers exercise a great deal of influence over their players' choices. If a college team includes several individuals who have come together to organize a protest, "but the coach is saying, No, you're not kneeling, you're not walking out, you're not doing whatever it is—that's powerful," says Jennifer McGarry, a professor of educational leadership at Connecticut and a former athletic administrator.

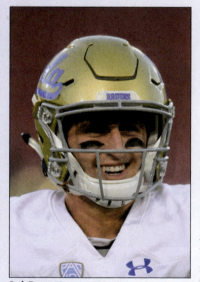
Josh Rosen Thearon W. Henderson/Getty Images

Last year Josh Rosen, the quarterback at the University of California at Los 15 Angeles, publicly criticized a new $280 million deal with the apparel company Under Armour. Mr. Rosen pointed out that while student athletes had effectively made the large contract possible, they would not benefit financially from it because they aren't paid. "We're still amateurs, though. . . . Gotta love non-profits."

#NCAA" he wrote on Instagram. Mr. Rosen is expected to be a top pick in next year's NFL draft.

After UCLA's coach, Jim L. Mora, admonished the player for making a contentious statement that distracted from the university's announcement, Mr. Rosen deleted the post.

At least one athletics director believes there's growing support among his colleagues for student activism. "The athletic director of today is a lot more knowledgeable about the right to free expression and the fact that this isn't the old-school old days anymore," says Ray Anderson, who serves in that role at Arizona State University.

Mr. Anderson stresses, though, that there's an important distinction to be drawn between a respectful, peaceful protest and a mean-spirited "intentional interference."

College officials also have to ponder the question of whether their athletes should be treated primarily as students with First Amendment rights or as athletes who represent the institution, he says. For him there's no question: They are students first and athletes second. So the job of colleges is to educate them about possible ramifications of speaking out, he says.

In sports, he says, "the memories go long."   20

Mr. Rosen, the UCLA quarterback, has had to learn some of those lessons firsthand. In April, he posted an Instagram photo of himself teeing off at a Trump golf course while wearing a bandana that profanely insulted Mr. Trump—which sparked a social-media firestorm and earned another public rebuke from his coach. "With Trump, I'm learning to evolve my message and understand how to convey the substance of it," he later told *Sports Illustrated*.

Despite the risks, Mr. Edwards believes the college athletics world will see more activism in the coming months. He specifically predicts more activity on the issue of athlete pay.

"It's almost inevitable, given the impact on activism that the Trump regime will have," he says. "Before a Final Four or a bowl championship series with four teams playing, some group of athletes or teams in the locker room is going to say, 'We'll take the court or field when someone talks to us about the damn money.'"

TAKEAWAY

Athletes take the field—and a knee

- Activism among college athletes swelled in 2016. Many were inspired by Colin Kaepernick, the NFL quarterback who knelt during the national anthem to protest racial injustice.

- College athletes can pack a powerful protest by leveraging their high profiles—and, in some cases, the revenue they generate. But the number of athlete activists remains small because protesting carries risks.

- Widespread opposition to President Trump is likely to inspire more college athletes to take stands on race and other issues in the coming months.

RESPOND●

1. What is your response to political activism by athletes? Have you seen it occurring on your own campus? Did this selection give you new ways of thinking about such activism as it relates to the issue of free speech?

2. This selection, which is from early 2017, makes strong predictions about what would happen in the future. Were these predictions borne out? Why or why not, do you think?

3. Given the leverage that student athletes potentially have, some would argue that they have an obligation to engage in activism of the sort described in this selection. Would you agree or disagree with such an argument? Why or why not? How does such an argument intersect with arguments about freedom of speech on campus or with membership in various groups?

4. **THINKING CRITICALLY**   Chapter 13 encourages you, as a critical reader and a writer, to pay special attention to word choice and the often subtle messages word choice conveys. In paragraph 23 of this selection, Professor Harry Edwards refers to "the Trump *regime*."

Investigate the connotations and denotations of that word *regime*, including possible synonyms Edwards might have used. What does his word choice tell readers about Edwards? Does that information influence how you assess Edwards's trustworthiness, or his ethos? Should it? Why or why not?

5. Paragraph 19 poses a question: Should student athletes be treated primarily as students with First Amendment rights or as athletes who represent the institution for which they play? Another paragraph offers the perspective of Ray Anderson, athletic director at Arizona State University, on that issue. What is your position and what has led you to that conclusion? Which of the two ways of characterizing student athletes do you believe should be privileged? What do you see as the consequences of assuming either perspective, or of trying to acknowledge the tension between the two and to honor that tension? **Write a causal argument** in which you state your position on this issue and explain the reasons that you hold it, that is, the evidence, experiences, or understanding of the situation that have caused you to see the issue as you do. (Chapter 11 will offer direction in how to construct a successful causal argument.)

▼ *In this selection, Catherine Nolan-Ferrell, an associate professor of Latin American history at the University of Texas at San Antonio, shares her experiences with the challenge of balancing free speech and civility in the classroom. It first appeared in* Academe, *the journal of the American Association of University Professors, an organization of professors and other academics in the U.S., in late 2017. As you read, reflect on your own experiences with this balancing act and consider how and why these issues may be experienced differently by students and by their instructors.*

Balancing Classroom Civility and Free Speech

CATHERINE NOLAN-FERRELL

Last fall, I began my modern Latin American history course with my usual introduction: "I am a historian of modern Latin America, with a particular emphasis on nationality and citizenship among marginalized peoples. My current research is on the Guatemalan refugee crisis of the early 1980s and its aftermath along the Guatemalan-Mexican border." I explained that the course focuses on themes of ethnicity, class, and how nations include or exclude marginalized peoples as citizens.

I always introduce myself like this at the beginning of any class I teach because students have the right to know who I am, what my interests are, and how my particular perspectives have influenced the choice of topics to be discussed. By acknowledging how my interests shape my teaching, I want to emphasize the importance of intellectual honesty. I cannot claim complete neutrality about the subject matter, but I do promise students that I will discuss multiple perspectives and explain how and why I reached my point of view. Although they may not remember the details of the **Mexican Revolution** or the causes and impacts of the **Dirty War** in Argentina, they will learn how to read critically and evaluate a wide range of primary sources. By assessing these sources, students develop the fundamental skills needed to build historical arguments. We may not always arrive at the same conclusion, but we have some basic agreement about what constitutes historical data. The challenge lies in teaching students how to contribute to the dialogue about how "facts" are made, or, more precisely, how people develop consensus about what constitutes factual information in the face of individual (and societal) choices to dismiss accepted facts that may conflict with particular worldviews.

Mexican Revolution: a series of armed struggles occurring in Mexico during the second decade of the twentieth century that continue to shape contemporary Mexican politics in complex ways.

Dirty War: the program of state terrorism in Argentina from the mid-1970s until 1983, during which some 30,000 people disappeared as the military, militia, and right-wing death squads "disappeared" those who did not share their political views or were suspected of not sharing them. It was part of a larger U.S. CIA-sponsored project during the Cold War, Operation Condor.

A demonstration of the Mothers of Plaza de Mayo, an association of Argentinian women whose children were "disappeared" during the Dirty War EITAN ABRAMOVICH/AFP/ Getty Images

Primary sources are the "raw data" of historical research. Broadly defined as documents or objects created at the time the historical events occurred, these sources provide direct or firsthand knowledge of past events. This knowledge is not yet "fact," though, because primary sources often reflect distinct perspectives on the past. History professors teach students to assess the validity of historical data by asking who produced the primary source, why he or she produced it, and what biases may have influenced the creator of the source. Researchers also **cross-reference** documents. They ask whether other primary sources **corroborate**, or at least mention, the subject in question. By discussing and debating primary sources, we construct general understandings of historical facts as concrete events that occurred at a particular time and place and involved specific people. Historians may debate some of the details, but they agree on the overall parameters of the historical event. This knowledge, along with understanding of **foundational** concepts of historical context, causality, complexity, **contingency**, and change over time, enables students to figure out why something happened in the way that it did.

The heart of any history class is not the memorization of names and dates but the process of historical analysis. Students quickly learn that patterns of human behavior often recur, not in the simplistic sense of "history repeating itself" but because history

---

cross-reference: here, compare documents dealing with same period or topic.

corroborate: provide support for or confirm the existence of.

foundational: forming the basis or foundation of.

contingency: here, how a range of events and circumstances work together to shape history; its opposite would be inevitability—that certain events necessarily occurred.

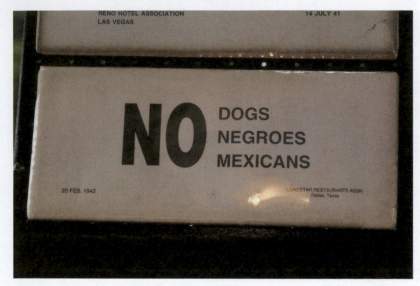

This 1942 sign distributed by Lonestar Restaurants in Texas represents the sort of indignities Mexican Americans and African Americans had to endure in Texas and elsewhere in the country before the Civil Rights era. Clark Brennan/ Alamy Stock Photo

"rhymes." Historians see echoes of past events in current conflicts, though we remain mindful of how unique times, places, and people affect experiences.

A Difficult Balance

The political situation that characterized the 2016 pres- 5 idential campaign posed multiple challenges to classroom civility and academic freedom in my class. These challenges were magnified by the demographics of the University of Texas at San Antonio, which is designated as a Hispanic-serving institution and has a student body that is nearly 50 percent Latino. The composition of my class mirrored that of the institution as a whole: 54 percent of the students were Latino (including Mexican American, Mexican-origin, and Guatemalan-origin students), 32 percent were **Anglo-American**, and the rest were a mix of international students and those who preferred not to define themselves by race, ethnicity, or nationality. Nearly half of those attending UTSA are first-generation college students. Many students work more than thirty hours a week and also have full-time school and family responsibilities.

Anglo-American: in Texas, the term *Anglo-American* applies to individuals who do not identify as or are not taken to be African American, Asian American, or Hispanic. Thus, someone whose ancestors immigrated to Texas from Germany or Czechoslovakia would be considered Anglo. Broadly, the term refers to non-Hispanic whites.

Given the composition of UTSA's student body, many students carry with them community memories that include a long legacy of racism and violence. Prior to the mid-1960s, **Jim Crow**–like segregation and federal redlining in San Antonio restricted many Mexican Americans to substandard housing and inadequate schools, ultimately excluding them from well-paying employment opportunities. Community members and leaders throughout south Texas, including politicians, activists, and artists, remind people not only of the **Chicano movement's** struggles for civil rights but also of previous deportation campaigns of Mexicans and Mexican Americans in the United States during the 1930s and 1940s. Although historians dispute the numbers of those who left and the level of coercion that was used, most agree that between four hundred thousand and five hundred thousand people of Mexican origin left the United States. Some were forcibly removed, others were pressured (with threats or incentives), and others voluntarily repatriated. Roughly 50 to 60 percent of those who went to Mexico were actually US citizens.

The Mexican American community's experiences of racism in south Texas, and in San Antonio specifically, made US presidential candidate Donald Trump's blanket characterization of Mexican immigrants as rapists and murderers particularly offensive to both students and faculty at UTSA. Trump's call to "build a wall" and "throw them out" also instilled in students fears of racial profiling. Several Mexican American students shared stories of being verbally harassed, being told that "you'll get sent home soon" or "we'll be cleaning up this country, so you'd better get ready," and "we don't want you 'illegals' who live off welfare." A Mexican American student in her late twenties came to my office before class one day, obviously distressed. She had overheard students talking about how Trump was going to "take back America" from the "illegals." In tears, she asked me how she should try to cope with these sorts of racist comments.

On the one hand, these are cases of free speech. A person can express opinions about political ideals or religious beliefs without censorship. According to the US Supreme Court's ruling in *Schenck v. United States*, such speech is protected unless it "incites actions that would harm others." Indeed, colleges and universities actively encourage diverse viewpoints. On the other hand, UTSA has an explicit policy on classroom civility that asserts "students share in the obligation to maintain a classroom environment that is conducive to learning. Accordingly, students are prohibited from engaging in any behavior that obstructs, disrupts, or interferes with any class."

How do faculty members draw the line between free speech and disruptive behavior? The 2016 election has made that question more difficult to answer. In almost any other year, students could wear clothing with political slogans, religious statements, or mottos that advocate for a certain cause without provoking any alarm. However, the toxic political climate of the election, particularly the use of polarized rhetoric that explicitly denigrated certain ethnicities, religions, or political belief systems, made "normal" political campaign slogans ambiguous.

Jim Crow: state and local laws and practices enforcing racial or ethnic segregation of African Americans in the southern United States from the post-Reconstruction period in the nineteenth century until the Supreme Court rulings responding to the Civil Rights movement in the 1950s and 1960s.

Chicano movement: a 1960s civil rights movement led by Cesar Chavez and Dolores Huerta focusing on the Mexican American community in the southwestern United States.

Schenck v. United States: 1919 Supreme Court case that was the first in a series of rulings that have shaped contemporary understandings of free speech in this country.

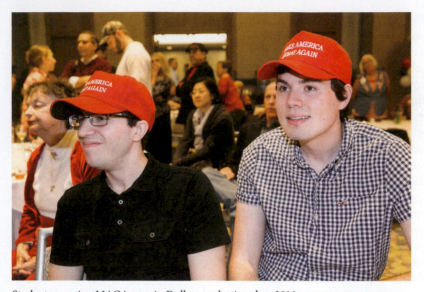

Students wearing MAGA caps in Dallas on election day, 2016 LAURA BUCKMAN/Getty Images

Shortly before the election, one student showed up 10 to class wearing a red "Make America Great Again" baseball cap. Was the person wearing the hat expressing disdain for the opposition political party or candidate? Or was the hat-wearer expressing more hostile beliefs, such as support for calls to "deport illegals"? In the absence of context—not knowing what the student meant to say—I had no good way to assess the student's intentions in wearing the hat. In contrast, I did know that another student viewed the hat as a threat to Mexican Americans. At the time, I decided that the hat disrupted the class, at least for some students, and I asked the person to remove it. The student immediately did so and apologized for wearing "distracting" clothing.

In the next class period, my students discussed the overall hostile atmosphere created by election rhetoric and the balance between protecting free speech and creating a safe learning environment. Since many students in that class wanted to become K–12 teachers or to work in business, we discussed how to handle such a situation in a professional setting. After much debate, students agreed that in a work environment, wearing overtly political clothing could be seen as either intimidating or inappropriate. As the class moved toward consensus, several students explicitly stated that they would not wear clothing associated with "their" candidate as long as the "other side" agreed to do the same.

Unfortunately, the **détente** lasted only until the day after the election. On that day, a different student

---

détente: easing of strained
relations or hostility
between two political
entities, often countries.

A mass grave from the Guatemalan Civil War in the 1980s being exhumed in Guatemala City AFP/Getty Images

wore his red "Make America Great Again" hat to class, but I failed to notice it because the hat was turned backward. After class, several students asked me why I did not make him take off the hat, clearly annoyed that the neutrality agreement had been violated. Then, on Thursday morning, I arrived at work to find that someone had slid a photocopy of a flyer from the "Texas State Vigilantes" under my office door. The flyer read, "Now that our man TRUMP is elected and republicans own both the senate and the house—time to organize tar & feather VIGILANTE SQUADS and go arrest & torture those deviant university leaders spouting off all this Diversity Garbage."

Without context, how was I to interpret the flyer's message? Was it from a student who was concerned about ensuring faculty free speech? Or was it from someone who wanted to intimidate a professor? Was it a "plant" from left-wing activists who sought to make conservatives look bad? Was it merely a bad joke? Given that Texas law allows concealed weapons on campus, should I be concerned for my personal safety?

How could I turn this disturbing incident into a "teachable moment"?

THINKING HISTORICALLY

By chance, the class was scheduled to discuss human 15 rights and the Guatemalan Civil War that day. During the early 1980s, Guatemalan military leaders, with support of the US government, unleashed massive waves of violence against any perceived opponents, murdering and "disappearing" thousands of civilians. The violence culminated in **genocide** against Mayan

---

genocide: the deliberate killing of a large group of people, generally people of a particular ethic, religious, or national group.

indigenous peoples. Faculty and students at the University of San Carlos, the most prestigious university in Guatemala, faced persistent threats. **Paramilitary** groups often sent flyers or spray-painted messages on doors to inform activists that they were targeted for disappearance or execution.

Because this sort of violence has never characterized academia in the United States, students here often take for granted their safety and their right to speak their minds. They sometimes fail to recognize the privileges and responsibilities that accompany our civil liberties. I showed students the flyer and asked them what they thought about it. How would they interpret it? Given the context of the class material, and the fact that some of them were honestly fearful about the new president, most interpreted the flyer as a threat.

One student, however, defended the use of intimidation tactics as sometimes necessary for the greater good. He argued that it was acceptable to "put people on notice" that "we" (I presume he meant Texans) would not tolerate "misbehavior down here." When I asked him what he meant by misbehavior, he said, "Well, you know, the kind of rioting and stuff that happens in California and New York, where people feel like it's okay to just break things, just because they've lost." Other students spoke out against the vandalism that accompanied postelection protests but said that people had a legitimate right to demonstrate. They pointed out that few protests turned violent and that demonstrations in Austin, Houston, and San Antonio were all peaceful. His response: "Yeah, well, you know they want to bring all that chaos here, and we'll shoot them before they do it." Someone asked, "Who's the 'they?'" He responded, "You know, the immigrants and the liberals and the

blacks who just want the government to baby them and take stuff from the people who work."

At this point, a very bright but quiet young woman interrupted him. She challenged his willingness to classify entire groups of people as "problems." Her family immigrated "with papers" and never requested government assistance. She was the first in her family to attend college, and although she had received some subsidized student loans as financial aid, she did not see such loans as "a handout from taxpaying citizens." In response to the "good immigrant" argument, someone else brought up Donald Trump Jr.'s "Skittles" analogy. (During his father's campaign, he said, "If I had a bowl of Skittles and I told you three would kill you, would you take a handful? That's our Syrian refugee problem.") The woman's family may be "good immigrants," but this student was not convinced that accepting immigrants was worth the risk of possibly welcoming terrorists.

At this point, I interrupted and asked students where they drew the line between free speech and civility. Clearly, given the very heated debate, students recognized that they were no longer respecting their classmates. Instead, students on all sides of the debate had fallen into the trap of treating their classmates as "the other."

In teaching genocide, we explicitly discuss the 20 process of "othering," of how extreme identity constructions of "us versus them" dehumanize particular groups that are perceived as inferior. The "others" carry markers of exclusion, such as ethnicity or race, religion, class, or gender. Othering, from its mildest forms of exclusion to its extremes of genocidal violence, not only enables people to

---

paramilitary: unofficial group often operating as if it were the military.

dismiss alternate viewpoints; it also enables them to deny the fundamental humanity of those who differ from them.

When the students realized that they had slipped into using dehumanizing language, they backed away from confrontation and remained quiet for the rest of class. This was not precisely the result I wanted; I wanted them to realize that they could disagree with one another but still recognize value in those who held different viewpoints. However, as the young woman from the immigrant family told me after class, "I just cannot keep talking to people who refuse to listen."

In "The Problem of Othering: Towards Inclusiveness and Belonging," John Powell and Stephen Menendian define "othering" as "a set of dynamics, processes, and structures that engender marginality and persistent inequality across any of the full range of human differences based on group identities." The divisive rhetoric from the political arena so polarized students that the classroom environment felt "unsafe" to both the pro-Trump students (who believed they were being unfairly labeled and marginalized as racists) and the anti-Trump students (who believed they were being subjected to racist stereotyping).

For the following month, the class continued to grapple with tensions that surfaced during the election. My modern Latin American history course overlapped closely with political debates surrounding the North American Free Trade Agreement (NAFTA), the drug wars, and immigration from Mexico and Central America. My constant challenge to students

was to think historically: find primary sources, carefully analyze them, and then construct historical arguments that could be supported by evidence. Why did **narcotraffickers** gain respect and support in some parts of Latin America? To answer this question, students grappled with the causes of corruption, political and economic alienation, efforts of impoverished peoples to earn a viable income, and cultural values such as "machismo," which students saw as a positive idea that values men's roles in providing for their families and as a negative idea that leads men to use violence to protect their honor and authority. We discussed causality and contingency by examining the impact of NAFTA on workers in both the United States and Mexico. Students assessed the decline of US manufacturing by evaluating the impact of cheaper Mexican labor, as well as dramatic technological changes that automated and improved the efficiency of factories.

As students increasingly challenged each other to provide evidence, two key patterns emerged. First, debate became more respectful, because it was harder to simplify human actions as "good" or "bad." The people we studied were humanized, and students began to see one another as complex individuals. Second, students began questioning the fundamental validity of primary sources. When I showed statistical data from the Department of Homeland Security about the high level of Mexican deportations between 2008 and 2014, one student objected, questioning whether the Obama administration would accurately report deportation numbers. A few students dismissed statements from

narcotraffickers:
individuals and groups
that buy and sell illegal
narcotics.

women and children who fled gang violence in Honduras or El Salvador as either exaggerations or complete fabrications. In order to contextualize these oral testimonies, students looked at murder rates and reports on gang violence gathered from US Department of State bulletins, the *Congressional Record*, and various human rights organizations. These usually well-respected sources are created by people who are experts in their field. Student responses to these primary sources varied from mild concern about inaccuracy or misinterpretation to complete dismissal of their validity.

How do we navigate a world where many in society have lost trust in shared data? How do we teach students to respect the evidence, even if it challenges their worldviews? And how do we do so in such a politically charged climate, when an inability (or perhaps refusal) to trust data creates an inability to engage in dialogue about fundamental social, economic, and political issues? When one of my students states that "the guy in the Trump hat" scares her, I may not necessarily agree that her reaction is reasonable, but I cannot deny the fear. How do I teach the student wearing the hat that his classmate's fear is real? How do I acknowledge the very real fears that many Trump supporters share about immigration, terrorism, or imminent economic collapse—even when, in my analysis, the evidence does not validate those fears? Biologically, fear inhibits rational thinking and provokes the **"fight-or-flight" response**. Our 25

society seems trapped by this **primal** reaction, and we cannot distinguish between perceived and actual threats. The constant barrage of information—true, false, and other—has created a collective deafness. One way to counter this is to listen only to things that are familiar and comfortable.

However, history offers another option. By enticing us to "hear the past," to acknowledge tensions between the need to find patterns of human behavior and acknowledge unique situations, we can extend our ability to hold complex information. Critical analysis of primary sources creates a "safe space" where students can encounter the other without reacting with fear. It allows them to see the fundamental humanity in those who hold different beliefs.

Confronting "Alternative Facts"

The "Statement on Standards of Professional Conduct" of the **American Historical Association (AHA)** describes "critical dialogue," "trust and respect," and "integrity of the historical record" as core values of the profession. Historians' raw data come from primary sources—documents and

Catherine Nolan-Ferrell argues in favor of greater respect and understanding across different political viewpoints, much like the rhetorical listening Krista Ratcliffe advocates, as discussed in Chapter 1.

LINK TO P. 7 ·

---

fight-or-flight response: a physiological response to a threatening situation, real or imagined, in which an animal, including a human, responds with aggression (fight) or by fleeing (flight).

primal: relating to an early stage of evolution.

American Historical Association: the oldest and largest professional association for historians.

artifacts such as diaries, letters, court transcripts, and photographs that were created during the particular period being studied. The historian interprets the data to explain why particular events occurred in the way they did or why people acted in the way they did.

It has been said that "history is an exercise in **empathy**." Historians attempt to see the world as those who lived in the past experienced it. Ours is fundamentally a collective enterprise—we build on each other's work and debate multiple perspectives in order to create an understanding of the past. In order to participate effectively in the critical dialogues that help historians contextualize and interpret sources, it is imperative that we trust each other to "respect the integrity of the historical record." We may debate the interpretation of historical data, but we must respect the evidence. I teach my students to follow the archival trail, even if doing so challenges their preconceived ideas about the past. (For example, students may have a romanticized view of a revolution—oppressed peoples rebel to free themselves from their tormentors—but the historical data often create a much more complicated picture. The idealistic revolutionary may end up selling out his **compatriots** in exchange for personal profit or to protect his or her own life.) Without this fundamental respect for the historical record—for historical data—our interpretations cannot be trusted. As the AHA states, "By practicing their craft with integrity,

historians acquire a reputation for trustworthiness that is arguably their single most precious professional asset." In other words, facts matter. Arguments must be supported by evidence.

What do these core values mean in a world of "fake news" and "alternative facts"? At the start of the spring 2017 semester, a student told me that he "didn't believe in facts" because everything was fundamentally biased. In his view, if all historical data are merely representations of what people thought and perceived at the time, nothing is "real"—what we call "facts" are an endless chain of biased information. This is the danger of so-called alternative facts. They exist outside of dialogue. There is no need to come to an agreement about data because data exist in isolation—not as a part of a broader interpretive narrative. The student's reasoning made me think about those who deny genocides. By taking the view that everything is merely "perception," one can deny or minimize the horrors of mass violence. But bodies are real. Mass graves are real. Evidence cannot be dismissed.

As academics, we are dedicated to understanding 30 both the historical world and the present by interpreting evidence. We may disagree about *how* to interpret evidence, but we believe that evidence exists. When people claim that they are working from "alternative facts," they are not just disputing an interpretation; they are rejecting the very foundation of knowledge.

---

empathy: the ability to perceive a situation from another's perspective.

compatriot: a person from the same country.

RESPOND

1. What is your response to Nolan-Ferrell's argument in this essay—both at the gut level and intellectually? Have you had classroom experiences like the ones she describes? How did you respond? How did your instructor respond (if the professor was aware of them)? What is your reaction to Nolan-Ferrell's argument against the notion of "false facts"? Why?

2. Nolan-Ferrell's essay is, in many ways, built around a series of narratives—stories she recounts from her experiences as a professor of history. Which of these narratives, if any, did you find especially effective for constructing or supporting the arguments she is making? What specific aspects of the narrative(s) were effective? (If you did not find any of the narratives effective in advancing the author's argument, explain why you did not.) As Chapter 4 notes, testimonies often function as logical appeals—"this is my experience; therefore, it counts as fact"—but they can also serve as ethical or pathetic appeals. In what ways does Nolan-Ferrell use narrative to serve all these purposes? (See Chapters 1–4 for discussions of logical, ethical, and pathetic appeals.)

3. Throughout this selection, Nolan-Ferrell builds up a definition of "primary sources" and their particular meaning and value for historians and historical methods of analysis. Collect the various definitions and characterizations of the term "primary sources," and characterize them according to the types of definition presented in Chapter 9.

4. **THINKING CRITICALLY**   As explained in the headnote, *Academe*, where this essay appeared, is the magazine of the American Association of University Professors. Hence, it is safe to assume that Nolan-Ferrell's intended audience is other professors. What evidence can you provide for Nolan-Ferrell's invoked audience, that is, the audience whose values are reflected and inscribed in the text? How would you characterize that audience? (Your response will likely be "She is writing for people who assume/agree that . . ." or "She is writing to people who are concerned with. . . .") Had Nolan-Ferrell been writing for an audience of only historians, how might her essay have been different? For example, is there information in the selection she might have assumed her audience shared? Had she been addressing students, rather than faculty, how might her essay have been different? (Chapter 1 discusses the notion of intended and invoked audience as well as the key role that audience plays in the construction of any argument.)

5. Nolan-Ferrell's essay raises many questions that she does not explicitly answer, one of the most interesting being where the line is or
should be drawn between free speech and civility, both highly valued
on American college campuses. **Write a definitional essay** in which
you seek to define or characterize this line in light of the selections in
this chapter, class discussions, and your own personal experience.
(Chapter 9 will help you think about constructing a definitional
argument.)

Glossary

academic argument writing that is addressed to an audience well informed about the topic, that aims to convey a clear and compelling point in a somewhat formal style, and that follows agreed-upon conventions of usage, punctuation, and formats.

accidental condition in a definition, an element that helps to explain what's being defined but isn't essential to it. An accidental condition in defining a bird might be "ability to fly" because most, but not all, birds can fly. (See also *essential condition* and *sufficient condition*.)

ad hominem **argument** a fallacy of argument in which a writer's claim is answered by irrelevant attacks on his/her character.

allusion an indirect reference. Saying "watch out or you'll create the next Edsel" contains an allusion to the Ford Edsel, a disastrously unpopular and unsuccessful product of the late 1950s.

analogy an extended comparison between something unfamiliar and something more familiar for the purpose of illuminating or dramatizing the unfamiliar. An analogy might, say, compare nuclear fission (less familiar) to a pool player's opening break (more familiar).

anaphora a figure of speech involving repetition, particularly of the same word at the beginning of several clauses.

antithesis the use of parallel structures to call attention to contrasts or opposites, as in *Some like it hot; some like it cold.*

antonomasia use of a title, epithet, or description in place of a name, as in *Your Honor* for *Judge.*

argument (1) a spoken, written, or visual text that expresses a point of view; (2) the use of evidence and reason to discover some version of the truth, as distinct from *persuasion*, the attempt to change someone else's point of view.

artistic appeal support for an argument that a writer creates based on principles of reason and shared knowledge rather than on facts and evidence. (See also *inartistic appeal*.)

assumption a belief regarded as true, upon which other claims are based.

assumption, cultural a belief regarded as true or commonsensical within a particular culture, such as the belief in individual freedom in American culture.

audience the person or persons to whom an argument is directed.

authority the quality conveyed by a writer who is knowledgeable about his/her subject and confident in that knowledge.

background the information a writer provides to create the context for an argument.

backing in Toulmin argument, the evidence provided to support a warrant.

bandwagon appeal a fallacy of argument in which a course of action is recommended on the grounds that everyone else is following it.

begging the question a fallacy of argument in which a claim is based on the very grounds that are in doubt or dispute: *Rita can't be the bicycle thief; she's never stolen anything.*

causal argument an argument that seeks to explain the effect(s) of a cause, the cause(s) of an effect, or a causal chain in which A causes B, B causes C, C causes D, and so on.

ceremonial argument an argument that deals with current values and addresses questions of praise and blame. Also called *epideictic*, ceremonial arguments include eulogies and graduation speeches.

character, appeal based on also known as an ethical appeal; a strategy in which a writer presents an authoritative, credible self-image in order to gain the trust of an audience.

circumstantial evidence in legal cases, evidence from which conclusions cannot be drawn directly but have to be inferred.

claim a statement that asserts a belief or truth. In arguments, most claims require supporting evidence. The claim is a key component in Toulmin argument.

classical oration a highly structured form of an argument developed in ancient Greece and Rome to defend or refute a thesis. The oration evolved to include six parts—*exordium, narratio, partitio, confirmatio, refutatio,* and *peroratio.*

confirmatio the fourth part of a classical oration, in which a speaker or writer offers evidence for the claim.

connotation the suggestions or associations that surround most words and extend beyond their literal meaning, creating associational effects. *Slender* and *skinny* have similar meanings, for example, but carry different connotations, the former more positive than the latter.

context the entire situation in which a piece of writing takes place, including the writer's purpose(s) for writing; the intended audience; the time and place of writing; the institutional, social, personal, and other influences on the piece of writing; the material conditions of writing (whether it's, for instance, online or on paper, in handwriting or in print); and the writer's attitude toward the subject and the audience.

conviction the belief that a claim or course of action is true or reasonable. In a proposal argument, a writer must move an audience beyond conviction to action.

credibility an impression of integrity, honesty, and trustworthiness conveyed by a writer in an argument.

criterion (*plural* criteria) in evaluative arguments, a standard by which something is measured to determine its quality or value.

deductive reasoning a process of thought in which general principles are applied to particular cases.

definition, argument of an argument in which the claim specifies that something does or doesn't meet the conditions or features set forth in a definition: *Pluto is not a major planet.*

deliberative argument an argument that deals with action to be taken in the future, focusing on matters of policy. Deliberative arguments include parliamentary debates and campaign platforms.

delivery the presentation of an argument.

dogmatism a fallacy of argument in which a claim is supported on the grounds that it's the only conclusion acceptable within a given community.

either/or choice a fallacy of argument in which a complicated issue is misrepresented as offering only two possible alternatives, one of which is often made to seem vastly preferable to the other.

emotional appeal a strategy in which a writer tries to generate specific emotions (such as fear, envy, anger, or pity) in an audience to dispose it to accept a claim.

enthymeme in Toulmin argument, a statement that links a claim to a supporting reason: *The bank will fail* (claim) *because it has lost the support of its largest investors* (reason). In classical rhetoric, an enthymeme is a syllogism with one term understood but not stated: *Socrates is mortal because he is a human being.* (The understood term is *All human beings are mortal.*) (See also *syllogism.*)

epideictic argument See *ceremonial argument.*

equivocation a fallacy of argument in which a lie is given the appearance of truth, or in which the truth is misrepresented in deceptive language.

essential condition in a definition, an element that must be part of the definition but, by itself, isn't enough to define the term. An essential condition in defining a bird might be "winged": all birds have wings, yet wings alone don't define a bird since some insects and mammals also have wings. (See also *accidental condition* and *sufficient condition.*)

ethical appeal See *character, appeal based on,* and *ethos.*

ethnographic observation a form of field research involving close and extended observation of a group, event, or phenomenon; careful and detailed note-taking during the observation; analysis of the notes; and interpretation of that analysis.

ethos the self-image a writer creates to define a relationship with readers. In arguments, most writers try to establish an ethos that suggests authority, fairness, and credibility.

evaluation, argument of an argument in which the claim specifies that something does or doesn't meet established criteria: *The Nikon D4s is the most sophisticated digital SLR camera currently available.*

evidence material offered to support an argument. (See also *artistic appeal* and *inartistic appeal.*)

example, definition by a definition that operates by identifying individual examples of what's being defined: *sports car—Corvette, Viper, Miata, Cayman.*

exordium the first part of a classical oration, in which a speaker or writer tries to win the attention and goodwill of an audience while introducing a subject.

experimental evidence evidence gathered through experimentation; often evidence that can be quantified (for example, a survey of students before and after an election might yield statistical evidence about changes in their attitudes toward the candidates). Experimental evidence is frequently crucial to scientific arguments.

fact, argument of an argument in which the claim can be proved or disproved with specific evidence or testimony: *The winter of 2016 was the warmest on record for the United States.*

fallacy of argument a flaw in the structure of an argument that renders its conclusion invalid or suspect. (See ad hominem *argument, bandwagon appeal, begging the question, dogmatism, either/or choice, equivocation, false authority, faulty analogy,* *faulty causality, hasty generalization, non sequitur, paralipsis, red herring, scare tactic, sentimental appeal, slippery slope, stacking the deck,* and *straw man.*)

false authority a fallacy of argument in which a claim is based on the expertise of someone who lacks appropriate credentials.

faulty analogy a fallacy of argument in which a comparison between two objects or concepts is inaccurate or inconsequential.

faulty causality a fallacy of argument making the unwarranted assumption that because one event follows another, the first event causes the second. Also called *post hoc, ergo propter hoc,* faulty causality forms the basis of many superstitions.

firsthand evidence data—including surveys, observations, personal interviews, and so on—collected and personally examined by the writer. (See also *secondhand evidence.*)

forensic argument an argument that deals with actions that have occurred in the past. Sometimes called *judicial arguments,* forensic arguments include legal cases involving judgments of guilt or innocence.

formal definition a definition that identifies something first by the general class to which it belongs (see *genus*) and then by the characteristics that distinguish it from other members of that class (see *species*): *Baseball is a game* (genus) *played on a diamond by opposing teams of nine players who score runs by circling bases after striking a ball with a bat* (species).

genus in a definition, the general class to which an object or a concept belongs: *baseball is a* sport; *green is a* color.

grounds in Toulmin argument, the evidence provided to support a claim and reason—that is, an *enthymeme.*

hard evidence support for an argument using facts, statistics, testimony, or other evidence the writer finds.

hasty generalization a fallacy of argument in which an inference is drawn from insufficient data.

hyperbole use of overstatement for special effect.

hypothesis a well-informed guess at what the conclusion of one's research will reveal. Hypotheses must be tested against evidence, opposing arguments, and so on.

immediate reason the cause that leads directly to an effect, such as an automobile accident that results in an injury to the driver. (See also *necessary reason* and *sufficient reason.*)

inartistic appeal support for an argument using facts, statistics, eyewitness testimony, or other evidence the writer finds rather than creates. (See also *artistic appeal.*)

inductive reasoning a process of thought in which particular cases lead to general principles.

infotention a term coined by Howard Rheingold to describe the digital literacy skills of managing the technology we use and synthesizing the information we find online.

intended readers the actual, real-life people whom a writer consciously wants to address in a piece of writing.

invention the process of finding and creating arguments to support a claim.

inverted word order moving grammatical elements of a sentence out of their usual order (subject-verb-object/complement) for special effect, as in *Tired I was; sleepy I was not.*

invitational argument a term used by Sonja Foss and Cindy Griffin to describe arguments that are aimed not at vanquishing an opponent but at inviting others to collaborate in exploring mutually satisfying ways to solve problems.

invoked readers the readers implied in a text, which may include some whom the writer didn't consciously intend to reach. An argument that refers to *those who have experienced a major trauma*, for example, invokes all readers who have undergone this experience.

irony use of language that suggests a meaning in contrast to the literal meaning of the words.

kairos the opportune moment; in arguments, the timeliness of an argument and the most opportune ways to make it.

line of argument a strategy or an approach used in an argument. Argumentative strategies include appeals to the heart (emotional appeals), to character (ethical appeals), and to facts and reason (logical appeals).

logical appeal a strategy in which a writer uses facts, evidence, and reason to convince audience members to accept a claim.

logos See *logical appeal*.

metaphor a figure of speech that makes a comparison, as in *The ship was a beacon of hope*.

metonymy a rhetorical trope in which a writer uses a particular object to stand for a general concept, as in referring to businesspeople as *suits* or to the English monarchy as *the crown*.

narratio the second part of a classical oration, in which a speaker or writer presents the facts of a case.

necessary reason a cause that must be present for an effect to occur; for example, infection with a particular virus is a necessary reason for the development of mumps. (See also *immediate reason* and *sufficient reason*.)

non sequitur a fallacy of argument in which claims, reasons, or warrants fail to connect logically; one point doesn't follow from another: *If you're really my friend, you'll lend me five hundred dollars.*

operational definition a definition that identifies an object by what it does or by the conditions that create it: *A line is the shortest distance between two points.*

oxymoron a rhetorical trope that states a paradox or contradiction, as in *jumbo shrimp*.

paralipsis a logical fallacy in which speakers or writers raise a point by saying they will *not* mention it, thus doing the very thing they say they're not going to do.

parallelism use of similar grammatical structures or forms for clarity, emphasis, and/or artfulness: *in the classroom, on the playground, and at the mall.*

paraphrase a restatement of the meaning of a piece of writing using different words from the original.

partitio the third part of a classical oration, in which a speaker or writer divides up the subject and explains what the claim will be.

patchwriting a misuse of sources in which a writer's phrase, clause, or sentence stays too close to the original language or syntax of the source.

pathos, appeal to See *emotional appeal*.

peroratio the sixth and final part of a classical oration, in which a speaker or writer summarizes the case and moves the audience to action.

persuasion the act of seeking to change someone else's point of view.

plagiarism the act of using the words, phrases, and expressions of others without proper citation or acknowledgment.

precedents actions or judgments in the past that have established a pattern or model for subsequent decisions. Precedents are particularly important in legal cases.

premise a statement or position regarded as true and upon which other claims are based.

propaganda an argument advancing a point of view without regard to reason, fairness, or truth.

proposal argument an argument in which a claim is made in favor of or opposing a specific course of action: *Sport-utility vehicles should have to meet the same fuel economy standards as passenger cars.*

purpose the goal of an argument. Purposes include entertaining, informing, convincing, exploring, and deciding, among others.

qualifiers words or phrases that limit the scope of a claim: *usually; in a few cases; under these circumstances.*

qualitative argument an argument of evaluation that relies on non-numerical criteria supported by reason, tradition, precedent, or logic.

quantitative argument an argument of evaluation that relies on criteria that can be measured, counted, or demonstrated objectively.

quantitative data the sort of data that can be observed and counted.

reason in argumentation, a statement that expands a claim by offering evidence to support it. The reason may be a statement of fact or another claim. In Toulmin argument, a reason is attached to a claim by a warrant, a statement that establishes the logical connection between claim and supporting reason. (See also *Toulmin argument*.)

rebuttal an answer that challenges or refutes a specific claim or charge. Rebuttals may also be offered by writers who anticipate objections to the claims or evidence they offer.

rebuttal, conditions of in Toulmin argument, potential objections to an argument. Writers need to anticipate such conditions in shaping their arguments.

red herring a fallacy of argument in which a writer abruptly changes the topic in order to distract readers from potentially objectionable claims.

refutatio the fifth part of a classical oration, in which a speaker or writer acknowledges and refutes opposing claims or evidence.

reversed structures a figure of speech that involves the inversion of clauses: *What is good in your writing is not original; what is original is not good.*

rhetoric the art of persuasion. Western rhetoric originated in ancient Greece as a discipline to prepare citizens for arguing cases in court.

rhetorical analysis an examination of how well the components of an argument work together to persuade or move an audience.

rhetorical questions questions posed to raise an issue or create an effect rather than to get a response: *You may well wonder, "What's in a name?"*

rhetorical situation the relationship among topic, author, audience, and other contexts (social, cultural, political) that determines or evokes an appropriate spoken or written response.

Rogerian argument an approach to argumentation based on the principle, articulated by psychotherapist Carl Rogers, that audiences respond best when they don't feel threatened. Rogerian argument stresses trust and urges those who disagree to find common ground.

scare tactic a fallacy of argument presenting an issue in terms of exaggerated threats or dangers.

scheme a figure of speech that involves a special arrangement of words, such as inversion.

secondhand evidence any information taken from outside sources, including library research and online sources. (See also *firsthand evidence*.)

sentimental appeal a fallacy of argument in which an appeal is based on excessive emotion.

signifying a distinctive trope found extensively in African American English in which a speaker or writer cleverly and often humorously needles another person.

simile a comparison that uses *like* or *as*: *My love is like a red, red rose* or *I wandered lonely as a cloud.*

slippery slope a fallacy of argument exaggerating the possibility that a relatively inconsequential action or choice today will have serious adverse consequences in the future.

species in a definition, the particular features that distinguish one member of a genus from another: *Baseball is a sport* (genus) *played on a diamond by teams of nine players* (species).

stacking the deck a fallacy of argument in which the writer shows only one side of an argument.

stance the writer's attitude toward the topic and the audience.

stasis theory in classical rhetoric, a method for coming up with appropriate arguments by determining the nature of a given situation: a question of fact; of definition; of quality; or of policy.

straw man a fallacy of argument in which an opponent's position is misrepresented as being more extreme than it actually is, so that it's easier to refute.

sufficient condition in a definition, an element or set of elements adequate to define a term. A sufficient condition in defining God, for example, might be "supreme being" or "first cause." No other conditions are necessary, though many might be made. (See also *accidental condition* and *essential condition*.)

sufficient reason a cause that alone is enough to produce a particular effect; for example, a particular level of smoke in the air will set off a smoke alarm. (See also *immediate reason* and *necessary reason*.)

summary a presentation of the substance and main points of a piece of writing in very condensed form.

syllogism in formal logic, a structure of deductive logic in which correctly formed major and minor premises lead to a necessary conclusion:

Major premise	All human beings are mortal.
Minor premise	Socrates is a human being.
Conclusion	Socrates is mortal.

synthesis a kind of critical thinking in which a writer identifies patterns, themes, and connections among sources and combines them to make a particular point or to support a claim.

testimony a personal experience or observation used to support an argument.

thesis a sentence that succinctly states a writer's main point.

Toulmin argument a method of informal logic first described by Stephen Toulmin in *The Uses of Argument* (1958). Toulmin argument describes the key components of an argument as the claim, reason, warrant, backing, and grounds.

trope a figure of speech that involves a change in the usual meaning or signification of words, such as *metaphor*, *simile*, and *analogy*.

understatement a figure of speech that makes a weaker statement than a situation seems to call for. It can lead to powerful or to humorous effects.

values, appeal to a strategy in which a writer invokes shared principles and traditions of a society as a reason for accepting a claim.

warrant in Toulmin argument, the statement (expressed or implied) that establishes the logical connection between a claim and its supporting reason.

Claim	Don't eat that mushroom.
Reason	It's poisonous.
Warrant	What is poisonous should not be eaten.

Acknowledgments

Sara Barbour. "Kindle vs. Books: The Dead Tree Society." First published in the *Los Angeles Times*, June 17, 2011. Reprinted by permission of the author.

Kate Beispel. "The Snacktivities and Musings of a Millennial Foodie." Reprinted by permission.

Sarah Brown. "Activist Athletes." *Chronicle of Higher Education*, February 26, 2017. Used with the permission of the *Chronicle of Higher Education*. Copyright © 2017. All rights reserved.

Melinda C. R. Burgess, Karen E. Dill, S. Paul Stermer, Stephen R. Burgess, and Brian P. Brown. "Playing with Prejudice: The Prevalence and Consequences of Racial Stereotypes in Video Games." *Media Psychology* 14.3 (2011): 289–311. Copyright © 2011. Reprinted by permission of Taylor & Francis Group Ltd., http://www.tandfonline.com.

James Carroll. "Who Am I to Judge?" *New Yorker*, December 23–30, 2013. Copyright © 2013. Reprinted by permission of the author.

Lauren Carroll. "Congress Let Internet Providers 'Spy On' Your Underwear Purchases, Advocacy Group Says." *PolitiFact*, March 30, 2017. Copyright © 2017. Reprinted by permission.

Stephen L. Carter. "Offensive Speech Is Free Speech. If Only We'd Listen." *Bloomberg View*, June 19, 2017. Used with permission of Bloomberg L.P. Copyright © 2017. All rights reserved.

Juliana Chang. Presentation about immigrant mother. Reprinted by permission of Juliana Chang.

D.K. "Shooting Guns: It's Rather Fun, Actually." *Economist*, February 13, 2015. Copyright © 2015 by The Economist Group Limited. Reproduced with permission of The Economist Group Limited in the format Educational/Instructional Program via Copyright Clearance Center.

James Dubick, Brandon Mathews, and Clare Cady. "Hunger on Campus: The Challenge of Food Insecurity for College Students." *studentsagainsthunger.org* (National Student Campaign Against Hunger and Homelessness), October 2016. This work is licensed under a Creative Commons Attribution 4.0 International License. To view the terms of this license, visit http://creativecommons.org/licenses/by/4.0.

Sophie Egan. "The American Food Psyche." Excerpted from pp. 14–20, 305–9 of *Devoured* by Sophie Egan. Copyright © 2016 by Sophie Egan. Reprinted by permission of HarperCollins Publishers.

Jorge Encinas. "How Latino Players Are Helping Major League Baseball Learn Spanish." © 2017 National Public Radio, Inc. News report as originally published on npr.org on March 26, 2017, and used with the permission of NPR. Any unauthorized duplication is strictly prohibited.

Franklin Foer. Excerpt from *World without Mind: The Existential Threat of Big Tech* by Franklin Foer. Copyright © 2017 by Franklin Foer. Used by permission of Penguin Press, an imprint of Penguin Publishing Group, a division of Penguin Random House LLC. All rights reserved. Any third-party use of this material, outside of this publication, is prohibited. Interested parties must apply directly to Penguin Random House LLC for permission.

Tal Fortgang. "Checking My Privilege: Character as the Basis of Privilege." *Princeton Tory*, April 2, 2014. Copyright © 2014. Reprinted by permission.

Gallup/Knight Foundation. "Free Expression on Campus: What College Students Think about First Amendment Issues." A Gallup/Knight Foundation Survey. Copyright © 2018 Gallup by Gallup, Inc. Reproduced with permission of Gallup Press in the format Educational/Instructional Program via Copyright Clearance Center.

Roxane Gay. "The Careless Language of Sexual Violence." *The Rumpus*, March 10, 2011. Copyright © 2011 by Roxane Gay. Reprinted by permission of the author.

Pascal-Emmanuel Gobry. "America's Birthrate Is Now a National Emergency." *The Week*, August 12, 2016. Copyright © 2016. Reprinted by permission.

Briahna Joy Gray. "The Question of Cultural Appropriation." *Current Affairs*, September 6, 2017. Copyright © 2017 by Briahna Gray. Reprinted by permission of the author.

Rob Greenfield. "An Argument against Veganism . . . from a Vegan." *robgreenfield.tv*, July 23, 2015, http://robgreenfield .tv/vegan/. Reprinted by permission.

Deanna Hartley. "Creative Ways to Get Noticed by Employers on Social Media." *CareerBuilder.com*, March 27, 2017. Reprinted by permission.

Cameron Hauer. "Appeal, Audience, and Narrative in Kristof's Wilderness." Reprinted by permission.

Amanda Hess. "How Privacy Became a Commodity for the Rich and Powerful." *New York Times Magazine*, May 9, 2017. Copyright © 2017 The New York Times. All rights reserved. Used by permission and protected by the Copyright Laws of the United States. The printing, copying, redistribution, or retransmission of this Content without express written permission is prohibited.

Michael Hiltzik. "Don't Believe Facebook: The Demise of the Written Word Is Very Far Off." *Los Angeles Times*, June 17, 2016. Copyright © 2016 Los Angeles Times. Reprinted by permission.

Japanese American Citizens League. "Power of Words Handbook: A Guide to Language about Japanese Americans in World War II." April 27, 2013. Reprinted by permission.

Index

Readings by Type of Argument

While it is likely the case that all texts ultimately feature aspects of multiple kinds of arguments, we have sought here to categorize the selections in Part 5 according to major type(s) of argument. At the same time, we're quick to acknowledge that many factors, including one's own position on the issues discussed or even a single word choice by an author, may make one reader's proposal another's evaluation.

Rogerian Argument

In addressing other vegans in particular, Greenfield seeks to find and build on common ground while simultaneously encouraging all his readers to examine seriously what it means to eat ethically.

Invitational Argument

These arguments are invitational in that even though their writers are strongly committed to a particular stance or position, both consider varying points of view fairly and openly and show the deep complexity of the issues involved.